Ashkelon 4

HARVARD SEMITIC MUSEUM PUBLICATIONS
Lawrence E. Stager, General Editor
Michael D. Coogan, Director of Publications

FINAL REPORTS OF THE LEON LEVY EXPEDITION TO ASHKELON

Series Editors
Lawrence E. Stager, Daniel M. Master, and J. David Schloen

1. *Ashkelon 1: Introduction and Overview (1985–2006)*
   edited by Lawrence E. Stager, J. David Schloen, and Daniel M. Master
2. *Ashkelon 2: Imported Pottery of the Roman and Late Roman Periods*
   by Barbara L. Johnson
3. *Ashkelon 3: The Seventh Century* B.C.
   by Lawrence E. Stager, Daniel M. Master, and J. David Schloen
4. *Ashkelon 4: The Iron Age Figurines of Ashkelon and Philistia*
   by Michael D. Press

THE LEON LEVY EXPEDITION TO ASHKELON

ASHKELON 4

The Iron Age Figurines of Ashkelon and Philistia

By

Michael D. Press

Winona Lake, Indiana
EISENBRAUNS
2012

Ashkelon 4:
The Iron Age Figurines of Ashkelon and Philistia

by Michael D. Press

Printed in the U.S.A.

Distributed by
Eisenbrauns
PO Box 275
Winona Lake, IN 46590-0275

http://eisenbrauns.com

Library of Congress Cataloging-in-Publication Data

Press, Michael D.
Ashkelon 4 : the Iron age figurines of Ashkelon and Philistia / by Michael D. Press.
pages ; cm. — (Final reports of the Leon Levy expedition to Ashkelon ; 4)
"This monograph is a revision of my 2007 dissertation, 'Philistine Figurines and Figurines in Philistia in the Iron Age'"—Ecip introduction.
Includes bibliographical references and index.
ISBN 978-1-57506-942-5 (alk. paper)
1. Ashkelon (Israel) 2. Ashkelon (Israel)—Antiquities. 3. Excavations (Archaeology)—Israel—Ashkelon. 4. Material culture—Israel—Ashkelon. 5. Figurines, Prehistoric—Israel—Ashkelon. 6. Iron age—Israel—Ashkelon. I. Title.
DS110.A76A752 2011
933′.49—dc23

2012034576

The paper used in this publication meets the minimum requirements of the American National Standard for Information Sciences—Permanence of Paper for Printed Library Materials, ANSI Z39.48-1984. ⊗™

Shelby White and Leon Levy

The Leon Levy Expedition to Ashkelon is indebted to the vision and support of Leon Levy and Shelby White. Its ongoing publications are underwritten by a grant from the Leon Levy Foundation.

CONTENTS

EDITORS' PREFACE

In 2007, Michael Press capped his splendid academic career at Harvard in the Department of Near Eastern Languages and Civilization with a "high honors" Ph.D. thesis entitled, "Philistine Figurines and Figurines in Philistia in the Iron Age." Now he has revised and expanded that work into *Ashkelon* 4: *The Iron Age Figurines of Ashkelon and Philistia*. This is the fourth volume in the publication series that constitutes the final report of the Leon Levy Expedition to Ashkelon.

Here, for the first time, he publishes the complete Iron Age corpus of terracotta anthropomorphic and zoomorphic figurines from the Leon Levy Expedition. Adapting a methodology of typology, iconography, and iconology pioneered by Erwin Panofsky, Press lays out in detail his theoretical framework for analyzing and understanding the figurines of Ashkelon and those from Philistine cultures. Press's exposition of his method and theory toward this particular corpus could easily be applied to the coroplastic art of many other cultures.

With an uncanny eye for form and detail, Press eliminates some old favorites, such as the "mourning figurine," and defines anew such dominant categories as the "standing lady with upraised arms" (Psi figurines) and the "seated or enthroned lady" ("Ashdoda").

Press's entire project rests on the many excavators and registrars who discovered the figurines addressed in this study. Just as their dedicated work created this set of figurines, Press's careful study honors their excavation work. Throughout this study, covering nearly six centuries of Philistine life, the archaeological contexts of the figurines are stressed as much as their form and decoration. To have an archaeological context for more than 200 figurines is in itself extremely rare and an extraordinary achievement thanks to the precise excavation and recording of these small objects by the Ashkelon field staff over the past 25 years.

All aspects of this volume have taken place under the auspices of the Leon Levy Expedition to Ashkelon. The work from 1985–2004 was sponsored by Leon Levy and Shelby White, and the work from 2007 to the present continues to be supported by the Leon Levy Foundation. The Leon Levy Expedition has also been sponsored by Harvard University, the Semitic Museum, and later by Boston College, Wheaton College, and Troy University.

Lawrence E. Stager
Concord, Massachusetts

Daniel M. Master
Wheaton, Illinois

J. David Schloen
Chicago, Illinois

August 2012

AUTHOR'S PREFACE

This monograph is a revision of my 2007 dissertation, "Philistine Figurines and Figurines in Philistia in the Iron Age." As a result, I must first of all thank the members of my dissertation committee—Lawrence Stager, David Mitten, and Peter Machinist—for their input and encouragement in having me convert the dissertation into a monograph. In particular I would like to single out Prof. Stager for his years of advice and patient guidance and for providing me a forum for publication within the series of studies of the Leon Levy Expedition to Ashkelon Final Reports. I should also thank Prof. Mitten for his unwavering support in the process of completing my dissertation and Prof. Machinist for his extensive set of constructive comments.

One of the most rewarding aspects of this project was interacting with a number of archaeologists who were particularly helpful and accommodating. Sy Gitin, Eliezer Oren, and Aren Maeir were gracious enough to allow me access to unpublished figurine collections from Tel Miqne-Ekron; Tel Sera^c, Tel Haror, and Ruqeish; and Tell eṣ-Ṣafi, respectively. In addition, they were always willing to discuss aspects of the terracottas and offer further suggestions. Aaron Burke and Martin Peilstöcker invited me to publish Iron and Bronze Age figurines from the Kaplan excavations of Jaffa and graciously allowed me to use them for this study prior to publication. Joe Uziel and Rona Avissar provided invaluable assistance in sorting through the Ṣafi collection. Anna de Vincenz took the time to help me sort through figurines from Miqne. Jacob Huster helped me with unpublished drawings and photographs of figurines from Ḥorvat Hoga and shared some of his unsurpassed knowledge of that site. Prior to the publication of their volumes, Yuval Gadot and Marta Guzowska graciously provided me with unpublished manuscripts and information concerning figurines from Aphek, Area X, and Ephraim Stern shared drawings and information on figurines from Dor.

I was also able to have access to unpublished or underpublished figurines from Philistia and its immediate vicinity in several museums and storage facilities, thanks to the help and cooperation of several colleagues. In particular, Alegre Savariego, curator of the Rockefeller collections, provided most valuable assistance in studying figurines (from Tell Jemmeh, Tell el-^{c}Ajjul, Tell el-Far^{c}ah [S], and Gezer) which were in storage in that museum. Debi Ben-Ami, Iron Age and Persian Period curator at the IAA Storehouses in Beth Shemesh, graciously helped me to view published and unpublished figurines from a variety of sites. I am indebted to Rachael Sparks, keeper at the Institute of Archaeology, University College, London, whose valuable support made it possible to both access and understand the large assemblage of figurines from Flinders Petrie's old excavations at Tell Jemmeh and Tell el-Far^{c}ah (S). I am also indebted to Felicity Cobbing, curator of the Palestine Exploration Fund, for allowing me to study figurines and figurine casts in their collection.

In addition, I have benefited immensely from discussions about the figurines with a series of colleagues and friends. Most valuable were correspondence and conversations with Assaf Yasur-Landau and David Ben-Shlomo; both of them offered valuable insights based on their detailed knowledge of the Iron I Philistine figurines in particular, and Philistine material culture more generally. Erin Darby was generous with her knowledge of Judean pillar figurines, and of figurines more generally. I am also happy to acknowledge helpful comments from and discussions with Adam Aja, Kate Birney, Brian Brisco, Susan Cohen, Jean-Baptiste Humbert, Ely Levine, Daniel Master, Dalit Regev, and Seong-Hyun Park.

A word of thanks is also due to the illustrators responsible for the drawings and photographs of the figurines. The figurine drawings were made by Anna Proctor, Cathy Alexander, and Noga Ze'evi; the photographs were taken by Zev Radovan. All drawings and photographs are courtesy of the Leon Levy Expedition to Ashkelon. I am most grateful to the Leon Levy Expedition and to these individuals for the use of this material.

Most importantly, I am privileged to be able to acknowledge the support of my family: my parents, my sisters, and my wife Arlene. Beyond their moral support and encouragement, I am grateful to my father Stephen for reading over much of the text of my dissertation in its final stages of preparation and to Arlene for assistance in formatting the tables and figures. Without their help, the completion of this project would not have been possible.

Michael D. Press
Fayetteville, Arkansas August 2012

ABBREVIATIONS

AA	*American Anthropologist*
AAA	*Athens Annals of Archaeology*
AASOR	Annual of the American Schools of Oriental Research
AJA	*American Journal of Archaeology*
AJBA	*Australian Journal of Biblical Archaeology*
ANET[3]	*Ancient Near Eastern Texts Relating to the Old Testament,* 3d ed. [= Pritchard 1969]
AM	*Mitteilungen des deutschen archäologischen Instituts: Athenische Abteilung.*
Annuario	*Annuario della R. Scuola Archeologica di Atene e delle Missioni Italiane in Oriente*
Ashkelon 1	*Ashkelon*, vol. 1, *Introduction and Overview (1985–2006)* [= Stager, Schloen, and Master 2008]
Ashkelon 3	*Ashkelon*, vol. 3, *The Seventh Century B.C.* [= Stager, Master, and Schloen 2011]
ASOR	American Schools of Oriental Research
BA	*Biblical Archaeologist*
BAR	*Biblical Archaeology Review*
BARIS	British Archaeological Reports, International Series
BASOR	*Bulletin of the American Schools of Oriental Research*
BCH	*Bulletin de Correspondence Héllenique*
BDB	*A Hebrew and English Lexicon of the Old Testament* [= Brown, Driver, and Briggs 2006 (1906)]
BSA	*Annual of the British School at Athens*
CAJ	*Cambridge Archaeological Journal*
EA	*Egyptian Archaeology: Bulletin of the Egypt Exploration Society*
EAEHL	*Encyclopedia of Archaeological Excavations in the Holy Land*
EI	*Eretz-Israel*
Ephemeris	*ΑΡΧΑΙΟΛΟΓΙΚΟΝ ΕΦΗΜΕΡΙΣ*
Ergon	*ΤΟ ΕΡΓΟΝ ΤΗΣ ΑΡΧΑΙΟΛΟΓΙΚΗΣ ΕΤΑΙΡΕΙΑΣ*
ESI	*Excavations and Surveys in Israel*
HTR	*Harvard Theological Review*
IAA	Israel Antiquities Authority
IEJ	*Israel Exploration Journal*
JANES	*Journal of the Ancient Near Eastern Society*
JAOS	*Journal of the American Oriental Society*
JBL	*Journal of Biblical Literature*
JCS	*Journal of Cuneiform Studies*
JHS	*Journal of Hellenic Studies*
JNES	*Journal of Near Eastern Studies*
JSOT	*Journal for the Study of the Old Testament*
LB	Late Bronze Age
MB	Middle Bronze Age
NEA	*Near Eastern Archaeology*
NEAEHL	*New Encyclopedia of Archaeological Excavations in the Holy Land*
NT	New Tomb (Ialysos)
OBO	Orbis Biblicus et Orientalis
OIP	Oriental Institute Publications
OJA	*Oxford Journal of Archaeology*
PEFQS	*Palestine Exploration Fund Quarterly Statement*
PEQ	*Palestine Exploration Quarterly* [continues *PEFQS*]
QDAP	*Quarterly of the Department of Antiquities in Palestine*
RDAC	*Report of the Department of Antiquities, Cyprus*
SIMA	Studies in Mediterranean Archaeology
TA	*Tel Aviv*
UCL	University College, London
UT	Ustinow Terracotta
VT	*Vetus Testamentum*
ZAW	*Zeitschrift für die alttestamentliche Wissenschaft*
ZDPV	*Zeitschrift des Deutschen Palästina-Vereins*

1. Introduction

My purpose in this study is to analyze the clay figurines dating to the Iron Age (ca. 1200–600 B.C.E.) from Philistia, the region of southwest Palestine settled and inhabited by the Philistines in this period. The main corpus I am dealing with is the group of roughly 200 Iron Age figurines excavated at the site of Ashkelon (during the current Leon Levy Expedition, 1985 to present), supplemented with material from neighboring sites. As with any study of figurines, a major goal is to classify them into basic types and then discuss the origin and meaning of these types. Beyond this, I will use this discussion to generate hypotheses concerning the function of these figurines, the meaning of their similarity or difference to figurines of neighboring regions, and how these factors may have changed over the course of the Iron Age. I will then try to test these hypotheses through additional analyses—an iconographic study of more general imagery relating to the figurines and an archaeological study of the context of the figurines.

Ultimately, my goal in such a work would be to produce a study along the lines of that by E. B. French (1971) on Mycenaean figurines: a thorough study of a large assemblage, with enough detailed typological and contextual work for me to trace the evolution of types over time, as well as reach new insights into how these figurines would have been used. As I began this study, however, I doubted that such goals were possible given the current state of research. To begin with, the region of Philistia is relatively small, resulting in a much more limited number of sites than those in the Mycenaean world studied by French (essentially the entire Aegean region). In addition, the number of excavated sites within this region is rather limited, and the progress of publication is slow. As a result, there is not nearly the amount of data available for a study of Philistine figurines that there was already 40 or 50 years ago for a study of Mycenaean terracottas.

Nevertheless, I have always seen great value in conducting such a study. Given the current state of research on Philistine figurines, even the relatively limited and provisional conclusions I originally anticipated would result in an advancement of knowledge. Moreover, after surveying and analyzing the data in detail, I have found to my surprise that broader conclusions are in fact possible to make. The wealth of finds from Ashkelon, along with those from other sites (most notably, Tel Miqne-Ekron), has multiplied the number of figurines in the Iron Age corpus of Philistia and opens up a series of possibilities for new analyses. In that respect, this study is simply a first step, albeit an important one.

As a result, I have focused a great deal of attention on the theoretical and methodological considerations that serve as the framework for such studies—considerations that most studies of Palestinian figurines, I believe, have largely ignored. As I see it, the theoretical issues are of two basic types: one dealing with the nature of figurines, and the other dealing with the nature of an archaeological culture (in this case, Philistine culture). It is these basic issues which I highlight in the following study. Beyond a discussion of their overall character, I also consider the practical means by which we can address these issues in a figurine study. In other words, I am developing a methodology specifically for the study of figurines.

Therefore, before I engage in the typology and discussion—the usual concerns of a figurine study—I must discuss a large amount of introductory material. This material constitutes chapters 2–4: a definition of the basic theoretical issues; a history of the research, which highlights not only the amount of work conducted on Philistine figurines but also how previous studies have addressed these theoretical issues; and the development of a methodology for the current study.

Figure 1. Map of Philistia and environs

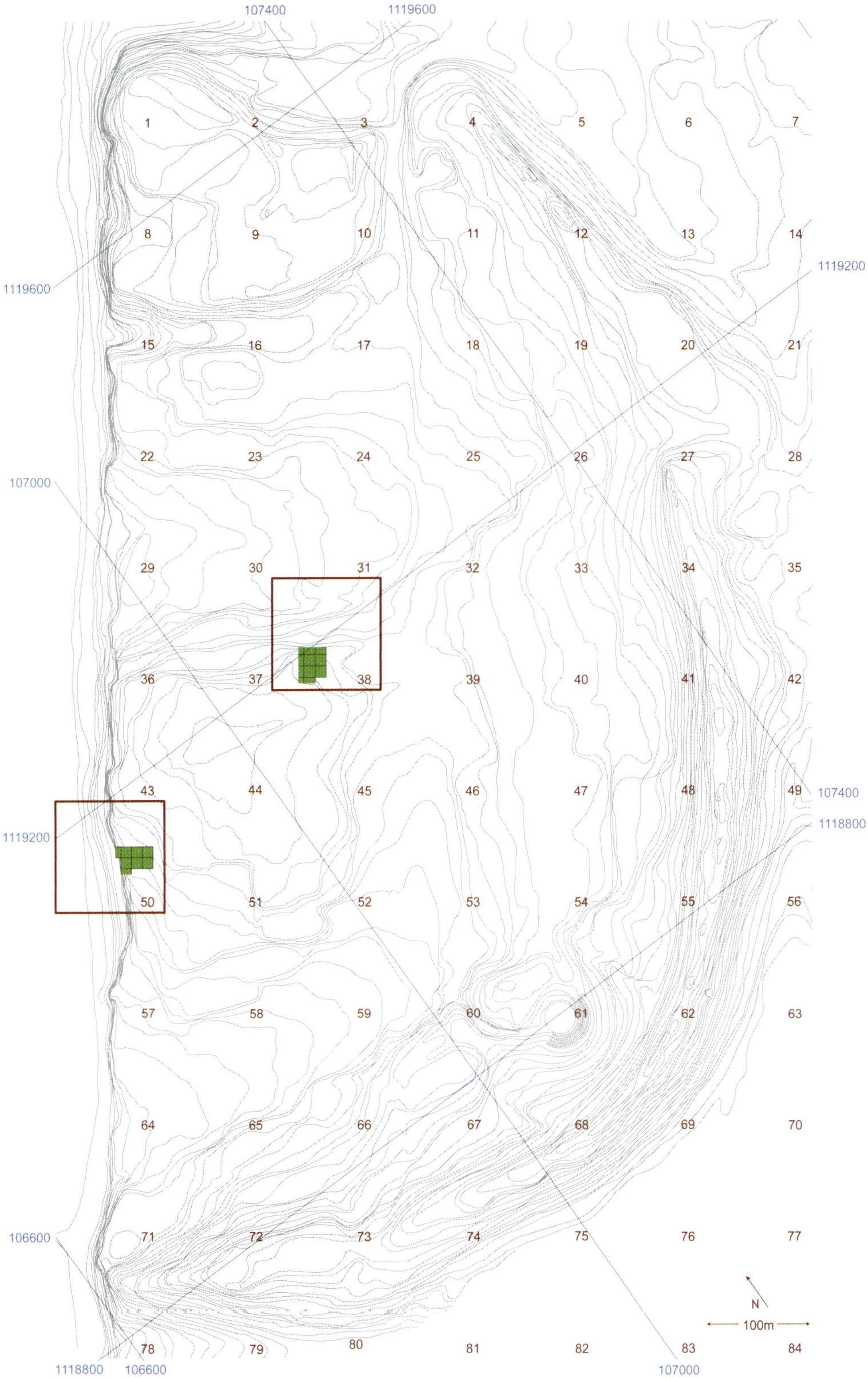

Figure 2. Map of Ashkelon with excavation areas (grids). The blue grid represents the local projected coordinate system, with coordinates given in the Old Israel Grid (OIG).

2. Theoretical Issues

The foundation of a proper study of figurines is a good theoretical and methodological framework; without this background, archaeologists often base their interpretations on general assumptions or miss crucial data.[1] Most discussions of Philistine figurines have lacked any treatment of the theory behind them.[2] As I see it, any discussion of Philistine figurines involves two basic sets of theoretical issues: one clustering around the concept of "figurine," the other clustering around the concept of "Philistine." I will treat each of these clusters separately in the pages below.

The Concept of "Figurine"

Basic questions such as "What is a figurine?" or "Why do we study them?" may seem fairly self-explanatory, but even here a review of what these objects are and the theoretical issues their study raises is in order. Such a process begins with what D. Bailey has called "definition" (1996:291–92).[3] Figurines are small objects made of various materials (such as clay, metal, stone, or bone) which serve as miniature representations, generally of humans (anthropomorphic figurines), animals (zoomorphic, or theriomorphic, figurines), or a group mixing the two.[4] In this study I will be dealing exclusively with figurines of fired clay (terracotta), representing both humans and animals.

As part of the process of description, Ucko (1968:67) and Voigt (1983:table 30) devised detailed lists of attributes of a (specifically anthropomorphic) figurine. These include (following Voigt 1983:table 30) material, technique of manufacture, dimensions, head form, form and position of torso and limbs, depiction of anatomical details, depiction of clothing and ornaments, and associated objects. I propose a simplified version of this list, highlighting four aspects of the figurine:

1. technique: whether handmade, moldmade, wheel-made, or some combination;

2. form: the overall shape of the figurine, as well as of specific parts (such as the head);

3. style: the manner in which the representation is rendered; for example, is it naturalistic or abstract? and

4. decoration: the use especially of paint, but also incisions, slip, etc.

These four basic categories should provide a sufficiently informative summary of the figurine's attributes and a useful basis for comparison with other figurines.

Figurines, and especially terracottas, have figured prominently in studies of the archaeology of the ancient Near East, and in material culture studies more generally, for two basic, related reasons: their relatively frequent occurrence in excavations and their particular significance for the study of religion (a favorite topic of research by archaeologists). Clay—unlike other materials such as metal—was easily accessible and therefore inexpensive in the ancient world; as a result, it was not only a common medium for manufacture but also one not needing to be recycled. Terracotta figurines, being made of clay, are rather fragile objects; once a figurine was broken, the fragments would not have been saved or reused but simply left where they fell or were discarded. In addition, despite the fact that whole figurines are fragile, once they have been broken the fragments are very sturdy and well-preserved in the archaeological record. Just as pottery is the most abundant class of material culture in excavations, so clay figurines are the most abundant class of figural representations.[5]

Given this relative abundance, scholars have relied on terracottas as a particularly valuable tool for understanding ancient societies, particularly the realm of

[1] See for example Bailey (1994; 1996) for a discussion of the significance of this framework and the effect that its absence has had on figurine studies in southeastern Europe.

[2] For an exception to this rule, see the recent study by Yasur-Landau (2001:330–31).

[3] If we take Bailey literally, we would replace the term "figurines" altogether with "durable three-dimensional miniature anthropomorphic representations" (1994:291). Such an action seems unnecessarily extreme, and not feasible, but it is still important to keep such elementary characteristics in mind to help sharpen our conclusions about how figurines could, or could not, have been used.

[4] Sometimes an additional class, tectomorphic figurines—those representing buildings—is included (Bailey 1994:291).

[5] That pottery is the most widely recovered material culture type recovered in excavations is recognized by archaeologists. This assertion is supported by my own involvement in the Leon Levy Expedition to Ashkelon. Similarly, at Ashkelon the ratio of clay figurines to those of metal and stone combined is roughly 100:1.

religion.[6] Their importance for the southern Levant is magnified due to the relative lack of other types of evidence concerning religious practices, notably large-scale cult statues and textual evidence. Figurines, then, have been perceived as a major source of information for cult in general and individual deities in particular. In this respect they are rivaled in their iconographic importance only by seals and seal impressions (Keel and Uehlinger 1998:10).

As I have implied in the brief discussion above, there are at least two significant assumptions or biases that scholars often make in analyzing figurines and that have had great effect on how they are understood generally. These are the differential treatment given to anthropomorphic and zoomorphic figurines and the belief that figurines are (primarily) religious objects. It is a general rule that the majority of figurines produced by cultures in the Levant are zoomorphic. For example, T. Holland, in his important survey of figurines from Iron Age Palestine in general, found that 1,555 out of 2,655 examples—58.6 percent—are representations of animals (1977:124). This trend has been confirmed in my study specifically of Philistine figurines.[7] Despite this basic fact, the vast majority of figurine studies, both for ancient Palestine and more generally, have dealt mainly if not exclusively with anthropomorphic figurines.[8]

Beyond superficial remarks about the bias of researchers toward human representations, I would offer two suggestions to explain this situation. First of all, it is generally true (certainly for the Philistine figurines) that zoomorphic terracottas are often less "interesting." A survey of the Iron Age corpus from Ashkelon, for example, demonstrates that: a) zoomorphic figurines are much less likely to be painted or otherwise decorated than anthropomorphic ones, and b) zoomorphic figurines were rarely if ever formed in molds, while anthropomorphic figurines were made in this technique quite often. Overall, it appears that the ancient people who produced these figurines paid more attention to the human representations than to the animal ones (perhaps reflecting a bias similar to that of modern researchers).[9] In addition, I think that the emphasis on anthropomorphic figures is explicable by the understanding of these objects as religious in nature. Despite the fact that various Near Eastern peoples at least sometimes imagined their gods in animal form (and sometimes imagined them with animal emblems), scholars studying figurines have generally identified the anthropomorphic, and only the anthropomorphic, figurines as representations of deities. Rightly or wrongly, there has clearly been a consensus among scholars that, in images, peoples of the ancient Near East tended to use the human form to depict their gods.[10]

[6] It is not surprising, therefore, that figurines have been a topic of long-standing interest, as well as a focus of recent discussion in the Iron Age archaeology of Palestine. See for example the work of Kletter (1996; 1999), as well as the attention they receive from Stern (2001) in his discussion of eighth- through fourth-century B.C.E. remains.

[7] At Ashkelon, the most common type by far is the horse figurine, which makes up about 39 percent (81 out of 210) of the Iron Age corpus. Figures for animal figurines in general are difficult to produce, as there are many unidentifiable fragments, but roughly 118 out of 210 figurines, or 56 percent, are probably zoomorphic.

[8] Even a brief survey of the titles of studies of figurines from ancient Palestine reveals an overwhelming focus on anthropomorphic figurines—and specifically on female figurines, which predominate among the human representations—from E. Pilz's "Die weiblichen Gottheiten Kanaans" (1924), through J. B. Pritchard's *Palestinian Figurines in Relation to Certain Goddesses Known Through Literature* (1943), to A. Yasur-Landau's "The Mother(s) of All Philistines?" (2001).

[9] Certain types of animal figurines in the Near East, for instance the horses found at many Phoenician sites, have much detail in the depiction of their heads, bridles, and other equipment, but these are an exception without parallel among most figurines in Palestine generally. For the Phoenician horses, see, e.g., E. Mazar 1990; 1993; see also the large number of horse and rider figurines from Cyprus (e.g., Karageorghis 1995:61–95).

[10] Ucko (1968:418) states that he can find only one instance where an archaeologist has suggested that animal figurines may have represented deities (G. Clark 1961:103); he is critical of the majority of researchers who have not hesitated to understand female figurines as deities and yet never suggest the same interpretation for zoomorphs, despite their often being found in precisely the same contexts. Kletter writes that "[a]lmost all scholars understood it would be ridiculous to see all the animal figurines as representations of gods, or as attributive animals of gods" (1996:78), but he provides no further discussion. Nevertheless, some researchers have indeed suggested that animal figurines, at least in certain cases, represented deities. The bull figurine found at Dhahrat et-Tawileh (broadly known as the "Bull Site") has been widely interpreted as a cultic object associated with a deity; this figurine is distinct, however, in being made of bronze and not clay, and even so scholarly opinion is uncertain as to whether to view the object as an actual representation of a deity or merely the deity's attribute or pedestal (e.g., A. Mazar 1982a:32; Coogan 1987:2; Ahlström 1990a:79–80). Nevertheless, Ahlström at least suggested that clay bull figurines indicate worship of a deity in the form of a bull (1990b: 579). Meanwhile, Macalister considered that at least some of the clay bovine figurines he discovered at Gezer probably represented a deity, along the lines of the golden calf (1912a: 411). May (1935:33–34) wondered whether the lack of male figurines at Megiddo suggested that gods were depicted as animals, or whether it reflected the aniconism of the ancient inhabitants. In either case, the suggestion reflects May's

This understanding of the figurines as religious objects, however, is itself a major assumption often not proven or even tested in the literature. From a survey of the literature on figurines, it appears that two main suggestions have been offered over the last century for their use: cult objects and toys.[11] The former label is almost universally applied to anthropomorphic figurines—which, in Near Eastern scholarship or historical archaeology more generally, are then identified with specific divine figures. The latter label is often given to the zoomorphic figurines (though often they too are thought to be religious in nature, not as images of actual deities but serving as votive substitutes for actual animals; see, e.g., May 1935:28). Even more recent comprehensive surveys, such as that of Kletter (1996), have, after a consideration of the different hypotheses, tended to dismiss the alternatives and focus on the traditional interpretations.

A major aspect of this problem of identification is the interpretation of female figurines. Even more than the divide between anthropomorphic and zoomorphic figurines, male vs. female figurines present a sharp contrast throughout the archaeological record. It is a remarkable fact that, in most regions and periods of the Near East, and even beyond, almost all anthropomorphic clay figurines are representations of women.[12] Traditionally, this situation was interpreted by recourse to the Goddess hypothesis: that female clay figurines in antiquity, like female images more generally, were representations of a Great (Mother/Earth/Fertility) Goddess particularly popular in prehistory. Starting with the work of Ucko (1968), this interpretation gradually came to be rejected. Following him, a large body of work on figurines has come to provide alternative interpretations: Voigt (1983:195) interprets Neolithic figurines from Iran as objects from magic rituals; Talalay (1993:84) suggests Neolithic figurines from Franchthi Cave in Greece served a variety of functions, notably as "identifying tokens"; Bailey (1994) suggests prehistoric figurines from Bulgaria represented individual persons; Haaland and Haaland (1996:296–97) similarly explain figurines of pregnant women from the Pavlovian, Kostenkian, and Gravettian cultures (29,000–23,000 B.P.) as symbolic representations of their "social selves." A common theme in many of these interpretations is identity, whether of the individual or of a society. Figurines studies in the last two decades have often focused on the use of the human body, and especially the female body, to map out social identities and relations (see, e.g., Bailey 2005; S. Clark 2007; Nakamura and Meskell 2009). Other proposals have also been made: Lesure, e.g., has suggested that the gender of figurines (at least for the Neolithic Near East and Mesoamerica) might simply reflect the gender of the user (2002:esp. 600).[13]

Ucko's study and most of those following him are distinguished, however, from the main body of work on Syro-Palestinian figurines in two basic and related respects: they approach the figurines from an anthropological (rather than humanistic) archaeological perspective, and they deal with prehistoric figurines. There are no texts relating to the use or identity of the figurines in these studies or in any way to the periods of their use. Thus, Ucko's and other anthropological archaeologists' theoretical reliance on ethnographic analogy, an important resource for anthropologists generally, is also due to necessity.[14]

---

assumption that figurines are cult objects (as reflected by their inclusion in his *Material Remains of the Megiddo Cult*), and specifically images of deities. In Judah in particular, the focus on anthropomorphic figurines appears to be connected to the scholarly assumption that they are objects of popular religion, given the assumed aniconism of the official cult (for a review and negative assessment of this argument, see van der Toorn 2002:47–51; cf. Kletter 1996:16–27).

[11] For more discussion, see chapter 3. For a survey of the explanations given to figurines from Palestine, and specifically the pillar figurines of seventh-century Judah, see Kletter (1996:73–77). For a survey of the explanations for prehistoric figurines from Egypt, Crete, and the Near East, see Ucko (1968:409–26).

[12] This observation is largely based on my study of figurine collections and publications covering Israel, the larger Levant, Cyprus, and the Aegean in the Bronze and Iron Ages. As a general observation (along with possibilities for interpretation), see also Moorey 2003:19–21. Thus, the predominant anthropomorphic type in Iron Age II Judah is the female pillar figurine (Kletter 1996; Darby 2011). For the wider Iron Age in Palestine, see Holland 1977:121–22, 124–25, fig. 1 (Types A–C). A similar pattern is visible at Ashkelon: only about 10 of the roughly 92 Iron Age anthropomorphic figurines can be classified as male. In Ashkelon and Philistia, as in the wider Levant in the Iron Age, the only male type of any popularity is the eighth- to sixth-century horse and rider. Cf. French (1971:148) on the rarity of Mycenaean male figurines; Ucko (1968); N. Hamilton (1996); Marcus (1996); and Haaland and Haaland (1996) on figurines in other regions and periods.

[13] For surveys of the range of interpretations given to figurines in the last 40 years, see also N. Hamilton (1996); Ucko (1996).

[14] More recently, the interpretations of anthropological archaeology have begun to have an impact on humanistic studies of Near Eastern figurines. Moorey, e.g., (2003:15–21) discusses the same issues of identity and miniaturization that are a focus of Bailey and others. This impact is part of a larger trend in humanistic archaeology, both in the Near East and in the Aegean, involving interpreting art as reflective of identity and social relations (e.g., Langdon 2008; Smith 2009).

The caution of anthropological archaeology, and its recognition of the wide range of possible explanations for the use of figurines,[15] are valuable examples to keep in mind. Thus, Fowler (1985), in discussing figurines of Palestine, suggests care in using them to identify cult places. He cites a particularly relevant example from Tell al-Hiba in Iraq: children would emulate the adults of the town in making objects of various types out of mud.[16] The children's examples, though of the same types as those of the adults, served an entirely different function—that of toys. On the basis of this example, Ochsenschlager concluded that the value of typical classification of figurines was quite limited (1974:174).

A study of Philistine figurines, unlike various recent anthropological studies, would at least in theory have textual evidence to aid in interpretation. Nevertheless, we must be careful not to rely on this additional class of evidence too much. While we should take advantage of this evidence when possible, we must be wary of swinging to the other extreme: the general assumption in Palestinian figurine studies that we must be able to relate our (often meager) archaeological evidence with our (also often meager) textual evidence. This assumption is problematic for multiple reasons. First, the attempt of scholars to relate archaeological and textual evidence in illuminating Near Eastern figurines has been used primarily to identify figurines with images of specific (and major) deities; there is little consideration of using textual evidence for making other types of identifications. It is worth noting that, in many cases in the Bronze and Iron Age Near East and Aegean where we have good iconographic and textual evidence for the identity of figurines, they represent either ordinary humans or minor deities: e.g., Mycenaean and later Greek mourning figurines, Egyptian shawabtis, and Neo-Assyrian *apkallu* figurines (see Press 2011:363–65 for further discussion). In addition, there is no reason that a god or goddess must be represented in the realm of small terracottas. This problem points to the types of questions that we might ask about the figurines. Typically, ancient Near Eastern scholarship deals with the identity of the figurines; the main questions of importance are usually seen to be "Who are they?" and "Are they human or divine?" Anthropological literature, on the other hand, often focuses on a somewhat different question: "What are the meanings, or functions, of these figurines?"[17] The lack of textual evidence for many anthropological studies has forced a subtle shift in how the figurines are treated, a shift which I believe is valuable even when questions of identity might possibly be answered.

A proper study of any group of terracottas, then, should focus on certain basic issues. The most fundamental of these, of course, is the question which has most interested researchers for the entire period of figurine study but with a shift in emphasis: What are the meanings (or identities) and functions of these figurines (to those who made and used them)? At the same time, however, we constantly need to keep in mind a related question: Is it possible, or to what extent is it possible, to reconstruct the meanings (or identities) and functions of these figurines?[18] The general assumptions made about terracottas are by no means necessarily wrong, but these assumptions should be treated not as givens but as hypotheses that need testing—through the analysis of archaeological context, and, in the case of Philistine figurines, the study of possible textual evidence. In addition, the traditional dichotomy between anthropomorphic and zoomorphic figurines, and their differential treatment, deserves reevaluation. Is there more that we can say about zoomorphic figurines? Were their uses and identities more varied than usually thought?

The Concept of "Philistine"

Just as the concept of "figurine" needed definition and elaboration, so too does the concept of "Philistine." This process involves, not simply a brief survey of Philistine culture and settlement history, but also—and perhaps more importantly—a review of the different ways that archaeologists have used the term, i.e.,

[15] See Ucko (1968:425–26); Voigt (1983:187–93) for a survey of ethnographic literature on the use of figurines.

[16] See Ochsenschlager (1974:164).

[17] Here I use the word "meaning" to indicate the set of beliefs or concepts that the figurine represented to its user—particularly, but not exclusively, the identity of the figure represented. By "function" I indicate the actual use of the figurine. (Talalay [1993:38] has already proposed the use of these same terms in an identical fashion.) Not only are these two concepts different, but they are also not always directly related; see Voigt (1983:188–89) for discussion. Thus, a figurine representing a deity would not have been necessarily used in a religious ceremony. For further discussion of the complex relationship between "meaning" and "function," see Keel and Uelhinger's critique (1998:7–10) of Dever's (1987) dichotomy of "belief" and "cult."

[18] Note in this context a group of articles published by archaeologists (N. Hamilton et al. 1996) entitled, "Can We Interpret Figurines?", dealing not simply with whether we can interpret them but what types of questions we should ask and can answer convincingly. On a more general archaeological level, see Schloen (2001) for a discussion of the "irreducible dialectic" between the "outer fact" (archaeologically, the artifact) and the "inner symbol" (the meaning to the ancients).

the different ways they have defined "Philistine." The tension between these various definitions is a problem which must be addressed before beginning any study of Philistine artifacts.

Despite occasional challenges (such as Brug 1985; Sherratt 1998), the traditional view of the Philistines, developed over the last hundred years through archaeological work in conjunction with analysis of the Bible and other texts, is still the generally accepted one.[19] Of Aegean origin, they settled along the southwest coast of Palestine (the region therefore known as Philistia) near the beginning of Iron Age I (ca. 1200–1000 B.C.E.), shortly after 1200 B.C.E. That settlement is understood as part of the movement of "Sea Peoples" at the end of the LB (Late Bronze Age, ca. 1550–1200 B.C.E.), based on their appearance (as *Peleset*) in the inscriptions and reliefs at Medinet Habu and in Papyrus Harris I. While their initial settlement involved the takeover of already existing LB Canaanite cities (the five cities known as the Philistine Pentapolis), they soon expanded north and east until coming into contact with the emerging Israelites (Stager 1998:340–44, 348). A long series of military engagements led eventually to Philistine defeat and retreat back to the heartland of the Pentapolis, where they remained until their cities were destroyed by the Assyrians and particularly the Babylonians, and they were deported to Mesopotamia. There is evidence, for a short time afterward, of settlements in Babylonia inhabited by persons from Ashkelon and Gaza (see Zadok 1978:61). No further record exists, however, of a people identifying themselves as "Philistine"; their particular ethnic identity seems to have been lost.[20]

Philistine culture is usually noted for its marked evolution over the course of a few centuries. When the Philistines first settled in Palestine, many elements of their material culture were quite distinct from those of the indigenous peoples and can clearly be traced back to the Mycenaean world of the LB. Most obvious among these elements is Philistine decorated pottery, but other elements including clay loomweights, Mycenaean-style figurines, architectural elements such as hearths, and the consumption of pig are also distinctive features of Philistine settlement in Iron I.[21] By the end of this period (roughly the early tenth century B.C.E.), however, many of these distinctive cultural elements had disappeared from the Philistine assemblage; this situation has typically been interpreted as the start of a process of "assimilation" (Bunimovitz 1990:219; T. Dothan 1982:1). Unfortunately, there are archaeological gaps of varying lengths over the following two centuries (roughly the ninth and eighth centuries B.C.E.) at many Philistine sites, notably Ashkelon and Miqne (see T. Dothan 1995:pl. IV; Stager 2006b:16; *Ashkelon 1*, pp. 279–82), as well as Batash (A. Mazar and Panitz-Cohen 2001:273–76), but, when more complete evidence reemerges in the seventh century B.C.E., the material culture found there is even more similar to that of the neighboring cultures. Historically, most archaeologists have interpreted this similarity as the continuing process of assimilation. For example, S. Gitin (1992:31; 1995:74–75; 2010:325) has stated that the Philistines lost their "cultural core."[22] More recent excavations at Tell eṣ-Ṣafi have added greatly to our knowledge of the earlier part of the Iron II in Philistia. These results, combined with what is known from the earlier excavations at Ashdod, have suggested that this process of cultural adaptation had been largely completed by the end of Iron I or early Iron II (Uziel 2007; Faust and Lev-Tov 2011).

An important counter to the view of assimilation was provided by B. J. Stone (1995), who argued that the process witnessed at Philistine sites is not "assimilation" but "acculturation." In this process, various

[19] For detailed elaboration of this view, see for instance T. Dothan (1982:1–24); B. Mazar (1986); Stager (1998). In this study, I will adopt this conventional view of the Philistines without attempting to prove it. Nevertheless, the analysis of the types and iconography of Iron I Philistine figurines in particular (chapter 6; see secondarily the contextual analysis of chapter 7) supports this traditional interpretation, as do recent studies of Philistine pottery (e.g., Dothan and Zukerman 2004; Killebrew 2000) and architecture (Aja 2009), among other cultural features.

[20] Peter Machinist has brought to my attention a relevant article by de Vaux (1972), dealing with the possibility of the survival of Philistine identity into the Hellenistic period. The particular issue discussed is the pattern of Greek terms used to translate Hebrew *Pelištîm*, "Philistines." de Vaux concludes, however, that the Philistines of the Iron Age were no longer residing in Philistia in the Hellenistic period or at least had lost their identity and ethnic markers (contra Machinist 2000:57). Thus, at least part of the reason that the Septuagint does not employ the term Παλαιστῖνοι, in use at least since Herodotus, for the Philistines is that it was understood that the inhabitants of Palestine were no longer the biblical Philistines (1972:188). Similarly, when Nehemiah (13:24) refers to the "Ashdodite" language, it is merely a Phoenician dialect (de Vaux 1972:191; Stager 2006c:383).

[21] Barako (2001:11–34; see also 2000:522–24) gives a detailed survey of the various classes of material culture with probable Aegean antecedents. To his list should be added the recent publication of Cypro-Minoan inscriptions from Ashkelon, pointing to Cypriot, if not Aegean, connections (see Cross and Stager 2006).

[22] In more recent publications, Gitin (e.g., 2003:287; 2010:346) has adopted the concept of "acculturation" for this process first popularized in Philistine studies by B. J. Stone (see below), while still suggesting that the Philistine "cultural core" (or "core culture") had been lost or diluted by the seventh century.

traits of the surrounding cultures would have been accepted by the Philistines, but the underlying thought patterns would still be distinct; the result would be the maintenance of a separate, "Philistine," identity (B. J. Stone 1995:8–9). For Stone, although Philistine culture had been "completely transformed" between the twelfth and seventh centuries, it remained distinct from all neighboring cultures (1995:24). This general understanding has been shared by scholars in more recent studies, whether adopting the term "acculturation" or using others, such as "cultural fusion" (Uziel 2007).

Stone's criticism, while valuable, points to a possibly more fundamental problem with our understanding of Philistine culture, one that has remained largely undiscussed in the literature. While Stone (1995:10–11) criticized the usual equation of Philistine identity with specific elements of Philistine material culture (such as Monochrome or Bichrome pottery)—and, therefore, the subsequent loss of Philistine identity with the disappearance of these elements—he, like Syro-Palestinian archaeologists generally, has collapsed or confused different classes of categories given the same label, "Philistine."[23] For him, the terms "culture" and "ethnicity" (or "ethnic group") are often interchangeable. Yet the understanding reached by anthropologists over the last half-century concerning ethnicity, culture, and related concepts such as language suggests that there are in fact sharp distinctions in type between these groups.

In order to understand these distinctions, and how they have been dealt with in the scholarship of Syro-Palestinian archaeology, it is necessary to trace briefly the evolution of the concept of ethnicity in anthropology and archaeology. The terms "ethnicity" and "ethnic group" themselves do not have a long history in anthropological literature; they have in fact appeared, at least in their current meaning, only since the mid-1950s in any frequency (Zenner 1996:393). Before that time, groups of people were described as "races," "peoples," or "cultures"; there was no real differentiation among these terms, however, and they would often be used interchangeably. In the emerging culture-historical approach of the late nineteenth and early twentieth centuries, archaeological cultures were identified with specific groups of people (and with specific eras of time); thus, cultures were identified archaeologically by ceramic types and other characteristic remains—that is, with a list of common traits to be checkmarked.[24] The first systematic statement of this idea was G. Kossinna's *Die Herkunft der Germanen*, published in 1911. While Kossinna's efforts were largely recognized as racist,[25] his ideas in general (without their racist overtones) were taken up by other archaeologists; among them was V. G. Childe, who advocated the identification of recurring archaeological assemblages with cultures and in turn with peoples in *The Dawn of European Civilization* (1925). Thus, this concept of "cultural monoliths" found a wide circulation in the early twentieth century.

This view of culture can only be properly understood when put in its proper context—a progressively increasing nationalistic feeling in Europe from the nineteenth century into the twentieth. The emergence of archaeology itself was intimately connected with the rise of nationalism. While Kossinna might be the most notorious example, the movement to identify the prehistoric ancestors of various groups was a pan-European enterprise and even spread beyond (Trigger 1989:174–81). Because modern nations were increasingly viewing themselves as discrete, homogeneous groups with their own isolated cultural history, the prehistory of these nations was viewed in the same way, and archaeology in turn came to provide a legitimation of this view.

In anthropology, similar issues revolved around a discussion of ethnicity. As stated above, the term "ethnicity" only came into common usage around the mid-1950s. In a sense, the term "ethnic group" emerged concurrently with a new understanding of "people" and "culture"; the use of this term somehow reflects the sense of difficulty this concept of monolithic cultures presented (Jones 1997:51). At the same time, however, "ethnic group" was commonly used merely as a substitute for "race" or "tribe," without any change in conceptual framework (Zenner 1996:393). In any case, discussion and debate about the definition of "ethnic group" and "ethnicity" accelerated in

[23] Thus, Bunimovitz (1990:217–18) criticized the "pots and people" equation—the idea that there is generally a simple and direct correlation between a specific type of pottery and a specific ethnic group—automatically made by many archaeologists but then argued that the "eclectic" cultural elements identified by T. Dothan (1982) and others in Iron I Philistia are in fact evidence for the presence of Egyptians, Canaanites, and other ethnic groups. Similarly, Stone (1995:16) cited Bunimovitz's rejection of the pots and people equation but then equated the Philistine culture group in a geographical area with Philistine presence at a site.

[24] See Trigger 1989:163–81 for a more expansive treatment of this approach.

[25] See Jones 1997:ch. 1 for discussion.

the late 1960s and 1970s.[26] While a multiplicity of definitions of ethnicity was presented at the time, certain general trends are definitely identifiable. These include notions of self-identity and (claims to) common descent. In other words, definitions moved from a materialist or behavioral realm into an ideological one—or from an "etic" (outside) to an "emic" (inside) one.[27] Hicks (1977:2) has suggested that "ethnicity can most usefully be seen as an attribute of role."[28]

This shift to the ideological realm in particular follows an influential essay by F. Barth (1969a). Barth gives the definition of ethnic group as "generally understood in anthropological literature" as a group which:

> 1. is largely biologically self-perpetuating;
> 2. shares fundamental cultural values, realized in overt unity in cultural forms;
> 3. makes up a field of communication and interaction; and
> 4. has a membership which identifies itself, and is identified by others, as constituting a category distinguishable from other categories of the same order. (1969a:10–11)

As Barth points out, this definition, or at least the first three components, is merely a sophisticated treatment of the race = culture = language equation. For Barth, the last component—that of "self-ascription and ascription by others"—is the key characteristic (1969a:13).[29] These issues of identity center on the maintenance of a boundary between different ethnic groups. Thus, the notion of discovering "ethnic groups" in the archaeological remains of isolated, homogeneous units must be discarded.[30]

Despite the fact that they frequently acknowledge the work of Barth and other anthropologists, Near Eastern archaeologists ultimately seem to disregard the substance of the anthropological arguments and the ethnographic evidence from which they derive. Indeed, Near Eastern archaeologists frequently fall back on the traditional culture-historical approach.

---

[26] For this, see the essays in Barth (1969c); A. Cohen (1974b); Glazer and Moynihan (1974); and Hicks and Leis (1977).

[27] The use of the terms "emic" and "etic" for "inside" and "outside" viewpoints was first introduced by the linguist K. Pike (1954), on the basis of the linguistic terms "phonemic" and "phonetic." This usage was imported by M. Harris (e.g., 1964) into anthropology, where they were applied to views of culture.

[28] A similar process has taken place in the field of linguistics. The classic Saussurean model of a homogeneous "community of speakers" (see Saussure 1916) came under attack in the 1960s, with the work of D. Hymes (1968), J. J. Gumperz (1968), and others. These sociolinguists challenged the assumptions of both the homogeneity of the speech community and the one-to-one correspondence between groups of people and languages. Significantly, they did this in the context of empirical, ethnographic data, wishing to reflect reality rather than pigeonhole groups of people into a classificatory system formulated a priori. Hymes, for instance, noted numerous examples where these established concepts failed among the complex situations in Australia and the Eastern Niger Delta. Language for them does not comprise a set list of traits but a "variable system of codes" (Hymes 1968:36). A speech community is characterized by shared rules for understanding these codes, a "shared set of social norms" (Gumperz 1968:220); compare Hicks's view of ethnicity.

[29] Emphasis on self-identity as the key component of ethnicity should not be seen as original with Barth; as Hicks (1977:3) indicates, Max Weber reached similar conclusions in the 1920s.

[30] This redefinition of ethnicity has met with some resistance. Some criticize this view as too subjective (van den Berghe 1974:5) or circular in its reasoning (A. Cohen 1974a:xii). Sometimes it is misunderstood: "Ethnicity tends to be conceived by this school of thought as an essentially innate predisposition," A. Cohen incorrectly summarizes (1974a:xii). Some (van den Berghe 1974; Hicks 1977) argue for a combination of "objective" and "subjective" factors. This debate centers on one issue, namely whether "ethnic group" is to be seen as emic or etic.

Alternatively, I might suggest that the problem stems from an argument over semantics; terms such as "ethnicity" in fact have different meanings for different people today. Thus, W. Petersen (1974:177) observes:

> In Europe, *nation* is ordinarily understood literally, as a community based on common descent. Many American scholars, on the contrary, seem reluctant to use the very terms of genetic differentiation: they are likely to interpret *nation* as meaning "state," to eschew *race* altogether and substitute the presumably less sullied "ethnic group" (from the Greek rather than the Latin for the same concept).

The current use of a term such as "ethnic group," then, has shifted from its original meaning. By relating "ethnicity" to self-identity, anthropologists such as Barth have in effect redefined the term to address a void, a category that terms such as "people" or "nation" or "culture" do not fill.

Regardless of the above criticisms, there are numerous ethnographic examples which demonstrate serious flaws with the traditional concept of ethnicity (and its relationship to other types of groups) and support the newer approach. See for example Barth (1969b); J. P. Blom (1969); L. Stone (1977). As a result, this shift in the understanding of "ethnicity," and the work of Barth in particular, have continued to be very influential in anthropology (see, e.g., Shennan 1994b; Vermeulen and Govers 1994b). Thus, Vermeulen and Govers correctly note that Barth's "central tenets [including his focus on boundaries and ascription] are clearly formulated and still stand" (1994a:1).

Influenced by Barth, Kamp and Yoffee (1980) attempted a critique of scholarship on ethnicity in order to understand how it might be expressed in the archaeological record. Their treatment criticizes trait-list approaches to ethnicity in favor of the "interactional" definition (1980:88). They continue by outlining a method for the proper archaeological identification of ethnic groups, centering on clusters of behavior, including those presumed to be learned among members of the ethnic group (such as domestic activities). This definition, however, is in reality just a more sophisticated statement of the trait-list approach to ethnicity. Similarly, W. Dever (1995) suggested that ethnic groups are not necessarily impossible or even difficult to trace archaeologically. For him, artifacts are material correlates of behavior. While using the recurrence of one or a few artifact types would be methodologically faulty, in his view the occurrence of consistent assemblages of types can be termed an archaeological culture; in turn, these cultures can then be labeled as ethnic groups with the aid of texts.

The redefinition of ethnicity, however, has enormous implications for Syro-Palestinian archaeology. As we saw above, the shift in definition to the ideological realm signifies a shift from an etic to an emic approach. This seems to contrast with the use of the term "culture." As first popularized by V. Gordon Childe (1925), the concept of an archaeological culture—a complex of material culture traits found in consistent association—was both an emic and an etic unit. For Childe, the archaeological culture was equivalent with what we now think of as an ethnic group. This model of the archaeological culture was undermined by anthropologists such as Barth: thus, K. Verdery (1994:41) refers to "Barth's partial liberation of ethnicity from culture." As a purely etic unit, however, the archaeological culture is still seen by anthropological archaeologists as having some value (e.g., Shennan 1994a).[31]

This difference between the archaeological culture and the ethnic group only highlights the fact that they are two entirely different kinds of groups. They should not be seen as overlapping, and sometimes equivalent, but rather as crosscutting. This implication, however, is not accepted or realized by most Near Eastern archaeologists. When A. Mazar questions the ethnic attribution of the pillared house or the collared-rim pithos (1992a:347),[32] he does not call into question the theoretical framework behind such an attribution. In fact, he seems to support it in that he discounts it only in this one instance and only because such attributes are found in places with other cultures (= ethnic groups), rather than on the basis of a fundamental theoretical objection. The case of these "Israelite" features is marked out as an exception, an aberration. The approach to the case of Kanesh (Kültepe), where an Assyrian trading colony is archaeologically indistinguishable from the native Anatolian population, is treated similarly by Near Eastern archaeologists (Özgüç 1963). For the most part, it is implicitly accepted that ethnic groups and cultural groups usually overlap.

If, however, we view the equation of ethnicity and culture (or, alternatively, the understanding of ethnicity as both emic and etic simultaneously) as a model, then we must reject this model. When a model or explanation is successful only sometimes, it is not retained; it is discarded in favor of a better one. Therefore the idea that ethnicity, race, language, and culture overlap or equate, even as a general rule with some exceptions, is not tenable. A new model is needed and has been provided by anthropology (and linguistics) in the past 40 years.

The "laboratory case" of the Philistines helps to maintain the old model: the evidence of archaeology, the Bible, and other ancient texts all seem to converge in suggesting that a Philistine ethnic group with, at least originally, its own culture, language (presumed), and self-identity inhabited the southwestern coastal plain of Palestine (i.e., Philistia). Thus, their material culture is presented as a discrete assemblage (see Dothan 1982). But surely the situation was more complex. In such presentations of "Philistine" material culture, emphasis is placed on the Aegean elements; the local ones which existed alongside are commonly omitted. From the ethnographic evidence, as

[31] Note in this context E. Bloch-Smith's contrast of the "Culture Area" and "Meaningful Boundaries" (the latter based on Barth's conception of ethnicity) approaches (2003).

[32] The traditional identification of Israelites in Iron I Palestine is a typical example of the culture-historical approach. W. F. Albright, in his excavations at sites such as Bethel and Tell el-Fûl, noted a ceramic type that he designated the "collared store-jar" (or collared-rim pithos) to be "so characteristic of early Iron I in central Palestine" (1934:12). Considering the geographic location of this type—precisely in the area considered to be the Israelite homeland—it was naturally identified as characteristic of the early Israelites (Amiran 1970:232). Similarly, the typical Iron I dwelling in the central hill country, the "pillared" or "four-room" house, was seen as a marker of Israelite ethnicity (Mazar 1992a:340–43). These recurring elements of material culture from the Iron I hill country were put together into a trait list of the early Israelite culture (and people), one which has been extremely influential in Syro-Palestinian archaeology. The idea has been disproved more recently, as it has been observed that both the collared-rim pithos and the pillared house have been found outside of the Israelite heartland in Palestine as well as in Transjordan (see for example Mazar 1992a:343–47).

well as the evidence of modern-day societies we can see around us, we can conclude that the inhabitants of Philistia would not have been a clearly bounded, homogeneous group; without doubt several ethnic groups called Philistia home. Yet how do we recognize them? The difference between local and foreign cultural traditions, as we have seen, cannot aid in distinguishing ethnic groups. Non-Philistine ethnic groups could have used Philistine pottery just as easily as the Philistines could have used non-Philistine pottery. Moreover, Philistines could certainly have lived outside of Philistia proper, just as easily as non-Philistines within Philistia.[33]

These questions point to a second implication of the shift in definition of ethnicity. Ethnic groups cannot be distinguished in the archaeological record without recourse to textual evidence. With the aid of texts that indicate the specific markers that ethnic groups used to maintain their boundaries, it might be possible to distinguish them in the archaeological record. Here, the case of the Israelites and the Philistines appears to work well. On the basis of the biblical evidence, if we admit it as valid, we can isolate certain markers (diet, circumcision) which the Israelites used to mark a boundary between themselves and the Philistines. We must be cautious in applying such a method, however. In addition, there are always difficulties in the use of texts. Even with the aid of texts, identification of ethnic groups is a difficult enterprise at best. On the other hand, at least study of the Philistines—unlike prehistoric archaeology—has this possibility.

I realize that this understanding of "ethnicity"—as separate from culture, as an emic, but not an etic unit—will not be accepted (at least fully) by most archaeologists working in Israel. Instead, the culture-historical approach is still seen as largely valid. This state of affairs may be gradually changing, with increased attention being given to issues of ethnicity and culture in ancient Israel (e.g., Killebrew 2005; Faust 2006). Thus, Faust, although including only a brief discussion of the anthropological theory of ethnicity and culture (2006:11–16), recognizes the fundamental fact that the post-processual approach to ethnicity from the 1960s on is a normative one (2006:14). Faust also recognizes that, while in some cases there may be a relationship between elements of material culture and ethnicity, this relationship can be an indirect one (2006:196). In addition, following the work of B. J. Stone (1995), several more recent studies have focused on Philistine ethnicity in particular and have helped to provide a more nuanced and complex understanding of this subject (e.g., Uziel 2007; Faust and Lev-Tov 2011).

[33] Thus, Bunimovitz's argument (1990) that the so-called eclectic culture of Iron I Philistia represents multiple ethnic groups is not necessarily correct; there is no direct correlation between the presence of multiple cultural assemblages and multiple ethnic groups.

Summary

A proper discussion of Philistine figurines needs to address two different sets of issues: one concerning the concept of "figurine," and one concerning the concept of "Philistine." The issues in the first set involve the nature of how anthropomorphic and zoomorphic figurines are treated and what range of interpretations figurines might have (i.e., are they simply to be viewed as either cult objects or toys, or are there additional possibilities?). Underlying this set of issues are the basic questions that the archaeologist should ask about figurines. The usual questions asked about the figurines of ancient Palestine are "What is the identity of the figure represented?" and "Is the figure human or divine?" Better are a different set of questions: "What are the meaning(s) and function(s) of these figurines?" and "To what extent can we identify their meaning(s) and function(s)?"

The second set of issues involves the problematic equation of ethnicity and culture. While anthropologists have come to redefine the former and separate these two concepts (the former being -emic, the latter -etic), Syro-Palestinian archaeologists still often view them—in practice even if not in theory—as identical. Moreover, ethnicity is difficult to identify in the archaeological record and depends upon textual evidence for support. Culture, meanwhile, must be clearly defined: when we discuss Philistine culture, do we mean the culture of Philistia? Or do we mean specific types or styles of artifacts, wherever they are found? The archaeologist should choose a definition that is single, clear, and consistent before embarking on a study of material culture. In the following two chapters, I will show how the success or failure in properly defining the term "Philistine" has fundamentally affected understandings of the figurines of Philistia.

3. History of Research

My purpose in this chapter is to give an overview of the research into Palestinian figurines. Of greatest importance to this present study is the work done on classifying and analyzing groups of Philistine figurines; in surveying the literature I will highlight the work that has, or has not, been done both in advancing the state of knowledge and in providing a usable framework for conducting such studies. Therefore I will not include a detailed look at excavation history or more general discussions of figurines and their functions. I will, however, include some of the significant surveys of Palestinian figurines more generally, both because of the methodological value they provide and, especially, because of their role in contributing to our understanding of Philistine and related types.

Within this survey, I will also investigate the theoretical backing for the different studies. Do they address all or any of the concerns highlighted in chapter 2? If they do address them, in what ways do they do so?

Early Research

Studies of Palestinian figurines can be traced back to the work of E. Pilz (1924). Pilz compiled an exhaustive catalogue of the female figurines excavated and published up to that point, dividing them by formal types. His listing, which included figurines from all periods and of materials other than clay (such as metal, stone, and faience), totaled 123 objects. Besides presenting his catalogue, Pilz discussed the origins of his various types and suggested identifications for the figures.

Pilz's study formed the basis, and set the general boundaries, for further research in the realm of figurines. Thus, Galling, in his brief entry on clay images of female deities (1937:230–32), did not provide a comprehensive study or even survey of the finds but merely updated Pilz's catalogue by including figurines published in the late 1920s and early 1930s. Albright, meanwhile, dealt with female figurines in a variety of works in the late 1930s and 1940s (e.g., 1939, 1942, 1943), based particularly on his important excavations at Tell Beit Mirsim. These were generally brief treatments, however, in the context of much broader questions of archaeology, history, and religion; Albright devoted only one article (1939) specifically to figurines, and this focused only on certain types he viewed as "hitherto insufficiently defined" (1939:108). He cited Pilz as exhaustive, although he noted that, given the state of knowledge at the time of Pilz's study, many of his chronological conclusions (which were tentative to begin with) were now seen as wrong (1939:108). He then proceeded to provide a refined chronology for his types.

The first researcher to attempt a fresh look at Palestinian figurines was J. B. Pritchard (1943). Pritchard was the first to devote an entire monograph to figurines, again focusing on representations of women. By this time, the number of published figurines had more than doubled from that available to Pilz—including many found in datable contexts, unlike a large portion of the earliest finds. Beyond this fact, as Pritchard himself recognized, the techniques of pottery dating had been refined, and the regions neighboring Palestine had provided a large amount of comparative material (1943:1). Like Pilz, he also embarked on a general discussion of the origins and identities of the types.

Summary of Early Research

The early research on Palestinian figurines displays several notable trends:

1. Perhaps most obviously, the majority of scholarly attention was devoted to female figurines. This state of affairs is certainly understandable, considering that representations of women tend to dominate among the anthropomorphic terracottas (as noted in chapter 2). Still, this does not explain the lack of attention given to zoomorphic figurines.[1] The result of this emphasis is a failure to discuss the full range of figurine types adequately. Pilz, though comprehensive in his treatment of female figurines (and so of anthropomorphic figurines generally), entirely ignored the zoomorphs. Pritchard, meanwhile, not only omitted the animal figurines, but provided only a selection of the total number of figurines excavated; he claims that this selection "is sufficiently large to represent a fair sample of the various types" (1943:84). He does not give any means to verify

[1] This lack of attention is particularly noteworthy, since representations of animals are more prevalent in the coroplastic repertory of Palestine than those of humans. As noted above in chapter 2, 1555 of Holland's corpus of 2655 objects were zoomorphic (1977:124). The most attention given to zoomorphic figurines in early research was by H. G. May in his discussion of figurine types found at Megiddo (1935:27–34), where he devoted one paragraph to them.

this claim independently, however; there is no list or indication of the total number (or percentage by type) of figurines found.

2. The figurines studied (i.e., the female figurines) were generally assumed to represent divinities.[2] Pilz, Albright, and Pritchard all referred to this view explicitly in the titles of their studies. Galling, meanwhile, included his survey of female figurines in his discussion of "female divine images." Pritchard alone offered caution in this identification. While he noted the consensus in the identification of the figurines, he himself concluded that there was no real evidence that these figurines could be identified with any of the major goddesses of Palestine or even that they represented goddesses at all (1943:86–87).

3. None of these early studies focused on the archaeological setting of the figurines. In his catalogue, Pilz provided a rough date for each figurine according solely to the stratum in which it was found. He completely ignored their context, however, or the finds associated with them. Even Albright limited his archaeological discussions to the strata of the finds and their chronological implications. It does not appear that a more detailed investigation of context was considered necessary or even important at the time; thus, Pilz could claim, in his subtitle, that he was providing "eine archäologische Studie."

4. A fairly standard procedure was established for figurine study: the body of the work begins with a typology and a catalogue arranged by type; following this is a discussion of origins and identities of figurines, by type. Pilz first established this format in his study; later it was expanded by Pritchard, who specifically focused on the imagery and its iconography and concluded by trying to relate the figurines to textual sources.

5. Finally, it is worth noting the general progress in the state of the knowledge over this period. In two decades the number of female figurines available for study more than doubled; thus, the length of a study dealing with them increased from an ordinary article to a short monograph. The primary reason for this progress, of course, was the continuing work of excavations and the increasing number of sites published. Despite this fact, however, none of these studies included any figurines from Philistia, as none of the sites of this region had yet been extensively excavated.[3]

Holland's Study

The last trend noted above—the steadily increasing knowledge of figurines through continuing and additional excavations—eventually left Pritchard's and Pilz's catalogues and conclusions outdated. By the 1970s, enough material had been collected that T. Holland (1975; see also 1977) was able to dedicate a doctoral thesis simply to Palestinian figurines of the Iron Age.[4] Holland's approach was therefore already different from previous studies, in focusing on figurines from a particular period. At the same time, Holland's work was notable as the first attempted study of the entire range of terracottas—including male and zoomorphic figurines—and not just a particular type or set of types. As with the preceding studies, Holland included figurines from the entire region of Palestine; given the increasing number of sites being excavated, however, Holland's corpus was representative of

[2] This consensus is not shared merely by those studying the figurines in detail. Pritchard (1943:2–3) provides an extensive survey of opinion up to that point, almost unanimously suggesting that the female figurines depict goddesses; in addition, a number of scholars provided opinions as to which particular goddess(es) are represented. Against this, H. G. May claimed (1935:1):

> Of late years there has been a tendency to decry the interpretation of archaeological finds in terms of religion or the cult. Mother-goddess figurines become dolls; animal figurines and rattles become toys; and the snake, dove, tree, and pomegranate motives become pure decoration.

[3] Petrie had worked at Tell Jemmeh (which he identified as Gerar) for one season, during which he recovered a large corpus of (mostly Iron II) figurines (1928:pls. 35–39); his extensive work at other sites in southern Palestine, notably Tell el-ᶜAjjul and Tell el-Farᶜah (S), produced little in the way of Iron Age terracottas. Excavation at the major Pentapolis sites consisted largely of soundings, such as Phythian-Adams's at Gaza and Ashkelon (1923a; 1923b).

[4] Holland's Ph.D. thesis (1975), despite its importance, has remained unpublished, and I have been unable to consult it extensively myself. Holland did publish a summary (1977), but the main focus of the article was on the eighth- and seventh-century figurines, particularly in relation to the important context of Cave 1 in Jerusalem.

Holland defined the Iron Age as the period from ca. 1200 B.C.E. to the mid-fourth century B.C.E. (Holland 1977:121); in the terminology adopted by the present study, this period is covered by Iron I and II and the Persian period. I will be concerned only with the period up to the end of the seventh century B.C.E. (the date of the destruction of the Philistine cities by Nebuchadnezzar II); reference will be made, however, to figurines of the early Persian period, as in some cases these continue earlier traditions.

the entire region. Holland was therefore the first researcher to include figurines from a subregion such as Philistia (the first major excavation of a Philistine site had begun at Ashdod only in 1962).[5] The wide scope of Holland's study, and the detailed typology he developed, allowed figurines such as those from Philistia to be placed in the wider context of Palestinian figurines as a whole; at the same time, this scope meant that any such subset could not be discussed in great detail.

Iron II Figurines

The developments reflected in Holland's work made a comprehensive study of Palestinian figurines no longer feasible; following Holland's thesis, and the steady increase in the corpus of figurines, no scholar has attempted to study the complete range of Palestinian figurines.[6] At the same time, these developments allowed for more attention to be given to particular subsets of Palestinian figurines: figurines of a certain period, such as the Iron Age, and also to certain subregions.[7] The area of greatest attention was the hill country, particularly the area of the kingdom of Judah. In particular, the Judean "pillar figurines" have become a major focus of study, largely because of interest in Judahite religion and the widely drawn connection between these figurines and the goddess Asherah.[8] Most noteworthy among these are the studies of Engle (1979) and Kletter (1996).

Engle's interest in the pillar figurines centers on their identification with Asherah; as a result, he highlights the textual evidence concerning the figurines. His study, then, is not primarily archaeological in nature and devotes little space to a discussion of the figurines in their contexts. One of the major problems with Engle's work is typological in nature. Unlike Holland (who catalogued the entire range of figurines and then divided them by types), Engle starts with a "classic" or "standard" type of pillar figurine (as exemplified by those found at Tell Beit Mirsim) and then proceeds to classify others by their resemblance to these figurines (1979:9). While Engle's corpus is fairly comprehensive, he ignores the full range of the data in focusing on a subset as "standard." Such a focus on "ideal types" is suspect, moreover, in that it circularly confirms the "classic" character of a specific group of figurines—those from Tell Beit Mirsim (cf. the critique of Hadley [2000:19, 197]). Another fundamental issue is Engle's use of a single criterion for classification: the shape of the eyes (1979:10). Such a choice assumes that the shape of the eyes would have been of primary significance to the ancient peoples who produced these figurines; it does not take into account what effect, for instance, the reuse and damage of particular molds might have. Thus, Engle's system is ultimately arbitrary and not particularly helpful for those studying Palestinian figurines.

Kletter's study (1996) discusses the same basic problem: the Judean "pillar figurine" (JPF, in his terminology) and its meaning. Whereas Engle's interpretations rested primarily on textual evidence, Kletter's study is primarily archaeological. It is also systematic. Kletter prefaces the body of his work with a history of the research (1996:10–27) in order to demonstrate the lack of an "updated, systematic catalogue" and the lack of evidence supporting a particular explanation (1996:27). He then continues with a typology, not just of the JPFs but of anthropomorphic Iron Age figurines from Palestine generally (1996:28–39); the dating of the JPFs (40–42); their distribution (both between Judah and other regions and among sites within Judah; 42–48); a study of their manufacture (49–53); breakage patterns (54–56); archaeological context (57–67); historical analogies (68–72); and finally their meaning and function (73–81). His appendices include a

[5] See Dothan and Dothan (1992) for a discussion of the progress of excavations at Ashdod and other Philistine sites.

[6] An exception to this general situation is the work of Keel and Uehlinger (1998). Keel and Uehlinger, however, are not interested specifically in figurines but all forms of iconography, as well as epigraphic evidence. They also do not simply survey the Iron Age material but begin with Middle Bronze IIB (ca. 1800) and continue into the Persian period, ca. 450, which they label the end of Iron III (1998:5). Their purpose is to survey the iconography of Palestine (Israel) as a whole and use iconographic and epigraphic sources together to answer a set of questions; these questions relate not to the specific identity of the deities but to their meaning and function (1998:2). Note that this formulation: a) assumes that the figurines and other iconography represent deities, and b) focuses on the roles and functions—i.e., the conceptualization—of the actual deities, rather than on how their representations were used. Thus, Keel and Uehlinger write that the main purpose of their study is an attempt "to reconstruct the religious system (*belief*)" (1998:10), as opposed to the cult or religious practices that express such beliefs.

[7] In addition to the works cited below, I should note the studies of M. Tadmor (1982; 1996) and P. Beck (e.g., 1986; 1990; and 1995, now collected in Beck 2002a). Their publications, however, generally focus on either LB figurines or types not generally found in Philistia and so are not directly relevant to the current study.

[8] For a survey of this opinion in the recent literature, see Kletter (1996:76–77). The pillar figurine, a common type in the later Iron Age, is a nude female figurine whose lower body is in the form of a column. The association of the goddess Asherah with the "sacred tree" has led to the identification of this figure with Asherah, based on the suggestion that the column or pillar is in fact meant to represent a tree trunk (e.g., by Hestrin [1991:57]).

catalogue of the JPFs and of other types (the basis for his typology in the body of the work). Notably, the range of topics covered in Kletter's study does not include iconography; he does not analyze the imagery represented in the JPFs in any great detail. Still, the multifaceted nature of Kletter's study is valuable as a model for future research on Palestinian figurines; specifically, his focus on archaeological issues, such as context, marks an important distinction from most previous work on figurines. Kletter is also more cautious than many previous researchers; he does not assume that the figurines represent a deity but concludes that they do (specifically, that the JPFs represent Asherah) after surveying and evaluating the range of suggested interpretations (1996:81). In addition, Kletter's typology of the JPFs is ultimately more useful than Engle's; after basing his main types on technique (handmade heads, A, vs. moldmade heads, B), he introduces a series of subtypes for the handmade heads that involve the application of different features to the head ("turbans," sidelocks, hats, etc.; 1996:29).

For the figurines of Philistia, on the other hand, the value of Kletter's work is naturally limited. He mentions Philistine figurines only in passing, mostly in the typology and catalogue, as well as in stray JPF finds in Philistia. Nevertheless, his exhaustive catalogue has value for anyone studying Palestinian figurines of the Iron Age.

While the pillar figurines have received a large amount of attention, other types and other regions in Iron II have been largely ignored. Thus, no large-scale work has been devoted to the Iron II figurines of Philistia, for instance. The only study of any type on this group of figurines is that published by E. Stern (2001). Although it is only a general discussion of the material culture of Palestine in the late Iron Age and Persian period, Stern's work provides analysis not available elsewhere. Stern surveys the various regions of Palestine (including Judah, Israel, Phoenicia, and Philistia) and identifies the major classes of figurines in each. He finds that the major classes in each region are largely of the same two basic types (the nude woman and the horse-and-rider)—a widely made observation. For him, this observation reflects the use of a common model—that of the Phoenicians—for clay figurines (as for other objects and realms) throughout Palestine, as well as the existence of a common major cult (2001:79). He also concludes, however, that there are regional variants of these basic types with noticeable differences between them.

Stern divides his discussion of material culture of the seventh century by region (or people); he introduces the main figurine types in his discussion of the Phoenician material culture, as he recognizes the Phoenician types as the model for all other regional variants in Palestine. This method of organization, however, leads him to tend toward repetition when dealing with the figurines of other regions (peoples) and to lack an integrated survey of Palestinian figurines overall. Nevertheless, the actual conclusions he reaches and the evidence he cites are important contributions to the study of Iron II Philistine figurines. He suggests, for instance, that the figurines of Ashkelon are in a local style found only in Philistia (2001:114). He compares the decoration of Ashdod figurines to that of the Ashdodite pottery and finds both similarities with the surrounding "nations" and distinct features among the published finds from Ashdod (2001:121). Meanwhile, he points to distinctive features of figurines from other Philistine sites, probably representing "local subtypes" as in other elements of material culture (such as script). As for the Philistine figurines, Stern not only identifies them as exhibiting these two basic types, but he also suggests the existence of subregional variants among the different parts of Philistia itself.

Because the figurines comprise only a small topic in Stern's entire work, he cannot go into much greater detail. Thus, he cannot provide a detailed typology, a step-by-step procedure for analysis, or even a comprehensive look at the figurines. He also does not have space to study the contexts of the figurines in any detail; still, Stern manages to draw distinctions among the different types both on a regional and a site level. As for Stern's interpretation of the figurines—that they belong in the realm of cult representations of deities—he for the most part simply accepts the traditional view without evaluation.

An additional problem appears in these Iron II studies. In the early studies on figurines, the corpus was defined as that coming from the entire region of Palestine. Because the corpus was bounded geographically, there was little need for discussion of ethnic and cultural issues. With the more limited bounds of these Iron II studies, however, these issues are of greater importance yet rarely addressed. Stern, for instance, simply identifies the material culture of each region with the people (i.e., the ethnic group) inhabiting it. Kletter, meanwhile, identifies the pillar figurines as characteristic of Judah. He notes that he is "speaking about Judah and the Judeans here as political (and not ethnic) entities" (Kletter 1996:45), but this merely emphasizes another aspect of the race = culture = language equation. Kletter's subsequent work, such as "Pots and Polities" (1999), makes this equation even more explicit.

Iron I Figurines

As with the Iron II material, no research was conducted on figurines of Iron I Philistia in the first half of the century. Therefore, the publication of T. Dothan's *The Philistines and Their Material Culture* in 1967 was a major step forward, even if it included only a brief discussion of the figurines (181–84). The English, updated version, published in 1982, included a greatly expanded discussion of the terracottas. Dothan devoted a chapter (32 pages) to "cult and cult vessels," within which she surveyed certain types of Philistine figurines. This chapter was the first published discussion devoted to Iron I Philistine figurines.[9] Because of these facts, and especially because of the effect that Dothan's work has had on the subsequent literature, it will be necessary to review this study in greater detail.

Dothan focused on a few specific figurines, particularly those that appear to have Aegean affinities.[10] She then used these as the basis of her categories (i.e., as if they were "ideal types"). Nowhere does she give an indication of the percentage of the total corpus of Iron I figurines that might belong to each of her types. Beyond this, she began her discussion with a selection of objects from the Gezer cache (first published by R. A. S. Macalister in 1912) which "appears to be an early assemblage of Philistine cultic vessels and figurines," both for their inherent value and to introduce the "principal types" (1982:219). Gezer, far from being a major Philistine center, was a peripheral site on the shifting border with Judah (see chapter 4). The "Gezer cache," then, is hardly the ideal group to use for an introduction to the range of Philistine types.

Dothan made an important contribution in distinguishing two basic types of female figurines in the Iron I (1982:234): seated figures (the "Ashdoda") and standing ones (particularly the "mourning figurine"). As with much of early Philistine material culture, Dothan traced both types back to the Mycenaean world of the Aegean; she found some parallels to the first type on the Greek mainland and Cyprus and compared the second type with a small group of figurines discussed by Iakovidis (1966; see Dothan 1982:234, 242–44). The exact definition of these types, however, is suspect to a greater or lesser degree. The "Ashdoda" type was identified on the basis of one (nearly) complete example. As for the standing type, her survey did not consider the entire range but dealt exclusively with those in a mourning gesture (i.e., with hands to the head). The "mourning figurine" type has six examples (there are photographs and drawings of only five of these), but most are too fragmentary or too crude to allow a detailed analysis; the actual identification of the type as a "mourning figurine" is based primarily on two examples, which had been earlier published by Dothan (1969; 1973). Neither of these examples, however, was found in an excavation: one was from the collection of the Israel Museum, the other in the personal collection of Moshe Dayan (for references, see Dothan 1982:240; 1969:42; 1973:120–21). The provenance of these figurines—both their place of origin and their date—is therefore unknown. Dothan cited neutron activation analysis (NAA) results for the clay of one of these figurines as sufficient evidence that they are from the tombs of Tell ᶜAitun; the NAA tests supposedly demonstrated that the clay of the figurine was from the Lachish region (the region of Tell ᶜAitun), as was (according to Dothan) the clay of pottery tested from these tombs (see Dothan 1982:237; but cf. Perlman and Asaro 1969; see discussion in chapter 6). She subsequently referred to them as "the ᶜAitun examples" without any further evidence. Even if this conclusion were correct, Tell ᶜAitun is, like Gezer, on the periphery of Philistia, and its very identification as "Philistine" in terms of culture, or political control, is questionable (see figure 1 and discussion in chapter 4). Meanwhile, the lack of provenance calls into question not only whether these figurines are Philistine, but whether they are even authentic. Any question about their authenticity would be supported by their stylistic uniqueness. While Philistine figurines tend to be even cruder and less naturalistic than the Mycenaean antecedents that have been identified, these two "mourning figurines" are in fact more naturalistic and completely unlike any other published Philistine examples. At any rate, even if these figurines are genuine, they are a very poor basis for the identification of a basic type.

Dothan's treatment of figurines focused almost exclusively on female representations. Males and animals are virtually absent; the only other figurines Dothan referred to are a lyre player from Ashdod (in connection with the Ashdod musician stand) and a single male figurine from Tell eṣ-Ṣafi. Thus, Dothan's survey of Philistine figurines is not comprehensive and focuses on anomalies as the basis of ideal types.

Dothan's work on the figurines, like that she conducted on Philistine material culture (of the Iron

[9] Previously, Iron I types had been discussed briefly by Hachlili (1971). Holland (1975) had included material from Philistia in his study of Iron Age figurines, which was finished between the Hebrew and English publications of Dothan's work; as a doctoral thesis, however, it was not officially published.

[10] For the Aegean affinities of Philistine material culture generally and their implications, see discussion in chapter 2 above and references there.

I) generally, was taken as authoritative. Some of its conclusions—especially that the two unprovenanced mourning figurines are definitely from Tell ᶜAitun and that the mourning figurine was a major Philistine type—entered the literature virtually unchallenged.[11] Thus, A. Mazar in *Archaeology of the Land of the Bible, 10,000—586 B.C.E.*, a standard textbook for courses in biblical archaeology and Syro-Palestinian archaeology, refers to a figurine "[f]ound in a tomb at Tel Eitun" (1992a:324), and includes only the "Ashdoda" and the "mourning" figurine as Philistine types with Mycenaean antecedents (1992a:323).[12] Dothan herself did not attempt a detailed analysis of figurine types and so did not conclude that the Ashdoda and mourning figurine were the only two types in existence in Iron I Philistia. In addition, she did more properly refer to seated and standing figurines in her work. Nevertheless, because of the acceptance of Dothan's work as definitive, these two types are generally seen as the exclusive Philistine types in Iron I.

There has been very little subsequent study of the Iron I figurines. Starting in the late 1990s, however, detailed studies began to appear. The first, by R. Schmitt (1999), focuses on Iron I types generally. Schmitt's study is the first to provide a systematic survey and analysis of the entire range of Iron I anthropomorphic figurines (with a catalogue of 112 items). It is also the first to note that all Iron I anthropomorphic figurines cannot simply be categorized as either Ashdodas or mourning figurines; alongside these he introduces the Ψ (Psi) type, as well as multiple types of male figurines. Still, the change from the consensus view is not great, as he assigns most of the female terracottas to the categories of mourning figurine and Ashdoda. It appears that Schmitt is in this regard simply following the designations of the individual excavation reports, rather than independently evaluating them and creating his own typology.[13] This process leads to inconsistent, and ultimately unsatisfactory, results.

As with other researchers conducting regional studies, Schmitt has difficulty defining the culture he is studying. He includes figurines from sites outside of Philistia in his catalogue (e.g., Megiddo and Beth-Shean). He therefore seems to define Philistine figurines as figurines of certain type (regardless of findspot) and then circularly uses this preselected group to determine type. While including the standard typology, and discussion of types, he only briefly considers their function and meaning. Moreover, while he surveys the finds site by site, he does not give any further consideration of archaeological context.

Of a different nature is the study by A. Yasur-Landau (2001). Yasur-Landau provides the first detailed study dedicated to a specific class of Philistine figurines, the Ashdoda. As such, it represents progress, in terms of both attention to Philistine figurines and our accumulation of knowledge. He begins his discussion with both the range of views on the Ashdoda in the scholarly literature of Palestinian Iron Age archaeology and a more general consideration of the interpretation of figurines. He then provides a procedure to answer essential questions about the Ashdoda given these theoretical considerations—including whether the Ashdoda represents a human or divine figure, in addition to the actual function of the figurines. The steps to this procedure include analyzing the iconography of the Ashdoda figurines themselves, analyzing the iconography of similar figures (in the art of the Aegean, the proposed origin of the Ashdoda form), and analyzing the find contexts of the figurines (2001:331). Before this, the first task Yasur-Landau embarks on is a basic typology and catalogue. He concludes with an attempt to relate the Ashdoda to textual material (specifically, the Ekron inscription mentioning the goddess *ptgyh*). Yasur-Landau suggests that the figurine is a goddess,

[11] Dothan herself has not clarified this situation in later years. Thus, in the popular account of the search for the Philistines (*People of the Sea*) that she wrote with her husband, Dothan states:

> Although Tell Aitun was relatively far from the main Philistine cities, the extent of Aegean influence on the burial customs was evident. Later, when I was able to locate a number of artifacts from the site in private collections, I recognized an unusual class of female figurines, isolated examples of which had previously been found at Ashdod, Azor, and other sites along the coast. (Dothan and Dothan 1992:200)

She gives no indication of the problematic nature of their provenance.

[12] See also Mazar 1992b:275 for a reference to mourning figurines found at cemeteries of Azor and Tell ᶜAitun. I can attest personally to the effect of this consensus on the Ashkelon excavations. Although not a single figurine has been found in a mourning gesture—i.e., with hands to the head—generally any small anthropomorphic (or possibly anthropomorphic) figurine from the Iron I is immediately labeled a "mourning figurine" (or else an "Ashdoda").

[13] For instance, the Qasile figurine that Schmitt classifies as part of Typ II (mourning figurines) is described as a "mourning woman" by A. Mazar (1986:14). Schmitt classifies two similar figurines from Ashdod (M. Dothan 1971:fig. 65.10; M. Dothan and Porath 1982:fig 34:2)—one of which is specifically compared to the Mycenaean Ψ figurines (Hachlili 1971:131)—as part of his Typ I (Ψ figurines); he places all of the other anthropomorphic terracottas from Ashdod, which are labeled as "Ashdoda" or simply as "head," under his Typ III (Ashdoda).

and he even attempts to identify that goddess (*ptgyh*/Gaia).[14] He also draws some conclusions, through his iconographic and contextual analyses, about the basic function(s) of the figurines within Philistine society.

In many respects, Yasur-Landau's work represents progress in the treatment of Philistine figurines. Although he can only provide a brief discussion of theoretical and methodological concerns, given the format and setting of the article, the very presence of this discussion is noteworthy as it is lacking in all prior studies. Beyond this, he outlines a detailed procedure before he begins his study. This procedure includes both iconographic analysis and discussion of archaeological context. Yasur-Landau does not challenge the traditional interpretation of female figurines as goddesses, but he does include iconographic evidence to support this conclusion (2001:332–35).

More recently, D. Ben-Shlomo has focused attention on a group of Philistine figurines almost completely neglected in prior studies: the zoomorphic figurines (e.g., Ben-Shlomo in press; see also Ben-Shlomo and Press 2009). Careful attention to this group has allowed him to identify previously unknown types in Philistia. In addition, his work parallels that of Yasur-Landau by including considerations of context.

[14] Unfortunately, it is not yet possible to identify the goddess *ptgyh*, and, thus, the correlation of *ptgyh* with Gaia is unfounded (Press 2012:16). Additionally, there is not always a direct correlation between the figurine assemblages of a cultural group and its pantheon (Press 2012:8).

Summary

The history of Philistine figurine studies can be divided into two major periods. The first, running from the 1920s to the 1960s, is essentially the "prehistory" of this field; finds from Philistia were in fact not generally included in these studies. Overall, the research was of a more general nature, focusing on the entire area of Palestine. Studies were selective within this corpus, however, focusing exclusively on female figurines, which were widely interpreted as representations of goddesses. The major components of these studies were a typology and a discussion of the types (mostly in terms of their origin). There was no attempt made to discuss theoretical problems in studying figurines or to cite the figurines within their archaeological contexts.

With the gradual increase in the number and range of figurines excavated, a second phase in Philistine figurine studies began. Holland (1975) provided the first comprehensive, detailed typology of figurines, focusing exclusively on one period (the Iron Age). Subsequent researchers limited their scope even more, both chronologically and by region. Kletter (in the study of Judean pillar figurines) and Schmitt and Yasur-Landau (with respect to Iron I types from Philistia) began to look more systematically and comprehensively at smaller groups of figurines. In these studies of the last fifteen years, we see the beginnings of a systematic, comprehensive approach to subsets of figurines and the development of appropriate methodology.

4. Method

As we saw in chapter 3, no exhaustive study has been conducted on Philistine figurines. Archaeologists have only begun detailed study of the Iron I corpus and have not conducted any detailed research on the Iron II material at all. Certainly, no work has attempted to combine the two periods, in order to understand the development and use of Philistine terracottas over the course of the Iron Age. With excavation having proceeded sufficiently far, then, a complete study of the Iron Age Philistine figurine corpus is both feasible and needed.

In addition to the lack of exhaustive surveys of Philistine figurines, archaeologists have, in my view, failed to develop sufficient methods to study these figurines. In chapter 2, I discussed a series of methodological issues relevant to a study of Philistine terracottas. I then highlighted in chapter 3 how scholars studying Philistine figurines (and Palestinian figurines generally) have approached these issues. Building on their work, I hope to develop an appropriate methodology for the current study.

In the process of evaluating the methodologies employed in previous studies and devising a methodology for this one, I have developed a set of criteria that I believe are essential for a thorough study of figurines (or for groups of artifacts more generally). These criteria include the following characteristics:

1. Bounded—The study must include a corpus that is clearly defined from the start; in theory, this could be in terms of a geographically defined region or by characteristics of the figurines themselves (form, style, etc.).

2. Comprehensive—The study must include all examples within the boundaries established for the corpus, or at least as many examples as possible. It should not focus simply on a few ideal types or special figurines, those assumed to be characteristic, or complete figurines, many of which may turn out to be anomalous.

3. Systematic—The study must proceed in a consistent, logical, predetermined manner; ideally, this system should be explicitly stated.

4. Archaeological—The study must not simply apply an iconographic-iconological/art historical method; rather, it should adapt this method to an archaeological corpus, considering all aspects of figurines as archaeological artifacts. This involves looking at figurines in context: as a tool to see how they may have been used, as well as to look for differing distribution patterns between/among groups or areas. Ideally, it also includes study of the figurines' clay, breakage patterns, wear patterns, etc.

In this chapter I will discuss in greater detail what I mean by these criteria. In the process (as well as in the following chapters) I hope to show how the flaws of prior figurine studies have resulted from incomplete use of these criteria, or their lack of use entirely—in particular focusing on T. Dothan's *The Philistines and Their Material Culture* (1982).[1] More importantly, I will use the discussion of these criteria to form a methodology for dealing with the figurines, one which I will lay out clearly at the end of this chapter and then apply over the following chapters of this study.

Bounded

It is essential that I begin by giving a clear definition of the corpus with which I will be working. This step has in fact typically been omitted in studies of Philistine figurines. As a result, T. Dothan (1982) and Schmitt (1999) both included material from peripheral regions or from sites outside of Philistia. In particular, the figurines emphasized by Dothan were mostly from sites on the periphery of Philistia since at the time of her study the figurine corpus from the Pentapolis was limited to Ashdod, as Ashkelon and Miqne had yet to be excavated. Dothan and Schmitt may perhaps have been defining "Philistine" in terms of formal characteristics of the figurines themselves rather than in terms of a geographic region or culture area called "Philistia," but, if this is the case, they do not make this definition explicit. The reader is largely left to guess.

My first step, then, is to define what I mean by the term "Philistine." As I discussed in chapter 2, the term "Philistine" has been used in a variety of ways, often with a combination of these intended at once: to describe an archaeological culture, an ethnic group, a political entity, a geographical area, and a language. Because these are different kinds of groups entirely, it is vital that the researcher state which meaning he is using. (It is precisely this lack of statement which

[1] I do not by any means intend to single out Dothan as the only researcher to ignore (what I view as) essential criteria of a figurine study. Rather, I will focus on Dothan's study because it is almost the only general study of Philistine figurines that has been made, and its conclusions have had a significant impact on subsequent discussions of the figurines.

leads to confusion in T. Dothan's and Schmitt's studies.) Normally in an archaeological study, the primary consideration used to bound the corpus would be a geographical one: a site or a culture region. In this case, "Philistine" would then refer to Philistine material culture as characteristic of the geographical region of Philistia, as archaeological cultures are generally defined over geographical areas (see chapter 2).

The majority of detailed work that has been done on Philistine boundaries, all of it for the Iron I, has focused on archaeological elements—elements of Philistine material culture. The most common type of artifact used for this procedure is Philistine painted pottery (Monochrome and Bichrome). Both Wright (1966:74–77) and Kenyon (1979:222–25) used the distribution of Philistine pottery to determine the extent of Philistine settlement, either in its initial stage or in its expansion;[2] Kenyon noted that while a "moderate" amount of Philistine pottery might simply reflect trade, a larger amount indicates that a site or area is "Philistine" (1979:222). For both Wright and Kenyon, the distribution relates not simply to settlement but to political control as well (Wright 1966:75 n. 13; Kenyon 1979:222). More recently, Stager (1998:342) has used a similar method to delineate the initial boundaries of Philistine boundaries (his Stage 1). Stager suggests that a rough border for Philistine territory (meaning both settlement and political control) can be drawn by plotting sites with 25 percent or more Myc IIIC (Monochrome) pottery in the early to mid-twelfth century.[3]

In addition to pottery, perhaps the most cited element of Philistine material culture in attempts to draw Philistine boundaries is the distribution of pig bones. The relationship of pig in Philistine diet to the Aegean origins of the Philistines is a commonplace and has already been mentioned above (chapter 2); see Barako 2001:20–28. Stager (1998:344) specifically notes the correlation of pig distribution (by percentage) with Iron I Philistine settlement (and its absence in Iron I highland—i.e., Israelite—settlement). Finkelstein (1997:230) has observed that pig remains are abundant not only at Philistine sites but also at an Ammonite site (although he points only to a single example) and so suggests that their absence at highland sites can help to demarcate ethnic boundaries (in this case, of the Israelites). In trying to argue for the correlation of pig absence and Israelite settlement, he shows that abundance of pig bones is not restricted to Philistine sites in Iron I Palestine. Thus, the value of pig distribution in determining cultural boundaries (let alone ethnic ones) is more limited than often supposed. This is the same conclusion reached by Hesse and Wapnish (1997), who suggest that pig bones might indeed be used to determine ethnic identity but in a more complex procedure than simply noting presence or absence (1997:263–64).

In sum, the use of material culture elements such as pottery and pig bones to determine Philistine settlement is not a straightforward procedure. Looking at the presence or absence of one culture trait does not provide a map of any ancient people, but used together, pottery and pig bones seem to provide a rough picture of the boundaries of Philistia.[4] An additional problem is (as alluded to above) the confusion of different types of groups and boundaries: ethnic, cultural, and political especially. Even the most well-founded studies of Philistine material culture have had difficulty determining sharp cultural boundaries in the Iron I, and yet scholars have tried to use these to determine other types of boundaries as well. Clearly, it is necessary to choose a single type of boundary and then to determine what types of evidence best relates to this boundary.

For the purposes of bounding the study, I will not use the culture region definition typical of artifact studies; as we have seen, there are some difficulties with this method. Instead, I will use the term "Philistine" to refer to a geographic area defined as a political unit—a geopolitical entity, as determined from textual sources.[5] I am using this definition for two reasons. First, I wish to avoid the circularity of using archaeological

[2] Albright (1963:114) had provided a similar but briefer discussion of Philistine pottery, to justify the designation of this pottery as "Philistine."

[3] Stager cites Bietak (1993) for the method. According to Bietak (1993:298), "In archaeological methodology, the plotting of artifacts plays an important part in the recognition of cultural or even political clusters and boundaries." With this method, Bietak plots the distribution of inscribed Egyptian objects in Canaan from Dynasty 19 vs. from Dynasty 20. Notably, these inscribed objects—unlike the pottery used by Stager (and others)—have a more explicit political dimension to them. Stager also cites Singer (1993:302–7), who employs a similar method and infers a similar boundary for the initial Philistine settlement. See also Singer 1985:114; A. Mazar 1992a:308–13.

[4] Thus, Stager (1991:18) commented on the difficulty in drawing clear cultural boundaries between Israelites and Philistines in the Iron I Shephelah. Similarly, A. Mazar (1992a:312) observeed that the material culture remains from Shephelah sites such as Batash (Timnah) and Beth-Shemesh do not fit the description of these towns in Judges and 1 Samuel. See also A. Mazar 1994:251; Bunimovitz and Lederman 1997.

[5] As mentioned above, the archaeological evidence that does exist, in my view, relates (contra Kletter [1996; 1999]) not directly to the area under Philistine political control but primarily to Philistine cultural and settlement boundaries.

criteria (including figurines) to define the corpus of Philistine figurines, which I will then try to use to determine the homogeneity of the corpus and its relationship to that of surrounding regions.[6] Second, there is clear textual evidence relating to Philistia's boundaries at different points in the Iron Age. In addition, this definition of "Philistine" as a geopolitical unit will allow me to test Kletter's hypothesis that the distribution of artifacts such as figurines is directly related to political boundaries (Kletter 1996; 1999). Are the figurines found within the political entity of Philistia a uniform group, distinct from those from neighboring polities?

Despite the fact that the textual evidence for Philistia's boundaries does indeed exist, to my knowledge there is no survey devoted exclusively to this material.[7] Discussions of Philistia's boundaries have focused primarily on archaeological and cultural criteria and largely on the early history of Philistine settlement in Iron I (see below). It is therefore necessary for me to survey the available textual evidence before I can arrive at a set of boundaries for Philistia. Considering that I am investigating the state of Philistia's boundaries over the entire Iron Age—roughly 600 years—it is obvious that these boundaries would most likely have shifted many times. My goal, therefore, is not to note every shift in these boundaries but only to define that area which was under Philistine political control for an extended period.[8]

In my survey, I will consider the different groups of textual sources (Egyptian, Assyrian, and biblical) separately, and then discuss modern scholarship on the issue, before coming to final conclusions. In the textual sources, I will look for two separate but related types of information: information confirming the existence of Philistia specifically as a political entity (throughout the entire period) and information concerning the boundaries of this entity.

[6] Cf. Tappy's review (1998:87) of Kletter (1996): as Tappy notes, Kletter begins by defining his figurine types according to region (thus, Judean pillar figurines) and then concludes on the basis of his analysis that the pillar figurines are specifically Judean.

[7] Various studies of Philistine history, as well as the history and geography of ancient Israel more generally, have dealt with some or all of the textual evidence (e.g., Aharoni 1979; Noort 1994; Ehrlich 1996; Machinist 2000; Rainey et al. 2006, Cogan 2008; the studies of N. Naʾaman, collected in Naʾaman 2005/06). My discussion of Philistine boundaries below relies on these studies to varying extents, as well as the important studies of H. Tadmor (1958; 1966; 1969).

[8] There is also potential for confusion between references to "Philistia" as purely a geographical term and "Philistia" as some sort of political unit; it is not clear, however, that the term "Philistia" was used at any point in the Iron Age as a purely geographic term, as will be seen below.

Egyptian Sources

The Egyptian sources concerning Philistia and its boundaries are the least informative and pertain almost exclusively to the early Philistine settlement in Palestine.[9] The most widely consulted Egyptian sources on the Philistines, Papyrus Harris I and the Medinet Habu reliefs and inscriptions, refer to Philistines specifically as an ethnic group (as opposed to using a geographical or political term) and do not give any real indication of where they settled. In fact, for the whole of Iron I there are only two Egyptian documents that have been cited by scholars as even hinting at the nature and area of Philistine settlement (cf. Rainey et al. 2006:110): the Onomasticon of Amenope (Gardiner 1947) and the *Tale of Wenamun* (see Wilson 1955:25–29; Schipper 2005).

The Onomasticon of Amenope was dated by Gardiner to the end of the 20th Dynasty, around 1100 B.C.E. (1947:24), a conclusion generally accepted in the literature (e.g., Redford 1992:292; Rainey et al. 2006:110; followed by T. Dothan [1982:3], who cites a date of late twelfth or early eleventh century). The Onomasticon is simply a long series of words and phrases, loosely grouped by type of entity (Gardiner 1947:35). Included in its listing of foreign peoples are the terms ʾIsknrn, ʾIsdd, and G<u>d</u>t, interpreted as Ashkelon, Ashdod, and Gaza (Gardiner's nos. 262–64; Gardiner 1947:191*), followed not long afterward (but not directly) by the three peoples [Š]rdn, <u>T</u>kr, and Prst (nos. 268–70; Gardiner 1947:194*–200*)—Sherden, Sikils, and Philistines, three of the Sea Peoples fought by Ramesses III. The amount of information that can be gleaned from this document is quite limited; there is no strict order in the arrangement of the terms (as can be seen by the order of the three Pentapolis cities, listed from central one to northernmost to southernmost) and no clear association between the cities and the following peoples or any of the intervening or surrounding terms (cf. Schipper 2005:141).[10]

[9] Over the course of the twelfth century, Egyptian control of Palestine became increasingly tenuous, so that references to particular regions or other details in the country become intermittent in Egyptian texts.

[10] While some have suggested that Gardiner's no. 265, ʾIsr, represents biblical Asher (e.g., S. Yeivin; Aharoni [1979:270]; see Yeivin 1971:31–32 for discussion of ʾIsr in 19th Dynasty sources), there is no supporting evidence for such an identification; Gardiner himself favored interpreting the term as "Assyria" (1947:191*) and the following no. 266, Sbry, as [S]ubaru (following S. Smith; Gardiner 1947:193*). Regardless of the correctness of these suggestions, they indicate consensus and basic lack of knowledge concerning these terms, as well as the clear lack of tight geographical organization in the document. (For a discussion of

The *Tale of Wenamun* comes from the same general period as the Onomasticon of Amenope, but its exact date has been a matter of debate, one intimately connected to the interpretation of the text as either administrative/historical or literary fiction (see Schipper 2005:6–40). As Kitchen (1986:17, 251) has pointed out, the date "Year 5" within the text indicates year 5 of the Renaissance Era (Year 23 of Ramesses XI, ca. 1076 B.C.E.). Similarly, Wilson (1955:25) gives a date of the early 21st Dynasty (eleventh century) for the manuscript, while suggesting that the events of the manuscript themselves would have taken place slightly earlier, ca. 1100 B.C.E. (see also Goedicke 1975:4–5). This interpretation has been influential in studies by Levantine scholars trying to understand relations with Egypt in this period, who have therefore used the text rather uncritically for historical information on the late 20th Dynasty (e.g., Albright 1975:513; B. Mazar 1986:65; T. Dothan 1982:4; Stern 2000:198, 207; cf. Sass 2002:248). Studies of the text itself, however, have placed its composition anywhere from the late 20th Dynasty to the early 22nd Dynasty (i.e., early twelfth to late tenth century; see survey in Schipper 2005:6–40; summary in Sass 2002:247–48). Recent opinion in fact has tended to favor a literary interpretation and a date in the eleventh century (e.g., Schipper 2005, esp. 329–33).

For our current purposes, the chief value of the *Tale of Wenamun* lies in identifying Dor as the principal site of the Sikils (1.8–1.9; Wilson 1955:26 n. 5; Schipper 2005:171–72). Based on this text, in conjunction with the evidence from the Onomasticon of Amenope, scholars have been able to draw some conclusions about the general areas of settlement of some of the Sea Peoples on the Levantine coast (for recent discussion, see Rainey et al. 2006:110). From these documents, it is clear that the northern border of Philistine settlement must have been somewhere south of Dor. It is impossible, however, to learn much concerning Philistine settlement and boundaries from the *Tale of Wenamun*; beyond the problematic nature of the text as a historical document, neither the Philistines nor their land is mentioned anywhere in this text.[11]

There is one other piece of Egyptian textual evidence that pertains to Philistia as a geopolitical entity. G. Steindorff (1939) published a Middle Kingdom statue on which he identified an inscription added in some later period. This inscription most likely dates to the 22nd Dynasty (latter half of tenth to late eighth centuries).[12] It refers to a certain ᶜApy as *wpwty n p3-Knᶜn n Plst*, "commissioner (or messenger) of Canaan and Philistia (or Canaan of Philistia)" (Steindorff 1939:31; Singer 1994:330). The exact meaning of the phrase *p3-Knᶜn n Plst* is not clear, nor is the exact nature of the title *wpwty* (i.e., whether ᶜApy is an emissary of Canaan/Philistia to Egypt, or vice versa).[13] What is significant, however, is that *Plst* here appears not as the name of a people but as a geographical (or geopolitical) term, Philistia. This usage is unique in Egyptian texts (Aḥituv 1984:155). Given the context—that this term occurs in the inscription of a government official, I would follow Singer (1994:330) in suggesting that *Plst* refers specifically to Philistia as a geopolitical entity, composed of all the Philistine city-states. Thus, it appears we have textual evidence for a geopolitical unit known as Philistia in the early Iron II.

Assyrian Sources

The Assyrian sources pertaining to Philistia are more numerous than the Egyptian ones but are limited solely to the eighth and seventh centuries.[14] They

the problems posed by ᵓIsr and Sbry, see Alt 1950:66–67.) As a result, the value of this document for an understanding of the geopolitical and ethnic makeup of Palestine in Iron I is in fact fairly limited.

[11] A notable effort was made by W. F. Albright (see Albright 1975:513 n. 4) to identify three persons named in the *Tale of Wenamun*—Mkmr (1.16), Wrt (1.16), and Wrktr (2.2)—as Philistine kings (of the cities of Ashdod, Ashkelon, and Gaza). In this Albright has been followed by other scholars (e.g., B. Mazar 1986:65; T. Dothan 1982:4; Stern 2000:198). There are serious problems with this interpretation, however. First, Egyptologists have proposed a wide set of identifications for these three names, with Albright's interpretation, which was based on understanding the names as non-Semitic, not generally followed (see survey in Scheepers 1991:41–51). There is also the question of the historicity of the text. Perhaps most significantly, there is no indication in the *Tale of Wenamun* that these three figures are in fact kings, nor is there any hint that they are Philistine or associated with the Philistines in any way (as the Philistines are never discussed in the tale). The hypothesis only follows if we make an a priori assumption that the Onomasticon of Amenope and the *Tale of Wenamun*, the only two extant Egyptian texts to deal with the Levantine coast in the Iron I, must be connected, and therefore the three figures in the *Tale of Wenamun* must be associated with the set of three cities in the onomasticon. (For a similar critique of this hypothesis see Singer 1994:296.) In any case, Albright's suggestion does not affect the problem of Philistine boundaries.

[12] So Steindorff (1939:33), whose dating has become the consensus. See, e.g., Aḥituv (1984:155); Singer (1994:330).

[13] For discussion of the geographical terms, see Steindorff (1939:32); Aḥituv (1984:155); Singer (1994:330). For discussion of the title, see especially Singer (1994:330).

[14] As with the Egyptians, the Assyrians only made note of the political situation in Palestine when they were in direct contact with it. The advance of the Assyrian empire first came to the Levant in the ninth century and was a consistent

consist of the annals and other historical sources of the Neo-Assyrian kings (specifically, Adad-nirari III, Tiglath-pileser III, Sargon II, Sennacherib, Esarhaddon, and Ashurbanipal; for a recent edition of all of these texts with commentary, see Cogan 2008). Significantly, they include multiple references to Philistia as a geopolitical unit. The inscriptions of the Neo-Assyrian rulers refer to Philistia first as *Palaštu* and later as *Pilista* or *Pilišta* (H. Tadmor 1969:46). As Tadmor showed (1969:46), the spellings of these terms (*Pa-la-aš-tu*, *Pi-lis/liš-te*) contrast with that used for the people "Philistines," *Pilistaya* (*Pi-lis-ta-ayya*, *Pi-lis-ta-a-a*—see H. Tadmor 1958:81). The renderings of these terms in some translations as "Palestine" (for instance Oppenheim 1955:281, 282, 287) is incorrect. In this period, Assyrian inscriptions refer to Palestine (together with Syria) by the geographical terms Hatti and Amurru (H. Tadmor 1969:47; Cogan 2008:35). Moreover, it is clear from the contexts of these terms that "Philistia" is not simply a geographical term but a geopolitical unit: for example, Prism A of Sargon refers to the "rulers of [Philistia] (*Pi-lis-te*), Judah (*Ia-ú-di*), Ed[om], Moab . . ." (Oppenheim 1955:287). As in the Egyptian inscription of ᶜApy, then, Philistia appears in the Assyrian records as a geopolitical entity (grouping the individual Philistine city-states together) in the eighth and seventh centuries.

There is unfortunately little information in these inscriptions concerning the nature of Philistine boundaries at this time. The descriptions of certain campaigns against Philistia, however (particularly those of Sargon and Sennacherib), provide some valuable evidence by listing some of the cities and towns belonging to the different Philistine city-states. Most important among these texts are those describing the campaign of Sennacherib against Philistia in 701 B.C.E., when Sennacherib also invaded Judah and besieged but did not take Jerusalem. According to the Prism of Sennacherib, among the cities conquered by Sennacherib in this campaign were "Beth-Dagon, Joppa, Banai-Barqa [Bnei Braq], and Azuru [Azor], cities belonging to Sidqia [king of Ashkelon]" (Oppenheim 1955:287; Cogan 2008:114). This passage clearly indicates that Ashkelon controlled an area around the basin of the Yarkon (some 30 km north of the northernmost Pentapolis sites, Ekron and Ashdod), despite the relative distance of this area from Asheklon. Subsequently, this area was incorporated into the Assyrian empire. In the reign of Esarhaddon, neighboring Aphek (*Ap-qu*) appears at the border of the Assyrian province of Samerina (Oppenheim 1955:292; H. Tadmor 1966:99; Cogan 2008:143; Rainey et al. 2006:248). This is the northernmost region that appears as part of Philistia in any Assyrian inscription.

presence in the southern Levant only in the eighth and seventh centuries.

References to the eastern and southern borders of Philistia are less clear. In H. Tadmor's reconstruction of Sargon II's campaign against Philistia in 712 B.C.E. (Tadmor 1958:83), the Assyrian army moved against Gath (*Gi-im-tu*),[15] Gibbethon (*Gab-bu-tu-nu*), and Ekron (*Am-qa-[ar]-ru-[na]*) before reaching Ashdod (and its port Ashdod-Yam, *As-du-di-im-mu*). This reconstruction is only tentative, however. Sargon's Annals (Annals, 258; Display Inscription, 104; see Oppenheim 1955:286; Cogan 2008:83) mention only the conquest of Ashdod, Gath, and Ashdod-Yam; the sieges of Gibbethon and Ekron are depicted only on the wall reliefs of Room V of Sargon's palace at Khorsabad (see H. Tadmor 1958:83; Cogan 2008:85). In addition to the difficulties of reconstructing this campaign (or campaigns), our knowledge of the geographical region(s) referred to is incomplete; besides the difficulties presented by Gath, the location of Gibbethon is unknown (though it must have been situated in the coastal plain south of Jaffa [see the Danite town list in Josh. 19:40–46], and presumably not far from Ekron).[16] The Prism of Sennacherib provides additional evidence for the area around Ekron, the northern Shephelah, in Sennacherib's campaign of 701; it portrays the Assyrian army as progressing from the Yarkon basin to the plain of Eltekeh (*Al-ta-qu-ú*), where Sennacherib defeated the Nubians, and proceeding to conquer Eltekeh and Timnah (*Ta-am-na-a*) before moving on to Ekron (Oppenheim 1955:287–88; H. Tadmor 1966:97; Cogan 2008:114). Eltekeh and Timnah are closely associated in Sennacherib's Prism with Ekron and appear to be its fortresses (so

[15] "Gath" in both the Assyrian and biblical sources is problematic: not only is the identity of the Pentapolis city Gath uncertain, but this Gath is only one of several Gaths mentioned in the Bible, and in many instances it is unclear which Gath is mentioned. For this problem, see especially B. Mazar 1954. The most widely accepted identification for Philistine Gath is Tell eṣ-Ṣafi, near Gath in the northern Shephelah (e.g., Aharoni 1979:271; see the detailed discussion in Rainey et al. 2006:154–56); this site is currently being excavated by Aren Maeir, and its remains make it a good candidate. This identification is not certain, however. Stager (1998:343), for instance, suggested Tel Haror in the southern Shephelah. If this latter identification is correct, then the Gath conquered in Sargon's campaign of 712 must be Gath-Gittaim (or some other Gath); if the identification with Tell eṣ-Ṣafi with Philistine Gath is correct, then it is unclear which Gath is mentioned here.

[16] One possibility is Tel Malot (Tell Melat), discussed in Rainey et al. 2006:195; Ehrlich 1996:66; Cogan 2008:85.

H. Tadmor 1966:97), though the text is not explicit on this point. Timnah has been fairly certainly identified with Tel Batash in the Sorek Valley (see Kelm and Mazar 1982:2; 1995:4). The exact location of Eltekeh is unknown (see Rainey et al. 2006:48), although one proposal is Tel Shalaf (Tell esh-Shalaf; see Cogan 2008:119; Rainey et al. 2006:242, with references). Ekron's territory therefore constitutes some portion of the northern Shephelah, centered on the Sorek; on the basis of the Assyrian texts, it is impossible to give a more precise description.

Assyrian inscriptions attest to campaigns along the southern edge of Philistia in the reigns of Sargon II and Esarhaddon. Sargon's activity in this region includes defeating the forces of Hanno, king of Gaza, and the Egyptians at Rafiah (*Ra-pi-ḫu*; Display Inscriptions, 23–26; see Oppenheim 1955:285; Cogan 2008:82); resettling people in the "City of the Brook of Egypt," near the city of Laban (a prism fragment from Nineveh, 79-7-8, 14; see H. Tadmor 1958:77–78); and (in an enigmatic description) "open[ing] the sealed harbor [*kāru*] of Egypt" (Annals, 18; Nimrud Prism 46–48; see H. Tadmor 1958:34; Cogan 2008:89). The identity of Rafiah (modern Rafa) is not in question, but the other references are difficult to interpret. The "Brook of Egypt" (Naḥal Muṣur; biblical Naḥal Miṣrayim) has been traditionally identified with the Wadi el-ᶜArish, about 40 km southwest of Rafiah (e.g., Aharoni 1979:64; Oren 1993a:103). While this identification is still generally accepted, N. Naᵓaman has notably suggested that the "Brook of Egypt" instead be identified with the Naḥal Besor (the Wadi Gaza) (1979; also Naᵓaman and Zadok 1988:46; for arguments against this identification, see Rainey et al. 2006:35, 247–48). The identifications of the "City of the Brook of Egypt" and the "sealed harbor of Egypt," meanwhile, are widely debated.[17] In the reign of Esarhaddon, the Assyrian army attacked the town of Arṣa, located on the border with Egypt (see Oppenheim 1955:292; H. Tadmor 1966:79; Cogan 2008:132). This city is otherwise unknown from Assyrian sources, and its identification is also debated.[18] Regardless of the identification of these places, it is not at all clear in the inscriptions that they are actually part of Philistia. The Assyrian sources, then, shed little light on the southern border of Philistia in this period.

Biblical Sources

The biblical texts provide the greatest body of evidence for reconstructing the borders of Philistia. Even so, the information they provide is frustratingly incomplete. To begin with, the dating of the relevant texts is far from secure.[19] Aharoni (1979:81) notes an additional problem: the Bible, focusing on the people Israel, treats other peoples and regions—including Philistia—peripherally. Nevertheless, it is possible to

[17] Alt (1953 [1945]: 227–28) identified the "City of the Brook of Egypt" with Rafiah. Noting that this site is too far from the Wadi el-ᶜArish to be called the "City of the Brook of Egypt," H. Tadmor (1958:78), followed by Ephᶜal (1982:103–4) suggested Qalᵓat el-ᶜArish, which he identified with Assyrian Arṣa, and associated it with the "sealed harbor of Egypt." For the "sealed harbor," R. Reich (1981) suggested Tell Abu Salima, near Sheikh ez-Zuweid. E. Oren excavated a large fortified site at Ruqeish and identified it with the *kāru* (1993a:103; see also Stern 2001:113). A. Mazar (1992a:547) considered both Abu Salima and Ruqeish to be possible. For further discussion, including the city of Laban in Sargon's Annals and its identification with the "City of the Brook of Egypt," as well as with biblical Laban (= Libnah), see Aharoni 1979:377; Aḥituv 1984:129; Cogan 2008:89–92.

[18] H. Tadmor (1958:78) suggested that this was the same as the "City of the Brook of Egypt," which he located on the Wadi el-ᶜArish. B. Mazar (1952) proposed that Arṣa was identical with Yurṣa of New Kingdom sources and should be located at Tell Jemmeh (on the Naḥal Besor). This identification has been widely followed, for instance by Naᵓaman (1979:73), Aharoni (1979:401), and van Beek (1983). Aḥituv (1984:202–3) saw this identification as "untenable," as it relied on Naᵓaman's far from universally accepted identification of the "Brook of Egypt" with the Naḥal Besor. In fact, as Naᵓaman pointed out, if Yurṣa is Tell Jemmeh, then either the Besor is the "Brook of Egypt," or Yurṣa and Arṣa cannot be equated (1979:72). Thus, Rainey has recently argued for the identification of Tell Jemmeh as Yurṣa but for Arṣa as Rhinocolura on the el-ᶜArish (for him, the "Brook of Egypt"; see Rainey et al. 2006:75, 247, 283; cf. Cogan 2008:134–35).

[19] The traditional view espoused especially by the Albright school—that the Pentateuchal sources J and E date to the tenth to eighth centuries, and Dtr was composed in the seventh to sixth centuries (see the expression of this view by Friedman 1987)—has become increasingly marginalized. Following the work of scholars such as van Seters (1975) and H. H. Schmid (1976), these tenets began to be increasingly questioned. The idea that the compositional history of the text may start with Dtr in the seventh and sixth centuries and that the Pentateuch as a whole is largely Persian period in date is now widely followed (for surveys of research, see, e.g., Ska 2006; Nicholson 1998). These uncertainties lead to problems in the use of various biblical passages in the following discussion, problems which cannot be sufficiently addressed here. The result for our purposes is that the following conclusions are somewhat tentative, although still have some value as the biblical texts—even if composed after the Iron Age—must be based to a significant extent on earlier sources.

glean some information about Philistia and its boundaries from a survey of the relevant material.

The Bible uses two names for this land. One, "the land of the Philistines" (*ereṣ Pelištim*), occurs in Genesis (21:32–33). The other, "Philistia," is the more commonly used (e.g., Ex. 15:14; Isa. 14:29–31). The Hebrew word, *Pelešet*, is the same word used for "Philistine" (cf. Egyptian *plst*, generally "Philistines," but "Philistia" in the ᶜApy inscription); it is clear from context, however, that a geographical area is meant instead of a people.[20]

The borders of the land inhabited by the Philistines are indicated broadly in Joshua 13:2–3, in the description of the "land that yet remains." The Philistines, along with the Geshurites, are said to inhabit the area from the Shihor in the south to the "territory (*gĕbûl*) of Ekron" in the north. This area is then described as composed of the peoples of the Pentapolis sites (Gaza, Ashdod, Ashkelon, Gath, and Ekron) and the Avvites to the south (cf. Deut. 2:23, where the Avvites are said to have lived in *ḥăṣērîm* around Gaza but to have been wiped out and replaced by the Caphtorim; see Naᵓaman and Zadok 1988:45 n. 49). Here, and in the more detailed border descriptions (and town lists) of Joshua 13–19, the area north of Ekron is not accounted as Philistine but is part of Israel (allotted to Dan, and perhaps to Judah?). Thus, in Joshua 19:40–48—a passage often considered, as we shall see, as a fragment from the second district of the Solomonic province list (1 Kgs. 4:8–19)—the territory of Dan is said to include Bene-beraq and "the waters of the Yarkon," as well as Eltekeh and Timnah (and Ekron!).[21] In the story of the capture of the Ark by the Philistines and its return to the Israelites (1 Sam. 5–6), the border between Israelite and Philistine territory runs between Ekron and Beth-Shemesh. Similarly, in the Samson cycle, the Philistia-Judah border is located between Philistine Timnah and Israelite Zorah and Eshtaol (Judg. 13:25–14:1; see Aharoni 1979:274). While Timnah is fairly securely identified with Tel Batash (Tell el-Batashi), the locations of Zorah and Eshtaol are uncertain; still, it is clear that they must not be far to the east of Timnah (see discussion in Rainey et al. 2006:144).

The biblical view of Philistia, at least as seen in the book of Joshua (and also 1 Samuel), is composed of little more than the area of the Pentapolis. Aharoni (1979:81) observed that "[e]xcept for the five Philistine capitals there is practically no information about other population centres in Philistia; important towns in that region such as Beth-ᶜeglaim (Tell el-ᶜAjjul)[22] and Yurza (Tell Jemmeh?) are not mentioned at all." Nevertheless, there are hints concerning other Philistine towns—including those outside the area of the Pentapolis—at least for certain periods. As has often been noted (e.g., Noth 1960:165; Aharoni 1979:273), Aphek is mentioned in 1 Sam. 4:1 and 1 Sam. 29:1 as the mustering point from which the Philistines would campaign against the Israelites; it therefore appears that, c.1000 B.C.E., Aphek was near the border of Philistia and Israel. There is also some indication of other settlements in Philistia as satellites of the Pentapolis cities—described as *ḥăṣērîm* ("villages") or *bānôt* (literally "daughters")—but generally without details (see, e.g., T. Dothan 1982:18).

Another of these Philistine towns is Ziklag. Oren (1982), followed by Borowski (1988:24) and Singer (1994:305), has identified Ziklag with Tel Seraᶜ (Tell esh-Shariᶜa). While it appears on the basis of biblical references (1 Sam. 27, 30; see Borowski 1988:24) that Ziklag was in the Negev and in the vicinity of the Naḥal Besor, its exact location, however, is far from certain. Oren further suggests that the entire area of the western Negev witnessed Philistine expansion in the twelfth to eleventh centuries, based in part on the reference to this area in 1 Sam. 30:14 as the "Negev of the Cretans."[23] Again, however, the exact referent of this phrase is unclear. In any case, Ziklag, while in the sphere of Gath at the end of the eleventh century, is described as belonging to Judah from the time of David on (1 Sam. 27:6).

An enigmatic but important passage is the Danite town list of Josh. 19:40–48, referred to above. Unfortunately, the nature and date of this list are a matter of debate. First, it is worth noting that all scholars discussing this passage have seen in it a genuine reflection of some historical period. Alt (1925), followed by Noth (1971:121–22) and Strange (1966), dated the

---

[20] De Vaux (1978:4, 509) also discusses the Hebrew *Pelešet* and its relationship to the term "Philistia" in Egyptian and Assyrian texts.

[21] Aharoni's emendation (1979:299, 312) of "Timnah and Ekron" to Timnat-Ekron, or "Timnah of Ekron," has been generally accepted (e.g., Rainey et al. 2006:178–79), as Ekron is not realistically considered to have been a part of Israel. Contrast this with the inclusion of the territory of Ekron, Ashdod, and Gaza "to the Brook of Egypt" in the boundary list of Judah (Josh. 15:45–47), generally rejected as a historically authentic passage (see below).

[22] Kempinski's identification (1974) of ᶜAjjul as the Sharhon of Egyptian sources (and biblical Sharuhen) has not been universally accepted; cf. Rainey et al. 2006:64.

[23] Literally, "Negev of the Cherethites." The Cherethites, on the basis of parallelism in prophetic passages (Ezek. 25:16, Zeph. 2:5), are often concluded to be synonymous with Caphtorim—i.e., Cretans (see, e.g., T. Dothan 1982:13).

list to the time of Josiah. Cross and Wright (1956) attributed it to the reign of Jehoshaphat (mid-ninth century). The most widely held view, however, is that it reflects the situation of the United Monarchy (Aharoni 1978:298; Kallai 1958:139; de Vaux 1978:777). In particular, Kallai and Aharoni saw the list as a fuller reflection of the Second Solomonic Province of 1 Kgs. 4:9.[24] Aharoni (1979:313) has also noted that the Septuagint version of this passage substitutes Azor for Jehud; with this, along with Bene-beraq and "the border near Joppa," this town list would also seem to correspond to the Ashkelon enclave in the Yarkon region in the time of Sennacherib. In addition, Singer (1985:116) has argued that this area existed as a unit prior to being settled by the Philistines, as a "Canaanite enclave" with its capital at Gezer (as reflected in Judg. 1:29). Singer cites Naʾaman's work on the area in the Amarna period (fourteenth century B.C.E.), when (as Naʾaman observed) the borders of the kingdom of Gezer closely resembles the Danite town list. Significantly, in the tribal boundary system, Gezer itself is included within the territory of Ephraim but is described as still inhabited by Canaanites (Josh. 16:10; see also Judg. 1:29). According to 1 Kgs. 9:15–17, Gezer was part of the Solomonic kingdom but only as part of the dowry that the Egyptian Pharaoh gave to Solomon when the latter married Pharaoh's daughter. The area of the Danite town list, then, would seem to have been in Canaanite and then in Philistine hands and to have belonged to Israel only briefly, in the time of the United Monarchy.

For the Iron II, the changing nature of the borders of Philistia is clearly indicated in the books of Kings and Chronicles. The Solomonic province list (1 Kgs. 4:9) includes the area of the northern Shephelah that was part of Dan's allotment in Josh. 19 as part of Solomon's second province (Aharoni 1979:311). This includes Beth-Shemesh, which also appeared as part of Israelite territory in the story of the return of the Ark (1 Sam. 6). Under Nadab (ca. 900 B.C.E.) and Zimri (ca. 875), Israel laid siege to Gibbethon, now described as a Philistine town (1 Kgs. 15:27; 16:15–17). The reference to Libnah as a city that Judah lost to the Philistines under Jehoram (2 Kgs. 8:22; 2 Chr. 21:10) presumably indicates that the boundary with Philistia moved eastward here (Aharoni 1979:340). 2 Kgs. 12–13 describes the campaign of Hazael against Israel and Philistia (ca. 815 B.C.E.); there is little information concerning the boundaries of Philistia at this point, except for an interesting note in the Septuagint addition to 2 Kgs. 13:22, giving Aphek as a border point in Philistia which Hazael conquered.[25]

Further information concerning the wars of Philistia and Israel is contained in 2 Chronicles.[26] Under Uzziah, Judah invaded deep into Philistine territory: "He went forth to fight the Philistines, and breached the wall of Gath and the wall of Jabneh and the wall of Ashdod; he built towns in [the region of] Ashdod and among the Philistines" (2 Chr. 26:6).[27] Later, under Ahaz, Judah in turn lost much territory to the Philistines:

> And the Philistines made forays against the cities of the Shephelah and the Negeb of Judah; they seized Beth-Shemesh and Aijalon and Gederoth, and Soco with its villages, and Timnah with its villages, and Gimzo with its villages; and they settled there. (2 Chr. 28:18)[28]

---

[24] The major obstacle to this suggestion is the inclusion of Ekron. Aharoni (1979:315) has made the valuable suggestion that Ekron should be read together with the preceding entry in the list, Timnah, as Timnath-Ekron. As Aharoni points out, there are multiple towns named Timnah in the Bible, and in such cases a second element is typically added to indicate the location (i.e., in relationship to a larger city). With this change, this direct relationship between the Danite list and the Second Solomonic Province remains plausible (though it should be noted that the list in 1 Kgs. 4:9 is short, consisting of only four towns, and so its exact relationship to the Danite town list cannot be determined with certainty).

An even more problematic passage than this list is the passage in the boundary list of Judah (Josh. 15:45–47) naming Ekron, Ashdod, and Gaza. This passage is generally held to be fiction, as most scholars do not believe that Judah ever controlled this territory (see, e.g., Cross and Wright 1956:205, 218). Kallai (1958:137–39), however, argued that this passage might be located in the historical reality of Hezekiah's late eighth century expansion. This attempt has not met with much agreement, however.

[25] See Noth 1960:239; Aharoni 1979:342; cf. 2 Kgs. 13:17, referring to a victory of Israel over Aram at Aphek. Aphek appears to have been the border point of Philistia and Israel in this period.

[26] The reliability of Chronicles for descriptions of boundaries and events in the Iron Age is more controversial than that of the Deuteronomic History. The books of Chronicles are generally dated to the Persian or early Hellenistic period; the degree to which the Chronicler relied on earlier sources is debated (see Knoppers 2003:118–28). The information provided by Chronicles on Philistine boundaries, then, should be regarded as questionable, although recent assessments are more positive (Knoppers 2003; Rainey et al. 2006:214). Regardless, this situation does not significantly affect my survey of Philistia's borders, however, as I base no significant conclusions on these data (beyond the shifting nature of the border in Iron II, which is in any case a given).

[27] English translations of biblical passages are from the NJPS (New Jewish Publication Society) version.

[28] For further discussion of these passages and their implications for shifting boundaries in the northern Shephelah, see

Modern Scholarship

The work of modern scholars on the borders of Philistia is similar to the work done on Philistine figurines; the treatment of Philistine issues has been largely peripheral, with most effort going into defining the tribal and provincial boundaries of Israel. In this case, however, there may be more justification for such an emphasis than simply the bias of investigators. As noted above (and previously observed by Aharoni [1979:81–82]), the main source of information is the Bible, and the clear emphasis of the biblical texts is on Israel. The discussion of neighboring states and their borders is secondary and only in relation to Israel itself.

The few discussions of this issue that include any detail (Kenyon, Stager, and Singer; see above) are based on a combination of textual and archaeological evidence and do not strictly relate to Philistia as a geopolitical unit. Otherwise, scholarly opinion is rendered briefly, without supporting evidence given at all. In general, this opinion breaks down into two main views (following Singer 1985:115): one, that the Philistines settled the entire area between the Yarkon and the Naḥal Besor upon their arrival in Palestine (Noth 1960:36; de Vaux 1978:509; Aharoni 1979:273), and two, that initially Philistine settlement comprised only the Pentapolis plus hinterland, with expansion to the south and especially north and east only much later, in the mid- to late-eleventh century (Albright 1963:113–14; B. Mazar 1975:273).[29] A compromise view—one that is generally accepted and best accounts for the available evidence—has been put forth most clearly by Stager (1998, etc.). He has suggested two stages for Philistine settlement—the first (Monochrome phase) only in the area of the Pentapolis and the second (Bichrome phase) expanding beyond it—but with the second stage following relatively shortly after the first, at the time of the collapse of Egyptian power in Canaan in the mid- to late twelfth century. Again, this view is based largely on material culture remains, and so while it may be connected with expansion of the political entity Philistia, it does not relate directly to this entity but rather to the spread of Philistine settlement and especially Philistine culture more broadly.

For the Iron II, relatively little scholarly attention has been paid to Philistine boundaries. The most comprehensive study devoted to Philistia as a political entity in this period was made by H. Tadmor (1966); he does not, however, give much consideration to the specific issue of Philistine borders. Aharoni (1979) provides some information and suggestions for this period, but these are scattered among the discussion of the geography of Israel and Judah, his main focal points. Similar scattered references can be found in other discussions of biblical geography or Philistine history (e.g., Rainey et al. 2006; Noort 1994; Ehrlich 1996). Stern (2001:102–4) devoted some space to the political characteristics of Philistia in this period. He details the four "semiautonomous political units" of Ashdod, Ashkelon, Gaza, and Ekron and the territory of each, stretching in all from Jaffa and the Yarkon to Gaza and el-ᶜArish. Stern does not, however, give clear documentation for the sources of these kingdoms; they seem to be based on a combination of textual sources (such as the Assyrian description of Sennacherib's campaign of 701) and archaeological excavations. Oren (1993a) studied the particular situation of the "kingdom of Gaza," consisting of the western Negev. Again, his conclusions, while not explicitly sourced, appear to be based on a combination of textual and archaeological evidence.

Conclusions

The most obvious conclusion to draw from the above survey is that Philistia's boundaries (as would be expected with any entity over several hundred years) were fluid, continually changing depending on the political and military fortunes of Philistia itself as well as its neighbors (specifically Israel and Judah). This is hardly a novel observation to make. Given this fact, it is of course impossible to delineate detailed boundaries for an unchanging entity known as Philistia: the very meaning of that name, both as a general geographic designation and as a specific geopolitical term, probably changed over time along with its boundaries. Nevertheless, for the purposes of this study, I feel it is important to circumscribe a set area and label it "Philistia." To do so, I will try to consider that area under Philistine control for an

especially A. Mazar 1994; see also T. Dothan 1982:18; Kelm and Mazar 1982:3; 1995:5; A. Mazar 1992a:532–35.

[29] T. Dothan presents a mixture of both possibilities, suggesting at one point (1982:16) that the initial Philistine settlement occurred only in the Pentapolis area proper, following Josh. 13:2–3, and at another (1982:296) that the "main wave" of Philistine settlement encompassed the entire area from the Yarkon to the western Negev. The confusion seems to result from her advocacy of a two-wave hypothesis, where a first wave of (non-Philistine) Sea Peoples settled in the Pentapolis area (as represented by Monochrome pottery), and a second wave of Philistines (manifested in bichrome remains) settled the larger area (1982:295–96; see also M. Dothan 1979; Dothan and Dothan 1992:161–69). For refutations of the two-wave hypothesis, see A. Mazar 1985a; Stager 1985:61*–62*.

extended period. Based on the discussion above, this includes essentially the Pentapolis area, plus the coastal plain up to the Yarkon (where Philistine control is attested textually in the eleventh century in the books of Samuel, again in the tenth to ninth centuries in Kings, and in the eighth century in the inscriptions of Sennacherib). To the south, the border is mostly safely identified at the Naḥal Besor (just south of Gaza, the southernmost of the Pentapolis cities), regardless of whether Naʾaman's identification of this as the "Brook of Egypt" is to be accepted. The Yarkon and the Besor are both fairly significant natural boundaries in the region as well. To the east, however, there is no clear natural border as the landscape gradually changes from coastal plain to foothills and then to highlands. It is perhaps not surprising, then, that this area—especially the northern Shephelah, along the northeast corner of the area of the Pentapolis—was the most hotly contested between Philistia and Israel/Judah. Sites like Beth-Shemesh and Lachish to the south generally appear in the sources as part of Israelite territory; on the other hand, Timnah (though sometimes a part of Judah) was under Philistine control both in the Iron I (in the Samson cycle) and again in the time of Sennacherib.[30]

As I stated above, it is important to come up with a single, clearly defined area and work from there. While there are no definitive boundaries based on the sources available, this procedure is still of great value. First, it is essential to come up with some clear set of boundaries, to set definite limits on the corpus of figurines; in addition, the boundaries I have defined are far from completely arbitrary. Still, I will not overlook the figurines of the neighboring areas; I will therefore examine the figurines from sites in the Shephelah such as Gezer and Beth-Shemesh particularly closely as comparative material. If there are discrepancies over time in the distribution of "Philistine" figurines, possible historical explanations can be cited (direct or indirect ties to boundary changes, for example), but also we can cite movement of peoples, of goods (trade), or of ideas without referencing conquest.

Comprehensive

A figurine study should consider the entire corpus of figurines (or at least as much of this corpus as possible) from the area under consideration. This method offers the best chance to view the entire range of types within a corpus and then to identify certain figurines or types as standard, or anomalous. Too often in the early research on Palestinian figurines, comprehensiveness was overlooked; even Pilz and Pritchard, who presented the most comprehensive studies of the time, catalogued only a selection of the full corpus available. This characteristic is perhaps the most critical shortcoming of T. Dothan's study (1982). By focusing on a few special examples rather than examining the full body of artifacts, Dothan ended up presenting figurines which are by no means typical of the Philistine repertoire. Thus, in the case of the mourning figurines, Dothan was unable to see that this type represents only a small fraction even of the Iron I female figurines and emphasized this type out of proportion to its frequency. This problem has since been magnified by archaeologists, who have generally failed to recognize that Dothan's study is not comprehensive and so have come to label all small Iron I female torsos as "mourners." (For further discussion, see chapter 6 below.)

I have already indicated the starting point for achieving this criterion of comprehensiveness (in the previous section). I have defined a clearly bounded region that I am investigating, and I have attempted to include the figurines of every site within this region. For each site, I have considered (as much as possible) the entire corpus of Iron Age figurines. The starting point for this procedure is the previously unpublished collection of figurines from Ashkelon. I have catalogued the 200-plus Iron Age figurines recovered by the Leon Levy Expedition from 1985 to 2004. Of next importance are the other securely identified and excavated Pentapolis sites (Ashdod and Miqne).[31] Table 4.1 presents a complete list of sites, with references for their figurine assemblages, for the area that (for the purposes of this study) I am designating as "Philistia."

[30] It is definitely worth noting that the boundaries I am drawing for the Philistine political entity on the basis of textual sources are roughly the same as those determined by archaeological means (for example by Kenyon [1979:224–25], who locates Philistine settlement in the coastal plain and Shephelah between the Wadi Gaza and Jaffa). This is not surprising, since the scholarly consensus on Philistine settlement is based partly on the textual evidence, but more importantly suggests that there is an expected relationship (even if not direct) between Philistine settlement, Philistine cultural penetration, and Philistine political control. Nevertheless, I believe the exercise undertaken above is valuable, for these kinds of relationships should not simply be assumed but be tested. In addition, I think that through the use of the textual sources I have, in places and at times, been able to draw boundaries more sharply.

[31] Of the Pentapolis sites, only Ashdod, Ashkelon, and Ekron have been identified and extensively excavated. For the problem of Gath, see above. The site of Gaza is located underneath the modern city and so has not been investigated, other than soundings by Phythian-Adams (1923a).

Table 4.1: List of Sites in Philistia included in study, with references to figurines

Site	*References*
1. Ashkelon	Catalogue, chapter 5; *Ashkelon 3*, chapter 16 by S. Cohen
2. Ashdod (er-Ras)	M. Dothan and Freedman 1967; M. Dothan 1971; M. Dothan and Porath 1982; M. Dothan and Porath 1993; M. Dothan and Ben-Shlomo 2005; personal inspection at IAA storehouse, Beth Shemesh
3. Miqne (Khirbet el-Muqanna^{c}; biblical Ekron)	Ben-Shlomo 1999; 2006; 2010; in press; Ben-Shlomo and Press 2009; personal inspection at W. F. Albright Institute of Archaeological Research, Jerusalem
4. Tell eṣ-Ṣafi (Tel Zafit; Gath of the Philistines?)	Personal inspection at Bar-Ilan University, Ramat Gan; T. Dothan 1982; Schmitt 1999
5. Tell Qasile	A. Mazar 1980; 1986; B. Mazar 1950/51
6. Tell Jerishe (Tel Gerisa)	Herzog 1984; 1993
7. Aphek (Ras el-^{c}Ein)	Guzowska and Yasur-Landau 2009; Kochavi 1989
8. Jaffa (Yafa)	Personal inspection at Jaffa Museum*
9. Azor (Yazur)	T. Dothan 1982
10. Yavneh (Yibnah)	Ziffer and Kletter 2007; Kletter, Ziffer, and Zwickel 2010
11. Tel Shalaf (Tell esh-Shallaf)	Fischer and Taxel 2006
12. Tel Ḥamid (Ras Abu Hamid)	Wolff 1998; Wolff and Shavit 1999
13. Tel Batash (Tell el-Batashi; Timnah)	A. Mazar and Panitz-Cohen 2001; A. Mazar 2006
14. Tel Ṣippor (Tell et-Tuyur)	Negbi 1966
15. Netiv Ha-^{c}Asara	Shavit and Yasur-Landau 2005
16. Tell el-Hesi (Tel Ḥasi)	Bennett and Blakely 1989
17. Tel Sera^{c} (Tell esh-Shari^{c}a)	Oren 1978; 1993b; personal inspection at Ben Gurion University of the Negev, Beersheba
18. Tel Haror (Tell Abu Hureira)	Oren et al. 1991; personal inspection at Ben Gurion University of the Negev, Beersheba
19. Ruqeish (Tell er-Reqeish)	Personal inspection at Ben Gurion University of the Negev, Beersheba
20. Tell Jemmeh (Tel Gamma)	Petrie 1928; personal inspection at University College, London, and the Rockefeller Museum, Jerusalem
21. Tell el-^{c}Ajjul	Petrie 1931; 1932; 1933; Mackay and Murray 1952; personal inspection at the Rockefeller Museum, Jerusalem
22. Tell el-Far^{c}ah (S; Tel Sharuhen)	Personal inspection at University of College, London, and the Rockefeller Museum, Jerusalem
23. Ḥorvat Hoga (Khirbet Huj)	Gophna 1970; Kletter 1996; unpublished drawings and photographs courtesy of Jacob Huster and the Israel Antiquities Authority
24. Mefalsim A	Gophna 1970; Kletter 1996
25. Tel Milḥa (Tell el-Muleihah)	Personal inspection at IAA storehouse, Beth Shemesh

A note on site names: The commonly used form is given first, whether Hebrew, Arabic, or English; this is then followed in parentheses by the Arabic or Hebrew name and, in some cases, by the biblical or other ancient identification.

* I am currently preparing the Bronze and Iron Age figurines from Kaplan's excavations at Jaffa for publication.

Among all of these sites, I consider both anthropomorphic and zoomorphic figurines, complete examples as well as fragments, in order to gain as complete a picture of the Philistine corpus as possible. By being comprehensive, then, I am able both to present this as a broad overview and to isolate standard and nonstandard types and individual examples in this study.

Systematic

Any proper figurine study, or in fact any artifact study in general, requires an appropriate procedure and has that procedure stated at the outset. This may seem an obvious remark, but it is one that has not been generally followed. The fairly simple procedure followed by Pilz (1924), who provides a catalogue of his corpus followed by a discussion of types focused on their imagery (i.e., the human or animal figures depicted, their gestures, symbols, and associations) and parallels, is still followed today in the majority of artifact studies in the field (including studies of figurines); a perusal of current excavation reports will bear this observation out. Beyond lacking consideration of additional types of analysis, this procedure is usually not explained. The archaeologists make no attempt to justify why this procedure is used; it is simply an accepted heritage of prior scholarship. The alternative is provided by T. Dothan (1982), who offers no explicit method at all. I believe it necessary, then, to develop a proper methodology—or, perhaps better, to modify existing ones—and state it before I begin the study itself. I am not undertaking this work in isolation; my methodological suggestions are paralleled and influenced by similar work in recent studies of Palestinian figurines, such as Kletter (1996) and Yasur-Landau (2001); in particular I will draw on their use of multiple avenues of analysis, some not typically employed in artifact studies (see below).

My method is essentially an adaptation of the traditional art-historical study of iconography and iconology developed in large part by Erwin Panofsky.[32] While Panofsky expressed these ideas in many of his writings, his system of interpretation was crystallized in his essay, "Iconography and Iconology: An Introduction to the Study of Renaissance Art," originally published (as "Introductory") in his book, *Studies in Iconology* (1939; reprinted in a collection of his essays, *Meaning in the Visual Arts*, in 1955). Panofsky identified three levels (or "strata") of meaning in a work of art: the primary, or natural, subject matter ("pre-iconographical description"); secondary, or conventional, subject matter ("iconographical analysis"); and intrinsic meaning, or content ("iconological interpretation"). Briefly, the pre-iconographic level involves identifying forms, and their general character or mood, as artistic "motifs"; iconographical analysis involves connecting these motifs with themes or concepts (for instance, identifying specific saints or mythological figures by their attributes); and iconological interpretation involves connecting these themes and concepts with underlying attitudes of a period or group of people, as expressed by the individual artist (i.e., by the artist's personality). For Panofsky, each successive level of meaning is a deeper and more fundamental layer; iconological interpretation, then, is the ultimate goal of his studies of art—it is "intrinsic," a "unifying principle" (Panofsky 1955b:28). Beyond distinguishing these levels, Panofsky also suggested a set of "correctives" for each level of interpretation, which involves an intimate knowledge of the history of style, of types, and of symbols. In each case these correctives consist of knowing how (in a given period) artists tended to use elements from one level to express those of the next.

Panofsky's scheme is open to multiple types of serious criticism, especially postmodern criticism.[33] One of these is the problem of relativism; Panofsky's scheme assumes that the researcher can operate successively in the mindsets of other cultures and periods. This assumption, however, underlies essentially all work in humanistic disciplines and is not specifically characteristic of Panofsky's work.[34] A critique more central to my adaptation of Panofsky's scheme is that of circularity. There is an element of circularity in the relationship between Panofsky's levels of meaning; in practice it is impossible to distinguish fully among description, iconography, and iconology. As I. Gaskell (1992:184) points out, this idea of separation in interpretation has been reevaluated by the work of postmodernist theorists, such as Roland Barthes and Michel Foucault, who in discussing the parallel semiotic concepts of denotation and connotation have shown that the two cannot in fact be separated. Gaskell even argues that this new realization has "superseded" Panofsky's model. In addition, there is an explicit circularity in the application of Panofsky's correctives; in order to interpret a part, or one work of art, it is necessary to understand the whole, or the collective works of an artist or period, and vice versa.

Significantly, these critiques were largely anticipated by Panofsky himself. He clearly realized that true

[32] I am by no means the first researcher outside the field of art history to attempt to apply Panofsky's method. See the group of articles concerning applications in archaeology, anthropology, history, and other fields in Lavin 1995; especially Kelley (1995:118) for the application of this method to classes of artifacts (such as gravestones). Panofsky's method as well as more general art-historical conceptions of iconography have in fact been applied to specific studies of Near Eastern and Aegean art and archaeology: e.g., Petty 2006:21–42 (on Bronze Age Syrian figurines); Lesure 2002 (on different groups of prehistoric figurines); Ahlberg 1971:17–19 (on mourning scenes in Greek Geometric art); Keel 1992:267–73 (on method in Near Eastern art generally).

[33] See Erwin 1991 and Mitchell 1991 for some examples of postmodern critiques on aspects of Panofsky's views of art historical interpretation (specifically of Panofsky 1955b) which are not directly relevant to this study.

[34] Moreover, that all of us engage in this type of work means that for all of us this assumption is more or less a given and does not need to be defended to great extent here.

objectivity in interpretation is impossible.[35] In fact, it was to control for this lack of objectivity that Panofsky developed his correctives; he intended them to correct for the researcher's own cultural baggage by grounding him in the culture of the society in question. As for circularity, according to Panofsky "the beginning of our investigation always seems to presuppose the end" (1955a:9). He acknowledged the hermeneutic circle present in his approach but considered it not a flaw but a strength. For Panofsky, the circle was not vicious but what he termed (citing T. M. Greene) an "organic situation" (Panofsky 1955a:9). Thus, while Panofsky's levels (or "spheres of meaning") may appear to be successive stages, Panofsky (and I, following him) merely presented them in this manner to make them more readily understood. Panofsky's own view was quite different; these levels are part of "one organic and indivisible process" (Panofsky 1955b:39).[36] As D. R. Kelley points out (1995:119), Panofsky did not need to read Barthes or Foucault to appreciate the intertwined nature of the different levels of interpretation; he had already reached similar conclusions decades earlier.

I am not as optimistic as Panofsky in approaching this circularity; I believe that it compromises the complete integrity of the investigative process. Nevertheless, this simply means that our investigations into the past cannot be completely successful; following Panofsky, I still see great value in them and in the many incomplete successes that we can achieve. Panofsky too, as I discussed above, saw some limitations in the process of interpretation; his "candor" concerning these limitations has in fact been remarked upon in postmodern critiques of his interpretive approach, and is considered one of its most "up to date" features (see, e.g., Mitchell 1995:217).

My adaptation of Panofsky's approach for studying Philistine figurines runs as follows: The first phase of my research involves the formulation of a typology for Philistine figurines. This typology is centered on a catalogue of the terracottas from Ashkelon. Over 200 figurines have been recovered from Iron Age levels at Ashkelon by the Leon Levy Expedition, starting in 1985, and this study provides an opportunity to publish the Iron Age corpus comprehensively.[37] I then develop the typology using not only the Ashkelon catalogue but also comparisons with finds from other Philistine sites. Thus, I arrive at a comprehensive description of the different types of figurines present at Ashkelon specifically, and in Philistia in general. The description of the figurines in this catalogue is the "purely formal perception" that Panofsky (1955b:26) describes as necessary grounding for pre-iconographical description—in this case the figurine typology. Next I move to iconographic analysis; this involves aspects of the imagery depicted in the figurines, as paralleled in other media, as well as in other cultures. In addition, I consider textual evidence concerning the identity of the figures represented in the terracottas. These analyses, then, constitute an investigation into what I have described above (chapter 2) as the meaning of the figurines. I then move on to the figurines' function in what corresponds (to some extent, but far from perfectly) to Panofsky's iconological analysis. This process might involve techniques such as using analogies suggested by both ancient texts and modern ethnographic research; in the present study, I will concentrate on a consideration of the archaeological aspect of the figurines—specifically, the figurines in their contexts (see below).

The above method involves some modifications of Panofsky's approach. Most important is my adaptation of his levels of interpretation. While, as I discussed above, for Panofsky these interpretive levels were part of an integrated, "organic" whole, I will treat them as discrete stages of interpretation, each building on the last. Again, in my view (as well as that of postmodernist critics, and even Panofsky himself) this separation of stages can only be ideal. The circularity inherent in this approach cannot be avoided. For instance, by labeling one type of terracotta "mourning figurines," I am already drawing conclusions concerning the meaning and function of this type. To do otherwise, however, would be absurd. The label "mourning figurine"

[35] "Even when dealing with the remote past, the historian cannot be entirely objective" (Panofsky 1955c:321). Elsewhere, Panofsky noted, "There is no such thing as an entirely 'naïve' beholder" (1955a:16).

[36] For examples of how Panofsky applies this process of interpretation, see the individual studies in Panofsky 1939. In these Panofsky does not analyze works of art by proceeding through successive levels but moves readily back and forth between spheres to give a synthetic view of the whole process, always with the larger iconological realm in greatest focus. In this way his work is echoed in the hermeneutic method for archaeological study advocated by Schloen (2001), with its approach to the dialectic of fact and symbol involving simultaneous study of the whole and the parts—as one can only be understood by the other (2001:10). It also bears similarity to the ideas of postprocessualist archaeologists such as Hodder (e.g., 1992:213–40), who redefines the hermeneutic circle as a "hermeneutic spiral"; Hodder sees the movement between different levels of analysis and interpretation as a strength, as long as it is acknowledged.

[37] From this group, about 95 of the seventh century B.C.E. figurines have now been published by S. Cohen in *Ashkelon 3*.

is already well established in the archaeological literature, and there is no reason to abandon it given that careful iconographic and contextual analysis proves it to be correct. It is impossible and pointless simply to "unlearn" the previous accumulation of knowledge concerning Philistine and related figurines. While a certain amount of circularity is therefore unavoidable, in my view it is important to limit this circularity as much as possible by separating the stages of interpretation and by explicitly acknowledging when this separation cannot be maintained.

As my example above suggests, then, I have not been able to follow completely the exact order of the interpretive stages. Nevertheless, I believe that these stages are of great value, in providing important controls on how we look at a set of artifacts. As long as we recognize the limitations in our approach (as in any approach), and work within them, the interpretive process is ultimately sound.

Archaeological

Another significant modification involved in adapting Panofsky's method to a figurine study is accounting for the archaeological nature of this class of objects. The works of art that Panofsky analyzed differ in (at least) two important respects: artworks, notably those in a museum, are typically divorced from their original contexts, and the primary method of reconstructing the worldviews (the *mentalités*) of the artists is textual. Archaeology adds an additional dimension not generally present in the art-historical study of paintings or sculptures—figurines, and artifacts in general, are given meaning by their contexts. These contexts include both what type of building or structure—e.g., domestic, cultic, funerary—an artifact is found in, as well as what other artifacts are found associated with it (note that some Renaissance and Baroque paintings are similarly given meaning by context; e.g., as an altarpiece in a church). At any rate, very often the context is our primary or even only means to understand the function of the figurine. Texts even indirectly related to iconographic and iconological aspects of Palestinian figurines, or those of the ancient Near East more generally, are meager or non-existent.[38] From these contexts we might be able to test hypotheses generated from textual evidence or ethnographic analogy.

In devoting a section of this study specifically to contextual analysis, I am following the work of Kletter (1996:57–67) and Yasur-Landau (2001:335, table 2); see chapter 3. Through this method, beyond trying to determine the functions of the figurines, I also try to reveal patterns of distribution among them, patterns that either correspond to the initial typology or crosscut it. These patterns are of two major types: temporal and spatial. The spatial patterns involve a general distinction between distribution in the Iron I (ca. 1200–1000 B.C.E.) and in the Iron II (ca. 1000–600 B.C.E. for Philistia); in addition, they involve possibilities for a more refined chronology of figurines. The spatial patterns of distribution involve three levels: interregional (between Philistia and the neighboring regions of Palestine), intra-regional (between different sites or areas in Philistia), and intra-site (between different types of contexts—domestic, industrial, cultic, etc.). Investigating distribution patterns in these different levels will allow me to study whether the figurine corpus of Philistia is uniform or exhibits regional variation, whether the corpus is unique to Philistia or shared with adjacent regions, and how these relationships change over time.

As for intra-site contexts, these do not simply involve the identification of gross categories (domestic, funerary, cultic) and determination of figurine distribution within these categories. Their investigation also involves the identification of figurine clustering or concentration, along both spatial and temporal lines, and the investigation of other artifacts associated with figurines. On another level, identification of contexts allows for studying the entire use and disposal history of figurines: how figurines came to be where they are on a site and in their present state of preservation. In this study, the major analysis of use and disposal will be based on a division between primary and secondary contexts, as it is in much archaeological literature. A primary context is a living surface such as the floor of a building, occupational debris (buildup on the floor from use over time), courtyard surface, or a street; these are the contexts in which ancient people were living and using objects such as figurines. At the same time, it is important to be aware of more complex issues of site formation processes and the life history of artifacts such as figurines. The use-life of a figurine was typically longer than simply its active (or primary) use in a house. Meanwhile, a broken figurine, even if found on a floor, is not in the condition, or necessarily in the location, of actual use; various processes, both cultural and non-cultural, affect the condition and placement of artifacts subsequent to their main use (see Schiffer 1972; also 1976; 1985; 1987). Following Schiffer, a broken object could alternatively be de facto refuse (if not explicitly discarded), primary refuse (if discarded at the location of use), or secondary refuse (if discarded at another location; see Schiffer

[38] An exception is the group of Neo-Assyrian apotropaic figurines; note, beyond the texts describing these figures in Assyrian thought, there are texts describing the manufacture of the figurines themselves. See Wiggermann 1992.

1972:160–62). Often material found on a floor is treated by archaeologists as de facto refuse (Schiffer 1985) and therefore used uncritically by archaeologists to reconstruct activities on that floor, when in fact it has been through some discard process. These objects, then, are no longer in what we might call a primary use context; we might label the context instead a secondary use context. Even with this problem, however, study of the location of fragments allows us to see how figurines were disposed of—if there is any patterning to the treatment of figurines, whether of specific types or in specific periods, etc.

Ideally, considering figurines as archaeological artifacts would involve other types of analysis: use-wear (how handling of figurines during use affects the preservation of modeled, painted, or incised features); breakage patterns (whether fragments are broken along structurally weak points or in anomalous patterns suggesting deliberate breaking); and composition (study of the clay and ware of figurines, either with the naked eye or through elemental analysis—petrography, neutron activation analysis [NAA], or other techniques). I will not devote much attention to these analyses, although at certain points I will highlight aspects of breakage patterns or characteristics of figurine clay.

These, then, are the major components of my proposed figurine method. In the remainder of the study, I hope to demonstrate the usefulness of their application to the Iron Age figurines of Ashkelon and of Philistia more generally.

5. Catalogue

This catalogue includes all Iron Age figurines found in the Ashkelon Excavations, Leon Levy Expedition (1985–2010).[1] The category "Iron Age figurines" can be defined in two ways: figurines found in Iron Age levels (regardless of their date of manufacture/use) and figurines of Iron Age type (regardless of the phase or level of their findspot). For the purposes of this catalogue, I have chosen an inclusive definition of "Iron Age figurines," encompassing both definitions. I have not included, however, any seventh-century figurine types from post-Iron Age levels, as the major seventh-century types (or close variants of these types) continue into the Persian period, and it is impossible (based on present knowledge, at least) to distinguish between them.

Based on the above, it is evident that there are difficulties in applying the method described in chapter 4 exactly as designed. Simply determining which figurines are Iron Age figurines involves a knowledge not only of the description of the figurines but beyond; it is necessary to know the full range of a type, and to know something of the iconography associated with it, in order to be able to date figurines properly and classify them into types. Some level of circularity is unavoidable. The necessity of such a process, however, overcomes any limitations that it produces. Some Iron Age types found in post-Iron levels are significant examples of unusual styles or subtypes not found among figurines from strictly Iron Age levels, and therefore their inclusion is worthwhile. The same difficulties are found in naming figurine types. If we return to an example from chapter 4, it would be unreasonable to discard the label "mourning figurine" for the purely descriptive "small standing female figurine with arms raised to the head," for several reasons: the label "mourning figurine" is already in wide use, it is considerably less awkward than the alternative, and, ultimately, it is correct. This difficulty is what Panofsky's "correctives" attempted to address; for Panofsky, only a thorough grounding in the types and styles of the period in question could help the researcher limit the influence of his own subjective viewpoint. Such a grounding allows us to determine that "mourning figurine" is an appropriate label for a certain class of figurine, even at the outset of a study. Certainly it would be more confusing, or misleading, to use a purely descriptive label and then pretend to discover the term "mourning figurine" as an appropriate label of the type after investigating its meaning and function than to adopt the label from the outset.

Format

The basic format for catalogue entries is the following:

- Registration Number
- Findspot
  (Grid.Square.Layer/Feature.FineGrid.Bucket #)
- Year of Excavation
- Context
- Dimensions (height, width, thickness, diameter)
- Description

Some of the terms used in the catalogue require further explanation.[2]

Registration Number

Every piece of material culture, or artifact, is given its own registration number. This number belongs to a sequence numbered according to the order in which it was registered; it is a single sequence running for the entire span of the excavation. Also, the fact that the artifacts are numbered by order of registration means that the numerical sequence only roughly reflects their order of excavation; artifacts were usually registered within a few days of their excavation but, in some cases, not for weeks or even years. In some cases, registration numbers were never given to figurines, and I have not found it necessary to assign new numbers at this point, as the catalogue number provided in this chapter as well as the findspot information (see below) are sufficient for purposes of identification.

[1] I have modified the catalogue from its original form in my Ph.D. dissertation. Six objects (reg. nos. 43781, 46089, 46273, 46733, 51913, and 52418) have been reassigned as legs of zoomorphic vessels (to be published in Press forthcoming), and one (reg. no. 49560) is a fragment of a Mycenaean vessel. Fifteen figurines, meanwhile have been added: cat. nos. 16, 32, 70, 172, 190, 203–6, and 210 were discovered in the 2007–2009 seasons, after the completion of the dissertation; cat. nos. 81, 87, 116, and 118 were missing when I compiled my catalogue originally but have since been located; and cat. no. 209 was reinterpreted as a figurine (instead of as an anthropomorphic vessel).

The figurines from other Philistine sites will not be catalogued. For a discussion of the types found at other Philistine sites, see chapter 6; see chapter 7 for discussion of contexts.

[2] For more on the grid system and recording system at Ashkelon, see chapter 11 of *Ashkelon 1*.

Findspot

For purposes of excavation and recording, the Leon Levy Expedition to Ashkelon has applied a grid system to the entire site. This grid system consists of 84 squares of 10,000 m^2 each (100m x 100m), running 7 squares across and 12 squares down. The grid system runs parallel to the coast, with the numbering of the grid squares starting in the northwest and running row by row (see figure 2). Each of these 100m x 100m squares is referred to as a "Grid." Each grid is then divided into 100 squares, each 10m x 10m; these are numbered similarly from northwest to southeast. Each of these squares is called a "Square."

The Ashkelon system essentially follows the Wheeler-Kenyon method of detailed stratigraphic analysis, as developed by M. Wheeler and applied by K. Kenyon at Jericho and Jerusalem.[3] Typically, each type of layer[4] and feature[5] receives its own number, as appropriate. In some cases, where a feature and its fill are associated, the designation of layer-feature (LF) is given. Each square has its own numbering system; if a layer or feature spreads across multiple squares, it will have a separate number in each square (each of which is then noted by the supervisors to be equivalent). This numbering system continues from year to year. Originally, there were separate sequences for layers and features, but this system was changed early in the history of the excavation so that layers and features share a single sequence; note, however, that the original separate sequences were still retained for the earliest seasons and not changed retroactively.

For certain significant layers and features—usually floors and occupational debris—excavation and recording are recorded by fine grid: each 10m x 10m square is divided into 100 fine grids of 1m x 1m each, numbered in the same manner as the squares. This procedure allows the possibility of reconstructing activities in different parts of a room. Because this procedure is used for only some of the layers and features, many figurines do not have a fine grid number.

Through the 2004 season, each square kept a running sequence of pottery buckets (B) used for each season. At least one pottery bucket is used for each layer and feature (and each fine grid when applicable) for each day of excavation. Every item of material culture is then associated with the pottery bucket in use for the layer or feature in use when and where the item was found. Starting in 2007, a single sequence of pottery buckets has been used for the entire excavation, and this sequence is not restarted each season.

Context

This line gives the local phasing (the phasing of the individual grid) for the findspot and a brief description. I believe having the contextual information presented along with the catalogue provides a more useful reference than separating this information, as in a purely descriptive catalogue, which leaves contextual analysis for a separate chapter.

Typology

For this study I have devised a typology of Philistine figurines.[6]

I. Anthropomorphic Figurines
- A. Female Figurines
  - 1. Small standing handmade figurines
    - a. miniature
    - b. standard
  - 2. Large (seated) handmade figurines ("Ashdoda" and similar types)
    - a. miniature
    - b. standard
    - c. with arms
  - 3. Composite figurines
  - 4. Plaque figurines
  - 5. Hollow moldmade figurines
  - 6. Miscellaneous
- B. Male Figurines
  - 1. Riders
  - 2. Miscellaneous

II. Zoomorphic Figurines
- A. Horses
  - 1. With riders
  - 2. Without riders
- B. Lions
- C. Bulls
- D. Birds
- E. Miscellaneous

[3] See Wheeler 1954; Kenyon 1952. For discussion of its influence on the American excavations at Gezer, see Dever, Lance, and Wright 1970:9–10.

[4] Layers of dirt: deliberate or natural fill, occupational debris, destruction debris, etc.; "L" in the catalogue.

[5] Feature or structure: wall, pit, well, floor, etc.; "F" in the catalogue.

[6] Though separate, it is partially based on those of previous studies. Thus, the basic divisions of figurines (anthropomorphic vs. zoomorphic, male vs. female) and identifications of major types (standing figurines, seated figurines/Ashdodas, etc.) follow those of earlier studies. On the other hand, the exact order of the types, some of their names, and their subtypes are unique to this study. This typology is also unique in that it is focused on figurines from Philistia and is comprehensive for the entire Iron Age assemblage from Philistia.

This typology includes all types of figurines from Philistia, not just those found at Ashkelon. I have organized the catalogue according to figurine type in this typology (meaning that certain types are skipped if they are not attested in finds from Ashkelon). For further discussion of the typology, see chapter 6.

Catalogue of Philistine Figurines

I.A.1.a. (Miniature Small Standing Female Figurines)

Catalogue no. 1

Registration no.:	40293
Findspot:	50.59.L427.B265
Year excavated:	1992
Context:	Ph. 9 natural fill
Height:	3.0 cm
Width:	2.6 cm
Thickness:	1.4 cm
Description:	A head and upper torso, probably female. The nose is pinched; the eyes are formed by two incised dots, and the mouth is also incised. The headdress is a typical *polos* with a concave top. The arms are broken off. Brown clay, gray core, 0.25–1.00 mm grits.

Scale 1:1

Catalogue no. 2

Registration no.:	53755
Findspot:	38.84.L685.B15
Year excavated:	2000
Context:	Ph. 19A street
Height:	2.6 cm
Width:	3.7 cm
Thickness:	2.0 cm
Description:	A neck and upper female torso (with raised breasts). The arms and head are broken off. Orange clay, with horizontal and vertical red-brown lines painted on front and back. Black core, 0.25–0.50 mm grits.

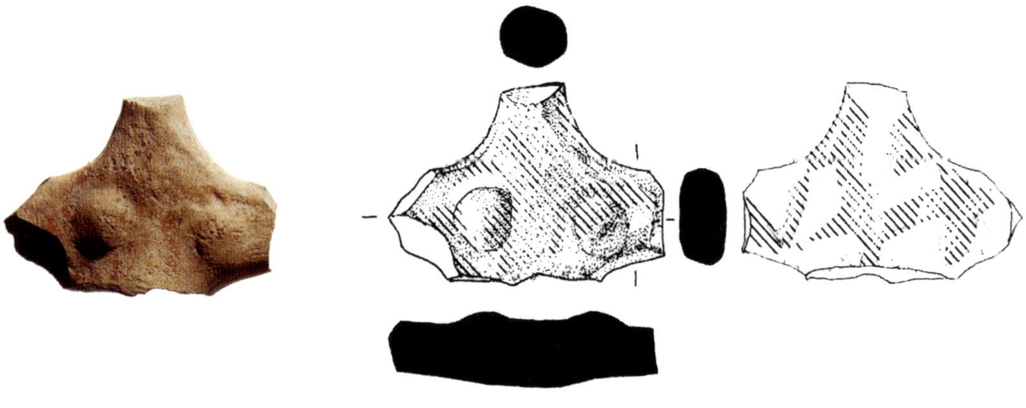

Scale 1:1

Catalogue no. 11

Registration no.:	53503
Findspot:	38.84.LF638.B286
Year excavated:	1999
Context:	Ph. 17C deliberate fill
Height:	3.6 cm
Width:	3.5 cm
Thickness:	2.1 cm (at base)
Diameter:	0.8 cm (of hole)
Description:	A human torso, possibly female: there are no breasts or other anatomical features emphasized. The head is broken off. There is a hole running from the neck through the bottom of the torso, suggesting that this figurine might have been attached to a vessel (or other object) by a dowel. Reddish clay, light gray slip, with black painted lines: there is one around the waist, one partially preserved around the base, and one on top of each arm. Clay-colored core, 0.25–1.00 mm grits.

Scale 1:1

Catalogue no. 12

Registration no.:	53647
Findspot:	38.75.L148.B18
Year excavated:	2000
Context:	Ph. 17A deliberate fill
Height:	3.6 cm
Width:	3.5 cm
Diameter:	1.6 cm (of neck); 2.3 cm (of top: outer); 1.7 cm (of top: inner)
Description:	A human head, with a hole in the top and another in the neck; these may have originally been one continuous hole, but there is clay blocking them in between. There are applied pellets for eyes and applied pieces of clay on the sides of the head (perhaps representing hair). The nose is small and raised and partially broken; there are ridges on the sides of the head, probably representing ears. There is no mouth. Red-brown clay, cream slip. Light-colored core, 0.25–0.50 mm grits.

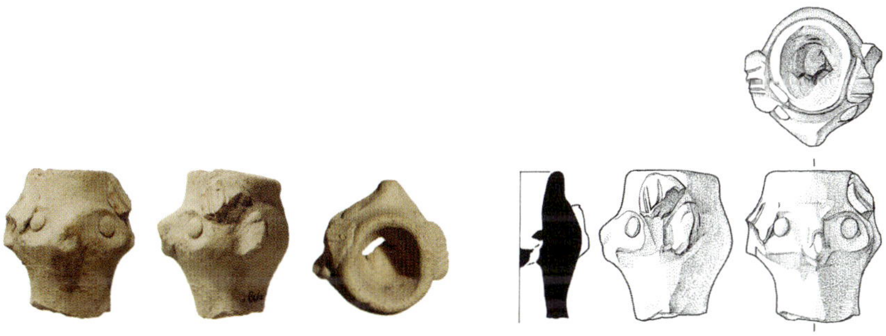

Scale 1:2

Catalogue no. 13

Registration no.:	54271
Findspot:	38.83.L464.FG90.B39
Year excavated:	2000
Context:	Ph. 19A courtyard
Height:	3.0 cm
Width:	1.8 cm
Thickness:	2.3 cm
Description:	A human head, probably female. There is a small applied pellet for one eye (the other is missing) and a pinched nose; there is no mouth. The *polos* is concave and tilted down toward the back; there is a round piece of clay on top of the headdress. Light brown clay, clay-colored core, 0.25–0.75 mm grits.

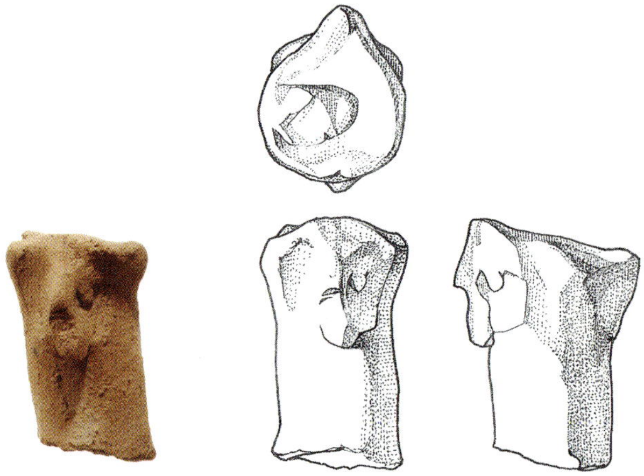

Scale 1:1

Catalogue no. 14

Registration no.:	55679
Findspot:	38.83.L488.FG47.B103
Year excavated:	2000
Context:	Ph. 19B occupational debris
Height:	8.6 cm
Width:	4.9 cm (at hands); 2.9 cm (of body)
Thickness:	1.8 cm (of body)
Description:	A cylindrical female figurine. The head has incised dots for eyes and a small pinched nose which is largely missing. The headdress (*polos*) is concave and tilting slightly backward. The torso has scars from the breasts, with a small hole incised in each. Most of the lower body is preserved, without legs differentiated. Red-brown clay, cream slip, with horizontal black lines over most of the front (but not continuing onto the back), running from the base up to the face. Black core, 0.25–3.00 mm grits.

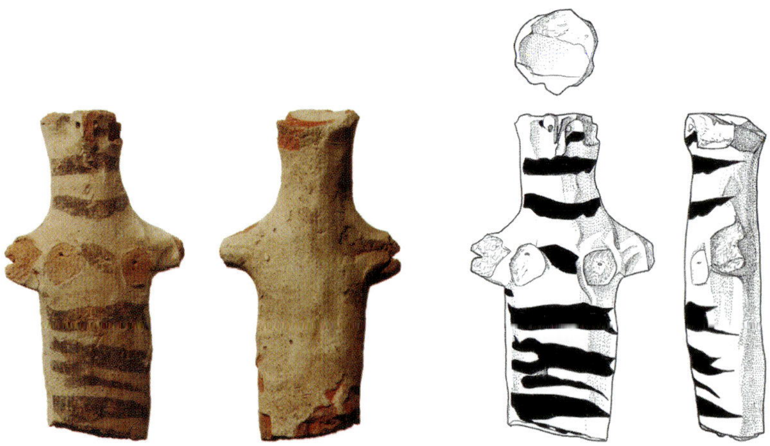

Scale 1:2

Catalogue no. 15

Registration no.:	56375
Findspot:	38.83.L536.B14
Year excavated:	2004
Context:	Ph. 19A pit
Height:	2.5 cm
Width:	1.6 cm (of neck); 2.4 cm (of *polos*)
Thickness:	2.0 cm
Description:	A human head, probably female. The *polos* is slightly concave and slanting backward. The entire face is formed by a depression, with ridges for eyebrows and another ridge for the chin or mouth. The nose is pinched, and the eyes are incised. The top of the headdress is entirely painted; there is also a painted ring around the entire circumference of the neck. Brown clay, with red paint. Brown core, few if any grits.

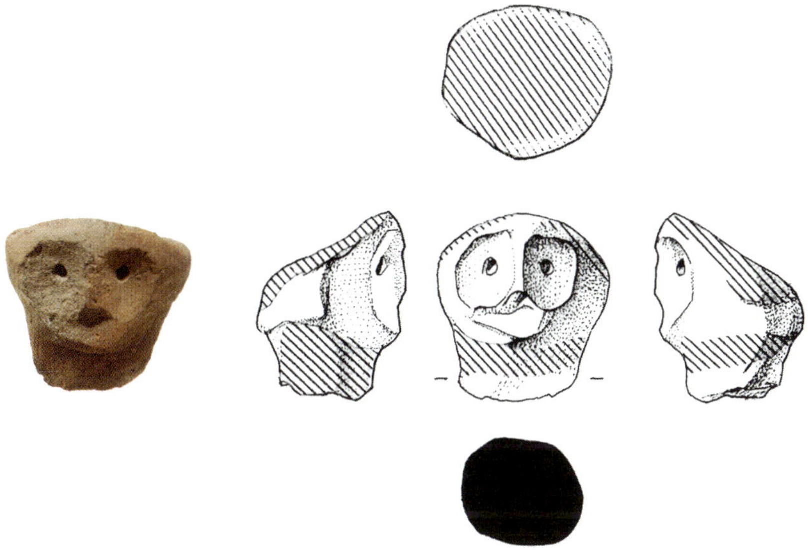

Scale 1:1

Catalogue no. 16

Registration no.:	57469
Findspot:	38.84 [North baulk].B1891
Year excavated:	2007
Context:	N/A
Height:	7.7 cm
Width:	7.2 cm (at arms)
Thickness:	3.0 cm
Description:	A female torso, with arms out to sides. The breasts are relatively large applied pieces of clay, not pellets. Black paint, including a necklace, zigzag line down the chest, and ringed breasts. There are incised lines down the back. Red-brown clay, with a cream-colored surface; no clear core; white grits, 0.25–2.00 mm.

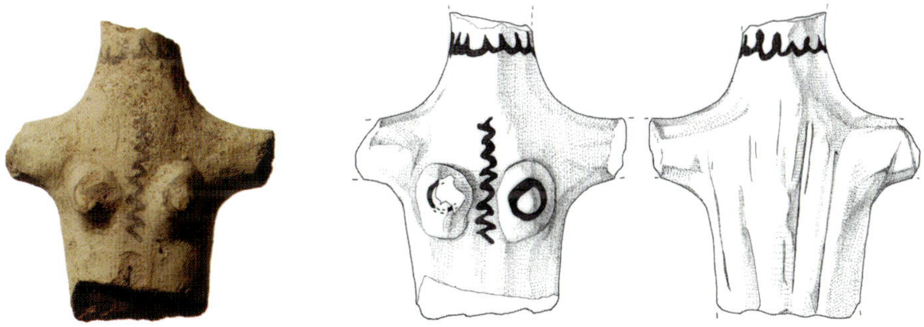

Scale 1:2

Catalogue no. 17

Registration no.:	Unregistered
Findspot:	50.49.L440.B168
Year excavated:	1994
Context:	Ph. 7 quarry fill
Height:	3.9 cm
Width:	3.6 cm (of head); 2.0 cm (of neck)
Thickness:	2.8 cm
Description:	An anthropomorphic head. There are applied pellets for eyes, a pinched nose, and ears pinched at the sides of the head. The *polos* is concave and tilted down toward the back, with a ridge all the way around but especially pronounced on the front and by the ears on the sides. The neck is mostly preserved. Reddish-brown clay, cream slip.

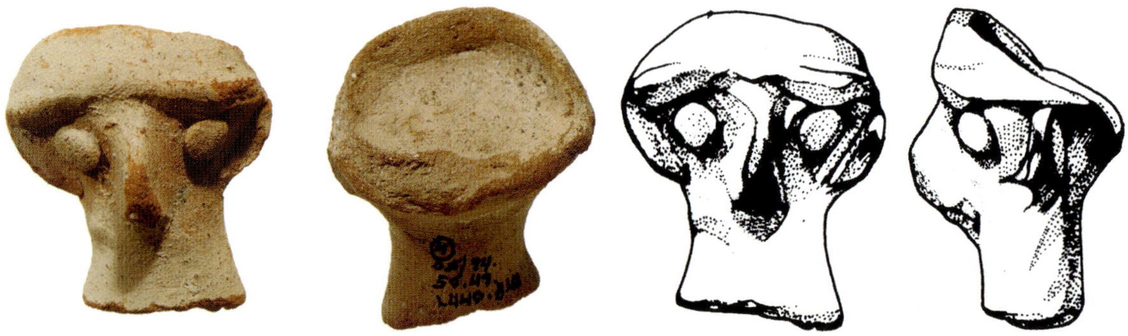

Scale 1:1

I. A. 2. (Large [Seated] Female Figurines; "Ashdoda" and Similar Types)

Catalogue no. 18

Registration no.:	43782
Findspot:	38.74.LF563.B60
Year excavated:	1994
Context:	Ph. 16 pit
Height:	4.0 cm
Width:	7.8 cm
Depth:	5.1 cm
Description:	An Ashdoda chair fragment: only the front of the "couch" is preserved, with the two front legs complete. There is a partial scar from one of the back legs, with the rest of the back of the seat missing. Brown clay, black core, 0.25–0.50 mm grits.

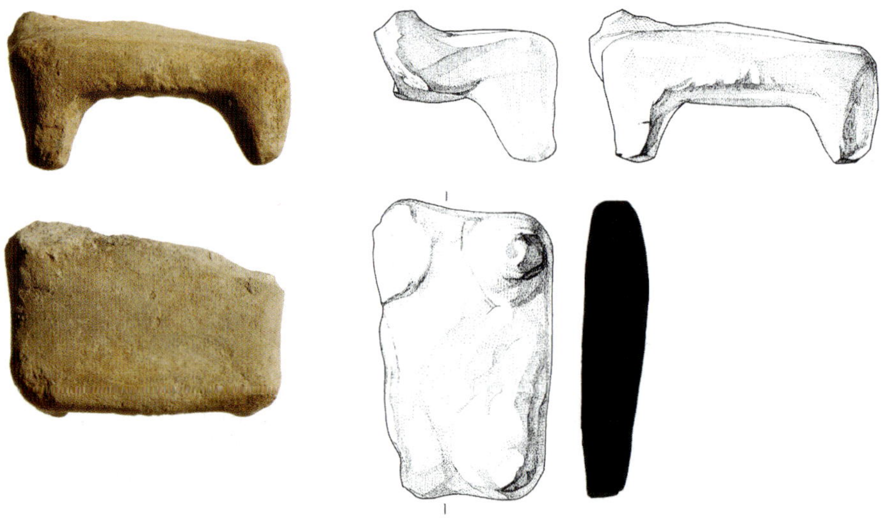

Scale 1:2

Catalogue no. 19

Registration no.:	44919
Findspot:	50.58.L318.B22
Year excavated:	1994
Context:	Ph. 7 quarry fill
Height:	8.2 cm
Width:	7.9 cm
Thickness:	2.2 cm
Description:	An Ashdoda torso: fragment of a torso/back with two breasts. The bottom is broken off as it is curving and thickening (the top of the Ashdoda "seat") and broken off at the neck. There is a clear neck scar. Reddish-brown clay with cream slip and red paint: an "x" across the center of the chest between the breasts and circles around the breasts. Black core, 0.25–1.00 mm grits.

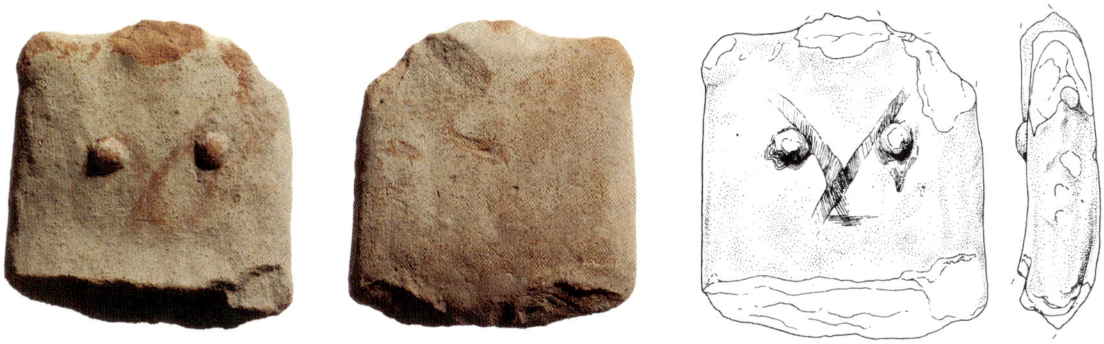

Scale 1:2

Catalogue no. 20

Registration no.:	45403
Findspot:	2.65.L5.B12
Year excavated:	1995
Context:	Ph. 8 deliberate fill
Height:	6.3 cm
Width:	7.1 cm
Thickness:	1.5 cm
Description:	A probable anthropomorphic torso. The head is broken off, the neck is partially preserved, and the base is completely missing. Protrusions from the upper corners of the torso may represent raised arms. This figurine is similar to the Ashdoda torso, but thinner and without any breasts. Light brown clay, black core, 0.25–3.00 mm grits.

Scale 1:2

Catalogue no. 21

Registration no.: 46097
Findspot: 38.84.L446.B185
Year excavated: 1995
Context: Ph. 14 robber trench
Height: 7.7 cm
Width: 9.0 cm
Thickness: 2.3 cm
Description: An Ashdoda torso: a complete torso/back with two breasts (one broken off). There is a ridge on top, with the two upper corners broken off but appearing to protrude slightly. There is a possible neck scar on the top, but it is relatively thin. Red-brown clay, with traces of white slip. Black core, 0.25–3.00 mm grits.

Scale 1:2

Catalogue no. 22

Registration no.: 48701
Findspot: 38.74.L724.B63
Year excavated: 1997
Context: Ph. 17C deliberate fill
Height: 2.7 cm
Width: 10.0 cm
Depth: 5.8 cm
Description: An Ashdoda chair fragment: most of the "couch" is preserved, but the back of the seat and the two rear legs are missing. The two front legs are largely broken off. Brown clay, black core, 0.25–5.00 mm grits.

Scale 1:2

Catalogue no. 23

Registration no.:	50559
Findspot:	38.84.L496.FG86.B73
Year excavated:	1998
Context:	Ph. 18A occupational debris
Height:	6.6 cm
Diameter:	2.3 cm (of neck); 2.1–2.6 cm (bottom of fragment); 3.8 cm (of head)
Description:	An Ashdoda head and neck. The head has applied pellets for eyes and a thick pinched nose. There is a typical *polos*, tilted down toward the back, but it is flat instead of concave. The neck is long and broken off at the point of the body join. Light brown clay, with traces of white slip. Clay-colored core, 0.25–1.00 mm grits.

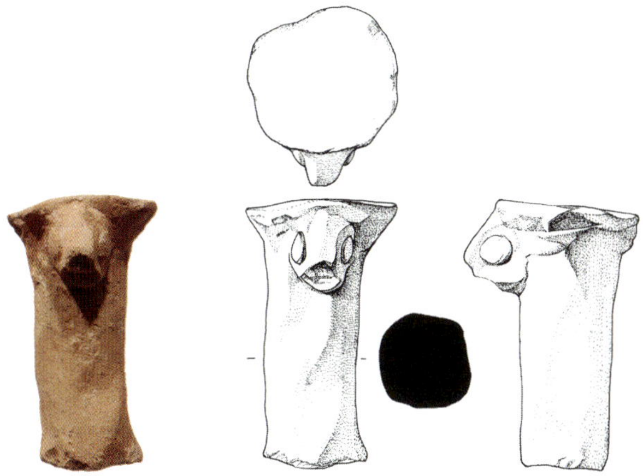

Scale 1:2

Catalogue no. 24

Registration no.:	50647
Findspot:	38.84.L591.B52
Year excavated:	1998
Context:	Ph. 17C deliberate fill
Height:	6.1 cm
Width:	3.7 cm
Thickness:	3.1 cm
Description:	A large human head, probably female. The eyes are applied pellets incised with dots (for pupils). The triangular nose is largely broken off. There are ears pinched on the sides of the head and an incised mouth. A ring of clay extends around most of the neck but does not extend around all of the back. The *polos* is concave and tilted downward toward the back, with small incisions along the front edge (representing either headdress decorations or hair). Gray colored clay, with white slip. Black core, 0.25–1.00 mm grits.

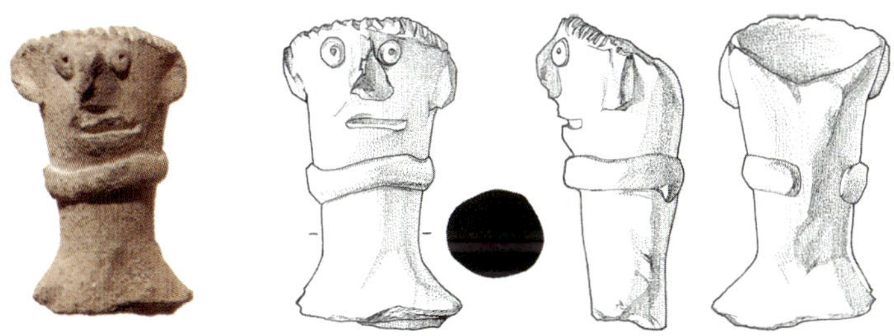

Scale 1:2

Catalogue no. 25

Registration no.:	50766
Findspot:	38.84.L496.FG88.B35
Year excavated:	1998
Context:	Ph. 18A occupational debris
Height:	6.1 cm
Width:	2.7 cm
Thickness:	1.5 cm
Diameter:	3.6 cm (of head)
Description:	A large human head and neck, possibly female. The face is very poorly preserved with no features visible. There are large ears on the sides of the head. The *polos* is flat and tilting toward the back, with a ridge on the front half. Light brown clay, gray core, 0.25–1.00 mm grits.

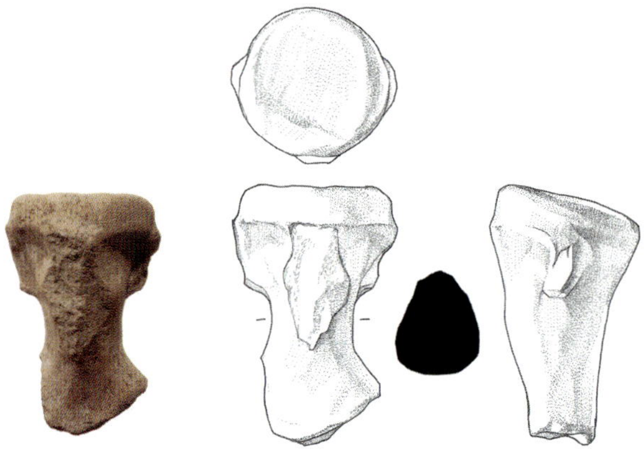

Scale 1:2

Catalogue no. 26

Registration no.:	52435
Findspot:	38.84.L686.B98
Year excavated:	1999
Context:	Ph. 18A deliberate fill
Height:	5.8 cm
Width:	9.0 cm
Depth:	7.6 cm
Description:	An Ashdoda chair and torso fragment: all of the seat is preserved, as is the bottom of the torso/back. All four legs are broken off. Gray clay with cream slip. Gray to black core, 0.5–2.5 mm grits.

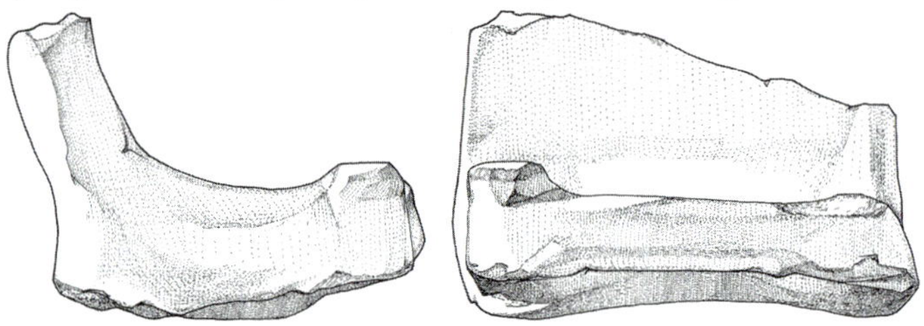

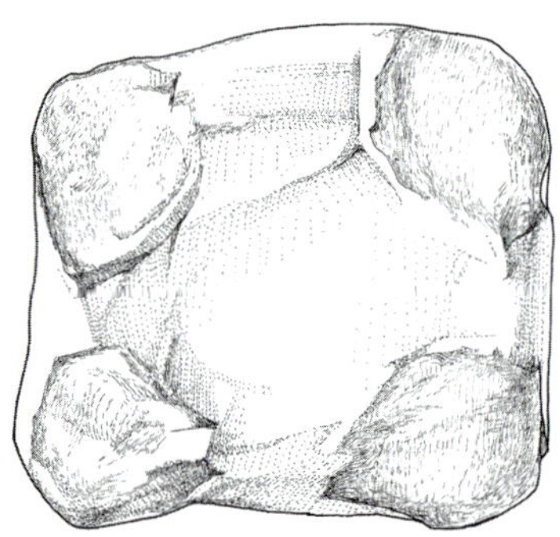

Scale 1:2

Catalogue no. 27

Registration no.:	53100
Findspot:	38.84.L693.B183
Year excavated:	1999
Context:	Ph. 18A deliberate fill
Height:	8.0 cm
Width:	8.7 cm
Thickness:	2.2 cm
Description:	An Ashdoda torso. The torso/chair back is mostly extant. The breasts are relatively close together. There is a scar on the top from the broken-off neck. Reddish-brown clay with cream slip, and black and red paint: there are black and red horizontal lines painted across the torso, and the breasts and the space in between them is painted solidly red. Black core, 0.25–5.00 mm grits.

Scale 1:2

Catalogue no. 28

Registration no.:	56867
Findspot:	38.63.L759.B5
Year excavated:	1996
Context:	Ph. 17A deliberate fill
Height:	4.1 cm
Width:	7.2 cm
Thickness:	1.4 cm
Description:	A partial Ashdoda torso. The fragment is broken off just below the breasts, one of which is completely preserved while the other is partially preserved. There is a neck scar. The left side has part of an arm preserved, ending in what appears to be a hand cupping the left breast. Reddish-brown clay with white slip preserved fairly well on the front, and less well on the back. Gray core, 0.25–1.00 mm grits.

Scale 1:2

Catalogue no. 29

Registration no.:	56954
Findspot:	50.49.L428.B12
Year excavated:	1994
Context:	Ph. 7 foundation trench
Height:	5.5 cm
Width:	3.9 cm
Thickness:	2.0 cm
Description:	An Ashdoda torso fragment. One half of the torso/chair back is preserved, with one breast. The breast is closer to the upper corner of the torso than on the other examples of this type. Brown clay, dark brown core, 0.50–2.00 mm grits.

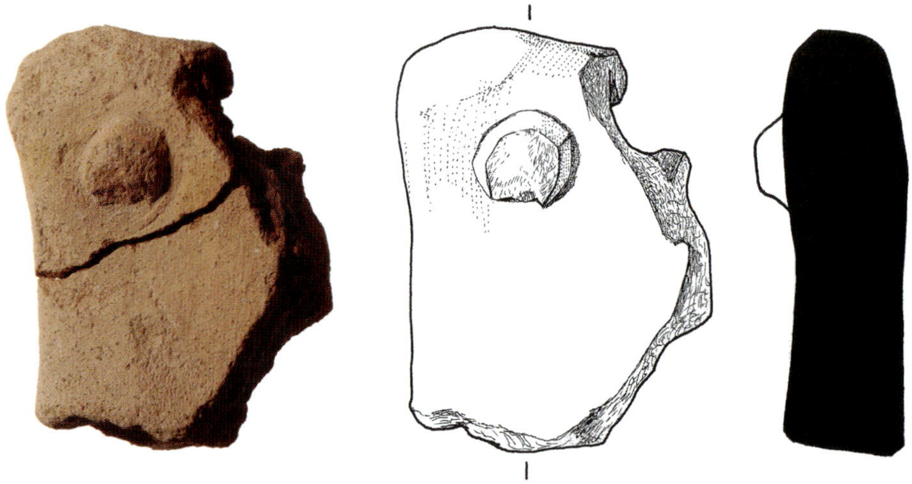

Scale 1:1

Catalogue no. 30

Registration no.:	40638
Findspot:	50.48.LF151.B435
Year excavated:	1992
Context:	Byzantine well
Height:	7.7 cm
Diameter:	4.4 cm (of head); 2.3–2.7 cm (of neck)
Description:	A large human head and neck. There are pellets applied for eyes, but most of the rest of the face (including the nose and possible mouth) is broken off. There is a large rectangular ear on the left side of the head; the right ear is broken off. The headdress is slightly convex, with a central ridge running front-to-back across it, and is level instead of being tilted downward toward the back. A fairly long neck is preserved. Reddish-brown clay, cream slip, gray core, 0.25–2.00 mm grits.

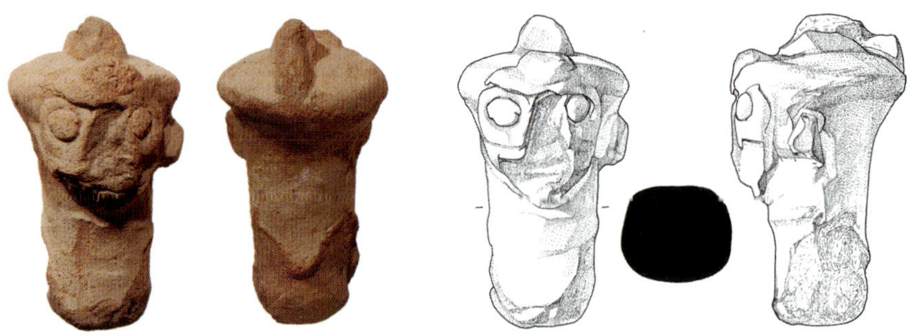

Scale 1:2

Catalogue no. 31

Registration no.:	56064
Findspot:	38.83.L355.B26
Year excavated:	1996
Context:	Ph. 17A courtyard
Height:	2.1 cm (actual thickness: 1.6 cm)
Width:	6.2 cm
Depth:	5.6 cm
Description:	An Ashdoda seat fragment: the front part of the "couch" is preserved, with scars from the two front legs. Reddish-brown clay, with white slip, clay-colored core, 0.10–0.50 mm grits.

Scale 1:2

Catalogue no. 32

Registration no.:	57585
Findspot:	38.84 [East baulk].B2005
Year excavated:	2007
Context:	N/A
Height:	8.0 cm
Width:	9.5 cm
Length:	8.7 cm
Description:	An Ashdoda seat and lower back fragment. Most of the seat is preserved, with two legs complete; there is a scar from the third, while the fourth corner is missing. Brown-red clay, with white slip, black core; white grits, 0.25–1.00 mm.

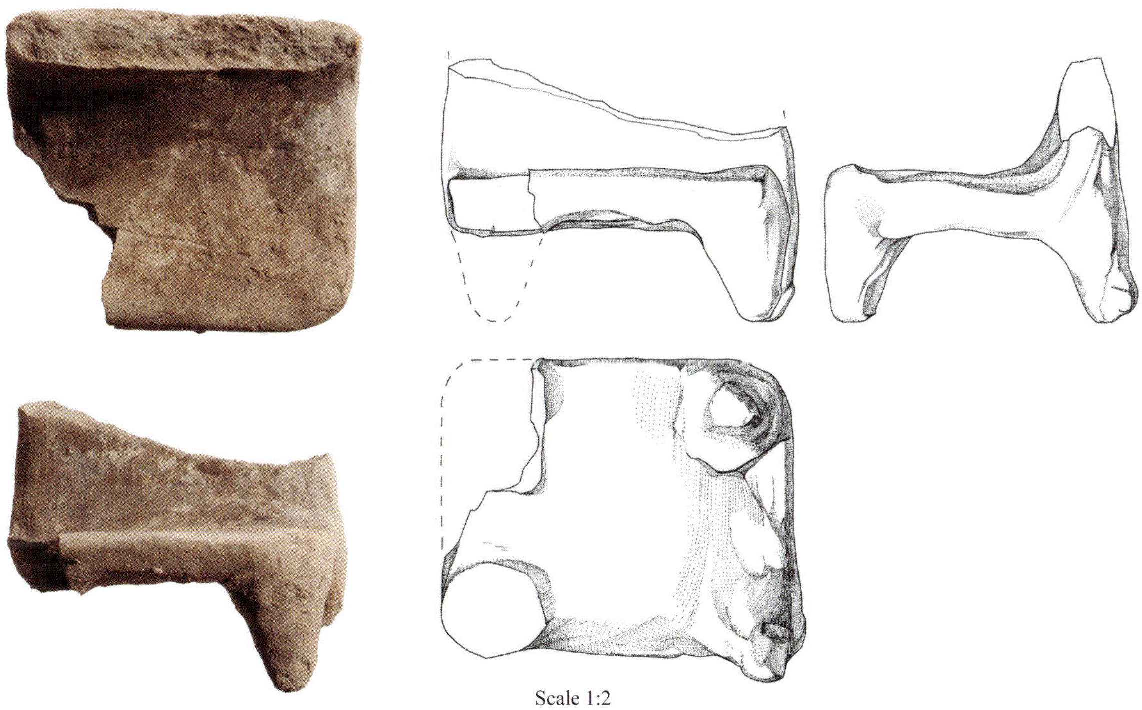

Scale 1:2

I.A.3. (Composite Female Figurines: Solid Moldmade Heads, Hollow Bodies)

Catalogue no. 33

Registration no.:	40174
Findspot:	50.49.L376
Year excavated:	1992
Context:	Ph. 7 occupational debris
Height:	5.9 cm
Width:	3.0 cm
Thickness:	1.7 cm
Description:	A female head with tang. The face is moldmade, with Egyptian features (the hair or headdress, plus the almond eyes and shape of the eyebrows), but the eyes also have pupils. The pupils are not simply outlined, but are formed by solid circular depressions. The rest of face is broken off; the head is relatively shallow, flat, and oval in shape (others of this type are more rounded). Brown clay, with traces of white slip, especially around the eyes. Clay-colored core, 0.25–0.50 mm grits.

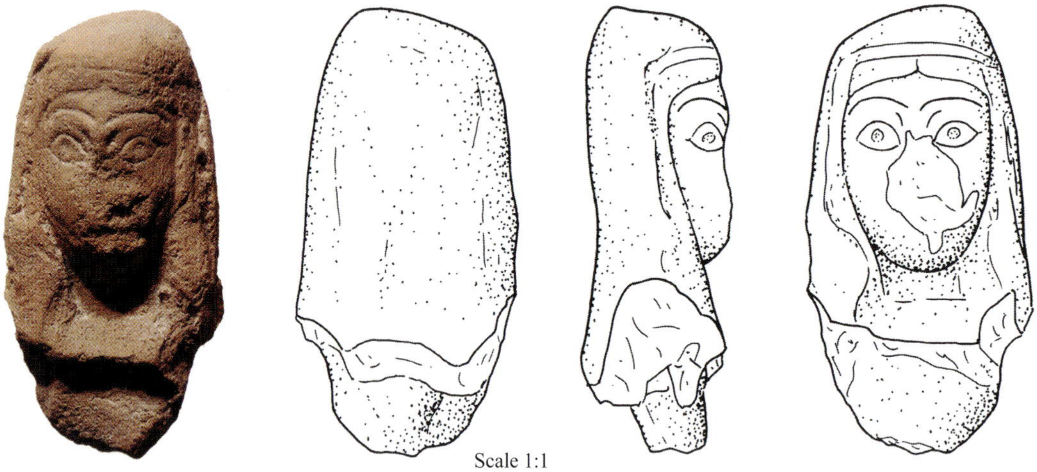

Scale 1:1

Catalogue no. 34

Registration no.:	40439
Findspot:	50.58.L302.B421
Year excavated:	1992
Context:	Ph. 7 street surface
Height:	4.2 cm
Width:	3.0 cm
Thickness:	2.3 cm
Description:	A female head without tang. The face is moldmade, with Egyptian hair/headdress and Egyptian eyes. The nose and mouth are broken off; the head is of medium roundness. Brown clay, with gray slip for the head, and traces of white slip (especially around the eyes). Black core, 0.25–1.00 mm grits.

Scale 1:1

Catalogue no. 35

Registration no.:	44344
Findspot:	50.58.L302.B9
Year excavated:	1994
Context:	Ph. 7 street surface
Height:	6.3 cm
Width:	3.2 cm
Thickness:	2.6 cm
Description:	A moldmade female head with tang. The eyes are oval with solid raised pupils; the nose is partially broken. The hair or headdress is much less wide than on most figurines of this type, with the face covering almost all of the head: it appears that the hair/headdress is an extra layer of clay handpacked onto the molded face, rather than part of the mold itself. The layer continues down around the tang as well. Brown-red clay, with traces of white slip. Gray core, 0.25–0.50 mm grits.

Scale 1:2

Catalogue no. 36

Registration no.:	44449
Findspot:	50.57.L256.B75
Year excavated:	1994
Context:	Ph. 7 quarry fill
Height:	6.1 cm
Width:	4.1 cm
Thickness:	3.8 cm
Description:	A large female head without tang. The face is moldmade, and the head is hollow. The eyes are worn but appear to be fairly large. The nose is thin, and the face is rounded. The hair/headdress may have a faint part in the center of the head. Brown clay with traces of white slip, especially around the sides. Clay-colored core, 0.25 mm grits.

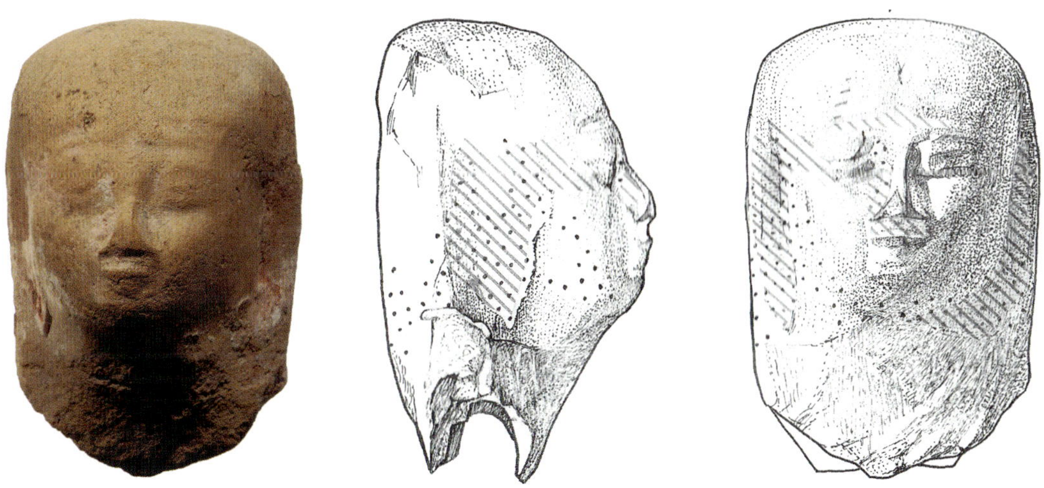

Scale 1:1

Catalogue no. 37

Registration no.:	44450
Findspot:	50.48.L448.B83
Year excavated:	1994
Context:	Ph. 7 quarry fill
Height:	7.4 cm
Width:	6.5 cm (at arms); 3.0 cm (of body)
Thickness:	2.9 cm
Description:	A female head and torso. The face is moldmade with pronounced Egyptian features (the headdress, and the eyes as thin ovals tapering off to extended lines on the sides). The headdress is a rounded veil. The torso is broken off just below the breasts. The arms are mostly broken off, but the left arm is clearly extending forward, and the right arm is extending out to the side. Light brown clay, with traces of white slip, gray core, 0.25–0.50 mm grits.

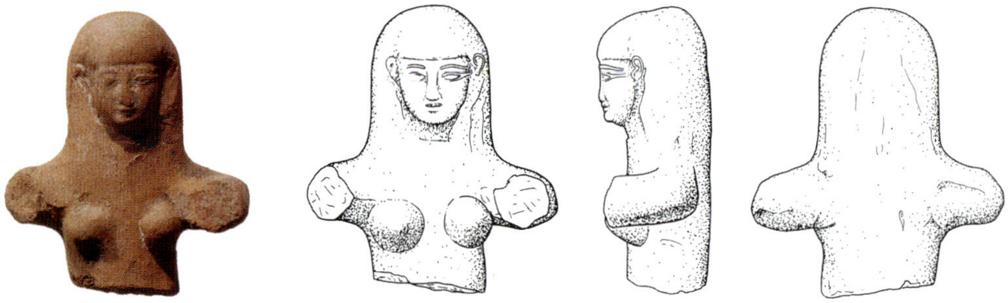

Scale 1:2

Catalogue no. 38

Registration no.:	44535
Findspot:	50.48.L439.B67
Year excavated:	1994
Context:	Ph. 7 quarry fill
Height:	6.3 cm
Width:	3.0 cm
Thickness:	2.6 cm
Description:	A small female head with tang. The eyes are the typical almond shape, and the hair (or wig) ends in bulbs along the sides below the face. Ears are clearly indicated on each side. Brown clay, clay-colored core, 0.25–1.00 mm grits.

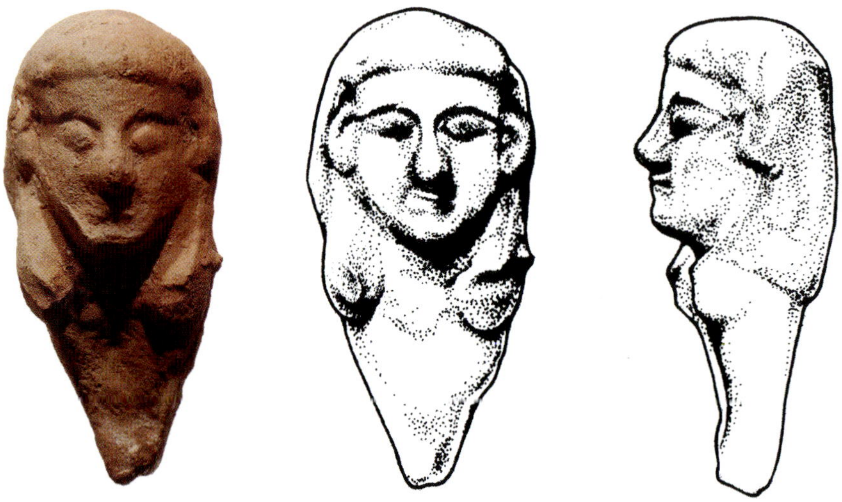

Scale 1:1

Catalogue no. 39

Registration no.:	45164
Findspot:	50.48.L446.FG48.B181
Year excavated:	1994
Context:	Ph. 7 quarry fill
Height:	6.0 cm
Width:	3.4 cm
Thickness:	2.8 cm
Description:	A female head with tang. The face is moldmade, but its features are worn. The hair (or wig) appears to come down on the sides below the face. Brown clay, gray core, 0.25–1.00 mm grits.

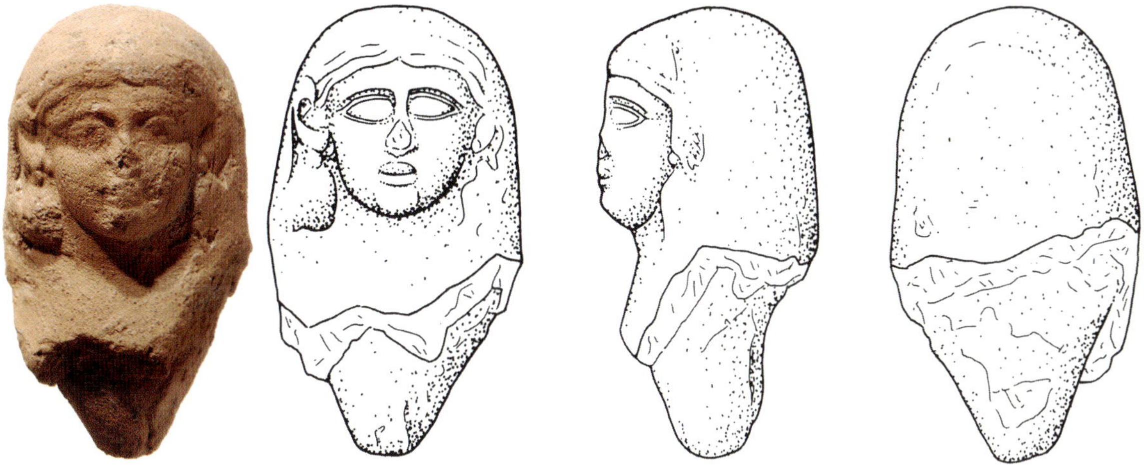

Scale 1:1

Catalogue no. 40

Registration no.:	45172
Findspot:	50.49.L440.B126
Year excavated:	1994
Context:	Ph. 7 quarry fill
Height:	5.9 cm
Width:	3.5 cm
Thickness:	2.8 cm
Description:	A small moldmade female head with tang. The features are worn, the face is round, and the nose is relatively slender. The headdress is a rounded veil. Brown-red clay, with traces of white slip, clay-colored core, 0.25 mm grits.

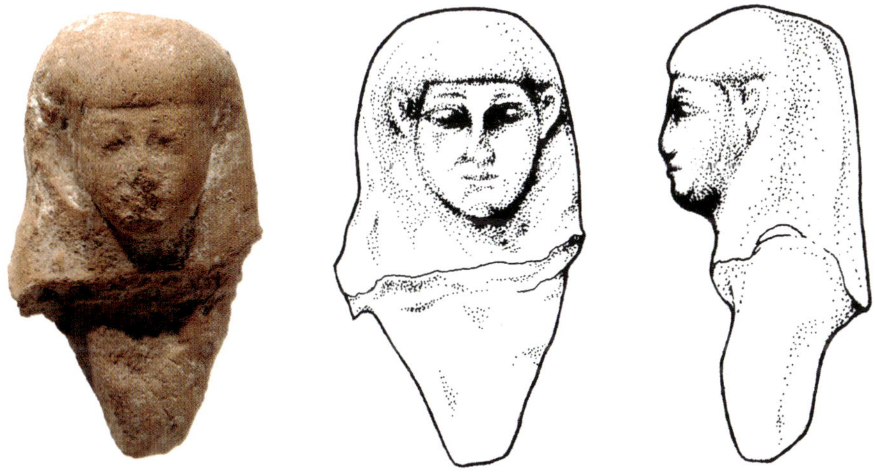

Scale 1:1

Catalogue no. 41

Registration no.: 45176
Findspot: 50.48.L449.FG58.B197
Year excavated: 1994
Context: Ph. 7 quarry fill
Height: 5.1 cm
Width: 3.4 cm
Thickness: 2.8 cm
Description: A small female head with tang. The face is moldmade, but the features are worn; the face is small and rounded, and the headdress is a rounded veil. Brown clay, gray core, 0.25 mm grits.

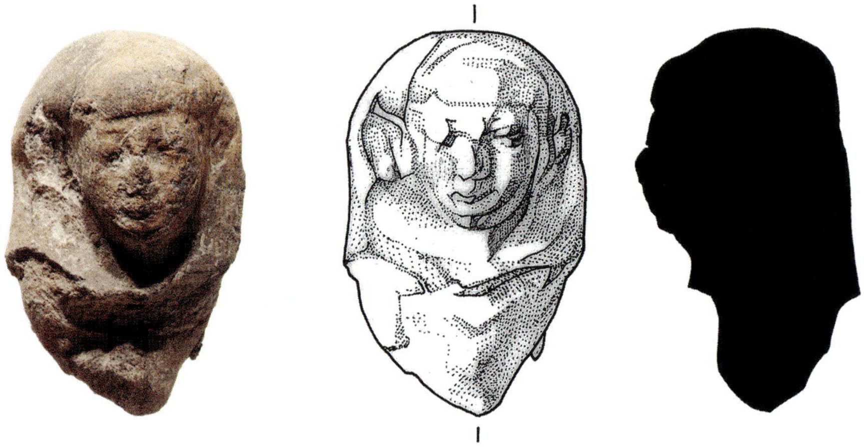

Scale 1:1

Catalogue no. 42

Registration no.: 45329
Findspot: 50.48.L452.B7
Year excavated: 1995
Context: Ph. 7 quarry fill
Height: 6.2 cm
Width: 4.1 cm
Thickness: 2.9 cm
Description: A moldmade female head with tang. The features of the face are particularly well preserved, and the execution of the face (particularly the eyes) follows the typical Egyptian style. The eyebrows are thick lines, slightly curved. The bottom half of the face is chipped. There are well-defined ears on the sides of the head. The headdress is a rounded veil. Brown clay, gray core, 0.25–0.50 mm grits.

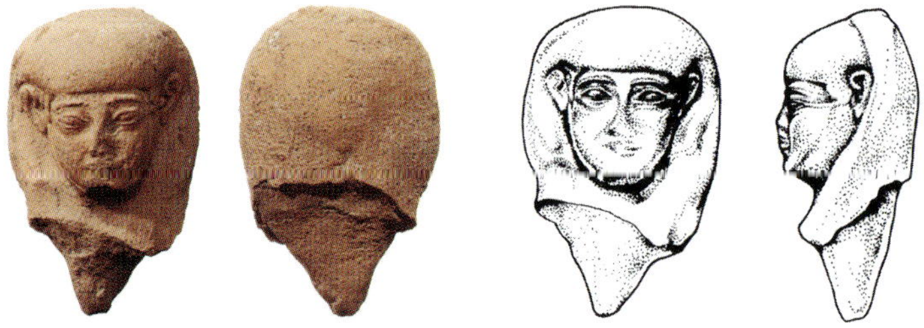

Scale 1:2

Catalogue no. 43

Registration no.: 45496
Findspot: 50.48.L452.B52
Year excavated: 1995
Context: Ph. 7 quarry fill
Height: 5.8 cm
Width: 3.4 cm
Thickness: 3.2 cm
Description: A female head with tang. The face is moldmade with solid circular eyes in relief and a large bulbous nose. The headdress is the hair/wig as opposed to the veil but is not worn. The neck and top of the body are preserved. The tang is worn and rounded. Brown clay, traces of white slip, clay-colored core, 0.25–0.50 mm grits.

Scale 1:1

Catalogue no. 44

Registration no.: 45524
Findspot: 50.48.L452.B62
Year excavated: 1995
Context: Ph. 7 quarry fill
Height: 5.9 cm
Width: 3.0 cm
Thickness: 2.7 cm
Description: A moldmade female head with tang. The eyes are solid circles in relief, with thin lines for eyebrows just below the ridge of the hair/wig, and the nose is large and bulbous. The headdress is the hair/wig but is not well preserved; it was not formed in a mold but hand-modeled around the face. Brown clay, with traces of white slip, black core, 0.25–1.00 mm grits.

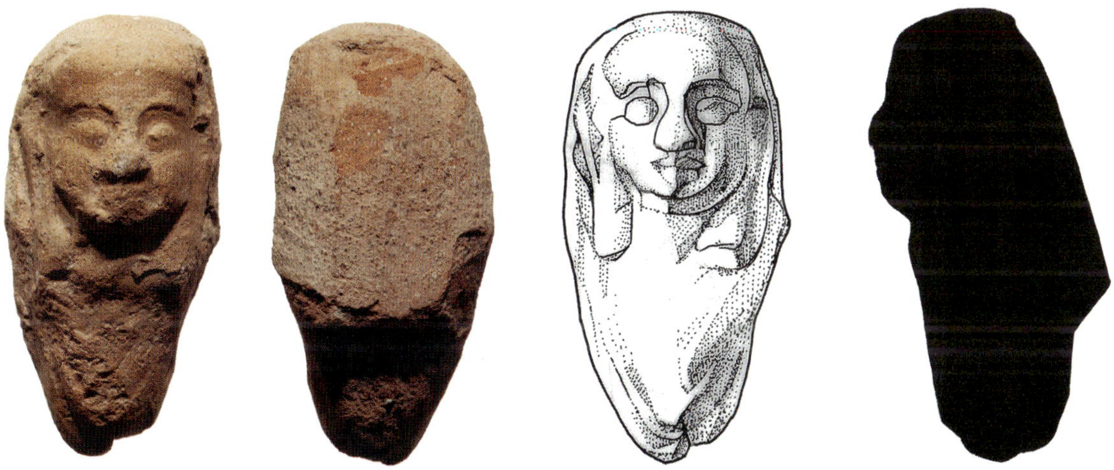

Scale 1:1

Catalogue no. 45

Registration no.: 45575
Findspot: 50.48.L452.B89
Year excavated: 1995
Context: Ph. 7 quarry fill
Height: 3.9 cm
Width: 3.2 cm
Thickness: 1.7 cm
Description: A small moldmade female head. The features of the face are very worn. The headdress is a veil which comes to a point at the top. There is no tang preserved. Brown clay, clay-colored core, 0.25–1.00 mm grits.

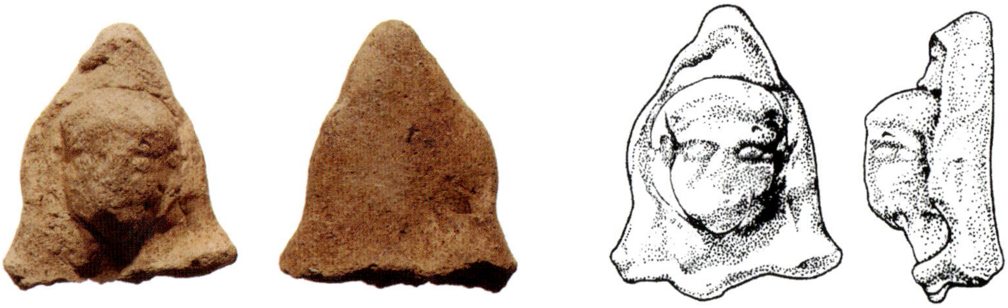

Scale 1:1

Catalogue no. 46

Registration no.: 46683
Findspot: 50.49.L451.B21
Year excavated: 1996
Context: Ph. 7 quarry fill
Height: 5.5 cm
Width: 3.6 cm
Thickness: 1.9 cm
Description: A moldmade female head with tang. The face and head have atypical features: the eyes are more rounded (instead of the more usual Egyptian style), and there is a band on the forehead with a row of small squares and circles below, perhaps representing curls. The hair extends to the bottom of the face, where it ends in straight strands instead of bulbs. The head is relatively flat. Brown clay with traces of white slip (especially around the eyes, nose, and headdress). Black core, 0.25–0.50 mm grits (few grits).

Scale 1:1

Catalogue no. 47

Registration no.: 46687
Findspot: 50.48.L462.B21
Year excavated: 1996
Context: Ph. 7 quarry fill
Height: 3.6 cm
Width: 2.7 cm
Thickness: 1.8 cm
Description: A small moldmade female head. The face is very worn. The headdress is rounded at the top but broken off at the sides. The neck or possible tang is not preserved. Cream-colored clay with traces of white slip (especially around the eyes). Gray core, 0.25–1.00 mm grits.

Scale 1:1

Catalogue no. 48

Registration no.: 46688
Findspot: 50.49.L451.B21
Year excavated: 1996
Context: Ph. 7 quarry fill
Height: 4.1 cm
Width: 3.7 cm
Thickness: 3.2 cm
Description: A moldmade female head without tang. The head is very deep and round; the face appears to have the typical Egyptian (almond or thin extended oval) eyes, but the facial features are fairly worn. The nose is partially broken off. There is a trace of a right ear, but the left ear is not depicted. The headdress is a rounded veil, with the clay around the neck area hand-modeled against the moldmade face: this process may have obscured the left ear. Brown clay, with few traces of white slip. Clay-colored core, 0.25–0.50 mm grits.

Scale 1:1

Catalogue no. 49

Registration no.:	46689
Findspot:	50.48.L462.B21
Year excavated:	1996
Context:	Ph. 7 quarry fill
Height:	5.6 cm
Width:	3.2 cm
Thickness:	2.8 cm
Description:	A moldmade female head with tang. The head is fairly round. The face is worn, but the wide oval lines of the eyes and eyebrows are visible, as is a thin nose. The headdress appears to be hair or a wig coming down to the level of the chin, with possible lines representing strands of hair across the forehead. Red-brown clay, with traces of white slip (especially around the eyes and eyebrows). Black core, 0.25–2.00 mm grits.

Scale 1:1

Catalogue no. 50

Registration no.:	46974
Findspot:	50.49.L451.B71
Year excavated:	1996
Context:	Ph. 7 quarry fill
Height:	5.8 cm
Width:	2.7 cm
Thickness:	3.2 cm
Description:	A small moldmade female head with tang. The face is so worn that most of the features are not distinguishable. The headdress is a rounded veil, with no distinguishable features other than a ridge across the forehead. Brown clay, with a few traces of white slip, clay-colored core, 0.25–1.00 mm grits.

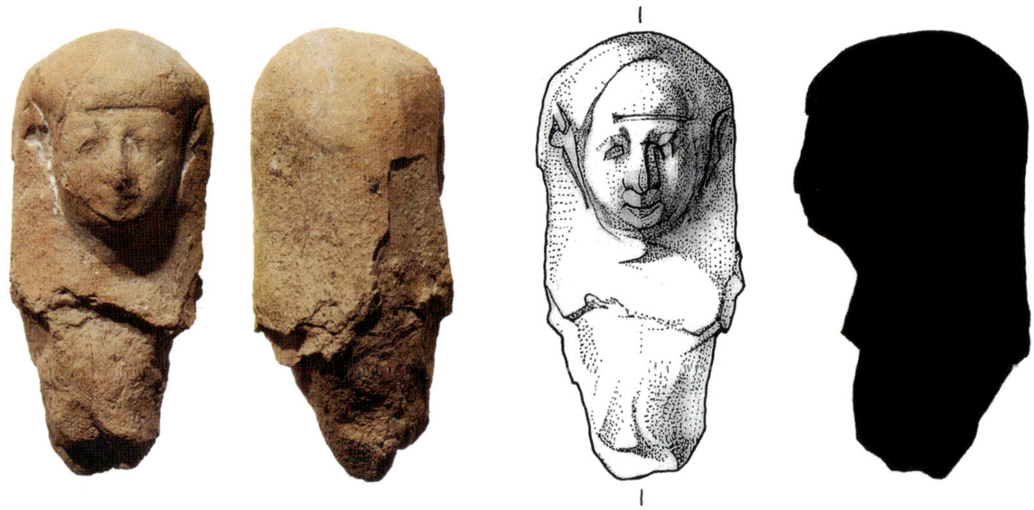

Scale 1:1

Catalogue no. 51

Registration no.:	49530
Findspot:	38.75.L54.B127
Year excavated:	1997
Context:	Ph. 14 deliberate fill
Height:	6.1 cm
Width:	3.5 cm
Thickness:	3.1 cm
Description:	A moldmade female head with tang. The face is very worn, and the individual features are not visible. The face is very round and deep. The headdress appears to be a rounded veil. Reddish-brown clay, gray core, 0.25–2.00 mm grits.

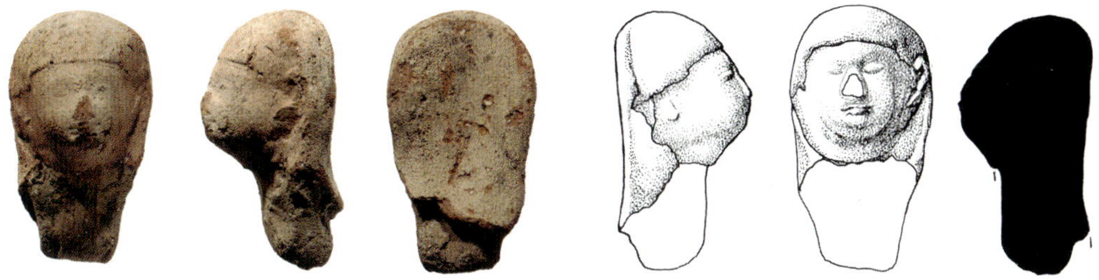

Scale 1:2

Catalogue no. 52

Registration no.:	51305
Findspot:	38.65.L48.B44
Year excavated:	1998
Context:	Ph. 14 deliberate fill
Height:	4.6 cm
Width:	3.1 cm
Thickness:	2.6 cm
Description:	A small moldmade female head. The eyes are almond-shaped, and the eyebrows are thick and raised. The nose is partially broken. The headdress is a veil that comes to a point on the top toward the back. There is no trace of a tang. Light brown clay, gray core, 0.25–0.75 mm grits.

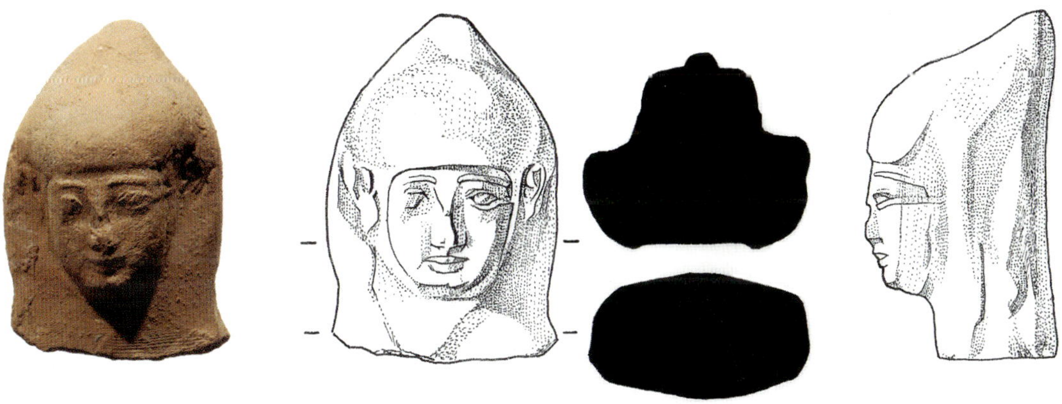

Scale 1:1

Catalogue no. 53

Registration no.: 51609
Findspot: 50.48.L452.B18, 22
Year excavated: 1995
Context: Ph. 7 quarry fill
Height: 3.4 cm
Width: 2.5 cm
Thickness: 1.7 cm
Description: A very small moldmade female head with tang. The face is very worn. The headdress is a veil which appears to come to a point, but it is also worn. The tang is a rounded stub, apparently also worn. Reddish-brown clay, gray core, 0.25–0.50 mm grits. (Note the combined pottery buckets for this figurine.)

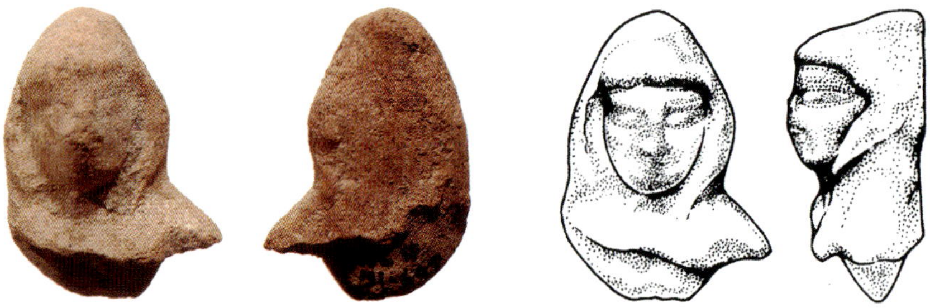

Scale 1:1

Catalogue no. 54

Registration no.: 51613
Findspot: 50.49.L453.B131
Year excavated: 1996
Context: Ph. 7 quarry fill
Height: 5.5 cm
Width: 3.3 cm
Thickness: 2.8 cm
Description: A moldmade female head with tang. The face is worn, the eyes are wide ovals, and the nose is large and bulbous. The headdress is a rounded veil. Both ears are depicted. The tang is large and rounded. Reddish-brown clay, gray core, 0.25–0.50 mm grits.

Scale 1:1

Catalogue no. 55

Registration no.:	44362
Findspot:	50.49.F354.B2
Year excavated:	1994
Context:	Ph. 7 wall
Height:	4.6 cm
Width:	3.1 cm
Thickness:	0.7 cm
Description:	A possible partial torso: a fragment of a hollow ceramic piece, which may belong to a human torso or to a pottery vessel. Part of one arm is preserved. One wheelmark is visible on the inside. Brown clay, clay-colored core, 0.25–0.50 mm grits.

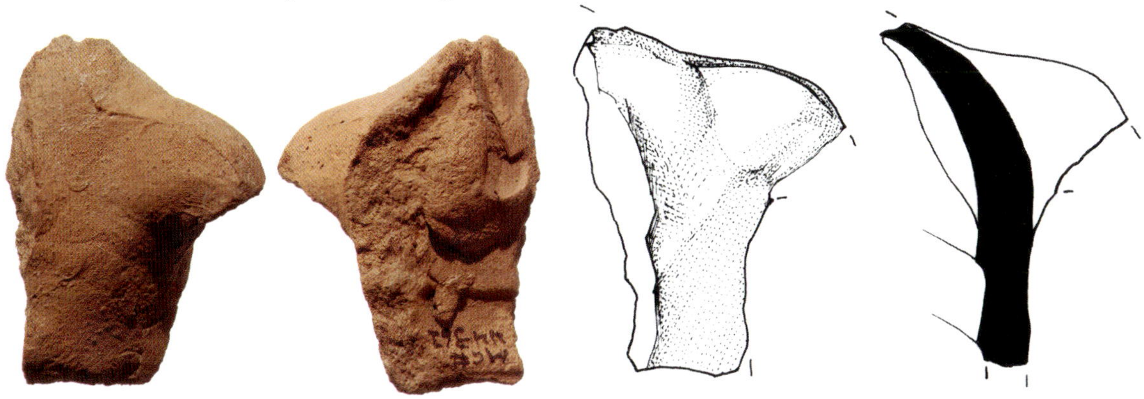

Scale 1:1

Catalogue no. 56

Registration no.:	44616
Findspot:	50.48.L448.B99
Year excavated:	1994
Context:	Ph. 7 quarry fill
Height:	6.0 cm
Width:	3.9 cm
Thickness:	4.5 cm (at breast)
Description:	A hollow female torso. The body is wheelmade (with clear wheelmarks on the interior). The sides of the torso are fairly straight but slightly widening toward the bottom (on the better preserved side). On top this fragment is broken at the neck. One breast is preserved, and there is a scar where the other has broken off. There are no arms preserved. Brown-red clay, with traces of white slip, clay-colored core, 0.25–4.00 mm grits (few grits).

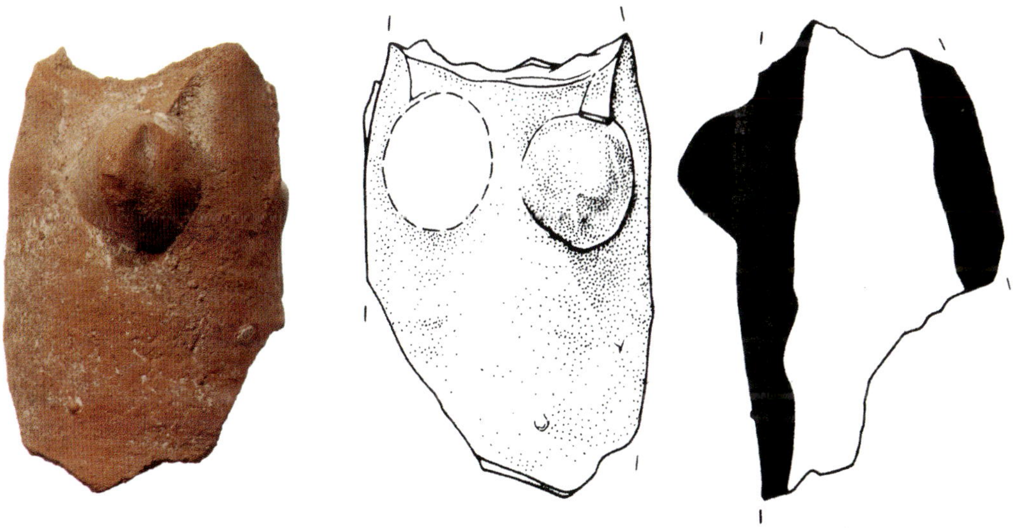

Scale 1:1

Catalogue no. 57

Registration no.:	44660
Findspot:	50.58.L302.B11
Year excavated:	1994
Context:	Ph. 7 street surface
Height:	3.5 cm
Width:	3.1 cm
Thickness:	0.7 cm
Depth:	1.9 cm
Description:	A possible fragment of a hollow female torso. Two breasts are preserved. There are no wheelmarks visible. Brown-red clay, black core, 0.25–1.00 mm grits.

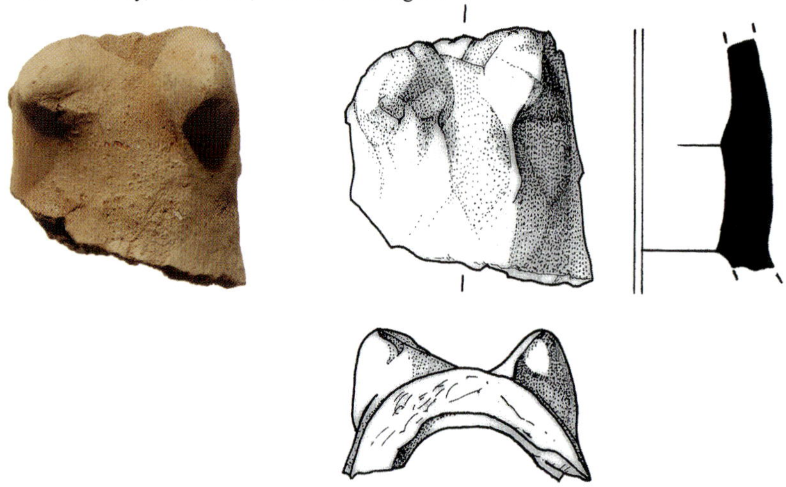

Scale 1:1

Catalogue no. 58

Registration no.:	44698
Findspot:	50.57.L259.B112
Year excavated:	1994
Context:	Ph. 7 quarry fill
Width:	4.0 cm
Thickness:	3.0 cm
Description:	A possible torso fragment. This may be the neck and upper torso of a female figurine, with part of the tang remaining in the neck. The fragment is probably handmade. Brown clay, black core, 0.25–1.00 mm grits.

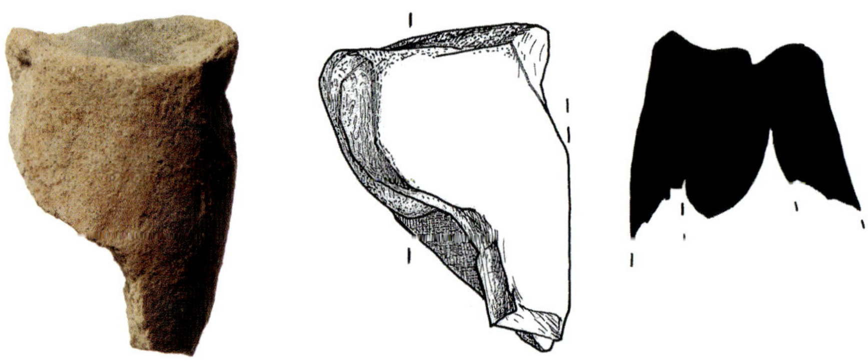

Scale 1:1

Catalogue no. 59

Registration no.: 45521
Findspot: 50.48.L452.B62
Year excavated: 1995
Context: Ph. 7 quarry fill
Height: 5.5 cm
Width: 8.1 cm
Thickness: 3.2 cm
Description: A female torso fragment. The fragment is hollow and wheelmade (there are several wheelmarks on the interior). The breasts are emphasized. The sides of the torso are straight; handmade arms are attached to the shoulders, and the arms cradle a child. The child is handmade, and is preserved completely except for the head. The left arm of the child is holding onto the female torso above the left breast. The torso is broken off just below the left arm of the female. The torso is broken at the neck; in the hollow interior, a piece of the triangular head of the tang is preserved. Reddish-brown clay, with traces of white slip, gray core, 0.25–1.00 mm grits.

Scale 1:2

Catalogue no. 60

Registration no.: 46596
Findspot: 50.48.L462
Year excavated: 1996
Context: Ph. 7 quarry fill
Height: 6.0 cm
Width: 4.2 cm
Thickness: 2.4 cm; 4.1 cm (of legs)
Description: A torso and upper legs of a handmade seated female figurine. The head and neck are missing. The legs are broken off below the knees. The right arm is completely missing; the left arm is bent at the elbow and extending out, but the hand is broken off. The breasts are shown, but the figure appears to be wearing a dress, as the legs are not differentiated on the front of the figurine; there is simply a slight depression between them. On the underside of the figurine, the legs are clearly separate where the surface clay is broken off and the core is visible. Brown clay, with traces of white slip, black core, 0.25–0.50 mm grits.

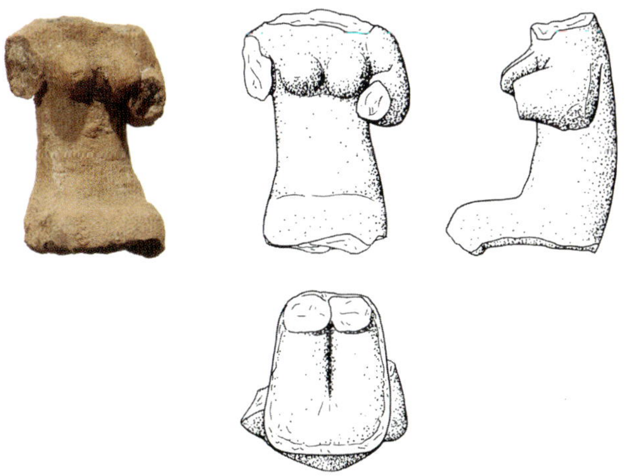

Scale 1:2

Catalogue no. 61

Registration no.: 46709
Findspot: 50.48.L462.B21
Year excavated: 1996
Context: Ph. 7 quarry fill
Height: 4.8 cm
Width: 3.7 cm
Thickness: 6.0 cm
Description: A fragment of a seated figurine: only the lower legs, feet, and pedestal of the figurine are preserved. The figure is wearing a dress that extends down to the feet. The feet were made separately from the dress and the pedestal. Light brown clay, with traces of white slip, light-colored core, 0.25–2.00 mm grits.

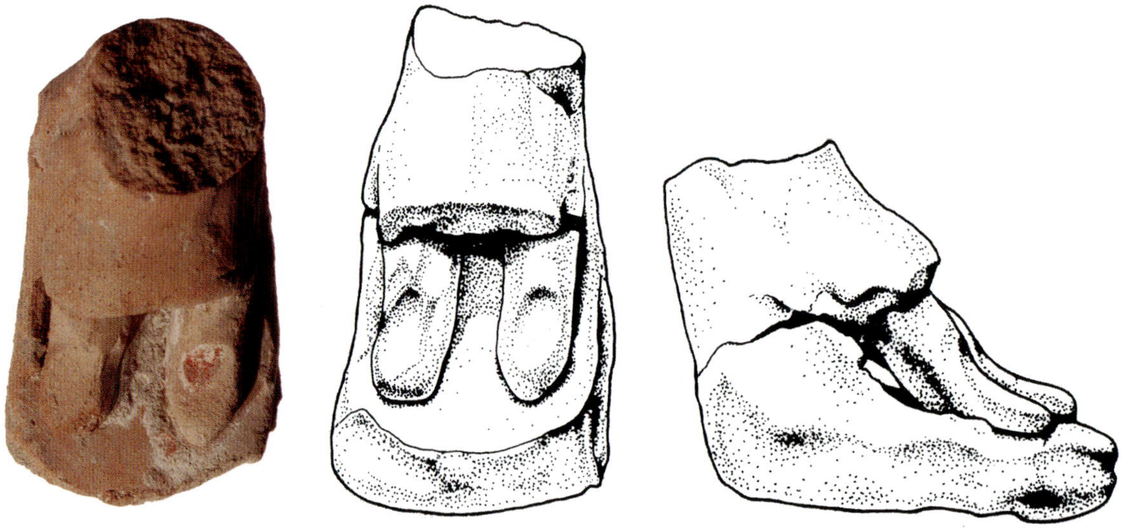

Scale 1:1

Catalogue no. 62

Registration no.: 50425
Findspot: 38.75.L57.FG53.B66
Year excavated: 1998
Context: Ph. 14 deliberate fill
Height: 7.1 cm
Width: 6.1 cm (at arms)
Thickness: 4.3–4.7 cm (at bottom of body)
Description: A torso, possibly of a female. The fragment is broken at the neck and waists. Only stumps of the arms remain. No features of the torso, such as breasts, are preserved. There is a small depression (made by a finger) at the bottom center of the torso. The figurine is hollow, with a piece of clay stuck through the neck (probably from the tang of a moldmade head). The sides of the body slope slightly outward. Reddish-brown clay, with traces of white slip; black core; 0.25–0.50 mm grits (few grits).

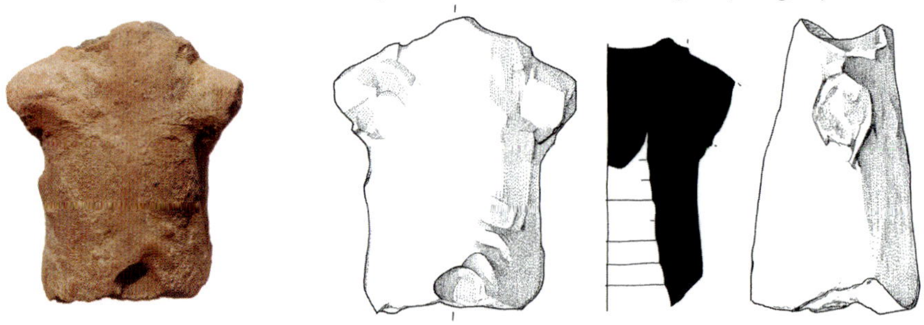

Scale 1:2

Catalogue no. 63

Registration no.:	Unregistered
Findspot:	50.49.L432.B32
Year excavated:	1994
Context:	Ph. 7 quarry fill
Height:	7.0 cm
Width:	9.2 cm
Thickness:	4.6 cm (bottom - outer); 3.6 cm (bottom - inner); 2.6 cm (top - outer); 1.7 cm (top - inner)
Description:	A wheelmade body fragment of a standing nude female figurine. The figurine is broken at the neck and the bottom of the torso. Handmade arms were attached separately; the arms bend back toward the body, and the hands cup the breasts. Wheelmarks are visible on the interior. Brown clay, with white slip; gray core; 0.25–1.50 mm grits.

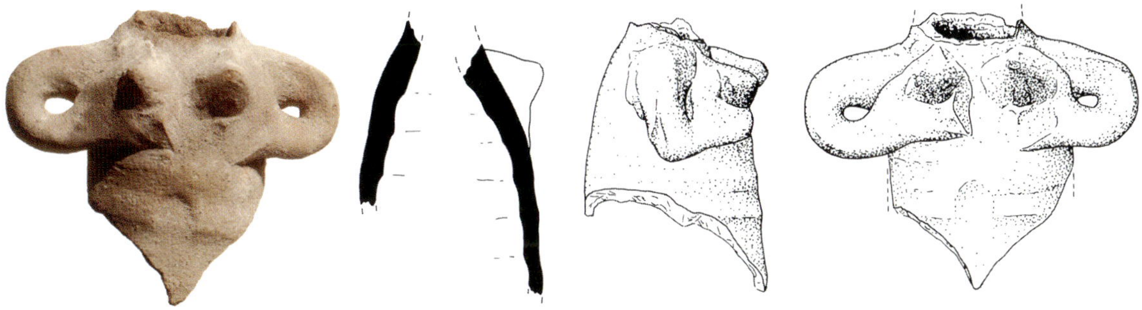

Scale 1:2

I.A.4. (Female Plaque Figurines)

Catalogue no. 64

Registration no.:	39266
Findspot:	50.59.L370.B20
Year excavated:	1992
Context:	Ph. 7 deliberate fill
Height:	9.4 cm
Width:	4.6 cm
Thickness:	2.3 cm
Description:	A standing nude female plaque figurine. The figurine is largely complete, consisting of the torso and legs; the head and neck are missing. There is a ridge along each side of the figurine, indicating the arms (and hands) at the sides and the legs below them. The breasts and the stomach are raised; there is a depression in the middle of the raised stomach. A raised upside-down triangle below the stomach may represent an emphasized pubic area, but the figurine is worn here. Red-brown clay, with traces of white slip, black core, 0.25–1.00 mm grits.

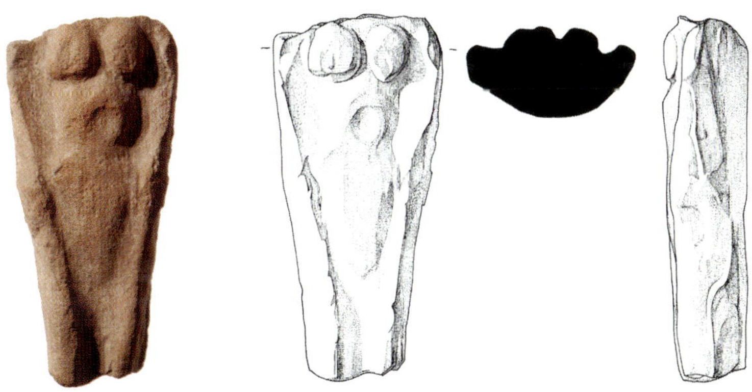

Scale 1:2

Catalogue no. 65

Registration no.:	39692
Findspot:	50.58.L262.FG41.B138
Year excavated:	1992
Context:	Ph. 7 destruction debris
Height:	4.9 cm
Width:	4.5 cm
Thickness:	2.0 cm
Description:	A head and upper torso of a female plaque figurine. The face is worn; a curved vertical incision may represent the mouth. The headdress is the typical hair or wig, reaching down to the shoulders. The figurine is broken at the shoulders. Gray-brown clay, with traces of white slip, gray core, 0.25–0.50 mm grits.

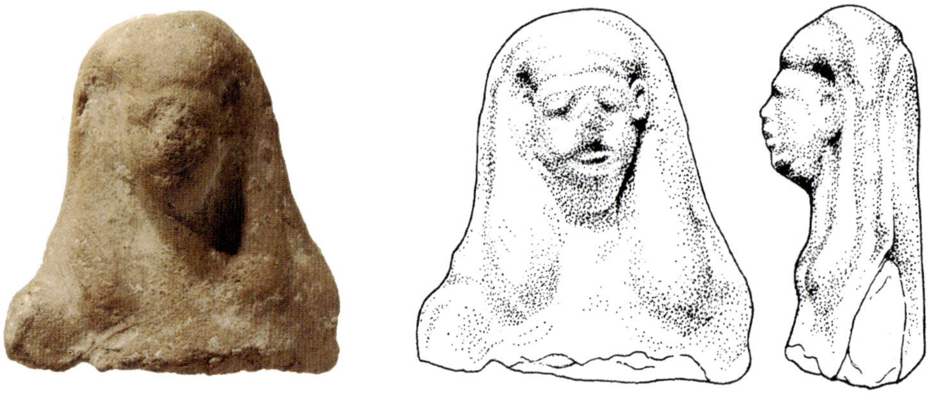

Scale 1:1

Catalogue no. 66

Registration no.:	46274
Findspot:	50.48.L462.B241
Year excavated:	1995
Context:	Ph. 7 quarry fill
Height:	6.4 cm
Width:	4.3 cm
Thickness:	2.2 cm
Description:	A mother and child plaque figurine. The torso and most of the legs are preserved. The arms are stretched across the body, cradling a child on the left side. The child's head and visible arm are covering the mother's left breast; the right breast is visible. The entire figurine was moldmade as a single piece, with the breast, arms, and child in low relief. The legs are not differentiated. There is a thin ridge along the edge of the figurine which indicates the edge of the mold. Brown clay, gray core, 0.25–0.50 mm grits.

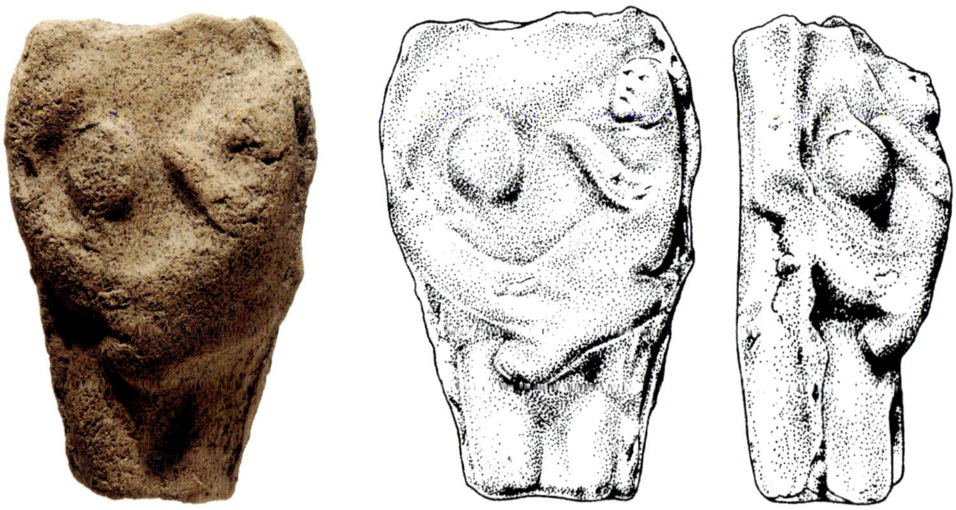

Scale 1:1

Catalogue no. 67

Registration no.:	49501
Findspot:	50.49.L482.B169
Year excavated:	1997
Context:	Ph. 9 deliberate fill
Height:	8.0 cm
Width:	4.4 cm
Thickness:	2.0 cm
Description:	Legs and feet of a nude female plaque. The figurine is very worn, and the legs are barely visible. There is a thick ridge along the sides of the figurine indicating the edge of the mold. Light brown clay, black core, 0.25–3.00 mm grits.

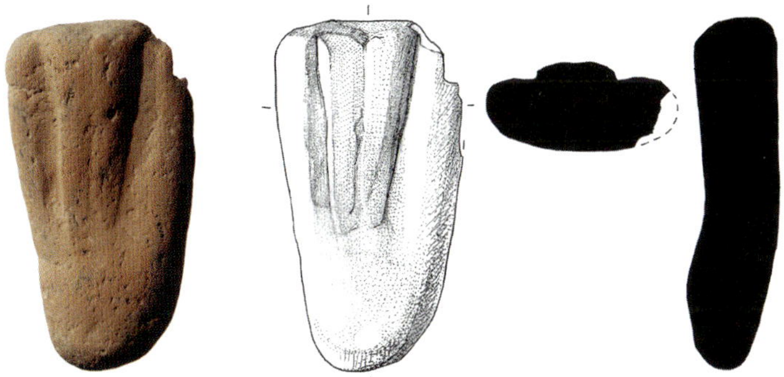

Scale 1:2

Catalogue no. 68

Registration no.:	52341
Findspot:	38.74.L848.B57
Year excavated:	1999
Context:	Ph. 18B floor
Height:	7.3 cm
Width:	3.5 cm
Thickness:	2.1 cm
Description:	A standing nude female plaque figurine. The head and neck are missing. The arms are bent, with the hands cupping the breasts. The right arm has incisions along the wrist, probably representing bracelets. The pubic area is emphasized (as an upside-down triangle). There is a fairly large clay backing to the raised figurine. Gray clay, black core, 0.25–2.00 mm grits.

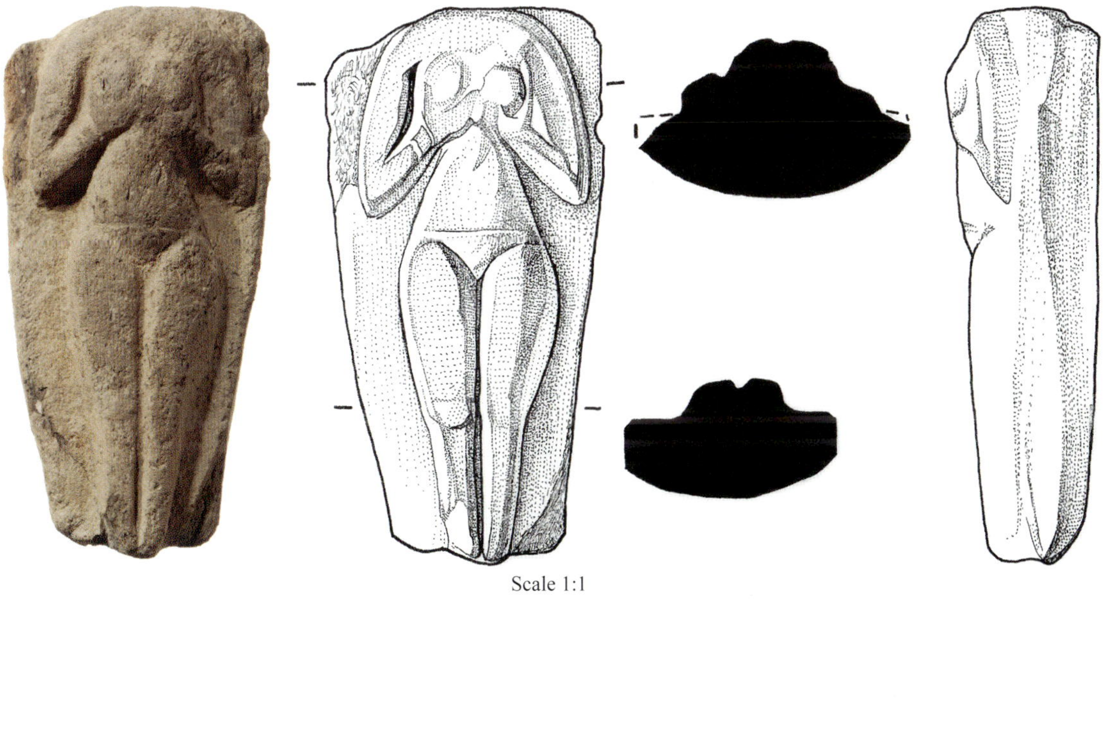

Scale 1:1

Catalogue no. 69

Registration no.:	56516
Findspot:	38.84.L973.B239
Year excavated:	2004
Context:	Ph. 20 street
Height:	2.6 cm
Width:	4.6 cm
Thickness:	2.2 cm
Description:	A fragment of a nude female plaque figurine: part of the left arm, shoulder, and part of the torso are preserved. The left breast is preserved. The locks of hair run along each side of the figurine along the chest. There are raised emblems on the body: a caprid (possibly an ibex) next to a tree on the shoulder, and around the neck area is possibly the bottom of a human figure with a zigzag pattern running down below.

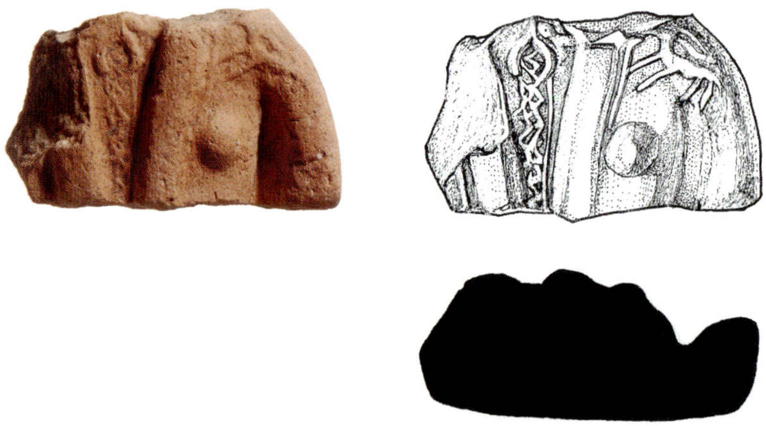

Scale 1:1

Catalogue no. 70

Registration no.:	57146
Findspot:	38.75.U317.B1307
Year excavated:	2007
Context:	Ph. 17A deliberate fill
Height:	3.7 cm
Width:	2.8 cm
Thickness:	2.1 cm (at arm)
Description:	Left side of the torso of a female figurine. The left arm is preserved, reaching toward the left breast, but the hand is broken off. The locations of the hand and breast are marked by depressions on the body. While the form is essentially a typical plaque figurine with the back flat, the figurine appears to be handmade and not moldmade. Red-brown clay, cream surface (slip?) on back; gray core, white grits (0.10–1.00 mm).

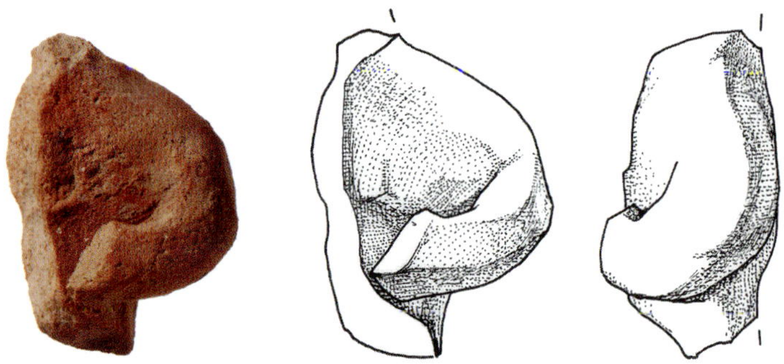

Scale 1:1

I.A.5. (Hollow Moldmade Female Figurines)

Catalogue no. 71

Registration no.: 44973
Findspot: 50.57.L259.B121
Year excavated: 1994
Context: Ph. 7 quarry fill
Height: 5.0 cm
Width: 3.5 cm
Thickness: 4.0 cm
Description: Half of a moldmade head. The figurine was made fully (three-dimensionally) in a mold. The left side of the face is preserved, with the left ear, and the left eye appears to be worn but faintly visible. Light brown clay, with red paint one ear and below the neck (possibly representing a necklace, but not enough of the neck is preserved to see); gray core, few if any inclusions.

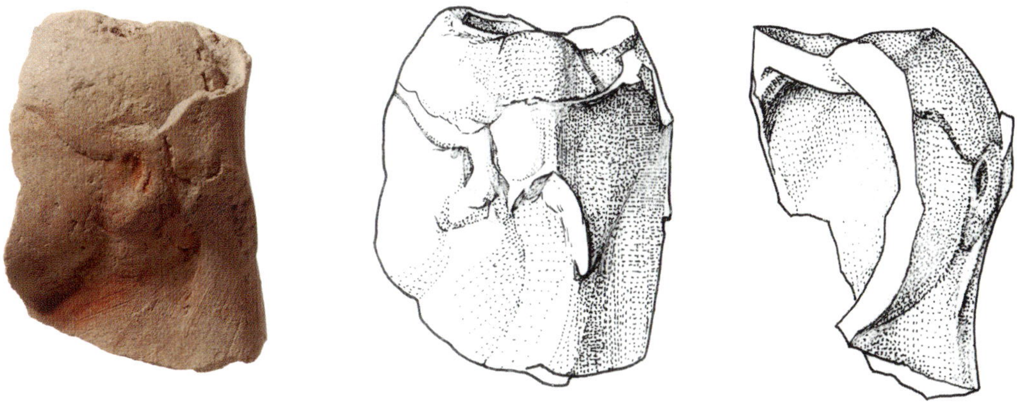

Scale 1:1

Catalogue no. 72

Registration no.: Unregistered
Findspot: 50.49.L436.FG9.B102
Year excavated: 1994
Context: Ph. 7 quarry fill
Height: 3.3 cm
Width: 2.9 cm
Thickness: 0.4 cm
Description: A fragment of a moldmade figurine. Only part of the back of the head is preserved. There are wavy lines representing the hair. Brown-red clay, with black and brown paint; clay-colored core, few if any inclusions.

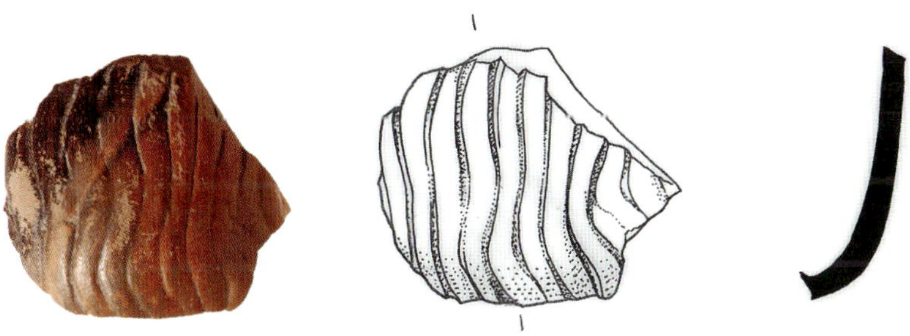

Scale 1:1

Catalogue no. 73

Registration no.: Unregistered
Findspot: 50.49.L421.B421
Year excavated: 1993
Context: Ph. 7 quarry fill
Height: 3.3 cm
Width: 4.0 cm
Thickness: 0.7 cm
Diameter: 3.1 cm
Description: A fragment of a completely moldmade figurine. Only the feet and the base are preserved; the figure was presumably seated. Light brown clay, with traces of red paint around right foot; clay-colored core, 0.25–0.50 mm grits.

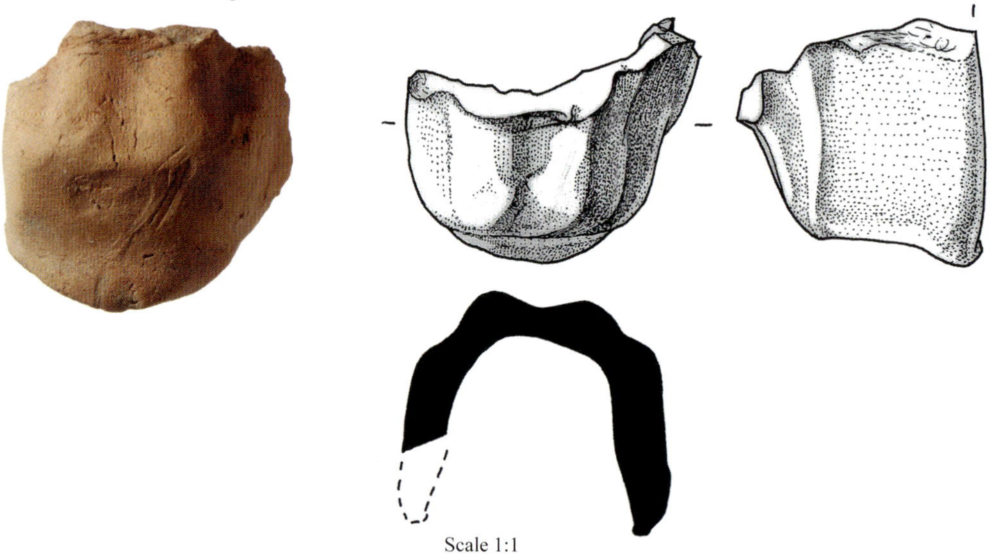

Scale 1:1

I.B.1. (Male Rider Figurines - See under Horses, II. A.2 [Nos. 160–64])
I.B.2. (Miscellaneous Male Figurines)

Catalogue no. 74

Registration no.: 32007
Findspot: 38.64.LF700.B510
Year excavated: 1990
Context: Ph. 10 floor
Height: 6.0 cm
Width: 4.1 cm
Thickness: 3.4 cm
Description: A head, neck, and partial torso of a human figurine, probably male. The right arm is completely missing; the left is preserved only as a stump. The eyes appear only as depressions, without eyeballs or pupils indicated. There are incised holes for the nostrils and an incised line for the mouth. The ears are flat ridges on the sides of the head. There is a raised circular ring around the top of the head, forming the line of a possible headdress. Light brown clay with cream slip; burnishing is visible on the neck. There are black lines painted from the back of the headdress to the front below the neck; there are traces of white slip on the body. Gray core, few if any grits.

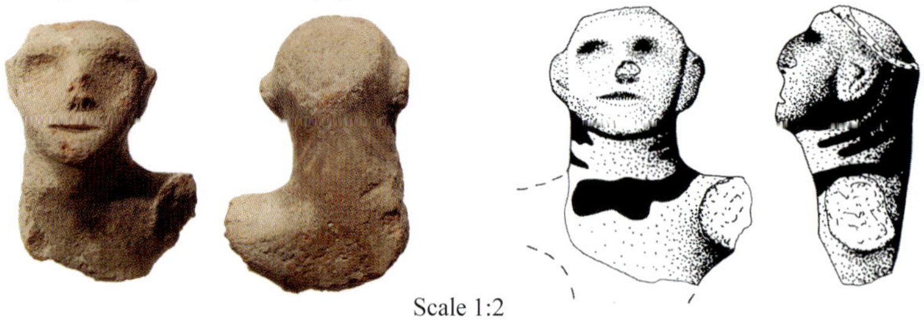

Scale 1:2

Catalogue no. 75

Registration no.:	45580
Findspot:	38.73.F429.FG20.B26
Year excavated:	1995
Context:	Ph. 17A hearth
Height:	7.7 cm
Width:	5.0 cm
Thickness:	2.5 cm
Description:	A torso, possibly of a nude male figurine. The figurine is very crude, and it is unclear what it represents. There are four limbs plus a possible phallus, or tail, on the bottom. There is a pinched line of clay on top, possibly representing a head. Brown clay, clay-colored core, 0.25–1.00 mm grits.

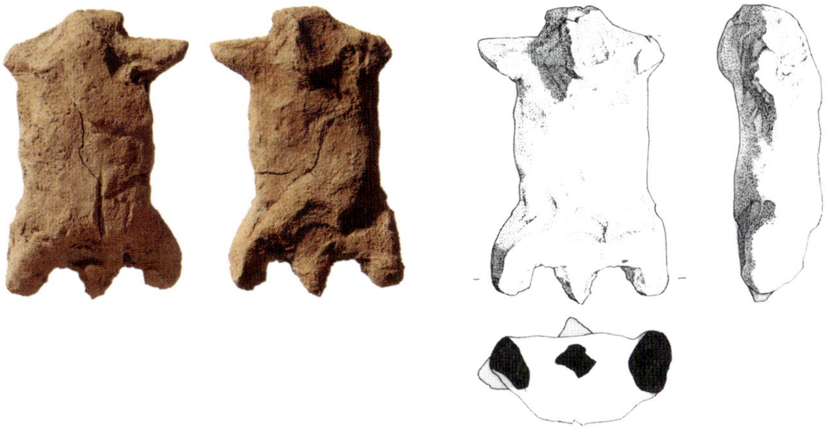

Scale 1:2

Catalogue no. 76

Registration no.:	48223
Findspot:	38.63.L788.B15
Year excavated:	1997
Context:	Ph. 18A deliberate fill
Height:	5.2 cm
Width:	3.3 cm
Thickness:	2.7 cm
Description:	A male head and neck. The head is moldmade, with round eyes, arched eyebrows, a slender nose, and mouth clearly visible. The figure wears a headdress, possibly a crown, with a series of horizontal lines. The headdress is partially broken. Reddish-brown clay, clay-colored core, 0.25–1.00 mm grits.

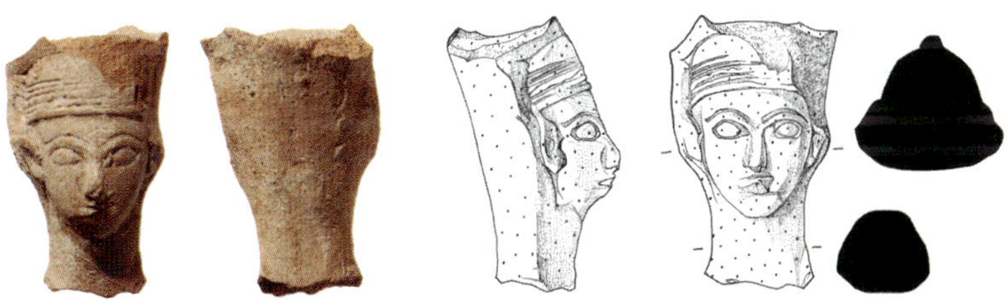

Scale 1:2

Catalogue no. 77

Registration no.:	45388
Findspot:	38.74.L624.B45
Year excavated:	1995
Context:	Ph. 17B street
Height:	3.4 cm
Width:	4.5 cm
Thickness:	2.2 cm
Description:	A human lower torso and upper legs, possibly of a female; a depression in the center may represent the pudendum. Grayish clay, clay-colored core, 0.25–2.00 mm grits.

Scale 1:1

Catalogue no. 78

Registration no.:	52537
Findspot:	38.84.L690.B112
Year excavated:	1999
Context:	Ph. 18C deliberate fill
Height:	4.4 cm
Width:	2.1 cm
Thickness:	1.8 cm
Description:	A human head and neck, possibly of a male. The head is small, with applied pellets for eyes, a concave head (or headdress) tilted down toward the back, a pinched nose, and applied spirals for the ears (the left is partially broken). Applied strips of clay along the sides and bottom of the face may represent a beard. Brown-red clay, with traces of white slip, gray core, 0.25 mm grits.

Scale 1:1

II.A (Horse Figurines)

Catalogue no. 79

Registration no.:	40173
Findspot:	50.58.L274.B418
Year excavated:	1992
Context:	Ph. 7 destruction debris
Height:	5.0 cm
Width:	2.3 cm
Thickness:	3.5 cm
Description:	A horse head and neck: the shape is typically rounded and slender. The end of the muzzle is broken off; the left ear is completely missing, and the right ear is mostly missing. The neck has a triangular section with a ridge for the mane on the back. There is a depression in the bottom of the broken neck. Brown clay, with traces of white slip, black core; 0.25–0.50 mm grits.

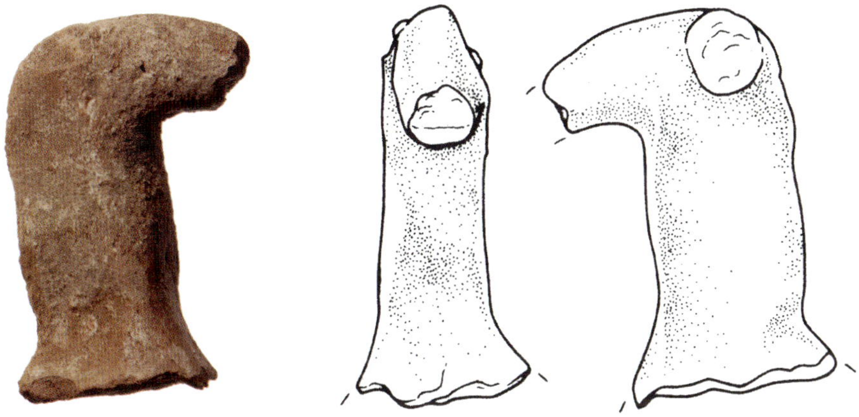

Scale 1:1

Catalogue no. 80

Registration no.:	40396
Findspot:	50.58.L302.B424
Year excavated:	1992
Context:	Ph. 7 street surface
Height:	4.4 cm
Width:	2.2 cm
Thickness:	3.6 cm
Description:	A horse head and neck: the shape of the back of the head and the muzzle is typically rounded and slender. The left ear is mostly missing; the right ear is pointed, jutting up and out from the head. The neck has a triangular section formed with the ridge of the mane. Brown clay, with traces of white slip, black core, 0.25 mm grits.

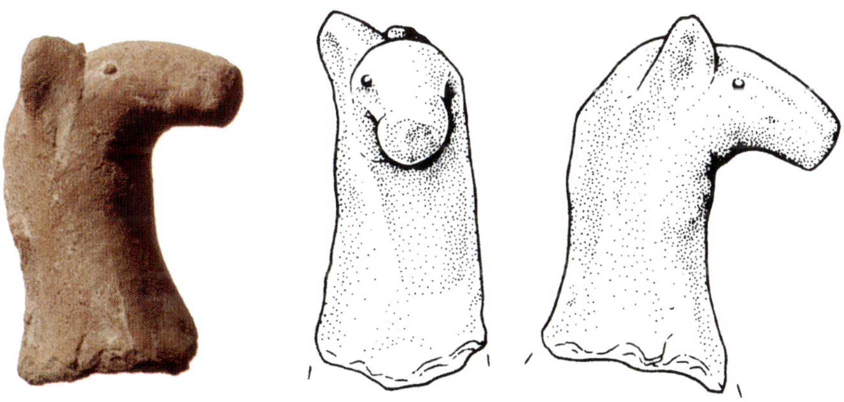

Scale 1:1

Catalogue no. 81

Registration no.: 42427
Findspot: 50.48.L405.FG36.B32
Year excavated: 1993
Context: Ph. 7 quarry fill
Height: 5.6 cm
Width: 2.0 cm
Thickness: 3.4 cm
Description: A horse neck and head. The snout is missing; there is a mane as a ridge on the back of the neck (forming a triangular/teardrop section), ending at the back of the head. The left hand of a rider may be preserved on the neck. Red-brown clay, black core, traces of white slip; white grits, up to 0.25 mm.

Scale 1:1

Catalogue no. 82

Registration no.: 42654
Findspot: 50.48.L405.FG37.B39
Year excavated: 1993
Context: Ph. 7 quarry fill
Height: 5.2 cm
Width: 2.0 cm
Thickness: 2.7 cm
Description: A zoomorphic neck, probably of a horse. Only the back of the head is preserved. One ear is partially broken. The neck and mane form a triangular section. Brown-red clay, black core, 0.25–0.75 mm grits.

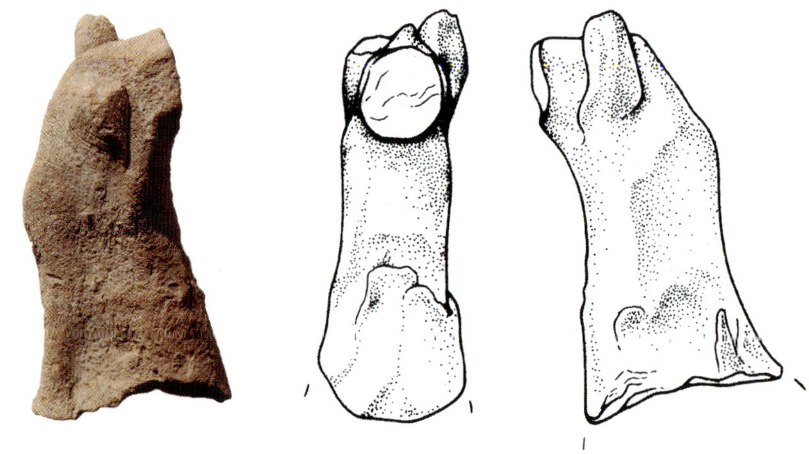

Scale 1:1

Catalogue no. 83

Registration no.: 42847
Findspot: 50.49.L419.FG9.B82
Year excavated: 1993
Context: Ph. 7 wall fall/destruction debris
Height: 4.5 cm
Width: 2.0 cm
Thickness: 3.7 cm
Description: A horse head and neck: the shape is typically slender and rounded, though the edge of the muzzle comes to a small point. The ears are partially broken. The neck and mane ridge form a triangular section. Red-brown clay, with traces of white slip, clay-colored core, 0.25 mm grits.

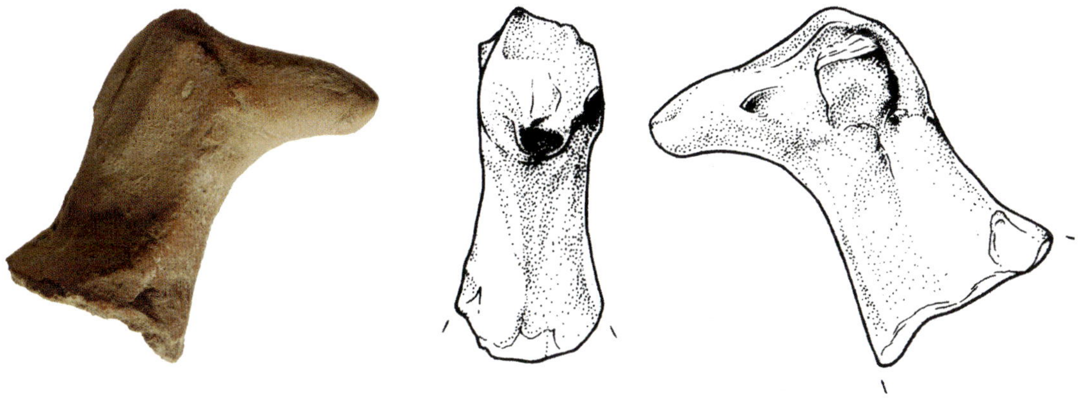

Scale 1:1

Catalogue no. 84

Registration no.: 42856
Findspot: 50.49.L420.B53
Year excavated: 1993
Context: Ph. 7 quarry fill
Height: 4.6 cm
Width: 1.8 cm
Thickness: 3.3 cm
Description: A horse head and neck: the head and neck shape are typically rounded and slender, though the edge of the muzzle comes to a near point; the back of the neck has the usual mane. The right ear is completely missing; the top of left ear is broken. Brown-red clay, with traces of white slip, black core, 0.25–1.00 mm grits.

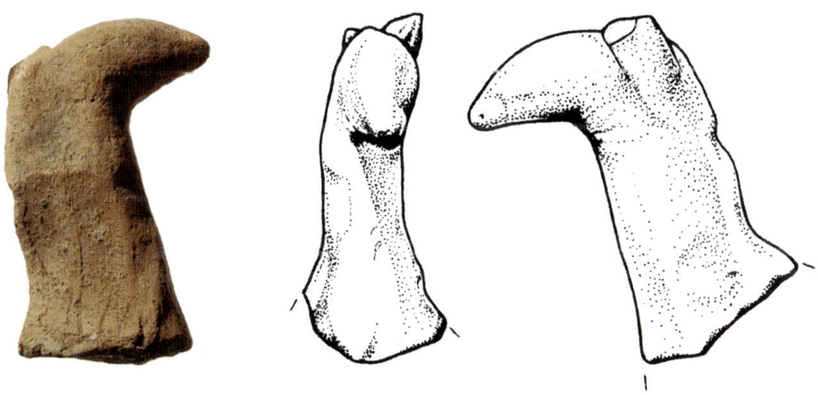

Scale 1:1

Catalogue no. 85

Registration no.:	42901
Findspot:	38.74.L493.FG90.B42
Year excavated:	1993
Context:	Ph. 14 alley surface
Height:	1.8 cm
Width:	1.2 cm
Thickness:	3.6 cm
Description:	A horse head: the neck is missing; the muzzle has the typical rounded shape. The right ear is missing; the left ear is protruding out and above the head. The back of the figurine shows the beginning of a mane. Brown clay, gray core, 0.25–0.75 mm grits.

Scale 1:1

Catalogue no. 86

Registration no.:	42946
Findspot:	50.49.LF423.B95
Year excavated:	1993
Context:	Ph. 7 floor
Height:	3.3 cm
Width:	2.1 cm
Thickness:	3.0 cm
Description:	A horse head and neck: the muzzle is broken off, and both ears are largely missing. There is a ridge for the mane on the back of the neck. Circular pellets are applied to the face for eyes. Brown clay, with traces of white slip, gray core, 0.25–0.50 mm grits.

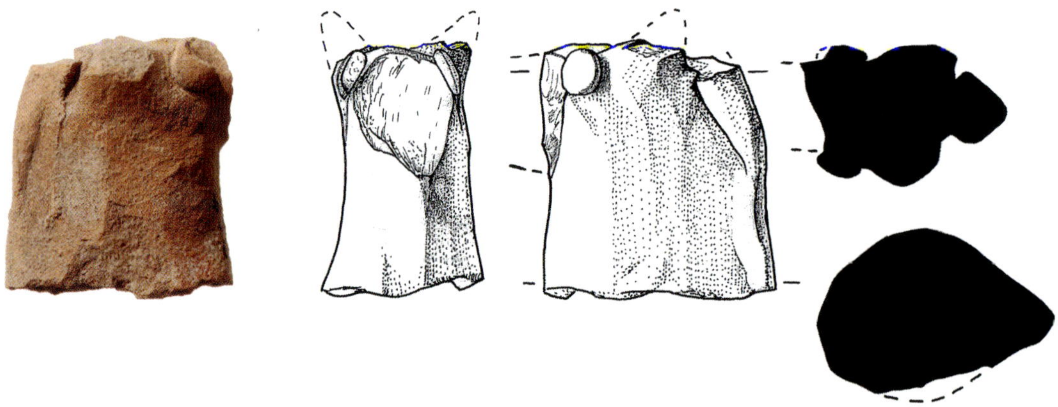

Scale 1:1

Catalogue no. 87

Registration no.:	43539
Findspot:	50.48.L405.B113
Year excavated:	1993
Context:	Ph. 7 quarry fill
Height:	4.7 cm
Width:	4.2 cm
Thickness:	2.1 cm
Description:	A horse head and neck: the left ear is missing; the snout is rounded. There is a ridge for the mane at the back of the neck (with a triangular/teardrop section). Brown clay, gray core, traces of white slip; white grits, 0.25–0.50 mm.

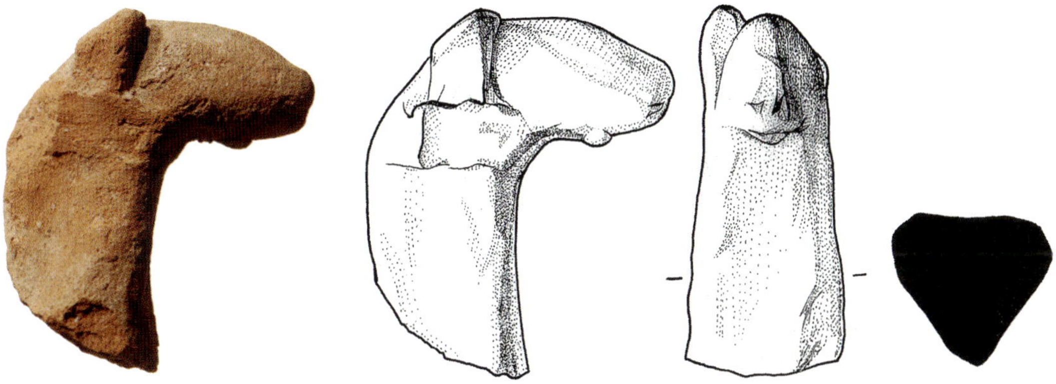

Scale 1:1

Catalogue no. 88

Registration no.:	44176
Findspot:	50.47.LF278.B33
Year excavated:	1994
Context:	Ph. 7 deliberate fill
Height:	8.0 cm
Width:	3.4 cm
Thickness:	4.1 cm
Description:	A horse head and neck: the head and neck shape is typically rounded; the muzzle is missing. The neck and mane ridge form a triangular section; the mane continues onto the top of the head and ends there in a rounded edge. The ears are large and protrude outward from the head. The front edge of the torso, along with the tops of the two front legs, is preserved. Reddish brown clay, black core, 0.25–5.00 mm grits.

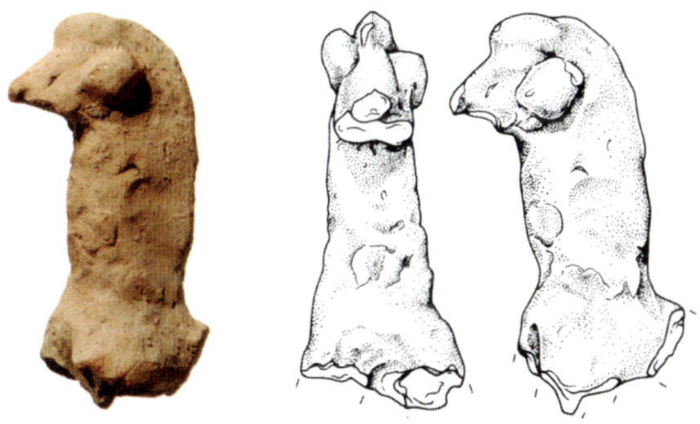

Scale 1:2

Catalogue no. 89

Registration no.:	44552
Findspot:	50.48.L448.B81
Year excavated:	1994
Context:	Ph. 7 quarry fill
Height:	2.7 cm
Width:	1.4 cm
Thickness:	2.5 cm
Description:	A horse head and neck: the shape of the head and neck is typically rounded; the muzzle is missing, as is the bottom of the neck. The left ear is missing; the right ear is pointed and protruding away from the head. The neck and mane form the typical triangular section. Brown clay, black to gray core, 0.25–0.50 mm grits.

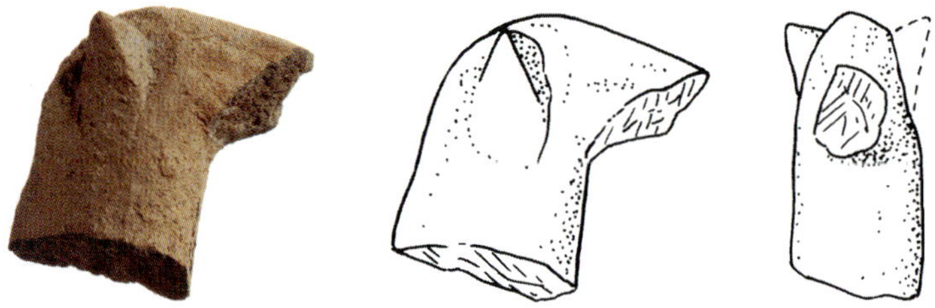

Scale 1:1

Catalogue no. 90

Registration no.:	44562
Findspot:	50.48.LF421.B90
Year excavated:	1994
Context:	Ph. 7 floor
Height:	5.8 cm
Width:	3.0 cm
Thickness:	3.0 cm
Description:	A zoomorphic neck and partial head, probably of a horse: the head and neck shape is rounded; the muzzle is missing. The neck is complete, down to the beginning of torso and the tops of the front legs. The right ear is missing, and the left ear partially broken. Two pieces of clay attached below and behind the ears may represent the hands of a rider. Brown clay, with traces of white slip, gray core, 0.25–0.50 mm grits.

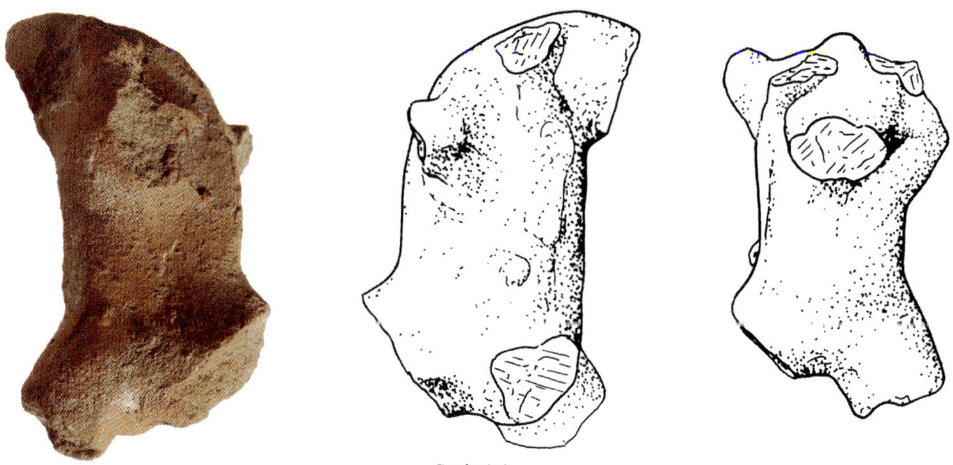

Scale 1:1

Catalogue no. 91

Registration no.: 44566
Findspot: 50.58.L316.B15
Year excavated: 1994
Context: Ph. 7 quarry fill
Height: 2.7 cm
Width: 1.5 cm
Thickness: 3.7 cm
Description: A horse head: the shape of the head is typically rounded and slender, and the muzzle has a rounded edge. Only the very top of the neck is preserved, but the mane ridge is visible and forms a triangular section with the neck. Most of each ear is missing. Brown clay, with traces of white slip, gray core, 0.25–0.50 mm grits.

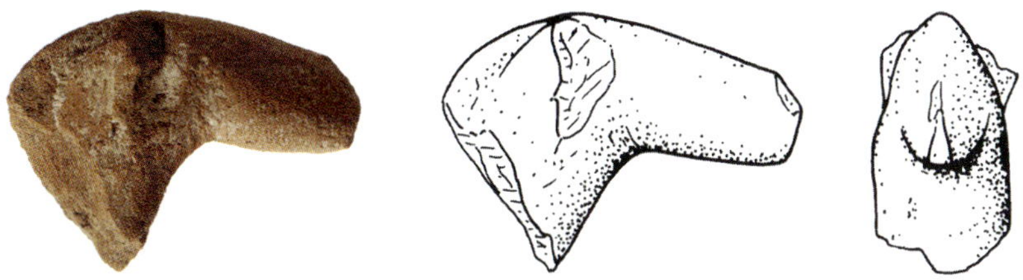

Scale 1:1

Catalogue no. 92

Registration no.: 44576
Findspot: 50.49.L436.FG29.B88
Year excavated: 1994
Context: Ph. 7 quarry fill
Height: 4.9 cm
Width: 2.9 cm
Thickness: 4.0 cm
Diameter: 1.8 cm (of neck)
Description: A zoomorphic head and neck, probably of a horse: the head and neck have the typical rounded and slender shape. The end of the muzzle is relatively flat. The right ear is mostly preserved, and the left ear is partially broken; on the right ear there are two separate pieces (one perhaps representing a horn). Brown-red clay, with a few traces of white slip; black core, 0.25–0.75 mm grits.

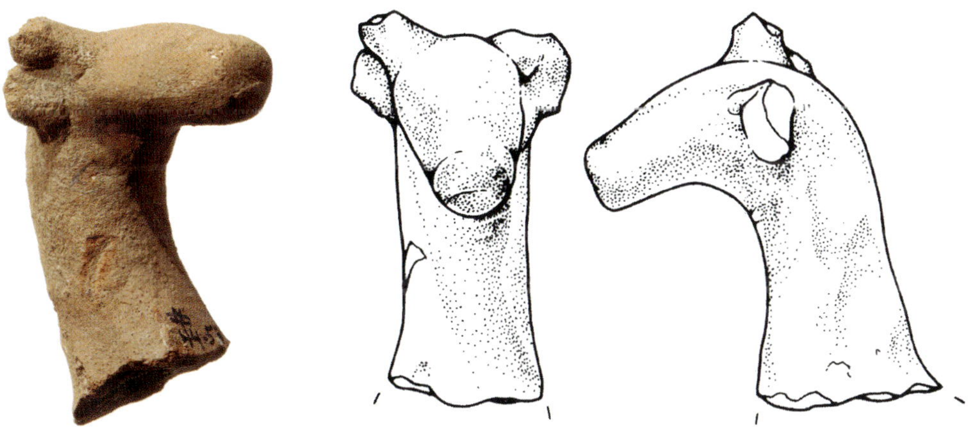

Scale 1:1

Catalogue no. 93

Registration no.: 45078
Findspot: 50.48.L448.B87
Year excavated: 1994
Context: Ph. 7 quarry fill
Height: 3.6 cm
Width: 1.9 cm
Thickness: 4.2 cm
Description: A zoomorphic head and neck, probably of a horse: the head and neck are typically rounded and slender, but the muzzle is short and comes to a pronounced point. The ears are large circular pieces applied flat against the back of the muzzle. There is a small ridge along the back of the neck for a mane, though the section it forms with the neck is barely triangular. Brown clay, with traces of white slip; black core, 0.25–0.50 mm grits.

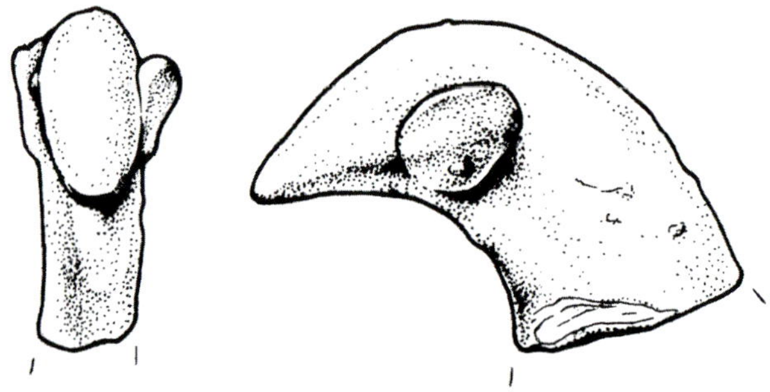

Scale 1:1

Catalogue no. 94

Registration no.: 45163
Findspot: 50.57.L258.B148
Year excavated: 1994
Context: Ph. 7 quarry fill
Height: 4.7 cm
Width: 1.7 cm
Thickness: 3.7 cm
Description: A horse head and neck: the shape of the head and neck is typically slender and rounded; the muzzle comes to a relatively flat end. There is a ridge for the mane, forming a triangular section with the neck. The left ear is partially broken, but the right ear is fully preserved; the ear is relatively thin and pointed and protruding away from head. Brown clay, with a few traces of white slip; black core, 0.25 mm grits.

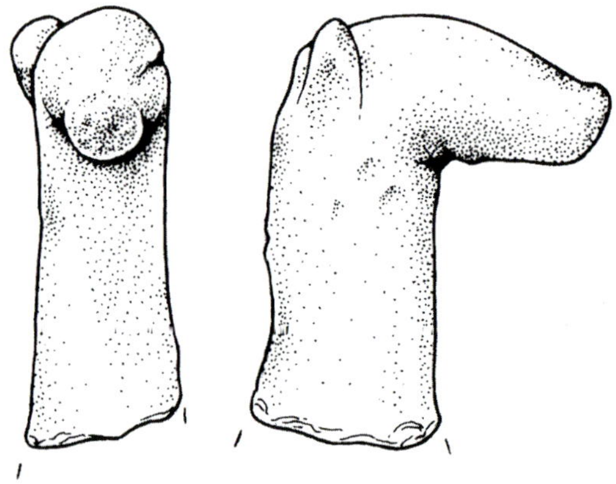

Scale 1:1

Catalogue no. 95

Registration no.:	45356
Findspot:	50.48.L452.B11
Year excavated:	1995
Context:	Ph. 7 quarry fill
Height:	5.0 cm
Width:	2.0 cm
Thickness:	4.1 cm
Description:	A zoomorphic head and neck, probably of a horse: the shape of the head and neck are typically slender and rounded, but the end of the muzzle curves up to a point. The neck and the ridge for the mane form a triangular section, but the mane ends on the back of the head as a low-lying horizontal piece. Each ear is partially broken. Brown clay, with traces of white slip; black core, 0.25–1.00 mm grits.

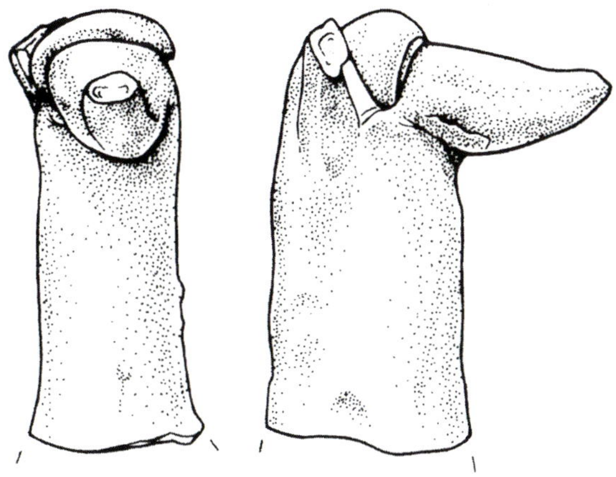

Scale 1:1

Catalogue no. 96

Registration no.:	45497
Findspot:	50.48.L452.B52
Year excavated:	1995
Context:	Ph. 7 quarry fill
Height:	5.2 cm
Width:	2.6 cm
Thickness:	4.3 cm
Description:	A horse head and neck: the shape is typically rounded and slender. The end of the muzzle curves downward almost to a point. There is a ridge for the mane on the back of the neck (with the usual triangular section). The left ear is missing; the right ear is a long, thin strip of clay with a rounded tip, jutting just above the top of the head. Brown clay, clay-colored core, 0.25–0.50 mm grits.

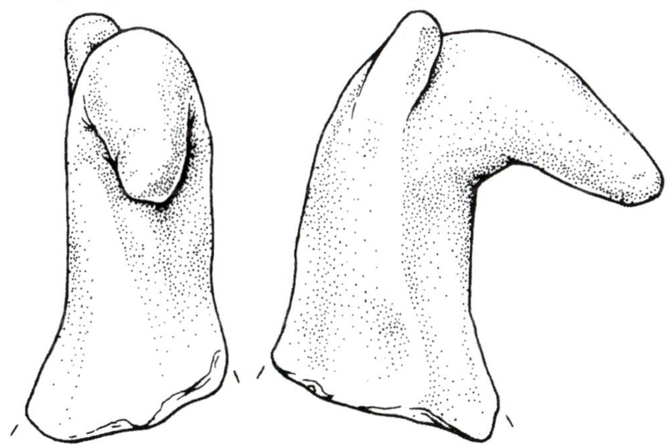

Scale 1:1

Catalogue no. 97

Registration no.:	45512
Findspot:	50.48.L452.B44
Year excavated:	1995
Context:	Ph. 7 quarry fill
Height:	4.4 cm
Width:	1.9 cm
Thickness:	3.8 cm
Description:	A horse head and neck: the shape is typically rounded and slender. There is a ridge on the back of the neck for the mane, forming a triangular section with the neck; the mane continues up (as a thin strip of clay) onto the back of the head. Only the left ear is preserved; it protrudes away from the head. Brown clay, with traces of white slip; clay-colored core, 0.25–1.00 mm grits.

Scale 1:1

Catalogue no. 98

Registration no.:	45601
Findspot:	50.48.L452.B76
Year excavated:	1995
Context:	Ph. 7 deliberate fill
Height:	3.1 cm
Width:	1.7 cm
Thickness:	3.7 cm
Description:	A horse head and neck: the shape is typically rounded and slender. The back of the neck has a ridge for the mane, forming a triangular section with the neck. The muzzle ends in a near point (which is partially chipped). The neck is partially broken; the ears are mostly missing. Brown clay, with traces of white slip; black core, 0.25–1.00 mm grits.

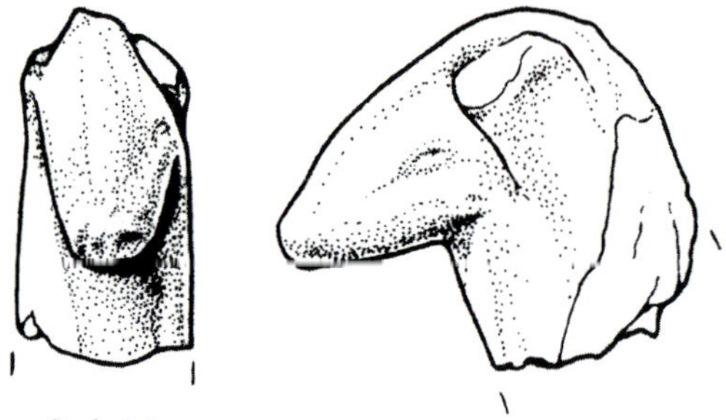

Scale 1:1

Catalogue no. 99

Registration no.:	45603
Findspot:	50.48.L452.B88
Year excavated:	1995
Context:	Ph. 7 quarry fill
Height:	4.6 cm
Width:	1.6 cm
Thickness:	4.0 cm
Description:	A horse head and neck: the shape is typically rounded and slender, but the neck is particularly curved. The ears are large, thin strips of clay ending in points and protruding away from the head. The back of the neck has a mane, forming a triangular section with the neck. Reddish-brown clay, with some cream slip preserved; gray core, 0.25–1.00 mm grits.

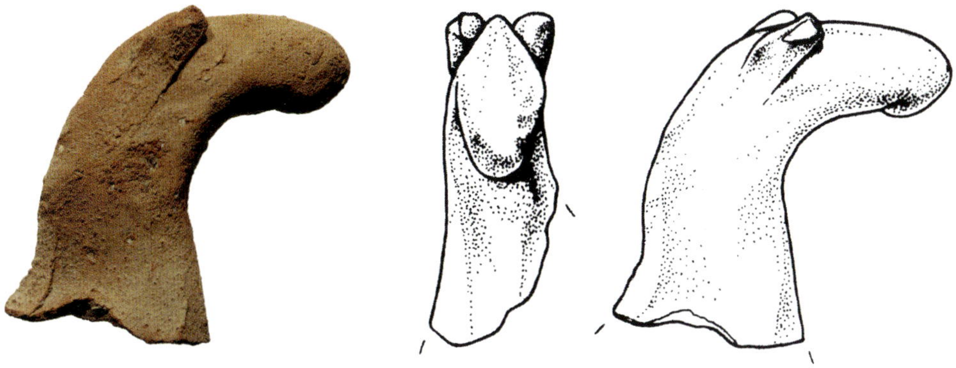

Scale 1:1

Catalogue no. 100

Registration no.:	45736
Findspot:	50.48.L452.B107
Year excavated:	1995
Context:	Ph. 7 quarry fill
Height:	4.7 cm
Width:	1.7 cm
Thickness:	2.5 cm
Description:	A horse neck and partial head: only the back of the head is preserved; the shape is typically rounded and slender. The left side of the neck is broken off. The top of the right ear is broken, and the left ear is missing entirely. There is a ridge for the mane on the back of the neck, forming a triangular section with the neck. Brown clay, gray core, 0.25–0.50 mm grits.

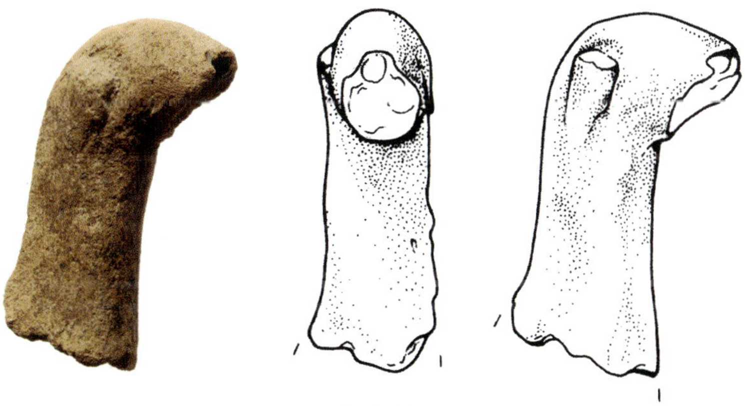

Scale 1:1

Catalogue no. 101

Registration no.:	45998
Findspot:	50.48.L452.B179
Year excavated:	1995
Context:	Ph. 7 quarry fill
Height:	5.6 cm
Width:	1.9 cm
Thickness:	3.4 cm
Description:	A horse head and neck: the shape is typically rounded and slender. The ears are large and semicircular and applied perpendicularly (rather than parallel) to the head, rising high above it. The back of the neck has a ridge for the mane, forming a triangular section with the neck. Brown clay, with traces of white slip; black core, 0.25–1.00 mm grits.

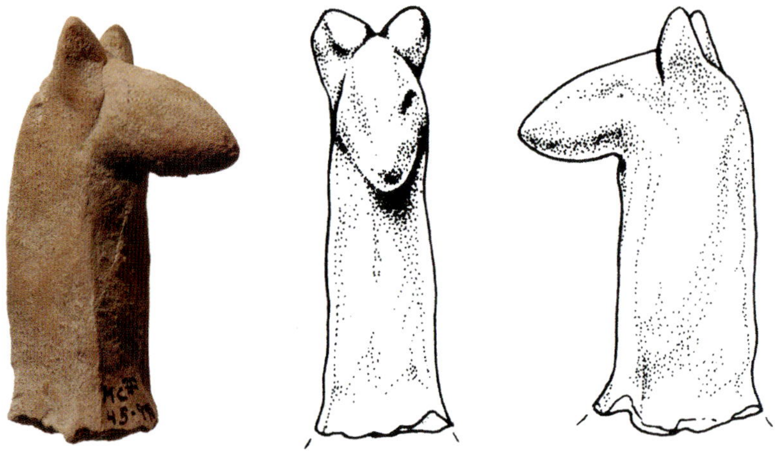

Scale 1:1

Catalogue no. 102

Registration no.:	46086
Findspot:	50.48.L461.B193
Year excavated:	1995
Context:	Ph. 7 quarry fill
Height:	4.3 cm
Width:	2.5 cm
Thickness:	4.0 cm
Description:	A horse head and neck: the shape is typically rounded and slender, but the neck is particularly curved. The ears are mostly preserved. The back of the neck has a ridge for the mane, with the usual triangular section. Brown clay, with traces of white slip; gray core, 0.25–0.50 mm grits.

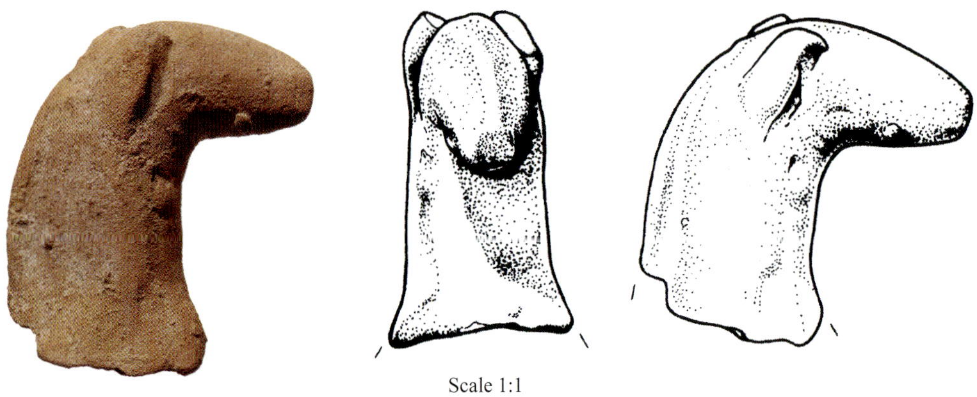

Scale 1:1

Catalogue no. 103

Registration no.: 46100
Findspot: 50.57.L256.B96
Year excavated: 1995
Context: Ph. 7 quarry fill
Height: 2.4 cm
Width: 1.3 cm
Thickness: 3.3 cm
Description: A horse head and neck: the shape is typically rounded and slender, but the muzzle curves to a point. The bottom of the neck is not preserved. The left ear is partially broken; the right ear is fully preserved. The neck and the ridge of the mane form a triangular section. Reddish-brown clay, with traces of white slip; clay-colored core, 0.25–0.75 mm grits.

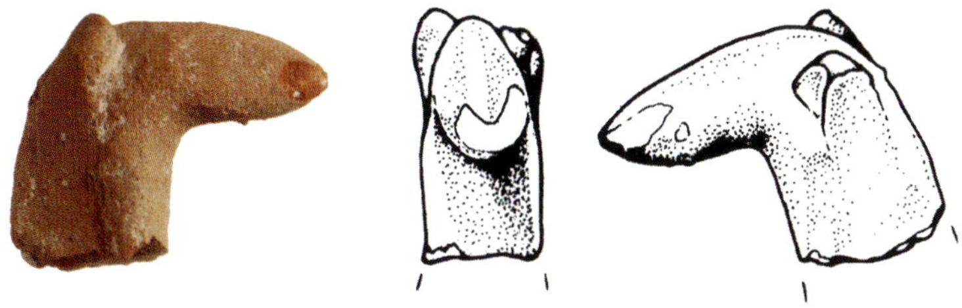

Scale 1:1

Catalogue no. 104

Registration no.: 46602
Findspot: 50.49.L449.B7
Year excavated: 1996
Context: Ph. 7 quarry fill
Height: 5.0 cm
Width: 1.7 cm
Thickness: 4.4 cm
Description: A horse head and neck: the shape is typically rounded and slender, but the tip of the muzzle is chipped. The ears are thin strips of clay lying flat against the head. The neck has a ridge for the mane; on each side of the neck is an applied circle, probably representing the hands of a rider. Brown clay, with traces of white slip; black core, 0.25–0.75 mm grits.

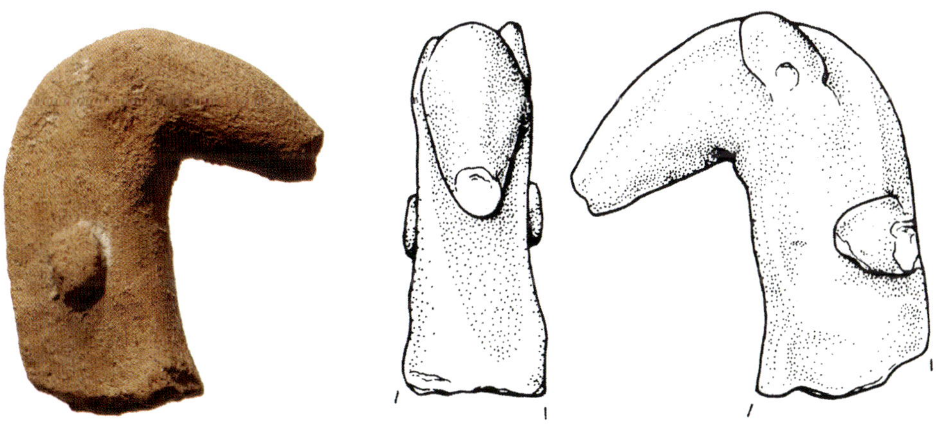

Scale 1:1

Catalogue no. 105

Registration no.: 46686
Findspot: 50.49.L451.B34
Year excavated: 1996
Context: Ph. 7 quarry fill
Height: 4.3 cm
Width: 1.7 cm
Thickness: 2.2 cm
Description: A horse head and neck: the shape is typically rounded and slender, but the muzzle is missing. The ears are large, set perpendicularly at the very back of the head, and rise above it. There is a ridge for the mane on the back of the neck. Brown clay (with traces of burning), clay-colored core (also with burning), 0.25–1.00 mm grits.

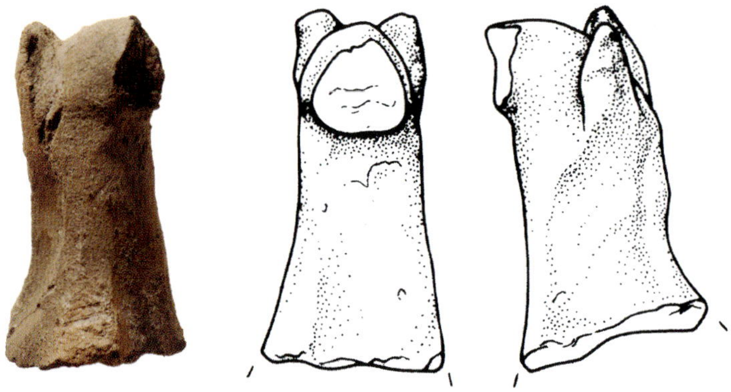

Scale 1:1

Catalogue no. 106

Registration no.: 46909
Findspot: 50.48.L453.B92
Year excavated: 1995
Context: Ph. 7 quarry fill
Height: 6.5 cm
Width: 2.7 cm
Thickness: 3.0 cm
Description: A zoomorphic neck and partial head, possibly of a horse: the muzzle is broken off. The right ear is a large rounded lump of clay at the back of the head; the left ear is missing. There are large applied circular pellets for eyes. Peach-colored clay, with traces of red paint; gray core, 0.25–5.00 mm grits.

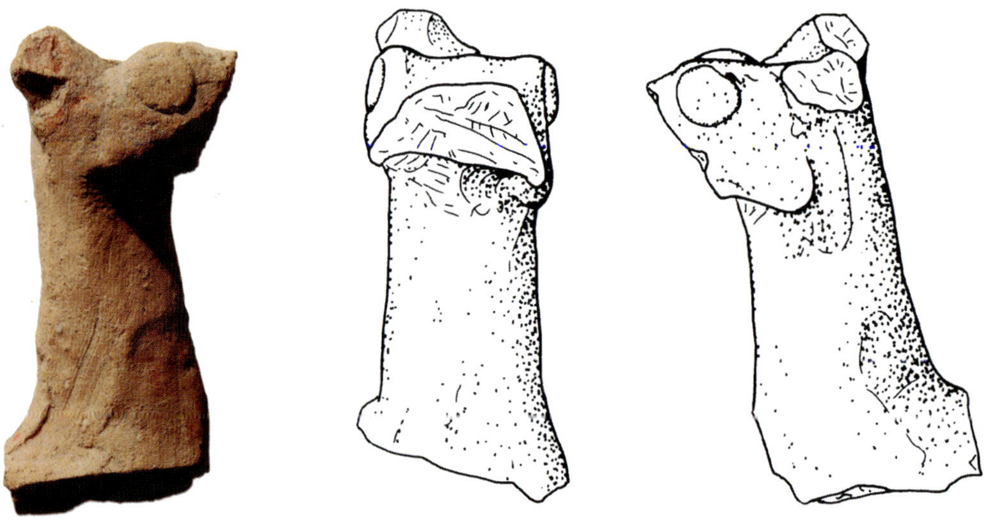

Scale 1:1

Catalogue no. 107

Registration no.: 51614
Findspot: 50.49.L453.B123
Year excavated: 1996
Context: Ph. 7 quarry fill
Height: 4.8 cm
Width: 1.9 cm
Thickness: 4.5 cm
Description: A horse head and neck: the shape is typically rounded and slender. The muzzle is long and has a flattened end. The right ear is small and set low on the back of the head; the left ear is not preserved. The back of the neck has a ridge for the mane. Brown clay, with traces of white slip; clay-colored core, 0.25–0.75 mm grits.

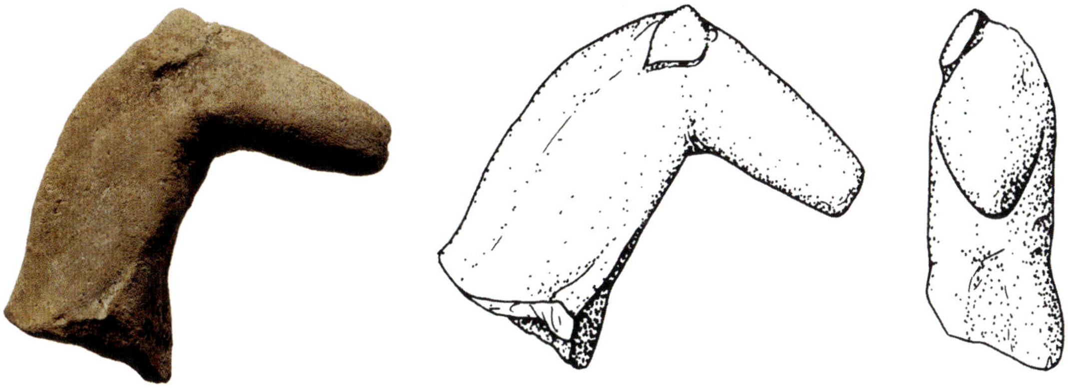

Scale 1:1

Catalogue no. 108

Registration no.: 56063
Findspot: 50.48.L384.B304
Year excavated: 1992
Context: Ph. 7 natural fill
Height: 4.7 cm
Width: 2.3 cm
Thickness: 2.7 cm
Description: A zoomorphic neck and partial head, probably of a horse; only the very back of the head is preserved. The neck is curved and has a ridge for a mane on the back. The ears are broken off. Brown-red clay, with traces of white slip; gray core, 0.25–0.50 mm grits.

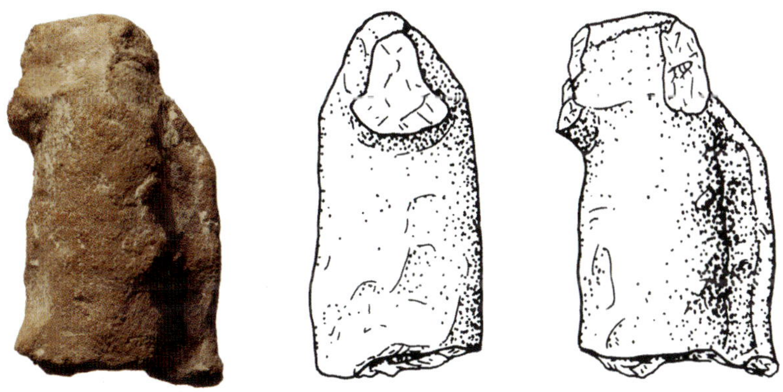

Scale 1:1

Catalogue no. 109

Registration no.: 38823
Findspot: 50.58.L252.B7
Year excavated: 1992
Context: Ph. 7 floor
Height: 2.6 cm
Width: 6.4 cm
Thickness: 3.4 cm
Description: A zoomorphic torso, probably of a horse. The torso itself is complete, and stumps of all four legs (especially the hind legs) are preserved. The tail, head, and neck are completely missing. Brown clay (with traces of burning); clay-colored core, 0.25–1.00 mm grits.

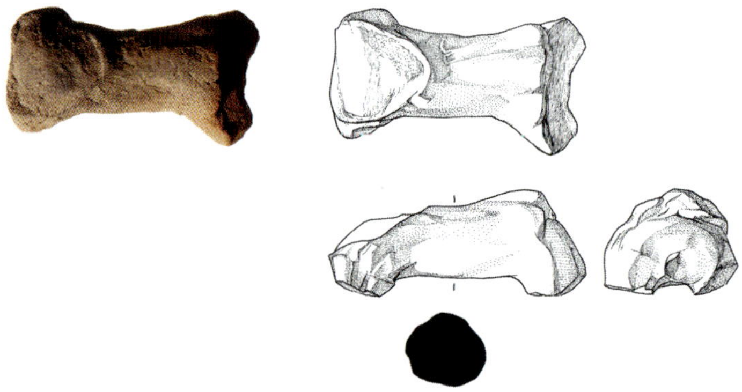

Scale 1:2

Catalogue no. 110

Registration no.: 40249
Findspot: 50.49.L373.FG3.B182
Year excavated: 1992
Context: Ph. 7 floor
Height: 1.8 cm
Width: 3.0 cm
Length: 3.8 cm
Description: A horse torso fragment. Scars from two of the legs are visible. On each side of the body a small circular piece of clay is attached, probably representing the legs of a rider. Red-brown clay, with traces of white slip; clay-colored core, 0.25–1.00 mm grits.

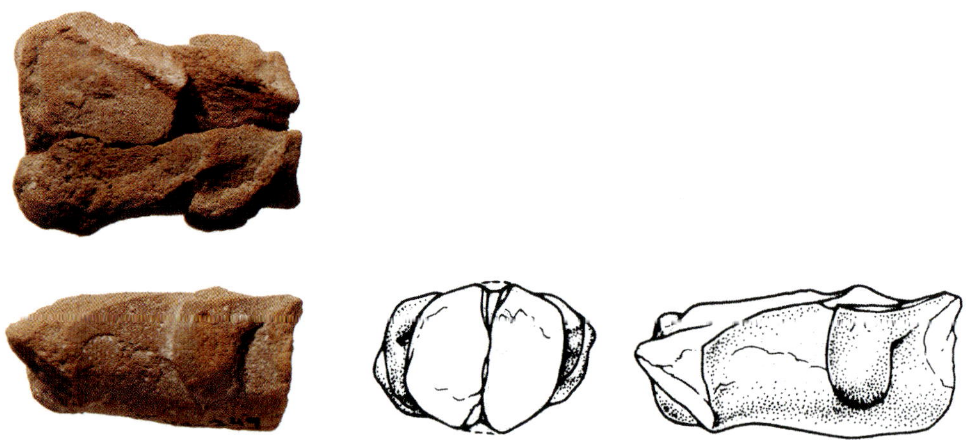

Scale 1:1

Catalogue no. 111

Registration no.: 40281
Findspot: 50.58.L274.B398
Year excavated: 1992
Context: Ph. 7 destruction debris
Height: 2.2 cm
Width: 3.3 cm
Length: 5.7 cm
Description: A zoomorphic torso, probably of a horse. The torso itself is complete, and stumps of all four legs, as well as part of the tail, are preserved. The head and neck are completely missing. Gray-brown clay, with traces of white slip; black core, 0.25–2.00 mm grits.

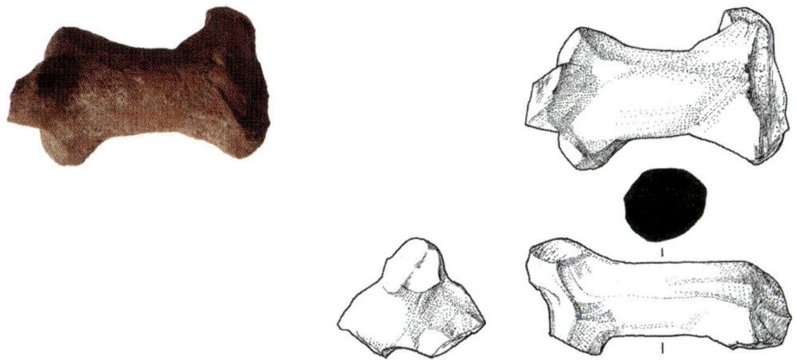

Scale 1:2

Catalogue no. 112

Registration no.: 40395
Findspot: 50.58.L302.B424
Year excavated: 1992
Context: Ph. 7 street surface
Height: 2.9 cm
Width: 3.1 cm
Length: 6.5 cm
Description: A zoomorphic torso, probably of a horse. The torso is complete, and stumps of all four legs and part of the tail are preserved. There is a neck scar in the front. Red-brown clay, with two red stripes painted across the back, and traces of white slip; black core, 0.25–2.00 mm grits.

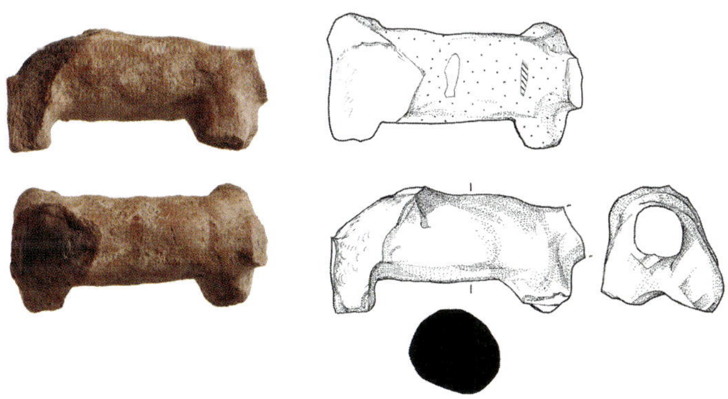

Scale 1:2

Catalogue no. 113

Registration no.:	40397
Findspot:	50.58.L302.B424
Year excavated:	1992
Context:	Ph. 7 street surface
Height:	2.4 cm
Width:	3.1 cm
Length:	3.5 cm
Description:	A zoomorphic torso fragment, probably of a horse: the forequarters, with partial front legs, are preserved; there is a neck scar on top. Brown clay, with traces of white slip, black core, 0.25–0.50 mm grits.

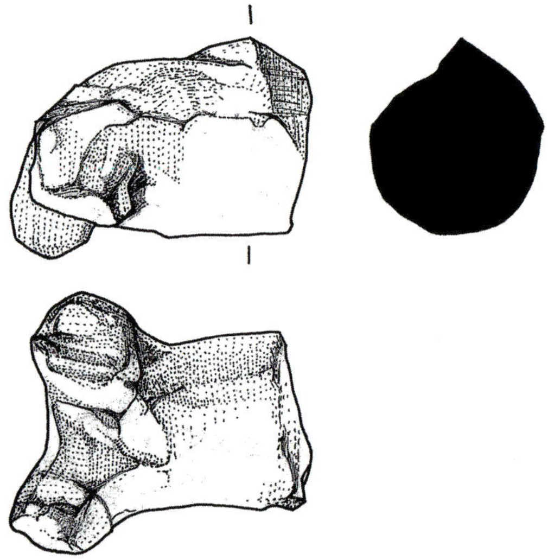

Scale 1:1

Catalogue no. 114

Registration no.:	40731
Findspot:	50.48.L388.B442
Year excavated:	1992
Context:	Ph. 7 deliberate fill
Height:	6.7 cm
Width:	3.7 cm
Length:	7.5 cm
Description:	A horse torso and neck: the torso is complete; the right hind leg is partially preserved, but the others are almost completely missing; the tail is partially preserved; the neck is complete up to the back of the head, with the left ear largely preserved. There is a ridge on back of the neck for the mane. Light brown clay, with a few traces of white slip, and traces of two red stripes across the back; clay-colored core, 0.25–0.75 mm grits.

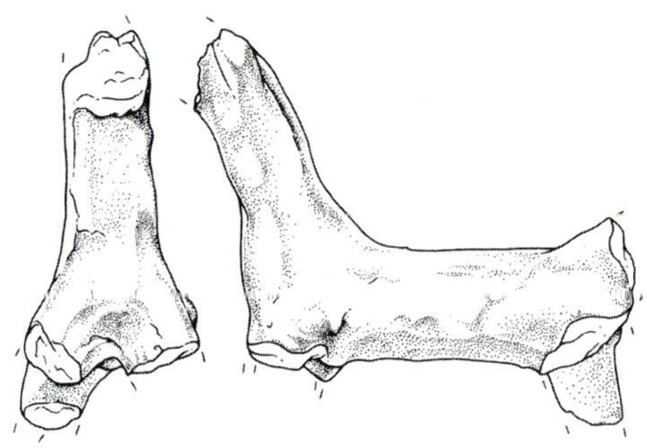

Scale 1:2

Catalogue no. 115

Registration no.:	42312
Findspot:	50.49.L389.B14
Year excavated:	1993
Context:	Ph. 7 street surface
Height:	4.4 cm
Width:	4.4 cm
Length:	8.1 cm
Description:	A zoomorphic torso, probably of a horse: a complete body with the two left legs mostly preserved and the right hind leg partially preserved. The tail is also mostly preserved. There is a neck scar on the top front of the body. Brown-red clay, with traces of white slip, black core, 0.25 mm grits.

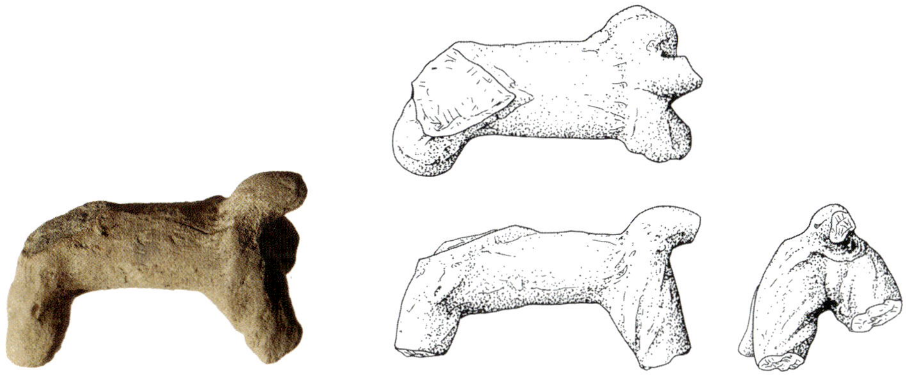

Scale 1:2

Catalogue no. 116

Registration no.:	42570
Findspot:	50.57.L240.B68
Year excavated:	1993
Context:	Ph. 7 quarry fill
Height:	4.4 cm
Width:	2.9 cm
Thickness:	5.0 cm
Description:	A zoomorphic torso, probably of a horse: part of the torso, probably the rear, with two legs complete; the tail(?) is mostly broken off. Red-brown clay, no clear core, traces of white slip; no clear grits.

Scale 1:1

Catalogue no. 117

Registration no.:	43029
Findspot:	50.57.L239.B47
Year excavated:	1993
Context:	Ph. 7 quarry fill
Height:	3.1 cm
Width:	4.6 cm
Length:	6.8 cm
Description:	A zoomorphic torso, probably of a horse: the body is complete; the legs are only preserved as stumps, and the tail is completely missing. There is a neck scar on the top front of the body. Red-brown clay, with traces of white slip; brown core, 0.25–0.50 mm grits.

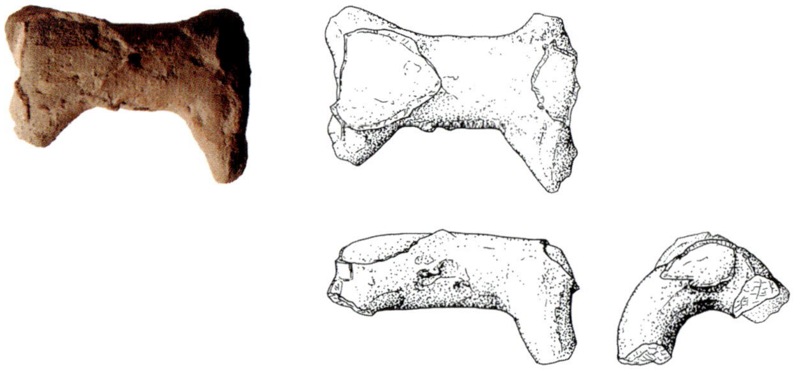

Scale 1:2

Catalogue no. 118

Registration no.:	43549
Findspot:	50.48.L405.FG23.B59
Year excavated:	1993
Context:	Ph. 7 quarry fill
Height:	1.9 cm
Width:	3.7 cm
Length:	5.2 cm
Description:	A zoomorphic torso, probably of a horse: the front part of the body, with the left front leg partly preserved, and the right front leg missing. There is a scar for the neck. Brown clay, gray core; white and black grits, 0.25–2.00 mm.

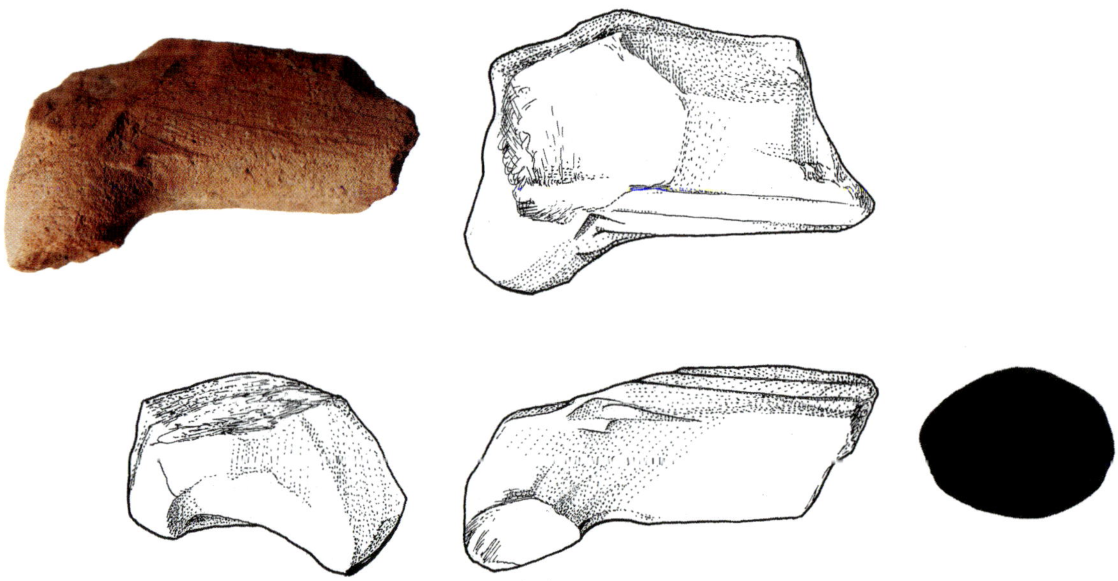

Scale 1:1

Catalogue no. 119

Registration no.:	43935
Findspot:	38.74.L591.B141
Year excavated:	1994
Context:	Ph. 14 deliberate fill
Height:	1.9 cm
Width:	2.9 cm
Length:	6.5 cm
Description:	A zoomorphic torso, probably of a horse. The torso is complete; there are scars from all four legs, and from the neck. Red-brown clay, gray core, 0.25–1.00 mm grits.

Scale 1:1

Catalogue no. 120

Registration no.:	44119
Findspot:	50.49.L425.B33
Year excavated:	1994
Context:	Ph. 7 quarry fill
Height:	1.7 cm
Width:	2.6 cm
Length:	6.1 cm
Description:	A zoomorphic torso, probably of a horse: the body is complete and the tail is partially preserved; there are scars from all four legs. There is no visible neck scar. Dark brown clay, clay-colored core, 0.25–0.75 mm grits.

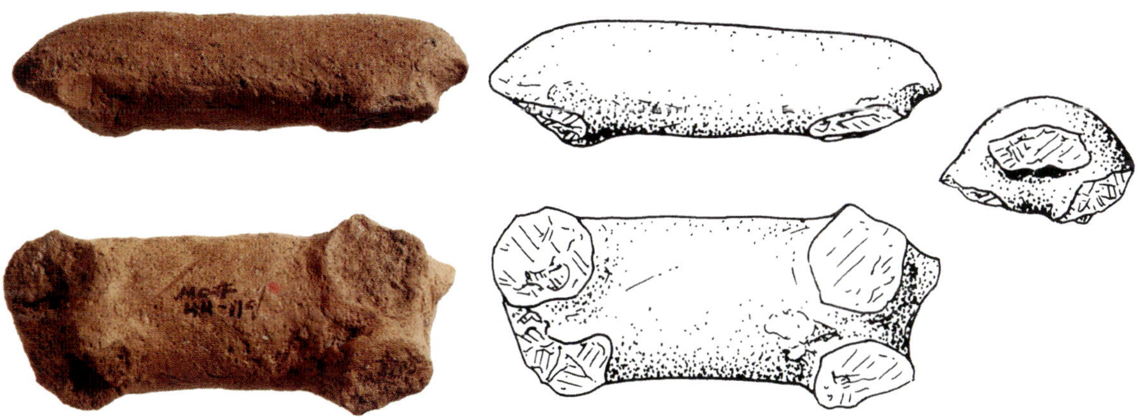

Scale 1:1

Catalogue no. 121

Registration no.: 44409
Findspot: 50.49.LF427.B70
Year excavated: 1994
Context: Ph. 7 foundation trench
Height: 2.7 cm
Width: 3.7 cm
Length: 6.8 cm
Description: A zoomorphic torso, probably of a horse: the complete body is preserved, but the tail is mostly broken. The right rear leg is partially preserved; the right front and left rear legs are preserved only as tiny stumps; there is only a scar of the front left leg. There is also a neck scar on the top front. There is a ridge extending slightly along back of the horse. Brown clay, with traces of white slip, gray core, 0.25–0.50 mm grits.

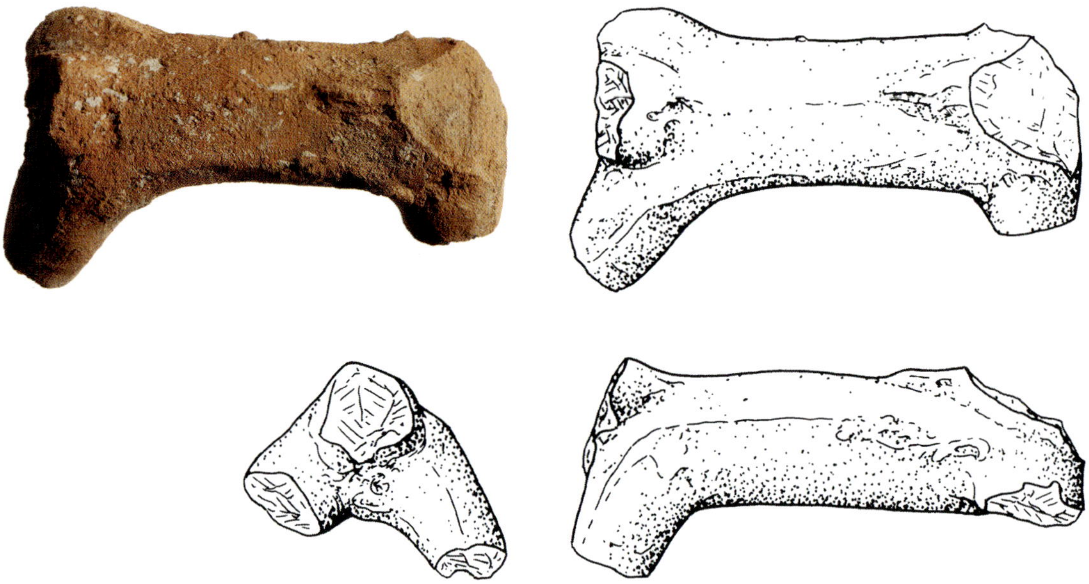

Scale 1:1

Catalogue no. 122

Registration no.: 44474
Findspot: 50.48.L439.B65
Year excavated: 1994
Context: Ph. 7 quarry fill
Height: 3.5 cm
Width: 4.4 cm
Length: 9.2 cm
Description: A zoomorphic torso, probably of a horse: the body is complete; the right rear leg is partially preserved, but the others are almost completely missing. There is a neck scar on the top front, with a possible shallower scar just behind. The tail is partially preserved. Brown clay, with traces of white slip, gray core, 0.25–1.00 mm grits.

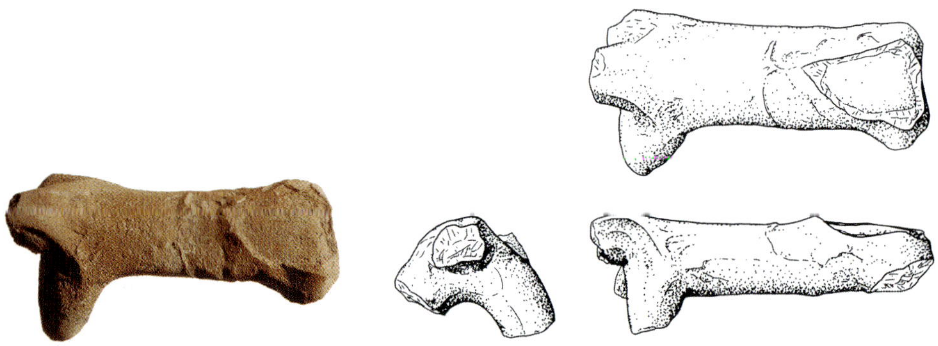

Scale 1:2

Catalogue no. 123

Registration no.: 44501
Findspot: 50.57.L256.B93
Year excavated: 1994
Context: Ph. 7 quarry fill
Height: 1.5 cm
Width: 2.0 cm
Length: 2.9 cm
Description: A zoomorphic torso fragment, probably of a horse: the front half of the torso is preserved, with stumps of the front legs. There is a neck scar on top. Dark brown clay, black core, 0.25–1.00 mm grits.

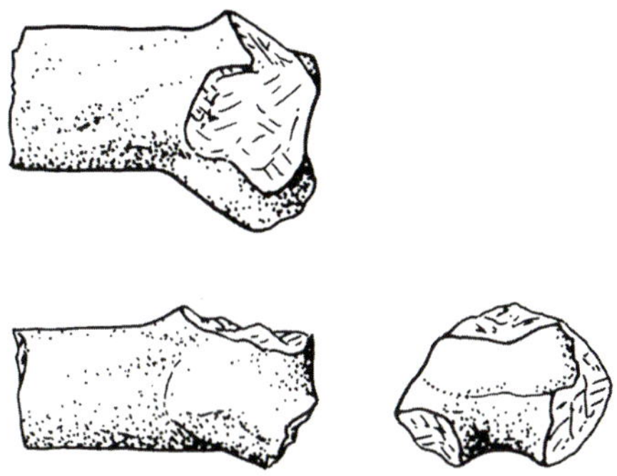

Scale 1:1

Catalogue no. 124

Registration no.: 44627
Findspot: 50.49.L436.FG29.B88
Year excavated: 1994
Context: Ph. 7 quarry fill
Height: 3.3 cm
Width: 3.0 cm
Length: 8.2 cm
Description: A zoomorphic torso, probably of a horse: the body is complete; none of the legs are preserved. There is a neck scar on top. The tail rises up behind and then curls down along the rear of the body, but the end is chipped. Brown clay (with traces of white slip, and traces of burning); clay-colored core, 0.25–2.00 mm grits.

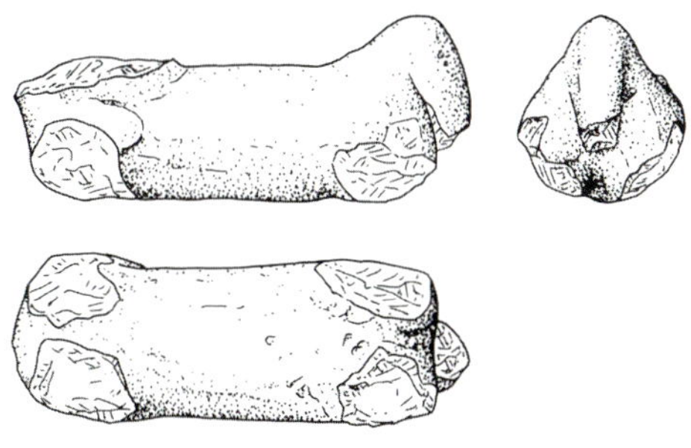

Scale 1:2

Catalogue no. 125

Registration no.:	44652
Findspot:	50.48.L439.B53
Year excavated:	1994
Context:	Ph. 7 quarry fill
Height:	4.5 cm
Width:	3.6 cm
Length:	4.7 cm
Description:	A horse body fragment: the front half of the torso, parts of the front two legs, and part of the neck are preserved. There is a mane on the back of neck. Gray clay (with traces of burning), clay-colored core, 0.25–5.00 mm grits.

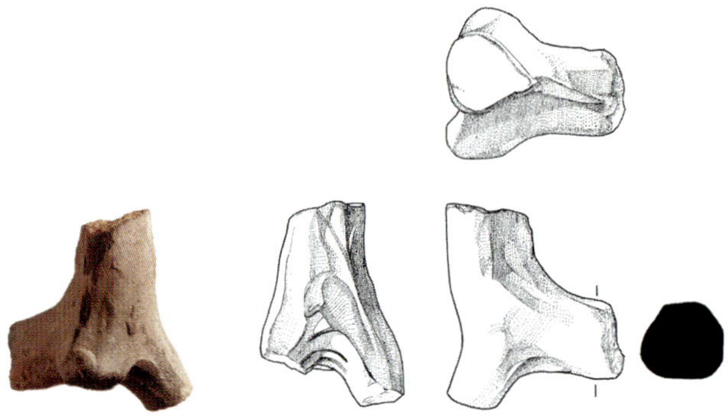

Scale 1:2

Catalogue no. 126

Registration no.:	44993
Findspot:	50.47.L285.B72
Year excavated:	1994
Context:	Ph. 7 quarry fill
Height:	2.9 cm
Width:	2.6 cm
Length:	4.8 cm
Diameter:	1.6–1.9 cm (of body)
Description:	A zoomorphic torso fragment, probably of a horse: the rear half of the torso is preserved, with stumps for the rear legs. The tail is partially preserved. There is a possible scar from a rider on the front end of the fragment. Brown clay, with traces of white slip, black core, 0.25–0.50 mm grits.

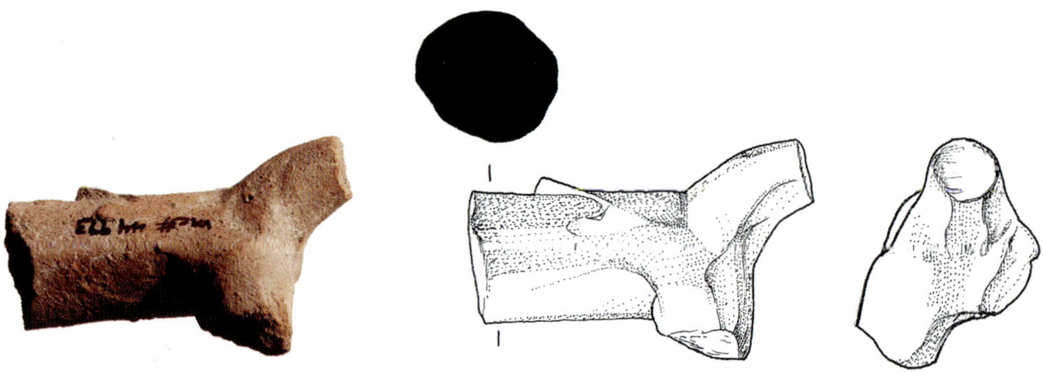

Scale 1:1

Catalogue no. 127

Registration no.:	45070
Findspot:	50.48.LF422.B189
Year excavated:	1994
Context:	Ph. 7 deliberate fill
Height:	3.2 cm
Width:	4.3 cm
Length:	7.2 cm
Description:	A zoomorphic torso, probably of a horse: the body is complete, and the legs are partially preserved. There is a neck scar on the top front of the figurine. Brown-red clay, with traces of white slip, black core; 0.25–5.00 mm grits.

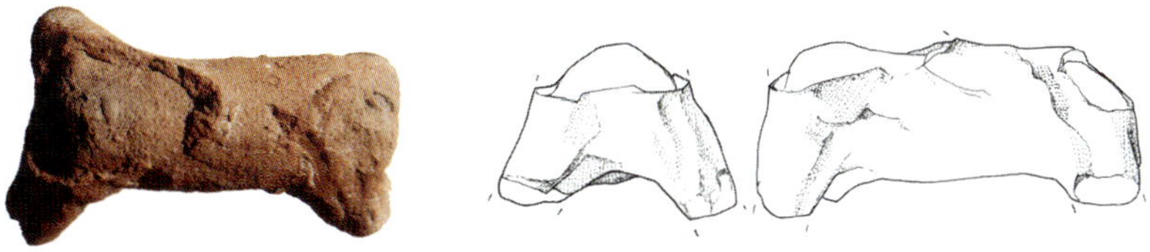

Scale 1:2

Catalogue no. 128

Registration no.:	45084
Findspot:	50.49.L440.B167
Year excavated:	1994
Context:	Ph. 7 quarry fill
Height:	2.8 cm
Width:	3.8 cm
Length:	7.7 cm
Description:	A zoomorphic torso, probably of a horse. The body is mostly complete, except for the front left end. The front leg is completely missing; the others are preserved only as stumps. The tail is partially preserved. There is a neck scar on the top front. Brown clay, clay-colored core, 0.25–1.00 mm grits.

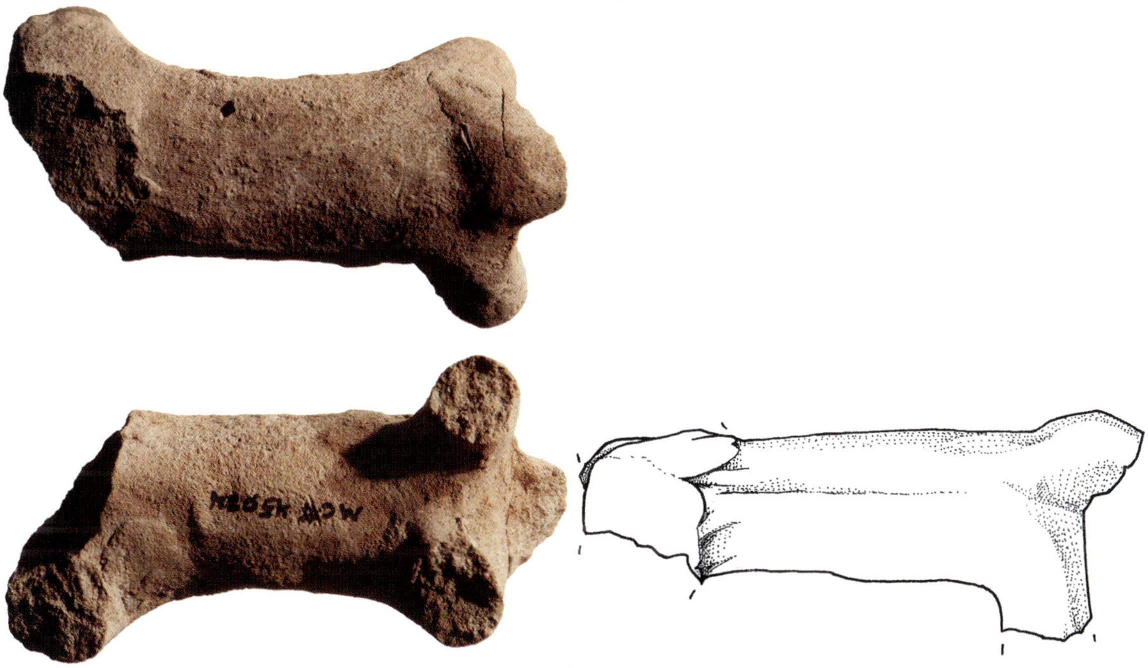

Scale 1:1

Catalogue no. 129

Registration no.:	45144
Findspot:	50.49.L443.B172
Year excavated:	1994
Context:	Ph. 7 quarry fill
Height:	2.6 cm
Width:	3.5 cm
Length:	7.9 cm
Description:	A zoomorphic torso, probably of a horse: the body is complete; the legs are mostly broken off. The tail is partially preserved. There is a neck scar on the top front of the body. Brown clay, with traces of white slip, clay-colored core, 0.25–4.00 mm grits.

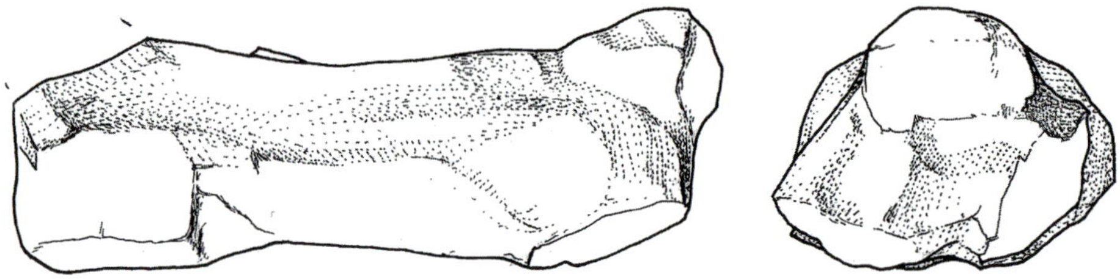

Scale 1:1

Catalogue no. 130

Registration no.:	45310
Findspot:	50.58.L335.B20
Year excavated:	1995
Context:	Ph. 8 deliberate fill
Height:	5.9 cm
Width:	6.2 cm
Length:	6.1 cm
Description:	A zoomorphic torso fragment, probably of a horse: the front half of the torso is preserved, with the front legs complete. The bottom of the neck is also preserved. Brown clay, black core, 0.25–4.00 mm grits.

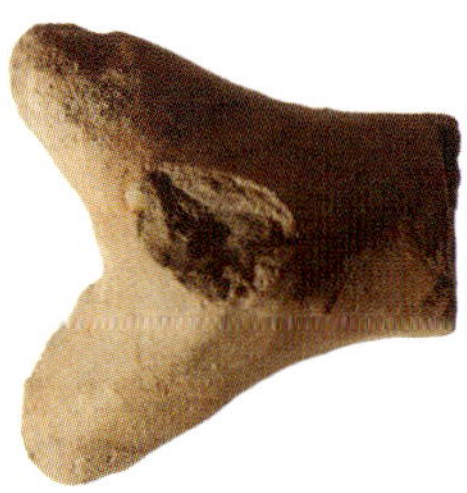

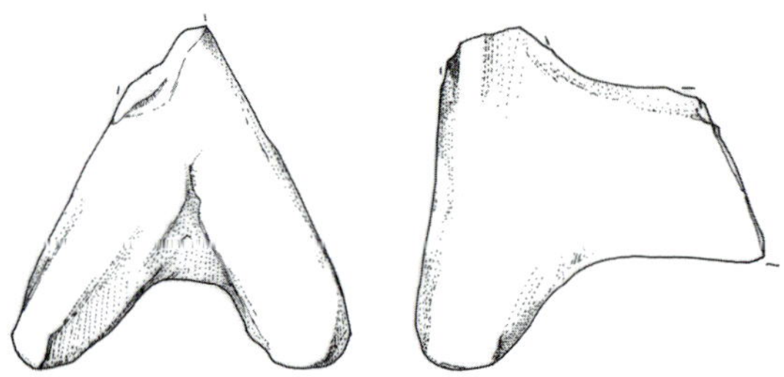

Scale 1:2

Catalogue no. 131

Registration no.:	45495
Findspot:	50.48.L452.B52
Year excavated:	1995
Context:	Ph. 7 quarry fill
Height:	1.9 cm
Width:	2.7 cm
Length:	3.4 cm
Description:	A zoomorphic torso fragment, probably of a horse: the rear half of the body is preserved, with the end of the tail broken off. The rear legs are almost completely missing. Dark brown clay, black core, 0.25–0.75 mm grits.

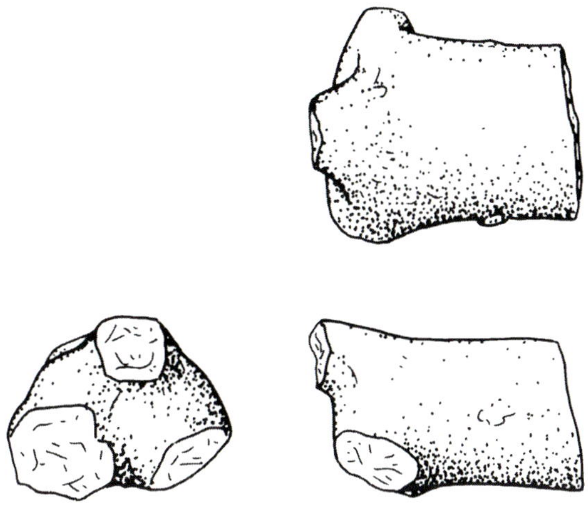

Scale 1:1

Catalogue no. 132

Registration no.:	45999
Findspot:	50.48.L452.B182
Year excavated:	1995
Context:	Ph. 7 quarry fill
Height:	2.8 cm
Width:	3.9 cm
Length:	2.5 cm
Description:	A zoomorphic body fragment, probably of a horse: the front half of the body is preserved, with parts of the front legs. There is a neck scar on the top of the figurine. Dark brown clay, with traces of white slip, black core, 0.25–1.00 mm grits.

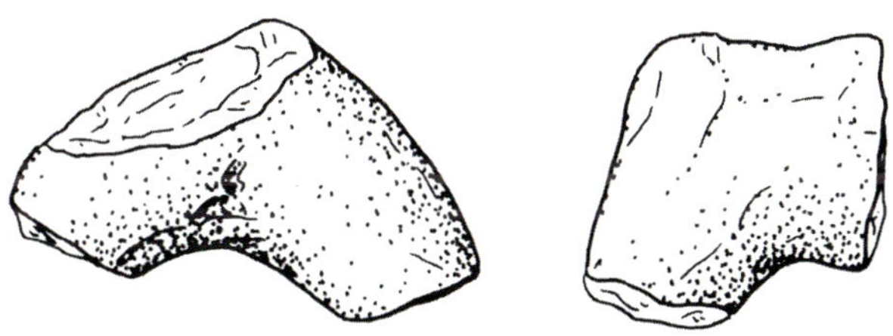

Scale 1:1

Catalogue no. 133

Registration no.:	46087
Findspot:	50.48.L461.B193
Year excavated:	1995
Context:	Ph. 7 quarry fill
Height:	3.2 cm
Width:	3.7 cm
Length:	6.8 cm
Description:	A zoomorphic torso, probably of a horse: the body is complete; the front left leg is partially preserved, while the others are completely broken off. The tail is completely missing. There is a neck scar on the top front of the body. Reddish-brown clay, with traces of white slip; gray core, 0.25–0.75 mm grits.

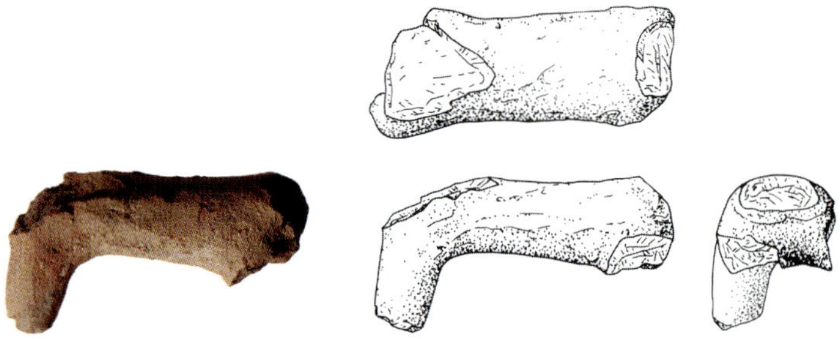

Scale 1:2

Catalogue no. 134

Registration no.:	46227
Findspot:	50.48.L461.B223
Year excavated:	1995
Context:	Ph. 7 quarry fill
Height:	2.2 cm
Width:	4.0 cm
Length:	6.2 cm
Description:	A zoomorphic torso, probably of a horse: the body is complete; the front legs are partially preserved, while the rear legs are completely missing. The tail is broken off. There is a neck scar on the top front of the body. Brown clay, with traces of white slip; gray core, 0.25–1.00 mm grits.

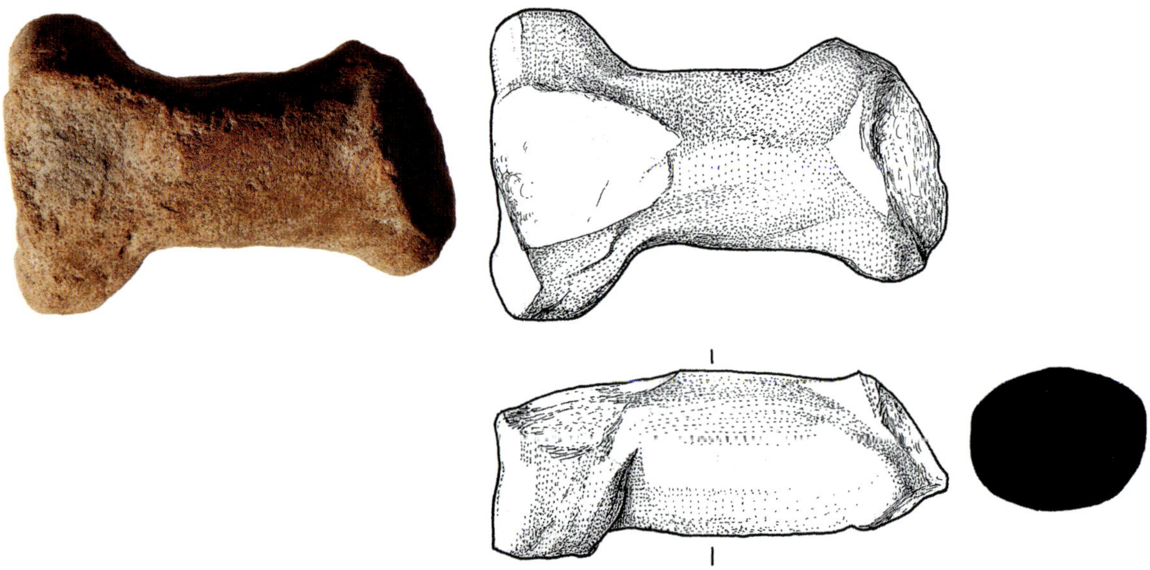

Scale 1:1

Catalogue no. 135

Registration no.: 46272
Findspot: 50.48.L462.B241
Year excavated: 1995
Context: Ph. 7 quarry fill
Height: 4.7 cm
Width: 4.5 cm
Length: 6.9 cm
Description: A zoomorphic torso, probably of a horse: the body is complete; the front right leg is largely preserved, while the left legs are preserved as stumps and only a scar remains of the right rear leg. The tail is broken off. There is a neck scar on the top front of the body. Light brown clay, with traces of white slip; black core, 0.25–2.00 mm grits.

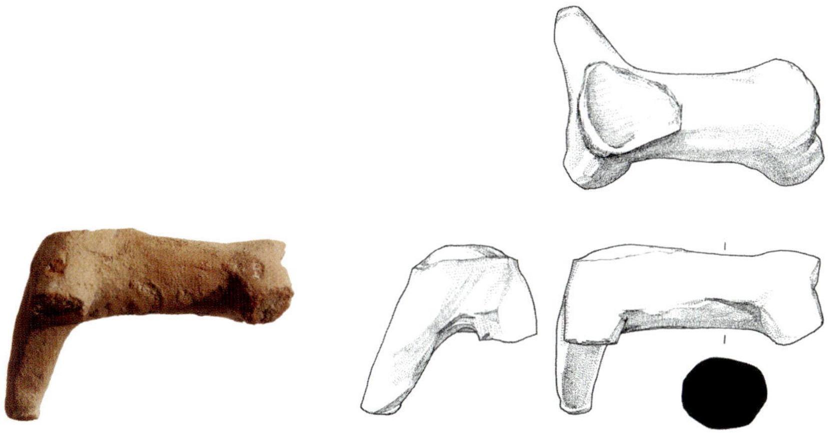

Scale 1:2

Catalogue no. 136

Registration no.: 46493
Findspot: 50.48.F460.B243
Year excavated: 1995
Context: Ph. 7 quarry fill
Height: 3.5 cm
Width: 3.8 cm
Length: 7.0 cm
Description: A zoomorphic torso, probably of a horse: the body is complete, with all four legs preserved as stumps. The lower part of the neck is preserved. The tail is almost completely broken off. Reddish-brown clay, with traces of white slip; black core, 0.25–1.00 mm grits.

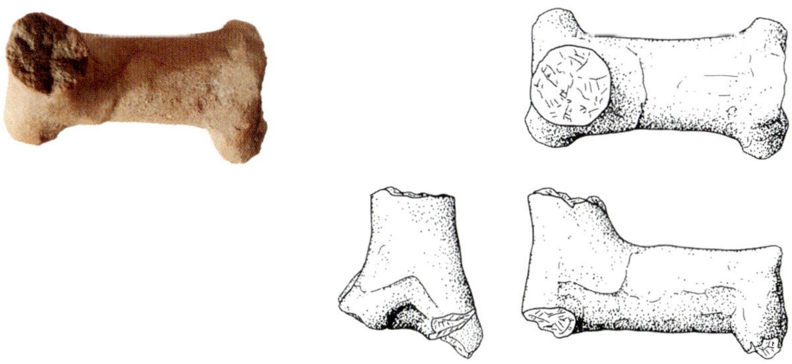

Scale 1:2

Catalogue no. 137

Registration no.:	46744
Findspot:	50.48.L467.B69
Year excavated:	1996
Context:	Ph. 7 quarry fill
Height:	3.6 cm
Width:	3.8 cm
Length:	6.5 cm
Description:	A zoomorphic torso fragment, probably of a horse: the body is largely complete, but the hind section with the two rear legs is missing. The front two legs are preserved as stumps. The bottom of the neck is preserved. Brown clay, gray core, 0.25–1.00 mm grits.

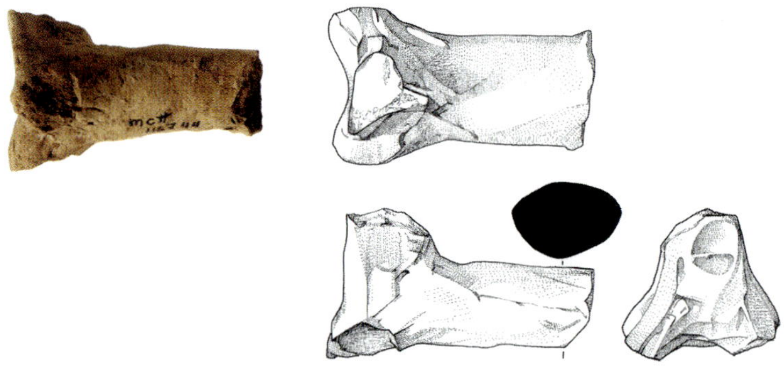

Scale 1:2

Catalogue no. 138

Registration no.:	46907
Findspot:	50.48.L453 (B# unknown)
Year excavated:	1995
Context:	Ph. 7 quarry fill
Height:	2.7 cm
Width:	3.5 cm
Length:	7.8 cm
Description:	A zoomorphic torso, probably of a horse: the torso is complete; the left front leg is partially preserved, a small portion of the right hind leg is preserved, and the other legs are completely missing. The tail is broken off. There is no neck scar, as the surface of the figurine is slightly eroded. Dark brown clay, with traces of white slip; black core, 0.25–2.00 mm grits.

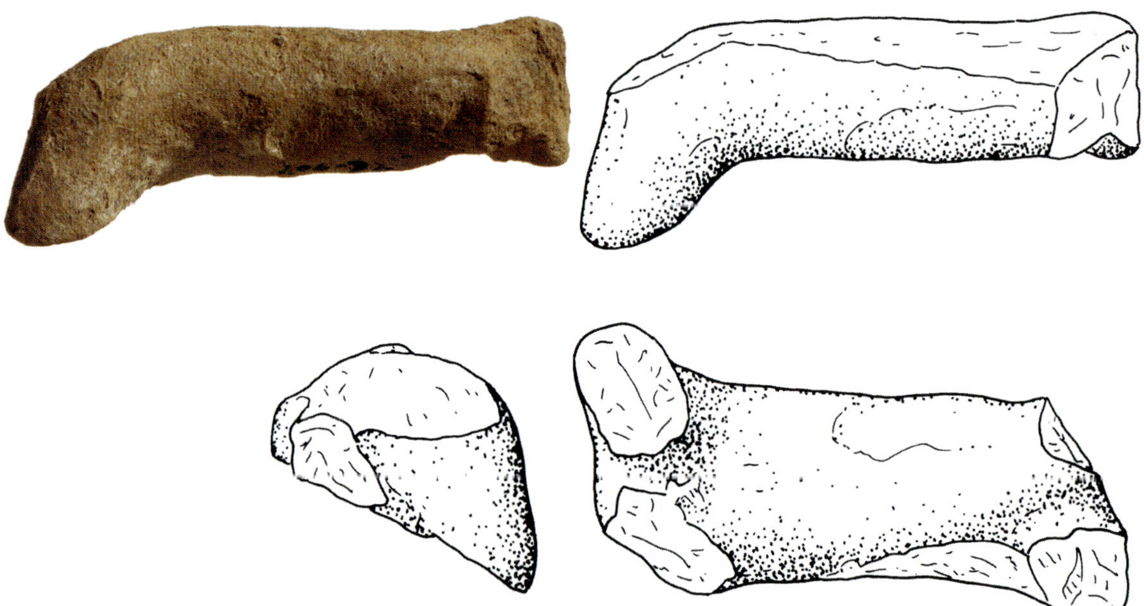

Scale 1:1

Catalogue no. 139

Registration no.:	47815
Findspot:	50.49.L451.B146
Year excavated:	1996
Context:	Ph. 7 quarry fill
Height:	4.4 cm
Width:	4.1 cm
Length:	10.0 cm
Description:	A zoomorphic torso, probably of a horse: the body is complete; three legs are complete (the right rear leg is completely missing). The tail is partially preserved. There is a neck scar on the top front of the body. Brown clay, with traces of white slip; light-colored core, 0.25–1.00 mm grits.

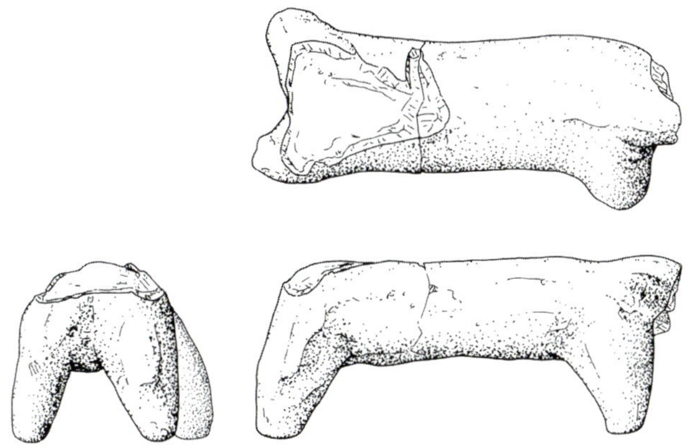

Scale 1:2

Catalogue no. 140

Registration no.:	47946
Findspot:	50.48.L453.B8
Year excavated:	1997
Context:	Ph. 7 quarry fill
Height:	5.5 cm
Width:	5.3 cm
Length:	9.8 cm
Description:	A zoomorphic torso, probably of a horse: the body is complete; the left rear leg is complete, but the others are preserved only as small stumps. The tail is partially preserved. There is a neck scar on the top front of the body. Brown clay, gray core, 0.25–1.00 mm grits.

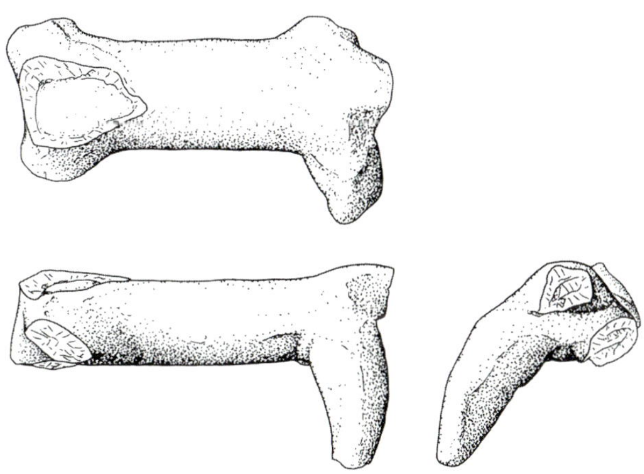

Scale 1:2

Catalogue no. 141

Registration no.:	48558
Findspot:	50.57.L274.B8
Year excavated:	1997
Context:	Ph. 7 quarry fill
Height:	5.1 cm
Width:	4.1 cm
Length:	4.2 cm
Diameter:	2.6 cm (of body)
Description:	A zoomorphic body fragment, possibly a horse torso. This may be the rear section of a horse, with the left rear leg preserved (and the right rear leg completely missing). The tail is partially preserved. Red-brown clay, black core, 0.25–3.00 mm grits.

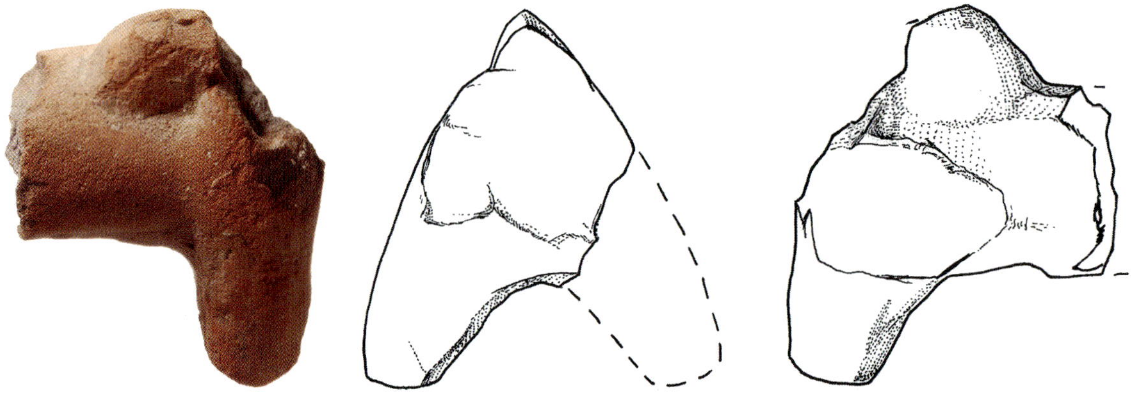

Scale 1:1

Catalogue no. 142

Registration no.:	49068
Findspot:	38.94.L296.B25
Year excavated:	1997
Context:	Ph. 14 destruction debris
Height:	2.3 cm
Width:	2.6 cm
Length:	6.5 cm
Description:	A zoomorphic torso, probably of a horse. The torso is complete; the left rear leg partially preserved, the left front is leg mostly missing, and the others are completely missing. The tail is partially preserved. There is a neck scar on the top front of the body. Brown clay, with traces of white slip and traces of burning; black core, 0.25–1.00 mm grits.

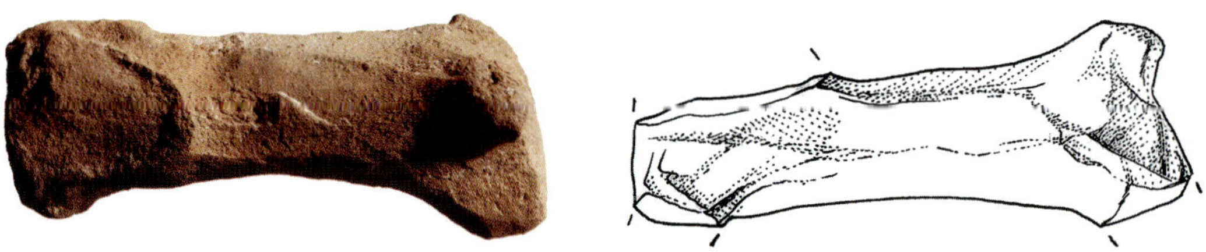

Scale 1:1

Catalogue no. 143

Registration no.: 49198
Findspot: 38.94.L299.FG16.B35
Year excavated: 1997
Context: Ph. 14 floor
Height: 4.2 cm
Width: 4.5 cm
Length: 4.2 cm
Description: A zoomorphic torso fragment, probably of a horse: the rear of the body is preserved, with the right rear leg complete. The left rear leg is preserved as a tiny stump. The tail is missing. Brown-gray clay, with traces of white slip; black core, 0.25–2.00 mm grits.

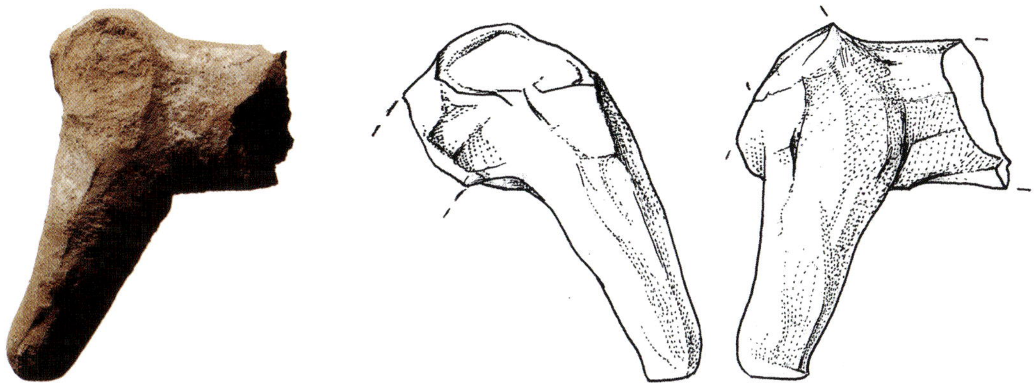

Scale 1:1

Catalogue no. 144

Registration no.: 51610
Findspot: 50.49.L451.B100
Year excavated: 1996
Context: Ph. 7 quarry fill
Height: 2.7 cm
Width: 4.3 cm
Length: 6.1 cm
Description: A zoomorphic torso fragment, probably of a horse: the front half of the body is preserved; of the legs, only a piece of the front right leg is extant. There is a neck scar on the top of the body. Brown-red clay, with traces of white slip; gray core, 0.25–1.00 mm grits.

Scale 1:2

Catalogue no. 145

Registration no.:	51611
Findspot:	50.49.L453.B85
Year excavated:	1996
Context:	Ph. 7 quarry fill
Height:	3.5 cm
Width:	5.1 cm
Length:	4.5 cm
Description:	A zoomorphic torso, probably of a horse: the front part of the torso is preserved, with the right front leg complete and the left front partially broken. The base of the neck is preserved. Brown-red clay, with traces of white slip; gray core, 0.25–0.50 mm grits.

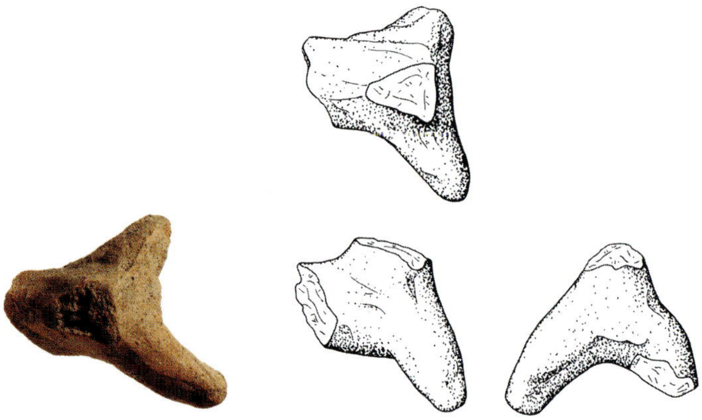

Scale 1:2

Catalogue no. 146

Registration no.:	51612
Findspot:	50.49.L449.B33
Year excavated:	1996
Context:	Ph. 7 quarry fill
Height:	3.0 cm
Width:	3.7 cm
Length:	8.7 cm
Description:	A zoomorphic torso, probably of a horse: the body is complete; none of the legs is preserved. There is a short tail on the rear of the body. On the top front of the body is a scar from the neck break. Brown clay, with traces of white slip; gray core, 0.25–2.00 mm grits.

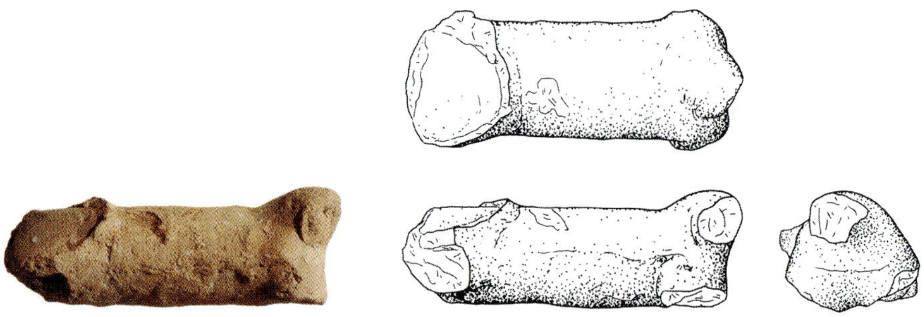

Scale 1:2

Catalogue no. 147

Registration no.:	56951
Findspot:	38.84.L569.B29
Year excavated:	1998
Context:	Ph. 14 deliberate fill
Height:	2.6 cm
Width:	3.3 cm
Length:	6.4 cm
Description:	A zoomorphic torso, possibly of a horse: the majority of the body is preserved, except for the very rear and two rear legs. The two front legs are broken off. There is a neck scar on the top front of the figurine. Brown clay, with traces of white slip; gray-brown core, 0.25–0.50 mm grits.

Scale 1:1

Catalogue no. 148

Registration no.:	56953
Findspot:	50.49.L440.B158
Year excavated:	1994
Context:	Ph. 7 quarry fill
Height:	2.0 cm
Width:	3.2 cm
Length:	6.4 cm
Description:	A zoomorphic torso, probably of a horse: the entire body is preserved, except the very rear; all four legs are broken off. There is a neck scar on the top front of the body. Light brown clay (with traces of burning on top), light brown core, 0.50–1.00 mm grits (few grits).

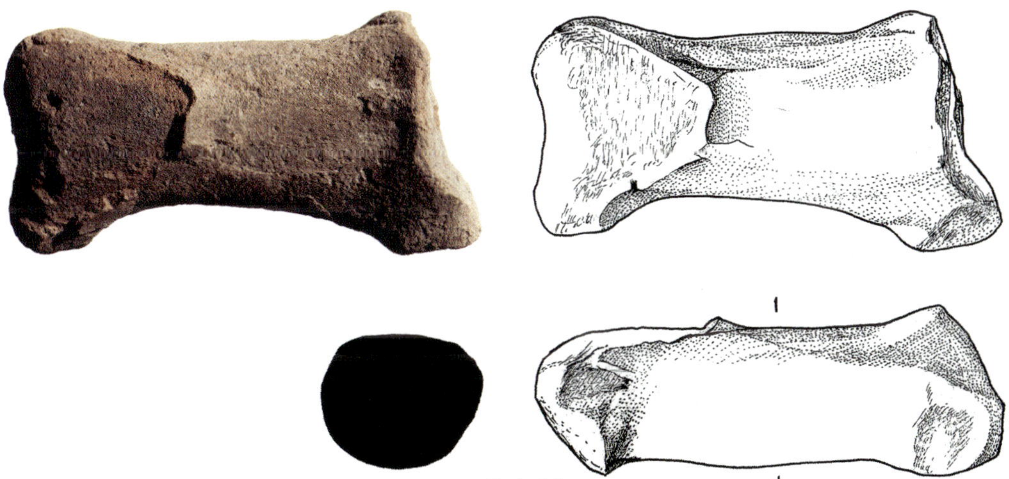

Scale 1:1

Catalogue no. 149

Registration no.: 38445
Findspot: 38.83.LF272.B67
Year excavated: 1991
Context: Ph. 14 robber trench
Height: 4.3 cm
Diameter: 1.3–1.4 cm (of wider end)
Description: A zoomorphic leg, probably of a horse. The leg tapers to a near-point at the bottom and is slightly curved. Red-brown clay, gray core, 0.25–0.50 mm grits.

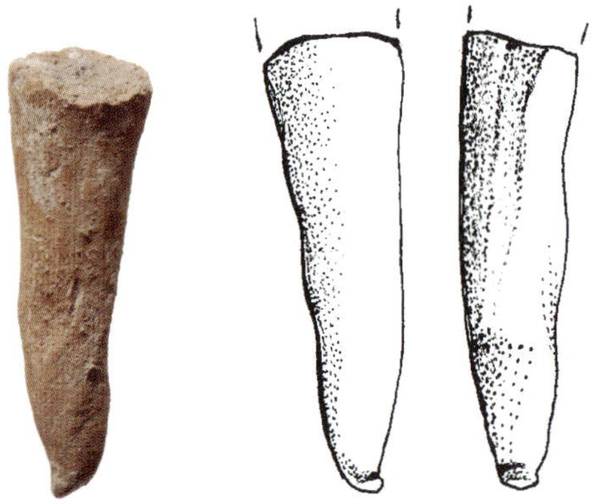

Scale 1:1

Catalogue no. 150

Registration no.: 44482
Findspot: 50.48.L444.B16
Year excavated: 1994
Context: Ph. 7 quarry fill
Height (Leg 1): 4.1 cm
Diameter: 1.5–1.7 cm (of wider end)
Height (Leg 2): 3.3 cm
Diameter: 1.5–2.0 cm (of wider end)
Description: Two zoomorphic legs, probably of a horse. One leg is longer and tapering down to a rounded tip; the shaft is straight but the clay looks to have been twisted. The other leg is shorter and slightly curved, with a flat tip; part of the shaft is smoothed and flattened. Both legs: brown clay, with traces of white slip; black core, 0.25–1.00 mm grits.

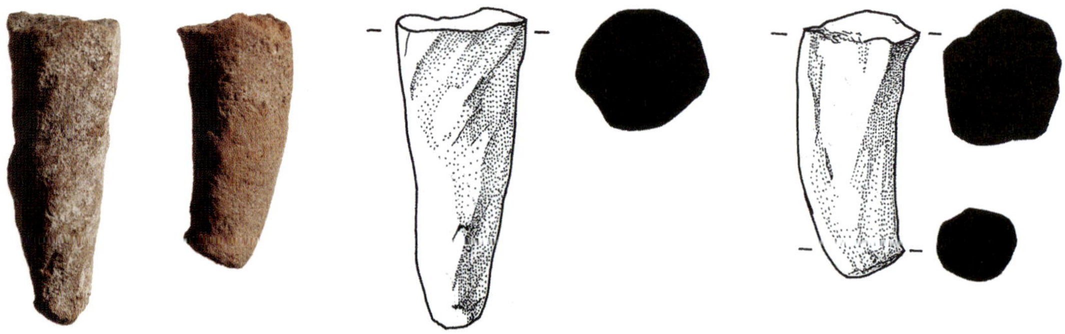

Scale 1:1

Catalogue no. 151

Registration no.: 44677
Findspot: 50.57.L259.B112
Year excavated: 1994
Context: Ph. 7 quarry fill
Height: 2.7 cm
Diameter: 1.5–1.8 cm (of wider end)
Description: A zoomorphic leg, probably of a horse (or a possible horse muzzle): the shaft tapers to a flat end. Brown clay, gray core, 0.25–1.00 mm grits.

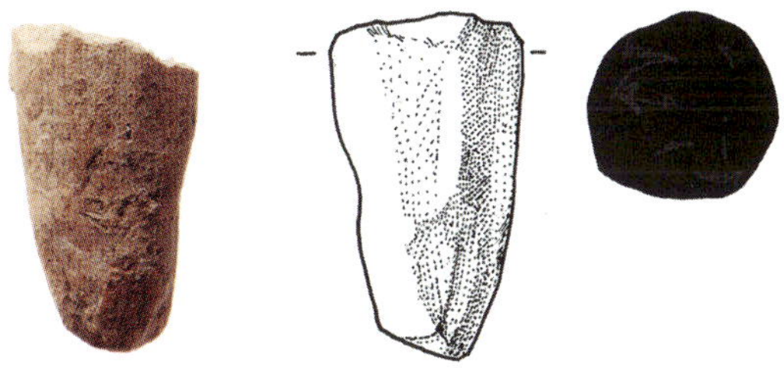

Scale 1:1

Catalogue no. 152

Registration no.: 44820
Findspot: 50.57.L259.B121
Year excavated: 1994
Context: Ph. 7 quarry fill
Height: 3.3 cm
Diameter: 1.4 cm (of wider end)
Description: A zoomorphic leg, probably of a horse (or a possible horse muzzle); the shaft tapers to a near point. Gray-brown clay, with traces of white slip; gray core, 0.25–0.50 mm grits.

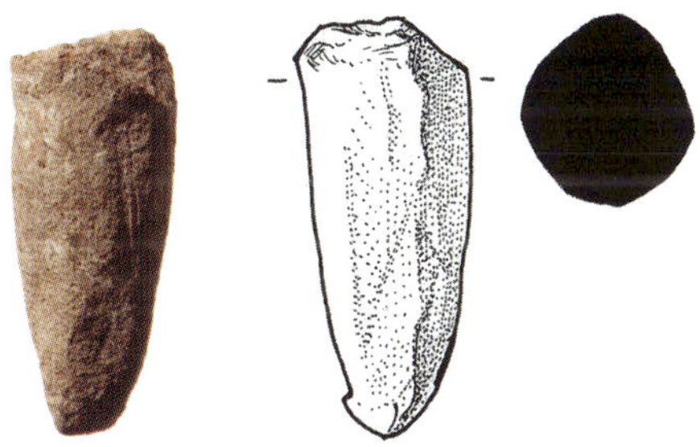

Scale 1:1

Catalogue no. 153

Registration no.: 44972
Findspot: 38.84.L299.FG54.B256
Year excavated: 1994
Context: Ph. 14 destruction debris
Height: 2.6 cm
Diameter: 1.5 cm (at base)
Description: A possible zoomorphic leg, probably of a horse (or a possible horse muzzle). The fragment tapers to a rounded end. Red-brown clay, with traces of white slip; gray core, 0.25–1.00 mm grits.

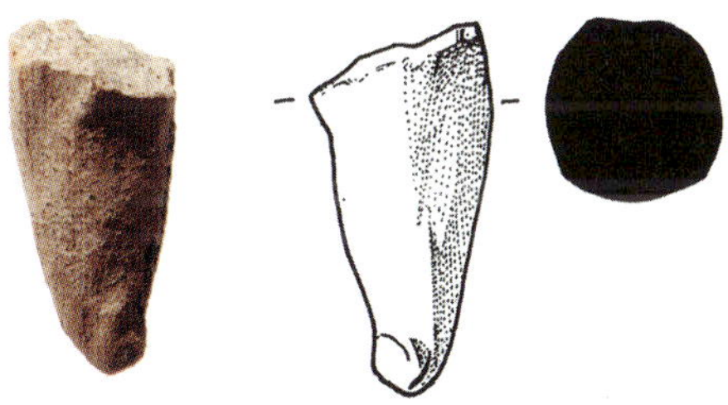

Scale 1:1

Catalogue no. 154

Registration no.: 45196
Findspot: 50.57.L259.B115
Year excavated: 1994
Context: Ph. 7 quarry fill
Height: 2.8 cm
Diameter: 1.2–1.4 cm (of wider end)
Description: A zoomorphic leg, probably of a horse (or a possible horse muzzle): the shaft tapers to a near point. Brown clay, with traces of white slip; black core, 0.25 mm grits.

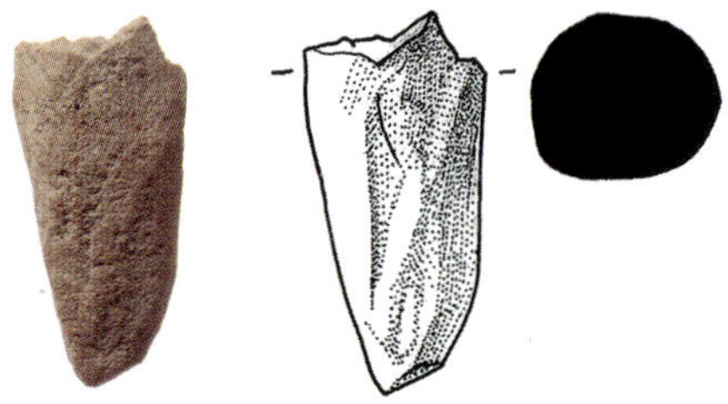

Scale 1:1

Catalogue no. 155

Registration no.: 45747
Findspot: 50.48.L452.B23
Year excavated: 1995
Context: Ph. 7 quarry fill
Height: 3.1 cm
Diameter: 1.5–1.9 cm (of wider end); 1.0 cm (of other end)
Description: A zoomorphic leg (or a possible horse muzzle): triangular section at wider end, tapering and curving to rounded narrower end. Brown clay, black core, 0.25–0.75 mm grits.

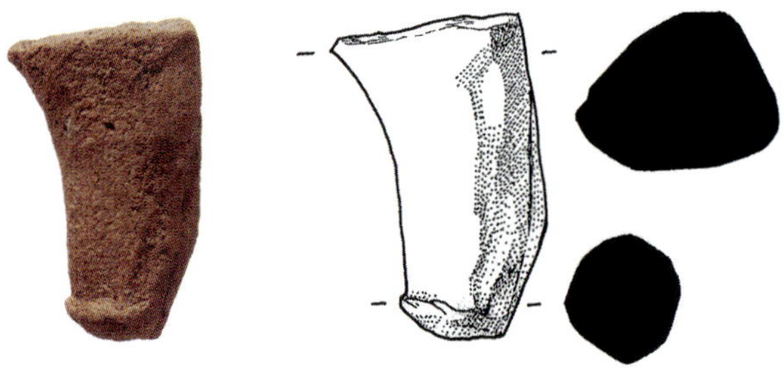

Scale 1:1

Catalogue no. 156

Registration no.: 45748
Findspot: 50.48.L452.B23
Year excavated: 1995
Context: Ph. 7 quarry fill
Height: 1.9 cm
Diameter: 1.2–1.4 cm (of wider end)
Description: A possible zoomorphic leg, probably of a horse (or a possible horse muzzle). The fragment is cone-shaped, tapering to a near point. Brown clay, gray core, 0.25–0.50 mm grits.

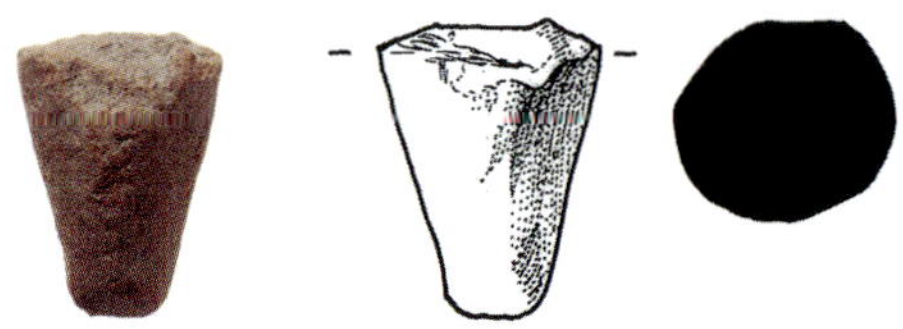

Scale 1:1

Catalogue no. 157

Registration no.:	45749
Findspot:	50.48.L452.B23
Year excavated:	1995
Context:	Ph. 7 quarry fill
Height:	3.3 cm
Diameter:	1.6–1.8 cm (of wider end)
Description:	A zoomorphic leg, probably of a horse: the shaft tapers to a flattened end. Brown-red clay, gray core, 0.25–0.50 mm grits.

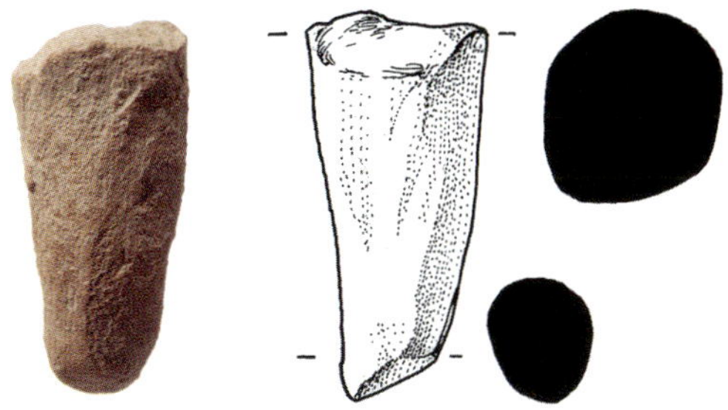

Scale 1:1

Catalogue no. 158

Registration no.:	45870
Findspot:	50.48.L453.B120
Year excavated:	1995
Context:	Ph. 7 quarry fill
Height:	6.7 cm
Diameter:	3.0 cm (of wider end)
Description:	A zoomorphic leg, probably of a horse. The leg is completely preserved, with a piece of the body attached as well as a partial scar from a second leg. Peach-colored clay; black core, 0.25–5.00 mm grits.

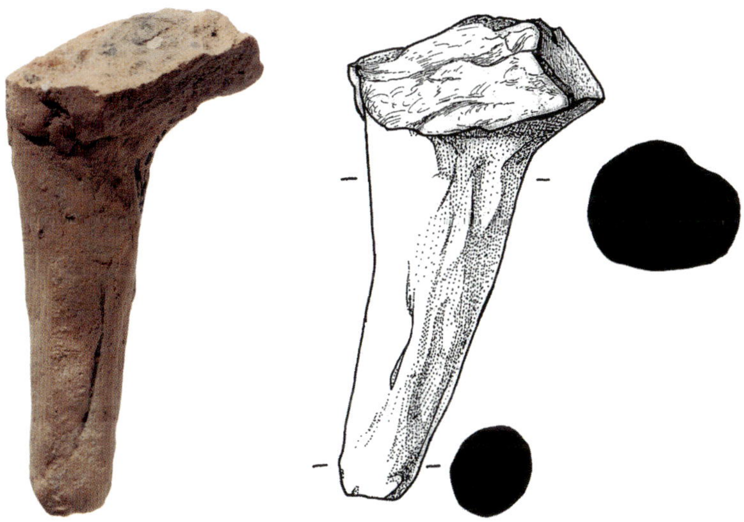

Scale 1:1

Catalogue no. 159

Registration no.:	46685
Findspot:	50.48.L467.B52
Year excavated:	1996
Context:	Ph. 7 quarry fill
Height:	3.7 cm
Diameter:	1.2 cm
Description:	A possible zoomorphic leg, probably of a horse: a thin curving cylinder, rounded at one end. Gray-brown clay, with traces of white slip; clay-colored core, 0.25–0.50 mm grits.

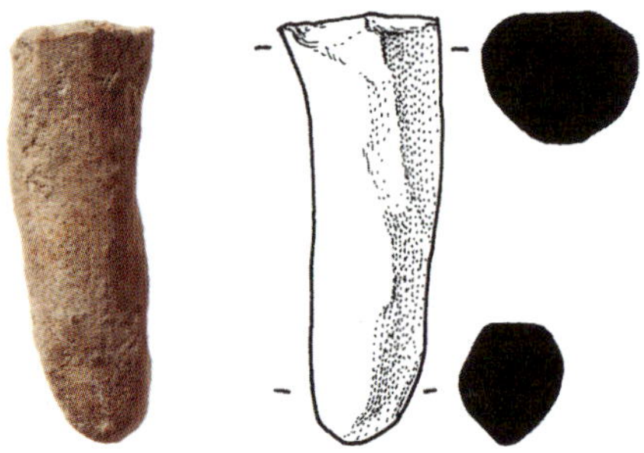

Scale 1:1

Catalogue no. 160

Registration no.:	42426
Findspot:	50.49.L389.B7
Year excavated:	1993
Context:	Ph. 7 street surface
Height:	4.0 cm
Width:	3.3 cm
Thickness:	1.6 cm
Description:	A torso, probably of a rider: broken at the neck and at the waist (where the figurine attached to the horse). The arms are bent at the elbows and curving downward, but the forearms are missing. Brown clay, clay-colored core, 0.25–1.50 mm grits.

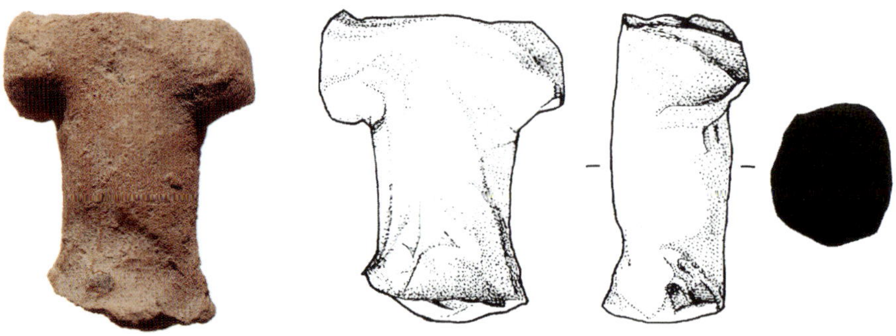

Scale 1:1

Catalogue no. 161

Registration no.: 44893
Findspot: 50.49.L440.B143
Year excavated: 1994
Context: Ph. 7 quarry fill
Height: 4.5 cm
Width: 4.2 cm
Thickness: 1.7 cm (of body); 3.6 cm (at arms)
Description: A torso, probably of a rider (possibly a zoomorphic torso). The head and neck are missing. The figurine is broken at the waist, where it attached to the horse. The arms are partially preserved. Dark brown clay, with traces of white slip; black core, 0.25–0.75 mm grits.

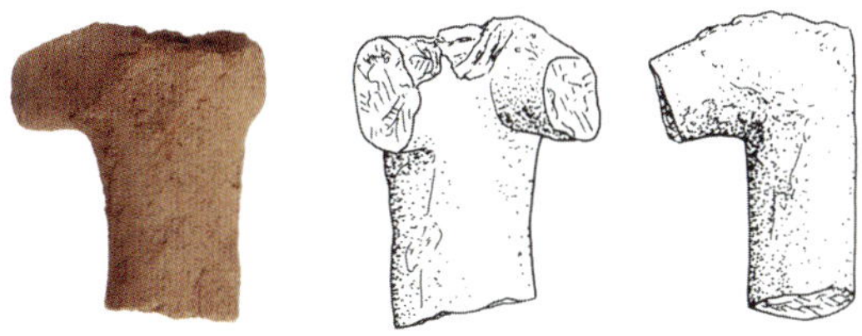

Scale 1:2

Catalogue no. 162

Registration no.: 45082
Findspot: 50.57.L258.B145
Year excavated: 1994
Context: Ph. 7 quarry fill
Height: 3.4 cm
Width: 2.1 cm
Thickness: 1.6 cm
Description: A small torso, probably of a rider. The head is broken off; the arms are bent at the elbows and curving downward, but the forearms are missing. The beginnings of legs are present at the base. Brown-red clay, with traces of white slip; clay-colored core, 0.25 mm grits.

Catalogue no. 163

Registration no.: 45494
Findspot: 50.48.L452.B52
Year excavated: 1995
Context: Ph. 7 quarry fill
Height: 3.5 cm
Width: 3.7 cm
Thickness: 2.8 cm
Description: A torso of a rider: the arms extend forward but are mostly broken off; the head is missing. The figurine is broken at the waist, where it attached to the horse at the waist. The torso is leaning forward. Dark brown clay, with traces of white slip; clay-colored core, 0.25–1.00 mm grits.

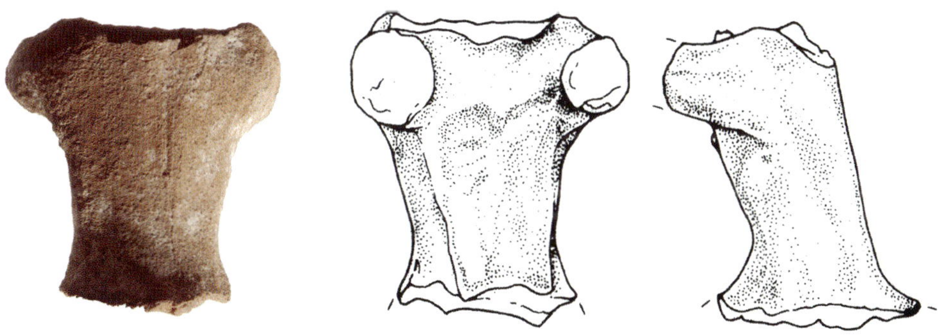

Scale 1:1

Catalogue no. 164

Registration no.:	45527
Findspot:	50.48.L452.B25
Year excavated:	1995
Context:	Ph. 7 quarry fill
Height:	5.3 cm
Width:	2.5 cm
Thickness:	2.3 cm
Description:	An anthropomorphic moldmade head, probably male. Originally this was probably the head of a rider. The face is very worn, but the facial features (eyes, nose, and mouth) are visible; there is also a possible beard, but this is unclear because of the wear. The figure wears a pointed cap. The back of the head is flat. Brown clay, gray core, 0.25 mm grits.

Scale 1:1

II.B. (Lion Figurines)

Catalogue no. 165

Registration no.:	17725
Findspot:	50.57.L50.B282
Year excavated:	1988
Context:	Unknown context, post-Iron Age
Height:	2.1 cm
Width:	1.9 cm
Length:	3.5 cm
Description:	A zoomorphic head, probably of a lion (called a lioness in the registration books). There is a deep recess in the muzzle for a mouth, with two pierced holes for the nostrils. Two small circular ears are partially raised above the head; each has a hole pierced in the center. The eyes are painted on. There is a thin piece of clay, probably for a mane, on the top of the head. The neck is partially preserved. Reddish-brown clay with black and red painted lines: there are black ovals for eyes with dots for pupils; red horizontal stripes along the back of the head; a red stripe on each side of the snout running up to the mouth, with a black line just below; a black circle around each ear; and black lines along the top of the mane and the top of the snout. Gray core, 0.25–1.00 mm grits.

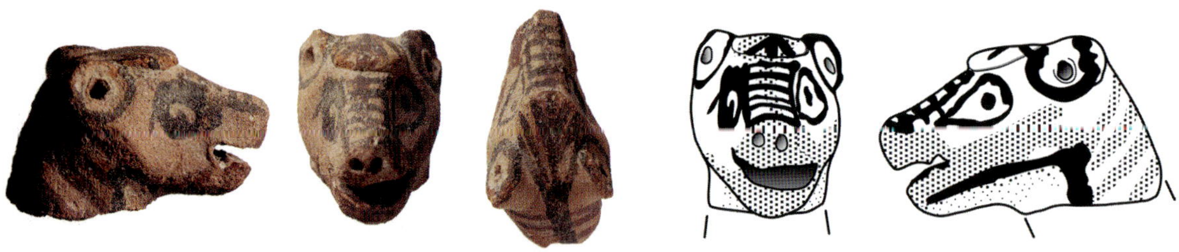

Scale 1:1

Catalogue no. 166

Registration no.:	45778
Findspot:	50.48.L452.B89
Year excavated:	1995
Context:	Ph. 7 quarry fill
Height:	4.2 cm
Width:	3.4 cm
Thickness:	2.6 cm
Description:	A zoomorphic head, possibly a lion. There is an incised line in the snout for a mouth; there is a long thin string of clay along the top of the head, possibly part of a mane. There is one applied pellet, possibly an eye, on one side of the face. The back of the figurine is flat. The figurine is broken at the neck. Brown clay, gray core, 0.25–1.00 mm grits.

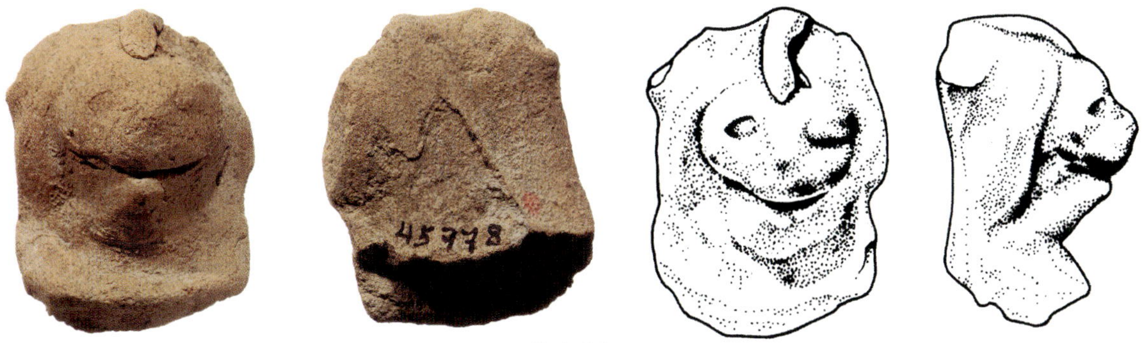

Scale 1:1

II.C. (Bull Figurines)

Catalogue no. 167

Registration no.:	39844
Findspot:	50.48.L384.B320
Year excavated:	1992
Context:	Ph. 7 natural fill
Height:	2.8 cm
Width:	5.4 cm
Length:	4.7 cm
Description:	A bull head: there are pierced holes in the snout for the eyes and nostrils; the mouth is an incised line across the front of the snout. The horns curve outward from the sides of the head; the left one is partially preserved, while the right is almost completely missing. The figurine is broken at the neck. Reddish-brown clay, black core, 0.25–1.00 mm grits.

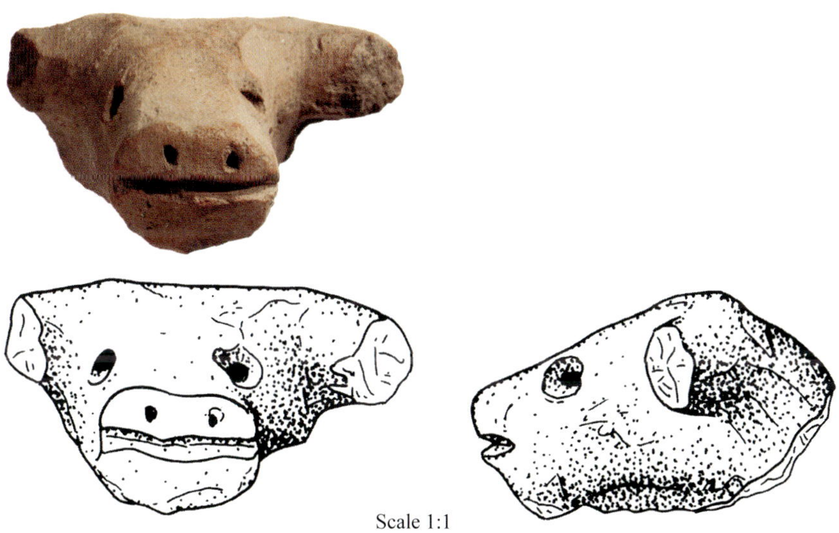

Scale 1:1

Catalogue no. 168

Registration no.:	44376
Findspot:	50.47.L281.B16
Year excavated:	1994
Context:	Ph. 7 quarry fill
Height:	3.5 cm
Diameter:	2.2 cm (of leg); 1.8–2.2 cm (of foot)
Description:	A foot and partial leg, possibly of a bull. The foot is small and stubby. Light brown clay, black core, 0.25–3.00 mm grits.

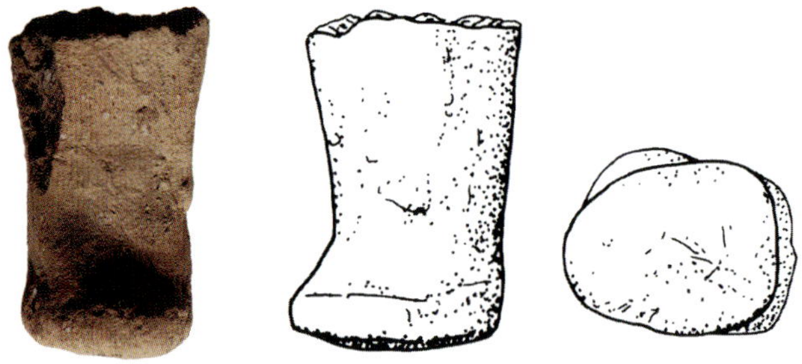

Scale 1:1

Catalogue no. 169

Registration no.:	48826
Findspot:	50.59.LF520.B126
Year excavated:	1997
Context:	Ph. 9 floor
Height:	4.6 cm
Width:	2.3 cm
Length:	3.8 cm
Description:	A zoomorphic figurine, probably of a bull: the head, front half of the torso, and parts of the front legs are preserved. The horns are preserved as stubs curving outward from the side of the head. The muzzle ends in a flat snout. Gray clay (with a greenish tint), with traces of black painted lines: one around the neck, a horizontal one across each leg, and possibly one along the muzzle. Clay-colored core, 0.25–1.00 mm grits.

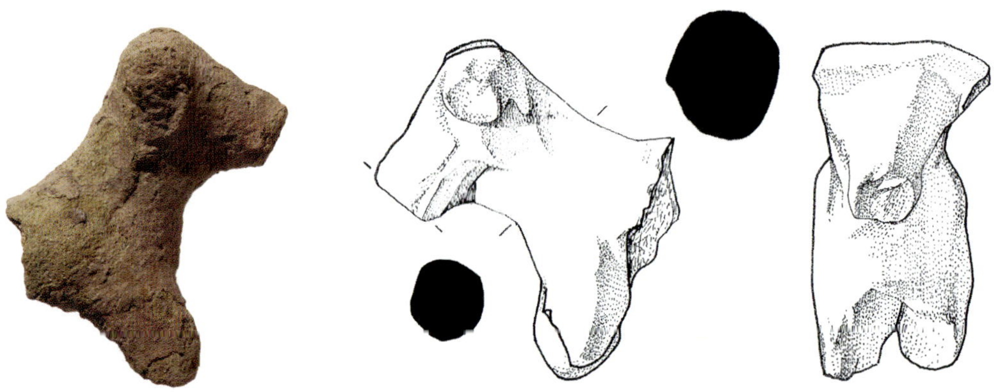

Scale 1:1

Catalogue no. 170

Registration no.:	51165
Findspot:	38.64.L900.B79
Year excavated:	1998
Context:	Ph. 18B pit
Height:	3.8 cm
Width:	2.3 cm (of head)
Thickness:	2.7 cm (of head)
Diameter:	1.6–2.1 cm (of neck); 1.9–2.4 cm (of base)
Description:	A zoomorphic head and neck, probably of a bull. The head has two small horns, or ears, which are mostly broken off. There are two incised lines for the eyes. The snout extends out in a straight line from the back of the head; at the end there are two incised holes for nostrils and an incised line for the mouth (with another incised hole in the middle). Gray-brown clay, black core, 0.25–0.50 mm grits.

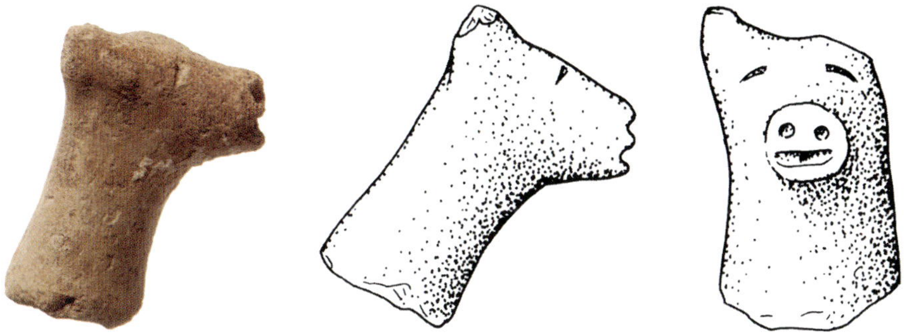

Scale 1:1

Catalogue no. 171

Registration no.:	52415
Findspot:	38.75.L97.B76
Year excavated:	1999
Context:	Ph. 14 deliberate fill
Height:	3.7 cm
Width:	1.3 cm
Thickness:	0.9 cm
Description:	A zoomorphic leg, probably of a bull. The leg is thin and curved, and there appears to be some musculature defined; the calf is clearly visible, as is the hoof. Brown clay (with traces of burning), black core, 0.25–1.00 mm grits (few grits).

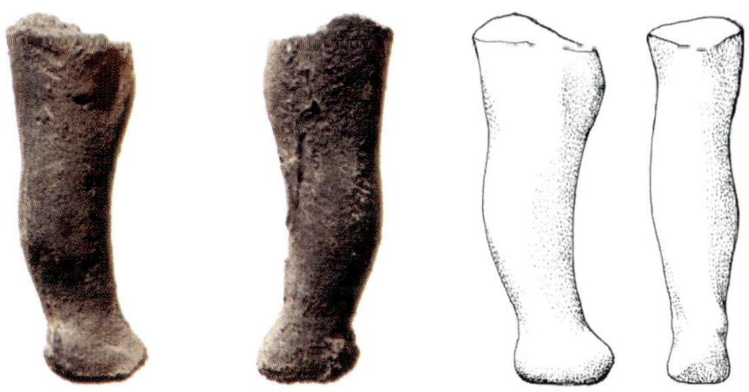

Scale 1:1

II.D. (Bird Figurines)

Catalogue no. 172

Registration no.: 60918
Findspot: 38.75.U601.B4747
Year excavated: 2009
Context: Ph. 19B occupational debris
Height: 4.2 cm
Width: 1.4 cm
Length: 3.3 cm
Description: A head and neck of an apparent bird figurine. The beak of the bird is flattened like a duck bill; the head is pinched in around the eyes and widens at the bill. Reddish clay, clay-colored core, white grits (few), 0.05 mm.

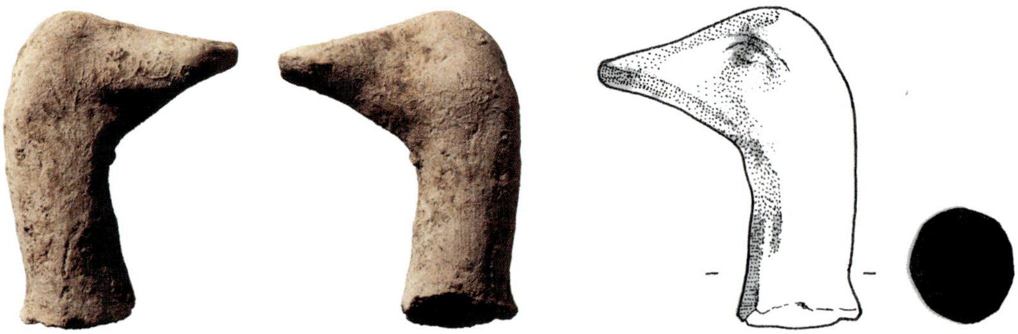

Scale 1:1

II.E. (Miscellaneous Zoomorphic Figurines)

Catalogue no. 173

Registration no.: 38610
Findspot: 50.59.L356.B189
Year excavated: 1991
Context: Ph. 9 deliberate fill
Height: 4.1 cm
Diameter: 2.2–2.3 cm (of wider end)
Description: A possible zoomorphic leg. The tip is rounded. Red-brown clay, with a few traces of white slip, 0.25–3.00 mm grits.

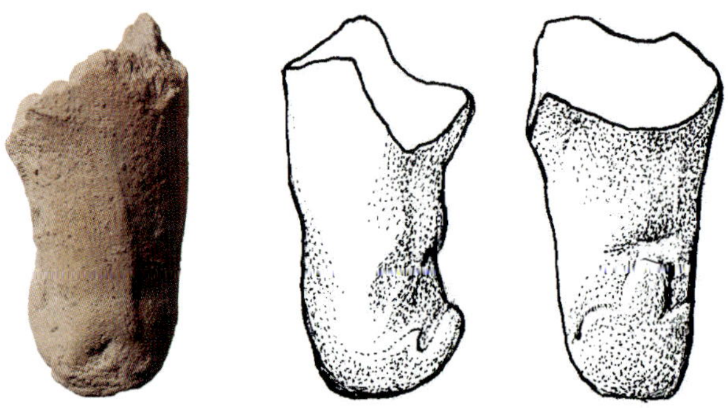

Scale 1:1

Catalogue no. 174

Registration no.:	43827
Findspot:	38.74.LF567.B76
Year excavated:	1994
Context:	Ph. 16 courtyard
Height:	5.8 cm
Diameter:	2.0 cm (of neck)
Description:	A possible zoomorphic neck: similar to horse necks, but with one bump along the back (possibly the back of the face). This could also be a partial handle. Brown-red clay, black core, 0.25–0.50 mm grits.

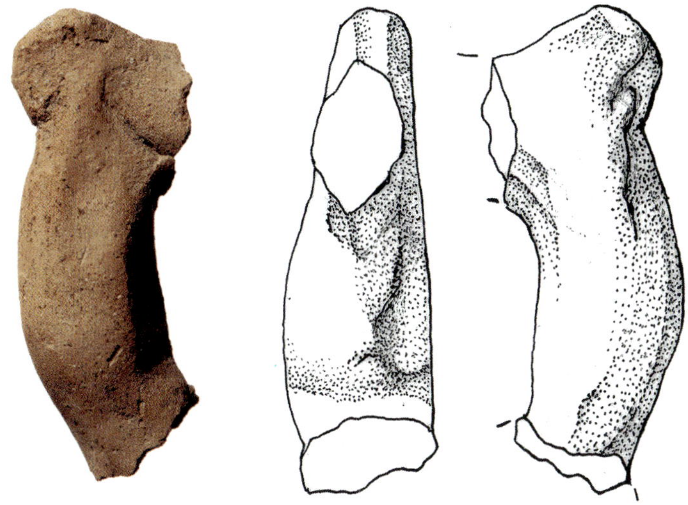

Scale 1:1

Catalogue no. 175

Registration no.:	44733
Findspot:	50.58.F317.B21
Year excavated:	1994
Context:	Ph. 8 wall
Height:	5.1 cm
Width:	4.2 cm
Length:	7.3 cm
Description:	A probable zoomorphic head, possibly of a horse: the figurine is hollow (but not a vessel as the interior is stopped up). The muzzle is missing. On top of the head is a piece of clay with two small cone-shaped bumps. The neck appears to have a ridge along the back, possibly for a mane. Peach-colored clay, clay-colored core, 0.25–2.00 mm grits.

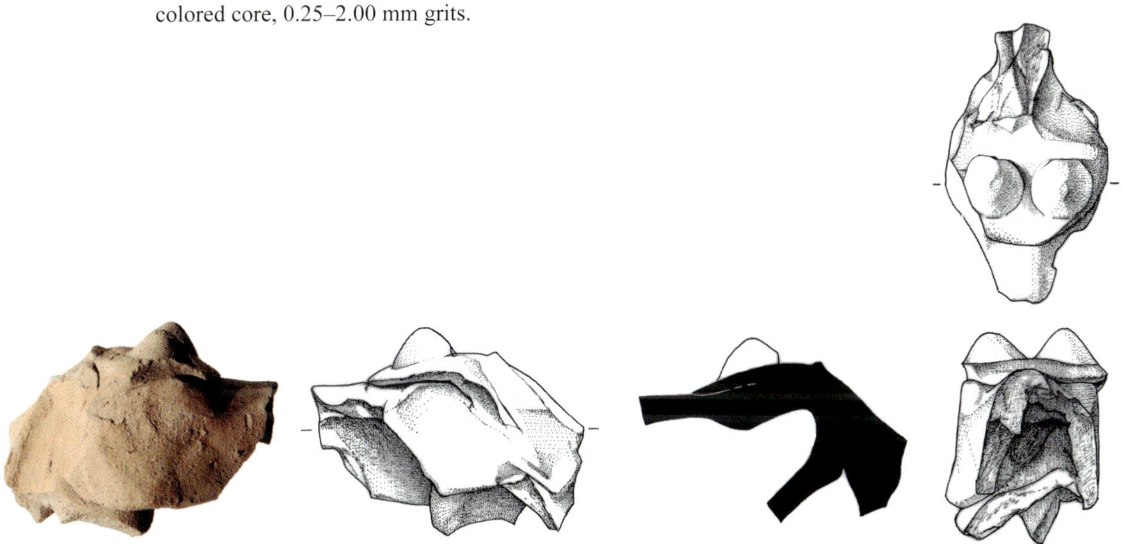

Scale 1:2

Catalogue no. 176

Registration no.:	45138
Findspot:	50.49.L443.B173
Year excavated:	1994
Context:	Ph. 7 natural fill
Height:	7.3 cm
Width:	3.5 cm
Thickness:	2.8 cm
Description:	An animal seated on its hind legs. The face is worn, but the eyes appear handmade as circular depressions; there are large rounded ears on top of the head. The area of the mouth is chipped. The arms (forelegs) are broken at the shoulders but are clearly protruding forward. The chest or stomach area is rounded and bulging out. The legs (hind legs) are curving downward over a base; the left one is mostly missing, the right one is largely preserved. Between the legs is a pierced hole. The base is broken off in front. The back of the figurine is flat. Brown clay, with traces of white slip; clay-colored core, 0.25–0.50 mm grits.

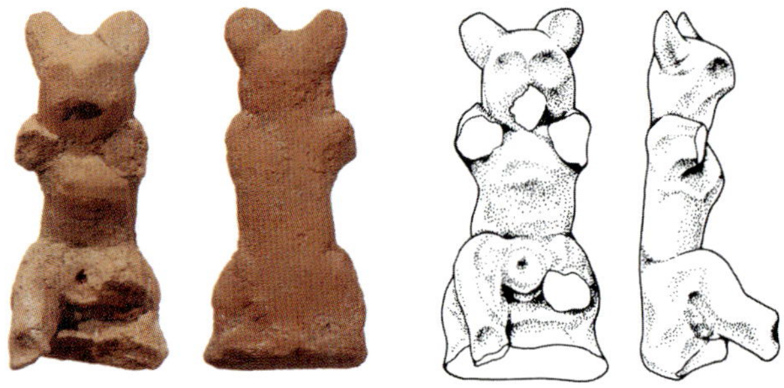

Scale 1:2

Catalogue no. 177

Registration no.:	45750
Findspot:	50.48.L452.B23
Year excavated:	1995
Context:	Ph. 7 quarry fill
Height:	5.6 cm
Diameter:	4.0 x 3.6 cm (of wider end); 2.4–2.6 cm (of other end)
Description:	A possible zoomorphic leg. The shape is roughly cylindrical, with the top attached to a large flat piece of clay (a possible body); the cylinder is bent in the middle and has a relatively flat end. Brown clay, black core, 0.25 mm grits.

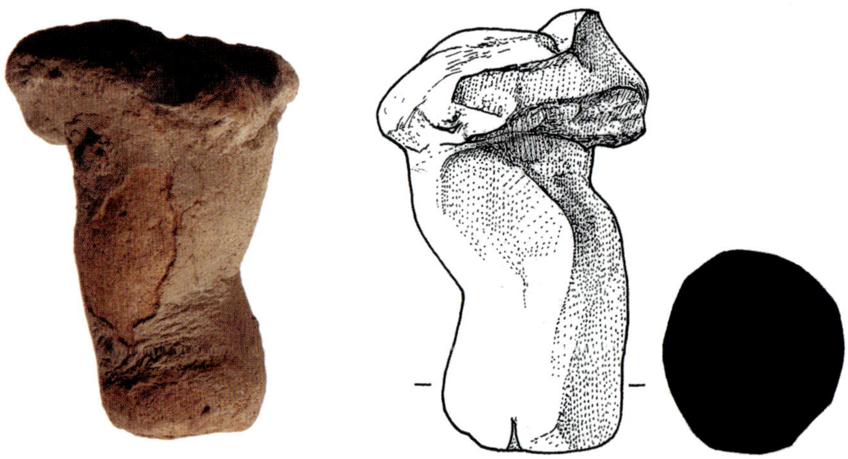

Scale 1:1

Catalogue no. 178

Registration no.:	46303
Findspot:	38.84.L407.B207
Year excavated:	1995
Context:	Ph. 14 deliberate fill
Height:	2.9 cm
Width:	1.7 cm
Length:	3.1 cm
Description:	A possible torso and arm fragment: a thin rectangular piece of clay, with a long thin strip of clay wrapped around (for arms or legs). Brown clay, with traces of white slip; gray core, few if any inclusions.

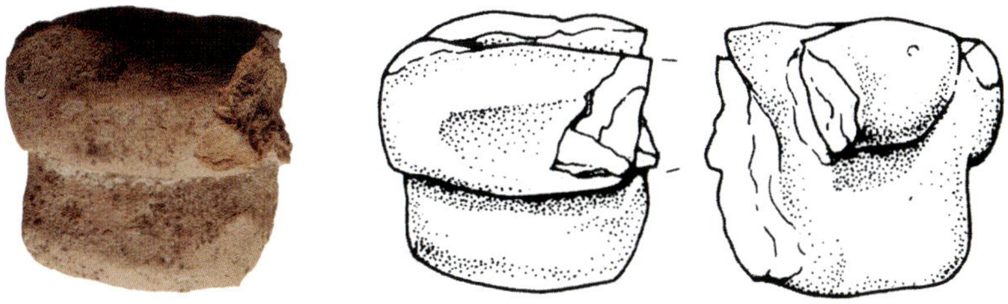

Scale 1:1

Catalogue no. 179

Registration no.:	46603
Findspot:	50.49.L449.B6
Year excavated:	1996
Context:	Ph. 7 quarry fill
Height:	5.0 cm
Width:	2.6 cm
Thickness:	3.0 cm
Description:	A complete zoomorphic figurine (possibly a hyrax or a bear): the animal is siting on its hind legs, with its forelegs not represented. The neck and head are round and slender, with the snout coming to a rounded end. The ears are small and rounded and placed at the back of the head. The hind legs are rounded. The tail is curling up and attached to the body. The front of the figurine—including the area of the forelegs—is partially hollowed out. Brown clay (no core visible), 0.25–1.00 mm grits.

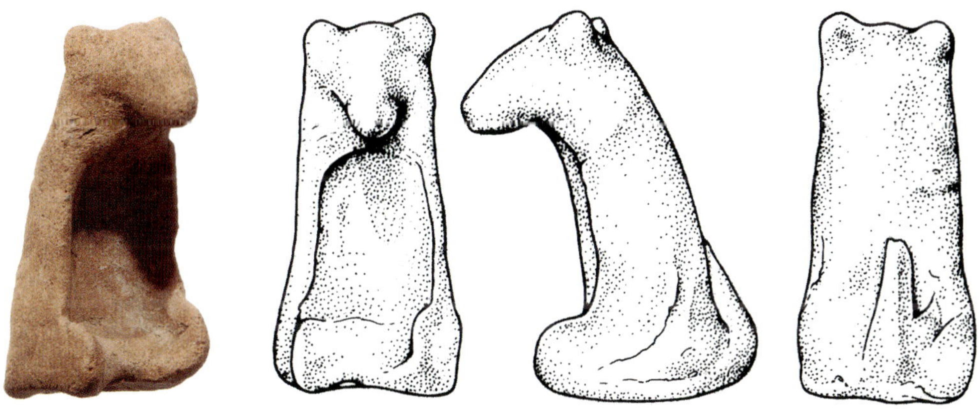

Scale 1:1

Catalogue no. 180

Registration no.: 46872
Findspot: 38.74.L681.FG51.B90
Year excavated: 1996
Context: Ph. 17B courtyard
Height: 3.8 cm
Width: 2.3 cm
Thickness: 1.9 cm
Description: A possible zoomorphic leg: a fragment with a pointed end attached to a slightly wider section. Light brown clay, with black painted vertical lines, and traces of white paint; gray core, 0.25–0.50 mm grits.

Scale 1:1

Catalogue no. 181

Registration no.: 46999
Findspot: 50.47.L302.B55
Year excavated: 1996
Context: Ph. 7 natural fill
Height: 3.8 cm
Diameter: 2.4 cm (of wider end); 2.1 cm (of other end)
Description: A possible zoomorphic leg fragment: a cylindrical stump. Peach-colored clay, with a red stripe along the length of the fragment; clay-colored core, 0.25–0.75 mm grits.

Scale 1:1

Catalogue no. 182

Registration no.: 47494
Findspot: 50.48.L475.B193
Year excavated: 1992
Context: Ph. 7 quarry fill
Height: 4.1 cm
Width: 3.6 cm
Length: 6.9 cm
Description: A zoomorphic body fragment: the rear of the body is preserved, along with parts of the tail and two rear legs. The body is thick and round. Reddish-brown clay, with white slip and black stripes: one around the body just in front of the rear legs, the other around the tail. Gray core, 0.25–1.00 mm grits.

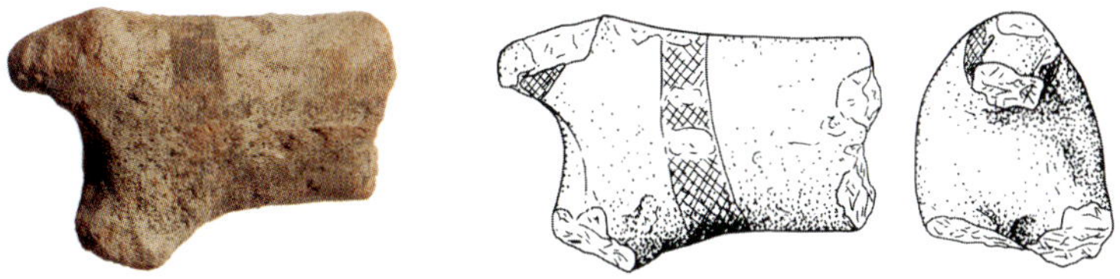

Scale 1:2

Catalogue no. 183

Registration no.: 48280
Findspot: 38.63.L788.B15
Year excavated: 1997
Context: Ph. 18A deliberate fill
Height: 2.9 cm
Diameter: 1.0–1.8 cm (of wider end)
Description: A possible zoomorphic leg: a cylindrical shaft tapering to a point. Light brown clay, black core, 0.25–1.00 mm grits.

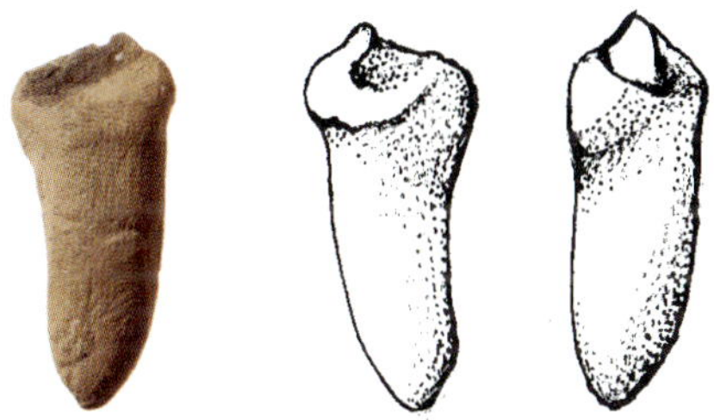

Scale 1:1

Catalogue no. 184

Registration no.: 50645
Findspot: 38.84.LF514.B42
Year excavated: 1998
Context: Ph. 18A street
Height: 4.0 cm
Width: 4.5 cm
Length: 7.5 cm
Description: A zoomorphic body fragment: the rear half of the body is preserved. The two rear legs are preserved as stumps; the tail is partially preserved, curving along the rear of the body. Below the tail, on the rear of the body, a circle is incised. Brown clay, with traces of white slip; black core, 0.25–1.00 mm grits.

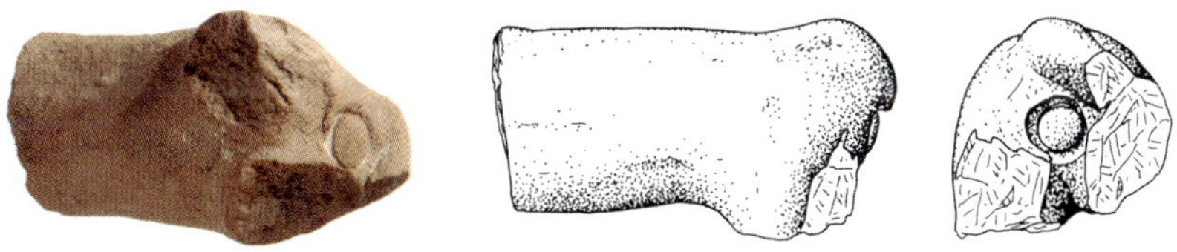

Scale 1:2

Catalogue no. 185

Registration no.:	53374
Findspot:	38.74.L963.B261
Year excavated:	1999
Context:	Ph. 18B deliberate fill
Height:	2.1 cm
Width:	1.3 cm
Thickness:	0.6 cm
Description:	A possible zoomorphic leg or horn (or possibly an arm of an anthropomorphic figurine): a thin and flat fragment, triangular in shape. Dark brown clay, black core, 0.25 mm grits.

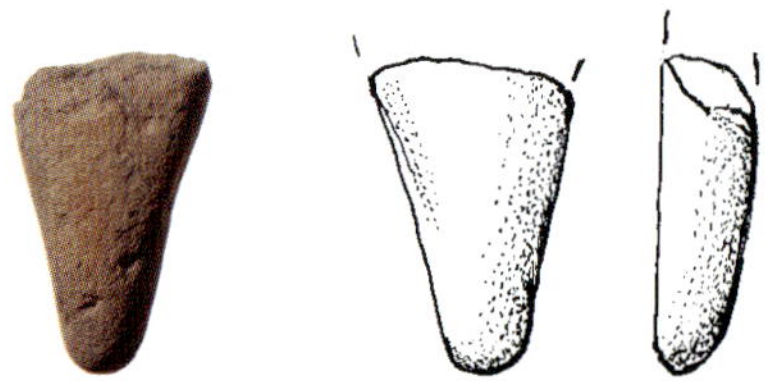

Scale 1:1

Catalogue no. 186

Registration no.:	54478
Findspot:	38.84.L791.B115
Year excavated:	2000
Context:	Ph. 18B deliberate fill
Height:	4.8 cm
Width:	2.9 cm
Thickness:	2.5 cm
Description:	A cylindrical fragment, representing a torso. This may be the torso of an anthropomorphic figurine, with part of the right hand on the upper edge of the figurine and a representation of the pubic area and genitalia below. Reddish-brown clay, black core, 0.25–1.00 mm grits.

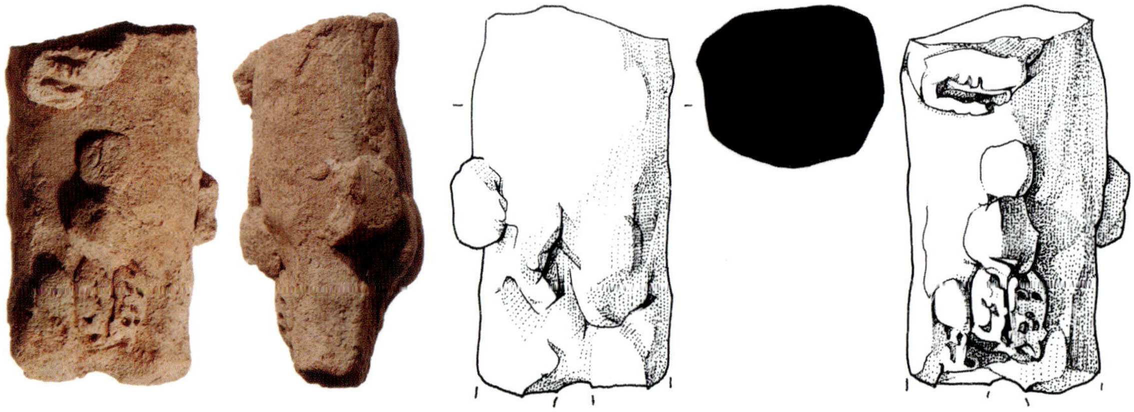

Scale 1:1

Catalogue no. 187

Registration no.: 55505
Findspot: 38.74.L1008.B113
Year excavated: 2000
Context: Ph. 18B pit
Height: 3.1 cm
Diameter: 1.0 cm (of wider end); 0.5–0.6 cm (of other end)
Description: A possible zoomorphic leg: a thin cylindrical shaft, tapering toward the bottom, and broken at both ends. Dark brown clay, with one painted black line along the length of the shaft; also one incised line next to it. Black core, 0.25 mm grits.

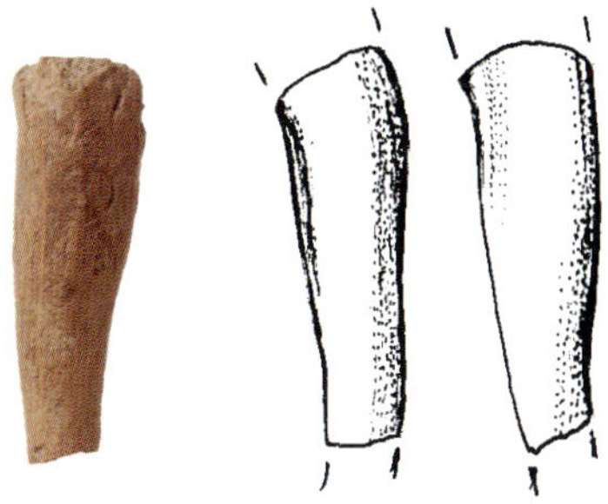

Scale 1:1

Catalogue no. 188

Registration no.: 55735
Findspot: 38.65.L116.B125
Year excavated: 2000
Context: Ph. 18A street
Height: 4.1 cm
Width: 3.3 cm
Length: 3.9 cm
Description: A possible zoomorphic torso: the front half of the body, with scars from the front two legs and the neck. The body is thick and has a ridge along the top of it. Brown clay, black core, 0.25–1.00 mm grits.

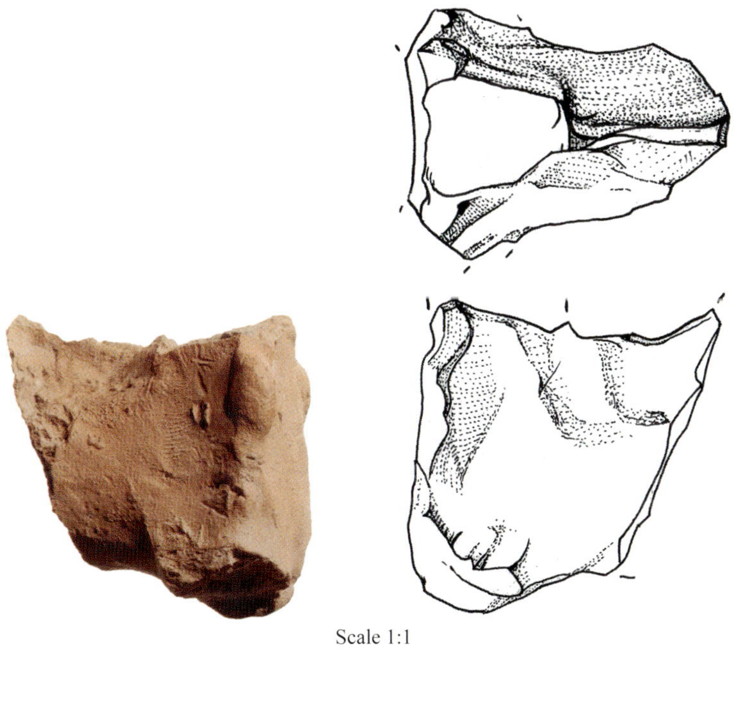

Scale 1:1

Catalogue no. 189

Registration no.:	56189
Findspot:	38.74.L699.FG73.B190
Year excavated:	1996
Context:	Ph. 17B occupational debris
Height:	5.1 cm
Diameter:	2.8–3.2 cm (of wider end); 1.6 cm (of other end)
Description:	A possible zoomorphic leg: a cylindrical shaft, slightly curving and tapering to a rounded end. Brown clay, black core, 0.25–0.50 mm grits.

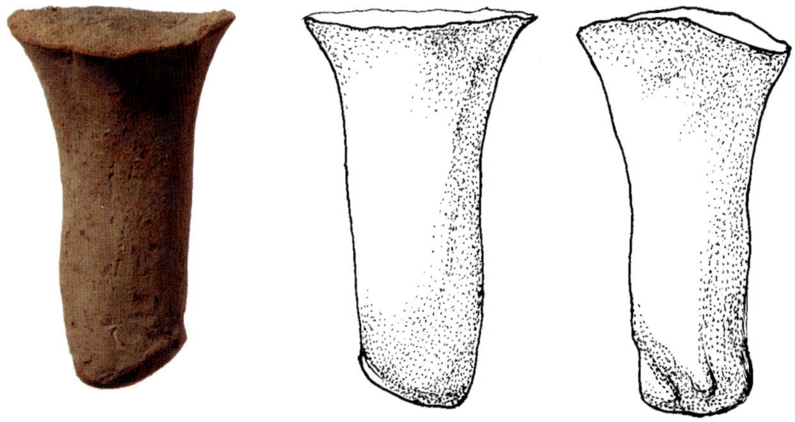

Scale 1:1

Catalogue no. 190

Registration no.:	58934
Findspot:	38.65.U232.B3482
Year excavated:	2008
Context:	Ph. 18 deliberate fill
Height:	3.3 cm
Width:	2.0 cm
Thickness:	1.0 cm
Description:	A probable zoomorphic leg (type unclear). The upper part is wider, narrowing toward the foot; the foot has a flat end. Brown-red clay, gray core, white and black grits (up to 0.25 mm).

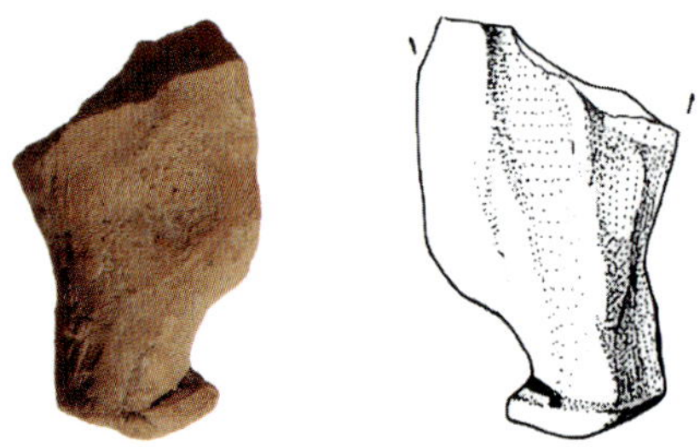

Scale 1:1

Catalogue no. 191

Registration no.:	Unregistered
Findspot:	38.64.L808.B40
Year excavated:	1994
Context:	Ph. 17A deliberate fill
Height:	4.2 cm
Width:	1.5 cm (of wider end)
Description:	A possible zoomorphic leg: a cylindrical shaft, tapering to a near point. Gray clay (with a greenish tint).

Catalogue no. 192

Registration no.: 56956
Findspot: 38.65.L146.B81
Year excavated: 2000
Context: Ph. 17B deliberate fill
Height: 2.3 cm
Width: 2.8 cm
Length: 4.6 cm
Description: A possible zoomorphic figurine fragment or seat of an Ashdoda-type figurine: part of an apparent seat is preserved, with a groove around the top edges. There are two legs in front and two broken off in the back. Reddish clay, black core, 0.25–1.00 mm grits.

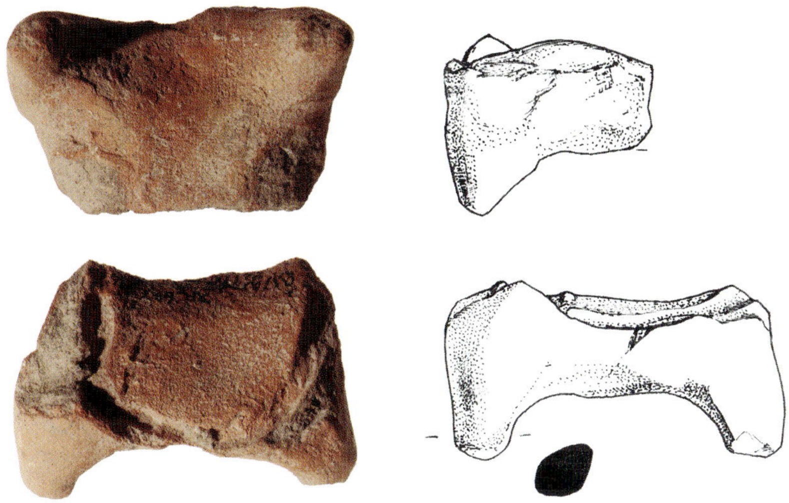

Scale 1:1

Catalogue no. 193

Registration no.: 56911
Findspot: 50.58.LF318.B157
Year excavated: 1995
Context: Ph. 7 quarry fill
Height: 5.4 cm
Width: 4.0 cm
Length: 4.9 cm
Description: A zoomorphic body fragment: the front part of the torso, the tops of the two front legs, the neck, and the back of the head are preserved. The ears are mostly broken off. The head is tilted back (as opposed to the typical horse head, which tilts downward). Red-brown clay, with traces of white slip; dark brown core, 0.50–1.00 mm grits.

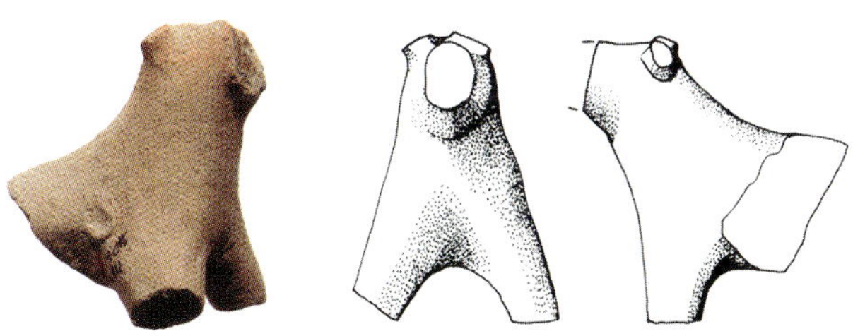

Scale 1:2

Non-Iron Age Types (Found in Iron Age Levels)

Catalogue no. 194

Registration no.: 46096
Findspot: 50.57.L256.B92
Year excavated: 1995
Context: Ph. 7 quarry fill
Height: 5.6 cm
Width: 4.7 cm
Thickness: 2.3 cm
Description: A Mycenaean Psi figurine: the upper half of figurine, from the headdress to the torso below the breasts. The headdress is a high *polos* with a concave top; the headdress tapers into a thin head and neck with a pinched nose. The arms are upraised, though not very far. The torso is thin, with the breasts in low relief. Cream-colored clay, with black or dark brown paint: a line around the rim of the *polos*, with circles running just below it; a line around the bottom of the *polos*, with lines running down from it (for hair or part of the headdress); dots for eyes; lines down the back of the neck for a long braid of hair; along the edge of the nose; two horizontal stripes running from arm to arm across the torso, with small vertical lines in between; and a single vertical stripe running from this pattern downward. Gray core, 0.25 mm grits.

Catalogue no. 195

Registration no.: 49030
Findspot: 50.49.L473.B166
Year excavated: 1997
Context: Ph. 9 courtyard/alley
Height: 2.7 cm
Diameter: 1.0–1.2 cm (of wider end)
Description: A Mycenaean figurine fragment: possibly an arm of a Psi figurine or a horn of a zoomorphic figurine. A cone-shaped shaft tapering to a rounded point. Cream-colored clay, with three red painted lines along the length of the shaft; clay-colored core, 0.25 mm grits.

Catalogue no. 196

Registration no.: 49804
Findspot: 38.63.L789.B22
Year excavated: 1997
Context: Ph. 18A deliberate fill
Height: 3.7 cm
Width: 1.6 cm
Length: 3.0 cm
Description: A Mycenaean zoomorphic figurine fragment: the front part of the body and part of the neck are preserved. Only the tops of the legs are present. Light gray clay, with traces of black paint. Clay-colored core, 025–0.50 mm grits.

Catalogue no. 197

Registration no.: 50563
Findspot: 38.84.L580.B3
Year excavated: 1998
Context: Ph. 17B deliberate fill
Height: 1.7 cm
Width: 2.7 cm
Length: 2.6 cm
Description: A Mycenaean zoomorphic figurine fragment; the front half of the body is preserved. There is a neck scar on the top front; the two front legs are preserved as stumps. Cream-colored clay with brown painted lines: vertical stripes on the outside of the legs, a line running along the back of body, with shorter vertical lines coming down from it. Clay-colored core, 0.25 mm grits (few grits).

Catalogue no. 198

Registration no.:	51166
Findspot:	50.58.L456.B145
Year excavated:	1998
Context:	Ph. 9 wall fall
Height:	4.6 cm
Width:	5.7 cm
Length:	3.3 cm
Description:	A Mycenaean bull figurine head: the head is complete (except for part of the horns that have been chipped off), and the top of the neck is preserved. The muzzle is a thin cylinder protruding outward; the horns are large and curved outward, ending in points. (Note: this head is now joined to reg. no. 53022, assigned to an LB stratum.) Cream clay with brown painted lines: a circle on the flat end of the snout, horizontal lines across the top of the muzzle, long horizontal lines running from horn to horn across the top of the head; and a thick stripe along the neck. Clay-colored core, 0.25 mm grits (few inclusions).

Catalogue no. 199

Registration no.:	52434
Findspot:	38.74.L734.B134
Year excavated:	1999
Context:	Ph. 17B pit
Height:	4.5 cm
Diameter:	1.2 cm
Description:	Bottom half of a Mycenaean Psi (or Tau) figurine: part of the base is broken off; at the other end the very bottom of the torso is preserved. The legs are a cylindrical shaft. Cream-colored clay, with three painted brown stripes running along the legs (as a dress). Clay-colored core, few if any inclusions.

Catalogue no. 200

Registration no.:	55487
Findspot:	38.83.L487.B74
Year excavated:	2000
Context:	Ph. 19A deliberate fill
Height:	3.2 cm
Diameter:	1.0 cm (of base)
Description:	A Mycenaean zoomorphic leg or possibly an arm of a Psi figurine: a cylindrical shaft tapering to a near point. Cream-colored clay with brown painted lines across the top of the fragment. Clay-colored core, few if any inclusions.

Catalogue no. 201

Registration no.:	55566
Findspot:	38.84.L685.B113
Year excavated:	2000
Context:	Ph. 19A street
Height:	3.8 cm
Diameter:	1.2–1.7 cm (of base)
Description:	A possible Mycenaean zoomorphic leg or an arm of a Psi (or Tau) figurine: a long cone-shaped fragment ending in a rounded tip. Light gray clay, with four brown painted lines along the length of the fragment. Clay-colored core, 0.25 mm grits (few grits).

Catalogue no. 202

Registration no.: 55635
Findspot: 38.74.L1029.B157
Year excavated: 2000
Context: Ph. 20A deliberate fill
Height: 2.7 cm
Width: 3.6 cm
Thickness: 2.2 cm
Description: Rear half of a Mycenaean zoomorphic figurine. The two rear legs are preserved as stumps; the tail is complete and hangs down along the rear of the figurine. Cream-colored clay with brown painted lines: stripes running along the body and down the legs, a vertical line on each side of the tail (continuing down the back of the legs), with short horizontal lines across the tail in between. Clay-colored core, few if any inclusions.

Catalogue no. 203

Registration no.: 58926
Findspot: 38.75.U377.B3312
Year excavated: 2009
Context: Ph. 19B deliberate fill
Height: 1.7 cm
Width: 1.9 cm
Length: 2.9 cm
Diameter: 0.9 cm (of snout)
Description: A Mycenaean zoomorphic fragment, probably a snout (from a bull figurine). A cylindrical fragment with a flat end; broken as widening into the face. Gray clay with black stripes, one along each side of the snout to the tip, with two small stripes extending down from a horizontal stripe on each side (on the left side, the horizontal stripe is thick and the two vertical ones are less distinct from it); also a dot of black on the flat end of snout. Gray-brown core, no visible grits.

Catalogue no. 204

Registration no.: 59241
Findspot: 38.75.L519.B3757
Year excavated: 2009
Context: Ph. 19 deliberate fill (for bowl-lamp-bowl deposit)
Height: 4.9 cm
Width: 3.2 cm
Diameter: 2.2–2.4 cm (of *polos*)
Description: A head and upper torso of a Mycenaean Psi figurine: the *polos* is fairly low and tilting back, with a thick bottom line separating it from the face. There is an applied plait on the back. Cream clay, no core, no visible grits.

Catalogue no. 205

Registration no.: 59690
Findspot: 38.65.U251.B3988
Year excavated: 2009
Context: Ph. 19 occupational debris/courtyard fill
Height: 2.6 cm
Width: 2.4 cm
Length: 5.7 cm
Description: A Mycenaean bull torso, mostly complete. Light brown-cream clay, orange stripes (vertical stripes down from a central line on the back); no visible core, white grits (few), up to 0.25 mm.

Catalogue no. 206

Registration no.: 61377
Findspot: 38.75.U601.B5078
Year excavated: 2009
Context: Ph. 19B occupational debris
Height: 2.3 cm
Width: 3.3 cm
Thickness: 1.2–1.4 cm (of trunk)
Description: A lower torso and waist of a Mycenaean Psi figurine. Gray clay, black paint; slightly darker gray core; black and white grits, up to 0.25 mm.

Catalogue no. 207

Registration no.: Unregistered
Findspot: 50.59.L523.B223
Year excavated: 1997
Context: Ph. 9 deliberate fill
Height: 3.0 cm
Width: 4.0 cm
Diameter: 1.5–1.6 cm (of body); 1.4 cm (of neck); 1.4 cm (of legs)
Description: Front half of a Mycenaean zoomorphic figurine: the front legs are mostly broken off, and only the bottom of the neck is preserved. Gray-brown clay, with light brown slip and orange-brown stripes: one ringing the bottom of the neck, and vertical ones descending the neck down the legs and diagonally down the body. Clay-colored core; 0.10–0.25 mm grits (few grits).

Catalogue no. 208

Registration no.: Unregistered
Findspot: 38.64.LF190.FG56.B124
Year excavated: 1989
Context: Ph. 20A floor
Height: 2.4 cm
Width: 0.6 cm (of face)
Thickness: 1.6 cm (of head)
Diameter: 2.3 cm (of *polos*)
Description: A head of a Mycenaean Psi (or Tau) figurine: the top of the headdress is tipped, and the figurine is broken just below the nose. The headdress is a low *polos* with a concave top. Gray clay, with brown painted lines: a band around the rim of the *polos*, with semicircles hanging down from it; a ring around the bottom of the *polos*, with vertical stripes descending from it (for hair, or fringes from the headdress); a painted dot for each eye; a line down the ridge of the nose; four short horizontal stripes along the back of the head, for a braid of hair. Gray core, no grits.

Catalogue no. 209

Registration no.: 54803
Findspot: 38.74.F1013.FG17.B91
Year excavated: 2000
Context: Ph. 19A beaten earth floor
Height: 2.9 cm
Width: 2.5 cm
Thickness: 1.2 cm (at breast)
Description: A body fragment from a hollow Late Cypriot female figurine. One breast preserved with hand below it, with three incised lines for the fingers. Clay: brown-red surface with gray interior; white grits, up to 0.25 mm.

Catalogue no. 210

Registration no.: 58895
Findspot: 38.75.U418.B3622
Year excavated: 2008
Context: Ph. 19 cobble installation
Height: 5.3 cm
Width: 2.2 cm
Thickness: 5.1 cm
Description: Part of the head and neck of a hollow Late Cypriot female figurine: right side of the face, from nose to ear. Pointed ear; eye as concentric circles, formed from applied ring with incised lines inside for pupil. Brown surface, gray interior. Purple and brown (or black) paint: brown on the top of the head, eyebrows, interior circle of the eye; brown and purple alternating on the neck, three stripes preserved. White grits, 0.25–0.5 mm.

6. Typology and Iconography

In chapter 5, I presented a catalogue of the complete corpus of Iron Age figurines from Ashkelon. I also provided an introduction to my overall typology of Philistine figurines by organizing the catalogue according to type. This typology, however, is based not simply on the Ashkelon figurines but also on those from the other sites in Philistia (whose figurines have been published or were made available to me by the excavators and curators). Since much of this material is unpublished, I have not been able to present a detailed catalogue of these figurines; in any case, such a catalogue would make this study very unwieldy. Instead, I have chosen to use this chapter to present the overall corpus of Iron Age terracottas from Philistia. This discussion is again organized by type. I will provide a basic discussion of the technique, form, style, and decoration of each type, with reference to specific examples from the Ashkelon catalogue as well as to examples from other Philistine sites (both published and unpublished). By this procedure, I will be able to discuss the basic trends in the Philistine figurines, while still drawing attention to unusual and exceptional examples.

In the discussion of each type, I will follow the general description of the type with a discussion of its iconography, based on parallel figurines from throughout the eastern Mediterranean and Near East, as well as representations in other media and relevant textual evidence. In doing so, I will begin to address the issues of the meaning and function of these figurines: how were they used, and what did they represent to the people who made and used them? I have chosen to combine some of the descriptive and iconographic stages of analysis in this chapter, rather than strictly following the outline provided in chapter 4, for several reasons. First, the greater part of the descriptive stage has already been presented in the catalogue in chapter 5. Second, whatever exact method I choose will not remove the circularity of the analysis completely, beyond this combination of description and iconography. As it is, at various points in this chapter I will refer to the contextual analyses of chapter 7 and to some of their results. In the discussion below, I will try to separate the descriptive and iconographic analysis of each type as much as possible. As I have discussed in chapter 4, however, this circularity cannot be avoided entirely; the most I can do is to acknowledge and try to minimize it. It would also be futile to try to ignore the basic contextual and chronological conclusions that have already been made in previous studies of the figurines, and so I will discuss issues such as the general dating of the figurines (e.g., Iron I vs. Iron II). The result of this organization will, I hope, be a more coherent and comprehensible discussion of the iconography than what would be possible if it were detached completely and presented as a separate chapter.

Typology (repeated from chapter 5 above):

- I. Anthropomorphic Figurines
  - A. Female Figurines
    - 1. Small standing handmade figurines
      - a. miniature
      - b. standard
    - 2. Large (seated) handmade figurines ("Ashdoda" and similar types)
      - a. miniature
      - b. standard
      - c. with arms
    - 3. Composite figurines
    - 4. Plaque figurines
    - 5. Hollow moldmade figurines
    - 6. Miscellaneous
  - B. Male Figurines
    - 1. Riders
    - 2. Miscellaneous
- II. Zoomorphic Figurines
  - A. Horses
    - 1. With riders
    - 2. Without riders
  - B. Lions
  - C. Bulls
  - D. Birds
  - E. Miscellaneous

I.A.1. and 2. Iron I Handmade Female Figurines (Cat. Nos. 1–32)

Most anthropomorphic figurines in the Iron I are female, and these types (I.A.1 and 2) are the most common Iron I female figurine types. They are also the types most commonly seen as characteristic of "Philistine figurines" (see, e.g., Mazar 1992a:323) and the types most commonly studied (see T. Dothan 1982; Schmitt 1999; Yasur-Landau 2001). In all major respects they are very distinct from previous Palestinian figurines, especially the predominant type of the LB, the plaque figurine (see, e.g., Pritchard 1943; Albright 1939:114–17; Moorey 2003:37–38). By considering and comparing the characteristics of these different types of figurines, we will be able to highlight the distinctiveness of the Iron I figurines (see discussion of Bailey's concept of "description" in chapter 2).

The contrast between the LB plaque figurines and the predominant Iron I female types can be seen in all four main categories listed above in chapter 2: technique, form, style, and decoration:

1. In terms of technique, the plaque figurines are moldmade; the front of the figurine is pressed in a mold, while the back is left flat. The Iron I figurines, meanwhile, are completely handmade.[1] The result of this difference in technique is that the plaques had to lie flat, while the Iron I figurines were free-standing; the Iron I types, unlike the plaques, could be viewed from all sides and generally were meant to be, as indicated by the decoration and surface treatment on front and back. (Nevertheless, it appears that the front view was the primary focus of the figurine; cf. Ashkelon Catalogue No. 14, with a series of horizontal stripes on the front but no paint on the back.)

2. The forms of the figurines are also distinct from each other: this distinction is partly a function of the technique used but is particularly related to the differing gestures of the figurines. The LB plaques are of standing women with a few major types of gestures or poses: arms extended with hands holding stalks or serpents, hands over the genital region, hands down along the sides of the body, hands cupping the breasts, or arms cradling a child (see, e.g., Pritchard 1943; compare the similar Iron Age plaque gestures on Ashkelon figurines, Catalogue Nos. 62–67). The Iron I handmade types may occasionally show the hands cupping the breasts (Catalogue Nos. 10, 27) but more commonly have their arms outraised (the exact gestures of the Iron I types are often unclear; for further discussion see below). In fact, figurines of I.A.2 ("Ashdodas" and perhaps other related types) are typically depicted as seated and without arms.

3. The style of the LB plaque figurines is generally naturalistic: the bodies largely display typical human proportions and tend to be slender and curved. The Iron I handmade figurines, on the other hand, are (almost universally) crude and abstract, with bodies not displaying features such as waists. Similarly, the LB plaques tend to emphasize the breasts and genitalia. Types I.A.1 and 2, on the other hand, never indicate the genitalia, and, while indicating the breasts, generally do not emphasize them to the extent that the plaques do.

4. Finally, in terms of decoration, the LB plaques are unpainted (some may have been decorated with a slip; cf. Catalogue Nos. 62–63); the Iron I handmade types, however, generally have a white slip and often painted decoration. This painting consists of various geometric patterns (such as circles or triangles) and especially stripes, in black and/or red paint. The color of these designs matches that of Philistine Monochrome and Bichrome pottery. Similarly, the specific motifs are also paralleled in Philistine pottery; for instance, the series of horizontal stripes on Catalogue No. 14 is typical of many Iron I Philistine handles, particularly on stirrup jars (T. Dothan 1982:ch. 3, figs. 14–17, pls. 26–32) and various jugs and juglets (T. Dothan 1982:ch. 3, figs. 58.1, 59, pls. 94–95).

[1] To my knowledge, there are almost no handmade anthropomorphic figurines in LB Palestine. See, e.g., the catalogue in Pritchard 1943 (where the basic handmade type is the pillar figurine, of the eighth-seventh centuries). An exception is Pritchard's type IV.A ("Archaic Type of Figurine: Pierced Ear Examples"; cat. nos. 151–55, fig. 13). This handmade type, with a "grotesque" or "bird" face, large applied eyes, and multiple earlobes with earrings, is rare in Palestine but common on Cyprus in the LB, where it is made in a ware similar to Base-ring ware. It appears to have originated in the late third–early second millennia in Syria and Mesopotamia and was the predominant female type in Syria in the MB; it was replaced there, however, by moldmade plaques by the beginning of the LB (though an adaptation continued as the predominant human figurine type on LB Cyprus, Karageorghis's Type A). See Badre 1980:135–36; Pritchard 1943:52–53; Albright 1939:108–10; Marchetti and Nigro 1997:22; Marchetti 2001; Karageorghis 1993a: 1–10, 21–22, pls. I–VII; Moorey 2003:34–35, pl. 9. Some of the examples from Palestine, dating to LB I, are apparently Cypriot imports (e.g., R. W. Hamilton 1934:55 nos. 320–21), as are rare examples of Karageorghis's (1993a) Type B (similar to Type A, but with a "normal" face and dating to LB II; see Ashkelon Catalogue No. 210; also Hamilton 1934:54 no. 319; Ben-Tor, Zarzecki-Peleg, and Cohen-Anidjan 2005:fig. I.5.15; Schmitt 1999:591, Kat. Nr. 3). Occasional examples of the Syrian type are also found in Palestine in MBII–LBI (e.g., Lapp 1969:fig. 30; see Badre 1980:134). Lapp also found variants of the "grotesque" type in MB IIC–LB I levels at Taanach (1964:41, fig. 22.8–11; 1969:45, fig. 30, TT 1300), apparently a local continuation of the MB Syrian tradition that was soon replaced by the typical LB plaques (see Moorey 2003:35). In any case, these figurines had long ceased to be made and used in Palestine by the Iron Age; in addition, although they are handmade, the "grotesque" figurines display the typical stylistic features of the LB plaques—emphasis of the pubic area, wide hips—in contrast to the main Iron I types from Philistia.

On the other hand, there are a few characteristics shared by the LB plaques and the main Iron I female types: they are roughly the same size, they both depict women, and both tend to emphasize the breasts. Nevertheless, in all major aspects of figurine production, the Iron I types are markedly different. In fact, they are to my knowledge completely unparalleled among locally made LB female figurines generally. Clearly, they represent an entirely new phenomenon. T. Dothan (1967:184) identified these figurines as of Mycenaean origin, and most subsequent studies (Hachlili 1971; T. Dothan 1982; Schmitt 1999; Yasur-Landau 2001) have followed this analysis.[2] Given the current consensus concerning the origin of the Philistines, the parallels of various other Philistine material culture elements (most notably pottery) to Mycenaean antecedents, and the relationship mentioned above between the decoration of the figurines and that of Philistine pottery, it appears beyond doubt that these are Mycenaean-derived types.

Beyond these general observations, however, there is a great deal of confusion in the literature concerning the basic types and their characteristics. As a result, these figurines tend to be misidentified by archaeologists. There is, to my knowledge, no study that properly distinguishes the major types and subtypes of the Iron I female figurines. Ultimately, these problems can be traced back to the chapter on "Cult and cult vessels" in T. Dothan's *The Philistines and Their Material Culture* (1982); as mentioned in chapter 3, this work contains the first significant discussion of these types (it is a greatly expanded and modified version of the 1967 Hebrew original) and has been generally followed in the literature, and in the field, as the definitive treatment of the topic. Therefore, before I survey the major types themselves, I believe it necessary to examine this work critically.[3]

Dothan (1982:234, 237) identified two major types of Iron I female figurines: standing figurines and seated ones. In this I believe she is entirely correct (for further discussion, see below). Her more detailed analysis, however, is questionable; in particular, her emphasis of mourning figurines as a major Philistine type is suspect for several reasons. While initially suggesting (1982:237) that there are additional standing figurine types besides mourning figurines, Dothan includes no discussion of these other types. As mentioned in chapter 3, this problem of emphasis has been compounded by the lack of critical analysis of Dothan's work, resulting in a widespread belief that mourning figurines, along with Ashdodas, are the principal Iron I figurine types.

There are several problems with Dothan's analysis. The first is a lack of comprehensiveness. Her entire survey of standing figurines includes only six examples (only five of these are illustrated; an example from Tell Jerishe is mentioned but not illustrated or referenced). Moreover, just two of these figurines, the so-called ᶜAitun examples (Dothan 1982:237), serve as the basis for the identification and elaboration of the entire mourning figurine type. While it is true that Dothan did not have nearly as much evidence to study as exists now—due in large part to the subsequent excavations of Tel Miqne and Ashkelon—the material from Ashdod was readily available (M. Dothan and Freedman 1967; M. Dothan 1971; etc.). If Dothan had surveyed and analyzed the entire corpus of female figurines, she might have reached very different (or at least more complete) conclusions. Instead, her focus on special examples leads to an unhelpful emphasis of anomalous figurines.

Dothan's reliance on just two of these anomalous figurines—the so-called ᶜAitun examples—is particularly problematic. These two figurines, which Dothan herself had first published in two earlier articles (1969; 1973), were not found in excavations but first identified by Dothan in collections. Thus, even their authenticity is not beyond question. Assuming that they are in fact genuine, we cannot securely assign them a provenience or date. Dothan's only evidence for the suggestion that these figurines were from Tell ᶜAitun is the neutron activation analysis (NAA) conducted on one of the figurines (Figurine A). According to Dothan, the analysis showed that the figurine "matches" the pottery from Tell ᶜAitun, indicating that it was made at least in the Lachish region, if not specifically at ᶜAitun (T. Dothan 1982:237).[4] It is unclear, however, that

[2] A few studies (e.g., Brug 1985:185–88, 202; Vanschoonwinkel 1999:90–91) have suggested that Iron I Philistine figurines are partially (if not completely) Canaanite in origin; generally, however, these discussions are brief, are not thorough in their presentation of parallels, and rely principally on the problematic presentation in T. Dothan's *The Philistines and Their Material Culture* for their understanding of the Philistine figurines themselves.

[3] While chapter 3 contained a similar critique, the discussion below is much more detailed and comprehensive.

[4] Tell ᶜAitun is a site in the Shephelah near Lachish; it is therefore at best a site on the periphery of Philistine settlement and culture. Besides the tell itself, the site is noteworthy for a series of tombs. The common identification of ᶜAitun as a "Philistine site" is based largely on the Philistine pottery found in the tombs (see T. Dothan 1982:44; A. Mazar 1992a:312). The tombs were thoroughly looted, however, so that few other objects were found there (see T. Dothan 1982:44). T. Dothan (1969:42 n. 3; see also Dothan and

this is a correct characterization of the NAA results. While to my knowledge the NAA results have never been published in full, Perlman and Asaro discussed a sample of five sherds from the ᶜAitun corpus in comparison with a sample of Philistine pottery from Ashdod (Perlman and Asaro 1969:36–37, table VII; see also T. Dothan 1969:120–21). They concluded that, according to the statistical analysis, the pottery of each group (Ashdod and ᶜAitun) is identical and was all made at Ashdod, or at another coastal site (Perlman and Asaro 1969:37).[5] If indeed the analysis of the mourning figurine produced identical results to that of the pottery, as Dothan stated, then it was apparently not made at Tell ᶜAitun but along the coast. In any case, the analysis of the clay merely shows where the figurine would have been made and not where it was used; these two places were by no means necessarily the same (see discussion in chapter 7). The origin of these figurines is a mystery after all.

There are several problems, then, just with the use of the "ᶜAitun examples": their authenticity is not beyond doubt; their provenience is, despite Dothan's attempts, unknown; in any case, the site Dothan suggests for their origin is a peripheral Philistine site, and so it is not clear that they are in fact elements of Philistine material culture;[6] and the lack of contextual information means that it is impossible to date the figurines.[7] Beyond all of this, these two figurines are completely anomalous among the entire corpus of Philistine terracottas. Dothan (1982:237) notes the fairly naturalistic rendering of these two figurines and compares them to LB plaque figurines; for her, the "ᶜAitun examples" represent a hybrid of Myceanean and Canaanite elements (specifically, Mycenaean form and Canaanite style) similar to that of Philistine Bichrome pottery (Mycenaean forms and some Mycenaean motifs combined with a decorative style derived probably from local LB bichrome). This style, however, is completely different from that of every other known Philistine figurine. Philistine figurines of Mycenaean-derived types are always (at least apart from the two "ᶜAitun examples") crude and abstract, like their Mycenaean antecedents; if anything, the Philistine examples tend to be rendered more crudely than the Mycenaean ones.[8] Thus, the issue of style further highlights the dubious reliability of these two figurines, along the lines of the other problems mentioned above. At the very least, it is clear that these figurines should not be used, as Dothan has used them, as the sole basis for a major Philistine terracotta type.

There are additional indications that the mourning figurine is not a common Philistine type, contra Dothan and subsequent researchers (see, e.g., Schmitt 1999:600–7). First is the context of the figurines. All of the Mycenaean mourning figurines were found in

Dothan 1992:199–200) has remarked on the flood of objects that came to the attention of Israeli archaeologists after 1967, many thought to be from the tombs at Tell ᶜAitun; this is in fact the only initial explanation she gives for concluding that these two mourning figurines were from Tell ᶜAitun (1969:42 n. 3).

At the time of initial publication, Dothan's Figurine A (T. Dothan 1969; 1982:ch. 4, fig. 10A, pl. 23) had been acquired by the Israel Museum from the collection of Moshe Dayan, while Figurine B (T. Dothan 1973; 1982:ch. 4, fig. 10B, pl. 24) was in Dayan's collection. According to both an Israel Museum catalogue of a 1970 exhibition on figurines (Israel Museum 1970:17, cat. no. 75) and Dayan (1978:42), Figurine A was found at Azor. Presumably it is suggested to have been among the finds illegally excavated by Dayan from that site (for this activity, see Dayan 1978:132; Kletter 2003:2.5). D. Ben-Shlomo (pers. comm.) reports that there were no figurines recorded among the finds from M. Dothan's excavations at Azor; as there is no discussion of the circumstances of discovery of the figurines in either the Israel Museum catalogue or Dayan's book, however, this supposition cannot be proven. T. Dothan (1969; 1982) does not mention this problem in her discussion of the provenance of these figurines, although this is the same figurine on which the NAA was conducted. She does note briefly (1969:42 n. 2) that this figurine (Figurine A) was purchased by the Israel Museum from the Dayan collection.

[5] In her discussion of ᶜAitun as a Philistine site (elsewhere in *The Philistines and Their Material Culture*), T. Dothan suggests that Edelstein and Glass reached the same conclusion in their petrographic analysis of the ᶜAitun pottery (1982:44 n. 119). In fact, Edelstein and Glass (1973) identified two groups of pottery at Tell ᶜAitun: the decorated ("Philistine") pottery, which was made in the coastal plain, and the plain ware, which was made locally in the vicinity of ᶜAitun. It is possible that Dothan is referring to the results of the petrographic analysis in identifying the "locally made ware," but this is entirely unclear.

[6] Dothan presumably concluded that they are "Philistine" based on the form of the figurines, particularly the gesture of hands to the head and its apparent connection with Mycenaean mourning figurines (1982:237–49).

[7] Again, they are assumed to be Philistine (and therefore from Iron I) on the basis of the form. T. Dothan (1969:42; 1973:120; see also Dothan and Dothan 1992:200) has emphasized the twelfth- and eleventh-century tombs of Tell ᶜAitun in connection with the figurines but elsewhere (1982:44) notes that the tombs range from twelfth to eighth century in date.

[8] In addition, as I will discuss below, the other apparent examples of hybrid figurines—displaying a combination of Mycenaean and local Levantine features—completely reverse the combination of influences. Whereas the "ᶜAitun examples" appear to combine Levantine style with Mycenaean form/gesture, all other hybrids combine Levantine form/gesture with Mycenaean style.

tombs;[9] on the other hand, few if any of the Iron I Philistine figurines are from tombs (the only exceptions are perhaps the two figurines Dothan cites from Azor [1982:237, ch. 4, fig. 12.2, pls. 25, 27][10] and the "ᶜAitun examples"). Certainly none of the figurines from the Pentapolis sites, which have yielded the vast majority of Philistine terracottas, is from a funerary context. Iron Age cemeteries have not been found at any of these sites, although a communal tomb from the Iron I–early Iron II has recently been excavated at Tell eṣ-Ṣafi (see Faerman et al. 2011; further discussion in chapter 7). Second, the Mycenaean mourning figurines are themselves a minor type. These figurines are found only in the twelfth century B.C.E. and only in a restricted area in the central Aegean region (the LH IIIC "miniature Mycenaean *koine*," as labeled by Desborough [1964:20]); they have been found mainly at the three sites of Perati (in Attica on the Greek mainland), Kamini on Naxos, and Ialysos on Rhodes (Iakovidis 1980; Kontoleon 1961; Maiuri 1923/24).[11] Altogether about a dozen of these figurines are known. Much more common are the so-called Phi, Psi, and Tau (Φ, Ψ, and T) figurines, of which thousands have been found at Mycenaean sites.[12] However, the major typologies of Mycenaean figurines do not distinguish the mourning figurines as a separate type. Furumark (1941b:87–88) included the mourning figurines within his Ψ2 type and made no mention of their unique character. Similarly, French (1971:137) included them in her Late Psi type (essentially equivalent to Furumark's Ψ2), although she does give them brief attention as a separate group. It is therefore likely that most of the Philistine figurines that have been identified as "mourners" are in fact Psi figurines or perhaps Tau figurines.[13]

The identification of at least some Philistine figurines as Psi figurines is not new. T. Dothan, in her original Hebrew version of *The Philistines and Their Material Culture*, identified all of the figurines from (or thought to be from) Azor and Jemmeh as belonging to Furumarks's Ψ2 type (1967:184). In *Ashdod II–III*, R. Hachlili (1971:131) suggested that at least one figurine fragment from Ashdod (M. Dothan 1971:fig. 65.10) might have had its arms raised like a Mycenaean Psi figurine. Schmitt (1999) labeled his Type I "Ψ-Figurinen." In these cases, however, the mourning nature of all or most of the figurines was emphasized. In her original discussion, T. Dothan briefly referred to the classification of her examples as Psi figurines, focusing instead on their mourning

[9] The type was revived in the Aegean in the eighth century B.C.E. and was in use over the following few centuries; almost every known example of these later Greek mourning figurines is also from a tomb. See Iakovidis 1966:45; T. Dothan 1982:249; Cavanagh and Mee 1995; and Kurtz and Boardman 1971 for further discussion and references; see also below.

[10] These two figurines have not been published elsewhere. They are said to be from Azor, but no further information is provided. While the results of excavations under M. Dothan have yet to be published, D. Ben-Shlomo, who has worked on the material for publication, states that no figurines were found in the excavations themselves (pers. comm., January 2007); much of the material from the site, meanwhile, had been looted previously. One of the figurines (T. Dothan 1982:ch. 4, pl. 15, fig. 12.2), with one hand on its head (in the typical mourning gesture) and the other just below its breast, is said to be from the collection of the Israel Department of Antiquities and Museums but without further information. The other (T. Dothan 1982:ch. 4, pl. 17) is said to be from the Weisenfreund Collection. While one arm of this figurine is clearly upraised, both arms and the head are broken off, and so it is unclear if the arms were in the mourning gesture.

[11] Occasionally there are other reports of LH mourning figurines, but in these cases the examples are unpublished, of later date, or of uncertain type. T. Dothan (1969:60; 1982:244) cites a mourning figurine from a twelfth-century context at Iolkos, the major Mycenaean center in Thessaly. This figurine has a hole perforated in the base (suggesting attachment to a vessel or another object), but the arms are broken; while clearly upraised, there is no clear indication that they attached to the head (Theocharis 1960:60, fig. 72). Dothan (1969:44; 1982:242–44) states that a group of mourning figurines was found in a tomb in eastern Crete; in fact, these figurines (H. E. Schmid 1967:168–71) were purchased from an antiquities dealer who could only identify their origin as "eastern Crete," and the decoration on the figurines is not typically Mycenaean and suggests a later date. (Dothan [1982:244] similarly observes that several features of these figurines are "approaching the style of the Sub-Minoan period.") A similar group to these Cretan examples was found at Elateia in central Greece in a Protogeometric context; while they display some relationship to the LH IIIC examples, Alram-Stern concludes (rightly, in my opinion) that they were not just deposited but made in the Protogeometric period (1999:217–20, esp. 220). Vermeule suggests possible finds of mourning figurines at Argos and Tiryns (1964:303; 1965:142), but to my knowledge no such figurines have been published.

[12] The standard typology, naming the three basic types after the Greek letters they resemble, was developed by Furumark (1941b:86–89), although the basic types had already been distinguished by Tsountas (1888:168). The definitive study is by E. French (1971), whose elaboration of Furumark's scheme has been universally accepted. Archaeologists have frequently noted how common these figurines are at Mycenaean sites starting in LH IIIA1 (ca. 1400; e.g., Mylonas 1966:114; French 1971:106).

[13] I should note that D. Ben-Shlomo (pers. comm., April 2006) independently concluded that the mourning figurines are a minor Philistine type and that most of the small standing figurines are of the Psi type. See now Ben-Shlomo and Press 2009.

aspect (1967:181–84); this focus only increased after her publication of the so-called ᶜAitun examples (T. Dothan 1969; 1973) and dominated her lengthy discussion of standing figurines in her influential study (1982:237–49). This focus has been followed even in those studies that have included the Psi identification: thus, Schmitt (1999) includes only four figurines in his Type I (Psi figurines) but 11 in his Type II (mourning figurines). As discussed in chapter 3, the emphasis on mourning figurines has skewed the discussion of Iron I Philistine figurines in the wider literature (e.g., A. Mazar 1992a:323) and their identification in the field (as witnessed by the Ashkelon fieldbooks and registration books).

If the major types of Iron I Philistine female figurines have been improperly identified in previous research, then what are the major types? I have examined closely the roughly 32 examples of these types from Ashkelon and compared them with those from other Philistine sites (particularly Ashdod and Tel Miqne). From examining the Ashkelon examples, I initially concluded that there are two major types of female figurines in the Iron I, based on their sizes. These types would correspond to the two general categories (standing and seated) that T. Dothan identified (1982:234, 237): the smaller figurines appeared to be standing figurines, while the larger ones were seated. This was apparent in the different types of torsos: the larger, flat Ashdoda torsos versus the smaller, more rounded torsos of standing figurines (which were generally labeled "mourning figurines" in the Ashkelon registration books and supervisor notebooks). In addition, there seemed to be two basic ranges of sizes for the heads. It appeared, however, that most of these heads, which had been called Ashdoda heads in the Ashkelon registration books and supervisor notebooks, were of the smaller group and belonged to standing figurines.[14]

In order to test these initial impressions, I took a set of specific measurements to compare the different Iron I heads and torsos in the Ashkelon corpus. In almost every case, the fragment consists simply of a head or a torso; as part of my test, then, I would need to compare the measurements of these different types of fragments. The best measurement for comparison is the diameter (or, perhaps more accurately, width) of the neck, as this is not only related to the other dimensions of the head and neck but also provides a helpful comparison with the sizes of the torso (especially of the neck scar on the torso). The results of this analysis are presented in table 6.1.

The torsos clearly divide into two groups, and these two groups correspond exactly to the two basic figurine forms: the rounded torsos of the standing figurines range up to 1.7 cm in neck diameter, while the flat Ashdoda torsos range from 2.5 cm up. The neck measurements of the heads fall into a narrower range, but it is still possible to discern two clusters: one group forms a cluster around 1.5–1.7 cm, and a small second group over 2.0 cm. Again, these clusters correspond to the formal characteristics of the figurines. The figurines of the smaller group have short necks (even though the necks are broken, it is clear that they are broken at the join with the body as they widen appreciably at the break); those of the larger group all have long necks. There is some overlap in between these two clusters, however. The nearly complete standing figurine (cat. no. 14) has a neck diameter of 2.0 cm, while one of the large heads with long necks (cat. no. 25) has a neck diameter of 1.9 cm. The ranges for each type appear to be wide and overlap at their ends. Nevertheless, two basic groups are clear: the standing figurines tend to have neck diameters under 2.0 cm (clustering around 1.5–1.7 cm), while the seated (Ashdoda) figurines tend to have neck diameters over 2.0 cm.

In addition to these clusters, there are a few outlying figurines. On the upper end are one or two Ashdoda torsos (cat. nos. 27, 28); their large neck diameters can be related to the nature of their neck scars, which include part of the upper torso in the break. There are also two outliers on the lower end (cat. nos. 1, 2). These form a separate group of miniature standing figurines, which will be discussed in more detail below.

These basic trends are matched among the Iron I figurines at other sites. The neck diameters of the Miqne and Ashdod figurines also fall into two basic groups, with some exceptions (these will be discussed further below).[15] T. Dothan's general identification of two types of figurines, standing and seated, is clearly correct; moreover, these types are also generally distinct in size. (Again, I should mention that it is unclear if all of the larger heads belong to seated figurines.

[14] In addition, my initial conclusions were based on the principle that the main head and body types should go together. If most of the smaller heads were indeed "Ashdoda heads," then these heads would have no corresponding bodies, while the standing figurine bodies would have no corresponding heads. I would like to thank Seong Park for observing the relevance of this principle.

[15] My measurements of the Ashdod figurines are generally only approximate. I was not able to inspect most of them in person, and so the measurements are based largely on the drawings and photographs in the volumes of the site report. Nevertheless, the basic trend of two types, based both on size and on characteristics of form, is clear and was confirmed by my study of a selection of the Ashdod figurines (after the completion of my dissertation in 2007), courtesy of the Israel Antiquities Authority.

Table 6.1: Neck Diameters of Iron I Female Heads and Torsos (Types I.A.1 and 2) from Ashkelon

D (cm)	*Catalogue No., Heads*	*Catalogue No., Torsos*
0.9	0	No. 2
1.0	No. 1	0
1.1	0	0
1.2	0	0
1.3	No. 6	No. 3
1.4	0	0
1.5	No. 7	0
1.6	Nos. 9, 12, 13, 15	Nos. 5, 8, 11
1.7	No. 17	Nos. 4, 10
1.8	0	0
1.9	No. 25	0
2.0	No. 14	0
2.1	0	0
2.2	0	0
2.3	No. 23	0
2.4	0	0
2.5	No. 30	No. 19
2.6	No. 24	No. 21
2.7	0	0
2.8	0	0
2.9	0	0
3.0	0	No. 27
3.1	0	0
3.2	0	0
3.3	0	0
3.4	0	0
3.5	0	0
3.6	0	No. 28

Diameters were measured to the nearest tenth of a centimeter. For many of the figurines, the neck does not have a true diameter as the width varies, both from the top to the bottom of the neck and from the front-to-back width to the side-to-side width. While the larger torsos have only a neck scar, some of the smaller torsos have part of the neck preserved. Not only is there a small difference in the neck width (between the width at the break and that at the bottom of the neck) in these cases, but the measurements of neck width are not exactly equivalent to the measurements of neck scars on the larger torsos, as these tend to include small portions of the body as well. In all of these cases, the value for neck width is an average.

* Two figurines (cat. nos. 1, 14) had both head and torso preserved; they were included in the head column. Eight figurines of Types I.A.1 and 2 (cat. nos. 16, 18, 20, 22, 26, 29, 31, 32) were not included: two (cat. nos. 16, 32) were found in 2007, after the measurements were taken; one (cat. no. 29) is of an unusual type; and the others are Ashdoda seat fragments and so do not have necks (as is cat. no. 32, found in 2007).

Some of them are unique examples, and the only example of a larger head attached to a torso is the complete Ashdoda. I would still argue that it is most likely that all of these larger figurines were seated, as the only large figurine base fragments are of Ashdoda-type seats.)

Having confirmed the identification of two basic types, I can now describe each type in greater detail.

I.A.1. Standing Figurines (Philistine Psi)

As mentioned above, the standing figurines appear to be very closely related to the Mycenaean figurines of the thirteenth and twelfth centuries, particularly the Psi and Tau types. Like the latter, the Philistine standing figurines are all handmade; all (or most) appear to be abstract representations of women, and they are generally around 10 cm high. These characteristics have been recognized previously (see, e.g., T. Dothan 1967: 181–84; 1969:43; Hachlili 1971:125, 131), though they have not been noted in any systematic study of these figurines as a group.[16] With the addition of

[16] Many ideas relating to this point and to the reconstruction of the major features of this Philistine Psi have now been published in Ben-Shlomo and Press 2009:42–49; the discussion below, however, is much more systematic and detailed.

the unpublished material from Ashkelon and Miqne/ Ekron to the corpus of Iron I female figurines, we now have enough examples to attempt a reconstruction of all of the major features of this figurine type—in conjunction with the antecedents and parallels from the Aegean and Cyprus.

Gestures

1. Psi. Most of the Philistine standing figurines have only stumps preserved for arms. Based on a comparison with the Mycenaean examples, however, it is likely that most were Psi figurines; that is, they had a gesture of arms upraised (but not touching the head). The Psi is the most common female terracotta type from LHIIIA on (especially in the thirteenth and twelfth centuries; see French 1971). The cumulative evidence of the Philistine figurine fragments seems to support this suggestion. Of the few standing figurines from Pentapolis sites with any significant portion of its arms preserved, perhaps the most noteworthy is Miqne obj. no. 140 (see Gitin and Dothan 1987:203; T. Dothan 1995:fig. 3.12; Ben-Shlomo and Press 2009:fig. 15.1): its left arm is clearly extended slightly upward but not toward the head. A few other figurines from Miqne are also notable in this regard: obj. no. 5158 (a miniature; Ben-Shlomo and Press 2009:fig. 14), obj. no. 57, and obj. no. 1703. A fragment from Ṣafi (basket 460100) may represent a partial torso and complete arm of a Psi figurine, but it is too fragmentary to be certain. No figurine head from the Pentapolis sites shows any trace of a hand, either in terms of a preserved piece or of a scar from a broken-off hand. At the same time, on the torsos that have enough of the arms preserved, it is clear in most cases that they were upraised or extended out to the sides. This is particularly clear when the head and torso are preserved together: e.g., cat. no. 1; Ashdod S50 (M. Dothan 1971:fig. 65.10); Ashdod H702/1 (M. Dothan and Ben-Shlomo 2005:fig. 3.36.2); Miqne obj. no. 5080 (Ben-Shlomo and Press 2009:fig. 1.1).

2. Tau. Possibly a few of the Philistine figurines are of the Tau type; that is, they have their upper arms extending outward at the sides but with their forearms turned back toward their bodies and their hands on their breasts. This type, though less common than the Psi type, is also attested at thirteenth- and twelfth-century Mycenaean sites (see, e.g., French 1971:125–26; Furumark 1941b:87–88). There is no clear example of this type in Philistia, however. One possible Tau figurine is cat. no. 14: the preserved portion of the arms extend out (but not up), and both the front sides of the arms and the breasts are chipped off. These observations suggest that this figurine might have had a separate piece of clay for each forearm, bent back toward the breast. The evidence is not clear, however.

3. Mourning. As mentioned above, this type is found in the Aegean (and Cyprus; see Karageorghis 1993a:29, pl. XVIII.1–2) in the twelfth century but not earlier. There are no known examples of this type from a Pentapolis site; in fact there are no clear examples of this type with a certain provenience. Besides the so-called ᶜAitun examples,[17] the only other Philistine figurine clearly displaying a similar gesture is a figurine said to be from Azor, with one hand to the head and the other just below the breast (Israel Museum 1970:17, cat. no. 75; T. Dothan 1982:ch. 4, pl. 25, fig. 12.2); as mentioned above, however, the exact provenience and circumstances of discovery for this figurine are unclear. T. Dothan suggests that a figurine from Tell Jemmeh (Petrie 1928:pl. XXXVI.2; see T. Dothan 1969:46, fig. 8; 1982:ch. 4, pl. 26, fig. 12.1) also belongs to this group. The arms of this figurine, however, are broken, and it is unclear from Petrie's and Dothan's photographs if the figurine actually had remnants of the hands on its head, as reconstructed by Dothan.

4. Miscellaneous. A complete figurine from Tell Jerishe (Herzog 1984:pl. 7e; 1993:483) has both of its hands just below the breasts. Cat. no. 10 may also share this pose: while its arms are only partially preserved, they appear to be turning back toward the body at the "elbows," and a large scar below the breasts might suggest that the hands were originally placed here. This gesture may be related to the Tau type; see discussion below.

Overall, it appears that the vast majority of I.A.1 figurines had their arms upraised. As a result, I propose using the phrase "Philistine Psi" as a general label for the type, while recognizing that a few examples may have been "Philistine Tau" figurines, mourning figurines, or other types. As a result, this label is perhaps not entirely satisfactory; nevertheless, in my view it is important to offer a name which is more representative than the misleading but still widely used "mourning figurine." The use of the term "Psi" indicates the

[17] If the figurines are indeed from Tell ᶜAitun, they fall outside the bounds of my study and so for my purposes cannot be labeled "Philistine." On the other hand, they may have been made at Ashdod, in which case they would be directly relevant. Of course, these two possibilities are not mutually exclusive.

connection of these figurines to the Mycenaean Psi type, while the use of the qualifier "Philistine" emphasizes the fact that they are locally made and not Mycenaean imports.

Bases

1. Freestanding. Most Philistine Psi figurines were probably freestanding, with a column or "pillar base." This suggestion is based largely on analogy to the Mycenaean figurines, where a column base is found on the vast majority of figurines (see French 1971; Furumark 1941b:87–88; cat. no. 199). This type of base is preserved on a few of the Philistine examples, the clearest of which are Ashdod H721/1 (M. Dothan and Ben-Shlomo 2005:fig. 3.36.2) and one of the figurines said to be from Azor (Israel Museum 1970:17, cat. no. 75; T. Dothan 1982:ch. 4, pl. 25, fig. 12.2). Other examples probably belong to this type, but in these cases it cannot be ruled out that the figurines were somehow attached to another object (see discussion below): e.g., Miqne obj. no. 140 (Gitin and Dothan 1987:203; T. Dothan 1995:fig. 3.12; Ben-Shlomo and Press 2009:fig. 15.1) and Ashdod H1159/1 and H1742/2 (M. Dothan and Ben-Shlomo 2005:figs. 3.80.4, 3.115.5). In some cases, we have pillar bases which may have been part of Psi figurines, but the objects are too fragmentary for certainty: see Miqne obj. no. 1703 and obj. no. 2702.

2. Modeled onto the rim of a vessel. This is the reconstruction suggested by T. Dothan (1982:237, ch. 4, fig. 11) based on the so-called Tell ᶜAitun figurines: Figurine A preserves part of the vessel (krater?) rim to which it would have been attached, while Figurine B (according to Dothan) preserves the "negative impression of an identical rim" (1982:237). Because of the uncertain nature of these figurines, however, I would refrain from using them to reconstruct Philistine figurine types. Beyond these two examples, there is very little evidence that Philistine figurines were attached to vessels in this manner. Certainly it is a rare technique in the Aegean, attested only for some of the mourning and Tau figurines from Ialysos and a Tau figurine from Elateia (Alram-Stern 1999:216, fig. 9);[18] it is also found in a few cases on twelfth-century Cypriot examples (Karageorghis 1993a:29, pl. XVIII.1–3). Among the Pentapolis sites, the only such figurine I can identify is cat. no. 3; the base of the figurine is clearly attached to some other object, which may well be a vessel rim.[19]

3. Peg figurine. Some of the Philistine Psi figurines clearly had a lower body tapering to a point, for insertion into another object. This is certain on the figurine mentioned above from Tell Jemmeh (Petrie 1928:pl. XXXVI.2; see T. Dothan 1982:ch. 4, pl. 26, fig. 12.1), one of the fragmentary figurines said to be from Azor, regardless of whether it was a mourning figurine (T. Dothan 1982:ch. 4, pl. 17), and the Tell Jerishe figurine mentioned above (Herzog 1984:pl. 7e; 1993:483). There is no clear example, however, from a Pentapolis site. Miqne obj. no. 1298 (Ben-Shlomo and Press 2009:fig. 8.6) is probably a peg figurine, but it is not entirely certain that it represents a female body. Some torso fragments from Ashdod could conceivably have had such a base (e.g., H1281/1; M. Dothan and Ben-Shlomo 2005:161, fig. 3.62.2); in such instances, however, the base may simply have been a tapered freestanding base (see below).

4. Attached to a vessel separately by a dowel. This method of attachment was first suggested by Iakovidis for the mourning figurines from Perati, based on an observation of S. Marinatos (Iakovidis 1966:43–44, pls.15.4, 16.7). On these figurines, the bases were perforated with a hole (about 2–2.5 mm in diameter) that matched holes on the rims of the vessels (bowls with wide conical stems, variously referred to as *kalathoi* or *lekanai*) found in association with the figurines.[20] A dowel, perhaps of wood, could then have been inserted on one end into the base of the figurine and on the other into the rim hole of the *lekane* (*kalathos*), in order to attach the figurines.[21] None of the mourning figurines discussed above has such a perforation on the base. There are, however, a few fragments from Tel Miqne that may be the bases of such figurines, each

[18] Also note the later (ninth century) Geometric (Subprotogeometric in Euboean terminology) example from Lefkandi (Popham and Lemos 1996:Plate 126f).

[19] T. Dothan has written that the base of one of the mourning figurines said to be from Azor (Israel Museum 1970:17, cat. no. 75; T. Dothan 1982:ch. 4, pl. 25, fig. 12.2), "which is broken, seems to have been attached to a pot" (1982:246). From the photograph of this figurine, however, the nature of the base is unclear, and Dothan's suggestion seems speculative.

[20] The term *lekane* (pl. *lekanai*) was used by Iakovidis in his study of the Mycenaean mourning figurines (1966) and followed by T. Dothan in her discussion of mourning figurines in Philistia (1982:237–49). In Mycenaean studies today, this type of deep conical bowl is generally referred to as a *kalathos* (pl. *kalathoi*; see, e.g., Mountjoy 1986:152, 205).

[21] A similar hole was pierced in the base of the figurine from Iolkos mentioned above.

pierced with a small hole (ranging from approximately 2–4 mm in diameter): obj. nos. 4487, 5641, and 4485. In each case, however, only the base of the figurine is preserved, and so it is unclear if the upper part was in fact a female figurine.

5. Suspension. Miqne obj. nos. 1400 and 5158 (Ben-Shlomo and Press 2009:fig. 14) each have a hole pierced in their mid-section, suggesting they were meant to be suspended, perhaps as a pendant on a necklace. Such piercing is rare on Mycenaean Psi and related figurines. French (1971) does not identify this feature on any figurines. Hägg (1981:38) could identify only a group of figurines among those from the Marmaria area at Delphi (the site of the Sanctuary of Athena Pronaia; Demangel 1926:14–28, esp. fig. 16.d–e). These were generally pierced just above the breasts (versus the mid-section on the Miqne figurines). Hägg (1981:38) suggested that these figurines might have been hung on tree branches, but M. Krogulska has highlighted an Archaic figurine type from Boeotia, often painted with a necklace that has a pendant in the shape of a Phi figurine (1968:230, figs. 28, 31; see also Szabó 1994:figs. 64–71). While Hägg accepted that the Marmaria figurines might also have been worn in this way, he pointed out that the figurines did not have to be pierced in order to be worn as amulets; they may simply have had string tied around them (1981:38–39 n. 28). I would also emphasize that the figurine with a painted Phi pendant was Archaic, and so that the use of figurines as amulets may have been a post-Mycenaean phenomenon. Nevertheless, the two Miqne examples were found in Iron I contexts and suggest that some of the Philistine Psi figurines—whether pierced or not—could have been used as amulets.

Miniatures

In my analysis of the neck diameters of the Ashkelon figurines, I noted the presence of a miniature Psi type (cat. nos. 1–2).[22] This type of miniature is well known among the major types of Mycenaean figurines (French 1971:124, 131; cf. the twelfth-century figurines from Ialysos NT 15, with three freestanding figurines 7–8 cm high and three others attached to the rim of a *lekane*, of unstated height but smaller than the former group [Maiuri 1923/24:88, 174, figs. 99, 101; Benzi 1992:Tav. 18a, c–e]). A small number of examples from the other Pentapolis sites are also miniature variants of the Philistine Psi type: Miqne obj. no. 140 (Gitin and Dothan 1987:203; T. Dothan 1995:fig. 3.12; Ben-Shlomo and Press 2009:fig. 15.1), obj. no. 999, obj. no. 1703, obj. no. 5158 (Ben-Shlomo and Press 2009:fig. 14), Ashdod H1281/1 (M. Dothan and Ben-Shlomo 2005:fig. 3.62.2), and (perhaps) H702/1 (M. Dothan and Ben-Shlomo 2005:fig. 3.36.3). Unlike the applied eyes typical of the Philistine Psi figurines (see below), cat. no. 1 and Miqne obj. nos. 999 and 5158 (Ben-Shlomo and Press 2009:fig. 14) all have incised dots for eyes (and two have an incised mouth). This technique of decoration may have been typical of the miniature Philistine Psi figurines, presumably out of necessity given the small size of the heads.

Distinctions

In the above discussion, I have highlighted various features in which the Philistine figurines seem to parallel the Mycenaean Psi (and other standing) figurines closely. While on a general level this resemblance is fairly strong—particularly when viewed in contrast to the LB Canaanite tradition of moldmade plaques—there are several distinctions in technique between the Philistine figurines and the classic Mycenaean IIIB Psi of the thirteenth century (e.g., as seen in three examples from Ashkelon: Catalogue Nos. 191, 197, 202; see also French 1971). The most obvious is the fabric: Nos. 191 and 197 have the characteristic Mycenaean cream-colored clay and slip, while No. 202 has the less common but still attested gray clay and slip. Generally speaking, the clay of the locally made Philistine Psi figurines is not nearly as well levigated as the Mycenaean clay, instead containing a large amount of inclusions (as opposed to the fine and smooth fabric of the typical Mycenaean pottery; see Ben-Shlomo and Press 2009:45–47). The figurines are also not nearly as well fired, resulting in a gray or black core. These characteristics, however, are typical of the locally made Philistine pottery as well; they merely represent the differences in clays and techniques between the Mycenaean world of the thirteenth century and the southwest coastal plain of

[22] I am not certain that cat. no. 2 is a Philistine Psi as opposed to an imported Mycenaean Psi. While the surface is not well preserved, the clay appears to be similar to the typical cream color of Mycenaean clay, and the breasts are pinched rather than applied. On the other hand, miniature Mycenaean Psi figurines are rare if not unattested outside of the Aegean, and the figurine has a noticeable black core, which is also rare for Mycenaean figurines and vessels.

Palestine in the twelfth. Beyond these, though, there are several distinctions in the form and decoration of the Mycenaean and Philistine figurines:

1. The headdress: the IIIB figurines have a high *polos*;[23] the Philistine Psi examples either have a low *polos* (giving the appearance of a head with concave top; see, e.g., all of the Ashkelon heads; Ashdod H1845/1 [M. Dothan and Ben-Shlomo 2005:fig. 3.62.1]; and Miqne obj. no. 140 [Ben-Shlomo and Press 2009:fig. 15.1]) or are missing the headdress altogether (e.g., Ashdod H702/1 [M. Dothan and Ben-Shlomo 2005:fig. 3.36.3], with simply a rounded head).

2. The eyes: the eyes of the IIIB figurines are always painted; on almost all of the Philistine Psi examples, the eyes are applied pellets. There are a few exceptions: cat. no. 9 has painted eyes and mouth, and, as mentioned above, a few examples have incised eyes.

3. The neck: while the IIIB figurines have a short neck, the neck on some of the Philistine Psi figurines is relatively long (e.g., cat. no. 13; Ashdod A1725/2 and B644/1 [M. Dothan 1971:figs. 7.20, 36.10]; Miqne obj. no. 5080 [Ben-Shlomo and Press 2009:fig. 1.1]). This feature may be related to feature no. 1 above. While the Mycenaean IIIB figurines have short necks, they tend to have long faces and high headdresses, resulting in a high thin stem between the top of the head and the torso. Some of the Philistine heads/necks have a very similar profile to the Mycenaean IIIB examples; in those cases, however, the headdress is low, and the face is short, with most of the stem being taken up by the elongated neck.

4. The breasts: the breasts on the IIIB figurines are slightly raised bumps formed as a piece with the torso (i.e., pinched breasts); the breasts of the Philistine Psi figurines, on the other hand, are almost always applied separately.

5. The lower body: the IIIB figurines have a straight columnar stem, while on the Philistine Psi figurines the stem often tapers toward the bottom (e.g., Miqne obj. nos. 5080, 2107 [Ben-Shlomo and Press 2009 fig. 1.1–2]; Ashdod H1159/1 [M. Dothan and Ben-Shlomo 2005:fig. 3.80.4]; and the peg figurines). This feature appears to be connected to the angle at which the arms are coming into the body.

6. The base: the columnar base of the Philistine Psi figurines is sometimes much wider than the narrow stem of the IIIB figurines (e.g., cat. no. 14; Ashdod H721/1 [M. Dothan and Ben-Shlomo 2005:fig. 3.36.2]).

7. The decoration: the decoration on the IIIB figurine bodies is very standardized, composed of a series of vertical lines on the torso down to the waist line, with usually two to four vertical lines running from the waist down the length of the stem to the base. The Philistine Psi figurines, on the other hand, have a variety of decorative patterns: some (e.g., Ashdod 1925 [M. Dothan and Porath 1982:fig. 34.2]) have a crosshatched or checkerboard pattern on the torso; at least one example (cat. no. 14) has a series of horizontal stripes running across the front of the figurine from its base all the way to the head; and other examples are undecorated.

On the other hand, while none of these variant characteristics are typical of the IIIB figurines, all of them are found, to a greater or lesser extent, on French's Late Psi type (Furumark's Psi 2), which is the typical Mycenaean figurine of the late thirteenth and twelfth centuries (French 1971:133–39, fig. 1; Furumark 1941b:87–88). French specifically highlights, among the features of the Late Psi figurines, the presence of a "slight polos" (1971:137, 139) or the absence of a *polos* altogether (1971:135–36), the general use of applied pellets for breasts (1971:133, 135), and a variety of decorative patterns (1971:133, 135).[24] All of these features, as well as most of the others mentioned above, can be seen among some of the main collections of Late Psi figurines, e.g., from Mycenae,

[23] The *polos* is the name typically used for the common headdress of the Mycenaean female figurines, usually a high hat with a concave top and flaring rim. The name is taken from that used for the cylindrical headdress of many later Greek depictions of goddesses (see Müller 1915), but it is unclear if there is a relationship between this headdress and the Mycenaean one.

[24] Similarly, Furumark (1941b:87) made the following observation:

> The later type [of Psi figurine] is much coarser in the execution: the decoration is different, purely ornamental, and the shape is heavier, the headgear is atrophied, the arms are shorter and less graceful, and the stem is also shorter and much thicker.

Amyklai, Athens (the north slope of the Acropolis), and Delphi (the sanctuary of Apollo and the Marmaria) (see French 1971:pls. 20–24; Morgan 1935; Perdrizet 1908:figs. 57–60; Demangel 1926:figs. 16–31). These examples are not provided to indicate any special links with these sites; I could list other examples as well, but these sites include some of the largest groups of IIIC figurines and show all of the significant characteristics.

The Philistine Psi figurines, then, fit well within the mainstream trends of LH IIIC (the twelfth century B.C.E.), as represented by the Late Psi (Psi 2) type. All of the seemingly unusual features of the Philistine Psi figurines are paralleled in Late Psi examples. Beyond this, several of the Philistine examples are as a whole more or less indistinguishable from the Late Psi examples; they would not be considered at all out of place at Mycenaean sites. For example, Ashdod H1845/1 (M. Dothan and Ben-Shlomo 2005:fig. 3.62.1), a head outlined in red paint, is very reminiscent of some figurines from Mycenae with "ringed face" (French 1971:140, pl. 21b nos. 13, 19). The torso Ashdod M1925 (M. Dothan and Porath 1982:fig. 34.2) is paralleled closely by the hatching design on some of the Marmaria torsos (Demangel 1926:fig. 22.4–6). Another Ashdod torso, S50 (M. Dothan 1971:fig. 65.10), matches examples from Amyklai (French 1971:pl. 22a). Miqne obj. no. 2107 (Ben-Shlomo and Press 2009:fig. 1.2), with its painted "x" pattern across the torso and horizontal stripes below, is very similar to Late Psi figurines from Phylakopi (French 1985:fig. 6.2, pl. 38a–b); note, however, that on the latter these decorative patterns are found on the front of the figurines, whereas on the Miqne example the pattern is on the back of the figurine, with the front unpainted. The nearly complete Ashkelon figurine (cat. no. 14) has a shape and overall appearance very similar to some of the figurines from the house shrine at Asine, with their "ill-shaped long columnar bodies from which tiny pointed arms extend at the top" (French 1971:139; see Nilsson 1968:fig. 32; Persson 1938:figs. 206, 212; cf. French 1971:pl. 20d, figurines from Mycenae). The decorative pattern of cat. no. 14, meanwhile, is very close to the series of horizontal stripes on another terracotta from Asine (Persson 1938:fig. 213.5), as well as some of the figurines from Amyklai (French 1971:pls. 21c no. 18, 22d no. 22), the Marmaria (Demangel 1926:figs. 23.1, 8, 24.6, 26.4), and Ialysos on Rhodes (e.g., T 15/13 [Benzi 1992, 2:tav. 18a; Maiuri 1923/24:fig. 101]; T 32/59 [Benzi 1992, 2:tav. 61q]).

A special group of Philistine figurines, which I have not yet discussed, is a set of what D. Ben-Shlomo has labeled "bird-headed" figurines from Ashdod (K1070/1; M. Dothan and Ben-Shlomo 2005:fig. 3.115.6) and Miqne (especially obj. no. 576 [Ben-Shlomo and Press 2009:fig. 12]; also obj. nos. 4517, 4774, and 5080 [Ben-Shlomo and Press 2009:figs. 11, 10.4, 1.1, respectively]). These figurines are characterized by a long neck; applied eyes; a rounded or concave head; lack of decoration; and a generally long, low ridge for the nose, sometimes incised for a mouth. Most of these heads lack bodies, but based on the neck diameters (ranging from 1.0–2.0 cm) and the torso of Miqne obj. no. 5080, I believe that this type is simply a subtype of the Philistine Psi. The facial appearance of these figurines is particularly close to many of the Mycenaean examples; in many respects they are even closer than the other Philistine Psi figurines. For instance, Miqne obj. no. 576 is essentially indistinguishable from the head of a Late Psi figurine from Amyklai (French 1971:pl.22a no. 26). In general these Philistine heads fit completely within the range of types found at Amyklai, the Marmaria, and elsewhere. The incised mouth, however—dividing the facial ridge into nose, mouth, and chin—is unparalleled both among the IIIC figurines and the other Philistine examples; those figurines among the latter group with incised mouths are all incised below the ridge of the nose.[25]

In general, then, the Philistine Psi figurines fit perfectly within the corpus of Mycenaean Late Psi figurines from the twelfth century. In my opinion it would in fact be appropriate to classify the group of Philistine Psi figurines as Mycenaean IIIC or Late Psi figurines. Certain features of some of the figurines—the incised eyes and mouths, and possible applied noses on a few examples (e.g., cat. no. 7)—mark a divergence from the normal Late Psi trends but can be seen as a direct development from the IIIC tradition. For this reason it is perhaps best to keep the label "Philistine Psi" for the group as a whole. Nevertheless, it is clear that the Philistine Psi figurines display a very close relationship to the twelfth-century figurines of the Aegean.

Iconographic Discussion

Development of the Figurines. At this point, it would be worth discussing the development of the Mycenaean figurines in greater detail.[26] The Mycenaean figurines are thought to have developed from Cretan prototypes in late LH II, i.e., the late fifteenth century. The earliest Mycenaean figurines, in a somewhat naturalistic style, follow Minoan prototypes fairly closely, but as they become more popular, in LH

[25] Note however cat. no. 13, which appears to have an applied piece of clay representing nose, mouth, and chin, except that the mouth does not appear to be an incised line but rather a depression in the clay.

[26] This summary relies heavily on the work of French (1971).

IIIA2 (mid- to late fourteenth century), they gradually become more abstract and more purely Mycenaean in character. By this point, their popularity far exceeds that of the Cretan figurines at any point. Of the three major types—Phi, Psi, and Tau—the Phi figurines were the first to develop, in LH IIIA but were no longer in use by the end of IIIB (late thirteenth century).[27] The Psi and Tau types both emerged at the end of IIIA and continued through LH IIIC. Furumark and especially French have identified various subtypes of these figurines; it is not necessary to discuss these here but merely to point out that while some subtypes are found throughout the Mycenaean world, others are restricted to the centers on the Greek mainland. In the thirteenth century in particular, the IIIB Psi figurines are found at various sites around the eastern Mediterranean, generally following the distribution of Mycenaean pottery; their presence is most notable at major ports along the Levantine coast (Ugarit, Tell Abu Hawam, Ashkelon). All of these examples at foreign sites show the typical standardization of the IIIB figurines: they demonstrate the same form, decoration, and fine clay as the mainland examples. These examples, then, are fairly clearly not of local Levantine production but made presumably on mainland Greece; when found in relatively large numbers, as they are at the large Levantine ports, they are sometimes thought to reflect the physical presence of Mycenaean merchants (e.g., French 1971:131, 175).

In the twelfth century, however, the situation is quite different. French notes that the figurines are found at fewer sites but that these sites are scattered over a much wider area. Thus, late examples of the Tau type, which had generally not been very commonly distributed in the thirteenth century, are found at sites like Ialysos on Rhodes. French concludes that the wider distribution of the IIIC figurines reflects the population movements of the twelfth century, with the destruction or abandonment of many sites on the Greek mainland. This pattern also seems to be reflected on Cyprus (especially on the southeast coast, at sites such as Enkomi and Kition)—and in Philistia, where as we have seen the figurines follow closely in the twelfth-century Mycenaean tradition but are now locally made.

Dress. Most of the figurines of the three main types (Phi, Psi, and Tau), and especially the standardized figurines of LH IIIB (thirteenth century B.C.E.), have a basic referent which is clearly identifiable: they represent a woman in a dress (or blouse and skirt) with headdress and necklace (cf. French [1971:175–76], suggesting a "long and enveloping" robe along with necklace and headdress). The painting on these figurines, then, is representational, depicting details of women's dress. On some of the Philistine Psi figurines the decoration echoes this Mycenaean tradition. For instance, an Ashdod Psi (S/50) has painted waist and neck lines from garments (or necklace) and sleeves (M. Dothan 1971:fig. 65.10). Another example is a Psi torso from Qasile (Mazar 1986:14, fig. 6.2, pl. 3B; Mazar labels the figurine a "mourning woman"). In this case, however, the decoration was not painted but plastic; the neck has an indentation from a necklace, now missing, made from a separate piece of clay.

The fragmentation and loss of standardization that is found in the twelfth-century (LH IIIC) figurines in general is manifested specifically in their decoration and suggests a change in the function of the decoration. Among this variety of decorative patterns are some that fairly certainly do not represent garments; examples include the Mycenaean figurines with long vertical stripes (e.g., Demangel 1926:fig. 26.1) or horizontal stripes (e.g., Demangel 1926:figs. 23.1, 23.8, 24.6, 26.4; French 1971:pls. 21c no. 18, 22d no. 22). The Philistine figurines, as part of the mainstream tradition of LH IIIC figurines, demonstrate the same trend. The decorative pattern of cat. no. 14 is particularly noteworthy; it consists of a series of horizontal stripes on the front only (as opposed to painted decoration on the front and back, as is typical of the LH IIIB figurines), and the stripes run from the bottom of the preserved portion of the figurine (near the base) up to the head, with stripes even across the face of the figurine. In addition, the variety of decorative patterns noted above (no. 7 in the characteristics of Philistine Psi figurines vs. LH IIIB figurines), including checkerboard patterns and several undecorated examples, suggest that painting (or lack of it) no longer indicates specific characteristics of female dress. Both French (1971:137–38) and Furumark (1941b:87) have concluded that the decoration of the twelfth-century figurines was now ornamental instead of representational. The decoration of the Philistine figurines leads to the same conclusion.

Similarly, French has suggested that the *polos* of the Mycenaean figurines is simply a headdress representing current fashion (1971:176). The *polos* is missing from the earliest Mycenaean figurines but is fairly suddenly adopted at the end of LH IIIA (French 1971:121–24, 176); it is then ubiquitous on the figurines until LH IIIC. The shortening of the *polos* (so much so that some figurines appear to have simply a

[27] Note, however, that French identifies a special group of late Phi figurines, different from the rest but apparently connected to the Late Psi figurines, with features such as the "slight polos" and irregular decoration; French therefore dates this group to late IIIB–IIIC (1971:120–21).

flat or concave head, rather than a headdress), or the loss of the *polos* completely for a rounded bare head, parallels the loss of the standardized representation of dress at this time. These changes suggest that the makers of the figurines were no longer interested in portraying "current fashion" on them. It is also possible that the makers of the figurines were, to some extent, no longer certain exactly what the decoration represented; they may still have retained the tradition that standing figurines were to be made and decorated in this style but lost the meaning behind the decoration.

The Identity of the Figurines. The general identity of the Mycenaean figurines as female representations is clear. Moreover, it is clear that the Mycenaean figurines traditionally depicted women clothed in specific garments and wearing necklaces (and that this tradition only partially survived into the twelfth century in the Aegean and in Philistia). A more specific identification, however, requires further discussion. Do the figurines represent one or more divinities, or are they meant to depict humans? Scholars have tended to identify the figurines as divine representations, based largely on an assumption of the *polos* to be a divine crown (see above) and on the character of the distinctive gestures of the figurines (for further discussion, see below). In my view, the best method of settling this question is to consider the iconographic parallels to these figurines.[28] Very close iconographic parallels can be found in a group of larger terracotta statues generally referred to as "figures," as opposed to the smaller "figurines" (following French 1981:173).[29] While these figures have received much attention over the last few decades in literature on the Aegean Bronze Age, they have been rarely discussed by Syro-Palestinian archaeologists.[30] As a result, it is necessary to discuss their basic character here.

Large Mycenaean terracotta representations have long been known (e.g., the "Lord of Asine"; see Nilsson 1968:114; Persson 1938:218, figs. 206, 211) but have received much greater attention as a group over the last few decades, with discoveries in particular at Mycenae (Taylour 1969:91–92, pls. XI–XIII; Taylour 1970:271–73, pls. XXXVIII–XL; Moore and Taylour 1999:46–50), Tiryns (Kilian 1978:Abb. 17, 20, 21, 23; 1981:53–55), and Phylakopi (especially the famous "Lady of Phylakopi"; Renfrew 1981b; French 1985:211–22, figs. 6.2–6.8), as well as more recently at other sites such as Midea (Demakopoulou 1999; Demakopoulou et al. 1997/98:68, fig. 58). As with the figurines, E. French has made the most significant contributions toward classification of the figures (1981; 1985; 2001; see also Catling 1995), and her work has been generally followed in subsequent literature (see, e.g., Demakopoulou 1999:199; Moore and Taylour 1999:46). The figures represent humans—male, female, and perhaps sexless figures (French 1981:173; Moore 1988:222; Moore and Taylour 1999:101)—and animals. The group most relevant to understanding the figurines is a group of female figures among the finds at Mycenae, Tiryns, Phylakopi, and Midea, French's "Type A" (1981:173; 2001:275). They are hollow and wheelmade and range generally from 25 cm to 35 cm in height—roughly two to four times the size of the typical female figurines. In date they range from LH IIIA to LH IIIC (fourteenth to twelfth centuries), the heyday of the typical female figurines. While fragments of human and animal figures have been found in a variety of contexts, even occasionally in tombs (Moore and Taylour 1999:89; Catling 1995:190), the complete examples—especially for those of Type A—seem to be closely associated with sanctuaries (as at Mycenae, Tiryns, and Phylakopi; see Moore and Taylour 1999:90).[31] The consensus among archaeologists is that the figures in general were made for cultic purposes and that the Type A female figures served as cult images in shrines (Kilian 1981; French 1985:215;

[28] Perhaps the best known parallels are the Cretan "Goddess with Upraised Arms" cult images, common in Minoan shrines in LM III (for a recent summary, see Prent 2005:181–84; for further discussion and references, see Alexiou 1958; Nilsson 1968:99–103, 309–11; Renfrew 1981a:29). The relationship between these Minoan representations and the Mycenaean figurines, however, is at best indirect, and in style and dress they are quite distinct. These Cretan representations will be discussed further below, in the discussion of the different gestures of the figurines.

[29] For a fairly comprehensive catalogue of the Mycenaean figures, see Catling (1995:190–93).

[30] To my knowledge, A. Mazar (1980:81) is the only Syro-Palestinian archaeologist to discuss them in any detail, but he incorrectly refers to them as "anthropomorphic vessels." In his article on the Ashdoda, A. Yasur-Landau (2001:339, pl. XCIXc) referred to figures from Tiryns but does not discuss the special nature of the figures as distinct from the figurines; more recently (2010:306, fig. 8.7), however, he has pointed to their distinct status.

[31] Note also the 13 fragments of figures, coming from at least 10 different objects (mostly of Type A), found at the presumed Bronze Age sanctuary of Aphaia on Aegina (Pilafidis-Williams 1998:80–82). Moore (1999:89) notes that the figures found in other types of contexts are generally fragmentary, and so they probably represent not the primary use context of the figures but a secondary deposit (see chapter 4; cf. Mazow [2005:247, 388] on primary and secondary discard patterns and formation processes).

Renfrew 1985:415; Taylour 1995:58–59; Moore and Taylour 1999:90–92; Demakopoulou 1999:202).[32]

The Type A figures are closely connected to the female figurines in both form and decoration, as has often been noted (French 1981:173; Moore and Taylour 1999:87; French 2001:275); like the figurines they are also closely connected to Mycenaean decorated pottery. The Type A figures often wear a headdress similar to the figurines' *polos*. Stripes and other painted decoration are used to indicate garments, jewelry, and facial features. The complete or nearly complete figures display two basic gestures: arms upraised (the Tiryns examples, one from Mycenae, and probably the "Lady of Phylakopi") and hands on or just below the breasts (one Mycenae example and the Midea example). These gestures exactly parallel those of the typical thirteenth- to twelfth-century female figurines, the Psi and Tau; in addition, the earliest figurines—French's Naturalistic and Proto-Phi types—generally have arms, sometimes to the breasts (see, e.g., French 1971:104), suggesting that the Phi figurines (without arms depicted) may be connected with this gesture as well.

On the other hand, some of the details of the figures differ from those of the figurines. Only the Midea figure has a high *polos*; the others either have a low concave headdress (often with a central ridge running from front to back), a convex headdress, or none at all. The striped decoration of the figures takes on a variety of patterns, including a series of horizontal stripes for the skirt and multiple horizontal stripes on the neck, representing a set of necklaces. In general, the facial features of the figures are represented in a more naturalistic fashion than those of the figurines.

Nevertheless, it seems clear that the figurines, in general, served as abbreviated or shorthand versions of the Type A figures. Several scholars have made similar observations on their form and function: French (1971:174) highlighted the "summary nature" of the figurines, which she suggested were "intended to be a brief symbol"; Tamvaki (1973:258) suggested, as one of several possible functions of the figurines, that they were "cheap substitutes for large religious figures connected with everyday life and household cult." This relationship is illustrated by some of the Tiryns figures. Two in particular (Kilian 1978:Abb. 20, 21) are similar representations of a woman with upraised arms, but whereas one depicts the arms in a naturalistic manner with individual fingers rendered on the hands, the other depicts the arms and hands together as fin-like projections—in the exact style of the figurines. Also, while small female figurines are rarely found in the sanctuaries with female cult images, there appears to be a close connection between the few that have been found and the female figures. At Phylakopi, French (1985:231, 276–77) and Renfrew (1985:417) have suggested that the few Psi figurines found in the Phylakopi sanctuary were used only after the "Lady of Phylakopi" went out of use and served as substitute cult images receiving offerings. Similarly, Moore observes that the only two figurines present in the Mycenae Temple Complex were a Proto-Phi and an early Phi figurine (both dating to LH IIIA, before the temple was built), which he relates to the breast-cupping pose of the only complete figure found in the Temple Complex (Moore and Taylour 1999:50, 92–93). As for Midea (where the figure was found not in a sanctuary but in a storeroom or workshop), Demakopoulou and Divari-Valakou note that there was an unusual concentration of Tau figurines (20 in number) in the West Gate area, the vicinity of the figure (2001:185). Again, there seems to be a direct relationship between the gesture of the figure and that of the figurines in use in the same area.

[32] Identifying a cult image can be a difficult task, as in the cases of the Tiryns, Mycenae, and Phylakopi figures. Their association with shrines is a principal reason for identifying them as cult images; at the same time their identifications as cult images are major factors in labeling their associated buildings as shrines (compare Renfrew [1985:413] on the "recursive relationship" between sanctuaries and cult figures). Renfrew (1985:23–24) suggested five basic criteria for identifying a cult image, as opposed to another type of representation (such as a votive figure or a votary): scale and number, nature of role (asymmetrical for cult images), gesture, attributes/symbols, and association with supernatural elements (such as fantastic animals). Moore (1999:90–92) has applied Renfrew's criteria to the figures from the Mycenae Temple Complex and drawn a significant contrast between the Type A female figures and the larger Type B (male/sexless) figures. The Type A figures, Moore observes, are more individual, more limited in number, of generally higher quality, and (unlike the Type B figure in situ) serve as a focus of attention in the room; only in scale do the Type B figures better fit Renfrew's criteria. Moore therefore concludes that the smaller figures are cult images, while the larger ones represent votaries. In my view, Moore's claim that the Type A figures are more individual is debatable and ultimately subjective; Taylour (1970:278) emphasized the individuality of the Type B figures. Moore's other observations, however, are based on sound empirical data and support the general interpretation of the Type A figures.

Similarly, M. E. Caskey (1986:35–42) has suggested that the earlier Minoan-style figures from the Ayia Irini temple on Keos (LM I/LH II, fifteenth century B.C.E.), despite their large size (ca. 70–135 cm), represent cult worshippers. Most notably, the statues are large in number (a minimum of 32, with fragments of up to 50 additional figures likely) and nearly identical (lack of individuality). These analyses suggest that some of Renfrew's criteria (such as scale) may not be applicable, or that not all need to be present or positive (i.e., they should not be used as a simple trait list), but that his basic procedure can identify distinctive patterns.

In summary, the best explanation for the basic identities of the figurines is as schematic depictions of the divine figures represented, in more detailed form, by the cult images. The schematic nature of their depiction, along with their frequency, and standardization in LH IIIA–B, suggests that the figurines were intended as cheap icons with—as has often been proposed—a widespread popular or domestic use (see French [1971:174]; and Tamvaki [1973:258], as quoted above; Hägg 1981:39). Moore has suggested a parallel with modern icons; for him, the figurines were a

> cheap, mass produced and widely circulated expression of religious sentiment which might be expected to turn up anywhere. Similarly, in modern Greece, a cheap icon might equally be found in a chapel or hanging from the rear view mirror of a pick-up truck. (Moore and Taylour 1999:88; see also Vermeule 1964:291)

In a very different context, M. Voigt (1983:193) observed that, in some groups of figurines,

> variation within a functional class is related to the kinds of social context in which the members are used; for example, both ancient Mesopotamian and modern Catholic groups use relatively elaborate cult figures in ritual structures serving the community, and simpler, smaller, cheaper figures within domestic structures or household units.

Thus, the contrast between the individuality of the Type A figures and the heterogeneous nature of the small female figurines (see Catling 1995:188) is easily explained.[33]

Iconography of the Gestures. As I have discussed above, the identity of these figurines' referent as not simply a woman but a goddess or goddesses is supported to a large extent by the evidence. But what of the meaning of the specific gestures of the figurines? Can we determine the specific meanings of these gestures? Do they indicate a single figure or multiple goddesses? In order to answer these questions, it is necessary to look at the parallels to these gestures, in various media and (where possible) textual sources, more carefully.

Upraised Arms. The gesture of upraised arms has received by far the most discussion among Mycenaean scholars; this situation is not surprising, considering that this gesture is (as observed above) by far the most common among the Mycenaean terracottas. It is also known from Cretan iconography, particularly the series of late Minoan "Goddess with Upraised Arms" figures. Generally, the gesture has been interpreted as representing the epiphany of the deity (Prent 2005:181). Meanwhile, Mylonas related the gesture (at least for the Psi figurines) to one of blessing, interpreting the figure represented by the Psi figurines as the "Goddess of Blessing" (1966:154). Regardless, the gesture has been interpreted by most scholars as one of divinity. Renfrew (1985:23–24) provides a rare caution, suggesting that it is unclear whether the gesture represents epiphany or adoration—and that therefore the figure in this pose could be either divine or human. In most of these cases, however, the interpretation is generally offered with little empirical data for support and so does not rise far beyond the level of conjecture.

As for the development of the gesture, the definitive study was made by S. Alexiou (1958). Alexiou traced the gesture in Minoan iconography back to Middle Minoan but noted that the large figures with upraised arms—associated with shrines and likely cult images—appeared only in LM III. This period is contemporary with the highest popularity of the Mycenaean terracottas, and so some have argued that the Minoan "Goddess with Upraised Arms" figures were inspired by the Myceanean figurines (French 1981:173; Renfrew 1981a:29). French in particular has suggested that, while Crete served as the influence on the earliest Mycenaean figurines, the Mycenaean figurines in turn served as a counterinfluence on this large scale LM III sculpture; for her, while the iconography of the figure with upraised arms was of Minoan origin, its LM III terracotta form was partly influenced by Mycenaean trends (1981:173, 178).

This debate, then, centers on two fundamental issues:

1. the existence and extent of the pre-LM III iconography of the "Goddess with Upraised Arms"; and

2. the nature of Minoan-Mycenaean interaction in LM IIIA–B (chronologically, roughly the same as LH IIIA–B).

For the first issue, the predominant view is that the "Goddess with Upraised Arms" figure already had a long tradition in Minoan iconography by LM III. In my view, the extent of this tradition may well be exaggerated in some of the scholarship. For instance, a direct relationship is seen between this figure and the "Snake Goddess" known especially in the form of faience statues from MM Knossos (Alexiou 1958:180;

[33] For further discussion of this topic, see below and the contextual discussion in chapter 7.

Nilsson 1968:311–12; Prent 2005:181). The "Snake Goddess" figures, however, do not generally share the upraised arms gesture but have arms extended forward and down; even in the one example from Knossos with arms upraised, it is holding snakes in its hands. The snake, not the gesture, is the common symbol of the "Snake Goddess," and the snake is only one symbol (among many) sometimes associated with the "Goddess with Upraised Arms" figure. While the prevalence of figures with "upraised arm" gesture might sometimes be exaggerated, the existence of some Minoan tradition for this gesture is secure, as Alexiou has shown with an analysis of engraved gems (1958; see also French 1971:106). For the second issue, there is a question as to whether there was a strong Mycenaean influence on Crete in LM IIIA2–B. Many scholars counter the views of French and Renfrew, suggesting that this period is marked by a "Minoan Renaissance" and that the hypothesis of Mycenaean influence on Minoan statuary is not supported by the evidence in other forms of material culture (for summary, see Prent 2005:106–7, 196–97).

The Minoan-Mycenaean connections in this period, then, are ultimately too complicated to be clearly untangled, at least based on current evidence. In connection with the gesture of "upraised arms," the best conclusion is that it has its origins in Crete and passed from there to the Greek mainland, but that the Cretan representations in clay figures may have been influenced in turn by the Mycenaean figurines (and figures). Even if this is the case, it does not follow, however, that the Mycenaean Greeks adopted the concept of the figure with upraised arms wholesale: a borrowing of an outward form does not automatically imply a borrowing of the ideas behind it. Anthropologists have provided much ethnographic evidence to show that such borrowings are often "superficial" or that understandings of a single object or event can be unique to specific cultures (for a good discussion, see Gailey 1989; see also Sahlins 1983:529). Rather, imagery in such cases is generally adapted to fit the needs of the culture borrowing it. Indeed, the appearance of the figures themselves supports this concept. As I mentioned above, the style of the Mycenaean figures is typically Mycenaean: they are relatively abstract and painted in the general style of the Mycenaean figurines; in general they closely follow the decoration of Mycenaean pottery. On the other hand, the Minoan figures have tiaras with a series of symbols—birds, snakes, poppies, "horns of consecration," etc.—which are entirely within the Minoan tradition (Alexiou 1958:245; Prent 2005:181). Therefore, even determining the basic meaning of the Minoan gesture may be of little help in understanding what the gesture meant to Mycenaean Greeks (let alone to Philistines). In the end, a survey of the iconography of the upraised arms gesture provides little additional information; it is difficult to say more than that the gesture generally seems to be associated with deities.

Mourning. As opposed to the upraised arms, the gesture of the mourning figurines—arms raised to the head—has a clear iconographic and textual tradition that provides real insight into understanding its meaning. The gesture of hands to the head is a widespread, cross-cultural sign of mourning. It is found, for instance, throughout the history of Egypt, where clay mourning figurines were a common feature among grave goods in the Middle Kingdom (D'Auria, Lacovara, and Roehrig 1992:108–9). T. Dothan (1982:249 n. 58) and Cavanagh and Mee (1995:56) have noted that representations of mourners occur in examples as disparate as New Kingdom funeral scenes and the Ahiram sarcophagus. The specific features of the Philistine mourning figurines, however—especially their particular style and decoration—separate them from other Near Eastern representations of mourners, relating them instead to Mycenaean figurines and the Aegean world (as discussed above; see also T. Dothan 1982:249).

As I mentioned earlier, Mycenaean mourning figurines first appear in the twelfth century B.C.E. and are so far known from only three sites (Perati, Kamini, and Ialysos). Aside from occasional examples from the Sub-Mycenaean/Minoan and Protogeometric (from eastern Crete and Elateia in Locris; see above), the type is unattested in the Aegean until the late Geometric period (the second half of the eighth century). At that time they reappear in the central Aegean region (Attica, Cyclades, Rhodes), gradually increasing in popularity and becoming more widely distributed in the Archaic and surviving into the Hellenistic period (for a survey of some of these figurines, see especially Kurtz and Boardman 1971; also Iakovidis 1966:45; T. Dothan 1982:244). In almost every case they come from funerary contexts.

The large corpus of iconographic and textual parallels for these figurines provides further information concerning the meaning of the gesture. There are a number of Mycenaean painted representations of mourning women with hands to the head, especially on *larnakes* (sarcophagi) from the cemetery at Tanagra (in Boeotia) and elsewhere (Vermeule 1965; Iakovidis 1966:46–49; Spyropoulos 1969; 1970; 1971;

Cavanagh and Mee 1995:46–48, 60–61, figs. 1–10). Most depict simply a woman or group of women with this gesture, but some include a scene around what appears to be a bier with a corpse. This arrangement (female mourners with hands to the head, around a bier with a body laid out), is also found on a Mycenaean krater sherd from Agia Triada in Elis (Schoinas 1999:257, fig. 1). Remarkably similar to these paintings are scenes from the well-known Dipylon amphorae and kraters, the Geometric funerary urns from the Dipylon (Kerameikos) cemetery at Athens, although the latter were painted hundreds of years later (see, e.g., Karo 1943:pl. 11). From the later Geometric period on, painted depictions of mourners—like the terracottas—are commonly found in tombs, with a strong association of women and the gesture of hands to the head (for catalogues of these representations, see Zschietzschmann 1928; Boardman 1955; Ahlberg 1971; Cavanagh and Mee 1995:51–55). As on the Dipylon kraters and the earlier Mycenaean scenes, these painted representations focus in particular on *prothesis*, the official presentation of the body on the day after death (Ahlberg 1971:108).[34] Finally, Greek literature is full of references to mourning gestures, generally performed immediately upon death; there are several references to tearing the hair (*Iliad* 18.22ff., 22.77–78, 22.405ff., 24.710ff.; *Odyssey* 10. 567; Euripides: *Alkestis* 98ff.; *Andromache* 825ff.), as well as at least one to beating the head (*Iliad* 22.33).

The interpretation of the gesture of hands to the head, then, is clear: it is a mourning gesture (tearing the hair and/or beating the head) performed generally by women, either immediately after death or as part of the later official funerary rites. It is therefore clearly associated with humans. The painted scenes in particular indicate that this is an everyday ritual performed by ordinary Greeks, and all of the literary references to tearing the hair and beating the head show these gestures performed by mythological human, not divine, figures. This identification creates a problem, however. All of the Mycenaean mourning figurines follow the mainstream trends of the Late Psi figurines in style and decoration. The Perati mourning figurines, moreover, fairly closely echo the earlier LH IIIB tradition with the high *polos* and use of painting to indicate garments (although they are now partially depicted in the LH IIIC patterns). This situation means that attributes of the figurines such as the *polos* and dress, in which the figurines seem to copy the attributes of the terracotta cult images, cannot be interpreted as indicators of divinity; at least a small group of figurines with these attributes (the mourning figurines) are almost certainly human representations. It may be that these articles of clothing could be worn by either humans or deities; in this case, the only characteristic of the figurines that we can use to determine their identity is the gesture.[35]

Hands to the Breasts. Unlike the gestures discussed above, the gesture of hands to the breasts does not have a long Aegean pedigree. The figurines depicting this gesture (the Tau figurines), while not rare, are much less common than the Psi figurines. As mentioned above, the depiction of this gesture on the Mycenaean figures is also rare: one figure from Mycenae displays this gesture, while the Midea figure has its hands just below the breasts. French (1971:104) observed that, before the appearance of the early Naturalistic and Proto-Phi figurines with hands on or near the breasts, this gesture was "considered alien to Mycenaean iconography."[36] As with the general concept of small terracottas, French related certain iconographic features of the early Mycenaean figurines (such as occasional depiction of bare breasts) to Cretan influence (1971:104–5); R. V. Nicholls suggested that both the Phi and Tau gestures could be related to Minoan prototypes in clay and bronze (1970:3). At the same time, French suggested that the explosion in popularity of the Mycenaean terracottas, beginning in LH IIIA2, might be due to contact with Cyprus and the Levant, where terracottas had long been common (1971:106). Of course, the gesture of hands to the breasts was common in the LB Levant and Cyprus. It is possible that the origin or development of this gesture on mainland Greece is due to Near Eastern influence, although a form of the gesture appears on the Naturalistic and Proto-Phi figurines (which predate the period French was describing), and French did not make this suggestion herself. The origin of the Mycenaean gesture is ultimately problematic, and this problem leads in turn to confusion in the analysis of certain Philistine figurines. A good example is the figurine from Tell Jerishe discussed above (Herzog 1984:pl. 7e; 1993:483): the

[34] There are also occasional painted representations of *ekphora*, the carrying of the dead to the cemetery on the third day. Note also a clay model of *ekphora*, with figures accompanying the bier in the mourning gesture of hands to the head, from the cemetery of Vari in Attica (Kurtz and Boardman 1971:pl. 16).

[35] Similarly, A. Yasur-Landau (2001:332) observed that, in Aegean iconography, the jewelry and *polos* could be worn by either goddesses or women of high status.

[36] Note, however, that Moore has more recently compiled a brief catalogue of Mycenaean attestations of this gesture in other media; these include on gold plaques from the Shaft Graves at Mycenae (transitional MH–LH I), meaning that the appearance of the gesture in Mycenaean Greece must predate the figurines (see Moore and Taylour 1999:91).

hands are not on the breasts in the typical manner of the Tau figurines but on the body just below the breasts. In this case it is unclear whether the gesture is related to that depicted on the Midea figure or represents an example of a hybrid Aegean-Levantine type (see below).

The meaning of this gesture is also obscure. Moore, in discussing the connections of the Mycenae figure with hands to the breasts and the Naturalistic, Phi, and Tau figurines, suggests that it represents the pressing of the breast for milk during nursing (Moore and Taylour 1999:91). (Along the same lines, Mylonas [1966:115] interpreted the Phi figurines as divine nurses.) This interpretation seems speculative, however, for—while Moore notes that some Phi and Tau figurines are depicted as nursing—most figurines of these types are not *kourotrophoi*; certainly none of the Philistine standing figurines are. The Levantine (or Minoan) figurines cannot provide any additional help; even if the gesture was adopted from the Near East (or Crete), and even if the meaning of the Levantine (or Cretan) figurines was clear, there is no guarantee that the Mycenaeans would have borrowed the meaning along with the gesture.

In some cases, however, the interpretation of the gesture of hands to the breasts seems quite clear. In some of the tombs at Ialysos, there seems to be a direct connection between the Tau and mourning figurines. NT 15 included a *lekane* (T 15/13) with figurines attached: one is a Tau figurine, while a second has one hand to the head and the other to the side, or perhaps the breast (Maiuri 1923–24:174, figs. 99, 101; Benzi 1992:Tav. 18a). The same tomb also included three freestanding figurines (T 15/15–17), two mourning figurines and a Tau figurine (Maiuri 1923/24:174, fig. 99; Benzi 1992:Tav. 18c–e). A *lekane* from NT 21 had, among the two largely preserved figurines on its rim, a Tau figurine and another with upraised arms, either a mourning figurine or a Psi (T 21/31; Maiuri 1923/24:142, fig. 65; Benzi 1992:Tav. 38e). Another *lekane*, from Tomb 12 in Salzmann and Biliotti's excavation at Ialysos, has three figurines preserved on the rim: two are Tau figurines, and the third has its hands touching the neck (A 950; Forsdyke 1925:173, fig. 235). One of the figurines said to be from Azor (T. Dothan 1982:ch. 4, pl. 25, fig. 12.2) displays a similar connection: one hand is to the head, while the other rests just below the breast. Besides the gestures of tearing the hair and beating the head, Greek literary references to mourning mention beating or tearing the breasts (*Iliad* 18.50–51, 19.282ff.; Sappho 140a (L–P); Aeschylus: *Persai* 1054ff.; *Choephori* 423 ff.; Sophocles: *Elektra* 59ff.; Euripides: *Supplikes* 71ff., *Alkestis* 86ff.; Aristophanes: *Lysistrata* 387ff.) and tearing the neck (*Iliad* 19.282ff.). Thus, the gesture of hands to the breasts as depicted on the figurines at least sometimes seems to represent a gesture of mourning.[37]

The interpretation of the Tau figurines, then, is not straightforward. In some cases (on *lekanai*, or other examples from tombs) they seem pretty clearly to represent mourning women. As they—unlike the mourning figurines with hands to the head—are often found in non-funerary contexts, however, some of them must have a different interpretation; in these cases, they are presumably related to the Mycenaean figures with this gesture and were meant to serve as a schematic depiction of a deity. The following conclusions can therefore be drawn from this analysis:

1. not all Mycenaean figurines represent deities;
2. the *polos* headdress and decoration/dress cannot be automatically taken as indicators of divinity; and
3. even a single figurine type may have more than one referent (for instance, as both a human mourner and a goddess).

There are in fact few Mycenaean figurines (the mourning and Tau figurines from the tombs at Perati, Kamini, and Ialysos) that are demonstrably non-divine representations. Considering this, I should mention two possible explanations to be kept in mind. First, all of these figurines date to the twelfth century; it is therefore possible that, for most of the Late Bronze Age, all female terracottas were originally intended to represent deities, but that in the twelfth century their representational range changed or expanded. (Alternatively, this expanded range may only have applied in certain regions or in those regions only in the twelfth century.) Second, it may be that a deity (or

[37] One other mourning gesture is mentioned in the literary sources: tearing the cheek (Euripides: *Supplikes* 71ff., *Andromache* 825ff.). This gesture is occasionally depicted on later Greek figurines, for example from the Sellada necropolis on Thera (Kontoleon 1958:pl. 83) and the Papatislures Cemetery at Kamiros on Rhodes (Jacopi 1932/33:fig. 77). Some later Greek figurines also have red paint on the cheek as well as on the breast, representing blood (Higgins 1954:33 [Kamiros]; Kurtz and Boardman 1971:78 [Kerameikos]; see Karo 1943:pl. 16). Overall, then, there is a very close correspondence between the gestures of the figurines and those attested textually. Beyond this, the frequency of the different gestures on the figurines appears to match that of the literary sources: in each, the most common gestures are tearing the hair and beating/tearing the breast; tearing the cheek and tearing the neck are much rarer.

deities) may have been the primary referent of all of the figurines—even in the twelfth century—but that, in some cases, the figurines came to be used secondarily to represent humans. The case of the mourning figurines argues against the second suggestion. As for the first, even if true, it would mean that we cannot assume that the Philistine figurines represent deities, as they date to the twelfth century and later (and could also represent a localized development).

I.A.2. Ashdodas[38]

Unlike the small standing figurines, the complete form of this type is clear and generally uniform. Essentially, the Ashdoda depicts a seated woman, with the woman and the chair fused together. This basic form can be broken down into three parts:

1. The head and neck. The most characteristic feature of this part of the Ashdoda is the long neck. In addition, the eyes are always formed by applied pellets; generally, the top of the head is concave (forming a *polos*), the nose is relatively large and protruding, and there are ears on the sides of the head. These features are very similar to those of the Philistine Psi, but generally on a larger scale; the nose in particular is much larger than that of the Philistine Psi.

2. The torso/chair back. The torso of the figurine is a flat rectangle with two applied pellets for breasts. This section therefore appears to be more of a chair back than a human torso. It is sometimes decorated with various painted patterns.

3. The seat, or "couch." The couch is another flat rectangular piece, with four stubby legs in the corners on the bottom. No legs are depicted nor any other human body part. Overall, the figurine form is thus a chair with head, neck, and breasts.

Only one complete or nearly complete Ashdoda has been discovered;[39] nevertheless, every fragment, which generally consists of one of the three components of the Ashdoda (or a fragment thereof), shares the basic characteristics described above. A complete Ashdoda would have stood roughly 15–20 cm high. The one complete example is about 15 cm high; other examples, based on the constituent parts, would have been the same size or slightly larger (head and neck 6–7 cm; torso 5–8 cm; seat 4–5 cm)

As with the Philistine Psi type, the details of this type display a great deal of variation, and it is therefore difficult to isolate subtypes. Apparently (as with the Philistine Psi figurines) there was a wide range of possible expression. Of the multiple variations, two of them appear to be likely subtypes of the Ashdoda; it is difficult to generalize too much about these, however, as there are few examples of each. One subtype is, as with the Philistine Psi, a miniature variant (Ashdod H230/1 [M. Dothan 1971:fig. 91.1] and H1326/1 [M. Dothan and Ben-Shlomo 2005:fig. 3.80.2]). Notably, the complete Ashdoda, which is often seen as a typical Ashdoda and used in analyses as a stand-in for the entire type (see, e.g., Yasur-Landau 2001:331–32), is in fact a miniature variant. Compared to the main Ashdoda type, this variant is characterized most obviously by its smaller size. While the main Ashdoda type would have been roughly 18–20 cm in height (based on the measurements of the constituent parts), the one example of a miniature variant is about 15 cm high. There are, however, additional characteristics that distinguish the miniature variant from the main type: a rounder head; a more slender neck that tapers inward before curving outward again; a series of black and red (bichrome) horizontal stripes around the neck, representing necklaces; and eyes that are farther apart and flat along the face (while the larger Ashdodas tend to, though do not always, have eyes closer together and set against the sides of the nose). Also, the miniatures may be decorated more fully than the regular Ashdodas, not only on the neck, but on the torsos and seats. The relative lack of such decoration on other Ashdoda fragments may be due to poor preservation on these examples (Yasur-Landau 2001:331). The preservation of some slip and paint on several of the Ashkelon examples (paint on two torsos, cat. nos. 19, 27; slip on cat. nos. 21, 23, 24, 27, 28, 30, and especially 31 and 32) could support the idea that decoration on other examples has not been preserved, but on the regular Ashdoda examples the decoration is generally much simpler. If more elaborate decoration is indeed characteristic of the miniature Ashdoda, then the seat

[38] The nickname "Ashdoda" of course derives from the site name Ashdod, where the type was first identified (Hachlili 1971:129; M. Dothan 1971:21; T. Dothan 1982:234).

[39] In fact, while this example is generally referred to as complete (Hachlili 1971:129; T. Dothan 1982:234; Yasur-Landau 2001:331), it was originally found in multiple pieces and restored (Dothan and Dothan 1992:153; see the photographs in M. Dothan 1971:frontispiece, pl. LXXXII; T. Dothan 1982:ch. 4, pl. 19). It is also clear from the photographs, and especially the drawings, that some pieces of the figurine were not recovered and have been reconstructed (M. Dothan 1971:frontispiece, fig. 91.1; T. Dothan 1982:ch. 4, fig. 9). Nevertheless, the figurine is mostly complete and is the only case where the three main components of a single example have been found and fitted together.

fragments Ashdod H3/1 (M. Dothan 1971:fig. 91.4) and Miqne obj. nos. 3948 and 3949 (Ben-Shlomo and Press 2009:fig. 5.7–8) may be additional examples of this subtype; note that these fragments have the same series of bichrome stripes as the seat of the complete Ashdoda.

Some of the distinctive characteristics of the miniature Ashdoda heads—their small size, their relative roundness, and the position of the eyes—are similar to those of the main Philistine Psi type and can lead to confusion in distinguishing between the two types. This has certainly been the case in the Ashkelon registration books, where the Philistine Psi heads have generally been labeled as Ashdoda heads.[40] The necks of the miniature Ashdodas, however are clearly distinct from those of the Philistine Psi figurines, in their general form and especially in the series of painted rings around the neck.

The second Ashdoda subtype has an arm molded onto the torso. This subtype is represented by only two torsos (cat. no. 28 and Qasile No. 4952/1; see A. Mazar 1986:13, fig. 6.1, pl. 3A); it is therefore unclear whether the other components of the figurines had features distinct from those of the main Ashdoda type. In both cases it is the left arm which is depicted. On the Qasile example, the arm stretches across the torso below the breasts. The excavator, A. Mazar, suggested that it was a *kourotrophos* figurine (i.e., that it was holding a child), but there is no clear indication that it is cradling anything in its arm. The Ashkelon figurine is fragmentary; though the arm is partially chipped off, it appears that it has a hand which is cupping the left breast.

Beyond these two subtypes, it is generally unclear whether variations indicate additional subtypes or simply a wide range of possibilities within a basic unstandardized type. These variations include a *polos* with a higher lip or ridge: cat. no. 25 and Ashdod H3139/1 (M. Dothan and Ben-Shlomo 2005:fig. 3.80.1). In other cases, it is unclear whether the figurines represent variant subtypes or different types altogether. These cases include two unique heads from Ashkelon (cat. nos. 24, 30). It is unclear whether these heads represent females or if they would have belonged to seated figurines; as no other large figurine bases have been found at Ashkelon (or elsewhere), however, I believe that it is best to include them within the seated (Ashdoda) type. At least provisionally, I would suggest that all larger figurines were seated.

Another group of figurines includes three thinner, undecorated torsos without breasts (cat. no. 20, Ashdod H1158/1, and Ashdod K1378/1; M. Dothan and Ben-Shlomo 2005:figs. 3.62.4, 3.103.2). It is again unclear what the remainder of these figurines would have looked like, or if these even represent human figures. Both examples do have the bottom of a "neck" preserved, suggesting that there was indeed a human head attached. In addition, the bottom of the fragment Ashdod H1158/1 appears to be curving into a seat. The lack of breasts suggests that these three examples might represent a male subtype of the Ashdoda. At the same time, since the Ashdoda form is primarily not a human body but a chair, the lack of breasts may not be a clear indication of sex.

Finally, I should mention a distinct group of figurines from Ashdod, which I will refer to as the "Late Ashdoda" type (as these figurines come from Iron II deposits).[41] The main group is similar to the Ashdoda but with a very low chair back (see M. Dothan 1971:fig. 63.2–7); on some examples the sides of the seat are raised in the form of a ridge running the entire length of the seat from the chair back (Ashdod D1221/1 and D4343/1; M. Dothan 1971:fig. 63.2–3). D4343/1 has an arm and hand on the top of the seat; this feature may relate it to other "offering tables" with arms and hands along the side ridges of the seat, e.g., Ashdod K1295/1, also Ashdod D18 and D17 (M. Dothan and Ben-Shlomo 2005:fig. 3.103.1; M. Dothan and Freedman 1967:fig. 46.6–7). As with the last group discussed, there are no breasts or other female characteristics (as noted by Hachlili 1971:129). No head or neck has been found on any of these figurines. It is not entirely clear, in my opinion, that the "Late Ashdoda" represents a human figure seated in a chair, although it is noteworthy that most of the examples have breaks that look like neck scars (see M. Dothan 1971:fig. 61.2, 4–7). On the other hand, I believe that M. Dothan stretched the evidence too far in suggesting that these figurines represented "male cultic images" (in Dothan and Dothan 1992:156; emphasis in original). Although he did not elaborate on the evidence for this suggestion, he was presumably following Hachlili (1971:129) in observing the lack of female indicators (such as breasts) and her suggested association of the "Late Ashdoda" with the "Ashdodite" heads, presumed to be male (see discussion below,

[40] This also appears to be true for some of the heads from Ashdod, based on my inspection of a small number of examples at Beth Shemesh (see above and chapter 7).

[41] There also appears to be an unpublished example from Ḥorvat Hoga (IAA 73–5080); it consists of a seat with an arm on the top of the right side. Since the seat is otherwise typical of the regular Ashdoda—i.e., lacking the ridge characteristic of some of the "Late Ashdoda" examples—it is not entirely clear that this is a "Late Ashdoda" as opposed to an unusual example of the "regular" Ashdoda.

I.A.6/I.B), which were among the figurines found in the vicinity. There is, however, no direct evidence of a connection between the "Ashdodite" heads and the "Late Ashdodas." At the same time, if we follow the principle (as above with the Philistine Psi) that the distribution of heads should match that of bodies, we must conclude that at least some "Ashdodite" heads should belong to "Late Ashdodas." Even if this is true, however, it is not clear that the "Ashdodite" heads are male heads (see below). In addition, I would again point out that the basic form of the figurine is a chair, and therefore the lack of female markers may not be particularly significant.

Parallels/Iconography

A. Yasur-Landau (2001:332, table 1) has presented a brief but systematic iconographic analysis of the Ashdoda. From this analysis he concluded that the features of the Ashdoda derived largely from Aegean traditions, though he suggested that there were some Cypriot (and perhaps local Levantine) features incorporated as well. Because Yasur-Landau's analysis is the most significant published work of this type, it is a good starting point for a more detailed study. In addition, I will consider the relationship of the Ashdoda to the Philistine Psi figurines, a connection that Yasur-Landau did not discuss:

1. Headdress. Yasur-Landau suggests that the "slightly flaring headdress" (2001:332) of the Ashdoda is connected to the *polos* worn by Aegean women. The headdress, in fact a low *polos* or simply a concave head, is essentially identical to that of the Philistine Psi (and Mycenaean Late Psi) figurines.

2. Applied ears. This feature could be of either Mycenaean or Cypriot origin, as Yasur-Landau suggests. Applied ears are common on Late Cypriot figurines of the thirteenth to twelfth centuries (Karageorghis's Types B and C; see Karageorghis 1993a:pls. VII–X). On the other hand, they are rare on Mycenaean figurines, though they do appear especially on some Late Psi examples (e.g., Morgan 1935:fig. 1g). As Yasur-Landau (2001:table 1) points out, some of the Mycenaean female figures also have applied ears.

3. Applied eyes. For Yasur-Landau these, like the applied ears, could be equally Cypriot or Mycenaean. The eyes of the Ashdoda are, however, clearly distinct from those of the Cypriot female figurines (Karageorghis's Types A and B). On the LB Cypriot figurines, the eyes always indicate the pupil, which is formed by either a second applied piece of clay or by a deep incision in a single applied pellet (see Karageorghis 1993a:pls. I–X). Typically, the eyes of Mycenaean figurines are painted (as mentioned above), although those of the earliest Phi figurines closely resemble the Cypriot type (French 1971:116, pl. 15a, b). The eyes of the LH IIIC figurines, however, are simple applied pellets, just like those of the Ashdoda figurines. In fact, there is no difference between the eyes of the Ashdoda and those of the Philistine Psi, and both are therefore likely to be based on Mycenaean antecedents.

4. Large nose. This feature is essentially unknown on the Mycenaean and Philistine Psi figurines. The nose on the Mycenaean figurines (like that of many Philistine Psi figurines) is generally a low ridge formed by pinching the face. The Cypriot noses, however, are quite large and protruding and are formed by a separate piece of clay. In this respect they are very similar to the Ashdoda noses.

5. Long neck. As discussed above, this feature is typical of the LH IIIC figurines. There is no distinction between the Philistine Psi necks and the Ashdoda necks.

6. Applied breasts. Applied pellet breasts are also typical of LH IIIC (and Philistine Psi) figurines.

7. Painted decoration. Paralleling the LH IIIC and Philistine Psi figurines, there is a great deal of variety in decoration on the Ashdodas. Some have simple geometric designs, some have simply a white slip preserved, and others are undecorated. Only in the case of the miniature Ashdodas (and particularly the complete Ashdoda) is there an elaborate decorative scheme. Yasur-Landau focuses his analysis on the decoration of the complete Ashdoda, without emphasizing, however, that it is apparently atypical. Nevertheless, it will be worth discussing the painted features of the miniature Ashdoda briefly. The neck is decorated along its full length with a series of horizontal stripes in bichrome (black and red). These stripes are reminiscent of those on the necks of the thirteenth- and twelfth-century Cypriot figurines (Karageorghis's Type B), which are similarly in black and red; the latter figurines, however, have only three stripes, and these are thinner and do not cover the entire length of the neck. On the other

hand, a series of stripes can be found ringing the long necks of some of the Late Psi figurines (e.g., Demangel 1926:figs. 24.3, 26.5). The overall appearance of such heads is remarkably close to those of the Ashdodas.[42] (It may also be significant that the Mycenaean figures are generally decorated with multiple painted necklaces.)

The torso and chair of the miniature Ashdoda is also decorated in bichrome patterns, generally a series of stripes. Two particular motifs from the complete Ashdoda merit further discussion. The first is the pendant, probably representing a stylized lotus ("waz-lily") motif. There are examples on a Late Psi figurine from Tiryns (Kilian-Dirlmeier 1978/79:Abb. 2.22) and one of the Tiryns figures (Kilian 1978:Abb. 21), which, as I. Kilian-Dirlmeier has demonstrated, are related to pendants and other jewelry found in Mycenaean tombs (1978/79:34–35, Abb. 7, 8, 14, 16; Popham 1974:213 n. 14, fig. 11k).[43] The other Ashdoda motif is the set of bichrome triangles, which, as Yasur-Landau (2001:332) has pointed out, also occurs on Philistine pottery; he follows T. Dothan (1982:215) in interpreting this motif as a stylized lotus.

The general use of bichrome decoration parallels the Philistine Bichrome pottery, which may be related to the Levantine tradition of LB bichrome (T. Dothan 1982:215).

8. Seat. T. Dothan has traced the concept of a seated female figurine to various Mycenaean prototypes (1982:234; see Mylonas 1956). The typical thirteenth- and twelfth-century Cypriot female figurine was also sometimes depicted as seated (Karageorghis's Type C; Karageorghis 1993a:pl. X), as noted by T. Dothan (1982:234, ch. 4, pl. 22). The Ashdoda seat, however, is completely different from either the Mycenaean or Cypriot examples. On the Cypriot figurines there is no chair depicted at all, except for two rear legs; it is as if the figurine is seated on a two-legged stool. The Mycenaean chair or throne, on the other hand, has a high back but a very short seat, unlike the long Ashdoda seat. In addition, the Mycenaean chair is almost always three-legged: all of the 25 examples that Mylonas surveyed were three-legged (1956:118); French (1971:171) pointed to a four-legged example from Mycenae but noted that this type was very rare. Beyond a few Aegean examples from the end of the Late Bronze Age, there is at least one example of a figure seated on a four-legged chair from Cyprus (Karageorghis 1993a:14, 23, pl. XI.1). Not only is the chair of this example four-legged, but it has a long seat more like the Ashdoda seat than that of the typical Mycenaean throne. Furniture examples of four-legged chairs are known to have existed in the LB in the Aegean (Mylonas 1956:118; Rehak 1995:96; see also Younger 1995 for a survey of images of seated figures), but Rehak notes that the Aegean four-legged stool or throne is primarily a Minoan type (1995:96–97). Meanwhile, chair models (Karageorghis 1993a:23) as well as representations on cylinder seals (Theodossiadou 1995) suggest a four-legged type was also in use on Cyprus at this time. Besides chairs, the Ashdoda seat is also reminiscent, at least in some formal respects, of the Mycenaean model beds or biers (see French 1971:172).

On the basis of this analysis, I would modify Yasur-Landau's conclusion that the Ashdoda (or at least the head and neck) represents a real hybrid of Aegean and Cypriot elements (2001:332). Most of the elements can be explained as purely Mycenaean in origin—at least Mycenaean of LH IIIC, just as with the Philistine Psi figurines. The only element that is clearly alien to Mycenaean female figurines is the large protruding nose, which on the other hand is typical of Cypriot figurines; even the applied ears and four-legged chair, which do have Cypriot parallels, are found occasionally in the Aegean. The appearance of the head and neck is extremely similar to some of the Philistine Psi figurines and so in turn is fully within the LH IIIC tradition. French observed (1971:168) that the seated figurines are of the same type (Phi, Psi, and Tau) as the standing ones, and so it is not surprising to find this similarity in the Philistine figurines as well. For A. Mazar, the Batash figurine (E0863; A. Mazar 2006:pl. 82:15, photo 107) bears a "striking" resemblance to Karageorghis's Type B and C LB Cypriot figurines (2006:253; cf. Schmitt 1999:591). Following the above

[42] A figurine from Batash (E8063; A. Mazar 2006:pl. 82:15, photo 107) is probably a regular Ashdoda but is unusual in that it has similar red and black stripes (only the upper part of the neck is preserved). Mazar suggested that, while it might be an Ashdoda, it is different in several respects; one of the principal distinctions he draws, however, is the taller face of the Batash figurine, vs. a shorter face that is more clearly distinguished from the neck (2006:253). These latter features, however, are typical only of the miniature Ashdoda variant; the regular Ashdoda form does indeed have a taller head that is not well differentiated at all from the neck.

[43] For these motifs on Mycenaean pottery, see Furumark 1941a:148–49, 216–17 (Furumark Motif [FM] 11, 28).

analysis, I believe that the closest resemblance is actually to the Mycenaean figurines. Moreover, some of the elements of the Cypriot Type B and C figurines which are closest to the Philistine examples—such as the flat heads—are thirteenth-century innovations which have been plausibly interpreted as influenced by Mycenaean figurines (Karageorghis 1993a:22).[44] In the end, I would agree with T. Dothan's assessment of the Ashdoda in comparison to the Cypriot figurines: "The idea may be similar but stylistically the Ashdoda belongs to a different world—the Mycenaean" (1982:234).

At the same time, it is impossible to see the Ashdoda as a purely Mycenaean form. As I have just noted, there is at least one feature (the nose) that is more likely Cypriot than Mycenaean, and the form of the chair is extremely atypical. In addition, the overall form is ultimately distinct from any known Mycenaean (or for that matter Cypriot) figurine. No figurine from the Aegean or Cyprus displays such a fusion of figure and chair. The Mycenaean examples are often made as two pieces, chair and human figurine; even when in one piece there is always a clear demarcation between human body and chair, with the figure's legs always depicted as hanging over the edge of the seat. The closest example to a fusion is the Cypriot type, in which the two chair legs appear to be coming directly out of the figure's lower back. In this case, however, the figure appears in fully human form. In fact, the only signs of a chair are the two chair legs, suggesting that the type may not represent a human-chair hybrid but rather a figure seated on a stool.

The results of the analysis above suggest an important contrast between the Philistine Psi and the Ashdoda. The Philistine Psi is a clear continuation of the Late Psi form, in some cases with exact parallels in the Aegean. The Ashdoda, on the other hand, has no direct antecedent; it must represent one or more stages of development beyond the extant seated figurines from the Aegean and Cyprus.[45] Remarkably, while almost all of its individual elements can be interpreted as Mycenaean, the exact combination of those elements is unique.

The Ashkelon and Qasile examples with an arm modeled on the torso raise an additional issue. The arm of cat. no. 28 is partially chipped off, but it appears that the hand is cupping the left breast. If this is indeed correct, the figurine might represent a mixture of Aegean type and Canaanite motif (cf. discussion of cat. no. 10 above, under I.A.1). The Qasile example is more difficult to interpret. A. Mazar, the excavator, suggested that arm was cradling a child, but there is no clear indication that the arm is holding anything. If the figurine is in fact a *kourotrophos*, its origin is obscure. The motif is certainly attested in the Aegean (Mylonas 1956:119–20; French 1971:142–44; Olsen 1998; Pilafidis-Williams 2009), although its importance has often been overstated as it is relatively rare: Olsen (1998:384) counted a total of about 70 examples, while Pilafidis-Williams (1998:181) identified 78 examples, which is in either case a small number compared to the thousands of known Mycenaean figurines. While rare on seated Mycenaean figurines, French has noted it on at least two examples (1971:169). It is also found at least occasionally, however, on LB plaque figurines (Pritchard 1943:22–23; Nakhai, Dessel, and Wisthoff 1987/88:102, fig. 42).

Meaning

A. Yasur-Landau has written that his iconographic analysis strongly supports the identification of the Ashdoda as an Aegean earth goddess associated with vegetation and also as a "mother goddess" (2001:335, 338; 2010:305). In my view, the iconography proves nothing of the sort. Concerning the idea of the Ashdoda as a divine representation, there are good reasons for believing this to be true. The human elements of the Ashdoda figurine—the head, neck, and breasts—match those of the Philistine Psi figurines almost exactly in form, style, and decoration; this match is not

[44] Karageorghis (1993a:22) also suggests that the long pointed nose of the Type B and C figurines might derive from Aegean antecedents, such as the "Lord (or Lady) of Asine." To my eyes, however, the nose of the Asine figure is rounder and less protruding than that of the Cypriot examples; moreover, I have yet to see a nose of this type on a Mycenaean figurine.

[45] A possible link between the regular Psi form and the chair-torso of the Ashdoda is provided by a few LH IIIB2–IIIC Psi figurines with flatter triangular torsos from the Marmaria at Delphi (Demangel 1926:fig. 16d) and from Ialysos (T40/2, Maiuri 1923/24:195–96, Tav. 4; Benzi 1992:Tav. 72b). The shape of the torsos may be related to the tapering torsos of many Late Psi figurines, with the arms coming in to the body diagonally; the Marmaria and Ialysos examples may be a further step in this development. The Ialysos figurine is particularly interesting; it is large for a figurine (19 cm) and is reminiscent of the female figures particularly in its elaborate decoration, although smaller than most of the known figures mentioned above. It is almost a hybrid between the two. The decorative pattern includes dotted circles around each breast, and a possible neck pendant in between—details also found on the complete Ashdoda. In addition, compare fragments of two other larger figurines: one, from Asine (Persson 1938:309, fig. 212), is a head and upper torso, 11 cm in height, with two necklaces and a pendant; the other, from Phylakopi (Atkinson et al. 1904:202, pl. XXXIX.16), is a torso approximately 10 cm high, with three necklaces and ringed breasts.

surprising, since (as mentioned above) the Mycenaean standing and seated figurines share a similarly close connection (French 1971:168). It is therefore likely that the Philistine Psi and Ashdoda share the same referent (or referents). As I suggested above, it is likely that the basic referent of the Mycenaean standing figurines (and therefore of the Philistine Psi) is the goddess (or goddesses) depicted by the figures from Mycenae, Tiryns, Midea, and Phylakopi. At the same time, however, certain Mycenaean examples not only suggest but demand that at least some of the figurines (e.g., the mourning figurines) represent humans and not deities. Moreover, they suggest that few, if any, of the individual formal, decorative, or iconographic elements of the standing figurines are exclusive to representations of deities.

The only aspect of the Ashdoda that does not fall into this ambiguity is its chair, or throne. The seated position is well known to have been a position of superior status throughout the Near East and the Aegean; Yasur-Landau has observed that typical Aegean representations of seated women suggest representations of goddesses, as they are surrounded by animals—including fantastic ones such as griffins (2001:332, pl. C.a–e). Therefore, if the elements of dress displayed by the Ashdoda are suggestive of divinity, then the seated position makes this interpretation likely.

On the other hand, the interpretation of the Ashdoda as an earth, vegetation, and/or mother goddess finds little support in the iconography. Beginning with the Ashdoda itself, the only possible connection of its iconography with earth or vegetation is the appearance of lily and lotus flower designs on a single example, the complete Ashdoda. Even here, however, the imagery is probably not related to the role of a deity. As I discussed above, the lily motif is merely a typical motif depicted on pendants and other jewelry found in tombs and therefore not necessarily related to a fertility deity. In addition, both it and the lotus motif appear as purely decorative patterns on Mycenaean (and Philistine) pottery. Meanwhile, the only Ashdoda figurine that might have any connection with motherhood is the Qasile example. Even here, Mazar's interpretation of the figurine as a *kourotrophos* is questionable. Meanwhile, no other Ashdoda example (of over 35 I have identified) depicts a child, pregnancy, or any attribute that might be associated with motherhood. In the Aegean, Mycenaean seated figurines parallel the Ashdoda in rarely displaying any attribute that could be associated with earth, vegetation, or motherhood. Of the dozens of seated figurines surveyed by French, only two are *kourotrophoi* (1971:169); at the same time, this makes up a very small percentage of the total number of Mycenaean *kourotrophoi* (as noted above, about 70, according to Olsen [1998:384], or 78, according to Pilafidis-Williams [1998:181]). The motif is also rare on regular standing and group figurines, although even among those types there are more examples of it than among the seated type (French 1971:142–44). It is also worth repeating Pilafidis-Williams's observation (1998:30; 2009:113) that, while *kourotrophoi* are found in most types of Mycenaean female figurines, a notable exception is the Late Psi. Thus, it appears that the motif may have gone out of use in Mycenaean figurines by the beginning of the twelfth century.

Yasur-Landau bases his entire iconographic argument on a survey of a few painted and engraved scenes: the Tiryns gold ring, an LHIIIC krater from Tiryns; the Agia Triada sarcophagus; the Pylos "White Goddess"; and the LHIIIA Homage Krater (2001:333–34; 2002:238). Beyond sharing the image of an enthroned woman with a *polos*, the scenes depicted are quite diverse; they depict an array of associated symbols (birds, plants, snakes, etc.) and figures in procession (both humans and fantastic creatures). Despite this variety—and the fact that, as Yasur-Landau has acknowledged, the *polos* can be worn by multiple figures, humans and deities—Yasur-Landau interprets these figures as representing a single mother/earth/vegetation goddess. In my view, there is little evidence for such an all-embracing equation. None of these attributes can be directly associated with the Ashdoda, let alone all of them; alternatively, we cannot even be sure that the Ashdoda figurines all represent a single figure. Nevertheless, despite this lack of evidence, Yasur-Landau's interpretation agrees with the usual scholarly discussion of the Ashdoda (e.g., M. Dothan 1971:21; T. Dothan 1982:234; Dothan and Dothan 1992:157). This discussion makes it clear that the interpretation of the Ashdoda is ultimately influenced by the concept of an Aegean "Great Mother" goddess.[46]

[46] There is not the space to go into a detailed critique of the "Mother Goddess" hypothesis here (see Press 2012; for recent general discussions, see Moorey 2003:5–6; Budin 2006; and see Nilsson 1968:389–96 for a critique of this conception for the prehistoric Aegean). This hypothesis has, however, had far-ranging influence in Near Eastern scholarship. Its impact is evident in Schäfer-Lichtenberger's identification of the goddess of the Ekron inscription, *ptgyh*, as "Pytogayah," i.e., from a proposed Greek "Pythogaia," supposedly a form of the Greek "mother goddess" Gaia (2000). Despite several problems with this identification—among them the fact that, as Schäfer-Lichtenberger herself admits, there is no attestation of the alleged divine name "Pythogaia"—this identification has been rather widely accepted (see, e.g., Gitin 2003:286; Naʾaman 2003:82; Ziffer and Kletter 2007:12). Yasur-Landau (2001:337–38) has modified this identification, proposing instead "Pot[n]ia-Gaia"; while he can point to a few (rare) attestations for "Potnia

I.A.3. Composite Figurines (Cat. Nos. 33–63)

The major type of Iron II anthropomorphic figurine is quite distinct from the above Iron I types in all major respects (technique, form, style, and decoration). The technique is a composite one; the figurine is made in two main parts, head and body. Generally speaking, the head is made by pressing clay in a simple open-face mold, which forms the features of the face. The back of the head is then smoothed. The body is either hollow (wheelmade or handmade) or solid (handmade); if hollow, a triangular tang on the bottom of the head is inserted into the neck of the hollow body, with clay added to the neck area to complete the join. Occasionally the head is handmade. In this last instance the figurine is not truly a composite; since the body of the figurine generally follows the types found in the composite figurines, however, it is best to consider them within this same group.[47] Based on the rare complete or nearly complete examples of this type, as well as the measurements of head and body fragments, complete examples would have stood roughly 15–20 cm high; the head fragments are roughly 5–8 cm in height, with the bodies roughly 10–12 cm high.

It is therefore possible to develop a more detailed typology of these figurines by either head type or body type. Archaeologists classifying these figurines, and similar types from elsewhere in Palestine, have often tried to accommodate both criteria within a single typological system, resulting in somewhat convoluted schemes. Thus, for Gilbert-Peretz (1996:30), Type A1 consists of handmade heads and Type A2 of moldmade heads, while Type A3 includes the torsos of Types A1 and A2. Holland divides the figurines first by body type (solid vs. hollow), then by facial type (handmade vs. moldmade), and finally by the gesture of each body (1977:121–22). Kletter (1996) devises a detailed typology of moldmade heads (5.III), followed by a typology of handmade figurines (5.IV); within the latter he then includes bodies of the 5.III moldmade heads (5.IV.6). The problem with these typologies is that they do not treat the figurines as they originally existed but simply according to the fragments that are found. Of course, it is often difficult to reconstruct a complete form based on these fragments, and these typologies deal with the state of the evidence as excavated rather than with speculation. Nevertheless, I believe the ultimate goal of a typology should be to reconstruct the types actually in use by the ancient peoples. As a result, I will analyze the different head types and body types separately and then determine to what extent the subtypes of the two groups correspond with each other.

Head types

The major head types for the composite figurines are functions of the different molds used for the fronts of the heads. The treatment of the faces, however, is generally uniform; the most differences among types are found in the rendering of the hair, or headdress. It is often unclear if a hairstyle or a headdress is indicated; in some cases, locks of hair are distinguished, but these may simply indicate a wig as opposed to actual hair (cf. Kletter 1996:30 n. 3). I have been able to identify nine basic head types for Philistia:[48]

1. Veil (Kletter's 5.III.4).[49] This feature is sometimes referred to as a wig (Negbi 1966:12) or simply as a hairstyle (e.g., Dayagi-Mendels 2002:149–50, for Phoenician figurines from Akhziv).[50] Most of the Ashkelon figurines are of this type. The veil or hair

Gaia (or Ge)" (2001:338 n. 69), he cannot point to an example of this abbreviated form of the divine title "Potnia." Nevertheless, Yasur-Landau proceeds to equate this "Pot[n]ia-Gaia" with the Ashdoda (2001:338), again under the spell of the "Mother Goddess" hypothesis. This identification is tenuous, as is the textual and archaeological evidence for a single Great/Mother Goddess in antiquity (see Press 2012). Despite the meagerness of data supporting it, the Mother Goddess paradigm has continued to persist in the works of scholars of the Near East and Aegean, but ultimately it is unfounded and should be relegated to the "realm of scholarly myth" (Press 2012:17).

[47] This composite technique is often referred to in the literature as a "mixed technique" (D'Amore 1998:417; Ziffer 2010:66; Caubet, Fourrier, and Queyrel 1998:228, as "technique mixte"). S. Paz has independently used the terms "composite method" and "composite technique" (2007:121–22).

[48] Originally, in my 2007 dissertation, I identified six types. Since that time, I have been able to inspect roughly 200 additional Iron Age figurines of various types, many of them unpublished. In particular, being able to look at the figurines from Jemmeh in London and Jerusalem—many of which I had seen only in the small photographs in Petrie's *Gerar* publication (1928), and others unpublished—has allowed me to refine my typology.

[49] References to Kletter's typology are from Kletter 1996:ch. 3, Appendix 5.III, 5.IV. The terms "combed sidelocks," "finely molded," and "schematic" are his; I have used them here for the sake of consistency and easy reference to his types.

[50] According to Dayagi-Mendels, the Akhziv figurines have "parallel grooves" over the forehead indicating strands of hair. Such grooves are not apparent on the Ashkelon examples.

typically takes the form of an undifferentiated mass of clay surrounding the face and joining the head to the body (as shown by cat. no. 37). Occasionally the "veil" appears more clearly as hair, ending in "bulbs" at shoulder height (e.g., cat. no. 38). The veil is shown as separate from the forehead by means of a single, shallow incised horizontal line. The top of the veil or hair is usually rounded on top but occasionally pointed (cat. nos. 45, 52). There are a few miniatures (cat. nos. 45, 47, 53).

2. "Combed sidelocks" with bangs (part of Kletter's 5.III.3). Strands of hair (both in the "sidelocks" and on top of the head) are indicated by a series of vertical incised lines (see, e.g., Gitin 1995:fig. 4.17; 2003:fig. 4). The hair is often separated from the forehead by two horizontal lines, apparently representing a diadem or headband (see Gitin 1995:fig. 4.17). There are two subtypes: a) a large version (Gitin 1995:fig. 4.17; 2003:fig. 4), which is much larger than most other composite heads of any type; the head alone (without the neck) is about 6–7 cm high; and b) a small version (e.g., Petrie 1928:pl. XXXV.30), which is the same size as most other composite heads (about 4–5 cm in height for the head itself). Other than size, the two subtypes are largely identical. Cat. no. 46, the size of subtype b, is distinct in having a row of circles within the headband/diadem.

3. "Combed sidelocks" with part down the middle (part of Kletter's 5.III.2). Other than the part, the hair of this type is generally similar to that of Type 2. The most distinctive feature of these figurines is a necklace with a circular pendant or medallion in the center of the neck, decorated with a rosette (see Oren 1978:1069, second and third from left).[51]

4. Horizontal lines for "sidelocks" with bangs (Kletter's 5.III.1 and part of 5.III.2). This type can be either "finely molded" (Kletter's 5.III.2; e.g., Oren 1978:1069, first from left)[52] or cruder and more "schematic" (Kletter's 5.III.1; e.g., Gophna 1970:pl. VI.7). This type also has a necklace with pendant, which again appears to have a rosette decoration.

[51] The same photo appears in Oren 1993b:1333, but there the photo has been reversed. See also Oren 1982:159, second and third from left; Stern 2001:Ill. I.58, second and third from left.

[52] See also Oren 1993b: 1333, fourth from left; Oren 1982:159, first from left; Stern 2001:Ill. I.58, first from left.

5. Crude "combed sidelocks" with bangs. I have separated this type from Type 2 above because it is not only a cruder type artistically, but the facial features are also quite distinct. The face is smaller, and the eyes and mouth are ringed by thick ovals. The bangs are indicated by thick ridges. In addition, there is no double line above the forehead indicating a headband (e.g., Petrie 1928:pl. XXXVI.15, 18; 1933:pl. XVI.44). At Tell Jemmeh there may also be a mold of this type (Petrie 1928:pl. XXXVI.6).

6. Long "combed sidelocks" with part down the middle (part of Kletter's 5.III.3). This type has some similarities with Type 3, but the hair is longer (extending to the bottom of the neck), and there is no neck pendant (e.g., Petrie 1928:pl. XXXV.13, 17, 29; 1933:pl. XVI.43). The facial features are not well preserved on any of the extant examples.

7. Crescent hairstyle (Kletter's 5.III.5). The hairstyle forms a crescent around the head, similar to Type 8 but thinner and without circles for curls (e.g., Petrie 1928:pl. XXXV.14, 15, 23). The crescent extends down to the level of the chin.

8. Rows of curls (Kletter's JPF [Judean Pillar Figurine] Type B). This type is well known from Judah, as moldmade pillar figurine heads (Kletter 1996). The hairstyle is short, roughly down to the ear (as opposed to the previous types, whose hair/veil is chin- or shoulder-length). The hair is indicated by several rows of circles for curls (see, e.g., Miqne obj. nos. 3364, 6559). As with Type 4, there is also a cruder, more schematic form (e.g., Petrie 1928:pl. XXXVI.42). On the latter, the curls may be more rectangular and arranged along the lines of Type 4 above (Sera^{c} no. 1129; see Stern 2001:Ill. I.58, fifth from left).[53]

9. Handmade (Kletter's JPF Type A). This type is very simple in manufacture. The eyes are circular depressions and the nose is a thin ridge of clay; both are formed by pinching the clay (see Petrie 1928:pl. XXXVI.16; Gophna 1970:pl. VI.6). The tops of the heads are generally rounded and bare, but one (Petrie 1928:pl. XXXVI.16) wears a "turban" (Kletter's Type A.2), and another (Miqne obj. no. 6159/5965) has a "turban" and "sidelocks" (Kletter's Type A.3, or perhaps miscellaneous Type A.5).

[53] This latter type appears to consist of locally made JPF imitations unique to Philistia; see chapter 7.

One additional pattern among the above types is that Types 3 and 4 typically, if not always, have a neck pendant, while the other types never do.

Body Types

There are two main body types for the composite figurines. The first is a solid pillar body with emphasized breasts (Kletter's JPF Type C). Two examples from Philistia are complete, or nearly so (Miqne obj. no. 6159/5965; Ṣafi basket no. 110050/110650). In addition, the type is well known from Judah (Kletter 1996), so the basic form is clear. Most of the body is in the form of a fairly thin pillar or column, which flares out at the base in order to provide a secure stand. There is no differentiation of legs or any other body features in the column. The only body features indicated are the breasts, which are typically quite large, and the arms. The breasts and the arms are made as separate pieces of clay from the pillar body. All of these figurines display the same gesture: the hands rest under the breasts, with the arms supporting them.[54]

The second type of body is less uniform, and its complete form is not entirely certain. Unlike the first type, the body is typically hollow. There are no complete bodies of this hollow-bodied type preserved. An example from Miqne (Gitin 2003:fig. 4) is preserved below the waist and appears to be wearing a wide skirt. The entire form is essentially a straight-sided cylinder (with a nude torso and skirt below). It is likely that the other hollow-bodied examples had a similar skirt; at the break they still have a wide diameter and are not tapering to a pillar for the lower body (e.g., cat. nos. 59, 63). In fact, some examples (e.g., Petrie 1928:pl. XXXV.13) widen toward the bottom, giving the general appearance of a cone rather than a straight-sided cylinder; this body shape, however, is unusual. The upper bodies are nude, like the pillar type described above, and the most common gesture is also supporting the breasts (Petrie 1928:pl. XXXV.21; Gophna 1970:pl. VI.1), or cupping them (cat. no. 63). An example from Miqne (Gitin 2003:fig. 4) has the arms in two different positions along the torso; the right arm appears raised, but the hand is broken off. An Ashkelon example (cat. no. 59) cradles a child, also handmade. Finally, an example from Tell Jemmeh (Petrie 1928:pl. XXXV.14) and a second unprovenanced one from the area of Gaza (Humbert 2000:32–33) hold a large disc in front of the chest.

It appears that all figurines made in this technique are female and nude. There is to my knowledge only one example (cat. no. 62) of a torso without breasts depicted. In this case it is unclear whether the figurine was meant to represent a male, was represented as clothed, or if the breasts are somehow not preserved.

In addition, there are a few miscellaneous solid bodies. Cat. no. 37, a head and torso, has its arms only partially preserved, but they are clearly extending forward. Cat. no. 58 is a seated woman with the only preserved arm (the left arm) extending forward. The breasts are depicted, but the figure may be clothed. Cat. no. 61 also appears to be a seated figurine, but only the bottom of the legs and the base are preserved. All three of these bodies are handmade but otherwise do not seem to form a coherent type. The moldmade head of cat. no. 37 relates it to the hollow-bodied type above, but it is not clear if the seated figurines are similarly connected.

Overall, it is difficult to make a detailed assessment of the bodies, and particularly of their correspondence to the head types, because relatively few of them are known. At Ashkelon, for instance, where 22 heads were found in Iron Age levels, I can identify a total of only 9 bodies and possible body fragments. Even the more complete examples (cat. nos. 59, 63) were originally misidentified in the Ashkelon registration books, where they were labeled as "anthropomorphic bottles."[55] Given these difficulties, it is likely that some more fragmentary examples have been mislabeled or misplaced.

There are a few basic correspondences between the head types and the body types. The pillar body is found only with Type 8 and 9 heads, an observation which follows Kletter's work (his Type C bodies being associated with either Type A or B heads). The hollow cylinder bodies are associated with Type 1–7 heads (as apparently are the miscellaneous solid bodies). Beyond this, however, there does not seem to be a direct correspondence between gesture type and head type. The most common gesture, hands supporting or cupping breasts, is found with Type 2 heads (Miqne obj. no. 7133) as well as Type 4 heads (e.g., Gophna 1970:pl. VI.1). The gesture has not been found on any figurines with Type 1 and 3 heads, but this may simply be because no Type 1 and 3 heads have been found attached to a hollow body. The relationship of the gesture to the Type 5–7 heads is unclear, as only one or

[54] There are occasional pillar figurines in Judah with other gestures, such as holding a disc in front of the body (Kletter's Type C.1.d.; see Kletter 1996:fig. 4.3–4).

[55] In case there were any doubt as to the proper identification of these bodies, beyond the clear evidence of parallels in this technique from elsewhere in Philistia and in the wider Levant and Cyprus (see below), one need only look at cat. no. 59: the tang from a moldmade head is still present in the interior of the neck.

two examples of each type has even part of the body preserved. The other gestures on the hollow-bodied figurines are found only on single examples, and so no general conclusions about such correspondences can be made. Meanwhile, cat. no. 37 demonstrates that the Type 1 heads could also be used for solid-bodied figurines; the gesture of the arms is unclear, but is certainly distinct from the typical supporting or cupping the breasts.

Molds and Mass Production

The use of molds allowed for the production of large numbers of figurines quickly (cf. Karageorghis 1998:49; Kletter 1996:51; Dayagi-Mendels 2002:145). In addition, it allowed for standardization of types. It is to be expected, then, that sites in Philistia would produce groups of identical figurines—groups in which every figurine was made from the same mold. Of course, along with allowing a higher level of detail, this is a main purpose of the mold; it would not make much sense to produce a series of molds with each to be used once.

To this end, it appears that most of the Ashkelon heads were made in one of a small number of molds. In fact, of the 22 total heads of this type, 16 are likely identical with at least one other figurine (in some cases it is difficult to know for certain if figurines are identical, as some of the examples are very worn). I have been able to distinguish five different molds among these 16 heads. Two molds among these were particularly popular: 10 heads belong to one of these two molds, meaning that just two molds account for 45.5 percent of the total I.A.3 heads at Ashkelon. I have identified the five molds as follows:

1. Mold 1 (cat. nos. 37, 40, 41, 50, 52). The head is deep and round; the eyes are thin elongated ovals (in outline) tapering at the ends, and the eyebrows are relatively straight

2. Mold 2 (cat. nos. 33, 47). The head is flat, and the face thin and elongated; the eyes are wider than those of Mold 1, with high arching eyebrows.

3. Mold 3 (cat. nos. 34, 38, 43, 44, 54). The depth and roundness of the head, as well as the treatment of the eyes and eyebrows, fall between those of Molds 1 and 2; the face is circular, the eyes are solid raised circles, and the nose is large and "bulbous." This appears to have been the most popular mold at Ashkelon: besides the five examples listed above, there were two additional examples (reg. nos. 43556 and 43748) belonging to this mold but not included in the Iron Age corpus, as they were found (secondarily) in Persian period fill.

4. Mold 4 (cat. nos. 39, 49). The treatment of the eyes and eyebrows is similar to Mold 2, but the face is much rounder and deeper.

5. Mold 5 (cat. nos. 48, 51). The treatment of the eyes and eyebrows is similar to Mold 1, but the face is extremely deep and round.[56]

There is evidence that figurines made from the same mold were shared, not just within the same site, but between sites as well. The clearest example of this inter-site distribution is found in the relationship between figurines from Ashkelon and a small group from Tel Ṣippor.[57] Given that the relevant Ṣippor figurines have been dated to the Persian period, it is necessary to discuss the circumstances of this group in some detail. A cache of over 200 clay figurines was found in a *favissa* at the site and published in 1966 by O. Negbi. The *favissa* could not be dated stratigraphically, and so Negbi had to rely on the style of the figurines themselves for chronology. Negbi determined that the *favissa* dated to the Persian period based on the fact that most of the figurines were of Persian period style; additionally, she suggested a *terminus post quem* of the early fourth century for the actual date of deposit, as the latest figurines appeared to be of this date. While most of the figurines were clearly Persian period in style, Negbi dated a few (solid handmade horse and rider figurines and a plaque figurine) to the Iron Age (1966:8 n. 60–61). For the figurines in question (Negbi 1966:pl. 5 nos. 15–17), however, she suggested a date in the Persian period, as they were of a type distinct from the Iron Age composite figurines known at the time, the "Pillar-Astarte" type (Negbi 1966:8 n. 58, 12). The "Pillar-Astarte" type was in fact the well-known "pillar figurine" type, as defined especially by Albright (1939:120) and Pritchard (1943:23–27, 56–57). As these studies focused on the figurines from Albright's excavations at Tell Beit Mirsim, along with those from other sites dug in the early part of the twentieth century, their Iron II types were naturally biased

[56] After studying the Miqne figurines, I also concluded that several of those heads (e.g., Gitin 1995:fig. 4.17; 2003:fig. 4; obj. no. 7133) may well have been made from a single mold. S. Gitin (pers. comm., June 2006) suggests that these heads were the products of multiple molds; his suggestion, however, was based on inspection of the drawings alone, not of the figurines themselves. In any case, they are clearly very closely related not only in type but in style.

[57] Compare also the find of two Type 1 heads at Tel ᶜErani, discussed in chapter 7 below.

toward those of Judah (cf. chapter 3 above). It is therefore not surprising that Negbi was unable to locate Iron Age parallels for the Ṣippor figurines. Since Negbi published her work, however, excavations in other parts of Palestine have demonstrated that the "pillar Astarte" type is characteristic only of Iron Age Judah (Kletter 1996). Excavations at sites in the southern coastal plain in particular have shown that a variety of related but distinct types existed at this time, most significantly the examples discovered at Ashkelon in the 1990s. In addition, some of the figurines from Ben-Dor's excavations of the er-Ras cemetery at Akhziv, which Negbi cited as parallels for composite figurines from the Persian period (1966:8 n. 58), can now be dated to the Iron II on the basis of associated tomb finds (Dayagi-Mendels 2002:44, 77, 163).[58]

Certain heads from the Ashkelon excavations provide a particularly close parallel to Ṣippor nos. 15–17. They are so similar in form and style that it is likely they were produced in the same mold. In particular, Ṣippor no. 16 (and likely no. 17 as well) appears identical to figurines produced from Mold 3, the most popular mold at Ashkelon. Ṣippor no. 15 bears a close resemblance to the Mold 1 figurines, but in this instance it is less clear if they are in fact identical.[59] Ultimately, it is necessary to compare the figurines themselves before a secure identification can be made.[60]

R. V. Nicholls's work on moldmade figurines has provided additional insights into aspects of mass production in terracotta (1952). His work focused in particular on the "series," a group of figurines from a single archetype; he suggested that all figurines in a series were not necessarily from the same mold, but from second- (or third-, etc.) generation molds. In this case, a new mold would be produced from one of the figurines made in the original mold, and this mold in turn would produce a new set of (second-generation) figurines. Nicholls determined that, with each new generation, a certain amount of shrinkage would occur with air drying (and, to a lesser extent, with firing, 1952:220). According to Nicholls, the amount of shrinkage varies, depending on certain conditions: the clay, how it is prepared, and the shape of the mold; unfortunately, he did not suggest a range for the percent of shrinkage.[61] I attempted to apply Nicholls's procedure to the Ashkelon moldmade heads; in particular, Molds 1 and 3 provided two relatively large groups (series) of figurines to test. The process depends upon being able to take facial measurements consistently on a group of figurines (cf. Nicholls 1952:224 n. 47). Unfortunately, many of the Ashkelon figurines are so worn that their facial features are not well preserved; as a result, it was difficult even to find consistent points on the face from which to take the measurements. I ultimately took three sets of measurements: the distance from top of face to chin (one of Nicholls's two recommended measurements [1952:224 n. 47]), the width of face at eye level, and the distance from the ends of the two eyebrows. In many cases, however, I was unable to be certain about the points on the faces from which to take the measurements, due to the poor state of preservation. As a result, the measurements from two figurines would not even vary in the same direction: one measurement would be larger on figurine A, while another would be larger on figurine B. It was therefore impossible to determine if more than one generation of figurines was produced at Ashkelon. In any case, where they were clear the measurements generally did not vary beyond 15 percent. Based on Nicholls's (and Kelso and Thorley's) work, I would suggest that there were no more than two generations among the Mold 1 and Mold 3 heads, if that many.[62]

[58] Stern (1982:179) misstated Negbi's conclusions about the "Pillar Astarte" figurines from Ṣippor, stating that she had dated them to the Iron Age. Regardless, Stern, like Negbi, wrongly concluded that they were products of the Persian period, based on differences with the then-known corpus of Iron Age "pillar" figurines.

[59] L. E. Stager has suggested to me that this Ṣippor figurine is a pregnant woman typical of the Persian period. That figurine type, however, is hollow and completely moldmade (see I.A.5 below), and it appears that the body of the Ṣippor example is handmade; compare especially cat. no. 37.

[60] There are other possible instances in which figurines from different sites were produced in a single mold, particularly among the sites in southern Philistia. Originally in my 2007 dissertation I had suggested that a Type 2b figurine from Tel Seraᶜ (no. 1200; see Oren 1978:1069, fourth from left; 1993b:1333, first from left; Stern 2001:Ill. I.58, fourth from left) was extremely similar to the Miqne Type 2a heads, before realizing the difference in sizes between the two. On the other hand, Seraᶜ no. 1200 is very similar to certain Type 2b heads from Tell Jemmeh (esp. Petrie 1928:pl. XXXV.30); E. Oren (pers. comm., June 2006) also suggests that Seraᶜ no. 1200 may have been made in the same mold as a head from Tell el-Farᶜah (S).

[61] Kletter (1996:51) states that Nicholls had determined a shrinkage rate of 13–14 percent with each generation. In fact, Nicholls does not give a general value; Kletter has simply calculated the rate of shrinkage for the one series of figurines for which Nicholls provides data (1952:220). As Kletter notes, however, Kelso and Thorley (1943:138) estimated a shrinkage rate of about 15 percent between mold and figurine. These studies together suggest an approximate range for the rate of shrinkage.

[62] As Nicholls (1952:220) concluded that first-generation figurines were probably produced by the same workshop responsible for the original mold, while later generations could be made by anyone (allowing for export and diffusion of a single series), it is perhaps unsurprising that the

Origins/Iconography

The origin of the composite figurine technique is clear only in general terms: it was in some sense Cypro-Phoenician. The underlying problem is the complex and intimate relationship between Cypriot and Phoenician terracottas (see Vandenabeele 1985; 1986:351–56; Gubel 1991; see also chapter 7), which is complicated in turn by our incomplete knowledge of Iron Age Phoenician figurines (cf. Markoe 2000:143; Gubel 1983:23–24; Kletter 1996:53; see chapter 7 for further discussion). Birmingham stated that the technique was in use on Cyprus primarily in the eighth century, but that it was common in mainland Phoenicia and the Levant in the seventh century (1963:20). This suggestion follows the idea that use of the figurine mold on Cyprus began relatively early, perhaps in the ninth century; Vandenabeele (1986:351) suggested that it was brought by Phoenician colonists when they settled at Kition. More recently, however, it has become clear that the figurine mold was not introduced into Cyprus until after the start of the Cypro-Archaic period, i.e., in the late eighth or seventh century. Karageorghis (1998:49), in his detailed catalogue of Cypriot figurines, demonstrated that the earliest datable examples of moldmade terracottas—both large statues and small figurines—in the large corpus associated with the sanctuary at Ayia Irini can be assigned to ca. 670.[63] While these examples are among the earliest Cypriot figurines in the composite technique, Karageorghis's own excavations at Kition-Kathari yielded four examples of composite figurines from Floor 3 (Karageorghis 1999:pls. 14.3268A, 18.3345, 20.4624, 23.4937) and one more between Floors I and 3 (Karageorghis 1999:pl. 3.4645). These finds strongly suggest that the technique was introduced to Kition prior to the end of the eighth century, as the end of Floor 3 is dated to ca. 725 (Karageorghis 2005:103–7) or ca. 707 (Smith 2009, esp. xviii). Meanwhile, there is not a single moldmade figurine—even a plaque figurine—known from the preceding Cypro-Geometric period (ending in the mid-eighth century; see Karageorghis 1993a; Vandenabeele 1991).

The origin of this technique is now considered to be the Levant (cf. Kletter 1996:53), and most likely Phoenicia. Unfortunately, as mentioned above, the Iron Age figurines of Phoenicia are only imperfectly known, and so their exact chronology cannot yet be determined. Even with the limited data currently available, however, it is clear that the use of the technique in Phoenicia was fairly widespread by the second half of the eighth century. A composite frame-drum player (Bikai 1978:pl. 81.2) was found in Tyre Stratum II (second half of the eighth century). Shiqmona has produced a similar frame-drum player in this technique; although the results have not been fully published, preliminary reports state that the figurine and several other composite figurines were found in two strata dating to the late ninth and early eighth centuries (Elgavish 1993:1374–75; 1994:34, 67–68); based on the pottery published from the strata containing these figurines, however, a date in the mid- to late-eighth century for these two strata is likelier.[64] For Israel and Judah, it appears that the type likely originated in the second half of the eighth century. According to Kletter, Israelite sites not reoccupied after eighth-century destructions had few figurines of this type, while those that continued into the seventh century produced many more (1996:41).[65]

Given the probable Phoenician origin of the composite technique, it would not be surprising to find Phoenician influence on the imagery of figurines made in this technique. In particular, the treatment of the moldmade heads finds many parallels in Phoenician art. The "combed sidelocks," "bangs," and headband or diadem of the Type 2 heads are all paralleled by the female heads among the eighth- to seventh-century "Phoenician" ivories from Nimrud, including the famous "Woman at the Window" (Mallowan 1966:vol. I, figs. 153–54; vol. II: figs. 458, 549; Barnett 1982:50, pl. 50b; see also Pritchard 1954:fig. 131).[66] This relationship was pointed out by Dornemann (in connection with composite figurines from Transjordan), who also highlighted Egyptianizing elements of the ivories and figurines such as almond-shaped eyes (1983:132–34).

More recently, S. Gitin (2003:287) has pointed to parallels with another class of objects: the Phoenician protomes.[67] These objects, related to the well-known Phoenician masks, were terracotta female

figurines of a single site (Ashkelon) should not show clear evidence for multiple generations of figurines.

[63] For the date of the Ayia Irini sculptures, along with the important group of Cypriot terracottas from the Samian Heraion, and the implications for dating the composite technique on Cyprus, see Gjerstad et al. 1935:815–19; Gjerstad 1948:207, 334–35, 355; Schmidt 1968:4–8, 93–98; Karageorghis 1993b:6.

[64] A late eighth-century date for the Shiqmona drummer was first suggested to me by Avshalom Zemer (pers. comm., February 2011), although this suggestion was based simply on the figurine's similarity to the Tyre example and not on the date of its context.

[65] For further discussion of this problem, see chapter 7.

[66] See also a Phoenician ivory head from Shrine 1 at Sarepta, of roughly the same date (Pritchard 1975:fig. 43.1; 1988:fig. 29.26).

[67] Gitin, however, incorrectly refers to these protomes as figurines.

heads—roughly twice the size of a typical composite figurine head—often deposited in tombs (see C. G. Picard 1967; Culican 1975/76; Stern 1978; and Ciasca 1999 for discussions of this class of artifacts). They are best known from Phoenician (Punic) colonies in the western Mediterranean, having been found at Carthage, Motya (Sicily), and Tharros and Sulcis (Sardinia). As the protomes are made of clay, it is not surprising that they provide an even closer parallel to the composite figurine heads than the Phoenician ivories. Of particular importance is Stern's Type A, the protomes of "Phoenicio-Egyptian influence"; Stern himself compares this type to "the well-known 'Astarte' figurines" (1978:114). Stern's Type A can be divided into two groups, both dating to the seventh to sixth centuries. One, which Culican labels the "klaft" group, has a headdress rendered in two solid columns along the sides of the face (Culican 1975/76:79–81, figs. 24, 26); the other group is characterized by an Egyptian-type hairstyle or wig, with the hair "striated vertically" and with a diadem on the forehead (Culican 1975/76:81; Stern 1978:114; for examples, see Ciasca 1999:410, 414; Culican 1975/76:figs. 22, 28). While the hair or headdress of the first ("klaft") group is somewhat reminiscent of the Type 1 composite heads, the second group is extremely similar to the Type 2 heads in both imagery and style. Both Type 1 and Type 2 figurine heads, like both groups of Type A protomes, have Egyptianizing almond-shaped eyes and long, thin eyebrows, and have eyes and eyebrows in low relief. The stylistic and technical aspects of the second protome group, however, parallel the Type 2 heads almost exactly.[68]

While the Type 2 figurine heads and the protomes provide the closest set of iconographic parallels, additional connections can be drawn, both among other classes of Phoenician material culture and among the other types of composite figurine heads. For instance, the Egyptianizing elements found in the protomes and ivories are also paralleled in examples of Phoenician and Punic jewelry (see Pisano 1999:478–79 for examples from Tharros). The neck pendants of the Type 3 and 4 heads, meanwhile, are reminiscent of that on a gold plaque from a tomb in Lapithos (Cyprus), dated to CG III (Gjerstad et al. 1934:187, pl.51.2). The hairstyle of the figure on the plaque, including the horizontal "sidelocks," is similar to that of the Type 4 heads. The short curled hairstyle of the Type 8 (moldmade JPF) heads is also found on female figures on a series of pottery plaques (and a mold) of nude females flanking the door of a building (A. Mazar 1982; 1985b; Ward 1996). Unfortunately, these objects have not generally been found in excavations but purchased on the antiquities market, and so their date and provenance can only be guessed. At the time of purchase, the mold published by Mazar (1985b:12–13, figs. 20a–b) was said to be from the region of Gaza. Mazar suggests it was associated with a Phoenician colony in the vicinity of Gaza in the late Iron II (1985b:14; cf. Stern 2001:68–69), based on Culican's publication of a "Phoenician" cemetery at Tell er-Reqeish (Ruqeish, see Culican 1973). Ward suggested a broader range for the distribution of these objects, throughout the southern Levant and into Egypt (1996:15). Both, however, concluded that the artistic style is closely related to Phoenician art (A. Mazar 1985b:12; Ward 1996:15, 18).[69] Mazar (1985b:12) relates this hairstyle as well to the Phoenician ivories.

As for the iconography of the nude female and her gestures, these will be discussed below under I.A.4. This leaves one additional aspect of the composite figurines to be mentioned: the column base of the pillar body type. The pillar figurines are most commonly interpreted today as representations of Asherah (for discussion, see Kletter 1996:73–81, esp. 76–77).

[68] Note also a protome of this group from Akhziv (Dayagi-Mendels 2002:fig. 7.21).

[69] Ward also observed the Egyptianizing aspect of Phoenician art at work in this case. As he noted (1996:8 n. 3), the curled hairstyle of the plaques (and the Type 8 or moldmade JPF figurines) is paralleled in a series of Egyptian bronzes dating to the Third Intermediate Period and especially to the time of the 25th Dynasty (mid-eighth to mid-seventh centuries B.C.E.). For examples see, e.g., Fechheimer 1921:pls. 98–100, 102–3, 106–9; 1923:pl. 100. Thus, the curled hairstyle could have come into Judah (and Philistia) in the eighth century either directly from Egypt or indirectly from Egypt via Phoenicia. Ward also notes (1996:8 n. 3) that this short hairstyle may have ultimately derived from Old Kingdom models, although the Old Kingdom parallels occur exclusively on male figures.

Darby (2011:512–14) traces the curled hairstyle to a revival of Old Kingdom styles in the Third Intermediate Period, in turn influencing the art of Phoenicia and Syria in Iron IIB (ninth-eighth centuries). She notes that on seals, ivories, and metal reliefs, the hairstyle appears on both high-status humans and sphinxes—in contrast with representations of ordinary female hair in Judah, such as on the Lachish reliefs of Sennacherib—and therefore concludes that they are meant to represent (minor) divine or attending figures. However, in Syrian and Phoenician art at least some of the examples are male figures, whereas the Third Intermediate Period examples are all female and human (albeit apparently high status) rather than divine. The case may therefore not be as clear-cut as presented by Darby, although her observations deserve to be kept in mind for understanding the meaning and function of the figures with the curled hairstyle.

In the iconography of the figurines, however, there is little evidence in favor of such a connection. R. Hestrin (1991:57) popularized the idea that the pillar base represents a tree trunk, and so is related to imagery of Asherah (although the same suggestion had already been made by Kelso and Thorley [1943:138]). This explanation, however, is very unlikely. The pillar or column base is simply a solution—and a common one at that—to the problem of making a figurine free-standing (as also concluded by Kletter [1996:77] and Keel and Uehlinger [1998:331–32]). Many other types of figurines in the Aegean and Near East have a similar base: the Philistine standing figurines discussed above (I.A.1) and their Mycenaean antecedents are an obvious example. To this we can also add the trumpet or "funnel" base (Myres 1897:165, 167–68) ubiquitous on the thousands of examples of Cypro-Archaic female figurines (see Karageorghis 1998). These latter figurines provide close parallels for the Judahite pillar figurines, as many of them are the Cypriot versions of the composite figurines; yet no one would identify the Cypriot figurines as representations of Asherah. In the end, a purely functional interpretation of the pillar base is likely the best.[70]

I.A.4. Plaque figurines (Cat. Nos. 64–70)

The plaque figurine type has been found in most if not all phases of the Iron Age in Philistia (see chapter 7 below on distribution and questions concerning it); it is the only human figurine type to have such a long lifespan. It is the continuation of an LB type which was the predominant type of human figurine in the period.[71]

This figurine type, generally 10–15 cm high, was formed as a single piece in a mold, in essentially the same method used for the composite heads discussed above. Only the front of the figurine was formed in the mold; the back was left unfinished and later smoothed by hand (as with the composite heads). The result is a figurine, depicted in a full frontal view, that rises in relief from a flat background.

In Philistia, this type of figurine was used exclusively to represent women. Moreover, the women depicted are always nude. Most of the Iron Age plaques in Philistia depict women with a restricted number of gestures:

1. arms down at the sides (e.g., cat. no. 64);
2. hands to the breasts, usually cupping them (e.g., cat. no. 68; Miqne obj. no. 3235, 5667); and
3. arms cradling a child (e.g., cat. no. 66).

A combination of gestures 1 and 2 is also common: see, e.g., Ashdod D190/7 (M. Dothan and Freedman 1967:fig. 43.4) and Ashdod H436/1 (M. Dothan and Ben-Shlomo 2005:fig. 3.96.4). This hybrid type is generally depicted with a rounded stomach, suggesting pregnancy. There are a small number of figurines, however, that do not fit within the above groups.

As can be seen from the above list, there is a large degree of similarity between the gestures of the plaque figurines and those of the composite figurines; in particular, the gestures of cupping the breasts and cradling a child occur in both types. Cupping the breasts is easily the most common gesture in each type. The hairstyle of the plaque figurines is generally long and flowing, ending in "bulbs" at shoulder length (e.g., cat. no. 64; Ashdod D190/7 [M. Dothan and Freedman 1967:fig. 43.4]). This hairstyle is similar to that of the Type 1 and Type 2 composite figurine heads. Sometimes the figures wear necklaces or bracelets (e.g., Kochavi 1976:pl. 11c [= Kochavi 1989:fig. 75]); these features are not found on the composite figurines but do appear on the Phoenician parallels in ivory and metal. Overall, however, the similarities between the two types of figurines are quite strong and suggest that they shared a common referent (or referents). They also raise the possibility that both types had the same basic function (see chapter 7 for further discussion).

It has long been known that the ultimate origin of the plaque technique is Mesopotamia, where it is found already in the third millennium (Pritchard 1943:ch. 3, esp. 49; Riis 1949:49; Moorey 2003:27–28). Like the handmade female figurine type before it (see discussion at the beginning of the chapter), the moldmade technique for plaques spread from Mesopotamia west

[70] The only evidence that Hestrin offers in support of her interpretation is that there are three elements to the pillar figurine—pillar, breasts, and head—and while the last one may be handmade or moldmade, the first two are always handmade. She therefore concludes that the pillar and breasts are the most significant elements of the figurine, with both representing the life-giving aspects of the mother goddess (1991:57). This judgment is, of course, completely subjective. I could conclude at least as easily that, because the head is often moldmade, resulting in an additional attention to detail, it is the most significant element in the figurine. Moreover, on several eighth-century examples from Judah, the bodies of the JPFs are in fact not solid handmade pillars but hollow wheelmade cylinders (e.g., Holland 1977:fig. 7.6, 8–9 [Jerusalem]; Tufnell 1953:pl. 28.10, 13 [Lachish]).

[71] See the discussion at the beginning of this chapter concerning some basic aspects of the plaque figurines in contrast with the Iron I standing figurines (I.A.1–2).

to Syria and then down to Palestine, where it is present by the middle of the second millennium (Moorey 2003:34–35).[72] As in Mesopotamia, the one-piece mold was used in Palestine to produce plaque figurines of nude women (see, e.g., van Buren 1930:pls. III–XII). In Mesopotamia, however, the nude woman was only one of a series of figures that could be depicted on plaques (see, e.g., Moorey 2003:29); in Palestine, plaques were used exclusively for this figure.

Scholars have traditionally divided the LB plaque figurines from Palestine into two basic types (for discussion, see, e.g., Pritchard 1943; Keel and Uehlinger 1998:ch. 4; Moorey 2003:37–40). The first portrays the nude woman with her arms bent and forearms extending outward, holding various items such as serpents or lotus flowers. These attributes, along with the Hathor headdress that the figure often wears,[73] point to Egyptian influence. The second portrays the nude woman with arms at the breasts or down at the sides, without any attributes. Traditionally, the first type has been labeled "Qadesh" or "Qudshu," while the second type has been labeled "Astarte."[74] Moorey emphasizes that these names are merely conventional and do not indicate identification with specific goddesses (2003:38–39). Nevertheless, as Pritchard noted (1943:33–34), the name for the first type derives from a series of Egyptian reliefs with similar figures, where the figure is often identified as Qedeshet and described as a goddess (see Cornelius 2004:48–52, 123–29, nos. 5.1–5.10, 5.14–5.18; Pritchard 1954:figs. 471–74).[75]

Regardless, the "Qudshu" type seems to have disappeared from Palestine by the early Iron Age, coinciding with the collapse of Egyptian power in Canaan. Certainly, there are no known examples from Iron Age Philistia. The only plaque type that concerns us is the second, "Astarte" type. As with other female figurines, this type has been generally accepted in the scholarly literature as representing a goddess, usually considered to be a "fertility goddess" (see, e.g., Albright 1939:114; A. Mazar 1992a:273). Keel and Uehlinger have made a recent attempt to identify this figure as a goddess through iconographic analysis (1998:97–103). Others, however, have concluded that this figure is more likely a mortal woman. M. Tadmor (1982; 1996) suggested that at least some of the plaques (with a large flat background and with the figure's feet set together) represent a woman lying on a bed. This type is also known in Middle and New Kingdom Egypt (Pinch 1983:406; 1993:207–9). Moorey, who in general is cautious about identifying figurines as divine images, has argued that there is no clear evidence that the "Astarte" type represents a goddess (2003:40).

In order to address this problem more completely, it is necessary to survey the history of the nude female in Levantine iconography. Such a diachronic study can be full of pitfalls. As an example, let us consider Dever's evaluation of the nude female in the lowest register of the tenth-century cult stand found by Lapp at Taanach (Lapp 1969:42–44, fig. 29). Dever believes the evidence that this figure is the goddess Asherah to be "overwhelming" (2005:220). The evidence he presents, however, dates almost exclusively to the Late Bronze Age and mixes material from Egypt and different parts of the Levant (Dever 2005:220; 1984:28–29). In addition, none of the material directly equates any nude figure with Asherah. The problem in our case is compounded even further, as the history of the nude figure covers over a millennium and stretches throughout the Levant and Egypt. Keel and Uehlinger (1998:10–11) and Lipiński (1986) voice similar cautions in their review of U. Winter's monumental but problematic *Frau und Göttin* (1983). Lewis specifically notes the fundamental flaw in the frequent use of the Winchester College relief (see Edwards 1955), the New Kingdom Qudshu relief that features as a central piece of evidence in Dever's argument: Egyptian iconography "should not be privileged in reconstructing the Ugaritic pantheon" (Lewis 2005:72–73 n. 13). Any diachronic review, then, must be as careful as possible to separate iconographic and textual data by period and geographic area. In the following, then, I will briefly present the data period by period, attempting to see if we can reach any conclusions concerning the meaning(s) of the nude female(s) and to see if the meaning changed over time. It is of course impossible for me to cover the full range of objects or discuss them in much detail in this space. I will therefore highlight significant aspects of image types, as well as

[72] While the type is commonly found from LB I, Albright reported finding plaque figurines already in Stratum D (MB IIC) at Tell Beit Mirsim (1939:114; cf. Lapp 1969:45 for similar finds at Taanach).

[73] The so-called Hathor wig, or scroll wig, is thick and long, with the sidelocks curving inward along the neck and curling at the end around the shoulder. This hairstyle came to be associated with depictions of the head of Hathor and matches literary references to her flowing hair (see, e.g., Pinch 1993:134–35, 216).

[74] These were perhaps first suggested by Albright; see Albright 1939:118–19; 1942:75; 1943:26.

[75] In additon, there are a series of texts, especially from Ugarit, that appear to employ the word *qudšu* as an epithet of Astarte. These were already gathered by Albright (1938:118; 1942:196 n. 17); more recently, Maier (1986:81–96) concluded after a detailed textual study that *qdš* was rather an epithet of Aṯirat (see also Hadley 2000:127–28). At the same time, compare the survey of Qedeseht, Asherah, and other deities by Cornelius (2004:94–99), who observes that in the Egyptian texts Qedeshet is an independent goddess.

special examples or groups that are particularly crucial for understanding the iconography of the general type. In addition, I hope that such an analysis may begin to hint at the possible function(s) of these images, a more fundamental issue.

Keel and Uehlinger, among others, have traced the image of the nude female back to the Middle Bronze Age (1998:26–28; cf. Cornelius 2004:55–58). Ultimately, they find the source of the representation in Old Syrian cylinder seals. N. Marinatos, in her analysis of this figure on seals, has demonstrated that she is not directly involved in the main action of these seals but instead appears to represent a minor goddess functioning as a magical intermediary (2000:1–7). Meanwhile, on MBIIB scarabs there is a figure Schroer (1989) refers to as the "nackte Göttin" ("Naked Goddess") or "Zweiggöttin" (Branch Goddess; also Keel and Uehlinger 1998:26–28; Keel 1995:211). This figure is, as the name suggests, almost always (on 36 of 44 examples) associated with plant branches, one on each side (see Schroer 1989:97–99, nos. 1–44; also Keel 1995:Abb. 422–29; Keel and Uehlinger 1998:27, nos. 10–12c). She appears frontal and nude (while the breasts are rarely shown, the pubic triangle is almost always indicated), either with the face toward the viewer or to the side. Her gestures vary: she may hold the two branches, she may hold her hands on her chests (i.e., in the area where the breasts would be if depicted), or she may have her arms along the sides. While the association with the branches suggests the lotus flowers of the LB Qudshu plaques, it is significant that the other main gestures of the LB plaques—holding the breasts (rare on the Qudshu plaques) and arms along the sides (to my knowledge present only on the "Astarte" plaques)—are also depicted. Besides the fact that full frontal depictions and female nudity are rare not only on scarabs but in Egyptian depictions generally (at least, in the case of female nudity, for divine figures), the findspots of these scarabs are worth noting. Just three have been found in Egypt, and there only at the Delta sites of Tell ed-Dabᶜa and Tell el-Yehudiyeh—both sites strongly associated with Levantine influence or actual presence; the rest have either been found in Palestine or have an unknown provenance (Keel 1995:211; Keel and Uehlinger 1998:26). Therefore, it appears that this scarab type is typical of Canaan and not of Egypt.

Similar representations are found among metal figurines of women, apparently nude, holding their breasts (see, e.g., Negbi 1976:figs. 82–85, 92, 94, pls. 40, 42). These objects were produced and used in both the MB and LB. These should be considered likely cult images or other representations of deities due to their material as well as to their findspots, often associated with temples (see Keel and Uehlinger 1998:29–37; Negbi 1976). In addition, certain examples (e.g., Negbi 1976:fig. 93) show an alternate gesture of arms hanging down along the sides, and some (e.g., Negbi 1976:figs. 93–94) wear a horned headdress, an attribute widely associated with divinity.

Beyond these metal figures, there is a series of representations of a nude female in a variety of media—clay, metal, and stone—in the Late Bronze Age, from Egypt as well as the Levant. Looking at the clay plaques as part of this larger group, rather than on their own, we may no longer be tempted to divide them so starkly into two types (Qudshu and Astarte). Instead, it may be better to view these representations as a spectrum, showing a gradual transition from one type to the next:

1. On one end stand the Qudshu reliefs from Egypt, which explicitly identify the nude figure as the goddess Qudshu. These figures are nude, full frontal, holding a lotus and/or a serpent, and stand on a lion (Cornelius 2004:nos. 5.1–5.10, 5.14–5.18).

2. Similar to these are the gold plaques of a female figure standing on an animal (see Negbi 1976:99–100, 191, figs. 117–19, 128, pls. 53–54; Cornelius 2004:130–34, nos. 5.20–5.23, 5.27–5.30). Such objects are found throughout the Levant, from Minet el-Beida and Zincirli in the north to sites such as Akko in Palestine. Generally the animal is a lion, but on an example from Lachish (Clamer 1980; 2004), as well as a mold from Tel Qarnayim (Ben-Arieh 1983), the figure stands on a horse. While the figure(s) is not named, the representation is otherwise almost identical to the Qudshu reliefs: nude, usually full frontal (although not in the case of the Lachish plaque), and holding similar objects (lotus stalks and serpents, but also gazelles). Beyond the fact that the similar Qudshu reliefs are labeled, the pose of standing on an animal is widely associated with divinity in the ancient Near East (see Clamer's discussion [2004:1316, with references]; Cornelius 1994:195–97; 2004:50). Most of these figures have the Hathor headdress; the Lachish and Qarnayim examples, meanwhile, wear horned crowns, again suggesting divinity.[76] In addition, the Lachish horse is wearing armor. Stager offers an alternate explanation that the nude figure on the armored horse is Ishtar/Astarte, the Near Eastern goddess of sex and war (2000:6).

[76] Barrelet (1958) has also published two similar examples from the Louvre, of uncertain provenance but said to be from Syria; the female figure in one of these examples has a Hathor headdress and wings.

3. Among three LB clay plaques of nude females from Tel Ḥarasim, two are depicted holding lotus flowers and standing on a crouching animal, apparently a lion (Givon 1991a:24–25, pl. 7:1, 3, photos 3–4, nos. 2069, 2071; 1991b:146, fig. 163). Other than being produced in a more inexpensive medium (clay), these examples are largely identical to the Qudshu-type figures standing on lions in no. 2 above; the one example with a head preserved shows the Hathor headdress as well.

4. Other clay plaques from Canaan depict the same Qudshu type, but without a lion (see Cornelius 2004:52–57, 134–42, nos. 5.32–5.61a; Pritchard 1943:6–9, Type I). Often these figures hold lotus stalks (but not serpents or gazelles), as in nos. 2 and 3 above, but in rare cases they hold the breasts, with lotus stalks framing the edges of the plaque (Macalister 1912b:pls. CCXX.21, CCXXI.5 [Gezer]).

5. Finally, there are the clay plaques without the Hathor headdress ("Astarte" type; see Pritchard 1943:10–18, Types II–III), but often with the same gesture of holding breasts (others have the arms down along the sides of the body, or, rarely, holding a child).

There is no clear divide, then, between types and media, and while these may not represent the same figure, they are certainly a set of closely related representations. Note also that, while the "Naked Goddess" scarabs mentioned above date to the MB, the iconography of the scarabs—including the range of gestures—closely parallels that of the plaques and other LB representations, making it at least plausible that they represent the same figure(s).

At this point we must return to Tadmor's suggestion (1982; 1996) that at least some of the clay plaques from Canaan represent human women lying on beds. This interpretation, based on analogy with contemporary Egyptian examples (Pinch 1983:406; 1993:207–9), makes less sense for the Levantine plaques. The Egyptian plaques more clearly depict the background of the plaque as a bed. Perhaps more significantly, Egyptian iconography rarely represents goddesses as nude. In fact, the few instances of Egyptian depictions of nude goddesses—on Hyksos scarabs or Qudshu representations on reliefs—are generally considered to be of a Levantine figure or under Levantine influence (Pritchard 1943:86; Pinch 1993:216). Given that the nudity of Levantine goddesses is the issue under question here, and that there is greater evidence for such depictions, the analogy cannot be assumed. Instead, we may have an example of cross-cultural borrowing, where in Egypt the plaque type was reinterpreted.

For much of the Iron Age, the iconography of the nude female is much more limited, other than the small set of plaque figurines from Philistia, as well as examples from other parts of Palestine. In Iron IIA there are a few representations of deities standing on animals: a stone slab from Beth Shean, Level V and tenth- to ninth-century seals (Uehlinger 1997:104, 109–10; also Keel and Uehlinger 1998:141). It is not clear, however, if these figures were meant to be represented as nude. Beginning at this time are also a series of cult stands, shrine models, and plaques with entrances flanked by nude female figures (e.g., the Taanach cult stand [Lapp 1969:42–44, fig. 29; Beck 1994; Frick 2000:117–28, figs. 19–20]; a cult stand from Rehov [A. Mazar 2003:150–51]; and the Yavneh stands [e.g., Ziffer and Kletter 2007:Stands 2006-1046 and 1047; Ziffer 2010:66–67, 69, 75; Kletter, Ziffer, and Zwickel 2010:220–21, CAT28, 29]; see also the discussion of the shrine plaques above, with iconographic parallels for the composite figurine heads). The most common gesture on the large group of Yavneh cult stands is that of hands to the breasts (Ziffer 2010:66), with two of the Yavneh examples depicting such figures standing on lions (Ziffer and Kletter 2007:Stands 2006-1046 and 1047 [= Kletter, Ziffer, and Zwickel 2010:CAT28, 29]). These figures could plausibly be interpreted as protective deities guarding doorways, but direct evidence for their identity is lacking.

More relevant to the current discussion, perhaps, is a group of Iron II metal and ivory frontlets for horses from northern Levantine sites such as Tayinat and Zincirli, as well as exported examples at Samos and Miletus in the Aegean, depicting nude female figures holding their breasts (see, e.g., Kantor 1962; Ornan 2005:92–93). The Tayinat examples are also noteworthy for showing the female figures standing on lion heads (Kantor 1962:pls. XI–XIII). These objects could conceivably have served a protective function, for horses in battle. Also of note from this period is a seventh- or sixth-century bronze statuette from Cerro del Carambolo in Spain; it depicts a nude woman seated and has an inscription on the base identifying the figurine as a votive offering to Astarte (Solá-Solé 1966; see also Ammerman 1991:219, fig. 18).[77] Other than

[77] The inscription refers to *ʿštrtḥr, ʿAštarte-Ḥor*, which F. M. Cross (1971) translated as "Hurrian Astarte." This interpretation equates Astarte with Ishtar, the Near Eastern goddess of sex and war (Stager 2000:6). As J. Teixidor (1975) has pointed out, *ḫu-ru* in Egyptian texts refers to inhabitants of the Levant generally, while the third-century trilingual Decree of Canopus translates demotic "region of the Ḫors" in the Greek text as "Phoenician." Thus, the Spanish

its seated posture, the depiction is similar to that of the plaque figurines; there is an even closer similarity to the composite figurines, as the "combed sidelocks," "bangs," and diadem parallel the Type 2 heads closely. It is important to remember that the findspot of this statuette is Spain, and not the Levant. As Markoe points out, the Carambolo figurine is also unique in having an inscription (2000:125). Moreover, even the evidence of the inscription is ambiguous: as it merely identifies the figurine as an offering to Astarte, it cannot be stated with certainty that the figure represented is Astarte, as opposed to a worshipper. Nevertheless, the seated position—as noted above in the discussion of the Ashdoda—is one of authority.

The brief survey above demonstrates that there is solid evidence that, in multiple periods, the nude female figure represents a Levantine goddess (or goddesses). There is also some reason to believe that it may be a minor deity or deities, perhaps of a protective nature. Note that Darby (2011) and Meyers (2007) have recently proposed this interpretation for the Judean pillar figurines.[78] While many of these objects come from the northern Levant, or beyond, they suggest the continuation of a manner of representing female deities going back to the Bronze Age. At the same time, we do have representations of cult images of the Levant—and perhaps from Philistia itself—in Neo-Assyrian reliefs. Two reliefs in particular, one of Tiglath-pileser III from the South-West Palace at Nimrud (Layard 1849:pl. 65) and the second of Sennacherib from the South-West Palace at Nineveh (Layard 1853:pl. 50), depict the procession of captured cult images from cities in the west, and perhaps specifically from Gaza and Ashkelon (see Barnett 1985; Uehlinger 1997:124–28; Ornan 2005:94–95, esp. n. 285 with references). These figures, both male and female, are all depicted as dressed. However, we cannot use these images to generalize uncritically about the representation of all Levantine (or Philistine) deities: they may merely indicate Assyrian (mis-)representation of Levantine deities (note that many aspects of their iconography—symbols such as the ring, hairstyle, and horned headdress—reflect typical Assyrian representations of deities); they may represent only certain divinities, and not others, particularly not minor divinities; or they may represent deities in only certain contexts or forms. We might conclude, then, that for much of the Levant and throughout much of its history, the region contrasts strongly with Egypt (as well as with Mesopotamia) in that goddesses—at least minor goddesses, or goddesses in certain contexts—were more widely depicted as nude.

As to the character of the specific gestures, supporting the breasts has (along with general nudity and emphasis of the genital area) been interpreted as relating to fertility (as mentioned above). A comparison with the Egyptian plaques, however, may be illuminating. Pinch observes that most of the Egyptian types can depict children and so suggests that the figurines are generally associated with childbirth and child rearing, as opposed to simply with sexuality. The plaques from Palestine, and in particular the Iron Age plaques of Philistia, on the other hand, rarely depict a child; the female figure is almost always depicted in isolation. Many of the plaques, however, show a woman with a large rounded stomach, presumably to indicate pregnancy. Thus, many, but perhaps not all, of the plaque figurines from Philistia may be associated with fertility and child rearing on some level. It is possible, though, that the range in plaque figurines reflects more than one aspect of the figure, if not multiple figures as referents entirely. Some of the plaques, such as those with a figure cupping the breasts, may be associated more with sexuality than fertility.[79] At the same time, the survey of the iconography of the nude female shows that it is plausible that some such representations, particularly some of those supporting the breasts, may have had a protective function.

A few groups deserve special attention. One consists of a pair of figurines holding a disc against their bodies (Kochavi 1976:pl. 11c [= Kochavi 1989:fig. 75] [Aphek]; Miqne obj. no. 1250). These belong to a well-known Levantine and Cypriot type of disc-holding figurines, made both as plaques and as composite figurines (as in the Tell Jemmeh figurine; Petrie 1928:pl. XXXV.14).[80] The identity of the disc they hold has been a subject of great debate. The most common suggestions are a musical instrument (e.g., Keel and Uehlinger 1998:164–66; Karageorghis 1998:30; Dayagi-Mendels 2002:146; see esp. Hillers 1970; Paz 2007:71–74) and a cake (e.g., Petrie 1928:17, in discussing the Jemmeh composite figurine; Lapp 1964:40;

inscription may merely refer to "Phoenician Astarte," the Levantine love goddess. (See also Vance 1993.) However, the Astarte of the Levant lacks the military aspect possessed by Ishtar/Astarte, who is both goddess of sex and war (see Stager 2000). Therefore, the interpretation of the Spanish inscription as "Hurrian Astarte" is preferable.

[78] N. Marinatos (2000:12) argues more generally that images of nude female figures in the Levant are mostly protective devices, whether as figurines of clay or metal or as representations on toiletry items such as mirror handles.

[79] See Budin 2006:161 on recent archaeological trends in interpreting nudity as related to sexuality and eroticism, vs. simply "fertility."

[80] For general surveys of this type, see now Paz 2007 and Sugimoto 2008.

see also Keel and Uehlinger 1998:164).[81] Meyers made an important contribution in trying to distinguish different types of discs. She determined that there were two basic types: one held out in front of the body at a right angle to it (on the composite figurines, at least, but note also examples of Cypriot plaques holding a disc perpendicularly: J. Karageorghis 1999:pls. LIV–LV), and the other held flat against the body. For Meyers, the disc in the first type is a frame drum;[82] she did not suggest an identification for the disc held by the second type.[83] Karageorghis (1987:17–19) has suggested the second type represents a "tambourine-holder," as opposed to a "tambourine-player."

The situation, however, may be even more complicated. The disc held flat against the body is of varying sizes and held in different places (most commonly over the left breast or the lower torso; cf. Karageorghis 1998:pl. XVII–XX). It is not clear that all of these objects are identical.[84] The object held by the Aphek plaque figurine is much smaller and held at a lower height than that of the Jemmeh composite figurine. Nevertheless, the likeliest interpretations—musical instruments and cakes—suggest certain parameters for the discussion. Instruments such as frame drums are described in biblical and other sources as played by women (e.g., Ex. 15:20; see Keel 1997:339–40; Dayagi-Mendels 2002:145–46). The cakes would presumably represent offerings, along the lines of those to the "Queen of Heaven" (Jer. 7:17–18, 44:17–19; see Stager 2000).[85] Both items were used by mortal women, not goddesses, in acts of worship (although in the latter case, a goddess could be receiving an offering). Unfortunately, little more can be said concerning the figurines on a strictly iconographic level.

Another separate group consists not of figurines, but of figurine molds, from the site of Tel Batash (A. Mazar and Panitz-Cohen 2001:photos 132–35, pl. 30.1–3). Figurine molds have occasionally been found at other sites in Philistia: for instance, Petrie's excavations at Jemmeh produced a mold of either a composite figurine head or the head of a plaque figurine (Petrie 1928:pl. XXXVI.6). The Batash molds, however, form a separate group. Two are complete, while the third preserves only the head; it is not entirely certain that this is a plaque figurine mold, as opposed to a mold for a composite figurine head. Both of the complete plaques show a nude woman with shoulder-length hair. One has her arms at her sides, while the other has her hands cupping her breasts. In terms of iconography, then, the molds are entirely typical. The style of the molds, however, is unique in Philistia. A. Mazar (2001:207) noted the exceptional nature of the style and "physiognomy" of the molds and concluded that, while the molds may have been local products, they were based on master images (perhaps in ivory) which were of foreign, possibly Phoenician, origin. The faces, while distinct from the typical composite figurine heads described above, appear to have Egyptian (or Egyptianizing Phoenician) influence. In addition, the bodily proportions of the figurines—with their longer torsos and shorter legs—are reflective not of the Levantine tradition of plaque figurines that extends back to the LB (see, e.g., cat. no. 68), but rather of Egyptian sculpture as well as Greek korai (and kouroi) of the Orientalizing and Archaic periods.

The influence of Egyptian sculpture on Greek sculpture in the seventh century B.C.E. has been widely observed (e.g., Bothmer 1960:xxxviii; Levin 1964;

[81] For an early summary of suggestions see Pritchard 1943:55. Amiran (1967) suggested that the object was a solar disc, but this idea has not been widely adopted; see Keel and Uehlinger 1998:164 for a critique.

[82] Probably the object indicated by Hebrew *top*. As Meyers indicates, a frame-drum is more likely than a tambourine or timbrel, as no metal discs are depicted on the side of the instrument, and the tambourine is played differently than depicted on the figurines (1987:120; see also Keel 1997:339).

[83] Note that Meyers's distinction was already anticipated by H. G. May (1935:32), who differentiated between discs that (he thought) were clearly tambourines and others that he thought might be cakes, as well as by Bayer (1963:36). Unlike these observations, however, Meyers's work has been very influential in subsequent considerations of the problem.

[84] O'Bryhim (1997) has suggested that the disc held over the lower torso represents a baetyl. This suggestion seems unlikely for several reasons. O'Bryhim's evidence, including Hellenistic and Roman period authors and coinage, is overwhelmingly much later in date than the figurines. As Markoe points out, the Phoenician baetyl—or biblical *maṣṣebah*—was generally larger and rectangular (2000:122). Karageorghis (1998:30) suggests that Cypriot baetyls were spherical or conical, not flat discs.

[85] Jer. 44:19 suggests that the cakes were "made in her image" (*lĕhaᶜăṣibāh*), and indeed Karageorghis (2000) and Stager (2000) discuss four Cypriot molds depicting nude women that were likely not for making figurines but for making cakes. None of the molds comes from a stratified context, but Karageorghis (2000:4–5) suggests a date in the Cypro-Archaic period (ca. late eighth to mid-fifth centuries). They provide additional circumstantial evidence that the figurines of nude women—especially the composite figurines, with which they would be roughly contemporary—are representations of one or more goddesses, perhaps Astarte. In this connection, note the references in Herodotus (*History* 1.105, 4.59) and Pausanias (*Description of Greece* 1.14.7) to the worship of "Heavenly Aphrodite" among the Assyrians, the Ashkelonians, and the Cyprians.

Stewart 1990:345, 38, 106–8).[86] These parallels have been observed not only in the body proportions of the statuary but also in the stereotypical "archaic" smile and perhaps also the almond-shaped eyes. Moreover, for Greek art the earliest examples of Egyptian influence appear to be in clay figurines in the first half of the seventh century (the so-called Daedalic style figurines; see Levin 1964:24–26) and are sometimes thought to be based not directly on Egyptian but on Levantine ("Syrian") models (e.g., Cook 1967:24). It is not surprising, then, to find similar features on roughly contemporary Philistine figurines of the eighth to seventh centuries, not only in the Batash molds, but also in the composite heads as discussed above. As Markoe has noted (1990:22–23), the eighth century is a peak period of Egyptian influence on Levantine and especially Phoenician art, with a decline in the seventh; this chronology fits well with the Egyptianizing elements emerging in Philistine figurines of this period, and may suggest Phoenician intermediaries here as well.

A few plaque figurines, meanwhile, are of a completely different style. They are extremely crudely made, so much so that it is not entirely clear they were made in a mold, although they appear to have marks from the edges of the molds. Petrie encountered this type at Tell Jemmeh (1928:pl. XXXVI.34–35), where he described it as "a new type of moulded figures in one piece, of clumsy, thick style" (1928:17). Following Petrie's description, I will use the term "Thick Style" for this group. Other than the crudity of the style, the figurines appear similar to the other plaques: they represent nude women with arms down at the sides. Their proportions, with longer torsos and shorter legs, are reminiscent of the Batash molds, although they are not nearly as finely made.

Finally, a plaque fragment from Ashkelon (cat. no. 69) is notable for a raised emblem in the form of an ibex and palm motif. This and other features such as the hairstyle mark the fragment as a rare example of the type known only from a handful of sites, all in the southern coastal plain: a complete example from Kibbutz Revadim (Beck 1986; Margalith 1994; Ornan 2007), a fragment from Aphek (Guzowska and Yasur-Landau 2009:389, fig. 11.4 no. F4), and a second fragment from Tel Ḥarasim (Givon 1994:fig. 15.11).[87] The presence of the raised emblem on the shoulder, unlike the Revadim and Aphek examples, suggests that the Ashkelon fragment originated in a different mold. In any case, given the location of the parallels, the distribution of the type may well be restricted to Philistia. The date of the Aphek context suggests that the type is in fact LB, specifically thirteenth-century. The Ashkelon figurine was found in Grid 38 in a Phase 20 (early- to mid-twelfth century) context and is presumably residual. As a result, I will not deal further with this figurine type.

I.A.5. Hollow Moldmade Figurines (Cat. Nos. 71–73)

This type is represented in Philistia by three examples from Ashkelon. As they are all fragments, of different body parts, and made and decorated in different styles, they do not form a coherent group. One of the fragments (cat. no. 71) is particularly unusual in appearing to be part of a fully moldmade head; apparently, it was made in a bivalve (double-mold) technique. This method of manufacture is late; combined with the characterstics of the clay (micaceous, well-levigated) and the decoration (engraved wavy lines, black paint), it suggests it is a later Greek import that is intrusive in its seventh-century context.

The other two fragments may belong to a single type. One is half of a female head and neck, while the other is the base of a seated figurine with feet preserved. Unlike the fragment above, these appear to have been made in a single mold. In order to produce a hollow figurine, a thin piece of clay was pressed in a mold; the back was left open and later closed by strips of clay, creating a flat back (see, e.g., Stern 1989:27 for discussion of this technique). The date of introduction of this technique is unclear but was likely around the end of the Iron Age (see, e.g., Culican 1969; Stern 1989:27; Dayagi-Mendels 2002:148; see chapter 7 for discussion).

Intimately related to this chronological issue is the date and origin of the iconography. The technique appears to have been first used for a single type of figurine: a seated pregnant woman, or "Dea (Tyria) gravida" as Culican labeled it (1969). The type appears very standardized: it depicts a woman, dressed probably in a long robe, seated on a narrow chair with high back, and with a rounded, prominent stomach (see Culican 1969:35–37). Generally, the left hand is on the knee while the right hand is on the stomach; there are occasional variants of this pose, for instance with both

[86] Besides generally aesthetic observations, a series of statistical studies by Guralnick (1978; 1981; 1982; 1985) have demonstrated the adoption of the proportions of the "Egyptian second canon" by several Greek workshops in the late seventh to sixth centuries B.C.E.

[87] The identification of the Ashkelon figurine was first made by Brian Brisco during a visit to the Israel Museum in 2004, by comparison to the Revadim example; without his valuable assistance, the Ashkelon fragment might still remain an enigma.

hands on the knees (Prtichard 1988:fig. 12.39; Dayagi-Mendels 2002:fig. 7.6). The head is typically hooded, with the face slightly downturned, although there are variants of both of these features; sometimes a hairstyle or veil similar to that of the Type 1 composite heads is found (Dayagi-Mendels 2002:fig. 7.6).

The "dea gravida" is found most commonly in Phoenicia and Palestine (see, e.g., Culican 1969:37, 44, pl. V; Stern 1982:171, 272 n. 57); it appears in Cyprus but is largely restricted to the Phoenician colony of Kition (Vandenabeele 1986:351–52; Yon and Caubet 1988:13). Culican also noted two examples from the Dermech cemetery at Carthage (1969:37, pl. I.B). Given this distribution (along with the fact that the Akhziv and Sarepta examples are probably the earliest; see chapter 7), Phoenicia is the likeliest origin for the figurines.

Because the Ashkelon examples are so few and fragmentary, it is difficult to say more about their relationship to the main type or types of the "dea gravida." It is also difficult to conduct an iconographic analysis; any conclusions must be based on the parallels to this figurine beyond Philistia, and it is not entirely clear how closely the Ashkelon examples relate to these parallels. I would make three general observations, however. First, the figure is universally depicted as clothed, in contrast to all other Iron II types (I.A.3 and I.A.4). Second, the type shares the theme of pregnancy with several of the plaques discussed above. Finally, the style and imagery of the type are essentially Levantine, as opposed to the other Iron II types with their heavily Egyptian influence (see, e.g., Gubel 1983:33). Stern (1982:171) and Gubel (1983:33) can point only to the headdress, which they interpret as an Egyptian klaft wig, as an Egyptian element; yet Culican suggests that even this is more similar to the Punic "side-coils of hair" displayed by terracottas from Ibiza in Spain (1969:37).

As for the meaning of the figurine type, Stern has identified them with divine representations, perhaps Isis and (unborn) Horus (1982:272 n. 59). More generally, he has interpreted them along with other Phoenician figurines of the Iron Age and Persian Period as representations of the Phoenician divine triad: an adult male god (Baᶜal); a fertility goddess, sometimes pregnant (Astarte, identified in this period with Egyptian Isis); and a young boy (Stern 1989:8; Stern 2001:80–83, 493–95; 2003:313–15). Stern's interpretation rests on Moscati's discussion of a general Phoenician triad (1973:62), a concept widely discussed in reference to Phoenician religion (e.g., Bérard 1894:93, with references; Hajjar 1977/85; Gibson 1982:116). More recent scholarship on Phoenician religion has tended to reject this idea, however, seeing Phoenician religion as more complex, fluid, and regional (e.g., Clifford 1990:72). This basis for interpreting figurines such as the "dea gravida" is therefore undermined. In addition, Stern's view of Phoenician figurines as representing a divine triad relies on the reduction of all adult male and female figurines, with their variety of poses, gestures, and symbols, to a single pair of deities. The "dea gravida" itself has no signs of divinity, not even nudity. It is better, then, to follow Lipiński (2003:301–4) in viewing them, like the larger Phoenician corpus of figurines of this period, as representations of humans as worshippers or in other roles (see below).

I.A.6. and I.B. Male and Miscellaneous Figurines (Cat. Nos. 74–78, 186)

The remaining types of human figurines provide great difficulty in distinguishing sexes. Ultimately, the only conclusive criteria to use for this judgment are the depiction of breasts or male or female genitalia.[88] Even a protruding chin, generally taken to indicate a beard on a male figurine, can certainly be present on a female.[89] The many figurine heads without bodies preserved, then, pose a serious problem. With the types discussed above, it is generally easy to identify a head as female, based on similarity to more complete figurines and the inclusion of iconographic elements that tend to be characteristic of females, such as the *polos* or the veil. In many of the following groups, however, there are no clear indications; many have been identified as male for reasons that are not always sound. It is worth remembering that several researchers (e.g., Ucko 1968; Talalay 1993:17; French 1981:173) have considered that figurines in various cultures were sometimes made deliberately without any indication of sex. In these cases, however, it is difficult to tell whether this ambiguity is grounded in the *mentalité* of the makers and users of these figurines or simply reflects our inability to read the figurines properly.

The largest uncertain group of figurines which are generally identified as male are the so-called Ashdodite heads (e.g., M. Dothan 1971:figs. 62.4, 6–7, 63.1).[90]

[88] Even here, however, there is possible ambiguity. A plaque figurine from Tel ᶜIra has been interpreted by P. Beck (1990; 2002b) as a hermaphrodite, as it appears to have both breasts and a phallus. In this case, however, the "phallus" is not emphasized like the breasts and may be a product of an imperfectly made mold.

[89] French observes: "A figurine known as the 'bearded Aphrodite' from Cyprus indeed throws doubt on the whole series," as it clearly has both accentuated chin and breasts (1971:148).

[90] The name "Ashdodite heads" was given to this group by Kletter (1996:Appendix 5.IV.3), as most of the figurines he

Their technique and form is similar to handmade female figurines above (I.A.1 and 2) but without a *polos*. Instead, the head is always bare; it can be either rounded or flat.[91] In addition, the type generally has a more human-looking nose than the large bird nose of the Ashdoda or the thin low ridge of the Philistine Psi and often has an incision for the mouth. The full form of this type is unclear: Hachlili (1971:127) suggested that these heads may have been attached to the "Late Ashdoda," but no "Ashdodite head" has been found with a body.[92] A possible exception is a figurine of a lyre player from Ashdod, D756/1 (M. Dothan 1971:fig. 62.1; T. Dothan 1982:ch. 4, pl. 35). The head of the lyre player is similar to an "Ashdodite head" but is painted with a skullcap in black (cf. Hachlili 1971:126–27), marking it as separate from the group.

The group has generally been assumed to be male (e.g., Hachlili 1971:127; Dothan and Dothan 1992:171), although Kletter (1996:261) considered the sex to be uncertain. Certainly determining the sex of this group is problematic. Without bodies or iconographic elements as criteria, the judgment is ultimately subjective. The lyre player D756/1, if considered part of this group, might be helpful: the torso, without breasts, suggests it is male. There are also miniature figurines (Ashdod D4372/1 and D5021/1; M. Dothan 1971:figs. 62.2, 10) with similar heads whose torsos do not have any breasts (nor any indication of genitalia). On the other hand, the Tell Jerishe peg figurine (Herzog 1984:pl. 7e; 1993:483) presents a problem. The head of this figurine is typical of the "Ashdodite head" group: it has a bare, round head, applied pellet eyes, a more naturalistic nose, and an incised mouth. These features, along with a protruding chin, would by themselves suggest a male figurine. From the neck down, however, the figurine presents a completely different picture. The torso has applied breasts, which if anything are more emphasized than those of the typical Philistine Psi figurine (but cf. cat. no. 10); moreover, the figurine displays the gesture of supporting the breasts that is typical of many Levantine female types. Because of this figurine, I believe it is impossible to determine the sex of the "Ashdodite heads"; only with a torso is it possible to judge by the criteria laid out above. Still, I would suggest that these heads tend to represent females, given the predominance of female figurines both in the similar Iron I types (I.A.1 and 2 above) and the Mycenaean figurines (French 1971:esp. 148).[93]

Three figurines from Ashdod are unusual in their painted decoration. One of these is the lyre player discussed above, D756/1. It is covered in a red slip; besides the skullcap, black paint is used for rings around the eyes, stripes on the lower torso, and possibly a stripe along the chin (Hachlili 1971:126–27, but without mentioning the chin stripe). Hachlili suggests that the painted decoration on the body represents clothing (1971:127). The lack of breasts and possible beard indicate that the figurine probably represents a male. In many respects, the figurine is similar to the figurines in the round on the Ashdod musicians stand (T. Dothan 1982:ch. 4, pl. 33; M. Dothan and Ben-Shlomo 2005:figs. 3.76–3.78). The latter have bare heads that are rounded or flat and applied eyes; in these respects they are also generally similar to the "Ashdodite heads."[94] Kletter suggests that the lyre player as well may have belonged to a cult stand originally (1996:262).

The other two painted figurines are of a different type. One (D4375/1, M. Dothan 1971:fig. 62.8) is hollow, with black paint accentuating various features on the head: eyes, nose, and possibly a necklace. A net design painted in black on top of the head might represent a headdress (Hachlili 1971:127). The other figurine (D4185/1, M. Dothan 1971:fig. 62.3) has similar black paint accentuating facial features. It is unique, however, in having an elaborate headdress: the upper part is decorated with horizontal black and red stripes, while the lower part has a pattern of incised dots (Hachlili 1971:128). Scars on the chest appear to indicate breasts, but Hachlili (1971:128) suggested that an arc of incised circles along the chin might represent a

assigned to this group were from Ashdod. I use the label here primarily because it does not assume a gender for the type, as other labels do.

[91] A possible exception is Ashdod D1894/1 (M. Dothan 1971:fig. 62.5), which shares some similarities with this group (it is handmade, with applied eyes) but wears a (flat) headdress.

[92] At the same time, if we follow the principle stated earlier in this chapter about associating heads and bodies, at least some of the "Ashdodite heads" were likely associated with "Late Ashdodas." See the discussion of the "Late Ashdoda" above.

[93] A similar problem is presented by Ashdod H1845/1 (M. Dothan and Ben-Shlomo 2005:fig. 3.62.1), discussed above. It is a Philistine Psi head with *polos* but has painted decoration on the chin that might suggest a beard. Ben-Shlomo suggests it could be either male or female (M. Dothan and Ben-Shlomo 2005:161). As I suggested above, however, the painted decoration has close parallels among Late Psi figurines with "ringed face" (French 1971:140, pl. 21b nos. 13, 19). Again, French has observed that male Mycenaean figurines are rare, and even those with protruding chins are probably female (1971:148).

[94] Note that Ben-Shlomo compares their modeling to that of the Ashdoda figurines (M. Dothan and Ben-Shlomo 2005:181).

beard. As a result, the sex of the figurine is not entirely clear, although it may more likely be female.

T. Dothan published a head from Tell eṣ-Ṣafi (1982:229, ch. 4, pl. 12) that is somewhat similar to the "Ashdodite heads" but with more naturalistic modeling. The eyes are applied pellets, but modeling on the face indicates eyebrow ridges, cheeks, and the chin. Two holes are incised for the nostrils. The figurine is also notable for its headdress (or hairstyle), a ridge across the top front of the head incised with a series of vertical lines. Dothan compared it to a male head from the "Gezer cache" (a group of objects decorated in Philistine style), which was likely an ornamental handle of a vessel (1982:227–28, ch. 4, fig. 1.2). The Gezer head wears a flat cap painted with a series of vertical lines around the rim and a set of streamers down the back. Both heads are comparable to a fragment from Ashkelon (cat. no. 74). The latter figurine has a round head but a ridge of clay around the top edges of the head. A set of black lines descend from the back of the ridge and curve along the sides of the neck, perhaps corresponding to the streamers on the Gezer head. The face of the figurine is unusual for a Philistine piece: the eyes are simple depressions, and incisions are used for both the nostrils and mouth.

Another handmade head from Ashkelon (cat. no. 78) is very similar to the Philistine Psi heads described above: it has a concave head, applied pellets for eyes, and a long neck. There are applied strips of clay along the sides of the face and the chin, however, possibly suggesting a beard.

One more group needs to be discussed here: three crude figurines from Ashkelon (cat. nos. 75, 77, 186) that are best interpreted as nude torsos. Female genitalia appear to be highlighted on Catalogue Nos. 77 and 186. Of these, Catalogue No. 186 has a close parallel in an example from Enkomi (no. 1167; Dikaios 1969b:pls. 147.40–41, 177.6–7; Karageorghis 1993a:pl. XVII.6). Both cat. no. 186 and the Enkomi example are handmade, nude female torsos with applied pellets for the navel and genitalia; additionally, incised lines are used to indicate the fingers on the hand, which cups the breast. Cat. no. 186 is a significant find: it is, to my knowledge, the first figurine found in Philistia to parallel a non-Aegean-derived Cypriot figurine. If the figurine was in fact made in Philistia, it represents an important hybrid: a handmade figurine depicted nude, apparently with the gesture of one hand cupping the breast. On the other hand, if the figurine is Cypriot in origin, it is not such a radically new development; the use of molds for figurines did not begin on Cyprus (as discussed above) until centuries later, and nude, handmade female figurines (often with the gesture of cupping the breast) are typical of LB Cyprus. Dikaios therefore suggested the Enkomi example was a local type (1969a:291). Still, both the Enkomi and Ashkelon figurines display features not previously found in the LB Cypriot corpus. The body is more columnar than the LB Cypriot examples, and the hips are not nearly as wide. Perhaps most important is the depiction of the genital region. The LB Cypriot tradition was to indicate this by incised hatching; the Enkomi and Ashkelon examples, however, use an applied clay pellet with incised dots. The use of applied pellets is atypical of the Cypriot tradition, but as shown above is common in the Aegean, especially among LH IIIC figurines where they are used for the eyes and the breasts.[95]

Thus, I believe I have identified a new group of crude handmade female figurines in Philistia. While this type of crude figurine is common on Cyprus at sites like Enkomi and Kition (Dikaios 1969b:pls. 137.5–6, 8, 147.40–41; Courtois 1988:figs. 1.1, 5–7, pls. 42.1, 5; Karageorghis 1960:565, fig. 110; 1993a: 26–29, pl. XVII.1–7, Type K), it appears to be a minor type in Philistia. Moreover, this group presents a hybrid of local (Canaanite) and foreign (Mycenaean) elements: local form and underlying motif (gesture, nudity) combined with Aegean style (abstraction). A few of the figurines discussed under I.A.1 and 2 may represent a similar hybrid: cat. no. 28, an Ashdoda torso with hand cupping the breast; cat. no. 10, a Mycenaean-style torso with emphasized breasts, and possibly hands supporting them; and perhaps the Tell Jerishe peg figurine (Herzog: 1984:pl. 7e; 1993:483), although the gesture of this figurine may simply be related to those of the Tau type and the Midea figure.[96]

A later development of this hybrid type might be evident in the recently excavated group of 120 cult stands from a *favissa* at Tel Yavneh (Ziffer and Kletter 2007; Kletter, Ziffer, and Zwickel 2010). These stands, dated to the ninth century (Ziffer and Kletter 2007:9) or, based on a more detailed analysis of the pottery of the *favissa*, to the late ninth to early eighth century (Panitz-Cohen 2010), have a series of apertures in which figurines, made in the round, were stationed. This method of depicting figures is similar to that on most of the Ashdod musicians stand (T. Dothan 1982:ch. 4, pl. 33; M. Dothan and Ben-Shlomo 2005:figs. 3.76–3.78),

[95] Note that Dikaios (1969a:291) assigned the Enkomi figurine to a group in local style but with buff color clay, typical of Mycenaean figurines.

[96] If I have identified this hybrid type correctly, it is significant in that it is entirely distinct in nature from the hybrid identified by T. Dothan in the so-called ᶜAitun examples (1982:237); those figurines combined Mycenaean form (gesture) and local Canaanite style (naturalism).

but distinct from that of other more or less contemporary cult stands from Palestine. Thus, the Taanach cult stand from Lapp's excavations (Lapp 1969:42–44, fig. 29; Beck 1994; Frick 2000:117–28, figs. 19–20), as well as the Sellin stand from Taanach (Beck 1994:figs. 1–2; Frick 2000:117–19), have figures depicted in low relief (a technique used to a lesser extent on the Yavneh stands as well). A cylindrical stand from Tell Qasile (A. Mazar 1980:87–89, fig. 23, pl. 32.1–2; T. Dothan 1982:ch. 4, pl. 34) uses a cut-out technique to indicate figures, which is similar to that used for one figure on the Ashdod musicians stand.[97] The iconography of the Yavneh stands is purely in the Canaanite tradition: ibexes and palm trees are incised or stand in relief on the sides of many stands (e.g., Ziffer and Kletter 2007:Stands 2006-994, 1007, 1054, 998 [= Kletter, Ziffer, and Zwickel 2010:CAT90, 15, 86, 37]), while the figures display poses such as supporting the breasts, arms at the sides, or hands at the genital regions (e.g., Ziffer and Kletter 2007:Stands 2006-994, 998, 1033, 1036, 1047 [= Kletter, Ziffer, and Zwickel 2010:CAT90, 37, 79, 44, 29]). These gestures are particularly similar to those displayed by the plaque figurines (I.A.4, above). The figures, however, are crude, handmade figurines, in the manner of the Philistine Psi figurines. In addition, bodily features are often indicated by pellets of clay, especially in the case of applied eyes and applied breasts (see especially Ziffer and Kletter 2007:Stands 2006-1036, 1047 [= Kletter, Ziffer, and Zwickel 2010:CAT44, 29]).

At present, there is not a large enough group of hybrid figurines to allow for definitive identification of this type. In addition, it is important to consider that the important body of evidence from Yavneh involves figurines not meant to be freestanding but stationed on cult stands. It is certainly possible that different conventions were in use on cult stands, in which case they may not provide a direct parallel to the hybrid figurines; nevertheless, as I have tried to demonstrate above, the technique of attaching figurines in the round is unusual for cult stands. As a result, I offer the idea of hybrid figurine development as a suggestion, or a hypothesis for further testing.

The above miscellaneous groups include most of the male, or possibly male, figurines from Iron Age Philistia. Both few in number and diverse in type, they appear to have been much less standardized than the main female types. In fact, most types are represented by only one or two examples. As a result, I would suggest that male figurines—at least for most of the Iron Age—were not only rare but lacked defined types.

The one possible exception to the above statement is the rider of the horse and rider figurines. These will be discussed below with the horse figurines (II.A).

II. Zoomorphic Figurines

All of the zoomorphic figurines from Philistia are handmade. They also tend to be simplified renderings, crudely made, and most are undecorated, except at times a white slip. These general features of the figurines result in problems of identification. Identifying the referents of ancient depictions is often difficult. Representations are often stylized and generalized; in addition, we must acknowledge the fact that ancient cultures may not have used the same classificatory principles that we do (Daly, Hesse, and Perkins 1972; Yorkoff 1972:83; Wapnish 1985:11). These problems are magnified when dealing with the highly schematized representations found on many of the figurines. As a result, the best approach is to use general linguistic terms and to delay identification of unclear examples until further study (both of figurines and other representations, and of actual animals and their behavior) can be done (cf. Daly, Hesse, and Perkins 1972:80; Wapnish 1985:11).[98] In my typology I have suggested only four general types: equid (horses), bovine (bulls), leonine (lions), and avian (birds). Of these, only the first two appear in any large number and so are the subject of most of the discussion below.

II.A. Horses (Cat. Nos. 79–159, 175)

By far the most common type of animal figurine in Iron Age Philistia is the horse figurine, with or without a rider. This figurine type, clearly representing a quadruped of some sort, appears from certain details such as a mane on the back of the neck to be an equid. Furthermore, the combination of these details with iconographic parallels for these figurines, especially the many examples from Cyprus, makes it almost certain that they represent horses (see Karageorghis 1995:pls. XXIX–XLIX; Young and Young 1955:pls. 19–37).

This type is marked by a general standardization in its form and method of manufacture. Other than

[97] Another cult stand from Qasile (A. Mazar 1980:89–90, fig. 24, pl. 32:3–5) does have figurines made in the round, but they are modeled directly on the top end of the stand rather than stationed in apertures.

[98] The approach of Petrie (1928:18) is illustrative. Despite stating that many figurines are "too indeterminate" for a proper identification, he does not hesitate to label most of the figurines, even offering up the identification of "ichneumon?" (mongoose) for one unusual figurine (Petrie 1928:pl. XXXIX.8).

variations in size, there are few deviations from the standard. All of the horses are handmade and, with rare exception (e.g., cat. no. 175), completely solid; while none has been found complete, based on the fragments they would have been roughly 10–12 cm high and 7–9 cm long. The central section of the figurine is the torso, essentially a flattened cylinder with rounded ends. This is the portion of the figurine most commonly found at Ashkelon (cat. nos. 109–48). At one end of the torso a tail, usually short and curved, was attached; on the other, the head and neck were attached. The legs are four cylinders, all tapering toward the bottom to a small flattened end. The horses were often coated with a white or cream slip, but there is little evidence of any paint; Catalogue No. 112, however, has at least two red stripes painted across the back.

The above features are typical of virtually all the horses of Philistia. The only variation among figurines is found in two areas: the head and the inclusion of a rider.

The heads are of three main types:

1. Rounded snout (cat. nos. 79–108). The head and neck are slender and curved; the mane is indicated on the back of the neck by a thin ridge, giving the neck a triangular or teardrop shape in section.

2. Squared or box snout: a stockier, rectangular shape with generally flattened end (e.g., Ashdod M1926/3; M. Dothan and Porath 1982:fig. 34.7). This is the standard Judahite type (see chapter 7 for further discussion).

3. Intermediate type (e.g., Petrie 1928:pl. XXXVIII. 8–12). The head and neck are not very slender but rounded, although the end of the snout is flattened. This type is also distinguished from the others in having other facial features of the horse indicated. There are usually applied eyes and an applied or incised bridle, and sometimes the mouth is open.[99]

Note that, given the generally crude and schematic nature of animal figurines, it is often difficult to classify a fragment, or occasionally even a whole figurine. In the case of the horses, classification becomes very difficult if the piece does not belong to one of these three major types. It is therefore unclear whether there are additional types, but at the very least it is clear that these are the three major types of horse heads.

One exceptional horse head is cat. no. 175. The identification of this figurine would be uncertain if not for the fact that a nearly exact parallel was found at Tell Keisan (Paraire 1980:346, pl. 104.29). It is made of several separate strips of clay and is partially hollow. The front of the muzzle is broken off on the Ashkelon example, but based on the Keisan parallel it probably would have had an open mouth and a nostril indicated for the snout. Most distinctive is the piece of clay on the top back of the head, resembling a helmet or turban, with two rounded knobs projecting upward. From the Keisan example it is clear that these are representations of the ears. Cat. no. 175 is unique in Philistia, however, and does not constitute a common type like the three described above.[100]

Riders (Cat. Nos. 160–64)[101]

The horse type most common in the Iron II is a "horse and rider" figurine. In Philistia, however, relatively few

[99] It is not entirely certain that Type 3 is an Iron Age type. It is almost exclusive to Tell Jemmeh, where there are significant problems with the stratigraphy and dating of Petrie's excavation (see chapter 7). Unlike other Iron II types at Tell Jemmeh (the composite figurines, Thick Style plaques, and humped bovines), this type is not paralleled at most other sites in southern Philistia. There is one other possible example known to me, from Netiv Ha-ᶜAsara (Shavit and Yasur-Landau 2005:fig. 16; thanks are due A. Yasur-Landau for bringing this figurine to my attention). This figurine has an applied bridle and open mouth, as well as incised dots for nostrils. In addition, there is a small applied piece of clay on each side of the neck, probably representing the hands of a rider. While this figurine appears to be of Iron Age type, it was found in a Persian period context. At the same time, there are two arguments in favor of an Iron Age date for Type 3: 1) most of the overall Jemmeh figurine assemblage appears to consist of clear Iron Age types; and 2) this type is not paralleled among the known Persian period horse figurines in Palestine. In the end, I would conclude that this type very likely belongs to the Iron Age.

[100] Inspection of the clay confirms the conclusions reached here on technical and typological grounds. Dalit Regev (pers. comm. 2008) has looked at this figurine and notes that the clay, orange with some red inclusions, is typical of clays on the Phoenician coast from Akko to the north (cf. Master 2003:55). Regev has also suggested that the lack of a distinct core, in contrast to other Ashkelon horses, also suggests Phoenician manufacture.

[101] Besides the combination horse and rider figurines, there is one other similar type of combination figurine: the chariot. I will discuss this type only briefly here, as it is represented only by three examples from Tell Jemmeh (Petrie 1928:pl. XXXIX.12–14), as well as four possible chariot wheels (Petrie 1928:pl. XXXIX.15–18). It is not even certain that these are Iron Age figurines, due to the problems with the stratigraphy and dating of Petrie's excavation (see chapter 7). There are two arguments, however, for an Iron Age date: 1) most of the figurines at Jemmeh appear to be of eighth- to seventh-century types (see chapter 7); and 2) the human figure attached to one of the chariots (Petrie 1928:pl. XXXIX.14) has applied oval eyes very similar to some of the humped bulls from Jemmeh (e.g., Petrie 1928:pl.

riders have been found. There may be multiple reasons for this. Riders, like the horses, are crude and schematic; as a result, they have sometimes been mistaken for other types of figurines. It can even be difficult to distinguish between a rider body and a horse head or body.[102] All riders found in Philistia are fragmentary. They are most often noticed in their torso shape (widening toward the base as they were attached at the hips to the horse), the position of their arms (extending forward, and slightly down), and in the angle of the body (leaning forward, toward the horse's neck). In a few cases, remains of the rider's hands can be seen on the neck of the horse (cat. nos. 90, 104), or remains of the rider's legs are visible on the horse's torso (cat. no. 110; Petrie 1928:pl. XXXVIII.14).[103]

Still, the above examples account for only a small percentage of the figurines. If most horses had riders, we would expect to find more examples of rider legs and hands preserved on the horses themselves. It is possible that, in many cases, the rider was made without legs and stationed as if springing directly from the horse's back (as is common on Cyprus, for example; see Karageorghis 1995:61, pl. XXIX.4–7, XXX, etc.). If this were the case, however, we would expect to find a scar on the middle of the horse's back from the rider. I have been able to identify only one possible example with such a scar (cat. no. 126). Perhaps in some cases the rider was attached directly to or right behind the neck; in this case, the rider would have broken off along with the neck, leaving a single scar. Ciasca (1964:95) has suggested that, on some Judahite examples, black stains on the backs of the horses indicate the original presence of a rider: the horse and rider were modeled separately, but attached before firing, leaving the surface of the horse's back underneath the rider imperfectly oxidized. I have not been able to find any such black stains on the backs of the Ashkelon horses, however. One additional possibility is that the horse and rider were never attached but made in two entirely separate pieces. To my knowledge, however, there is no example of such a horse and rider figurine from the Levant or Cyprus. There is a real possibility, then, that most of the horses from Ashkelon, and from Philistia generally, did not have riders.

Identity and Iconography

Historically the horse and rider figurines, like most animal figurines, were commonly interpreted primarily as toys (e.g., Kelso and Thorley 1943:142; cf. May 1935:1). Recent debate has focused on the identity of the rider: is it a human or divine figure? Moorey, with typical caution, interprets these figurines as images of human worshippers (2003:63); Keel and Uehlinger, on the other hand, suggest that they might represent the "Host of Heaven" (1998:345). A fundamental issue in the interpretation of the figurines is the role of cavalry in the armies of the time. Stager (2006a:171) and Kletter (1999:39) have highlighted the problem of interpreting the Judahite riders as human, given that there is little evidence for cavalry in Israel and Judah at the time. The Assyrian cuneiform sources are unanimous in stating that Israel had only chariotry, unlike other Levantine kingdoms which had cavalry as well (Dalley 1985:38; Stager 2006a:171). Lemaire (1998) has tried to argue that Judah in fact did have a cavalry force, but he is forced to emend the Assyrian texts to support his argument. The sole positive piece of evidence he can offer is his translation of *pārāš* in the Tel Dan stele as "horsemen." Even this reading is uncertain, however; the term *pārāš* is problematic in that it can mean either "horseman" or "horse" (*BDB* 832; see Ap-Thomas 1983; Stager 2006a:171).

On the other hand, it is clear that cavalry was common in other Near Eastern armies in Iron II. As Stager observes (2006a:171), some biblical uses of *pārāš* can only be interpreted as "horseman" (e.g., Ezek. 23:6, 12), indicating their use in Assyrian and other armies. Certainly the Assyrian inscriptions refer to the cavalry of various Levantine states (Dalley 1985). Assyrian reliefs depict cavalry in increasing numbers from the ninth century on (Littauer and Crouwel 1979:130–39; Crouwel and Tatton-Brown 1988:83). Littauer and Crouwel (1979:137–39) have analyzed these reliefs, and have concluded that, in the late eighth and seventh centuries, the cavalry takes on a new role in Near Eastern warfare. They determined that cavalry had become more effective, with the development of the saddle cloth as a more secure seat for riders as well as a new reining system, and gradually replaced the

XXXVII.2), a type known from other Philistine sites in the eighth to seventh centuries (see below and chapter 7). Also note a possible chariot wheel from a seventh-century context at Ashkelon, reg. no. 40617, not included in the figurine catalogue.

[102] For instance, in the Ashkelon registration books cat. no. 160 was labeled as a zoomorphic torso.

[103] Another possible example of a partial rider preserved on a horse body comes from Tel Ṣippor (Negbi 1966:19, pl. 13 no. 85). Negbi considered this figurine one of the few in the *favissa* to date to the Iron Age, specifically the eighth to sixth centuries (1966:8 n. 60). Unlike Negbi's dating of the mold-made heads discussed above, I consider this suggestion to be likely. The typical horse and rider type in the Persian period is the "Persian rider" type, with distinctive features including a breastplate on the horse (see, e.g., Stern 1982:168, fig. 285) not found on this example from Ṣippor. Stern, however, suggested that the Ṣippor figurine dated to the Persian period (1982:179).

chariot as the principal mounted weapon. This new status is reflected in the depiction of horses with armor in the seventh century: ridden horses serve not merely a means of transport but take part in battle (Littauer and Crouwel 1979:137–39; see also Crouwel and Tatton-Brown 1988:83).

The horse and rider figurines themselves had been present in small numbers since the Bronze Age. They occasionally appear at MB sites in Syria (e.g., Marchetti 2001:Tav. 267.3–4 [Hama], 280.7 [Tell Rifaᶜat]); in Greece and Cyprus there are a few examples from the LB (French 1971:164–65; Karageorghis 1993a:16–17, pls. XII–XIV). They are then found periodically throughout the Cypro-Geometric period on Cyprus, becoming gradually more popular until they become a predominant figurine form in the eighth century (Karageorghis 1995:61). At the same time, they become popular throughout the Levant: not only in Philistia but in Judah, Transjordan, and Phoenicia (Kletter 1999:39; Dornemann 1983:137–40), as well as to the north in Syria (Riis and Buhl 1990:figs. 93.713–14, 94.720; Moorey 2003:58, pl. 13) and at Tarsus in Cilicia (Goldman 1963:figs. 158–61). While Cyprus is a possible source for the type, it may be that the Cypriot corpus is simply larger and better-known. In any case, the horse and rider type becomes prominent at approximately the same time as the rise of cavalry in Near Eastern warfare. Karageorghis (1995:61) associates the sudden popularity of the type on Cyprus with Assyrian influence, reflected in the introduction of accessories and breastplates for horses, and the associated rise of the aristocracy.

The iconography of the horse and rider might shed some additional light on the problem of the rider. As I mentioned above, in Philistia there is generally an absence of detail on the horses and riders, other than the applied eyes and bridle of one horse head type. Another exception to this might be cat. no. 164, which I suggest is the head of a rider. The head is most notable for its possible beard, suggesting that the rider is male, and especially the headdress, a high conical cap or helmet. The head is very thin, with a flat back, suggesting that it was not a freestanding human figurine. A very similar thin head, with the same conical pointed headdress, is found on a horseman from Akhziv, unfortunately of unknown provenience within the cemetery (Dayagi-Mendels 2002:fig. 7.13). Dayagi-Mendels (2002:152), citing Young and Young's (1955) work on the Kourion figurines, suggests that the conical headdress reflects Persian influence (cf. Thalmann 1978:80, fig. 21.F). In fact, this type of pointed cap or helmet was widely present in the Levant already in the Iron Age. This or a similar headdress is common on male figurines from Phoenicia (Paraire 1980:347, nos. 57–59; Bordreuil and Gubel 1988:fig. 19; Chéhab 1975:14). Excavators there have referred to it as the *lebbad* or *lebbadé*, a traditional Lebanese headdress (Chéhab 1975:14; Bordreuil and Gubel 1988:451; Badre et al. 1990:46), but this term seems to be applied to multiple headdresses: not simply a high conical cap but others that taper to a flat end (e.g., Badre et al. 1990:figs. 25a, 29b, 30g; Badre et al. 1994:275, figs. 15.d, e, g, 26). The high conical headdress is also known from Iron Age Cyprus (see, e.g., Karageorghis 1995:pls. XXX.9, XXXI.1, 2, etc.). Young and Young themselves observe that the pointed cap is common on seventh-century riders from Kourion; they suggest that it is of local origin but observe that it also appears on Neo-Assyrian reliefs (1955:197; see also N. A. Winter 1996:99–100).[104]

Among the finds from the cemetery at Tyre-Al Bass, Lehmann-Jericke published a horse and rider with a pointed helmet (2004:fig. 278). She observed that the helmet has two strips of clay attached: one extending downward on the left side, which she suggested is an earflap, and one extending upward on the right side, which she identified as a horn. As the horned helmet is often associated with deities, Lehnmann-Jericke concluded that the rider might be a god (2004:417). Metzger's brief survey of figures wearing similar pointed headdresses (2004:434) suggests that the type was common on deities only in the Bronze Age (with one later example from the Persian period). Meanwhile, as I have already discussed, this and similar headdresses were common on riders as early as the seventh century, particularly on the Cypriot riders. This type of headdress is also common among the seventh-century figures from the shrine at Ayia Irini (e.g., Gjerstad et al. 1935:pls. 189–96; see Karageorghis 1993b:7). These large terracotta figures are widely considered to have been votaries put in a position of continuous worship of the deity.[105] Thus, the elements of their costume, such as the pointed conical helmets, simply reflect elements of dress in the period (Karageorghis 1993b:86–87). It is therefore not

[104] See Dornemann 1983:138–39, figs. 87.1–3; Harding 1950:46–47, pls. 13.1, 15.12; and Burdajewicz 1993:1244 for riders with pointed headdresses from Transjordan. These are generally dated to the eighth and seventh centuries (Dornemann 1983:137; Harding 1950:45; Burdajewicz 1993:1244), although Stern (1982:167, fig. 286) suggests a sixth-century date.

[105] Using the criteria of Renfrew (1985:23–24) mentioned above, we see that only the scale of the figures might suggest divinity. On the other hand, the large number of figures, their lack of divine symbols or attributes, and the fact that they are not used as foci of attention all suggest that they represent worshippers.

necessary to follow Lehmann-Jericke in suggesting that the Tyre-Al Bass rider is a deity. The "horn" on the helmet of that figurine is simply a cheek-piece or earflap, turned upward.

To return to the riders from Philistia, there is no iconographic evidence to suggest that they represent deities. Analogy on the basis of the Cypriot and Phoenician examples is a strong argument in itself, though of course the meaning of the type could have changed for the Philistines. Beyond this, however, I am not aware of any image clearly showing a male deity riding a horse, at least for the Iron Age. Gods and goddesses are occasionally associated with horses as their symbols (as in Assyrian art), but in this case they are at most shown standing on top of the horse, as discussed above. There is a small series of Egyptian reliefs depicting a figure, apparently a deity, riding a horse (Pritchard 1943:57; 1954:305; Leclant 1960; Cornelius 1994:72–85). These depictions, however, are problematic for several reasons: they are Egyptian, and not Levantine; they date to the New Kingdom (i.e., to the Late Bronze Age); the figures are generally armed, unlike the Philistine riders; and, due to the fragmentary nature of the representations, the identity of the rider is unclear. Generally, scholarly opinion has favored an identity with Reshef (see survey of literature in Cornelius 1994:72–73); significantly, as Cornelius notes (1994:72–73), two of the reliefs have inscriptions mentioning Reshef. Leclant (1960), however, identified the figure instead with Astarte, including them in a much larger group of LB representations of the goddess on horseback (see Cornelius 2004:42–45, 117–23, nos. 4.1–4.26). Regardless of the identity, the images seem to have little relevance for understanding late Iron Age riders in Philistia.

Certainly, it may be significant that there are few clear rider fragments from Philistia, including at Ashkelon where the horse is the most common Iron Age type by far. Given the sudden popularity of the horse and rider in the eighth and seven centuries, this type can be linked—at least in Phoenicia and Cyprus—to the spread of cavalry. In many cases on Cyprus as well as in Phoenicia, they seem—like the composite figurines holding offerings or playing instruments—to have served as votive images left in sanctuaries as representations of worshippers. It may be that with both the composite figurine and the horse (and rider), the type was modified when adopted in Philistia in order to fit different cultural needs. As figurines do not appear to have been used widely as votives in sanctuaries in Philistia (see chapter 7), it appears that they may have been repurposed. Thus, the composite figurine type was used to represent a nude woman, carrying on the old Levantine tradition of representing a goddess or goddesses. Similarly, the horse may have been adopted without the rider in many cases, as there was no need to represent human cavalry.

II.B. Lion Figurines (Cat. Nos. 165–66)

Lion terracottas are best known in zoomorphic vessels, especially lion-headed cups (discussed in Press forthcoming), and appear as solid figurines attached to many of the Yavneh cult stands (Kletter, Ziffer, and Zwickel 2010). Freestanding lions, however, are rare. The two examples from Ashkelon vary greatly in both form and decoration. Beyond these, there are three possible examples from Tell Jemmeh (Petrie 1928: pl. XXXVIII.1–2, 7). The figurines do not appear to form a coherent group but are for the most part unique examples; given the small number of examples, it is impossible to draw further conclusions.

II.C. Bovine Figurines (Cat. Nos. 167–71)

The bull figurines of Philistia are for the most part even less detailed than the horses. They can be identified as bulls through the presence of horns. Some examples (e.g., cat. nos. 167, 170) have incisions for the eyes, nostrils, and mouth; otherwise, however, they are generally nondescript. Three groups can be isolated: 1) locally made Mycenaean-style bulls; 2) humped bulls; and 3) miniature undecorated bulls. D. Ben-Shlomo has identified a group of roughly a dozen bovine figurines notable for their painted decoration: it consists of a series of stripes along the body, in the same basic style and pattern as the Mycenaean bull figurines (see Ben-Shlomo and Press 2009:58–60, figs. 16–18), although sometimes including dots or other variations (e.g., Miqne obj. no. 620 [Ben-Shlomo and Press 2009:fig. 16.4]). In particular, the pattern is identifiable as French's Spine 2, which is found on Mycenaean examples of LH IIIB2 and LH IIIC (Ben-Shlomo in press; French 1971:151, 153). Besides the stripes along the body, paint is used to indicate the eyes (e.g., Miqne obj. no. 6646/6653 [Ben-Shlomo 2006:fig. 5.1.1; Ben-Shlomo and Press 2009:fig. 17]). Petrography and other chemical analysis conducted by Ben-Shlomo indicates that the figurine was indeed made in the vicinity of Miqne (2006:190). There are details to the modeling of these figurines, including a possible hump along the neck of some examples (e.g., Miqne obj. no. 6646/6653; Ben-Shlomo 2006:fig. 5.1.1; Ben-Shlomo and Press 2009:fig. 17) and a ridge on the neck apparently representing a dewlap (e.g., Miqne obj. no. 6646/6653 [Ben-Shlomo 2006:fig. 5:1.1; Ben-Shlomo and Press 2009:fig. 17] and obj.

no. 1739 [Ben-Shlomo and Press 2009:fig. 18]), that distinguish these figurines from most Mycenaean examples in the Aegean but are well paralleled on Cyprus (Ben-Shlomo and Press 2009:60; see esp. at Sinda, Furumark and Adelman 2003:pl. 37.4–5, 7–9 [= pl. 39.4–5, 7–9]; V. Karageorghis 1993a:pl. XXII.4–5).

The second distinctive group is characterized especially by a hump on the back of the neck; they are clearly identified as bulls by their horns (see Petrie 1928:pl. XXXVII).[106] These figurines are distinct from the Mycenaean-style bulls in several respects: their overall size, the size and position of the hump, decoration, and the treatment of facial features. The Mycenaean decorated bulls appear to be slightly smaller (approximately 7–8 cm high and 8–10 cm long) than this second group (approximately 8–10 cm high and 10–12 cm long). The Mycenaean decorated bulls have a less prominent hump, which may not even be present on all examples; in addition, it is located along the neck, whereas on this second group it is more prominent and usually located more toward the back than along the neck. The second group lacks decoration; in addition, the heads of these figurines—unlike those of the Mycenaean-style bulls, but like those of the regular undifferentiated type discussed above—may have incisions to indicate nostrils and mouth. They also generally have applied pellets for eyes.

The third group, also identified by D. Ben-Shlomo primarily at Miqne (see Ben-Shlomo 2010:114–18, figs. 3.61–62), consists of miniature figurines; while other animals besides bulls appear to be present, the bull is the predominant animal represented. Besides their size (roughly 3–5 cm long), they are distinct in their lack of decoration as well as the lack of indicated facial features. Some examples (e.g., Miqne obj. nos. 4708, 7004; Ben-Shlomo 2010:fig. 3.61.1–2) have humps on the back of the neck. This group is also notable in that many examples have traces of soot, which is much less commonly found on the other groups of bulls, and on other figurine types more generally. Again, as pointed out by Ben-Shlomo (2010:118), this type is paralleled in the Aegean and Cyprus in the twelfth century (in particular at Enkomi; see Dikaios 1969b:pls. 131.35, 38–40, 137.16a; V. Karageorghis 1993a:43, pl. XXII.8).

II.D. Birds (Cat. No. 172)

The role of the bird in the Philistine figurine corpus is unclear. Originally, in my 2007 dissertation, I did not discuss this type. Bird representations had long been known in Iron Age Philistia, but the only modeled examples in clay were heads and necks from the so-called bird bowls (see T. Dothan 1982:224–27, ch. 4, pls. 9–11), known especially from Ashdod (e.g., M. Dothan and Freedman 1967:fig. 35.1–2; M. Dothan and Ben-Shlomo 2005:figs. 3.36.5–6, 3.62.6–9) and Qasile (e.g., A. Mazar 1980:fig. 28). In 2009, the Leon Levy Expedition to Ashkelon discovered a bird head and neck (cat. no. 172) that is much smaller than the typical heads from the bird bowls. Small heads are also known from bird bowls or other apparent zoomorphic vessels (e.g., from Ashdod [M. Dothan and Freedman 1967:figs. 7:15, 42:18; M. Dothan 1971:fig. 66.7–8] and Qasile [A. Mazar 1980:figs. 29–30, 42b]), but these are invariably decorated with painted stripes, whereas the Ashkelon example is undecorated. It is therefore very possible that cat. no. 172 is the head and neck of a bird figurine. A possible indication of what such a bird figurine may have looked like is given by an example from Tell Jemmeh (UCL no. EXXXVI.8/65; Petrie 1928:pl. XXXIX.10–11); unfortunately, the date of the Jemmeh example is unclear, although it is likely to be Iron Age due to the nature of the larger assemblage. Unfortunately, any further discussion of the bird figurine type would be completely speculative.

Summary

The figurines of Iron Age Philistia belong to a series of types, some well-defined and some quite broad and unstandardized. There are a few significant types which account for the vast majority of the figurines: the Philistine Psi, Ashdoda, composite figurine, and horse. The remaining types—the plaque figurine, "dea gravida," hybrid human figurines, various male figurines, bull groups, and other miscellaneous animals—often consist of isolated examples; in some cases it is not even clear that a definite type has been identified. Most of the figurines, however, can be fairly securely assigned to a specific type.

As a general rule, much more attention was paid by the producers of these figurines to the anthropomorphic figurines than to the zoomorphic figurines. The only figurines for which molds—allowing for additional levels of detail—were used are anthropomorphic. All of the zoomorphic figurines are made by hand; no part of them is ever made on the potter's wheel, as are some of the anthropomorphic bodies. Other than the Mycenaean-derived bovine figurines, painted decoration is found only on rare examples; it occurs more often on anthropomorphic figurines, though here too mostly on figurines of Mycenaean derivation. These observations justify to some extent

[106] Note that zebu vertebrae have been identified in Palestine, for example at Tell Jemmeh (possibly from LB contexts; see Hesse 1997:442).

the focus of most modern scholars on the anthropomorphic figurines; this focus, it appears, was an aspect of figurine production in Iron Age Philistia, and is not just a bias of the modern researcher.

The most essential achievement of this chapter is the process of identification itself. This is an important step in the study of the Philistine figurines because it represents the first attempt to identify systematically the entire range of Iron Age types. The iconographic analyses of the different types have necessarily been brief; I have tried to focus particularly on areas where I could contribute original research and conclusions or at least research and conclusions which have not been featured in the scholarly literature on figurines of Palestine. In other cases, I have presented simply a summary of the major issues. The identification of the types, on the other hand, is important not only for the new contribution it represents. It will also serve as the basis of the analysis in the following chapter: a series of contextual analyses of the figurines, through which I will identify additional patterns corresponding to differences among types or crosscutting them.

7. Contextual Studies

In the previous two chapters, I have begun the process of analyzing the figurines through the steps of description and iconography. The current chapter is an attempt to continue this analysis on a level similar to Panofsky's "iconology." Through a contextual study of the figurines—an essential component of a study of figurines, as a group of archaeological objects—I will address questions of how the figurines were used. In addition, through identifying patterns of distribution I will be able to identify synchronic and diachronic differences: distinct cultural regions and changes over time, as reflected in the figurines.

As I have just suggested, there are two basic elements to this contextual analysis: chronological and spatial. The first involves looking at how the entire corpus of figurines differed from period to period, as well as how individual figurine types developed. The second involves in turn three levels of analysis:

1. inter-regional: between Philistia and its neighbors;

2. intra-regional (subregional, or inter-site): among the different subregions or sites of Philistia; and

3. intra-site: between different contexts at a site.

Thus, I will address questions of how the figurines were used at a site and how figurines may have been used differently by type. This spatial analysis also allows me to use the figurines as a test of the idea of a Philistine culture region, corresponding to the geographical and political borders of Philistia.

Chronological Study

A summary of the essential chronological data of figurine distribution is presented in table 7.1.

Before I discuss the data in detail, it is necessary to mention its limitations. This table gives only a rough indication of the chronological distribution of the main figurine types, as there are several problems with the data that had to be addressed. First, the table includes only the material from the three sites of Ashdod, Ashkelon, and Miqne. I have excluded material from the other sites for two main reasons: for the most part, they have only small numbers of figurines, and their stratigraphic sequences are not as complete or as well understood. Outside of these Pentapolis sites, only Tell Jemmeh has a large number of figurines: Petrie (1928) published over 150 terracottas from his excavation; most of these, along with several dozen more unpublished figurines are currently located at the Institute of Archaeology, University College, London (with some others in the collection of the Rockefeller Museum). Understanding the stratigraphy and chronology of Petrie's excavation, however, is a difficult task. In working at sites in southern Palestine, Petrie devised a chronology entirely independent of that used by other archaeologists in the region; instead, it was based solely on parallels (real or fictive) with Egyptian sites. As a result, Petrie's dates are generally unreliable.[1] The figurines from his excavations must be dated primarily on stylistic grounds and are therefore useless as independent evidence for the dates of figurine types.

The numbers given in the table are only approximate, as it is not always easy to identify types. This is particularly the case for Ashdod; I have not been able to inspect most of the Ashdod figurines personally and have therefore relied on the published drawings and photographs, which are not always clear. In addition, there are unpublished figurines from Ashdod which I could not include. It can be difficult to distinguish Ashdoda and Philistine Psi heads to begin with, and this problem is magnified by reliance on the drawings and photographs for the Ashdod examples.

Not all figurine types are present, as I do not have sufficient contextual data on certain types (e.g., the humped bovine figurines). The dates in the table are approximate; the absolute chronology of the strata and phases at these sites is known only to the level of decades. Beyond this, many strata and phases of course straddle centuries. The data from Ashdod, again, are especially problematic. There is an unusually large number of figurines from Ashdod that are surface finds or otherwise come from unstratified contexts. Even those whose loci are secure are often assigned not to a particular stratum but to a range of possible strata.[2]

Finally, the table combines primary contexts—floors or other surfaces with occupational buildup (in other words, where the figurines were being used)—and

[1] As Albright noted concerning Petrie's work at Tell el-ᶜAjjul:

> Archeologists have been very cautious in utilizing this rich new documentation, since the divergence between Petrie's chronology of Palestinian pottery and that of all other scholars is so great and since his historical deductions are in such sharp contrast to generally accepted views that no statement of Petrie's can be accepted without careful critical examination. (1938:338)

[2] Cf. Jacobs (1996:278–79) on the "confusion about the concept of 'stratum'" evident in *Ashdod V* (M. Dothan and Porath 1993).

Table 7.1: Distribution of Types at Pentapolis Sites, by Century

Catalogue Category	*Figurine Type*	*12th Cent.*	*11th Cent.*	*10th Cent.*	*9th Cent.*	*8th Cent.*	*7th Cent.*
I.A.1	Philistine Psi	9	15	3	0	0	4
I.A.2	Ashdoda	0	14	6	2	4	6
I.A.2	"Late Ashdoda"	0	0	0	0	1	6
I.A.3	Composite figurine	0	0	0	0	1	36
I.A.4	Plaque figurine	2	5	0	3	5	10
I.A.6/I.B	"Ashdodite head"	0	0	0	0	3	5
II.A	Horse/rider	0	0	0	0	1	85
II.C	Mycenean-style bovine	9	0	0	0	0	0

secondary contexts—for example, fills, in which figurines were deposited by various processes after they were no longer in use. Because of the manner in which contexts are reported in the Ashdod volumes, which may in turn reflect flaws in the original excavation and recording techniques, it is often difficult to distinguish between primary and secondary contexts at that site. Locus descriptions such as "room" do not differentiate between the living surface of the room itself and other contexts such as constructional and leveling fills, walls, and other built features. Other descriptions, such as "area," are even more vague. As a result, primary and secondary contexts can be reasonably identified only at Ashkelon and Miqne. In the analysis below, I will indicate where contexts are primary, or secondary, as appropriate.

On a general level, the data in table 7.1 confirm what has been widely known, or believed, about the figurines of Philistia. The Mycenaean-style female figurines (I.A.1–2) are characteristic of Iron I, while the composite female figurines and the horse (with or without rider; I.A.3 and II.A) are typical of (late) Iron II. The plaque figurine (I.A.4), already well established in Palestine in the LB, is found more or less throughout the entire Iron Age. An unusual aspect of this distribution is the large number of Mycenaean-style female figurines, especially Ashdodas, found in Iron II contexts. It is to be expected that a few Mycenaean-style figurines would be found in Iron II contexts; these can be discounted as residual and would normally appear in secondary contexts such as fills. The 12 Ashdodas present in post-tenth-century contexts, however, is a large number (relative to the total number of Ashdodas) for merely residual finds. An investigation of the individual contexts in this case is very illuminating. At Miqne, only one possible figurine of type I.A.1 or 2 was found in an Iron II context: obj. no. 57 is from pit fill of Stratum IA (a brief period of reoccupation after the Babylonian destruction). Ashkelon has a larger number of Iron I female figurines in late contexts. Three such Philistine Psi figurines—cat. nos. 3, 4, and 17—were found; two were from a massive layer of seventh-century fill in Grid 50, while the other was from the fill of a floor makeup in Grid 38. Of five Iron II Ashdodas, one came from this Grid 50 fill layer; one came from a seventh-century foundation trench in Grid 50; one came from seventh-century robber trench fill in Grid 38; one was from the fill of a tenth- or ninth-century pit in Grid 38; and one (a flat-chested Ashdoda) was from early Iron II fill in Grid 2.[3] All of the I.A.1 and 2 examples from Ashkelon and Miqne, then, are from secondary contexts; the same is true for all of the Iron II (specifically, seventh-century) Philistine Psi figurines from the Pentapolis as a whole. The remainders, then, are Iron II (and mostly ninth- and eighth-century) Ashdodas, all from Ashdod. Again, Ashdod is somewhat problematic in that primary and secondary contexts are difficult to distinguish; there is some issue concerning the assignment of figurines to specific strata, and there can be confusion with the separate "Late Ashdoda" type. Therefore, I would conclude that the Philistine Psi and Ashdoda figurines are characteristic of Iron I and found in Iron II only as residual artifacts in secondary contexts.

Moving beyond these initial impressions, it is best to study the data more closely by period.

Iron I

With the detailed stratigraphic sequences for the Iron I in Ashdod and especially Miqne and Ashkelon, it is possible to reach more detailed conclusions concerning the origin and development of figurine types. Table 7.2 lists the number of Philistine Psi and Ashdoda figurines from each Iron I stratum (or local phase) at each site.

[3] Another Ashdoda (cat. no. 30) was found in a Late Roman or Byzantine well in Grid 50.

Table 7.2: Distribution of Iron I Female Figurines at Pentapolis Sites, by Stratum/Phase

Date	*Site*		
Early/mid-twelfth century	Ashdod XIII 0	Miqne VII 0	Grid 38 Phase 20 0
Late twelfth century	Ashdod XII 3	Miqne VI 2	Grid 38 Phase 19 5
Early eleventh century	Ashdod XI 8	Miqne V 6	Grid 38 Phase 18 7
Late eleventh/early tenth century	Ashdod X 6	Miqne IV 5	Grid 38 Phase 17 7

Local phases are used for Ashkelon Grid 38, as this is the only area of the site where a detailed Iron I sequence has been revealed. Dates are only approximate. Moreover, the correlation among the strata/phases of the Pentapolis sites is not precisely set. Although four major strata or phases have been identified at each site, the chances that they are exactly synchronous are very small.

This table includes only the excavated Pentapolis sites (Ashdod, Miqne-Ekron, and Ashkelon). Sites outside of the Pentapolis have a limited number of Philistine Psi and Ashdoda figurines; in addition, they do not have the same detailed sequence covering the entire period of Iron I from the initial Philistine settlement (ca. 1175 B.C.E.).

The numbers of figurines are also only approximate for a number of reasons. At Ashkelon and Miqne, the final stratigraphic and contextual data are not fully published, and some small uncertainties remain (for this reason, there have been some changes to the Ashkelon data between the original publication of this study as a dissertation and its current form). At all sites, it is not always easy to classify Philistine Psi and Ashdoda fragments, especially head fragments that fall in the overlap range of the two types (see chapter 6). Finally, working from the drawings and photographs of the Ashdod figurines of these types—all of which may not be published—introduces additional uncertainty.

The data in the table reveal significant patterns in the chronology of these figurine types, patterns which for the most part were previously unknown. There are no Philistine Psi or Ashdoda figurines from the earliest (Monochrome) phase; while a small number have been discovered in the succeeding earliest Bichrome phase, there is an apparent sudden increase in their use around 1100 B.C.E. This popularity appears to be largely maintained over the course of the eleventh century. The absence of Mycenaean-style female figurines in the Monochrome phase may be a fluke, as we might expect an occasional example there as well.[4] What is clear is that there are few Mycenaean-style female figurines in the twelfth century overall, as opposed to a relatively large number after about 1100 B.C.E.[5]

It is necessary to address a few possible objections to this conclusion:

1. Ben-Shlomo (pers. comm., July 2006) has suggested that the chronological pattern might have to do with differentials in excavated areas among phases at each site. In Ashkelon Grid 38, however, there is little to no difference between the excavated areas in the earliest and latest phases; as of 2010, twelfth-century remains have been excavated in all four full squares and all four half-squares.

[4] Note that there are Mycenaean-style bovines in this phase from Miqne (Ben-Shlomo and Press 2009:30, table 4). Also, as first pointed out to me by D. Ben-Shlomo, the clay of two or three examples from Ashkelon (cat. nos. 2, 8) and Miqne (obj. no. 5080; Ben-Shlomo and Press 2009:fig. 1.1) is similar to the well-levigated clay of Philistine Monochrome pottery (see Ben-Shlomo and Press 2009:45). While none of these examples was found in a monochrome-phase context, they are among the earliest Philistine Psi figurines in Philistia, coming from Miqne VIB and Ashkelon Grid 38 Phase 19.

[5] To my knowledge, Yasur-Landau (2002:237) was the first to make this observation concerning the figurines, although he did not provide detailed evidence in support and did not have access to most of the Ashkelon material at the time. Note that at Ashkelon there is a relatively large number of later twelfth-century (Phase 19) Mycenaean-style female figurines, in relation to both contemporary strata at other sites and the numbers from subsequent phases at Ashkelon. Phase 19 is probably longer in timespan then the late twelfth-century strata at Ashdod and Miqne, which may at least partially explain the larger number of figurines. Since at least three of the five Phase 19 figurines come from Phase 19A, it appears based on the (admittedly limited) data that the frequency of these figurines was increasing toward the end of the twelfth century.

2. The sample size at each site, and in fact overall, is relatively small. Given that the same trend appears at each of the three sites, however, it is highly suggestive and likely significant statistically.

3. Table 7.2 combines primary and secondary contexts. It would be unusual, however, for the figurines made in a specific stratum to be more common in the fills of a later stratum than on the surfaces and in the fills of the stratum in which they were made. In addition, an analysis of only primary contexts (at Ashkelon and Miqne) reveals the same pattern. Most of the Philistine Psi and Ashdoda figurines from primary contexts at Miqne come from Strata V and IV. There is only one example from Miqne VI in a primary context: obj. no. 5080, from a hearth. On the other hand, there are one or two examples from primary contexts in Miqne V: obj. no. 140, from occupational debris, and obj. no. 1400, a possible Psi torso from occupational debris.[6] Three come from primary contexts in Stratum IV: obj. nos. 3948 and 3949, from surfaces, and obj. no. 4517, from an installation. At Ashkelon Grid 38, there are two figurines of these types in Phase 19 primary contexts (cat. no. 14, from occupational debris, and cat. no. 13, from a courtyard surface), while in Phase 18 three come from occupational debris (cat. nos. 9, 23, 25). In addition, analysis of the Ashkelon data reveals another pattern. There is only one Philistine Psi or Ashdoda figurine from a primary context later than 18A (the last subphase of Phase 18): cat. no. 31, from a 17A courtyard.[7] At Miqne, two of the five figurines from Stratum IV come from fill layers; in Stratum V, even many of those not from occupational buildup are from pits or a wall. These patterns, combined with the slight drop in Philistine Psi and Ashdoda figurines at Ashdod and Miqne over the course of the eleventh century (Ashdod XI to X, Miqne V to IV), suggest that by the late eleventh or early tenth century these two figurine types were declining in popularity.[8]

One more aspect of the chronology of the Mycenaean-style female figurines involves distinguishing between the Philistine Psi and Ashdoda types. In doing so, we see that there are no Ashdodas from the twelfth century (see table 7.1).[9] One example from Ashdod (M. Dothan and Y. Porath 1993:79, pl. 45.1) called an "Ashdoda" is attributed to Stratum XII, the late twelfth century. The figurine appears only in the plates; there is no drawing in the figures. From the photograph, it is clear that this is a Mycenaean-style head; as there is no scale indicated, nor any measurements given in the text, however, it cannot be confirmed on the basis of the publication alone that this is an Ashdoda head (as it is labeled), as opposed to a

[6] In addition, two Stratum V figurines (obj. nos. 2323, 999) come from walls and one (obj. no. 6088) from a pit; while not primary, these contexts may reflect a deposition closer to the time of use than simple constructional or leveling fill.

[7] Cat. no. 6 comes from 17B floor makeup, but this context almost certainly is the fill used to lay down a dirt floor and so is not primary.

[8] Note, however, that the one example of an Ashdoda from Qasile comes from the floor of a Stratum X (= Miqne IV/Ashdod X) building (A. Mazar 1986:12).

[9] There are various references in the literature to twelfth-century Ashdodas (or Mycenaean-style figurines generally), but further investigation reveals that, in most cases, the figurines under discussion were found in eleventh-century contexts. T. Dothan has written that the "complete" Ashdoda came from a floor in Ashdod Stratum XII (1982:234; see also Dothan and Dothan 1992:183; M. Dothan 1971:21). It is clear from the site report, however, that the figurine is from Area H local Stratum 4b, which equals (general) Stratum XI (M. Dothan 1971:161, fig. 91.1; see also M. Dothan and Ben-Shlomo 2005:186). T. Dothan's attribution may have been influenced by her attempt to associate the complete Ashdoda with the Area H apsidal building of Stratum XII, which she has interpreted as cultic (1982:41, 234). In fact, the Ashdoda was found in a building across the street from the apsidal structure (as observed by Yasur-Landau 2001:335).

T. Dothan and S. Gitin, the excavators of Miqne, have published various articles illustrating two Mycenaean-style female figurines that are labeled as from Miqne Stratum VII (T. Dothan 1995:fig. 3.12; Gitin and Dothan 1987:203; Dothan and Gitin 1994:10). As a result, the claim that Ashdoda and other Mycenaean-derived figurines have been found in the Monochrome phase at Miqne has begun to enter the literature (see B. J. Stone 1995:19; A. Mazar 2000:223; Yasur-Landau 2002:189–90). The attribution of these figurines to Stratum VII, however, seems incorrect. One of the figurines (Miqne obj. no. 140) is in fact known to have been found in Stratum V (S. Gitin, pers. comm., July 2006). The status of the other figurine is unclear, as S. Gitin has not been able to find its location or a record of it (pers. comm., December 2006). On inspecting the Miqne figurines in June 2006, I did not see a single example of a Mycenaean-style female figurine from Stratum VII. Similarly, D. Ben-Shlomo (pers. comm., July 2006) has stated that, to his knowledge, no such figurines were found in Miqne VII.

Finally, there are two Ashdoda seats from Area G at Ashdod (G112/2 and G741/1) whose date is unclear. One is said to be from local Stratum 7, which equals general Strata XII–XI, and the other from local Strata 7–6, equal to general Strata XII–X (M. Dothan 1971:figs. 75.1–2). Again, these attributions display the same problematic application of the term "stratum" that was observed above, and so these examples cannot be relied upon as evidence of twelfth-century Ashdodas. Nevertheless, in *Ashdod II–III* M. Dothan still described Ashdoda figurines as twelfth-century finds (1971:21).

Philistine Psi head.[10] A personal investigation of this figurine at the IAA storehouse in Beth Shemesh, however, has shown that the neck diameter of this figurine is 1.6–1.7 cm; it is likely, then, that the head was mislabeled an "Ashdoda" and is in fact a Psi head. In any case, there is no locus given for the figurine, so that its attribution to Stratum XII cannot be confirmed. It is likely, therefore, that no Ashdoda has been found in a twelfth-century context.

On the basis of the above data, I would suggest the following hypothesis: the Ashdoda is a later development than the Philistine Psi figurine and may not make its first appearance until around 1100 B.C.E. Besides the evidence of the contextual information, the iconographic analysis of the Ashdoda (see chapter 6) lends supporting evidence. While the Philistine Psi figurine is simply a continuation of the Late Psi form of Mycenaean figurine, the Ashdoda is a new development, unparalleled by any earlier finds in the Aegean or on Cyprus. It must represent one or more stages of development beyond any seated figurine form known from those areas. Beyond this, the popularity of the Ashdoda also seems to mark it as a distinct phenomenon. Table 7.1 shows that the Ashdoda figurines were roughly as popular as the Philistine Psi figurines at the Pentapolis sites and that these were the two main female figurine types in the Iron I. In the Aegean, however, Mycenaean seated figurines were relatively rare; while Olsen (1998:384) has counted about 70 examples of seated figurines, this number is dwarfed by the thousands of Psi, Phi, and Tau figurines that have been found.[11]

From the standpoint of the figurines, major changes appear to be taking place at the beginning of the eleventh century. Mycenaean-style female figurines suddenly become much more popular; along with this popularity, a new type—the Ashdoda—might be introduced. At the same time, the Mycenaean-style bovine figurines appear to have gone out of use; at Miqne, no example is found after Stratum VI (Ben-Shlomo and Press 2009:30, table 4). These developments may reflect more fundamental changes in Philistine society at this time. Yasur-Landau (2002:237) has referred to an "'explosion' in cult imagery" at the end of the twelfth century or the beginning of the eleventh; he based this observation partially on the increase in figurines but also on the appearance of cultic architecture and cult objects at Qasile and Miqne. L. Mazow has observed contemporary changes in the use of Philistine pottery at Miqne, suggesting a move from domestic utilitarian vessels to fineware for elite feasting; in her view, this reflects a change in Philistine identity from a purely ethnic one to an elite one (2005:451–52, 459–61).[12] The changes observed in the figurines, then, may well be related to other changes in Philistine material culture at the time and perhaps to changes in the very nature of Philistine identity (cf. Faust and Lev-Tov 2011).

At the same time, changes in the figurines may be connected to closer relations with Cyprus in the early eleventh century.[13] The Ashdoda, with possible Cypriot elements incorporated into the form (see chapter 6), points to Cypriot influence on Philistine terracottas. There is also the small group of undecorated human figurines that appear to represent a hybrid of local and Aegean elements. As I discussed in chapter 6, this type of hybrid is also found on Cyprus, where it is more common. In particular, there is the Ashkelon figurine (cat. no. 186) that closely parallels an example from Enkomi. The Enkomi figurine (no. 1167; Dikaios 1969b:pls. 147.40–41, 177.6–7; Karageorghis 1993a:pl. XVII.6) was found in Level IIIC, which dates to LC IIIB (late twelfth to early eleventh century; see Dikaios 1971:496). The Ashkelon figurine, meanwhile, was found in the fill of a sunken jar installation from Grid 38 Phase 18B (early eleventh century). While the amount of evidence for Cypriot influence on Philistine terracottas of the eleventh century is small, and should not be interpreted too broadly, it is nevertheless suggestive.

As I argued in chapter 6, these Cypriot-type hybrid figurines may also be related to hybrids among types I.A.1 and 2 (specifically, cat. nos. 10 and 28 and the

[10] See chapter 6 for the measurement of neck diameter as a criterion for distinguishing the Ashdoda and Philistine Psi types.

[11] French (1971:107; 2009:59) reported that over 1100 fragments were found at Mycenae in the 1939–1955 excavations alone, with another 1650 fragments from the 1959–1969 excavations, while noting that these amounts were exceptional. It is not unusual, however, for an excavation to produce over 100 Mycenaean standing figurines at a site: e.g., 175 at Midea (Demakopoulou and Divari-Valakou 2001:182) and 121 from Klenies, Haghia Triada in the Argolid (Kilian 1990:185, figs. 1–3).

[12] D. Master (pers. comm. 2006), in his analysis of the Iron I pottery of Ashkelon, has suggested the possibility of a large increase in the amount of characteristically "Philistine" pottery (in proportion to pottery in the local Canannite tradition) from Grid 38 Phase 19 to Phase 18. He has cautioned, however, that his results are preliminary.

[13] As suggested for other classes of material culture by A. Yasur-Landau (pers. comm., January 2007). It appears that maritime trade in the eastern Mediterranean in general was somewhat revived in this time, as reflected for example in Cretan influence on Cypriot figurines, pottery, and other artifacts (see, e.g., Karageorghis 1970, esp. 33 [on naiskoi]; 1982:54; 1993a:58; Vandenabeele 1991:58–59).

Table 7.3: Distribution of Plaque Figurines at Sites in Philistia, by Century

Gesture	*12th Cent.*	*11th Cent.*	*10th Cent.*	*9th Cent.*	*8th Cent.*	*7th Cent.*
Hands cupping breasts	0	1	0	0	3	0
Arms at sides	0	0	0	0	1	2
One hand cupping breast, one at side	0	0	0	0	1	2
Holding disc	0	0	1	0	0	1
Cradling a child	0	0	0	0	0	1

Tell Jerishe peg figurine). Both of the Ashkelon figurines were found in eleventh-century contexts: cat. no. 10 in an 18A street and cat. no. 28 in 17A deliberate fill. Although the true Mycenaean-derived types disappear after the early tenth century, the hybrid of Aegean style and local gesture continues well into the Iron II. The figurines from the Yavneh cult stands (Kletter, Ziffer, and Zwickel 2010) show that such hybrids existed in the ninth century. Even later, the "Ashdodite heads" appear to carry on the tradition of handmade heads with applied eyes, if now with more naturalistic features (for instance, a more human-looking nose). This type, along with the "Late Ashdoda," is found as late as the seventh century, suggesting that Aegean traditions of figurine production survived in some form until the end of Philistine settlement in Palestine.

Plaque Figurines

To judge by the known examples, the plaque figurine was never a particularly popular figurine type in Iron Age Philistia. For each of the Philistine Psi and Ashdoda types—which were produced over a period of roughly 200 years—there are more than 30 examples known from the Pentapolis sites. By contrast, these sites have produced only 22 known examples of plaque figurines from the whole of the Iron Age. It is therefore more difficult to draw sound conclusions about this type than about the Iron I handmade figurines.

Table 7.3 presents every plaque figurine from Philistia whose gesture is clear and whose context is fairly secure. I have organized the data by figurine gesture in order to try to reach some conclusions concerning the relative lifespans of different plaque figurine gestures. As the sample size is particularly small, these conclusions are necessarily limited but can at least provide a good starting point for discussion. I have not included the plaques from Tel Sera^{c} and Tel Haror, as their dates are not precise enough; according to E. Oren (pers. comm., June 2006), their contexts date between the eighth and sixth centuries, but I cannot narrow the range any further. I will, however, bring these figurines into the following discussion as appropriate. The plaque figurines from Tell Jemmeh, which likely date to the eighth to sixth centuries as well, will be treated in the same manner.[14]

The only gesture which is in evidence for both Iron I and Iron II is that of cupping the breasts, which is also the most common gesture. It appears already in a figurine from a Phase 18 floor in Ashkelon Grid 38 (cat. no. 68).[15] At the other end of the Iron Age, it is attested in eighth-century examples from Batash (mold E7051 [A. Mazar and Panitz-Cohen 2001:photos 132, 134, pl. 30.2], from a Stratum III floor) and Miqne (obj. no. 3235, from IIA occupational debris), as well as in a late eighth- or early seventh-century example from Miqne (obj. no. 5667, from occupational debris designated "Pre IB/C") . In addition, there is a cruder example (along the lines of the "Thick Style" plaques) from Tel Sera^{c} (no. 10114), dating to between the eighth and sixth centuries. That this gesture appears so

[14] Despite the problems with Petrie's chronology, this range of dates for the Jemmeh plaques to be discussed below—and for most of the figurines from Tell Jemmeh—is fairly secure. Wright, in his reassessment of Petrie's work at Jemmeh, concluded that almost all of the excavated remains dated to the tenth century or later (1939:460); a similar conclusion was reached by van Beek (1993:668–80). Beyond this, most of the figurines found at Jemmeh have close parallels at neighboring sites and so can be identified as examples of eighth- to sixth-century types.

[15] Note also cat. no. 70, from Phase 17A deliberate fill in Grid 38. It appears to have the left arm preserved, cupping the left breast; while it is likely that the right arm would have been cupping the left breast, the left side of the figurine is missing. In addition, while the fragment is a typical plaque form with flat back, it appears to be handmade instead of moldmade. Another example, from Ashdod (C176/1; M. Dothan and Freedman 1967:fig. 35.4), was found in a large pit (Area C Locus 2001). The material found inside was almost exclusively Iron I, with nothing later; on the other hand, only a few LB sherds were found and considered contamination (M. Dothan and Freedman 1967:108). The upper torso of the figurine is damaged, but the arms are clearly bent back toward the breasts.

early or so frequently is not surprising, given that it is the most basic gesture of the LB plaques (see Pritchard 1943:10–14).

None of the other gestures appears on an example datable to Iron I. The next gesture to appear is that of holding a disc. This is quite a rare type, appearing in only two examples: the first is from the tenth-century destruction in Aphek Area X (Kochavi 1976:52, pl. 11c; 1989:fig. 75), while the second (Miqne obj. no. 1250) is from occupational debris in Miqne IA (the post-Babylonian destruction reoccupation). The other gestures—arms at the sides, one hand cupping the breast and the arm at the side, and cradling a child—are attested only in the eighth and seventh centuries. Of these, cradling a child is found only once (cat. no. 66, from a late seventh-century fill layer). The others are attested multiple times, as the gesture of arms at the sides is particularly common on the "Thick Style" plaques from Jemmeh (see Petrie 1928:pl. XXXVI.34–35); it is also found on one example from Tel Haror (no. 18125).

Table 7.1 shows that the plaque figurines are the most common anthropomorphic type in the early Iron II (tenth to eighth centuries)—indeed, it appears to be the only human figurine type then commonly in use. Plaques showing a pregnant female are particularly common in this period and into the seventh century (see, e.g., Ashdod D868/1 [M. Dothan 1971:fig. 64.1]; H436/1 [M. Dothan and Ben-Shlomo 2005:fig. 3.96.4]). Only one gesture can be clearly identified on these figurines—the combination gesture of one hand cupping the breast, with the other arm down at the side; the other examples do not preserve the arms but are similar enough to the examples with combination gesture to suggest they may have shared it (Ashdod D/636/1 and D1022/1; M. Dothan 1971:fig. 64.2–3).[16] Unfortunately, it is difficult to make any further generalizations concerning the popularity of these plaque types. Besides the problem of the relatively small sample size, there is also the issue of provenience; most of the plaques—and figurines in general from this period—come from Ashdod. Ashkelon and Miqne both have limited remains in the areas of excavation between the early tenth and early eighth centuries (T. Dothan 1995:pl. IV; *Ashkelon 1*, pp. 275, 308; at Ashkelon, the gap extends into the late eighth or early seventh). Thus, at Miqne there is a total of two figurines, of all of the major types combined, coming from contexts dating between the mid-tenth and late-eighth centuries (one of them being a plaque, obj. no. 3235). At Ashkelon, there is only one such figurine (a possible horse body fragment; see below). As a result, the relative frequency of plaque figurines may not be representative of the early Iron II but instead representative of Ashdod. Nevertheless, the Batash molds and Miqne obj. no. 3235 demonstrate that, at least for the eighth century, the plaque figurine likely was the major anthropomorphic figurine type.

A. Yasur-Landau (pers. comm.) suggests that the plaque figurines from Iron I contexts in Philistia are residual—that they are merely secondary deposits of figurines made and used in the LB. He argues that the type is superseded by the new Mycenaean-derived female types. This is certainly possible given the small number of plaques in the period. Only four examples can be possibly assigned to the Iron I: cat. no. 68, discussed above; cat. no. 70, from Phase 17 fill; Ashdod C176/1, from a pit (though one with almost exclusively Iron I remains); and cat. no. 69, from a Monochrome period street. Cat. no. 69 is of a type clearly datable to the thirteenth century (see chapter 6) and so is almost certainly residual. The others, both with hands to the breast, are conceivably of Iron I type, but only cat. no. 68 comes from a primary context.

It is very difficult to argue for the survival of a type on the basis of one figurine. It is noteworthy, however, that plaque figurines are never found in large numbers, even in the Iron II (see Table 7.1); in the seventh century, when they clearly are in use, they form only a small proportion of the total number of female figurines, being dwarfed by the composite type. Nor are plaque figurines found in large numbers at any site in the southern coastal plain in the LB; at Ashkelon, for instance, there is only one plaque from a clear LB context. It is certainly difficult to conclude that Mycenaean-derived types superseded plaque figurines in the Iron I, since there were few plaques to be superseded, and more plaques have been found in Iron I contexts (even if mostly secondary) than in LB contexts. In addition, I consider it to be significant that, when plaque figurines are found in larger numbers in the Iron II, they appear in the same basic types as the earlier examples, especially with the gesture of hands to the breasts. Similarly, when the composite figurines appear in the eighth and seventh centuries, the people of Philistia adapted them to portray the same limited set of gestures (see chapter 6 and below). Thus, it appears that the small range of gestures found on these figurines, and especially the gesture of hands to the breasts, were deeply rooted in the regional culture. At the very least, the ideas behind the plaques must have survived through the Iron I, if not the figurines

[16] Other examples from unstratified contexts (e.g., Ashdod M1919/3; M. Dothan and Porath 1982:fig. 34.1) are depicted as pregnant and appear to display the same gesture and so can probably be assigned to this period.

themselves. This survival is also demonstrated by the Iron I hybrid figurines, which depict these same traditional gestures on Mycenaean-style figurines (e.g., cat. nos. 10, 28). Nevertheless, it is clear that—even if plaque figurines continued to be made and used in Iron I Philistia—they were at best a minor type.

Eighth and Seventh Centuries

The composite female figurine and the horse (with or without rider) are clearly the two most prevalent types in the late Iron Age. As I discussed in chapter 6, the origin of both types is likely to be found in Phoenicia. The Phoenician figurines, however, are too poorly known to provide a detailed chronology, beyond a starting point sometime in the eighth century. Kletter (1999:39) has concluded that the majority of datable horse and rider figurines of Palestine are from eighth-century contexts, though some can also be dated to the seventh century. Through a careful analysis of the dates of the Judahite pillar figurines, he has similarly concluded that this type was already common in the eighth century but continued through the rest of the Iron Age (1996:40–43). Kletter was unable, however, to reach any more precise chronological conclusions. Holladay tried to demonstrate that the earliest datable domestic "cult" assemblages, including composite figurines, appear in northern Palestine around the mid-eighth century and spread to Judah later at the end of the eighth century (1987:278–80; cf. Moorey 2003:58).[17] Holladay's analysis, however, was based on only one site each in the north (Hazor) and the south (Lachish). Despite the numerous examples, none of the finds from Philistia clarifies the problems of origin and diffusion. A large part of the problem is the gap in excavated remains at Ashkelon and Miqne, discussed above, which extends into the eighth century. Between the two sites, a total of three figurines can be assigned to the eighth century. Other sites are also problematic; the large corpus of figurines from Tell Jemmeh can be dated only on comparative evidence. As for Sera^{c} and Haror, currently the date of the figurines can only be given as a range between the eighth to sixth centuries.

Very few examples of the two types from Philistia can possibly be dated to the eighth century. A composite figurine head of Type 5 (obj. no. 6559) from Miqne was found in fill of Stratum IIB (early eighth century). This type, however, is the typical Judahite pillar figurine (JPF) moldmade head discussed in detail by Kletter and cannot be reliably dated before the latter part of the eighth century in Judah. It is possible that this find is intrusive.[18] Alternatively, it is noteworthy that P. James (2006; following certain ideas of Stager) has suggested lowering the dates of Miqne Strata II and I, with Stratum IIB being redated to the second half of the eighth century, but this idea remains speculative until complete publication of the material. A composite (pillar) body from Batash (reg. no. 1183; A. Mazar and Panitz-Cohen 2001:208, photo 136, pl. 57.15) comes from the street of either Stratum III or Stratum II, meaning that its date could range from the eighth to the early sixth century. A composite (JPF) figurine was found at Tell eṣ-Ṣafi (basket 110050) in level A3, dating to the late eighth or early seventh century (A. Maeir, pers. comm., May 2006). At Ashkelon, cat. no. 130 can be assigned to Grid 50 Phase 8, which should be dated to the late eighth or early seventh century. It is the front part of a zoomorphic body, which is perhaps likely but not certainly a horse. As a result, even if an origin in the eighth century (as in Phoenicia and Judah) is likely, there is no example of either the composite female figurine or the horse from a clear eighth-century context in Philistia.

While the origin of these types in Philistia is not clear, that they were used on a large scale into the late seventh century is certain. At Ashkelon, the majority of figurines of both types come from the large quarry fill of Grid 50, laid down in preparation for the construction of the marketplace in the late seventh century. The composition of this fill is unusual; while most fill layers contain artifacts from a range of preceding

[17] Holladay associated the dates of introduction of these domestic assemblages with Assyrian and Babylonian influence; its introduction in the south later than in the north, according to him, reflects the spread of Assyrian (and Babylonian) control over the region. We saw in chapter 6 that several scholars have tried to associate the rise of the horse and rider type in the Levant and Cyprus, and some of its specific iconography, with Assyrian influence. The case for the composite figurines is less convincing, however. Even if Holladay's data concerning the dates of the figurines by site are correct, there is no need to associate this pattern with increasing Assyrian influence. After all, these figurine types are not Assyrian in origin but from the Lebanese coast. A better explanation would be that northern Palestine, given its proximity to Phoenicia and Cyprus, was influenced by these figurine types before areas further south. In other words, if the pattern Holladay has observed is real, it may simply reflect the gradual spread of these types south from Cyprus and Phoenicia; Holladay himself suggested that the domestic cult was "revitalized" by foreign contact, particularly with Phoenicia.

[18] B. Mazar found a pillar figurine body in Area A at Tell Qasile (1950/51:206, fig. 13c); it was reported to be from Stratum VIII, which Mazar dated to the ninth century. A. Mazar later redated Stratum VIII to the tenth century (1980:11) but considered the pillar figurine to be from the seventh century (1980:114).

periods, the Grid 50 fill contains seventh-century material almost exclusively. In fact, much of it is clearly datable to the latter part of the century: there is a large amount of Greek imported pottery, including Wild Goat Style (cf. Stager 2006b:18; *Ashkelon 1*, pp. 309–12; *Ashkelon 3*, pp. 130–32, 244–81).[19] Therefore, while the contextual information of the majority of the horse and composite female figurines is useless for determining function, it provides a relatively precise chronological anchor in the late seventh century. In addition, several horse figurines were found in the 604 destruction debris, both in the winery in Grid 38 (cat. no. 142) and throughout the marketplace in Grid 50 (cat. nos. 79, 83, 109, 111). A plaque figurine head (cat. no. 65) was also found in the destruction debris of the marketplace.

As I discussed in chapter 6, the plaque figurines and the composite figurines share the same basic set of gestures: hands cupping the breasts, hands at the sides, and arms cradling a child.[20] Thus, it appears that these two figurine types had the same basic referent, or meaning—they represented the same figure (or figures). The possibility remains that they could have been used for different functions. The plaque is not freestanding, and so it must have been laid down on its back or propped against or hung on a wall; the composite figurine, on the other hand, stood on its own. Also, the plaque is not finished on its back, indicating—beyond the position in which it was displayed—that it was to be viewed from the front. The composite figurine could have been viewed from all sides (although usually more attention is given to decoration and finish on the front, indicating this was the focal point). These differences in technique and physical properties could have been connected to different types of uses.

The chronological distribution of these two types, however, argues against this conclusion. The plaque, as discussed in chapter 6, was the basic figurine type in the Late Bronze Age and continues to be found at sites in Philistia (and elsewhere) through the end of the Iron Age.[21] The composite figurine, on the other hand, was introduced to Palestine in the late Iron Age, probably around the middle of the eighth century, and probably continued into the Persian period. Therefore, it appears that these two types were used concurrently only for a fairly short period. It seems likely that the two figurine types had similar (if not the same) functions and that the composite type superseded the plaque, as the new technique came to be used widely in the Levant in the eighth and seventh centuries.

As for the other significant eighth- to seventh-century type, the humped bovine, its dating is less secure. The primary site at which they appear is Tell Jemmeh, which as I have discussed above is unreliable for chronology. In general they appear to be from the Iron II but cannot be dated much more precisely. They appear at Seraᶜ, Haror, and Ruqeish in eighth- to sixth-century contexts (E. Oren, pers. comm., June 2006), but the same problem involving the current lack of precision affects the dating of these figurines as it does the composite figurines. I can only conclude that, on the basis of their general association (in the same strata) as the composite figurines and the horse figurines, their lifespan is more or less the same as those types: i.e., they are primarily if not exclusively a seventh- (and perhaps eighth-) century type.[22]

Finally, I should mention the pregnant woman ("Dea gravida") type and the associated hollow moldmade technique. In chapter 6 I briefly referred to the uncertainty relating to the introduction of the type and the technique; a more detailed discussion is in order here. The type is often considered characteristic of the Persian period, as it is found in a number of cultic *favissae* from that time (see Negbi 1966:8, 12; Stern 1982:171, 272 n. 57; Pritchard 1988:51). In particular, it was long thought that the hollow moldmade technique was introduced from the Aegean in the sixth century B.C.E. (Negbi 1966:8 n. 57; Stern 1989:27). Some more recent discussions of this figurine type, however, have suggested that it had an earlier floruit: seventh to sixth centuries (Dayagi-Mendels 2002:148), or even eighth to sixth centuries (Gubel 1991:131; see also Gubel 1983:33–34). This revised dating follows that of Culican, who conducted the most detailed study of the type (1969). Culican, however, was very cautious in his dating, suggesting only that the type began about 600 B.C.E. (1969:39).[23]

---

[19] In my view, the likeliest explanation is that the fill was taken from a dump currently in use.

[20] Note also that this pattern holds for rarer gestures; both plaques and composite figurines displaying a woman holding a disc are rare in Philistia.

[21] Plaque figurines of women continued to be produced in Palestine in the Persian period (see, e.g., Stern 1982:165; Negbi 1966:10, pls. 1–2). These figurines, however, are rendered in Greek style, and the women are clothed. As far as I know, there are no plaque figurines—especially nude female plaques—from Ashkelon in the Persian period.

[22] As discussed above in chapter 6, there are also humped bulls among the crude, undecorated zoomorphic figurines from Iron I Miqne (see Ben-Shlomo 2010:114–16). These, however, form a separate group from the main collection of Iron II humped bovines, which are concentrated in southern Philistia. See below.

[23] Gubel (1983:34) cites a fragment from an eighth-century context at Kition, concluding that the type begins in the eighth century at the latest. In the final report of the excavation, however, Karageorghis reports the example as

Culican's caution—and, indeed, the general uncertainty about the date—stems from the fact that most examples of this type have been found in tombs or *favissae*, whose contents can generally not be dated with any precision (cf. Pritchard 1988:51). Culican suggests that the finds from the Akhziv cemetery might be the earliest known examples (1969:37, 39). Dayagi-Mendels's recent publication of Ben-Dor's excavations at the Akhziv cemeteries suggests that the cemeteries were in general use only through the seventh century, though with some continued use or reuse in the early Persian period (2002:163). The pregnant female figurine that she publishes (2002:148, fig. 7.6) comes from Tomb ZR XXVIII, whose finds only allow a general dating between the seventh century (or earlier) and the Persian period. The confusion about the date of the type is reflected in Pritchard's Sarepta publications (1975; 1988). At Sarepta, Pritchard excavated two superimposed shrines; originally, he suggested an eighth- to seventh-century date for Shrine 1, and sixth-to fifth-century for Shrine 2 (1975:40). At this time, Pritchard concluded that several fragments of seated pregnant women associated with Shrine 1 were contamination from the balk and originally associated with Shrine 2 (1975:36). Further excavation, however, revealed that the type was in fact associated with both shrines (1988:55). At this point, however, Pritchard appears to have revised his dating for the shrine, suggesting (on the basis of epigraphic evidence) only that Shrine 1 was in use by the second half of the seventh century but may have continued for some time (1988:54). In addition, the discovery of several figurines of this type at Kabri is very suggestive. While none of the examples comes from a good stratigraphic context, 9 out of 15 Iron Age figurines belong to this type (R. Oren 2002:350–51). This site is believed to have been destroyed ca. 600 B.C.E. and not reinhabited (Kempinski 2002).

The finds from Ashkelon, then, are of real significance, as they come from stratified contexts. There are only two examples (cat. nos. 71, 73), and both are fragmentary, so it is best not to draw wide-ranging conclusions based on them. Nevertheless, their seventh-century date is clear: both were found in the quarry fill laid in the late-seventh century in preparation for construction of the Grid 50 marketplace. The Ashkelon examples, therefore—combined with the evidence from other sites—confirm Culican's dating: the type must have begun around, or even somewhat before, 600 B.C.E.

Spatial Distribution: Philistia vs. Its Neighbors

Iron I

In my discussion of Types I.A.1 and 2 (Philistine Psi and Ashdoda) in chapter 6, I emphasized that a key distinguishing feature of the new Iron I types is the technique of manufacture; they are handmade, as opposed to the moldmade plaques ubiquitous in the LB. In comparison with the Iron I anthropomorphic corpus outside of Philistia, the same distinctiveness appears. Plaque figurines continued to be made outside of Philistia,[24] if at a more limited number of sites (e.g., Tell Beit Mirsim [Albright 1939:119; 1942:114–15; 1943:25–26] and Tel Zeror [Ohata 1967:pl. 47.3; see also A. Mazar 1992a:fig. 8.30]). The predominant type of plaque outside of Philistia appears to have been a nude woman, pregnant, with hands at her genitalia; Albright interpreted this figurine as depicting a woman in childbirth (1939:119; see also Albright 1941:115; Pritchard 1943:21–22, 55). This type is entirely absent from the corpus of Iron Age figurines in Philistia in general; in Iron I, if plaque figurines were being produced at all, they were simply a continuation of the common LB type with hands cupping the breasts.[25]

On the other hand, handmade anthropomorphic figurines, while predominant in Philistia, are extremely rare in other parts of Palestine in the Iron I. This is true of all types of handmade figurines generally but can be particularly demonstrated by the characteristic Iron I Philistine types, the Psi and the Ashdoda. Schmitt (1999:646, Kat. Nr. 646) has identified a likely Ashdoda head and neck from Tell Judeideh; unfortunately, the figurine has been lost, and only a sketch of it is available. In addition, there is an apparent example of an Ashdoda torso from Beth Shemesh (Grant 1934:pl. XXIII). These examples, along with two from Gezer (Dever, Lance, and Wright 1970:pl. 36.3; Dever 1986:pl. 62.18) and one probable example from Tel Ḥamid just to the northwest (Wolff 1998:782,

coming from Floor 2A, which he dates to ca. 725–550 B.C.E. (2003:87). This figurine, which in any case is only a single fragmentary find, could therefore date anywhere before the mid-sixth century B.C.E.

[24] As perhaps rare examples were inside Philistia; see above.

[25] The closest parallels to this type in the terracotta corpus of Philistia is the Revadim plaque (Beck 1986; Margalith 1994), with hands to the genitalia but no signs of pregnancy, probably dated to the thirteenth century on the basis of the parallel fragment from Aphek, and some of the figures on the Yavneh cult stands, with hands at the genital area (but no clear depiction of genitals; see Ziffer and Kletter 2007:Stand 2006-1033 [= Kletter, Ziffer, and Zwickel 2010:CAT79]), but these are from the ninth or early eighth century.

fig. 18; see also Wolff and Shavit 1999:69*, 105, fig. 162), mark the likely westward limit of the Ashdoda's distribution. According to my definition of Philistia as a geopolitical entity (see chapter 4), Gezer falls just outside; nevertheless, in terms of its pottery and other material culture it appears within the Philistine sphere in the Iron I. Finds at Gezer appear to mark the expansion of Philistine influence, if not actual settlement, in the late twelfth and eleventh centuries (see A. Mazar 1992a:311–12). Beyond these sites, the only possible example of an Ashdoda I have been able to identify is a head from Jerusalem, from Stratum 15 (Iron I) fill in Shiloh's City of David excavations (Gilbert-Peretz 1996:39, fig. 18.11, pl. 9.8–9). This fragment has the same flat head, applied eyes, and large nose of the Ashdoda. As Gilbert-Peretz (1996:39) notes, however, it is distinct in several ways; for instance, it is larger and coarser, with a headdress that flares out more widely. Regardless of the identification of this one example, the Ashdoda type appears as characteristic within Philistia but atypical or absent entirely outside of it. This finding supports my suggestions in chapter 6 and above in chapter 7 that the Ashdoda is a phenomenon peculiar to Philistia.

As for other Iron I handmade figurines outside of Philistia, I have been able to identify examples (or possible examples) from only a handful of sites (cf. Schmitt 1999:646–48; Kletter 1996:263–65): Khirbat Sitt Leila (in the Sharon; Aharoni 1959:fig. 1), Afula (M. Dothan 1956:fig. 15.19; see also Dothan and Dothan 1992:105), and Beth Shean (F. James 1966:figs. 107.7, 111.1–3; E. Oren 1973:figs. 50.12, 14–15, 76.2–4; A. Mazar 2009).[26] These figurines are widely diverse in style and type, and in many cases it is not clear that they are in fact handmade anthropomorphic figurines. The figurine from Khirbat Sitt Leila is, in my opinion, not clearly human and could represent a monkey or a similar animal (cf. Karageorghis 1993a:32–33, pl. XIX.5, for a Cypriot monkey figurine from LC III and possible parallels). The Beth Shean figurines form a separate group, many with arms in relief across their bodies; this type is otherwise unparalleled in Palestine, to my knowledge. One of the examples illustrated by James (1966:fig. 111.1) appears to be holding an object against its upper torso on the left side, and may be a disc-holding plaque. The other Beth Shean examples, however, are fairly clearly handmade.[27]

Another group of figurines from Beth Shean is problematic for different reasons. E. Oren illustrates three female figurines from the northern cemetery that he identified as imitations of the Mycenaean Psi and Tau types (1973:124, figs. 50.12, 14–15, 76.2–4). Schmitt (1999:587–88, 606, 629, Kat. Nr. 18, 102a–b), following Oren, included these figurines in his Philistine typology, labeling one (Oren 1973:fig. 50.12) a mourning figurine (in "naturalistic style"; Schmitt 1999:606). These figurines are quite distinct from the Philistine (and Mycenaean) Psi and Tau types: they are more naturalistic, especially in their treatment of the head, and differentiate the legs; between this latter feature and the gesture of one holding its breasts, it appears that these figurines are depicted as nude. As A. Mazar points out (1993:218–19), the northern cemetery is contemporary with Strata VII and VI on the tell (thirteenth to early twelfth centuries) and went out of use with the end of Egyptian control of Canaan during the Twentieth Dynasty. Given this fact, the figurines clearly predate any of the Philistine Psi figurines. Moreover, Oren reported that, according to the excavation notes (from the 1920s and early 1930s), the figurines all came from a single sarcophagus in Tomb 241, along with a *shawabti* (1973:124). The figurines may therefore be connected to Egyptian, as opposed to Philistine (or other Sea Peoples), influence; perhaps a similar Egyptian influence might be behind the other Beth Shean group discussed above, although that suggestion is more speculative.

This conclusion is confirmed by parallels for the figurines. The closest parallels I have been able to find, particularly in the rendering of the short hairstyle, are a group from Petrie's excavations at Tell el-ᶜAjjul (Petrie 1931:pl. 24; 1932:pl. 5; 1933:8, pls. 15, 16.38–39; Mackay and Murray 1952:19, pl. 28.7–9). The difficulty of interpreting Petrie's stratigraphy and recording techniques, however, has prevented a clear understanding of these figurines. Petrie (1933:8) stated that one of them (1933:pl.16.39) was found in an early

[26] Raban (1991:22) reports that Amitzur showed him a "mourning female" figurine from Tel Sham (Tell Shammam) in the western Jezreel, but to my knowledge this is unpublished. Raban (1991:23) also claims to have found a "broken figurine in Philistine style" in the surface survey of another Jezreel site, Tel Zariq (Tell Abu Zariq); he does not include this figurine, however, in his discussion of the site in the publication of Map 32 (Mishmar Ha-ᶜEmeq) of the Archaeological Survey of Israel (1999:54*).

[27] I had originally (in 2007) considered that the possible plaque (F. James 1966:fig. 111.1) suggested that the other Beth Shean figurines with arms in relief across the bodies might also be moldmade; however, inspection of the figurines from the 1989–1996 Hebrew University excavations made it clear that this group is in fact handmade. I would like to thank Amihai Mazar for allowing me to study these figurines and providing me with drawings prior to their publication.

Eighteenth Dynasty level (Petrie's "Palace V") and was probably Hyksos in origin.[28] Holland (1975, cited in Kletter 1996:258–59) and Kletter (1996:30, 32), in their detailed catalogues of Iron Age figurines, both considered them of Iron Age type.[29] Their suggested date (ninth to eighth centuries) fit Albright's reassessment of Petrie's results (1938:355–56, 358–59), in which he provisionally redated "Palace V" to the Iron Age, specifically the tenth to ninth centuries.[30] More recent analysis, however, has suggested that "Palace V," actually an Egyptian fortress, dates to the thirteenth to twelfth centuries (see, e.g., Kempinski 1993). Thus, both the Beth Shean figurines and their ᶜAjjul parallels can be identified, contra Holland and Kletter, as not Iron Age but LB in date and should be connected to Egyptian garrisons at those two sites, during the final period of Egyptian control in Palestine.

We are left, then, with very few figurines that might be related in any way to the Iron I female types of Philistia. In my view, only the Jerusalem example, as noted above, may be connected with the Ashdoda type. M. Dothan has connected the figurine from Afula with one discovered at Mycenae (see Dothan and Dothan 1992:105). I would suggest, however, that the closest parallels to this figurine are twelfth- and eleventh-century figurines from Cyprus (see Karageorghis 1993a:pls. XVII, XXVII.10–12).[31] In general, it is worth noting that the handmade human figurines outside of Philistia (other than the Jerusalem example) are concentrated in the north of Palestine. There are several possible explanations for this small and varied group; for instance, they could be finds related to the Philistines or other Sea Peoples (either made by these groups locally or traded to these areas) or could be local imitations of these foreign types. The connections, at least in some cases, with Cyprus are perhaps significant, suggesting connections with groups of Mycenaean immigrants other than the Philistines.

Overall, the figurine corpus of Philistia is a separate, unique phenomenon in Palestine—exactly what we might expect from an immigrant population. The Philistine Psi figurines reflect a connection not only with the LH IIIC culture of the Aegean but with Aegean immigrant cultures on the southeast coast of Cyprus (at Enkomi, Kition, and other sites), as well as perhaps in the Amuq.[32] Similarly, the Mycenaean-style bovine figurines, so far a unique find in Palestine, are paralleled by figurines from Enkomi and other sites in its vicinity (see, e.g., Karageorghis 1993a:35–40, pls. XXI.3–5, XXII.4–6). The Ashdoda type, however, marks the culture of Philistia as distinct from even Cyprus and the Amuq. In addition, the fact that these Mycenaean-style figurines do not seem to continue beyond LH IIIC in mainland Greece and the Dodecanese (see French 1971), along with their apparent rarity in Philistia in the twelfth century, suggest that the

[28] Keel (1997:347, 408) simply follows Petrie's dating by assigning this figurine to the Hyksos period (seventeenth to sixteenth centuries).

[29] Kletter (1996:30, 32) has suggested an Iron Age date for this group and placed them in his catalogue of Iron Age figurines under the heading, "Various Moulded Heads from the Coastal Plain" (1996:258–59, 5.III.8.17, 34, 37, 39). He notes (1996:259) concerning one head that, while Petrie dated it to the Bronze Age, there were a few figurines from Iron Age tombs at ᶜAjjul, according to Holland. Holland (1975:A.XII, cited in Kletter 1996:258–59) also included this group in his catalogue of Iron Age figurines, assigning them to type A.XII, "Miscellaneous Moulded Heads," except for the possible musician, which he assigned to type B.V., "Moulded Face; Arms Holding Some Object," and dated to the ninth to eighth centuries (Holland 1975, cited in Kletter 1996:258–59; see also Holland 1977:121–22). Schmitt discussed one figurine of this group (Petrie 1933:pl. 16.39), comparing it to the "pillar figurines" and dating it to Iron II (1999:580, 627, Kat. Nr. 98).

[30] Albright observed (1938:355–56) that only the foundations of Petrie's "Palace V" were preserved; his provisional dating relied largely on the abundant Iron Age material from the tombs at the site, most of which he dated to the tenth and ninth centuries (1938:358–59). Given the formal characteristics of the various ᶜAjjul figurines, it appears that settlement at the site continued through the end of the Iron Age.

[31] I would like to thank A. Yasur-Landau for suggesting a Cypriot parallel to this figurine. His particular suggestion of Karageorghis's no. K(i)4 (1993a:27, pl. XVII.4), however, differs from the Afula figurine in several respects: it is not painted, it has applied eyes and breasts, and it displays the gesture of hands to the breasts. Thus, M. Dothan identified the Afula figurine as male, whereas the Cypriot figurine is clearly female. Nevertheless, it is very close to the general types of anthropomorphic figurines on twelfth- and eleventh-century Cyprus. Indeed, the unusual head position of the Afula figurine, with upturned face, is characteristic of many Cypriot figurines from the eleventh century on (see, e.g., Karageorghis 1993a:pls. XXVII.3, 6–8, XXXVI.1–2, 4) and probably derived from Crete (cf. D'Agata 1999:Tav. 47–48, 73–77). I should also note that Schmitt (1999:580, 647) concluded that the Afula figurine was a Cypriot import.

Stern (2006:392–93), while noting Mycenaean and Cypriot prototypes for this figurines, describes it as a "typical Sikil object."

[32] A. Pruß (2010:200–2, Taf. 24.204–5; see also 2002:Abb. 6a–b) has identified two examples of (locally made) Psi figurines from Chatal Hüyük and Tell Judaidah in the Amuq; in addition, he has published at least one probable example of a locally made Mycenaean-type bull (2010:Taf. 69.513). The Chatal Hüyük example was published by Badre (1980:pl. XXIV.12). Otherwise, K. Birney (2007:393–94) reports that there is a general absence of Mycenaean-style figurines of any type from this region.

explosion in popularity in the eleventh century is a significant phenomenon and one unique to Philistia.

Tenth to Eighth Centuries

It is generally concluded that, with the disappearance of Mycenaean elements from Philistine material culture over the late twelfth and earlier eleventh centuries, Philistine material culture begins to resemble that of the surrounding regions of Palestine much more closely (e.g., T. Dothan 1982:296; A. Mazar 1992a:327–28; Stone 1995:19; Uziel 2007). It is difficult to test this idea for much of the Iron II, however, given the gap in excavated remains at Ashkelon and Miqne for the tenth to eighth centuries. Nevertheless, it is worth investigating to what extent the figurines of Philistia manifest such "acculturation," as B. J. Stone (1995) described this process (or "cultural fusion," as suggested by Uziel [2007]).

As I have demonstrated, the principal form of anthropomorphic figurine in this period was the plaque figurine. Plaques have not been found in large enough numbers to allow for wide-ranging conclusions. Nevertheless, I would offer a few preliminary observations. Among the most common gestures, those of hands cupping the breasts and arms to the sides (Holland's Types C.II and C.IV; Holland 1977:122), are well known outside of Philistia in this period, as seen for instance in the group of figurines from the cult center at Taanach (Frick 2000:107).[33] At least in the case of the Batash molds, however, these gestures are depicted in a style unparalleled elsewhere. On the other hand, one of the characteristic gestures of the period, the combination gesture (one hand to the breast, the other at the side), appears to be largely unique to Philistia. I have only been able to find one other possible example of a figurine with this gesture: a plaque fragment from the Samian Heraion, dated by Schmidt to the early seventh century (1968:17, Taf. 19.T2274).[34]

Two plaques from northern Philistia merit special attention. One is the female plaque holding a disc from Aphek. Other than a possible example from the post-destruction reoccupation at Miqne (obj. no. 1250), no additional plaque figurines holding a disc have been found. On the other hand, this type has been found at a wide variety of sites outside of Philistia, but this distribution includes figurines with different size discs and discs in different positions; there does not appear to be a consistent pattern of distribution to these types (see Beck 1990; 2002b). Similarly, a plaque figurine of a woman holding a child from Tel Shalaf (from a survey of the Yavneh area; Fischer and Taxel 2006:fig. 3) is unique in Philistia, not simply for its general artistic style, but particularly for the use of incised dots (for the eyes of woman and child as well as the breast). On the other hand, this figurine has several tenth- to ninth-century parallels outside of the region, particularly in the Beth Shean and Jezreel valleys (e.g., F. James 1966:fig. 112.3, 5–6; Beck 2002b:fig. 3, esp. 3.2–3), where the use of incised dots is found on women holding children and discs.[35] Northern Philistia (especially Aphek, on the northeastern periphery of the region) may therefore have had special connections to other regions in Palestine, particularly the north; such a suggestion on the basis of the Iron Age data, however, is largely speculative.[36]

---

[33] Both gestures also well attested among the large group of Cypriot plaque figurines from the Cypro-Archaic period (see J. Karageorghis 1999:pls. I–XXXIII).

[34] Pritchard (1943:13–14) includes a small group of plaque figurines with one hand holding the breast and the other over the genital area (II.D., nos. 100–5). These are mostly from Macalister's excavations at Gezer; some have their hand to their side instead of over the genitalia (though one of these holds an ankh symbol in this hand). The dating is unclear, but at least some of these (with their Egyptian attributes) must be LB. See also Kletter 1996:276 (5.V.8.20). A similar situation is found on Cyprus: while Cypro-Archaic plaques with both hands cupping the breasts or both arms at the sides are extremely common, there are few examples with only one hand on the breast. Moreover, most of these examples have the hand reaching across to the opposite breast and supporting rather than cupping it, with the other arm down at the side; a few have the hand cupping the near breast, but in those instances the other hand is not along the side of the body but over the genital area. See J. Karageorghis 1999:pls. XXXIV–XXXVI.

[35] I have also noted similar unpublished examples from Tel Rehov, which I was able to inspect courtesy of Amihai Mazar.

[36] Initially (in my 2007 dissertation) I had considered two Aphek figurines with rilled headdresses (now published in Guzowska and Yasur-Landau 2009:391 nos. F7, F8, figs. 11.7–8) as being Iron Age figurines (following Kletter [1996:272–73, types 5.V.3 and 5.V.5], who included them in his Iron Age catalogue). While both figurines were found in Iron IIA strata, they are in fact are examples of LB types: one typical of northern Palestine, especially Megiddo and Taanach (no. F7), the other typical of the Shephelah, especially Gezer (no. F8), an observation made by Guzowska and Yasur-Landau (2009:391). (On the former type, see now Kletter, Covello-Paran, and Saarelainen 2010.) Thus, for the LB at least, Aphek seems to have unusually close ties to other parts of the country, both to the Shephelah and the Jezreel, something not characteristic of the coastal plain to the south. Such a relationship could also conceivably be behind the presence of the tenth-century plaque holding a disc at Aphek (although in this case a similar figurine is known from a seventh-century layer at Miqne).

Eighth to Seventh Centuries

The most common types in Philistia in this period, the composite female figurine and the horse figurine, are of course ubiquitous in the Levant and Cyprus during this time. E. Stern suggested that each different region of Palestine—Israel, Judah, Transjordan—borrowed the basic Phoenician types, but developed its own regional variants (2001:69, 79). He identified the same pattern for Philistia as well (2001:121), but without providing a detailed analysis of the data to support his suggestion. The question to be investigated below, then, is: To what extent is Stern's idea correct?

I suggested in chapter 6 that the composite technique originated in Phoenicia in the eighth century and soon spread south to Palestine. In the process, various elements of Phoenician style and iconography, especially in the depiction of the head, were borrowed by the people of Philistia. Nevertheless, the basic head types of Philistia are distinct from the Phoenician examples. The Type 1 heads are closest to those of the Phoenician figurines; many of the Ashkelon heads, for instance, bear a strong resemblance to composite heads from Sarepta (Pritchard 1975:fig. 41.1–2, 4–5 [= Pritchard 1988:fig. 11.24–27]) and Akhziv (Dayagi-Mendels 2002:figs. 7.1–5, 9). In particular, the Phoenician heads share a rounded veil (or top of the head) separated from the forehead by a single horizontal line, with generally no indication of strands of hair over the forehead; the faces also share the Egyptianizing features, particularly in the rendering of the eyes and eyebrows.

The Phoenician heads, however, ultimately form a separate group. The hairstyle along the sides of the head is not treated like a veil, in the manner of the Type 1 heads (where clay is used to join the top of the head to the body with generally no indication of hair). This veil treatment can be found on Phoenician figurines in other techniques, for instance on hollow moldmade figurines of "Dea gravida" (Dayagi-Mendels 2002:fig. 7.6) or on the moldmade heads of otherwise handmade figurines of women performing daily activities (Dayagi-Mendels 2002:fig. 7.10). The composite heads attached to hollow bodies, however, are always treated differently. Separate strips of clay are often attached to the sides of the head, to indicate hair in one of two ways: 1) solid strips for long, flowing hair with rounded ends (called Würsten—"sausages"—by Schmidt [1968:50]) at shoulder length (Dayagi-Mendels 2002:figs. 7.1–3 [Akhziv]; Pritchard 1975 figs. 41.1–2 [= Pritchard 1988:figs. 11.24–25] [Sarepta]; Conrad 1997:figs. 1, 9 [Akko]), or 2) long braids extending below shoulder length (Bikai 1978:pl. 81.2 [Tyre]; Elgavish 1993:1374 [= Elgavish 1994:fig. 44] [Shiqmona]). On some examples, these clay strips are missing (whether broken off, or never attached in the first place); on these figurines the hairstyle or headdress simply appears particularly short, about ear length (Dayagi-Mendels 2002:figs. 7.4, 7.9 [Akhziv]; Pritchard 1975:fig. 41.4–5 [= Pritchard 1988:fig. 11.26–27] [Sarepta]). Occasionally the Type 1 heads imitate the first of the two hairstyles, with bulbs of hair at the shoulder (e.g., cat. no. 38). On these examples, however, the hair is shorter; more significantly, the hair is not formed by separate applied pieces of clay but modeled directly on the head.

There is an additional detail of technique that sharply distinguishes the Phoenician composite heads from the Type 1 (and other Philistine) heads. The Phoenician heads are remarkable in that they are always hollow, with an airhole located either in the back of the head or on one side of the head near the ear (see, e.g., Conrad 1997:54*, fig. 2; Brandl 2000:189, fig. 4; R. Oren 2002:350, fig. 10.2.4–5). This technical feature is almost unique to Phoenician composite heads; outside of Phoenicia it is found only on Cyprus, particularly in examples from Kition (Caubet, Fourrier, and Queyrel 1998:228–29).

As for the other composite head types from Philistia, none is paralleled in the figurine corpus of Phoenicia. In chapter 6, I surveyed the different media (clay protomes, ivory carvings, gold jewelry) in which the Phoenicians depicted similar female heads; no such depictions, however, are found on the figurines themselves. Gitin's claim (2003:187) that the Type 2 heads are found at Phoenician and Punic sites throughout the Mediterranean is incorrect. The parallels he has identified are in fact clay protomes, not figurines; the protome heads are roughly twice as large as the figurine heads and were never attached to a body (see chapter 6). Similarly, while neck pendants like those of the Type 3 and 4 heads are found in Phoenician and Cypriot art, I have never seen an example on a Phoenician or Cypriot figurine.[37]

A similar situation is found with the composite bodies. On a basic level, the Philistine bodies simply imitate the Phoenician examples: they are hollow and often wheelmade, with a hole in the neck for the

[37] The closest examples to the Philistine heads might be examples from Megiddo. Mold M4117 (May 1935:pl. 23) is similar to the Type 2 Philistine heads with its bangs and apparent "combed sidelocks," although the hair at the sides of the head is not as long or thick. In addition, it is very different stylistically from the Philistine heads—it is much less Egyptianizing in its facial features—and does not have a diadem over the forehead. M2213 (May 1935:pl. 24) has its hair parted in the middle similar to the Type 3 Philistine heads but is both stylistically distinct and lacking a neck pendant.

insertion of the head tang. The forms of the bodies, however, are quite distinct. The Philistine body, as described in chapter 6, is generally a straight-sided cylinder. The typical Phoenician body, however, is bell-shaped, gradually widening from the neck down to the base in the form of a cone (cf. Bisi 1999:380; Stern 2001:80; see, e.g., Dayagi-Mendels 2002:figs. 7.1–5, 7.7; Pritchard 1975:fig. 41.1 [= Pritchard 1988:fig. 11.24a–b]; Elgavish 1993:1374 [= Elgavish 1994:fig. 44]). In some cases, the Philistine body has a similar conical shape (e.g., Petrie 1928:pl. XXXV.13), but this shape is atypical. This basic formal difference is ultimately related to an essential iconographic difference; the Philistine figurines are depicted as nude, or at least with nude torsos, while the Phoenician figurines are depicted wearing a long dress. Thus, breasts are never depicted on the Phoenician bell-shaped figurines.[38] It appears that the Philistines, in borrowing the new Phoenician figurine technique, adapted it to represent the same nude figure(s) they had been representing on clay plaques, with the same traditional gestures. The Phoenicians, on the other hand, used the technique for entirely different types of figures: clothed women playing a variety of musical instruments (the frame drum, the double pipes, etc.) or holding offerings (birds, cakes?, etc.). There are occasional Phoenician figurines that are depicted as nude; these, however, are representations of women bathing (e.g., Dayagi-Mendels 2002:fig. 7.10) or women nursing or cradling a child (Chéhab 1975:14). In these cases, the bodies of the figurines are not hollow bells but solid, handmade, and more naturalistic; the figurines probably depict scenes from everyday life (cf. Dayagi-Mendels 2002:151).

The closest parallels to the Philistine straight-sided cylindrical body come from Cyprus.[39] A small number of the composite figurines are depicted as nude, sometimes with the arms supporting or covering the breasts (see Karageorghis 1998:pls. XXXII–XXXIII). A good example of a cylindrical body is Karageorghis's II(ii)1, from the Louvre (1998:pl. XXXII.1); this example, however, is of unknown provenance. Generally speaking, the bodies of the Cypriot figurines are narrower pillars or columns that flare at the base in a trumpet or "funnel" shape (cf. Myres 1897:165, 167–68; see Karageorghis 1998:pls. XXXII–LVIII). In some cases, the bodies approximate the bell shape of the Phoenician figurines. Usually, however, they are depicted, like the Phoenician figurines, as fully clothed and as either playing musical instruments or holding various offerings.

Turning to Judah, the typical composite figurine is the well-known pillar figurine, Kletter's JPF (1996). The bodies have a pillar or column base similar to those of the Cypriot figurines. The JPFs, however, are always depicted as nude or at least with a nude torso. As I discussed in chapter 6, several examples of JPF bodies have been found in Philistia, as have the JPF heads. It appears, then, that JPF figurines—identical to those of Judah—may have been relatively widespread in Philistia.[40] At the same time, there are examples of cruder imitations of the Judahite type, distinct from

[38] Stern (2001:80) claims that the bell-shaped bodies are used to depict nude women supporting the breasts. Among all of the published examples of Phoenician bell-shaped bodies, however, I have not been able to find a single clear example of a nude bell-shaped figurine. The possible exceptions are a small group from Sarepta (Pritchard 1988:figs. 10.3, 7, 13.54; see also Pritchard 1975:fig. 56.5, 8). These figurines are problematic, however, in two respects: they are fragmentary, and so their full form and gestures are generally unclear (although one is definitely holding a child), and their date is unclear (they could date to either the late Iron II or the Persian period). A hollow handmade body from Akhziv (Dayagi-Mendels 2002:fig. 7.8) has breasts depicted, but the figurine is crudely made, and the body is not bell-shaped. It may be that Stern is referring to plaque figurines of nude women (cf. Bisi 1999:380, with an illustration of such a plaque from Akhziv; see Stern 1989:23 for an Iron Age example from Dor).

Meanwhile, Darby (2011:483) suggests that the lack of breasts on Phoenician composite figurines may not be due to differences in iconography but simply to the difficulty of modeling both breasts and objects. While this is a plausible explanation, there are certainly cases where figurines with breasts depicted hold something in their hands, most notably a child (see, e.g., cat. no. 59). Regardless of whether the lack of breasts on Phoenician figurines indicates clothing, then, Darby is surely correct to conclude that these differences communicated distinct meanings and functions (2011:483).

[39] Other close parallels may come from northern Israel, specifically Megiddo (May 1935:pl. 24 nos. M4385, M2213, M4549). May himself (1935:pl. 24) noted the similarity of these bodies to Petrie's "pot figures," which he had identified at Tell Jemmeh (Petrie 1928:17). The Megiddo examples are depicted as nude; one (M4385) has its hands to the breasts, while the others had their arms extending outward. Stylistically the rendering of details such as the arms appears distinct from the Philistine bodies, although the general conception (a cylinder representing a nude torso) appears to be the same. Outside of Megiddo, however, local composite figurines in northern Israel are rare, and the Megiddo examples can therefore not be placed within a wider regional type at present.

[40] The Type 8 and 9 composite heads are Kletter's Type B and A heads, respectively (1996:29), and the pillar bodies are simply Kletter's Type C bodies (1996:30). Complete pillar figurines from Miqne (obj. no. 6159/5965) and Ṣafi (basket 110050) would not at all be out of place if found at a site in Judah (cf. Kletter 1996:fig. 4–5).

anything found in Judah itself (e.g., Petrie 1928:pl. XXXVI.42; Sera^c no. 1129).

The other basic Philistine composite body type—the cylindrical body—is entirely distinct from the Judahite pillars, however. Both types, unlike the Phoenician and Cypriot bodies, are depicted as nude (or at least with nude torsos). The Judahite bodies differ from the cylindrical Philistine figurines in several respects: most JPF bodies are solid, with only a small depression at the neck for the insertion of the head, whereas the Philistine bodies are typically fully hollow; some JPFs have breasts that are particularly emphasized, more so than on any Philistine composite body (although these JPF examples may be over-represented in published photographs; see Darby 2011:489–90); and the bottoms of the JPF bodies are relatively thin pillars, whereas the Philistine composites are wider cylinders. In sum, it appears that each region—Phoenicia, Cyprus, Judah, as well as Philistia—had its own local variant of the composite type.[41]

As for the horses and riders, at first glance the Philistine examples are quite similar to those of Phoenicia and other areas of the Levant. The bodies of all the Philistine horses are solid, handmade, and simple, with little or no decoration to indicate the harness and trappings. In this respect they are identical to examples from Judah (see Kletter 1999:fig. 9.1–2), Transjordan (Kletter 1999:fig. 9.3; see also Harding 1950:pl. 15.12; Burdajewicz 1993:1244), Phoenicia (Kletter 1999:fig. 9.4; see also E. Mazar 1990:107–8; E. Mazar 1993:ix, fig. 8; Dayagi-Mendels 2002:fig. 7.14; Pritchard 1988:fig. 14; Lehmann-Jericke 2004:figs. 278–80), and Cyprus (see Young and Young 1955:fig. 5, pl. 19; Karageorghis 1995:pls. XXIX–XLVIII), although the Cypriot examples are commonly painted with a series of stripes.[42]

The treatment of the horse heads, however, involves a much greater amount of variation. Of the three types of heads discussed in chapter 6, Type 2, with squared or box snout, is identical to the typical Judahite examples. The Type 3 heads, with their applied eyes and bridle, are very similar to a few Phoenician horse heads (e.g., Paraire pl. 104.34). The Type 1 heads, however, are to my knowledge unparalleled. They differ from the Judahite horse heads (= Type 2 Philistine heads) in being more slender and curved, with a rounded snout. The Type 1 heads, along with the Type 2 (Judahite) heads, differ from the main Phoenician types, particularly in their complete lack of painted decoration or applied features. Generally speaking, there are two types of Phoenician horse heads in the Iron Age. One type has applied eyes, incised nostrils, an open mouth, and (most distinctively) a "turban" or helmet on top of the head from which the ears protrude: e.g., Dayagi-Mendels 2002:fig. 7.15 (Akhziv); E. Mazar 1990:107–8 (= E. Mazar 1993:ix, fig. 8; Akhziv); Stern 2010:fig. 6.1 (Dor); Paraire 1980:pl. 104.28–31 (Keisan).[43] The second Phoenician type also has applied eyes, but it is distinguished by its mane, which curls over the top of the head in a "forelock" (Pritchard 1975:fig. 57.1–2; see also Pritchard 1988:fig. 14.11, 14 [Sarepta];

[41] Zevit (2001:271 n. 6) claims that the pillar figurines are not characteristic of Judah but are instead found simply in proportion to the length of Iron Age habitation at a site and the area excavated. He cites the fact that 15 pillar figurines were found in Ashdod as support for his conclusion. However, this number is greatly exaggerated. After having examined the Ashdod publication volumes multiple times, I would concur with Kletter (1996:147, 177, fig. 16) that there is only one clear JPF, a handmade head (my Type 6 composite head [= Kletter's Type A]) from the site (D1035/1; M. Dothan 1971:fig. 65.11). In addition, there is a possible second example (D1712/1; M. Dothan 1971:fig. 64.11); after inspection of this figurine courtesy of the IAA, I would suggest that this might be a moldmade JPF head, but because the face is completely worn, it is impossible to be at all certain. Rather than look at Kletter's data in detail, or survey the Ashdod volumes directly, Zevit used the number of figurines at the site from Holland's distribution chart (1977:fig. 1) for his Type A figurines, "Human Pillar Figurines with Solid, Hand-Modelled Bodies" (1977:121). Zevit has mistakenly concluded that Kletter's JPF type is equal to Holland's Type A (Zevit 2001:271), when in fact Holland's Type A is clearly a far broader category, encompassing figurines with any type of pillar base; this type of base is, as I discussed above, a very common type and found not only on the JPFs but on many other types. Moreover, as Kletter (1996:28) points out, Holland's Type A even includes seated figurines, peg figurines, and other non-pillar examples. Critiques similar to Zevit's have been made by Keel and Uehlinger (1998:327) and Hadley (2000:19). In neither case, however, did the author(s) have access to Kletter's work at the time of writing; instead, they were dealing with Engle's much less comprehensive and reliable study (1979). Thus, Keel and Uehlinger (1998:327) write that "[p]illar figurines shaped slightly differently have been found, albeit less frequently than in Judah, in Phoenician, northern Israelite, Philistine, and Transjordanian areas as well"—again based on Holland's distribution charts—when in fact pillar bases are rare for Levantine composite figurines outside of Judah.

At the same time, the possibility of a close relationship between the composite figurines of Philistia and northern Palestine (Israel), as suggested above (and also by Kletter [1996:32]), requires further study.

[42] Note that Kletter's figs. 9.3 and 9.4 are reversed (1999:39).

[43] Note that similar horse heads have been reported from Akko but are so far unpublished (see Dayagi-Mendels 2002:153). Messika illustrates one example (1996:pl. 4.50) in an unpublished master's thesis on Persian and Hellenistic period figurines from Akko; many figurines from her Persian period corpus, however—including this horse head—appear to be of Iron Age type.

Dayagi-Mendels 2002:fig. 7.16, with bridle applied [Akhziv]). The Type 1 heads are similar to a number of heads from Cyprus with simple, rounded snouts (see, e.g., the collection of horses from Amathus, Karageorghis 1987:pls. 19–26). Even these heads, however, are distinct from the Philistine examples in a variety of ways: besides the form of the mane, which generally rises in a high crest as is typical on Cypro-Archaic I examples (Tatton-Brown 1982:179–80), there is greater modeling on these Cypriot figurines, particular with indication of the eyes and cheekbones. Such modeling is entirely absent on the Type 1 (and Type 2) heads.

Beyond the three major types, there are occasional unique examples in Philistia, such as cat. no. 175. As I discussed in chapter 6, this example is nearly identical to one from Tell Keisan (Paraire 1980:346, pl. 104.29). The Keisan figurine is generally similar to the first type of Phoenician horse head, with "turban," mentioned above. Even in this group, however, it is atypical; for instance, there is no applied eye. I would therefore conclude that, while unusual Phoenician examples seem to have been traded to or copied in Philistia (cat. no. 175 and perhaps some of the Type 3 heads), the mainstream Phoenician trends are not found in the Philistine horses. Meanwhile, the Type 1 horses at least are to my knowledge unknown outside of Philistia. The horses, then, like the composite female figurines, display regional variations along the lines suggested by Stern (2001:121).[44]

The other, less common Philistine types from the eighth and seventh centuries also display traits distinct from the figurines of other areas of the Levant. Humped bovine figurines are occasionally found outside of Philistia, particularly on Cyprus in various periods (e.g., Karageorghis 1993a:figs. 5, 28, pls. XV.6–7, XXI.1–2, 4, XXII.4, 7, 9; 1996:pl. XVII.1).[45] The Cypriot examples, however, do not form a coherent group as do the late Iron II Philistine examples, as in any period a bull figurine may or may not display a hump. In addition, the Cypriot bulls tend to display more naturalistic modeling than the Philistine humped bulls. Meanwhile, types such as the "Late Ashdoda" and the "Ashdodite" heads appear to be developed from earlier (Iron I) Philistine figurines and are therefore found almost exclusively in Philistia.[46] Overall, then, the eighth- and seventh-century Philistine types, like the plaque figurines, reflect a new relationship between Philistia and its surroundings in the Iron II. Whereas the major types and techniques are borrowed from other areas of the Levant (especially Phoenicia), or simply continue traditional Canaanite themes, the specific details of the figurines are often unique to Philistia.

The Subregions of Philistia

Iron I

Table 7.4 presents the distribution of the major figurine types at Ashdod, Ashkelon, and Miqne. Numbers of figurines of each type are approximate, given the problems of identification already discussed in this

[44] This is the same conclusion reached by Kletter (1999:38, fig. 9), who identified three regional groupings among his four major types in Palestine: Judahite (Types 1 and 2), Phoenician (Type 3), and Transjordanian (Type 4). There are multiple shortcomings in Kletter's presentation, however. Kletter's table 1 (1999:41) shows the distribution of horse and rider figurine types by site; in this table Kletter identifies seven types, of which the last three are not discussed elsewhere in the article. Kletter's Types 1 and 2, meanwhile, are almost identical, except that Type 2 has applied eyes (on the horse). Although there are very few examples of Type 2 (nine or ten), a relatively high percentage (three or four) are from outside Judah; by isolating this type from Type 1, Kletter is able to present Type 1 as more fully Judahite (98 percent). In addition, Kletter's survey is not complete; for instance, he does not include the site of Ashdod, which has at least two examples of this Judahite horse head (my Type 2 head): M1926/3 (M. Dothan and Porath 1982:fig. 34.7) and D1588/1 (M. Dothan 1971:fig. 66.2). As a result, Kletter's results are somewhat exaggerated. Nevertheless, his general conclusion is entirely correct: the horses with box snout are ubiquitous in Judah and rare outside of it.

[45] There is a possible example among the figurines from the Samian Heraion (Ohly 1940:Taf. 61 no. 932), where a large group of Cypriot figurines was found (Schmidt 1968).

[46] Occasionally handmade heads similar to the "Ashdodite" heads are found elsewhere in Palestine: e.g., at Lachish (Tufnell 1953:pl. 31.16–17), Megiddo (May 1935:pl. 33 nos. M4334, M4553), and Samaria (Crowfoot and Sukenik 1957:pl. 11.5). The exact relationship of these figurines to the "Ashdodite" heads is unclear, however, as the Philistine type itself is not well defined. The Megiddo and Samaria figurines appear to form a separate group, with the top of the head depicted with a pointed cap.

Meanwhile, Schmitt (1999:621–22, Abb. 27a–e) cites as parallels a set of heads from Crete illustrated by Erlenmeyer and Erlenmeyer (1960:Abb. 80–85), dating to between 1050 and 750 B.C.E. (cf. D'Agata 1999:Tav. 86 no. D1.14). A relationship is possible but unclear without finds of more complete figurines. Schmitt also cites parallels from Cyprus and the Phoenician coast, but these are more problematic. An example from Enkomi (Dikaios 1969b:pl. 107.36, 38; see also Karageorghis 1993a:pl. XIX.2) is similar, but the eyes are not applied, and the figurine is much earlier (LC III). Supposed Phoenician parallels from Sarepta (Pritchard 1975:fig. 56.3, 6) and Tyre (Bikai 1978:pl. 82.7, 12) are often moldmade and generally wear the high pointed *lebbad*; they should be compared instead to the Ashkelon rider.

Table 7.4: Distribution of Iron I Figurine Types, by Site

	Site		
Figurine Type	*Ashdod*	*Ashkelon*	*Miqne*
Philistine Psi (standard)	18	15	9
Miniature Psi	2	2	2
Ashdoda (standard)	23	15	6
Miniature Ashdoda	3	0	2
Mycenaean bovine	0	0	11
Crude anthropomorph	1	2	1

chapter. I have included data only from these three sites, as there are very few Iron I figurines that are identifiable from other Philistine sites. In the following discussion, I refer to examples from other sites as relevant.

Analysis of the data shows that, in this period, Philistia was largely homogeneous from the standpoint of the figurines. All three sites have several examples of the two major female types, the Philistine Psi and the Ashdoda. On a general level, the only distinction is the relative number of each type at Ashdod; whereas at Ashkelon and Miqne at least as many Philistine Psi figurines have been found as Ashdodas, Ashdodas appear to be somewhat more common at Ashdod. Part of the problem here may be that, as I have indicated above, it is often difficult to distinguish between Ashdoda heads and Philistine Psi heads; it is particularly difficult to do so based on drawings and photographs, which I have relied upon for identification of most of the Ashdod figurines. This difficulty may result in some Philistine Psi heads being labeled Ashdoda heads (as happened in the Ashkelon registration books).[47] Regardless, both types are present in relatively large numbers at each of the three sites. Philistine Psi figurines have also been found at Qasile (A. Mazar 1986:fig. 6.2), Farᶜah (S) (UCL no. EVII.232/8), perhaps Jaffa (MHA 2362), perhaps Jemmeh (the peg figurine; Petrie 1928:XXXVI.2), and perhaps Azor (a peg figurine and a mourning figurine; T. Dothan 1982:ch. 4, pls. 25, 27, fig. 12.2). Ashdoda figurines have been found at Qasile (A. Mazar 1986:fig. 6.1), Batash (A. Mazar 2006:photo 107, fig. 82:15), ᶜAjjul (IAA 47-283; see Mackay and Murray 1952:pl. XXVIII.8), Jemmeh (UCL no. EXXXVI.7/84), Aphek (Guzowska and Yasur-Landau 2009:figs. 11.9–11), and perhaps Ṣafi (Schmitt 1999:646, Kat. Nr. 64).[48] The miniature variant of the Psi is also present at each of the Pentapolis sites, in small numbers.

There are, however, a few differences among the Pentapolis sites in figurine distribution:

1. The miniature Ashdoda. The miniature Ashdoda is clearly present only at Ashdod and Miqne, in four or five examples. At Ashdod, these include the "complete" Ashdoda (H230/1; M. Dothan 1971:fig. 91.1), a head fragment from Area H (1326/1; M. Dothan and Ben-Shlomo 2005:fig. 3.80.2), and possibly a seat fragment, also from Area H (3/1; M. Dothan 1971:fig. 91.4). Two Ashdoda fragments from Miqne (obj. nos. 3948, 3949) show red and black painted decoration (Ben-Shlomo and Press 2009:fig. 5.7–8); these appear to be additional examples of the miniature variant. It may be significant, however, that no miniature examples have been identified at Ashkelon.

2. Incised mouth. A few of the Psi heads from Miqne (e.g., obj. nos. 4517, 4774, 5080) have a pinched ridge for the nose with an incised mouth on the ridge, meaning that the ridge represents nose, mouth, and chin. This feature is present at no other sites; on other figurines, a mouth—if indicated at all—is depicted below the ridge, which therefore represents simply the nose.

[47] Indeed, I initially (in my 2007 dissertation) concluded that Ashdodas were much more common than Philistine Psi figurines at Ashdod. Since that time, however, I have had the opportunity to study several figurines from Ashdod, courtesy of the Israel Antiquities Authority, and have determined that some figurine heads labeled "Ashdoda" in fact have neck diameters under 2 cm and are likely Philistine Psi heads (see chapter 6 and above in this chapter).

[48] Note that the Batash and Aphek examples are heads that could theoretically be Philistine Psi heads instead of Ashdoda heads.

3. Mycenaean bovine. This type has been identified only at Miqne. Moreover, the total number of examples at Miqne (11) is relatively large considering the numbers of other Iron I types.

4. Miniature animal figurines. D. Ben-Shlomo has identified several figurines of this type at Miqne (see Ben-Shlomo 2010:114–16). There are few if any clear examples at other sites, however. I have been able to inspect, or otherwise note, only one possible example each from Ashdod (H1179/1; M. Dothan and Ben-Shlomo 2005:fig. 3.36.8), Ashkelon (reg. no. 61162, but from a context currently phased as LB), and Tell Jemmeh (UCL no. EXXXVI.51/98). Regardless of the correctness of these identifications, this type, like the Mycenaean bovine, clearly marks Miqne as distinct to some extent in the Iron I.

In general, however, it is very difficult to note differences between sites or regions of Philistia in the Iron I, given the small sample size of Iron I figurines and the apparent lack of standardization within the major types (as in the LH IIIC figurines of the Aegean). It is impossible, given the current data, to determine if many of the distinctions that I drew in chapter 6 are regular subtypes and therefore impossible to analyze the distribution of such subtypes. Even in the case of the distribution patterns mentioned above, further data may show that the different Pentapolis sites were more alike. In the case of the crude, handmade anthropomorphic figurines (of hybrid type) discussed in chapter 6, at first I identified this type only at Ashkelon (cat. nos. 77, 186). I have since located, however, representations of nude women with genitalia depicted, similar to the Ashkelon examples at least on a general level, from Iron I contexts at Ashdod (H1250/1; M. Dothan and Ben-Shlomo 2005:fig. 3.62.5) and Miqne (obj. no. 1400). Similarly, I was initially aware of the presence of the miniature Ashdoda only at Ashdod before D. Ben-Shlomo pointed to the two likely examples at Miqne. The best conclusion I can reach, therefore, is that the different sites in Philistia were largely similar with respect to figurine types in Iron I, with perhaps some minor differences between them.[49]

Tenth to Eighth Centuries

If it is difficult to judge inter-site variability in Iron I Philistia with respect to the figurines, then it is essentially impossible to do so for the greater part of Iron II. A major obstacle, as I have already discussed, is the gap in excavated remains at two of the three main sites (Ashkelon and Miqne) between the early tenth and the early eighth century at least, with a total of three figurines attributable to this period at the two sites. As a result, it is entirely unclear whether the material from Ashdod is typical of Philistia as a whole in the period or represents local developments. The evidence of the Batash molds and a plaque from Miqne IIA (obj. no. 3235) suggest that, as at Ashdod, the plaque figurine may have been the main anthropomorphic type in much of Philistia in this period or at least in the eighth century.[50] At the same time, the details of the plaques point to differences between sites; the style of the Batash molds is unparalleled in Philistia, and the combination gesture, which continues at Ashdod into the seventh century, is not found at any other site. Meanwhile, the tenth- to ninth-century plaques from Aphek and Shalaf may suggest unique connections between northern Philistia and other parts of Palestine, especially the north, but again this is a speculative statement.

Eighth to Seventh Centuries

Table 7.5 presents the distribution of composite figurines by site in Philistia. A few notes concerning the table are in order. The final column, "pillar body," equals Kletter's Type C (all JPF bodies; 1996:30). I have included in this column not only body fragments but also complete (or largely complete) figurines that could not easily be placed in Type 8 or Type 9 (Kletter's Types B and A, respectively) because the faces were not well preserved. The figurine totals given on the table are only approximate. A number of figurines from Gophna's (1970) survey of Ḥorvat Hoga and Mefalsim A remain unpublished; Kletter (1996:Appendix 5.III) has catalogued them, but mostly without illustration.[51] In addition, the figurine heads from Tell Jemmeh

[49] At the same time, it is not surprising that such minor differences might exist in figurine distribution. Compare the distribution of "bird bowls"—bowls with a bird's head and neck attached to the rim, presumed to be for cultic use. Such bowls, and the bird heads from them, are common especially at Ashdod and Qasile (for examples and discussion, see A. Mazar 1980:96–100; T. Dothan 1982:227; M. Dothan and Ben-Shlomo 2005:123). I have seen only one possible fragment of this type of bird's head from Ashkelon, however (see Press forthcoming).

[50] A plaque figurine from Naveh's survey of Tel Miqne (Naveh 1958:pl. 21.A–B) depicts a pregnant female with arms to the sides but very much in the style of the Ashdod plaques.

[51] Other figurines from Hoga, collected by nearby kibbutz residents, have been placed at my disposal courtesy of the Israel Antiquities Authority and Jacob Huster.

Table 7.5: Distribution of Composite Female Figurine Types, by Site

Site	*Type 1*	*Type 2a*	*Type 2b*	*Type 3*	*Type 4*	*Type 5*	*Type 6*	*Type 7*	*Type 8*	*Type 9*	*Pillar Body*
Ashkelon*	22	0	1	0	0	0	0	0	0	0	0
Sippor	3	0	0	0	0	0	0	0	0	0	0
Qasile	0	0	0	0	0	0	0	0	0	1?	1
Ashdod	0	0	0	0	0	0	0	0	1?	1	0
Miqne	0	3	0	0	0	0	0	0	2	0	1
Batash	0	0	0	0	0	0	0	0	0	0	1
Safi	0	0	0	0	0	0	0	0	0	0	1
Jemmeh**	0	0	3	0	9	2	4	6	1	1	0
Sera	0	0	1	3	1	0	0	0	1	0	0
Haror	0	0	0	0	0	0	0	0	0	0	1
H. Hoga	0	0	0	0	2	1	3	1	0	1	0
Mefalsim A	0	0	0	0	1	0	1?	0	0	0	0
Ajjul	0	0	0	0	0	1	1	0	0	0	0
Far^{c}ah (S)	0	0	0	0	0	0	0	0	1	0	0
Milha	0	0	0	0	1	0	0	0	0	0	0
Hesi***	0	0	0	0	0	1	1	0	0	0	0

* Note that the Ashkelon numbers include 1 veiled (Type 1) head from the British excavations of the early 1920s (Phythian-Adams 1923b: pl. II.9).

** The Jemmeh totals do not include the figurine mold (Petrie 1928:pl. XXXVI.6), possibly of Type 5.

*** The two Hesi figurines are from the publication of the Persian period (Bennett and Blakely 1989:fig. 208:3–4). While found in Persian period contexts, these two figurines are likely Iron Age types, as they are paralleled at Jemmeh and other sites in southern Philistia (although none of these figurines can be securely dated stratigraphically) and belong to the general range of composite head types in southern Philistia in the eighth to sixth centuries (contra Bennett and Blakely 1989:279).

(Petrie 1928:pls. XXXV–XXXVI) are not always easy to classify based on the published photographs; while I have been able to inspect many of these figurines (and additional unpublished examples) in person in London and Jerusalem, and thereby refine my original (2007) results, I have not been able to see all of the published examples in person. Meanwhile, no examples of Types 5 and 6 can be dated stratigraphically to the Iron Age. However, due to both their occurrence at multiple sites whose figurine assemblages are mostly if not exclusively Iron Age, and their general similarity to the other types which can be dated stratigraphically to the Iron Age, they are almost certainly Iron Age in type. As a result of the above issues, the table should serve only as a general indication of types and frequencies.

What is clear from the table is that, for the most part, the different composite figurine types have distinct geographical distributions within Philistia. Type 1 is exclusive to Ashkelon and Ṣippor; Type 2a is exclusive to Miqne, while Type 2b is concentrated at Jemmeh; and Types 3–7 are found only in the southern part of Philistia. Only Types 8 and 9, the Judahite types, have a distribution that significantly crosscuts these subregions. At least in some respects, then, the distribution of figurine types in seventh-century Philistia corresponds to boundaries of the Philistine city-kingdoms, as discussed by Stern (2001:102–4, 121–22). It is therefore worth looking more closely at the different regional corpora of figurines:

1. Southern Philistia (Tell Jemmeh, Tel Haror, Tel Sera^{c}, Ruqeish, Ḥorvat Hoga, Mefalsim A, Tell el-^{c}Ajjul, Tell el-Far^{c}ah [S], Tel Milḥa, Tell el-Hesi). This large area corresponds to Stern's kingdom of Gaza (2001:104). It is the most distinct subregion of Philistia in terms of the figurines, both the composite types and the other seventh-century types. The Type 4 heads are exclusive to this area (e.g., Petrie 1928:pl. XXXV.8–10 [Jemmeh]; Gophna 1970:pl. VI. 3, 7 [Ḥorvat Hoga, Mefalsim A]; E. Oren 1978:1333, first from left [Sera^{c}]); the Type 3 heads appear to be as well, but so far clear examples have been identified only at Sera^{c} (see, e.g., Oren 1978:1333, second and third from left). The same is true of the Type 5–7 heads, best known from Jemmeh but also with examples of each type

from Hoga. Certain composite bodies also appear to mark this region as distinct: it is the only region where the composite figurines hold a disc (Petrie 1928:pl. XXXV.14 [Jemmeh]; Humbert 2000:32–33 [unprovenanced]).[52] The "Thick Style" plaques are also unique to southern Philistia (Petrie 1928:pl. XXXVI.34–38 [Jemmeh]; Haror no. 18125). These plaques manifest a general carelessness concerning details of modeling, even on moldmade figurines, that is characteristic of the region: it is shared by the "schematic" Type 4 heads (Gophna 1970:pl. VI.1–3, 7; cf. Kletter 1996:252–53). Finally, the characteristic zoomorphic type of the region is the humped bovine (e.g., Petrie 1928:pl. 37 [Jemmeh]; Haror no. 16260; Sera^c nos. 1105, 3430, 3516; Ruqeish no. 16922). Horses have been found only at Tell Jemmeh (Petrie 1928:pl. XXXVIII.8–14), where despite several examples they are not nearly as numerous as the humped bovines, and possibly at Netiv Ha-^cAsara (Shavit and Yasur-Landau 2005:fig. 16); these examples belong largely or exclusively to Type 3 (see chapter 6), which appears to be unique to southern Philistia.

2. Ashkelon and Ṣippor. These sites form a "central Philistine" region similar to Stern's kingdom of Ashkelon, between the Naḥal Lachish and the Naḥal Shiqmah (2001:102). In fact, the figurine types of this region are known exclusively from Ashkelon, save for the three composite heads from the Persian period *favissa* at Ṣippor (Negbi 1966:pl. 5 nos. 15–17). These heads, and most of the Ashkelon heads, show that Type 1 was characteristic of this subregion.[53] In addition, Ashkelon is the only Philistine site to yield the Type 1 horse heads.

3. Northeastern Philistia (Miqne, Ṣafi, Batash). This subregion (similar to Stern's kingdom of Ekron [2001:102]) is characterized by relatively high Judahite influence (albeit of a small corpus). Judahite pillar figurines have been found at all three sites (Miqne obj. nos. 3364, 6159/5965, 6559; Ṣafi basket no. 110050/110650; Batash reg. no. 1183 [A. Mazar and Panitz-Cohen 2001:photo 136, pl. 57.15]). The Type 2 composite heads are characteristic finds at Miqne (Gitin 1995:fig. 4.17; 2003:fig. 4; Miqne obj. no. 2133). Relatively few zoomorphic figurines have been found. Even Miqne has relatively few zoomorphic figurines, especially compared to zoomorphic vessels found there; nevertheless, there is one horse head from the site (obj. no. 6891; Ben-Shlomo 2010:fig. 3.67.4), which is definitely of Judahite type (Type 2), and a second fragment that may also be a Judahite horse head (obj. no. 6068; Ben-Shlomo 2010:fig. 3.67.3).[54]

4. Ashdod. Ashdod appears to be unique, at least among excavated sites. There are no known composite figurines, with the exception of a likely Type 9 (handmade JPF, Kletter's Type A) head (D1035/1; M. Dothan 1971:fig. 65.11) and a possible Type 8 (moldmade JPF, Kletter's Type B) head (D1712/1; M. Dothan 1971:fig. 64.11).[55] The most common anthropomorphic type is instead the plaque figurine

[52] At the same time, it should be remembered that southern Philistia has the most examples of well-preserved composite bodies. Given the fact of fewer extant bodies generally from other parts of Philistia, the absence of disc holders in these subregions could be an accident of discovery.

[53] Also relevant are the finds from Tel ^cErani (Tell Sheikh el-^cAreini), about 5 km southeast of Ṣippor and roughly at the border of Philistia (as defined in chapter 4). Most of the published figurines from this site are typical Judahite pillar figurines (e.g., Yeivin and Kempinski 1993:420). Yeivin's *First Preliminary Report*, however, shows two figurines from Strata IV–V in Area A (seventh to early sixth centuries) that are clearly not typical JPFs (1961:pl. 2, third row, third and fourth from left). I have been able to inspect one of these figurines (fourth from left; IAA 57-598) in Beth Shemesh, courtesy of the IAA, and it is almost certainly made from the same mold as cat. no. 35; the photograph of the second is not detailed enough to allow for a definitive judgment, but it also appears to be a "veiled" Type 1 composite head. Given the proximity of ^cErani to Ṣippor, such a find is not surprising.

[54] D. Ben-Shlomo (pers. comm., March 2007) first suggested to me that these two fragments were Judahite horses.

[55] Note that there is a set of moldmade heads from Ashdod (e.g., M. Dothan and Freedman 1967:fig. 43.2 [D433/4]; M. Dothan 1971:figs. 64.10 [D838/1], 65.2 [D1990/1]; M. Dothan and Ben-Shlomo 2005:fig. 3.115.9 [H3337/1]), which taper to a break at the neck, for which it is difficult to tell whether they are composite heads or plaque heads. I have ultimately concluded that they are plaque fragments, for two reasons: 1) a plaque mold from Ashdod (D13, M. Dothan and Freedman 1967:fig. 46.3) is a close parallel, with the same hairstyle shown on the heads (ending in a triangle at mouth or chin level on each side) and a tapering neck, and 2) following the principle that extant heads and bodies should be related, these should be plaque heads as there are several Iron II plaque bodies from the site but only one possible composite body (A618/19, M. Dothan 1971:fig. 7.16).

These heads also have a set of close parallels among the material collected from Ḥorvat Hoga in southern Philistia (e.g., IAA 73-5075-6, 5078-9). In addition, note that the material from Hoga also includes the only "Late Ashdoda" found outside of Ashdod (IAA 73-5080; see chapter 6). These parallels might suggest some connection in the eighth to seventh centuries between the two sites. At the same time, this connection should not be pressed too far, given that the material from Hoga is not from archaeological excavation or survey but was collected by nearby residents; therefore the provenance of this material is perhaps not beyond doubt.

(see, e.g., M. Dothan 1971:fig. 64). There are no horses from stratified contexts, save for one possible example from Area D (D4973/1; M. Dothan 1971:fig. 66.3); on the other hand, there are two Type 2 (Judahite) horses from surface or unknown contexts (D1588/1 [M. Dothan 1971:fig. 66.2] and M1926/3 [M. Dothan and Porath 1982:fig. 34.7]).[56] Other types present at Ashdod, such as the "Late Ashdoda" (e.g., M. Dothan 1971:pl. 63) and unusual decorated examples (e.g., D4185/1; M. Dothan 1971:fig. 62.3), are unparalleled.[57]

Therefore, in many respects—as can best be seen by the finds in southern Philistia—the figurines are distributed along regional lines. This subregional patterning, however, is far from absolute. As I mentioned above, the Type 8 and 9 (Judahite) composite figurines crosscut these regions; they may be concentrated most heavily in the region of Miqne (where they make up a large percentage of the total number of composite figurines) but are also found at multiple sites in southern Philistia, and perhaps at Ashdod (M. Dothan 1971:figs. 64.11 [D1712/1], 65.11 [D1035/1]). In general, there appears to be some level of Judahite influence at almost every site, with the notable exception of Ashkelon. Still, it is possible to draw some distinctions between types of Judahite influence. In southern Philistia, some of the figurines of Judahite type are more crudely made and appear to be local imitations (e.g., Petrie 1928:pl. 36.42 [Jemmeh]; Stern 2001:Ill. I.58, fifth from left [Sera^{c} no. 1129]). Thus, at Tell Jemmeh, which has (along with Ashkelon) the largest collection of composite figurines, and of eighth- and seventh-century figurines in general, in Philistia, the only figurine truly in Judahite style is a pillar figurine with a Type 9 head (Petrie 1928:pl. XXXVI.16). Beyond this example, the only clearly Judahite figurine in this subregion of Philistia is a pillar body from Haror (no. 16934; E. Oren et al. 1991:17). On the other hand, at Miqne Judahite figurines make up 50 percent of the composite figurine corpus, and at Batash 100 percent (1 of 1). Thus, it appears that the concentration of Judahite figurines in the area of Miqne is attributable simply to its proximity to Judah, instead of to a geopolitical factor; in general, Judahite influence on the figurines is strongest in the Shephelah and gradually weakens toward the coast.[58]

In addition, there is little evidence for subregional styles or types in the vicinity of Miqne. Most of the material comes from Miqne itself, yet even in the small number of figurines from Batash and Ṣafi there are apparent distinctions. No Type 2 composite heads or cylindrical bodies have been found at either Batash or Ṣafi. Other than the one JPF body, the only anthropomorphic figurines from Batash in this period are the eighth-century molds, which are quite distinct in style from any plaques found at Miqne. Meanwhile, Type 2 heads (albeit the smaller Type 2b) have been found at Ashkelon (one example, cat. no. 46, although it is quite distinct in style), as well as at Sera^{c} (no. 1200; see, e.g., E. Oren 1978:1333, fourth from left), Jemmeh (e.g., Petrie 1928:pl. XXXV.30), and apparently Ḥorvat

[56] Although they do not come from stratified contexts, these horse heads almost certainly date to the eighth or seventh century. They are identical to the Judahite type, which was no longer produced after the end of the Iron Age. According to E. Stern (1989), Judah did not have horses (and figurines generally) in the Persian Period; Lachish, where such figurines were found, was outside the border of Yehud (the Persian province of Judah). In any case, finds from sites outside of Yehud—for instance, in the Shephelah at sites such as Lachish and Maresha—include the typical "Persian rider" type, which is very distinct from the Judahite horses with simple box snout (see, e.g., Tufnell 1953:pl. 33; Kloner 1991:71; Stern 1982:fig. 285). A survey of the Persian period horses from Ashkelon, meanwhile, suggests that they are of Phoenician type, similar to those from Dor (e.g., reg. no. 11890 [Stern 1995:fig. 7.3.9] and basket no. 152726).

[57] The unparalleled nature of the Ashdod corpus is also helpful in understanding the group of Iron Age terracottas among the collection of the Baron von Ustinow, collected by him while residing in Jaffa in the late nineteenth and early twentieth centuries (Skupinska-Løvset 1978). In trying to establish the provenience of the collection, Skupinska-Løvset (1978:17) suggested Ashkelon, based on the apparent provenience of the pottery from the collection (and from where it is historically established that other objects in the baron's collection derived; see Skupinska-Løvset 1976:17–21), and the fact that some of the figurines were paralleled at nearby Ashdod. At the time, of course, Ashkelon had not yet been systematically excavated. As can be seen in this study, however, the figurine corpus of Ashkelon is quite distinct from that of Ashdod for much of the Iron Age. In fact, none of the Iron Age types in the Ustinow collection (all Iron II) is known from Ashkelon, while all are attested at Ashdod: plaque with combination gesture (UT 3); Judean pillar figurine, moldmade (Type 8) and handmade (Type 9) heads (UT 4–5); plaque head with triangular hairstyle at chin length (UT 14); and Judahite (Type 2) horses (UT 25–27, 29–30). Some of these figurines, then, very likely came from Ashdod itself. The Judahite types could have come from any number of sites in Judah or its vicinity, but a provenience of Ashdod is certainly possible as well.

[58] At the same time, at least some of the instances of Judahite figurines in Philistia may be related to a political factor, specifically the border wars between Judah and Philistia in the Iron II (see discussion in chapter 4). Thus, even the presence of Judahite horses and pillar figurines at Ashdod could be understood in the context of a raid such as Uzziah's (2 Chr. 26:6), although the figurines are presumably dated later (seventh century) than Uzziah (mid-eighth century).

Hoga (not yet published; see Kletter 1996:253 no. 5.III.3.1, fig. 7.5).[59] The Sera^c and Jemmeh example listed above are particularly close in style to the Miqne heads, despite their smaller size. In addition, the area around the Yarkon, considered part of the kingdom of Ashkelon (Stern 2001:102; for more detailed discussion, see chapter 4), is represented only by a few figurines from Qasile (e.g., B. Mazar 1951/52:fig. 13c; A. Mazar 1980:fig. 42d–e). These figurines are typically Judahite and thus display no connection to the Ashkelon corpus.

In sum, the distribution of figurine types in Philistia is more complex than simply by city-kingdoms. There appear to be certain aspects of the figurines that reflect a common Philistine conception: the cylindrical composite bodies and perhaps the Type 1 horse heads.[60] Other aspects of the figurines reflect subregional distinctions that could be connected to geopolitical entities: e.g., the neck pendants on the Type 3 and 4 composite heads and the humped bovine figurines. In yet other respects, however, the figurine distribution reflects other kinds of subregional distinctions: e.g., between Miqne and Ṣafi or between Judahite influence in the interior and its absence on the coast.

Intra-Site Contexts

Historically, the relationship between figurines and contexts in archaeology, both in Philistia and beyond, has been a problematic one. The "recursive relationship" that Renfrew observed between sanctuaries and cult images (1985:413) is also operative for sanctuaries (or "cultic contexts" generally) and figurines. As Fowler has discussed, figurines are often cited in excavation reports for sites in Palestine as an automatic indicator of a cultic context (1985:333–34). Yet, as we will see, figurines are found in Iron Age Palestine—particularly in the eighth and seventh centuries—in a remarkable number of contexts, most of which can only be interpreted as domestic. This leaves open the possibility of domestic cult, of course (see below), but it also emphasizes the problematic nature of the identification of contexts. Moreover, Ucko (1968:420–26) and Voigt (1983:186–89, table 28), among others, have gathered a series of ethnographic parallels indicating a wide variety of uses for figurines, many of which have no religious connections, or questionable ones: e.g., toys, initiation figures, vehicles of magic. In the end, then, we cannot use figurines as indicators of use of contexts; we can only use contexts as indicators of use of figurines.

The situation at Ashkelon is worth exploring briefly. In table 7.6, I present all of the figurines for which a phase can be assigned, based on the type of context: primary (floor, occupational debris, or some other type of living surface, including courtyards and streets) or secondary (mostly fills from pits, robber trenches, or leveling activity).

The chart does not include five figurines from the catalogue; three (Cat Nos. 30, 74, 165) are from post-Iron Age contexts, and two (Cat Nos. 16, 32) are from balk removal and could not be assigned a phase. The percentages are calculated out of the 205 figurines that can be assigned an Iron Age phase. Percentages are rounded off to the nearest tenth of a percent (resulting in slight discrepancies in some of the totals). I have combined the subphases (A and B) for the Iron I in Grid 38.

Generally speaking, table 7.6 demonstrates that figurines are distributed randomly throughout the Iron Age phases of Ashkelon. The phase with the most figurines by far is Grid 50 Phase 7 (late seventh century B.C.E.), whose deposits are far deeper than any other phase. Overwhelmingly, the depth of these deposits is related to the massive quarry fill, which contains the vast majority of the figurines in secondary contexts in this phase (and in this phase overall). Beyond Phase 7, figurines are distributed rather evenly across the other well-preserved phases: Phases 19–17 and 14 in Grid 38, and (to a lesser extent) Phase 9 in Grid 50. On the other hand, ephemeral phases such as Grid 50 Phase 7 and Grid 38 Phases 15/16 have very few figurines. An exception appears to be Grid 38 Phase 20, which is relatively well preserved but yielded only three figurines. This anomaly may be connected to the gradual increase in Philistine Psi production over the course of the twelfth century and the late introduction of the Ashdoda, both trends being noted earlier in this chapter.

In comparing primary to secondary contexts, only 24.4 percent of figurines come from primary contexts, with 75.6 percent coming from secondary contexts such as fills. Again, this number is closely related to

[59] Kletter (1996:256 no. 5.III.3.3) also includes an example from Tell el-^cAjjul (Petrie 1933:pl. 16.43) in his group of heads with "combed double side-locks." The material from ^cAjjul is hard to assess, as discussed above. Nevertheless, Kletter's labeling of this figurine may well be correct, as far as I can tell from Petrie's drawing. While most of the ^cAjjul figurines probably date to the Late Bronze Age, a small number of other examples may be eighth- to seventh-century types: e.g., a horse head (Petrie 1931:9, pl. 24) that resembles the Ashkelon Type 1 heads and a humped bull figurine (Petrie 1933:8, pl. 17).

[60] Of course, beyond the large collection of Type 1 horse heads from Ashkelon, there are only questionable examples from Ashdod and Tell el-^cAjjul. At the same time, there have been relatively few horses found at all outside of Ashkelon, so additional data are needed to clarify this situation.

Table 7.6: Distribution of Figurines at Ashkelon by Iron Age Phase, Primary vs. Secondary

		Primary		*Secondary*		*Total*	
Grid	*Phase*	*Number*	*percent of Assemblage*	*Number*	*percent of Assemblage*	*Number*	*percent of Assemblage*
Grid 38	Phase 20	2	1%	1	0.5%	3	1.5%
	Phase 19	9	4.4%	5	2.4%	14	6.8%
	Phase 18	8	3.9%	11	5.4%	19	9.3%
	Phase 17	6	2.9%	11	5.4%	17	8.3%
	Phase 15/16	1	0.5%	1	0.5%	2	1%
	Phase 14	5	2.4%	9	4.4%	14	6.8%
Grid 50	Phase 9	2	1%	5	2.4%	7	3.4%
	Phase 8	0	0%	2	1%	2	1%
	Phase 7*	17	8.3%	109	53.2%	126	61.5%
Grid 2	Phases 8/7	0	0%	1	0.5%	1	0.5%
Totals		50	24.4%	156	75.6%	205	100%

*Note that the number of figurines from primary contexts in Grid 50 Phase 7 listed here (17) differs from the total of 15 given in *Ashkelon 3* (*Ashkelon 3*, p. 706, table 27.8). The difference appears to be due in part to several minor errors in the latter publication:

1. the omission of cat. no. 65 (reg. no. 39692) in Room 227 from the *Ashkelon 3* total;
2. the omission of two figurines from Room 373 (*Ashkelon 3*, fig. 27.17): cat. nos. 33 and 110;
3. the inclusion of two figurines in Room 426 (*Ashkelon 3*, fig. 27.15) when there should be only one, cat. no. 83 (reg. no. 42847); and
4. the omission of two figurines from the South Street (*Ashkelon 3*, fig. 27.24), cat. nos. 34 and 79.

the large number of figurines found in the Grid 50 quarry fill. Nevertheless, a predominance of secondary contexts is apparent in other phases. The exceptions to this trend are Phases 20 and 19 in Grid 38, each of which yielded more figurines in primary than secondary contexts. A closer inspection of the data, however, suggests that this pattern is not real. The two figurines in primary contexts in Phase 20 are cat. no. 69, a plaque figurine (of Revadim type; see chapter 6) which is probably a residual thirteenth-century example, and cat. no. 208, a Mycenaean Psi figurine head. These two examples, then, are likely both residual, and the excavation or classification of their contexts is perhaps flawed. Similarly, of the nine figurines in Phase 19 primary contexts, three (cat. nos. 201, 205–6) are Mycenaean figurines, and two (cat. nos. 209–10) are LB Cypriot female figurines. Again, these figurines should be residual, and there may be a problem with the designation of these contexts. These results, then, suggest that there is no significant distinction among phases in distribution between primary and secondary contexts.

To further illustrate some of these trends, I have plotted every figurine found in a primary context on a series of phase plans (figures 3–12; see Appendix). There are no figurines from primary contexts in Grid 38 Phase 20B or Grid 50 Phase 8, so I have not included plans for these phases. In addition, Grid 38 Phases 15/16 are two poorly preserved and poorly defined phases; between them there is one possible figurine from a primary context (cat. no. 174, a zoomorphic fragment from a possible courtyard). Given that this is a solitary figurine and that the definition of its context is unclear, I have not included a plan of these combined phases either.

For the most part, the same randomness of distribution discussed above is visible in the phase plans as well: the lack of patterning chronologically, between one phase and the next, is also visible spatially, among individual contexts within a phase. These results can be analyzed in multiple ways. First, let us look at a breakdown by figurine type. All major figurine types—Philistine Psi, Ashdoda, composite, plaque, and horse—are present in both primary and secondary contexts. Unidentifiable zoomorphic fragments also occur in both types of contexts. Meanwhile, LB Mycenaean and Cypriot figurines are both present in Iron I primary contexts; in fact, both Cypriot figurines in the catalogue occur in Iron I primary contexts. As noted above, the data here are problematic and suggest that most of these figurines are residual rather than having been used in the Iron I. Additionally, all figurines are fragmentary, meaning that in all cases we are dealing with secondary use contexts; there is no variation in this respect according to type. Therefore, there does not appear to be any significant difference in disposal patterns (or secondary use contexts) by type.

Second, let us move to an analysis of the clustering of figurines in primary contexts. There are three major figurine concentrations visible in the plans: in the South Street, Grid 50 Phase 7; in and around Building 406, Grid 50 Phase 7; and in and around Room 530, Grid 38 Phase 18A. The concentration in the South Street is the largest cluster of figurines in any Iron Age phase at Ashkelon: eight total objects, out of a total of seventeen for the entire grid in this phase. The significance of this cluster may be limited, however, as the South Street and its corner with the West Street formed the area with the heaviest concentration of artifacts throughout the seventh-century levels at Ashkelon (*Ashkelon 3,* p. 724). Thus, there are significant concentrations of artifacts such as jewelry and beads, bronze and stone weights, and Egyptian amulets in the same area. In addition, it appears that some of what was excavated as L302 (part of the South Street) may have been fill and bedding for a drain, and therefore the finds might not be entirely from a primary context. Beyond this observation, the South Street may simply have been a particularly busy area of activity and/or a particularly well-preserved area.

The other two concentrations are of a different nature: they do not consist of clusters from a single context (or set of closely related contexts) but are spread over a larger area. A total of six figurines were found in or immediately outside of Building 406 in the Grid 50 marketplace. However, the figurines were largely spread out in this area, with Room 373 the only room with more than one figurine (two total), and two more coming from the East Street just to the south of the building. The possibility therefore exists that there was a special use of figurines in this row of shops, as no other building in the marketplace yielded more than one figurine. The other possible concentration of figurines, in and around Room 530, consists of a group of five objects (out of seven total from primary contexts in Grid 38 Phase 18A): two (both Ashdoda fragments) from the room itself, with three more (two Philistine Psis and an unidentifiable zoomorphic fragment) in the street outside. This concentration might suggest a special use of figurines (and in particular the major female types) in Room 530, but any larger significance to this room cannot be pursued here.

Beyond these concentrations, figurines appear to be fairly randomly scattered across rooms. For instance, despite the clusters noted above, there is at least one figurine in every major building in the Grid 50 marketplace (Phase 7). I would note one exception to this pattern in the Iron I phases in Grid 38: while figurines are more or less randomly distributed among the rooms in the two buildings on the west side of the street (as well as in the courtyard between them), they are largely absent from the building on the east side of the street. The figurines that do appear in primary contexts are problematic, as noted above; most are residual LB types. The one exception is the bird figurine (cat. no. 172), an unusual type which again might suggest a difference between the two sides of the street. The possibility that the eastern building had a separate function from the buildings on the west side throughout the Iron I should be kept in mind, although it cannot be explored further here. The determination of a difference in function, and what that function might be, must wait for the full publication of the Iron I levels in Grid 38. Preliminarily, I would suggest that, since Philistine figurines (especially in Iron I) seem to have a largely domestic usage (see below), the eastern building—unlike those on the west side of the street—might not have been (primarily?) domestic in nature.

Overall, then, most figurines do not occur in clusters, and there is no clear significance to the clusters that do exist. All major types are represented, but they also occur in isolated cases. Neither does there appear to be any special association with other types of artifacts. I have not conducted an exhaustive study of artifact associations, but based on the spatial analysis conducted in *Ashkelon 3* (pp. 701–36), as well as my preliminary work on other contexts, there are no unique or recurring groupings of objects. For instance, figurines were found along with each of the two special clusters of Egyptian artifacts noted in the seventh-century levels (in Rooms 312 and 413 of the Grid 38 winery and in the corner of the West and South Streets in Grid 50; *Ashkelon 3,* pp. 706–8). These associations, however, do not appear to have special significance. The cluster of figurines in the South Street is matched by clusters of several different types of artifacts in the same area and seems instead to reflect either the state of preservation of the area or the general amount of activity, as noted above. Meanwhile, the figurines found in these clusters are not unique or specially preserved: they consist of the major seventh-century types, in their usual fragmentary state of preservation (composite head and body fragments, and horse heads, bodies, and a leg). These figurine types are by no means confined to these clusters, nor do they appear in these clusters in any greater frequency than any other non-Egyptian artifact class. It therefore appears that there are no special associations between figurines and other objects, although this issue should be investigated more closely once the Iron I levels of Ashkelon are fully published.

As is suggested in the above discussion, figurines at Ashkelon are found exclusively, or almost exclusively, in domestic and industrial contexts. It may be significant that, even if we view the Ashkelon figurines as primary and secondary refuse, they were consistently discarded in and around houses. At the same time, we should not exaggerate the importance of this observation; most of the Iron Age contexts at Ashkelon appear to be domestic or industrial, and figurines are found in almost all of them. Mycenaean-style female figurines and zoomorphics are found in Grid 38 Phases 19–17 (late twelfth and eleventh centuries) in both main buildings on the west side of the street, thought to have been primarily residential with some associated industrial activity (weaving, winemaking?; see Stager 2006b:14–16; *Ashkelon 1*, pp. 262–74), as well as the courtyard in between. In the seventh century, the two main types—the composite figurine and the horse—are found in the destruction debris and occupational debris in both the Grid 38 winery and the Grid 50 marketplace, in multiple rooms. At least from my initial survey, there is little patterning to this distribution. There may be two or three patterns of significance (figurines in Building 406, Grid 50 Phase 7; figurines in and around Room 530, Grid 38 Phase 18A; and lack of figurines in the eastern building in Grid 38 throughout the Iron I). Most figurines, however, do not fit any pattern of this sort. D. Ben-Shlomo has identified a similar lack of patterning at Miqne, for the zoomorphic figurines at least: they are randomly distributed across the site (1999; see also Mazow 2005:392).[61]

In fact, the limited nature of the Ashkelon contexts is characteristic to a large extent of the excavated remains in Philistia as a whole. There are in particular very few cultic or funerary contexts, which might otherwise give an indication of different types of functions for figurines. A brief survey of these special contexts within Philistia is called for here; this overview is only preliminary, as many of the contexts are still unpublished.

There are only two clear examples of cultic buildings in Iron Age Philistia:

1. The Qasile temples. A sequence of temples, forming the "sacred area" of the site, was excavated by A. Mazar in Area C (A. Mazar 1980:1). The three main strata of the temple, XII–X, extend from the late twelfth century to the early tenth century (A. Mazar 1980:11). A variety of objects of presumed cultic significance, such as cult stands and libation vessels, were found; some were located in a *favissa* associated with the temples (A. Mazar 1980:24–25), while others were located on and around a platform (A. Mazar 1980:38–39)—strongly supporting the interpretation of these buildings as cultic. There were, however, no figurines associated with the temples. The only figurines from Area C are a few unstratified finds (A. Mazar 1980:113–14); of these, only two are possibly diagnostic and are of eighth- to seventh-century type.

2. The Ekron temple. Temple Complex 650 at Miqne was found in Field IV, Strata IC–IB, dating to the seventh-century B.C.E. (Gitin 2003; Gitin, Dothan, and Naveh 1987). It is a monumental structure with a pillared sanctuary, the plan of which Gitin has compared to the Temple of Astarte at Kition (Cyprus; see Gitin 2003:284). The cultic nature of the complex is possibly suggested by the finds, including a series of incense altars in the auxiliary buildings. Most significant, however, is a dedicatory inscription explicitly identifying the sanctuary as built by the king of Ekron, Padi, for his "lady" *ptgyh*, who is asked to bless and protect Padi and the land (Gitin, Dothan, and Naveh 1997). A composite female figurine was found in the sanctuary; it has an unusual gesture of one arm across the lower torso, with the other broken but apparently bent with the forearm raised (Gitin 2003:287, fig. 4).

To these contexts I would add the *favissa* from Tel Yavneh, whose cultic nature is clear from the variety of cult stands found in it (Kletter, Ziffer, and Zwickel 2010). No freestanding figurines were found in the *favissa*; as already discussed, a number of handmade figurines were stationed in apertures of many of the stands. The Persian period *favissa* at Tel Ṣippor (Negbi 1966) contained three Type 1 composite figurine heads, but their presence in the *favissa* can be seen only as reflecting their meaning or use at the time of deposition (mid-fourth century), as opposed to the time of their manufacture (presumably the seventh century).

In addition to these, several contexts have been interpreted, particularly upon discovery, as cultic in nature (for a summary of arguments, see T. Dothan 2003):

1. Apsidal building, Ashdod, Area H, Stratum XII (late twelfth century). See M. Dothan and Ben-Shlomo 2006:23–25; Dothan and Dothan 1992:153–54. T. Dothan (1982:41, 234) interpreted this as a cultic

[61] Ben-Shlomo suggested clustering in Field IV, considered the "elite zone" throughout the Iron Age (see T. Dothan 1995:pl. IV), and in a room in Field INE, considered to be cultic, but statistics over time are not available (Ben-Shlomo 1999; see Mazow 2005:392–93).

structure and associated the "complete" Ashdoda with it. In fact, the Ashdoda was found in a Stratum XI building across the street (see Yasur-Landau 2001:335; 2002:239).

2. Cultic building, Ashdod, Area D, Strata VII/VI (seventh century). See Dothan and Dothan 1992:156; Yasur-Landau 2001:335; Holladay 1987:261–64. This building was interpreted as a shrine in a potters' quarter. A pit (L. 1067) in Room 1001 was interpreted as a *favissa* and contained kernos heads as well as a female plaque and two "Late Ashdodas."

3. "Open-air shrine," Ashdod, Area G, Stratum XIIIb (first half of twelfth century). See Dothan and Dothan 1992:166–67. T. Dothan (1982:37) suggested that this was a "high place," with a pillar base functioning as a stand for an "idol."

4. Buildings 351 and 350, Miqne, Field IV, Strata VII–VI, V–IV (twelfth, eleventh centuries). See T. Dothan 1995:43–45; 2002; Dothan and Dothan 1992:248. According to T. Dothan (1995:43–45), this was a "monumental public building" of the twelfth century with a "hearth sanctuary"; built directly over it was Building 350, an even larger eleventh-century structure. The building was located in the "elite zone," where public buildings continued to be built into the seventh century (the Ekron Temple Complex).

5. Superimposed shrines, Miqne, Field I, Strata VI–V (late twelfth to early eleventh centuries). See T. Dothan 1995:47; Yasur-Landau 2002:169. The Stratum V rebuild included white plastered benches and a floor.

6. Room F, Miqne, Field X, Stratum VII (first half of twelfth century). A room in Complex 200, with a plastered platform that Yasur-Landau (2002:189; 2010:279) labeled a *bamah*.

7. Room 16, Miqne, Field INE, Stratum VII (first half of twelfth century). See Meehl, Dothan, and Gitin 2006:34–41. This was the largest of 10 rooms or areas forming one or more buildings. Based on the presence of a stone bathtub, hearth, and a bench in different subphases of the room, the excavators interpreted the room as having a cultic function (Meehl, Dothan, and Gitin 2006:34–35, 41).

8. Industrial Cult Corner, Ṣafi, Area A, Stratum 3 (ninth century). See Hitchcock 2011:342–43. The finds of Building 23033, which contained oil and wine installations as well as weaving tools, included notched scapulae in association with an entrance and a bench as well as a painted chalice elsewhere in the building.

Significantly, most of these buildings have now been reinterpreted, particularly in recent studies by Yasur-Landau (2002; 2010) and Mazow (2005). For instance, Yasur-Landau has interpreted the open-air shrine remains in Ashdod Area G as a single large domestic complex, similar in plan to the Mycenaean *Korridorhaus* (2002:186–87; 2010:274). He also questions the cultic association of Room F in Miqne Field X on the basis of the finds (loomweights and pottery; see Yasur-Landau 2002:189). Mazow also interprets the Ashdod Area G buildings as a combination of domestic and workshop spaces; she understands Buildings 350 and 351 at Miqne in a similar way, as elite dwellings (2005:350). Similarly, I have suggested that Room 16 in Miqne Field INE was in fact the main room of a house (Press 2011:386). Yasur-Landau does allow for the Area D building to be a cult place with a *favissa* (2001:335) and agrees with the interpretation of the Miqne Field I structures as shrines (2002:189).

In general, the uncertain interpretations of these contexts underline the need for basic criteria by which we can judge the function of buildings. We cannot, as mentioned above, use figurines as indicators of sanctuaries. Instead, we must make a more rigorous attempt to define and identify cultic contexts. Elsewhere (Press 2011) I have made such an attempt, focusing not so much on specific types of artifacts or architecture as on traces of cultic behavior, as known from other examples in the same (or perhaps similar) cultures. The Qasile temples reveal such traces, especially in the large number of cult stands, anthropomorphic vessels, and other objects concentrated in the area of a raised platform and in a pit, as mentioned above; these concentrations relate to the known behaviors of leaving votive offerings on a platform or altar and collecting them in a *favissa*. The Ekron Temple, of course, has an inscription identifying it as a temple. On the other hand, the majority of "cultic" contexts described above are more problematic. Their reinterpretation is supported by the data from Grid 38 at Ashkelon—most of which was not available to Yasur-Landau and Mazow for their analyses. I will not attempt a detailed analysis of the architectural remains from the Iron I in Grid 38. It is worth noting, however, that the major architectural features or installations (hearths, both circular and keyhole, "bathtubs," and pillar bases) and material culture remains (pottery, bone, incised scapulae, figurines, loomweights, spindle whorls, etc.) of most of the "cultic" areas of Ashdod and Miqne are all typical of Grid 38 Phases 20–17. Not only every building, but nearly every room, of each phase 19–17 is characterized by these finds. There is nothing about these buildings that suggests a cultic use: they have been interpreted as residences and/or workshops (see Stager 2006b; *Ashkelon 1*, pp. 257–73).[62]

As for funerary contexts, most of these essentially come from the periphery of Philistia or even outside of it: Azor, Tell el-Farᶜah (S), and (perhaps) Tell ᶜAitun (see, e.g., T. Dothan 1982:27–33, 44, 54–57). At the Pentapolis sites themselves, no Iron Age cemetery has been found. Instead, most tombs consist of occasional graves, generally intramural burials of infants (see Stager 2006b:14–15; *Ashkelon 1*, pp. 262, 266, fig. 15.35); an important exception is an Iron I–early Iron II communal tomb excavated at Tell eṣ-Ṣafi in 2006 (Faerman et al. 2011). It may well be significant that no figurines have been recovered from any of the graves in these cemeteries. The so-called ᶜAitun examples, as I discussed in chapter 6, may in fact have come from Azor, and based on their mourning gesture we might expect them to come from funerary contexts, but it is impossible to draw conclusions from the current state of the evidence. D. Ben-Shlomo, who is preparing the results of the Azor excavations for publication, has indicated that there were no figurines found in the actual excavation (pers. comm., January 2007).

Thus, the need for more data is obvious. For now, we must rely on the contexts of parallel and antecedent figurines: Mycenaean figurines for the Iron I female types and Cypriot and Phoenician figurines for the eighth- and seventh-century types. For both groups of parallel figurines we indeed have a number of secure, identifiable contexts.

The Mycenaean figurines are very common and found in a variety of contexts. For many decades, scholarly discussion focused on their association with graves. Already Tsountas (1888:167) noted their occurrence in tombs, particularly poorer ones. Mylonas, while noting that they were also found in settlements and "sacred precincts" (1966:154), suggested that the majority came from tombs, particularly those of children (1966:114). As a result, he interpreted the Phi figurines at least as divine nurses (1966:115). More recent research, however, has suggested the need for a revision of these conclusions. Thus, Alram-Stern (1999:216) notes that all of the figurines from Elateia were found next to the burials of juveniles or adults, not children. More significantly, the number of tomb finds is now seen to be dwarfed by the numbers found in settlement contexts. As discussed above, French (1971:107; 2009:59) noted over 1100 fragments from the 1939–1955 excavations at Mycenae, with another 1650 fragments from the 1959–1969 excavations; similarly, Demakopoulou and Divari-Valakou (2001:182) reported 175 from Midea. Moreover, even in the major cemeteries, at least in the twelfth century, female figurines of all types were not common. According to Iakovidis (1980:74), the cemetery of over 200 graves at Perati produced a total of seven Psi figurines and seven mourning figurines. Similar numbers were found in the large Mycenaean cemetery at Ialysos (see Maiuri 1923/24; Benzi 1992). A few large deposits, meanwhile, are certainly votive in nature, being associated with cult places: for instance, at Amyklai, Kalapodi in Phocis, and Haghia Triada, Klenies (see French 1971:107, 139–42; Felsch 1981:87; Kilian 1990:185–90).

There are, then, three basic categories of contexts for the Mycenaean figurines: domestic, funerary, and cultic. As for cultic contexts, it is noteworthy that these are often associated with open-air sanctuaries (e.g., Haghia Triada) but not with the temples of the major centers. Thus, at Mycenae only two figurines were found in the Temple Complex, and these were of types that were made before the building of the temple (Moore and Taylour 1999:92–93). At Phylakopi, the only figurines found in the sanctuary were three Late Psi figurines, which were likely made after the "Lady of Phylakopi" went out of use. An exception is the site of Methana (see, e.g., Konsolaki 2002), where a shrine was found containing about 150 figurines on or around a bench. Here, however, the figurines were almost all bull figurines or other unusual types such as chariots and horse and rider figurines; Konsolaki emphasizes (2002:31) that there was only one female figurine and explicitly connects this fact to the scarcity of female figurines at other sanctuaries. It therefore appears that the figurines, or at least the female figurines, were not generally made for use in the sanctuaries and functioned there only in unusual circumstances; thus, French (1985:231) and Renfrew (1985:417) suggest that the Phylakopi figurines served as substitutes for the "Lady of Phylakopi." Alternatively, Mycenaean female figurines are not generally found together in the same cultic contexts as the larger figures.

The Mycenaean female figurines display a remarkable pattern of distribution. Early researchers appear

[62] Note also that most of the finds in the Grid 38 buildings are broken and scattered (fairly randomly) on the floors, suggesting that they result not from "primary discard behavior" (i.e., not constituting de facto refuse, or perhaps even primary refuse) but from "secondary formation processes" (following Mazow 2005:247, 388; cf. Moore 1999:89 on the contexts and state of preservation of the Mycenaean figures; see discussion in chapter 4).

to have overemphasized the finds in the tombs; presumably these were noticed in the early years of excavation because, unlike the much larger numbers in domestic contexts, these would have been complete (or relatively complete) examples. In general, the contexts suggest an association with "popular" religion, as opposed to the cult of the "official" sanctuaries; at the same time, given the relationship in iconography between the figures and the figurines (see chapter 6), the contrast should perhaps not be drawn too sharply. Meanwhile, my analysis of the Tau figurines in chapter 6 suggested that at least some figurines had different functions (and meanings?) based on context. In the case of the Tau figurines, they likely served as representations of mourners in tombs but perhaps as representations of goddesses (akin to the Mycenae Temple Complex and Midea figures) in other contexts. Thus, I would largely concur with French (1981:173) that the "figurines take their function from their context and not vice-versa, i.e., the same type of figurine has a discrete (though possibly related) function whether found in a tomb, an outdoor altar site or a domestic context."[63]

As for the major seventh-century types, they are known from Phoenicia and especially Cyprus. Unfortunately, as discussed in chapter 6, the Phoenician figurines are very imperfectly understood; as a result, it is difficult to draw definite conclusions concerning their contexts. Certainly, the largest and best-preserved figurine groups are from Shrine 1 at Sarepta (see Pritchard 1975; 1988)[64] and the Akhziv cemeteries (Dayagi-Mendels 2002; E. Mazar 1990; 1993; 2001; 2004); this distribution seems to parallel that on Cyprus, where the figurines are best known from tombs and especially sanctuaries (e.g., at Ayia Irini [Gjerstad et al. 1935:642–824], Kourion [Young and Young 1955; N. Winter 1996], and Kition [V. Karageorghis 1999; 2003; 2005]). Thus, it would be possible to explain the differences between the Cypro-Phoenician figurines and their Philistine parallels (dressed bell-shaped, or funnel-shaped, vs. nude cylinder) on the basis of contexts: the Cypriot and Phoenician figurines being known from tombs and sanctuaries, while the Philistine figurines are known primarily from residential contexts. It is significant, however, that excavations of Phoenician settlements (Tyre, Keisan, Akko, etc.) have turned up nearly identical figurines to those from Sarepta and Akhziv, if more fragmentary. As a result, it appears that the Phoenician (and Cypriot) figurines were used in cultic, funerary, and domestic contexts, and thus the differences between them and the Philistine figurines are indeed regional differences.

The distribution of the Cypriot and Phoenician figurines is therefore similar to that of the Mycenaean figurines. There is an important difference, however: whereas the cultic contexts of the Mycenaean figurines are open-air sanctuaries, those of the Cypriot and Phoenician figurines (Sarepta, Ayia Irini, etc.) are "official" shrines. It is clear from Cypriot sites like Ayia Irini that thousands of these figurines could be left at a sanctuary as votive offerings. While in many respect these, too, are domestic figurines, they can also be associated (perhaps unlike the Mycenaean figurines) with the elite.[65]

The Mycenaean, Phoenician, and Cypriot figurines allow for some basic conclusions to be drawn based on context. Unfortunately these conclusions provide little more than suggestions as to how the Philistine figurines might have been used; based on the small amount of evidence from Philistia, however, these suggestions are promising. Much has been made of the fact that no Mycenaean-style figurines were found in Area C at Qasile. Originally, Mazar (1980:119) emphasized the absence of Ashdoda and mourning figurines in an Iron I Philistine temple; he observed that mourning figurines were found only "in relation to burials" and so should not be expected in a temple or settlement. Based on the lack of Ashdoda figurines, Mazar concluded that Aegean traditions were not as strong at Qasile (as at Ashdod). After the publication of the sanctuary, however, Mazar's continued excavations at Qasile found two Mycenaean-style figurines—an Ashdoda torso and a Philistine Psi torso (called by Mazar a "mourning woman")—not in the temple precinct but in the settlement (Area A; A. Mazar 1986:13–14). At that time, Mazar contrasted their presence here and absence in the temples but considered this distribution "accidental" (1986:14). On the other hand, Yasur-Landau (2001:335; see also 2002:239) uses this distribution, together with the other finds of the Ashdoda in domestic contexts, to suggest that the figurine was used in domestic/popular cult rather than official temple cult.[66]

[63] This in turn supports the argument of Nilsson (1968:307–9) that the function of the figurines might vary widely depending on context (contra C. Picard 1948:247–48; Mylonas 1966:115).

[64] Note that the finds of Sarepta Shrine 1 counter Gitin's claim (2003:287) that the figurine from the sanctuary of Temple Complex 650 at Miqne is the only figurine from an independently defined cultic context in the Levant.

[65] Compare the find of typical Judahite figurines at Ramat Raḥel, interpreted as an elite residence (Aharoni 1962; 1964).

[66] But Yasur-Landau (2001:335) observes that, in Iron II, the "Late Ashdoda" appears associated with the cult place in

As for the seventh-century Philistine figurines, the one clear temple of the period (the Ekron Temple) did indeed have a composite figurine in the sanctuary. The fact that this figurine was found, like its Cypriot and Phoenician parallels, in an "official" sanctuary, while no Mycenaean-style figurines were found in the Qasile temples, is noteworthy. At the same time, this appears to be the only figurine from the Ekron temple (Gitin 2003:287), although a more complete understanding awaits the final publication of the temple. Of course, with such a small sample of data not much more can be said, but the patterns of distribution are beginning to be suggestive.

Area D, with two in L. 1067—probably a *favissa*. No example comes from a clear domestic context.

8. Synthesis: Summary, Conclusions, Prospects

Because of the method that I have employed for this study, the results and conclusions I have drawn have been presented in a somewhat disconnected fashion. Discussion of the description, meaning, and function of an individual figurine type spans sections of chapters 5–7. As a result, I believe it is useful to include a brief summary of my conclusions concerning the basic figurine types, synthesizing the material from my different analyses.

The Iron I figurines of Philistia include two major types: the Philistine Psi, often mislabeled as a mourning figurine, and the Ashdoda. Both types share close links with the typical Mycenaean figurines, but whereas the Philistine Psi is simply a continuation of the Mycenaean Late Psi type, the Ashdoda is an entirely new phenomenon. The Ashdoda appears to combine occasional Cypriot elements with the dominant Aegean ones; it represents a fusion of woman and chair not found in Aegean or Cypriot figurines, and it is much more popular in Philistia than any seated figurine is in the Aegean or on Cyprus. Moreover, the chronological distribution suggests—though the evidence is far from clear—that the Ashdoda was not produced before the beginning of the eleventh century, after several Philistine Psi examples are already attested. Thus, the origin and popularity of the Ashdoda suggest a uniquely Philistine phenomenon and one that might be connected with larger changes in Philistine religion and society. At the same time, female figurines in general (both Psi and Ashdoda types) see a sharp rise in popularity and appear to eclipse the bovine figurines.

While the Mycenaean-style female figurines appear to enjoy a heyday in the early eleventh century, they may already be in the decline before 1000 B.C.E. Certainly with the end of the Iron I, the standard Ashdoda and Philistine Psi forms disappear. Nevertheless, the Aegean legacy is likely carried on in certain special figurine types. This is already evident over the course of the eleventh century, with a new class of hybrid figurines likely arising. This class appears to represent nude female depictions (unlike the typically clothed Mycenaean figurines) and perhaps is influenced by Cypriot connections. This hybrid type continues into the Iron II in the form of the figurines on the Yavneh cult stands, dating to the late ninth and early eighth centuries. Moreover, the "Ashdodite heads" and the "Late Ashdodas" appear to manifest traces of Aegean influence, at least at Ashdod, into the seventh century.

With gaps of varying degrees in excavated remains at Miqne, Ashkelon, and Batash, determining the basic types of figurines in the earlier part of the Iron II (tenth to early eighth centuries) is difficult. Based on the Ashdod corpus in particular, it appears that the plaque figurine becomes the dominant anthropomorphic form at this time, although this trend may simply represent a local one at Ashdod.

In the mid- to late eighth century, or early seventh at the latest, new types of figurines become widespread in Philistia: the composite figurine and the horse. These types, especially the composite figurine and its new technique, are traceable to Phoenician influence. By the late seventh century, another new Phoenician type—the hollow moldmade figurine in the form of a pregnant woman—appears at Ashkelon; the fragments found there in the late seventh-century levels are important evidence for dating of the type.

Besides the changes in figurine types, the changes in how and where these figurines are used are significant. In the Iron I, the Philistine figurines—especially the Ashdoda—form a separate group from all other known figurines in Palestine, and the Levant generally. Moreover, while there may be small differences between the different sites and subregions of Philistia, the basic types are found throughout; one exception might be the decorated bovine figurines, which have so far been identified only at Miqne. By the tenth century, however, the figurines of Philistia begin to look much more like those of the neighboring regions. The plaque figurine, probably the most common type in Philistia from the tenth through the eighth centuries, is known through much of Palestine, continuing the old LB Canaanite traditions. The specific gestures of the Ashdod plaques, however—especially the combination of one hand to the breast and the other along the side—are unique to Philistia.

A similar situation occurs in the seventh century. While the basic types are of Phoenician origin, the specific forms that these types take are generally known only in Philistia. On the one hand there appear to be subregional distinctions with styles—and actual molds and figurine series—circulating among site subgroups. This is most apparent in southern Philistia, where not only styles of composite figurines are shared but also the "Thick Style" plaques and the humped bovines. At the same time, there also appear to be common Philistine conceptions of figurines, distinct from those of the neighboring areas (especially Judah and Phoenicia): the nude cylindrical composite figurine and perhaps the Ashkelon-type horses.

Beyond reaching a set of conclusions about the figurines, my analysis of the data has allowed me to test some basic hypotheses concerning Philistine figurines, and Philistine culture more generally:

1. The "common knowledge" that the Philistines become gradually more like their neighbors: in particular, that they have a distinct material culture in the Iron I, while by the seventh century their artifacts are regional variants of a broader type or are completely indistinct. Through an analysis of the figurines of the different subregions of Philistia, and a comparison with those of the neighboring regions, I have found that the situation is somewhat more complex. On a general level, the Philistine figurine corpus does indeed become much more similar to that of the surrounding areas of Palestine. At the same time, however, there are still common Philistine conceptions of figurines, subregional conceptions that approximate those of the different Philistine city-states, and other regional trends that cross-cut these.

2. Related to this commonly held view is Kletter's hypothesis (1996; 1999) that types of material culture such as figurines relate directly to political boundaries. Kletter seems to suggest this idea as an alternative to a connection between material culture and ethnicity, as if switching from ethnic groups to political groups removes the dangers of such correlations (1996:44). In fact, my study has been designed perfectly to test this idea; I began with a political (or geographic-political) definition of "Philistia" and proceeded to test whether it had a single, distinct corpus of figurines. Certainly much of the data suggests that such a distinct corpus does exist. For the Iron I, the Philistine figurine collection is largely uniform and distinctive; on the other hand, in the Iron II—when the sources (biblical and Assyrian) show an identity based more on individual cities—the Philistine corpus appears to contain a set of subregional variants. Again, however, the seventh-century corpus in particular appears far more complex, with some possible conceptions shared throughout Philistia, some apparently shared within city-kingdoms, and some not distributed along either of these boundaries. While we might conclude that there is, at least to some extent, a rough correspondence between the distribution of figurine types and political boundaries, this correspondence is ultimately superficial. On a theoretical level, I would argue that such a correspondence is generally not sound, except when dealing with specifically political or administrative elements of material culture: e.g., *lmlk* handles or Egyptian artifacts with cartouches (cf. Bietak 1993, concerning the distribution of 19th Dynasty vs. 20th Dynasty artifacts).

3. Another associated hypothesis is Gitin's conception of the unusually "eclectic" nature of Philistine material culture and his idea that, by the seventh century B.C.E., the Philistines had lost their cultural core and so could not retain a distinct identity (see, e.g., Gitin 1992:31; 1995:74–75; 2010:325). I must reject this idea on three grounds. First is a theoretical argument; the idea that the Philistines, or any ethnic group, have a "cultural core" and the connected idea of a direct relationship between material culture and ethnicity, are entirely unfounded. (This is the conception that I argued against in chapter 2.) The same point is also made by B. J. Stone (1995); ethnicity is a much more fluid concept, especially in its relationship to material culture. Thus, an identity (such as "Philistine") can be maintained over hundreds of years, despite various changes in the material culture produced and used by that ethnic group. My second argument is that the loss of Philistine identity was not (and is not) a unique occurrence that needs a special explanation. The same process can be seen with the conquest of the northern kingdom of Israel or with the subsequent critical events in the history of the Near East: the conquest of Alexander and Hellenization, the spread of Christianity, and the Arab conquest. Each of these major events was associated with large-scale changes in sociocultural, religious, linguistic, and/or ethnic changes. Viewed against history, the Philistines' loss of identity, especially after conquest and deportation, is hardly a unique event; rather, the maintenance of identity in the face of such events and processes—such as that of Judah—is the more peculiar event that needs explanation. Finally, as I have tried to show, the Philistine material culture—as seen from the figurines—was not unusually eclectic. On the one hand, the Philistines appear to have had some common cultural conceptions; for example, the Philistine composite figurines are not merely "Phoenician-type" figurines with close parallels at Phoenician sites, contra Gitin (2003:287; 2010:342). On the other hand, the amount of Phoenician (or other foreign) influence on Philistine material culture is not unusual either. As I have demonstrated, the Judahite pillar figurines (JPFs) are essentially as "Phoenician" in type as the Philistine composite figurines; they are both local variants of a Phoenician type or technique, but with both displaying a nude torso in place of the typically clothed Phoenician bell shape. The varieties of horses (especially the Ashkelon horses)

present a similar situation. Among other elements of material culture, the iconography of Israelite and Judahite seals reveals heavy Phoenician influence (Keel and Uehlinger 1998:248–62), and Judahite mortuary practices and beliefs incorporated elements from a variety of regions: Egypt, Philistia, Phoenicia, and Syria (Bloch-Smith 2002:129). Just like their neighbors, the seventh-century Philistines were open to outside influences, while still maintaining their regional distinctives. Thus, the cultural innovations in Philistia should not be viewed as the reason for the loss of Philistine identity after the Iron Age.

4. E. Stern (2001:79–85) offered the hypothesis that the figurines represent "official" religion, vs. the "popular" religion manifested in faience amulets. There are multiple arguments against this idea, however. First, if this were correct, it would suggest that "popular" Philistine religion (and Phoenician religion, for that matter) was in fact Egyptian religion; the amulets are used seemingly without exception to represent Egyptian deities and symbols, with the most common types (at Ashkelon at least) being the Udjat Eye (or Eye of Horus) and Bes. Beyond this, I have shown how Philistine figurines in all periods—along with their parallels and antecedents in Greece, Phoenicia, and Cyprus—are frequently found in domestic contexts. At least in some periods they may have close connections with "official" iconography; note the connection of the Mycenaean female figurines and the female cult images. Even in these cases, however, the use of the figurines demonstrates their distinctiveness from the "official" imagery: thus, for example, Mycenaean female figurines and larger figures rarely occur together. Moreover, even the meaning of these figurines—e.g., mourner vs. divine image—in different contexts could represent "official" vs. "nonofficial" interpretations, although this idea is more speculative.

Finally, this study as a whole has tested the idea that using a methodology along the lines I have developed can lead to new insights and a more complete understanding of the figurines, as well as new ideas about more general cultural issues. In that respect, I believe that I have achieved some measure of success. I have not always been able, as I have indicated, to follow my stated methodology exactly, and many of my conclusions are provisional; nevertheless, the application of this methodology to a large corpus of previously unstudied figurines has led, in the end, to a better understanding of the Philistine figurines.

APPENDIX

Chronological Charts

(all dates approximate)

Palestine (after *Ashkelon 1* and Mazar and Bronk Ramsey 2010)

Periods		*Dates*
Late Bronze Age (LB)	I	1550–1400 B.C.E.
	II	1400–1175 B.C.E.
Iron Age	I	1175–980 B.C.E.
	II	980–604 B.C.E.
Persian Period		525–290* B.C.E.

*Note that although 330 B.C.E. is the date normally assiged as the termination of the Persian Period, at Ashkelon there is evidence that the "Persian Period" phases last until 290 B.C.E.

Ashkelon: Local Phasing (adapted from *Ashkelon 1*, pp. 216–17)

Phases			*Dates*
Grid 38	*Grid 50*	*Grid 2*	
Phase 20			ca. 1175–1150 B.C.E.
Phase 19	Phase 9B		ca. 1150–1100 B.C.E.
Phase 18	Phase 9A		ca. 1100–1050 B.C.E.
Phase 17			ca. 1050–1000 B.C.E.
Phase 16		Phase 8	ca. 1000–800 B.C.E.
Phase 15	Phase 8		ca. 800–700 B.C.E.
Phase 14	Phase 7	Phase 7	ca. 700–604 B.C.E.

Cyprus (after Karageorghis 1993a:x; Dikaios 1971:496)

Periods		*Dates*
Late Cypriot (LC)	III	1200–1050 B.C.E.
Cypro-Geometric (CG)	I	1050–950 B.C.E.
	II	950–850 B.C.E.
	III	850–750 B.C.E.
Cypro-Archaic	I	750–600 B.C.E.

Mainland Greece (after Taylour 1995:30; Shelmerdine 1997:table 1)

Periods		*Dates*
Late Helladic (LH)	I	1650–1550 B.C.E.
	II	1550–1400 B.C.E.
	IIIA	1400–1300 B.C.E.
	IIIB	1300–1190 B.C.E.
	IIIC	1190–1065 B.C.E.
(Sub-Mycenaean		1100–1050 B.C.E.)
Protogeometric		1050–950 B.C.E.
Geometric		950–700 B.C.E.
Orientalizing Period		700–600 B.C.E.
Archaic		600–475 B.C.E.

Crete (after Taylour 1995:30; Rehak and Younger 1998:table 1)

Periods		*Dates*
Late Minoan (LM)	I	1650–1500 B.C.E.
	II	1500–1430 B.C.E.
	IIIA	1430–1300 B.C.E.
	IIIB	1300–1200 B.C.E.
	IIIC	1200–1100 B.C.E.
Sub-Minoan		1100–1000 B.C.E.

PHASE PLANS SHOWING FINDSPOTS OF CATALOGUED ITEMS

The schematic phase plans show the distribution of the catalogued figurines in their primary contexts. Each plan shows objects that were recovered from approximately contemporary stratigraphic contexts. Therefore, Iron Age figurines found in later Persian-period pits and fills are not included. The numbers in red represent the catalogue numbers of particular figurines (see chapter 5). Note that "phases" at Ashkelon are not site-wide "strata." Rather they refer to local architectural complexes and thus are numbered independently within each excavated area. See *Ashkelon 1*, pp. 185–94 for a general discussion of the stratigraphy of the excavated areas of the site. For a temporal correlation of the individual architecutral phases from one area to the next, see *Ashkelon 1*, pp. 216–17; see also the Appendix for a comparison of the phases at Ashkelon with Palestinian, Cypriot, Greek, and Cretan chronologies.

Figure 3. Findspots in Grid 38 Phase 20A (*Ashkelon 1*, pp. 257–61; 1175–1150 B.C.E.)

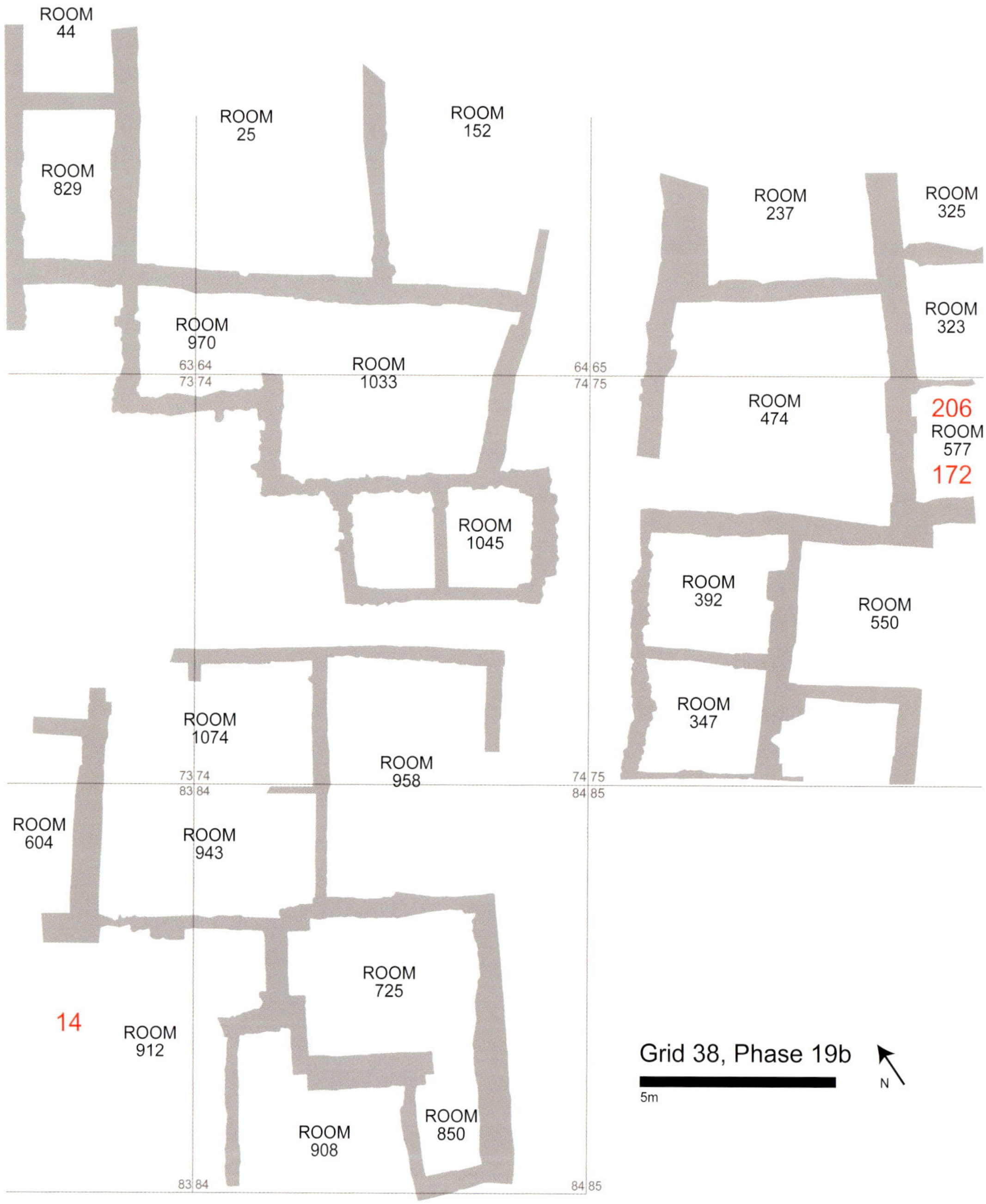

Figure 4. Findspots in Grid 38 Phase 19B (*Ashkelon 1*, pp. 262–66; 1150–1100 B.C.E.)

Figure 5. Findspots in Grid 38 Phase 19A (*Ashkelon 1*, pp. 262-66; 1150–1100 B.C.E.)

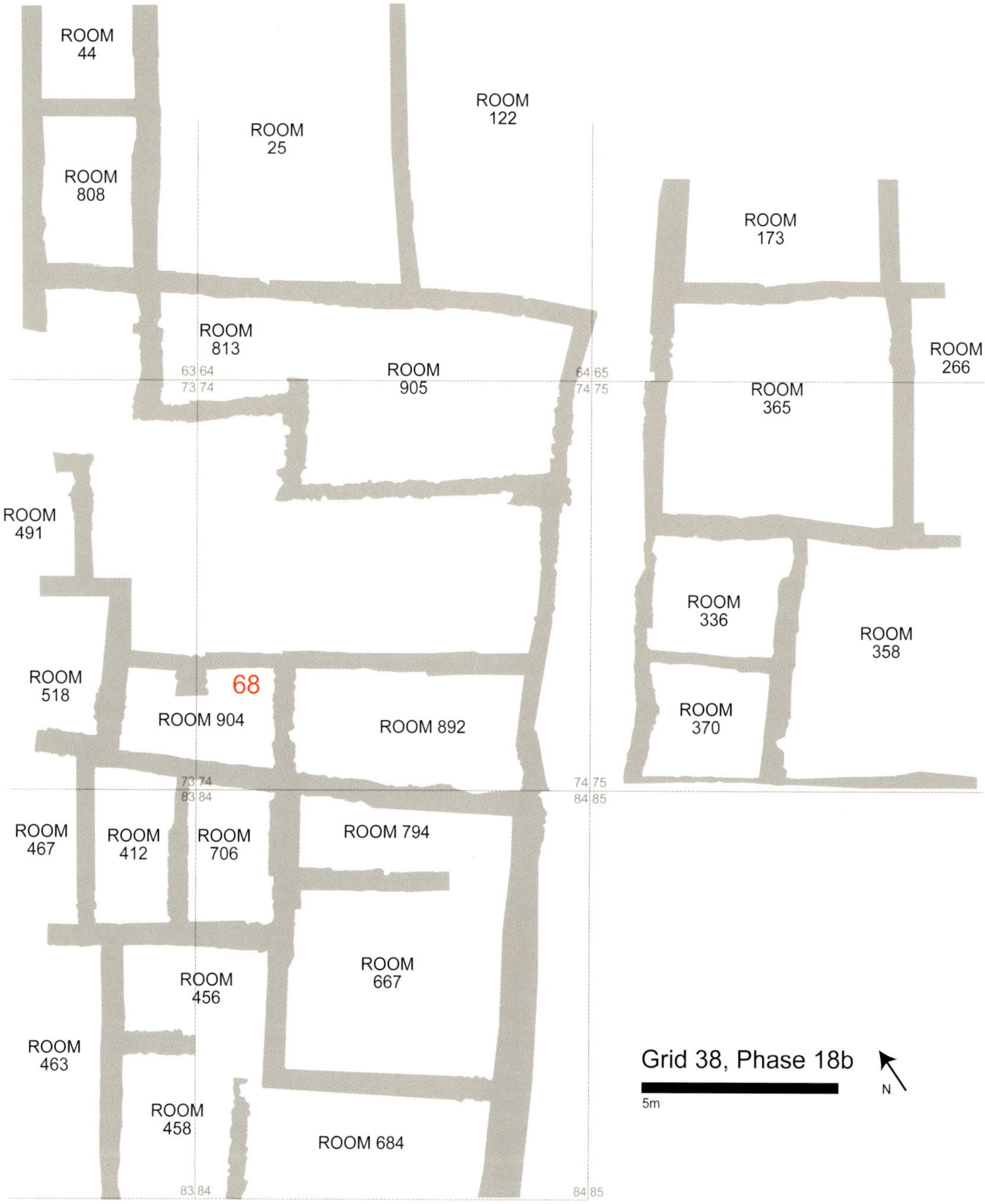

Figure 6. Findspots in Grid 38 Phase 18B (*Ashkelon 1*, pp. 266–71; 1100–1050 B.C.E.)

Figure 7. Findspots in Grid 38 Phase 18A (*Ashkelon 1*, pp. 266–71; 1100–1050 B.C.E.)

Figure 8. Findspots in Grid 38 Phase 17B (*Ashkelon 1*, pp. 271–74; 1050–1000 B.C.E.)

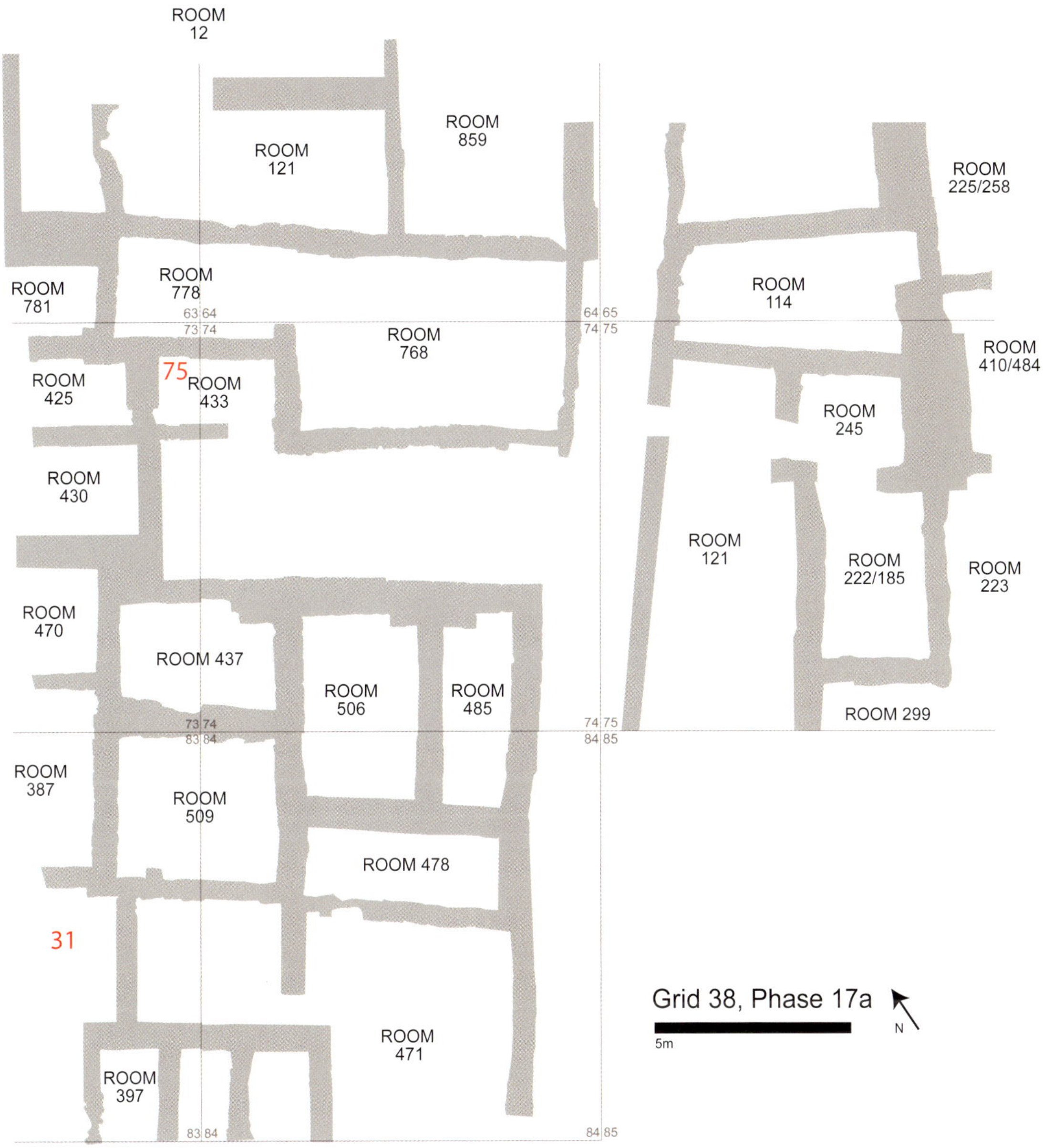

Figure 9. Findspots in Grid 38 Phase 17A (*Ashkelon 1*, pp. 271–74; 1050–1000 B.C.E.)

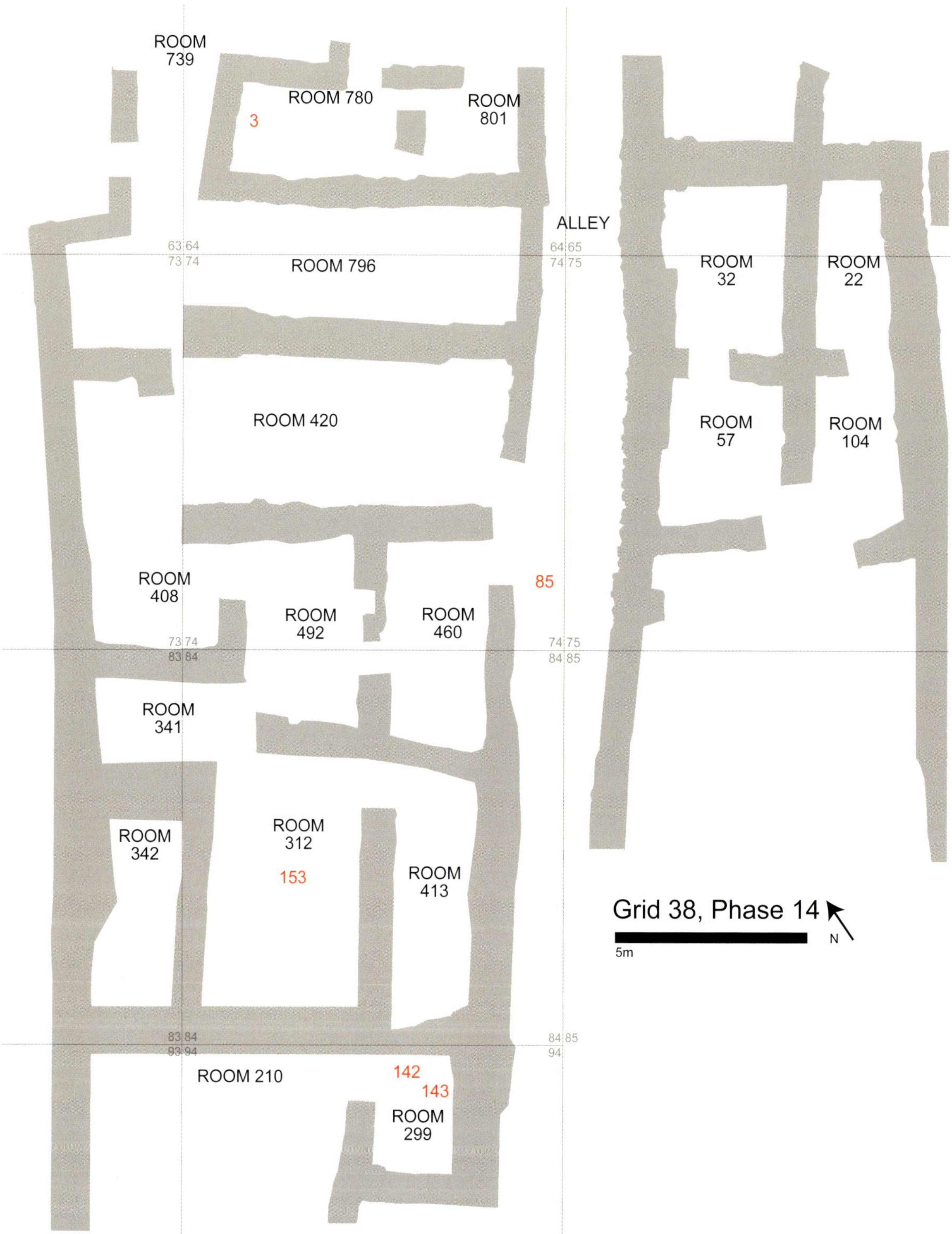

Figure 10. Findspots in Grid 38 Phase 14 (*Ashkelon 3*, chapter 2; 700–604 B.C.E.)

Figure 11. Findspots in Grid 50 Phase 9A (*Ashkelon 1*, pp. 306–7; 1100–1050 B.C.E.)

Figure 12. Findpots in Grid 50 Phase 7 (*Ashkelon 3*, chapter 3; 700–604 B.C.E.)

BIBLIOGRAPHY

Aharoni, Yohanan
1959 Zephath of Thutmose. *IEJ* 9:110–22.
1962 *Excavations at Ramat Rahel: Seasons 1959 and 1960*. Rome: Centro di Studi Semitici.
1964 *Excavations at Ramat Rahel: Seasons 1961 and 1962*. Rome: Centro di Studi Semitici.
1979 *The Land of the Bible: A Historical Geography*. Translated by A. F. Rainey. Revised and enlarged ed. Philadelphia: Westminster.

Aḥituv, Shmuel
1984 *Canaanite Toponyms in Ancient Egyptian Documents*. Jerusalem: Magnes Press, Hebrew University.

Ahlberg, Gudrun
1971 *Prothesis and Ekphora in Greek Geometric Art*. SIMA 32. Göteberg: P. Åström.

Ahlström, Gösta W.
1990a The Bull Figurine from Dhahrat et-Tawileh. *BASOR* 280:77–82.
1990b Review of *Asherah and the Cult of Yahweh in Israel*, by S. M. Olyan. *JAOS* 110:578–80.

Aja, Adam J.
2009 Philistine Domestic Architecture in the Iron Age I. Ph.D. diss., Harvard University.

Albright, William F.
1934 The Kyle Memorial Excavation at Bethel. *BASOR* 56:2–15.
1938 The Chronology of a South Palestinian City, Tell el-ᶜAjjûl. *American Journal of Semitic Languages and Literatures* 55:337–59.
1939 Astarte Plaques and Figurines from Tell Beit Mirsim. In *Mélanges Syriens offerts à René Dussaud*, 107–20. Paris: P. Geuthner.
1942 *Archaeology and the Religion of Israel: The Ayer Lectures of the Colgate-Rochester Divinity School, 1941*. Baltimore: Johns Hopkins Press.
1943 *The Excavation of Tell Beit Mirsim*. Vol. III, *The Iron Age*. AASOR 21–22. New Haven, Conn.: American Schools of Oriental Research.
1963 *The Archaeology of Palestine*. Rev. ed. Harmondsworth: Penguin.
1975 Syria, the Philistines, and Phoenicia. In *The Cambridge Ancient History*. Vol. 2, part 2, ed. I. E. S. Edwards et al., 507–34. 3d ed. Cambridge: Cambridge University Press.

Alexiou, Stylianos
1958 Η μινωικη θεα μεθ᾽ υψωμενων χειρων. *Kretika Khronika* 12:179–299.

Alram-Stern, Eva
1999 The Mycenaen Figurines of Elateia. In *ΗΠΕΡΙΦΕΡΕΙΑ ΤΟΥ ΜΥΚΗΝΑΙΚΟΥΚΟΣΜΟΥ.* Vol. 1, ed. H. Phroussou, 215–22. Diethnes Diepistemoniko Symposio, Lamia, 25–29 Septembriou 1994. Lamia: Ephoreias Proistorikon kai Klassikon Archaioteton.

Alt, Albrecht
1925 Judas Gaue unter Josia. *Palästinajahrbuch* 21:100–16.
1950 Syrien und Palästina im Onomastikon des Amenope. *Schweizerische Theologische Umschau* 20:58–71.
1953 Neue assyrische Nachrichten über Palästina. In *Kleine Schriften zur Geschichte des Volkes Israel.* Vol. II, 226–41. Munich: C. H. Beck'sche Verlagsbuchhandlung. (Originally published in *ZDPV* 67 [1945]:128–46.)

Amiran, Ruth
1967 A Note on Figurines with "Disks" [in Hebrew]. *EI* 8:99–100.
1970 *Ancient Pottery of the Holy Land: From Its Beginnings in the Neolithic Period to the End of the Iron Age*. New Brunswick, N.J.: Rutgers University Press.

Ammerman, Rebecca M.
1991 The Naked Standing Goddess: A Group of Archaic Terracotta Figurines from Paestum. *AJA* 95:203–30.

Ap-Thomas, D. R.
1983 All the King's Horses? A Study of the Term פרשׁ (I Kings 5. 6 [EVV., 4. 26] etc.). In *Proclamation and Presence: Old Testament Essays in Honour of Gwynne Henton Davies*, ed. J. I. Durham and J. R. Porter, 125–51. New corrected ed. Macon: Mercer University Press.

Atkinson, Thomas D., et al.
1904 *Excavations at Phylakopi in Melos, conducted by the British School at Athens*. London: Macmillan.

Badre, Leila
1980 *Les figurines anthropomorphes en terre cuite à l'âge du bronze en Syrie*. Paris: Librairie Orientaliste Paul Geuthner.

Badre, Leila, et al.
1990 Tell Kazel, Syria: Excavations of the AUB Museum, 1985–1987. Preliminary Reports. *Berytus* 38:9–124.

1994 Tell Kazel (Syrie). Rapport préliminaire sur les 4e–8e campagnes de fouilles (1988–1992). *Syria* 71:259–359.

Bailey, Douglass W.
1994 Reading Prehistoric Figurines as Individuals. *World Archaeology* 21/3:321–31.
1996 The Interpretation of Figurines: The Emergence of Illusion and New Ways of Seeing. *CAJ* 6/2:291–95.
2005 *Prehistoric Figurines: Representation and Corporeality in the Neolithic*. London and New York: Routledge.

Barako, Tristan
2000 The Philistine Settlement as Mercantile Phenomenon? *AJA* 104:513–30.
2001 The Seaborne Migration of the Philistines. Ph.D. diss., Harvard University.

Barnett, Richard D.
1982 *Ancient Ivories in the Middle East*. Qedem 14. Jerusalem: Institute of Archaeology, the Hebrew University of Jerusalem.
1985 Lachish, Ashkelon and the Camel: A Discussion of Its Use in Southern Palestine. In *Palestine in the Bronze and Iron Ages: Papers in Honour of Olga Tufnell*, ed. J. N. Tubb, 15–30. University of London, Institute of Archaeology, Occasional Publication No. 11. London: Institute of Archaeology.

Barrelet, Marie-Thérèse
1958 Deux déesses syro-phéniciennes sur un bronze du Louvre. *Syria* 35:27–44.

Barth, Fredrik
1969a Introduction. In *Ethnic Groups and Boundaries*, ed. F. Barth, 9–38. Boston: Little, Brown and Co.
1969b Pathan Identity and Its Maintenance. In *Ethnic Groups and Boundaries*, ed. F. Barth, 117–34. Boston: Little, Brown and Co.

Barth, Fredrik, ed.
1969c *Ethnic Groups and Boundaries*. Boston: Little, Brown and Co.

Bayer, Bathja
1963 *The Material Relics of Music in Ancient Palestine and Its Environs: An Archaeological Inventory*. Tel Aviv: Israel Music Institute.

Beck, Pirhiya
1986 A New Type of Female Figurine. In *Insight Through Images: Studies in Honor of Edith Porada*, ed. M. Kelly-Buccellati, P. Matthiae, and M. Van Loon, 29–34. Malibu: Undena.
1990 A Figurine from Tel ᶜIra [in Hebrew]. *EI* 21:87–93.
1994 The Cult-Stands from Taanach: Aspects of the Iconographic Tradition of Early Iron Age Cult Objects in Palestine. In *From Nomadism to Monarchy: Archaeological and Historical Aspects of Early Israel*, ed. I. Finkelstein and N. Naᵓaman, 352–81. Jerusalem: Israel Exploration Society.
1995 Catalogue of Cult Objects and Study of the Iconography. In *Ḥorvat Qitmit: An Edomite Shrine in the Biblical Negev*, ed. I. Ben-Arieh, 27–197. Tel Aviv: Institute of Archaeology, Tel Aviv University.
2002a *Imagery and Representation. Studies in the Art and Iconography of Ancient Palestine: Collected Works*. Tel Aviv: Institute of Archaeology, Tel Aviv University.
2002b A Human Figurine with Tambourine. In *Imagery and Representation. Studies in the Art and Iconography of Ancient Palestine: Collected Works*, ed. P. Beck, 437–46. Tel Aviv: Institute of Archaeology, Tel Aviv University. (Originally published in *Tel ᶜIra: A Stronghold of the Biblical Negev*, ed. I. Beit-Arieh, 386–94 [Tel Aviv: Institute of Archaeology, Tel Aviv University, 1999].)

Ben-Arieh, Sara
1983 A Mould for a Goddess Plaque. *IEJ* 33:72–77.

Bennett, William J., and Jeffrey A. Blakely
1989 *Tell el-Hesi: The Persian Period (Stratum V)*. Publications of the Joint Archaeological Expedition to Tell el-Hesi 3. Winona Lake, Ind.: Eisenbrauns.

Ben-Shlomo, David
1999 Zoomorphic Terracottas of the Early Iron Age (12th-10th c. BC) from Philistia, Focusing on Tel Miqne-Ekron and Ashdod. M. A. thesis, Hebrew University.
2006 Selected Objects. In *Tel Miqne-Ekron Excavations 1995–1996. Field INE East Slope: Iron Age I (Early Philistine Period)*, ed. S. Gitin, 189–205. Jerusalem: W. F. Albright Institute of Archaeological Research and Institute of Archaeology, the Hebrew University of Jerusalem.
2010 *Philistine Iconography: A Wealth of Style and Symbolism*. OBO 241. Fribourg: Academic Press.
in press Zoomorphic Terracottas from Tel Miqne-Ekron: Religious and Secular Aspects. In *Proceedings of the 3rd ICAANE Conference, Paris, May 2002*, ed. J. C. Margueron, P. de Miroschedji, and J. Thalmann. Winona Lake, Ind.: Eisenbrauns.

Ben-Shlomo, David, and Michael D. Press
2009 A Reexamination of Aegean-Style Figurines in Light of New Evidence from Ashdod, Ashkelon, and Ekron. *BASOR* 353:39–74.

Ben-Tor, Amnon, Anabel Zarzecki-Peleg, and Shlomit Cohen-Anadjar
2005 *Yoqneam II: The Iron Age and the Persian Period, Final Report of the Archaeological Excavations*

(1977–1988). Qedem Reports 6. Jerusalem: Institute of Archaeology, the Hebrew University of Jerusalem.

Benzi, Mario
1992 *Rodi e la civiltà micenea*. 2 vols. Rome: Gruppo Editoriale Internazionale.

Bérard, Victor
1894 *De l'origine des cultes arcadiens: essai de méthode en mythologie grecque*. Paris: Thorin et fils.

Bietak, Manfred
1993 The Sea Peoples and the End of the Egyptian Administration of Canaan. In *Biblical Archaeology Today, 1990*, ed. A. Biran and J. Aviram, 282–306. Proceedings of the Second International Congress on Biblical Archaeology, Jerusalem, June-July 1990. Jerusalem: Israel Exploration Society.

Bikai, Patricia M.
1978 *The Pottery of Tyre*. Warminster: Aris and Phillips

Birmingham, Judy
1963 The Chronology of Some Early and Middle Iron Age Cypriot Sites. *AJA* 67:15–42.

Birney, Kathleen J.
2007 Sea Peoples or Syrian Peddlers? The Late Bronze-Iron I Aegean Presence in Syria and Cilicia. Ph.D. diss., Harvard University.

Bisi, Anna Maria
1999 Terra-cotta Figures. In *The Phoenicians*, ed. S. Moscati, 380–404. New York: Rizzoli.

Bloch-Smith, Elizabeth
2002 Life in Judah from the Perspective of the Dead. *NEA* 65:120–30.
2003 Israelite Ethnicity in Iron I: Archaeology Preserves What is Remembered and What is Forgotten in Israel's History. *JBL* 122:401–25.

Blom, Jan-Petter
1969 Ethnic and Cultural Differentiation. In *Ethnic Groups and Boundaries*, ed. F. Barth, 74–85. Boston: Little, Brown and Co.

Boardman, John
1955 Painted Funerary Plaques and Some Remarks on Prothesis. *BSA* 50:51–66.

Bordreuil, Pierre, and Eric Gubel
1988 Bulletin d'antiquités archéologiques du Levant inédites ou méconnues, V. *Syria* 65:437–56.

Borowski, Oded
1988 The Biblical Identity of Tel Halif. *BA* 51:21–27.

Bothmer, Bernard V.
1960 *Egyptian Sculpture of the Late Period. 700 B.C. to A.D. 100*. Brooklyn: The Brooklyn Museum.

Brandl, Baruch
2000 Various Finds from Iron Age II and the Persian Period (Eighth–Fourth Centuries B.C.E.). In *Ramat Hanadiv Excavations: Final Reports of the 1984–1998 Seasons*, ed. Y. Hirschfeld, 187–210. Jerusalem: Israel Exploration Society.

Brown, Francis, Samuel Driver, and Charles Briggs.
2006 *The Brown-Driver Briggs Hebrew and English Lexicon*. Peabody: Hendrickson (1906).

Brug, John
1985 *A Literary and Archaeological Study of the Philistines*. BARIS 265. Oxford: British Archaeological Reports.

Budin, Stephanie L.
2006 Three Studies of Ancient Near Eastern Iconography. *AJA* 110:161–65.

Bunimovitz, Shlomo
1990 Problems in the "Ethnic" Identification of the Philistine Material Culture. *TA* 17:210–22.

Bunimovitz, Shlomo, and Zvi Lederman
1997 Beth-Shemesh: Culture Conflict on Judah's Frontier. *BAR* 23/1:42–49, 75–77.

Burdajewicz, Mariusz
1993 Rabbath-Ammon. In *NEAEHL*, ed. E. Stern, 4:1243–49. Jerusalem: Israel Exploration Society and Carta.

Caskey, Miriam E.
1986 *Keos*. Vol. II, part 1, *The Temple at Ayia Irini: The Statues*. Princeton, N.J.: American School of Classical Studies.

Catling, Hector W.
1995 A Mycenaean Terracotta Figure from the Menelaion. *BSA* 90:183–93.

Caubet, Annie, Sabine Fourrier, and Anne Queyrel
1998 *L'art des modeleurs d'argile: antiquités de Chypre coroplastique*. 2 vols. Paris: Réunion des musées nationaux.

Cavanagh, William, and Christopher Mee
1995 Mourning Before and After the Dark Age. In *Klados. Essays in Honour of J. N. Coldstream*, ed. C. Morris, 45–61. Bulletin of the Institute of Classical Studies Supplement 63. London: University of London, Institute of Classical Studies.

Chéhab, Maurice
1975 30 années de recherche archéologique au Liban. *Les dossiers de l'archéologie* 12:8–23.

Childe, V. Gordon
1925 *The Dawn of European Civilization.* New York: Knopf.

Ciasca, Antonia
1964 Some Particular Aspects of the Israelitic Miniature Statuary at Ramat Raḥel. In *Excavations at Ramat Raḥel, Seasons 1961 and 1962*, ed. Y. Aharoni, 95–100. Rome: Centro di Studi Semitici.
1999 Masks and Protomes. In *The Phoenicians*, ed. S. Moscati, 406–17. New York: Rizzoli.

Clamer, Christa
1980 A Gold Plaque from Tel Lachish. *Tel Aviv* 7:152–62.
2004 The Pottery and Artefacts from the Level VI Temple in Area P. In *The Renewed Archaeological Excavations at Lachish (1973–1994).* Vol. III, ed. D. Ussishkin, 1288–368. Tel Aviv: Institute of Archaeology, Tel Aviv University.

Clark, Grahame
1961 *World Prehistory, an Outline.* Cambridge: Cambridge University Press.

Clark, Sharri R.
2007 The Social Lives of Figurines: Recontextualizing the Third Millennium B.C. Terracotta Figurines from Harappa (Pakistan). Ph.D. diss., Harvard University.

Clifford, Richard J.
1990 Phoenician Religion. *BASOR* 279:55–64.

Cogan, Mordechai
2008 *The Raging Torrent: Historical Inscriptions from Assyria and Babylonia Relating to Ancient Israel.* Jerusalem: Carta.

Cohen, Abner
1974a Introduction: The Lesson of Ethnicity. In *Urban Ethnicity*, ed. A. Cohen, ix–xxiii. New York: Tavistock.

Cohen, Abner, ed.
1974b *Urban Ethnicity.* New York: Tavistock.

Cohen, Susan
2011 Terracotta Figurines. In *Ashkelon* 3:441–71. Winona Lake, Ind.: Eisenbrauns.

Conrad, Diethelm
1997 Two Figurine Heads and Their Parallels. *Michmanim* 11:53*–63*.

Coogan, Michael D.
1987 Of Cults and Cultures: Reflections on the Interpretation of Archaeological Evidence. *PEQ* 119:1–8.

Cook, R. M.
1967 Origins of Greek Sculpture. *JHS* 87:24–32.

Cornelius, Izak
1994 *The Iconography of the Canaanite Gods Reshef and Baʿal. Late Bronze and Iron Age I Periods.* OBO 140. Fribourg: University Press.
2004 *The Many Faces of the Goddess: The Iconography of the Syro-Palestinian Goddesses Anat, Astarte, Qedeshet, and Asherah c. 1500–1000 B.C.E.* Fribourg: Academic Press.

Courtois, Jean-Claude
1988 Enkomi (Fouilles Schaeffer 1934–1966): Inventaire Complémentaire (Suite): les objets en terre cuite et en pierre. *RDAC* 1988, part 1:307–18.

Cross, Frank M.
1971 The Old Phoenician Inscription from Spain Dedicated to Hurrian Astarte. *HTR* 64:189–95.

Cross, Frank M., and Lawrence E. Stager
2006 Cypro-Minoan Inscriptions Found in Ashkelon. *IEJ* 56:129–59.

Cross, Frank M., and G. Ernest Wright
1956 The Boundary and Province Lists of the Kingdom of Judah. *JBL* 75:202–26.

Crouwel, Joost H., and Veronica Tatton-Brown
1988 Ridden Horses in Iron Age Cyprus. *RDAC* 1988, part 2:77–87.

Crowfoot, Grace M., and Eleazar L. Sukenik
1957 Israelite Figurines. In *The Objects from Samaria*, ed. J. W. Crowfoot, G. M. Crowfoot, and K. M. Kenyon, 76–82. London: Palestine Exploration Fund.

Culican, William
1969 Dea Tyria Gravida. *AJBA* 1/2:35–50.
1973 The Graves at Tell er-Reqeish. *AJBA* 2/2:66–105.
1975–76 Some Phoenician Masks and Other Terracottas. *Berytus* 24:47–87.

D'Agata, Anna Lucia
1999 *Haghia Triada.* Vol. II, *Statuine minoiche e post-minoiche dai vecchi scavi di Haghia Triada (Creta).* Padova: Bottega d'Erasmo.

Dalley, Stephanie
1985 Foreign Chariotry and Cavalry in the Armies of Tiglath-pileser III and Sargon II. *Iraq* 47:31–48.

Daly, Patricia, Brian C. Hesse, and Dexter Perkins, Jr.
1972 Animal Domestication and Species Identification: Inferences from Ancient Art. *JANES* 4:79–80.

D'Amore, Paola
1998 The Iron Age Clay Figurines. In *Tell Afis (Siria): Scavi sull'acropoli 1988–1992*, ed. S. M. Cecchini and S. Mazzoni, 415–25. Pisa: ETS.

Darby, Erin D.
2011 Interpreting Judean Pillar Figurines: Gender and Empire in Judean Apotropaic Ritual. Ph.D. diss., Duke University.

D'Auria, Sue, Peter Lacovara, and Catharine H. Roehrig
1992 *Mummies and Magic: The Funerary Arts of Ancient Egypt*. Boston and Dallas: Museum of Fine Arts, Boston, Dallas Museum of Art.

Dayagi-Mendels, Michal
2002 *The Akhziv Cemeteries: The Ben-Dor Excavations, 1941–1944*. Israel Antiquities Authority Reports 15. Jerusalem: Israel Antiquities Authority.

Dayan, Moshe
1978 *Living with the Bible*. New York: William Morrow.

Demakopoulou, Katie
1999 A Mycenaean Terracotta Figure from Midea in the Argolid. In *Meletemata: Studies in Aegean Archaeology Presented to Malcolm H. Wiener as He Enters His 65th Year*. Vol 1, ed. P. P. Betancourt et al., 197–205. Aegaeum 20. Liège: Université de Liège.

Demakopoulou, Katie, and Nicoletta Divari-Valakou
2001 Evidence for Cult Practice at Midea: Figures, Figurines, and Ritual Objects. In *Potnia: Deities and Religion in the Aegean Bronze Age*, ed. R. Laffineur and R. Hägg, 181–92. Proceedings of the 8th International Aegean Conference/8e Rencontre égéenne internationale, Göteborg, Göteborg University, 12–15 April 2000. Aegaeum 22. Liège: Université de Liège.

Demakopoulou, Katie, et al.
1997–98 Excavations in Midea 1995–1996. *Opuscula Atheniensia* 22–23:57–90.

Demangel, Robert
1926 *Fouilles de Delphes*. Tome II, 5e Fascicule, *Topographie et architecture. Le sanctuaire d'Athènes. Troisième Fascicule (Texte). Topographie du sanctuaire*. Paris: École Française d'Athènes.

Desborough, Vincent R. d'A.
1964 *The Last Mycenaeans and Their Successors*. Oxford: Clarendon Press.

Dever, William G.
1984 Asherah, Consort of Yahweh? New Evidence from Kuntillet ᶜAjrûd. *BASOR* 255:21–37.
1986 *Gezer*. Vol. IV, *The 1969–71 Seasons in Field VI, the "Acropolis."* Jerusalem: Nelson Glueck School of Biblical Archaeology.
1987 The Contribution of Archaeology to the Study of Canaanite and Early Israelite Religion. In *Ancient Israelite Religion: Essays in Honor of Frank Moore Cross*, ed. P. D. Miller, P. D. Hanson, and S. D. McBride, 209–47. Philadelphia: Fortress.
1995 Social Structure in Palestine in the Iron II Period. In *The Archaeology of Society in the Holy Land*, ed. T. Levy, 416–31. New York: Facts on File.
2005 *Did God Have a Wife? Archaeology and Folk Religion in Ancient Israel*. Grand Rapids: William B. Eerdmans.

Dever, William G., H. Darrell Lance, and G. Ernest Wright
1970 *Gezer*. Vol. I, *Preliminary Report of the 1964–66 Seasons*. Jerusalem: Hebrew Union College Biblical and Archaeological School.

Dikaios, Porphyrios
1969a *Enkomi. Excavations 1948–1958*. Vol. I, *The Architectural Remains. The Tombs*. Mainz am Rhein: Philpp von Zabern.
1969b *Enkomi. Excavations 1948–1958*. Vol. IIIa, *Plates 1–239*. Mainz am Rhein: Philpp von Zabern.
1971 *Enkomi. Excavations 1948–1958*. Vol. II, *Chronology, Summary and Conclusions, Catalogue, Appendices*. Mainz am Rhein: Philpp von Zabern.

Dornemann, Rudolph H.
1983 *The Archaeology of the Transjordan in the Bronze and Iron Ages*. Milwaukee: Milwaukee Public Museum.

Dothan, Moshe
1956 The Excavations at Afula. *ᶜAtiqot* 1 [English series]:19–70.
1971 *Ashdod*. Vol. II–III, *The Second and Third Seasons of Excavations, 1963, 1965, Soundings in 1967*. ᶜAtiqot 9–10 [English series]. Jerusalem: Department of Antiquities and Museums.
1979 Ashdod at the End of the Late Bronze Age and the Beginning of the Iron Age. In *Symposia Celebrating the Seventy-fifth Anniversary of the Founding of the American Schools of Oriental Research (1900–1975)*, ed. F. M. Cross, 125–34. Cambridge, Mass.: American Schools of Oriental Research.

Dothan, Moshe, and David Ben-Shlomo
2005 *Ashdod*. Vol. VI, *The Excavations of Areas H and K (1968–1969)*. Israel Antiquities Authority Reports 24. Jerusalem: Israel Antiquities Authority.

Dothan, Moshe, and David N. Freedman
1967 *Ashdod.* Vol. I, *The First Season of Excavations, 1962.* ᶜAtiqot 7 [English series]. Jerusalem: Department of Antiquities and Museums.

Dothan, Moshe, and Yehoshua Porath.
1982 *Ashdod.* Vol. IV, *Excavation of Area M, The Fortifications of the Lower City.* ᶜAtiqot 15. Jerusalem: Department of Antiquities and Museums.
1993 *Ashdod.* Vol. V, *Excavation of Area G; the Fourth-Sixth Seasons of Excavations 1968–1970.* ᶜAtiqot 23. Jerusalem: Israel Antiquities Authority.

Dothan, Trude
1967 *The Philistines and Their Material Culture* [in Hebrew]. Jerusalem: The Bialik Institute and The Israel Exploration Society.
1969 A Female Mourner Figurine from the Lachish Region [in Hebrew with English summary]. *EI* 9:42–46.
1973 Another Mourning-Woman Figurine from the Lachish Region [in Hebrew with English summary]. *EI* 11:120–21.
1982 *The Philistines and Their Material Culture.* New Haven, Conn.: Yale University Press.
1995 Tel Miqne-Ekron: The Aegean Affinities of the Sea Peoples' (Philistines') Settlement in Canaan in Iron Age I. In *Recent Excavations in Israel: A View to the West*, ed. S. Gitin, 41–59. Dubuque, Iowa: Kendall/Hunt.
2002 Bronze and Iron Objects with Cultic Connotations from Philistine Temple Building 350 at Ekron. *IEJ* 52:1–27.
2003 The Aegean and the Orient: Cultic Interactions. In *Symbiosis, Symbolism, and the Power of the Past: Canaan, Ancient Israel, and Their Neighbors from the Late Bronze Age through Roman Palaestina*, ed. W. G. Dever and S. Gitin, 189–213. Proceedings of the Centennial Symposium, W. F. Albright Institute of Archaeological Research and American Schools of Oriental Research, Jerusalem, May 29–31, 2000. Winona Lake, Ind.: Eisenbrauns.

Dothan, Trude, and Moshe Dothan
1992 *People of the Sea: The Search for the Philistines.* New York: Macmillan.

Dothan, Trude, and Alexander Zukerman
2004 A Preliminary Study of the Mycenaean IIIC:1 Pottery Assemblages from Tel Miqne-Ekron and Ashdod. *BASOR* 333:1–54.

Edelstein, Gershon, and Jonathan Glass
1973 The Origin of Philistine Pottery Based on Petrographic Analyses [in Hebrew with English summary]. In *Excavations and Studies: Essays in Honour of Professor Shmuel Yeivin*, ed. Y. Aharoni, 125–31. Tel Aviv: Institute of Archaeology, Tel Aviv University.

Edwards, I. E. S.
1955 A Relief of Qudshu-Astarte-Anath in the Winchester College Collection. *JNES* 14:49–51.

Ehrlich, Carl S.
1996 *The Philistines in Transition: A History from ca. 1000–730 B.C.E.* Leiden: E. J. Brill

Elgavish, Joseph
1993 Shiqmona. In *NEAEHL*, ed. E. Stern, 4:1373–78. Jerusalem: Israel Exploration Society and Carta.
1994 *Shiqmona on the Seacoast of Mount Carmel* [in Hebrew]. Tel Aviv: Israel Exploration Society.

Engle, James R.
1979 Pillar Figurines of Iron Age Israel and Asherah/Asherim. Ph.D. diss., University of Pittsburgh.

Ephᶜal, Israel
1982 *The Ancient Arabs: Nomads on the Border of the Fertile Crescent, 9th–5th Centuries B.C.* Jerusalem: Magnes Press, Hebrew University.

Erlenmeyer, Marie-Louise, and Hans Erlenmeyer
1960 Über Philister und Kreter II. *Orientalia* 29:241–72.

Erwin, Timothy
1991 Modern Iconology, Postmodern Iconologies. In *Image and Ideology in Modern/Postmodern Discourse*, ed. D. B. Downing and S. Bazargan, 309–20. Albany, N.Y.: State University of New York Press.

Faerman, Marina, et al.
2011 ". . . In Their Lives, and In Their Death . . . ": A Preliminary Study of an Iron Age Burial Cave at Tell es-Safi (Tell eṣ-Ṣāfī), Israel. *ZDPV* 127: 29–48.

Faust, Avraham
2006 *Israel's Ethnogenesis: Settlement, Interaction, Expansion, and Resistance.* London: Equinox.

Faust, Avraham, and Justin Lev-Tov
2011 The Constitution of Philistine Identity: Ethnic Dynamics in Twelfth to Tenth Century Philistia. *OJA* 30:13–31.

Fechheimer, Hedwig
1921 *Kleinplastik der Ägypter.* Berlin: Bruno Cassirer.
1923 *Die Plastik der Ägypter.* Berlin: Bruno Cassirer.

Felsch, Rainer C. S.
1981 Mykenischer Kult im Heiligtum bei Kalapodi? In *Sanctuaries and Cults in the Aegean Bronze Age*, ed. R. Hägg and N. Marinatos, 81–89. Proceedings of the First International Symposium at the Swedish Institute in Athens, 12–13 May 1980. Stockholm: P. Åström.

Finkelstein, Israel
1997 Pots and Peoples Revisited: Ethnic Boundaries in the Iron Age I. In *The Archaeology of Israel: Constructing the Past, Interpreting the Present*, ed. N. A. Silberman and D. Small, 216–37. JSOT Supplement Series 237. Sheffield: Sheffield Academic Press.

Fischer, Moshe, and Itamar Taxel
2006 Yavne, Survey Map. *Hadashot Arkheologiyot—ESI* 118 (15/11/2006). http://www. hadashot-esi. org.il/report_detail_eng.asp?id=437&mag_id=111 (last accessed 10/24/11).

Forsdyke, E. John
1925 *Catalogue of the Greek and Etruscan Vases in the British Museum*. Vol. 1, part 1, *Prehistoric Aegean Pottery*. London: British Museum.

Fowler, Mervyn D.
1985 Excavated Figurines: A Case for Identifying a Site as Sacred? *ZAW* 97:333–44.

French, Elizabeth B.
1971 The Development of Mycenaean Terracotta Figurines. *BSA* 66:101–87.
1981 Mycenaean Figures and Figurines, Their Typology and Function. In *Sanctuaries and Cults in the Aegean Bronze Age*, ed. R. Hägg and N. Marinatos, 173–77. Proceedings of the First International Symposium at the Swedish Institute in Athens, 12–13 May 1980. Stockholm: P. Åström.
1985 The Figures and Figurines. In *The Archaeology of Cult: The Sanctuary at Phylakopi*, ed. C. Renfrew, 209–80. London: British School of Archaeology at Athens.
2001 The Mycenaean Figures. In *Potnia: Deities and Religion in the Aegean Bronze Age*, ed. R. Laffineur and R. Hägg, 275–76. Proceedings of the 8th International Aegean Conference/8e Rencontre égéenne internationale, Göteborg, Göteborg University, 12–15 April 2000. Aegaeum 22. Liège: Université de Liège.
2009 Mycenaean Figurines: 50 Years On. In *Dioskouroi: Studies presented to W. G. Cavanagh and C. B. Mee on the anniversary of their 30-year joint contribution to Aegean archaeology*, ed. C. Gallou, M. Georgiadis, and G. M. Muskett, 59–63. BARIS 1889. Oxford: Archaeopress.

Frick, Frank S.
2000 *Tell Taannek 1963–1968*. Vol. IV/2, *The Iron Age Cultic Structure*. Birzeit: Palestinian Institute of Archaeology, Birzeit University.

Friedman, Richard E.
1987 *Who Wrote the Bible?* Englewood Cliffs: Prentice Hall.

Furumark, Arne
1941a *The Mycenaean Pottery: Analysis and Classification*. Stockholm: Svenska Institutet i Athen.
1941b *The Chronology of Mycenaean Pottery*. Stockholm: Svenska Institutet i Athen.

Fururmark, Arne, and Charles M. Adelman
2003 *Swedish Excavations at Sinda, Cyprus: Excavations Conducted by Arne Furumark 1947–1948*. Stockholm: P. Åström.

Gailey, Christine W.
1989 "RAMBO" in Tonga: Video Films and Cultural Resistance in the Tongan Islands (South Pacific). *Culture* 9/1:21–32.

Galling, Kurt
1937 *Biblisches Reallexikon*. Tübingen: J. C. Mohr.

Gardiner, Alan H.
1947 *Ancient Egyptian Onomastica*. Vol. 1, *Text*. Oxford: Oxford University Press.

Gaskell, Ivan
1992 History of Images. In *New Perspectives on Historical Writing*, ed. P. Burke, 168–92. University Park: Penn State University Press.

Gibson, John C. L.
1982 *Textbook of Syrian Semitic Inscriptions*. Vol. III, *Phoenician Inscriptions, including the Mixed Dialect of Arslan Tash*. Oxford: Clarendon Press.

Gilbert-Peretz, Diana
1996 Ceramic Figurines. In *Excavations at the City of David, 1978–1985, Directed by Yigal Shiloh*. Vol. IV, *Various Reports*, ed. D. T. Ariel and A. de Groot, 29–84. Qedem 35. Jerusalem: Institute of Archaeology, the Hebrew University of Jerusalem.

Gitin, Seymour
1992 Last Days of the Philistines. *Archaeology* 45/3:26–31.
1995 Tel Miqne-Ekron in the 7th Century B.C.E.: The Impact of Economic Innovation and Foreign Cultural Influences on a Neo-Assyrian Vassal City-State. In *Recent Excavations in Israel: A View to the West*, ed. S. Gitin, 61–79. Dubuque, Iowa: Kendall/Hunt.
2003 Israelite and Philistine Cult and the Archaeological Record in Iron Age II: The "Smoking Gun" Phenomenon. In *Symbiosis, Symbolism, and the Power of the Past: Canaan, Ancient Israel, and Their Neighbors from the Late Bronze Age through Roman Palaestina*, ed. W. G. Dever and S. Gitin, 279–95. Proceedings of the Centennial Symposium, W. F. Albright Institute of Archaeological Research and American Schools of Oriental

Research, Jerusalem, May 29–31, 2000. Winona Lake, Ind.: Eisenbrauns.
2010 Philistines in the Book of Kings. In *The Books of Kings: Sources, Composition, Historiography and Reception*, ed. A. Lemaire and B. Halpern, 301–64. Leiden: Brill.

Gitin, Seymour, and Trude Dothan
1987 The Rise and Fall of Ekron of the Philistines: Recent Excavations at an Urban Border Site. *BA* 50:197–222.

Gitin, Seymour, Trude Dothan, and Joseph Naveh
1997 A Royal Dedicatory Inscription from Ekron. *IEJ* 47:1–16.

Givon, Shmuel
1991a The Figurines [in Hebrew]. In *The First Season of Excavations at "Tel Harasim" 1990. Preliminary Report 1*, ed. S. Givon, 24–29. Tel Aviv.
1991b Tel Ḥarasim—1990. *ESI* 10:145–46.
1994 *The Fourth Season of Excavation at Tel Harassim (Nahal Barkai) 1993. Preliminary Report 4* [in Hebrew and English]. Tel Aviv.

Gjerstad, Einar
1948 *The Swedish Cyprus Expedition.* Vol. IV, part 2, *The Cypro-Geometric, Cypro-Archaic and Cypro-Classical Periods*. Stockholm: The Swedish Cyprus Expedition.

Gjerstad, Einar, et al.
1934 *The Swedish Cyprus Expedition. Finds and Results of the Excavations in Cyprus, 1927–1931*. Vol. I. Stockholm: The Swedish Cyprus Expedition.
1935 *The Swedish Cyprus Expedition. Finds and Results of the Excavations in Cyprus, 1927–1931*. Vol. II. Stockholm: The Swedish Cyprus Expedition.

Glazer, Nathan, and Daniel P. Moynihan, eds.
1974 *Ethnicity*. Cambridge, Mass.: Harvard University Press.

Goedicke, Hans
1975 *The Report of Wenamun*. Baltimore and London: Johns Hopkins University Press.

Goldman, Hetty
1963 *Excavations at Gözlü Kule, Tarsus*. Vol. III, *The Iron Age. Plates.* Princeton, N.J.: Princeton University Press.

Gophna, Ram
1970 Some Iron Age II Sites in Southern Philistia [in Hebrew with English summary]. *ᶜAtiqot* 6 [Hebrew series]:25–30, 3*.

Grant, Elihu
1934 *Rumeileh being Ain Shems Excavations (Palestine)*. Part III. Haverford: Haverford College.

Gubel, Eric
1983 Art in Tyre During the First and Second Iron Age: A Preliminary Report. In *Redt Tyrus/Sauvons Tyr*, ed. E. Gubel, E. Lipiński, and B. Servais-Soyez, 23–52. Studia Phoenicia I. Leuven: Peeters.
1991 From Amathus to Zarephath and Back Again. In *Cypriote Terracottas*, ed. F. Vandenabeele and R. Laffineur, 131–38. Proceedings of the First International Conference of Cypriote Studies, Brussels-Liège-Amsterdam, 29 May–1 June, 1989. Brussels and Liège: A. G. Leventis Foundation.

Gumperz, John J.
1968 The Speech Community. In *International Encyclopedia of the Social Sciences*. Vol. 9, ed. D. Sills, 381–86. New York: Macmillan.

Guralnick, Eleanor
1978 The Proportions of Kouroi. *AJA* 82:461–72.
1981 Proportions of Korai. *AJA* 85:269–80.
1982 Profiles of Korai. *AJA* 86:173–82.
1985 Profiles of Kouroi. *AJA* 89:399–409.

Guzowska, Marta, and Assaf Yasur-Landau
2009 Anthropomorphic Figurines. In *Aphek-Antipatris*. Vol. II, *The Remains on the Acropolis. The Moshe Kochavi and Pirhiya Beck Excavations*, ed. Y. Gadot and E. Yadin, 387–95. Tel Aviv: Institute of Archaeology, Tel Aviv University.

Haaland, Gunnar, and Randi Haaland
1996 Levels of Meaning in Symbolic Objects. *CAJ* 6/2:295–300.

Hachlili, Rachel
1971 Figurines and Kernoi (Areas D, H, Trench C1). In *Ashdod.* Vol. II–III, *The Second and Third Seasons of Excavations, 1963, 1965, Soundings in 1967*, ed. M. Dothan, 125–35. ᶜAtiqot 9–10 [English series]. Jerusalem: Department of Antiquities and Museums.

Hadley, Judith M.
2000 *The Cult of Asherah in Ancient Israel and Judah: Evidence for a Hebrew Goddess*. Cambridge: Cambridge University Press.

Hägg, Robin
1981 Official and Popular Cults in Mycenaean Greece. In *Sanctuaries and Cults in the Aegean Bronze Age*, ed. R. Hägg and N. Marinatos, 35–39. Proceedings of the First International Symposium at the Swedish Institute in Athens, 12–13 May 1980. Stockholm: P. Åström.

Hajjar, Joseph N.
1977–85 *La triade d'Héliopolis-Baalbek*. 3 vols. Leiden: Brill.

Hamilton, Naomi
1996 The Personal is Political. *CAJ* 6/2:282–85.

Hamilton, Naomi, et al.
1996 Viewpoint: Can We Interpret Figurines? *CAJ* 6/2:281–307.

Hamilton, Robert W.
1934 Excavations at Tell Abu Hawām. *QDAP* 4:1–69.

Harding, G. Lankester
1950 An Iron-Age Tomb at Meqabelein. *QDAP* 14:14–48.

Harris, Marvin
1964 *The Nature of Cultural Things*. New York: Random House.

Herzog, Ze^cev
1984 Tel Gerisa, 1983. *IEJ* 34:55–56.
1993 Gerisa, Tel. In *NEAEHL*, ed. E. Stern, 2: 480–84. Jerusalem: Israel Exploration Society and Carta.

Hesse, Brian
1997 Cattle and Oxen. In *Oxford Encyclopedia of Archaeology in the Near East*, ed. E. M. Meyers, 1:442–43. New York and Oxford: Oxford University Press.

Hesse, Brian, and Paula Wapnish
1997 Can Pig Remains Be Used for Ethnic Diagnosis in the Ancient Near East? In *The Archaeology of Israel: Constructing the Past, Interpreting the Present*, ed. N. A. Silberman and D. Small, 238–70. JSOT Supplement Series 237. Sheffield: Sheffield Academic Press.

Hestrin, Ruth
1991 Understanding Asherah: Exploring Semitic Iconography. *BAR* 17/5:50–59.

Hicks, George L.
1977 Introduction: Problems in the Study of Ethnicity. In *Ethnic Encounters: Identities and Contexts*, ed. G. L. Hicks and P. E. Leis, 1–20. North Scituate: Duxbury.

Hicks, George L., and Philip E. Leis, eds.
1977 *Ethnic Encounters: Identities and Contexts*. North Scituate: Duxbury.

Higgins, Reynold A.
1954 *Catalogue of the Terracottas in the Department of Greek and Roman Antiquities, British Museum*. London: British Museum.

Hillers, Delbert R.
1970 The Goddess with the Tambourine. *Concordia Theological Monthly* 41:606–19.

Hitchcock, Louise A.
2011 Cult Corners in the Aegean and the Levant. In *Household Archaeology in Ancient Israel and Beyond*, ed. A. Yasur-Landau, J. R. Ebeling, and L. B. Mazow, 321–45. Leiden: Brill.

Hodder, Ian
1992 *Theory and Practice in Archaeology*. London and New York: Routledge.

Holladay, John S.
1987 Religion in Israel and Judah under the Monarchy: An Explicitly Archaeological Approach. In *Ancient Israelite Religion: Essays in Honor of Frank Moore Cross*, ed. P. D. Miller, P. D. Hanson, and S. D. McBride, 249–99. Philadelphia: Fortress.

Holland, Thomas A.
1975 A Typological and Archaeological Study of Human and Animal Representations in the Plastic Art of Palestine. Ph.D. diss., Oxford University.
1977 A Study of Palestinian Iron Age Baked Clay Figurines, with Special Reference to Jerusalem: Cave 1. *Levant* 9:121–55.

Humbert, Jean-Baptiste, ed.
2000 *Gaza Mediterranéenne: Histoire et archéologie en Palestine*. Paris: Errance.

Hymes, Dell
1968 Linguistic Problems in Defining the Concept of Tribe. In *Essays on the Problem of Tribe*, ed. J. Helm, 23–48. Proceedings of the American Ethnology Society, Annual Spring Meeting, 1967. Seattle: American Ethnological Society.

Iakovidis, Spyros E.
1966 A Mycenaean Mourning Custom. *AJA* 70:43–50.
1980 *Excavations of the Necropolis at Perati*. Los Angeles: Institute of Archaeology, University of California, Los Angeles.

Israel Museum
1970 *The Philistines and the Other Sea Peoples. The Israel Museum, Jerusalem, the Goldman-Schwartz Hall, Winter 1970, Cat. No. 68.* Jerusalem: Department of Antiquities and Museums and the Israel Museum.

Jacobs, Paul F.
1996 Review of *Ashdod.* Vol. V, *Excavation of Area G; the Fourth-Sixth Seasons of Excavations, 1968–1970*, ed. M. Dothan and Y. Porath. *JAOS* 116:278–79.

Jacopi, Giulio
1932–33 *Esplorazione Archeologica di Camiro*. Vol. II. Clara Rhodos 6–7.

James, Frances
1966 *The Iron Age at Beth Shan: A Study of Levels VI–IV*. Philadelphia: University Museum, University of Pennsylvania.

James, Peter
2006 Dating Late Iron Age Ekron (Tel Miqne). *PEQ* 138:85–97.

Jones, Siân
1997 *The Archaeology of Ethnicity: Constructing Identities in the Past and Present*. London: Routledge.

Kallai (Kleinmann), Zecharia
1958 The Town Lists of Judah, Simon, Benjamin and Dan. *VT* 8:134–60.

Kamp, Kathryn A., and Norman Yoffee
1980 Ethnicity in Ancient Western Asia During the Early Second Millennium B.C.: Archaeological Assessments and Ethnoarchaeological Prosepectives. *BASOR* 237:85–104.

Kantor, Helene J.
1962 A Bronze Plaque with Relief Decoration from Tell Tainat. *JNES* 21:93–117.

Karageorghis, Jacqueline
1999 *The Coroplastic Art of Ancient Cyprus*. Vol. V, *The Cypro-Archaic Period Small Female Figurines*. B. *Figurines Moulées*. Nicosia: A. G. Leventis Foundation.

Karageorghis, Vassos
1960 Fouilles de Kition 1959. *BCH* 84:504–88.
1970 Naiskoi de Chypre. *BCH* 94:27–33.
1982 The Late Bronze Age (Late Cypriote). 1600–1050 B.C. In *Footprints in Cyprus: An Illustrated History*, ed. D. Hunt, 37–57. London: Trigraph.
1987 The Terracottas. In *La nécropole d'Amathonte, Tombes 113–367*, ed. V. Karageorghis, O. Picard, and C. Tytgat, 1–52. Études Chypriotes IX. Nicosia: A. G. Leventis Foundation.
1993a *The Coroplastic Art of Ancient Cyprus*. Vol. II, *Late Cypriote II–Cypro-Geometric III*. Nicosia: A. G. Leventis Foundation.
1993b *The Coroplastic Art of Ancient Cyprus*. Vol. III, *The Cypro-Archaic Period Large and Medium Size Sculpture*. Nicosia: A. G. Leventis Foundation.
1995 *The Coroplastic Art of Ancient Cyprus IV. The Cypro-Archaic Period Small Male Figurines*. Nicosia: A. G. Leventis Foundation.
1996 *The Coroplastic Art of Ancient Cyprus*. Vol. VI, *The Cypro-Archaic Period Monsters, Animals and Miscellanea*. Nicosia: A. G. Leventis Foundation.
1998 *The Coroplastic Art of Ancient Cyprus*. Vol. V, *The Cypro-Archaic Period Small Female Figurines*. A. *Handmade/Wheelmade Figurines*. Nicosia: A. G. Leventis Foundation.
1999 *Excavations at Kition*. Vol. VI, *The Phoenician and Later Levels, Plates*. Nicosia: Department of Antiquities, Cyprus.
2000 Another Mould for Cakes from Cyprus. A. The Mould and Its Interpretation. *Rivista di Studi Fenici* 28:3–5.
2003 *Excavations at Kition*. Vol. VI, Part II, *The Phoenician and Later Levels*. Nicosia: Department of Antiquities, Cyprus.
2005 *Excavations at Kition*. Vol. VI, Part I, *The Phoenician and Later Levels*. Nicosia: Department of Antiquites, Cyprus

Karo, Georg
1943 *An Attic Cemetery*. Philadelphia: The Oberlaender Trust.

Keel, Othmar
1992 *Das Recht der Bilder gesehen zu warden: drei Fallstudien zur Methode der Interpretation altorientalischer Bilder*. OBO 122. Freiburg: Universitätsverlag.
1995 *Corpus der Stempelsiegel-Amulette aus Palästina/Israel: Von den Anfägen bis zur Perserzeit. Einleitung*. OBO, Series Archaeologica 10. Freiburg: Universitätsverlag.
1997 *The Symbolism of the Biblical World: Ancient Near Eastern Iconography and the Book of Psalms*. Translated by T. J. Hallett. Winona Lake, Ind.: Eisenbrauns.

Keel, Othmar, and Christoph Uehlinger
1998 *Gods, Goddesses, and Images of God in Ancient Israel*. Translated by T. H. Trapp. Minneapolis: Fortress Press.

Kelley, Donald R.
1995 Something Happened: Panofsky and Cultural History. In *Meaning in the Visual Arts: Views from the Outside. A Centennial Commemoration of Erwin Panofsky (1892–1968)*, ed. I. Lavin, 113–21. Princeton, N.J.: Institute for Advanced Study.

Kelm, George L., and Amihai Mazar
1982 Three Seasons of Excavations at Tel Batash: Biblical Timnah. *BASOR* 248:1–36.
1995 *Timnah: A Biblical City in the Sorek Valley*. Winona Lake, Ind.: Eisenbrauns.

Kelso, James L., and J. Palin Thorley
1943 The Potter's Technique at Tell Beit Mirsim, Particularly in Stratum A. In *The Excavations at Tell Beit Mirsim*. Vol. III, *The Iron Age*, ed. W. F. Albright, 86–142. AASOR 21–22. New Haven, Conn.: American Schools of Oriental Research.

Kempinski, Aharon
1974 Tell el-ᶜAjjul: Beth-Eglayim or Sharuhen? *IEJ* 24:142–52.

1993 ᶜAjjul, Tell el-. In *NEAEHL*, ed. E. Stern, 4:52–53. Jerusalem: Israel Exploration Society and Carta.
2002 *Tel Kabri: The 1986–1993 Excavation Seasons*. Ed. N. Scheftelowitz and R. Oren. Tel Aviv: Emery and Claire Yass Publications in Archaeology.

Kenyon, Kathleen M.
1952 *Beginning in Archaeology*. New York: F. A. Praeger.
1979 *Archaeology in the Holy Land*. 4th ed. London: Ernest Benn.

Kilian, Klaus
1978 Ausgrabungen in Tiryns 1976. Bericht zu den Grabungen. *Archäologischer Anzeiger* 4:449–70.
1981 Zeugnisse mykenischer Kultausübung in Tiryns. In *Sanctuaries and Cults in the Aegean Bronze Age*, ed. R. Hägg and N. Marinatos, 49–58. Proceedings of the First International Symposium at the Swedish Institute in Athens, 12–13 May 1980. Stockholm: P. Åström.
1990 Patterns of Cult Activity in the Mycenaean Argolid: Haghia Triada (Klenies), the Profitis Elias Cave (Haghios Hadrianos) and the Citadel of Tiryns. In *Celebrations of Death and Divinity in the Bronze Age Argolid*, ed. R. Hägg and G. C. Nordquist, 185–96. Proceedings of the Sixth International Symposium at the Swedish Institute at Athens, 11–13 June, 1988. Stockholm: P. Åström.

Kilian-Dirlmeier, Imma
1978–79 Zum Halsschmuck mykenischer Idole. *Jahresbericht des Instituts für Vorgeschichte der Universität Frankfurt a.M.*:29–43.

Killebrew, Ann E.
2000 Aegean-Style Early Philistine Pottery in Canaan During the Iron I Age: A Stylistic Analysis of Mycenaean IIIC:1b Pottery and Its Associated Wares. In *The Sea Peoples and Their World: A Reassessment*, ed. E. D. Oren, 233–53. Philadelphia: University Museum, University of Pennsylvania.
2005 *Biblical Peoples and Ethnicity: An Archaeological Study of Egyptians, Canaanites, Philistines, and Early Israel, 1300–1100 B.C.E.* Atlanta: Society of Biblical Literature.

King, Philip J.
2006 Gezer and Circumcision. In *Confronting the Past: Archaeological and Historical Essays on Ancient Israel in Honor of William G. Dever*, ed. S. Gitin, J. E. Wright, and J. P. Dessel, 333–40. Winona Lake, Ind.: Eisenbrauns.

Kitchen, Kenneth A.
1986 *The Third Intermediate Period in Egypt (1100–650 B.C.)*. 2d ed. with suppl. Warminster: Aris and Phillips.

Kletter, Raz
1996 *The Judean Pillar-Figurines and the Archaeology of Asherah*. BARIS 636. Oxford: British Archaeological Reports.
1999 Pots and Polities: Material Remains of Late Iron Age Judah in Relation to Its Political Borders. *BASOR* 314:19–54.
2003 A Very General Archaeologist: Moshe Dayan and Israeli Archaeology. *Journal of Hebrew Scriptures* 4:Article 5.

Kletter, Raz, Irit Ziffer, and Wolfgang Zwickel.
2010 *Yavneh*. Vol. I, *The Excavation of the "Temple Hill" Repository Pit and the Cult Stands*. OBO, Series Archaeologica 30. Fribourg: Academic Press.

Kletter, Raz, Karen Covello-Paran, and Katri Saarelainen
2010 Beautiful From All Sides: Twice-moulded Figurines of the Southern Levant. *Levant* 42:17–29.

Kloner, Amos
1991 Maresha [in Hebrew]. *Qadmoniot* 24/3–4:70–85.

Knoppers, Gary N.
2003 *I Chronicles 1–9. A New Translation with Introduction and Commentary*. Anchor Bible, vol. 12. New York: Doubleday.

Kochavi, Moshe
1976 Tel Aphek, 1975. IEJ 26:51–52.
1989 *Aphek-Antipatris: Five Thousand Years of History* [in Hebrew]. Tel Aviv: Kibbutz Hameuchad.

Konsolaki, Eleni
2002 A Mycenaean Sanctuary on Methana. In *Peloponnesian Sanctuaries and Cults*, ed. R. Hägg, 25–36. Proceedings of the Ninth International Symposium at the Swedish Institute at Athens, 11–13 June 1994. Stockholm: Svenska Institutet i Athen.

Kontoleon, Nikolaos M.
1958 Theräisches. *AM* 73:117–39.
1961 Naxos. Ergon for 1960. 185–92.

Kossinna, Gustaf
1911 *Die Herkunft der Germanen: zur methode der Siedlungsarchäologie*. Würzburg: C. Kabitzsch.

Krogulska, Maria
1968 Late Mycenaean Tradition in Boeotian Archaic Terracottas. In *Atti e memorie del 1° Congresso internazionale di micenologia, Roma 27 Settembre–3 Octobre 1967*, 228–31. Rome: Edizioni dell'Ateneo.

Kurtz, Donna C., and John Boardman
1971 *Greek Burial Customs*. London: Thames and Hudson.

Langdon, Susan H.
2008 *Art and Identity in Dark Age Greece, 1100–700 B.C.E.* New York: Cambridge University Press.

Lapp, Paul W.
1964 The 1963 Excavations at Taᶜannek. *BASOR* 173:4–44.
1969 The 1968 Excavations at Tell Taᶜannek. *BASOR* 195:2–49.

Lavin, Irving, ed.
1995 *Meaning in the Visual Arts: Views from the Outside. A Centennial Commemoration of Erwin Panofsky (1892–1968).* Princeton, N.J.: Institute for Advanced Study.

Layard, Austen H.
1849 *The Monuments of Nineveh: From Drawings Made on the Spot.* London: John Murray.
1853 *A Second Series of the Monuments of Nineveh.* London: John Murray.

Leclant, Jean
1960 Astarté à cheval d'après les représentations Egyptiennes. *Syria* 37:1–67.

Lehmann-Jericke, Kirsten
2004 The Terracotta Horseman. In *The Phoenician Cemetery of Tyre-Al Bass: Excavations 1997–1999,* ed. M. E. Aubet, 417–19. Bulletin d'Archéologie et d'Architecture Libanaises, Hors-Série I. Beirut: Ministère de la Culture, Direction Générale des Antiquités.

Lemaire, André
1998 Chars et cavaliers dans l'ancien Israël. *Transeuphratène* 15:165–82.

Lesure, Richard G.
2002 The Goddess Diffracted: Thinking about the Figurines of Early Villages. *Current Anthropology* 43:587–601.

Levin, Kim
1964 The Male Figure in Egyptian and Greek Sculpture. *AJA* 68:13–28.

Lewis, Theodore
2005 Syro-Palestinian Iconography and Divine Images. In *Cult Image and Divine Representation in the Ancient Near East,* ed. N. H. Walls, 69–107. Boston: ASOR.

Lipiński, Edward
1986 The Syro-Palestinian Iconography of Woman and Goddess. *IEJ* 36:87–96.
2003 Phoenician Cult Expressions in the Persian Period. In *Symbiosis, Symbolism, and the Power of the Past: Canaan, Ancient Israel, and Their Neighbors from the Late Bronze Age through Roman Palaestina,* ed. W. G. Dever and S. Gitin, 297–308. Proceedings of the Centennial Symposium, W. F. Albright Institute of Archaeological Research and American Schools of Oriental Research, Jerusalem, May 29–31, 2000. Winona Lake, Ind.: Eisenbrauns.

Littauer, Mary A., and Joost H. Crouwel
1979 *Wheeled Vehicles and Ridden Animals in the Ancient Near East.* Leiden: E. J. Brill.

Macalister, Robert A. S.
1912a *The Excavation of Gezer: 1902–1905 and 1907–1909.* Vol. II. London: John Murray.
1912b *The Excavation of Gezer: 1902–1905 and 1907–1909.* Vol. III. London: John Murray.

Machinist, Peter
2000 Biblical Traditions: The Philistines and Israelite History. In *The Sea Peoples and Their World: A Reassessment,* ed. E. D. Oren, 53–83. Philadelphia: University Museum, University of Pennsylvania.

Mackay, Ernest J. H., and Margaret A. Murray
1952 *Ancient Gaza.* Vol. V. London: British School of Archaeology in Egypt.

Maier, Walter A.
1986 *ᵓAšerah: Extrabiblical Evidence.* Harvard Semitic Monographs No. 37. Atlanta: Scholars.

Maiuri, Amedeo
1923–24 Jalisos—Scavi della Missione Archeologica Italiana a Rodi. *Annuario* 6–7:83–341.

Mallowan, Max E. L.
1966 *Nimrud and Its Remains.* 2 vols. London: Collins.

Marchetti, Nicolò
2001 *Materiali e Studi Archaeologici di Ebla.* Vol. V, *La coroplastica eblaita e siriana nel Bronzo Medio: campagne 1964–1980.* 2 vols. Rome: Università degli Studi di Roma La Sapienza.

Marchetti, Nicolò, and Lorenzo Nigro
1997 Cultic Activities in the Sacred Area of Ishtar at Ebla during the Old Syrian Period: The "Favissae" F. 5327 and F. 5238. *JCS* 49:1–44.

Marcus, Joyce
1996 The Importance of Context in Interpreting Figurines. *CAJ* 6/2:285–91.

Margalith, Othniel
1994 A New Type of Asherah-Figurine? *VT* 44:109–15.

Marinatos, Nanno
2000 *The Goddess and the Warrior: The Naked Goddess and Mistress of Animals in Early Greek Religion*. London and New York: Routledge.

Markoe, Glenn E.
1990 The Emergence of Phoenician Art. *BASOR* 279:13–26.
2000 *Phoenicians*. Berkeley: University of California Press.

Master, Daniel M.
2003 Trade and Politics: Ashkelon's Balancing Act in the Seventh Century B.C.E. *BASOR* 330:47–64.
2008 Grid System and Field Methods. In *Ashkelon* 1: 85–93. Winona Lake, Ind.: Eisenbrauns.

May, Herbert G.
1935 *Material Remains of the Megiddo Cult*. OIP 26. Chicago: University of Chicago Press.

Mazar, Amihai
1980 *Excavations at Tell Qasile*. Part One, *The Philistine Sanctuary: Architecture and Cult Objects*. Qedem 12. Jerusalem: Institute of Archaeology, the Hebrew University of Jerusalem.
1982a The "Bull Site"—An Iron Age I Open Cult Place. *BASOR* 247:27–42.
1982b Clay Plaques Depicting a Goddess Standing in an Architectural Facade [in Hebrew]. *Qadmoniot* 15:113–15.
1985a The Emergence of the Philistine Material Culture. *IEJ* 35:95–107.
1985b Pottery Plaques Depicting Goddesses Standing in Temple Facades. *Michmanim* 2:5–18.
1986 Excavations at Tell Qasile, 1982–1984: Preliminary Report. *IEJ* 36:1–15.
1992a *Archaeology of the Land of the Bible, 10,000–586 B.C.E.* New York: Doubleday.
1992b The Iron Age I. In *The Archaeology of Ancient Israel*, ed. A. Ben-Tor, 258–301. Translated by R. Greenberg. New Haven, Conn.: Yale University Press.
1994 The Northern Shephelah in the Iron Age: Some Issues in Biblical History and Archaeology. In *Scripture and Other Artifacts: Essays on the Bible and Archaeology in Honor of Philip J. King*, ed. M. D. Coogan, J. C. Exum, and L. E. Stager, 247–67. Louisville: Westminster John Knox.
2003 The Excavations at Tel Rehov and Their Significance for the Study of the Iron Age in Israel [in Hebrew]. *EI* 27:143–60.
2006 Clay Figurines and a Zoomorphic Vessel. In *Timnah (Tel Batash)*. Vol. III, *The Finds from the Second Millennium B.C.E.*, ed. N. Panitz-Cohen and A. Mazar, 251–54. Qedem 45. Jerusalem: Institute of Archaeology, the Hebrew University of Jerusalem.
2009 Clay Figurines and Cult Vessels. In *Excavations at Tel Beth-Shean, 1989–1996*. Vol. III, *The 13th–11th Century B.C.E. Strata in Areas N and S*, ed. N. Panitz-Cohen and A. Mazar, 530–55. Jerusalem: Institute of Archaeology, the Hebrew University of Jerusalem.

Mazar, Amihai, and Christopher Bronk Ramsey
2010 A Response to Finkelstein and Piasetzky's Criticism and "New Perspective." *Radiocarbon* 52: 1681–88.

Mazar, Amihai, and Nava Panitz-Cohen
2001 *Timnah (Tell Batash)*. Vol. II, *The Finds from the First Millennium B.C.E.* 2 vols. Qedem 42. Jerusalem: Institute of Archaeology, the Hebrew University of Jerusalem.

Mazar (Maisler), Benjamin
1950–51 The Excavations at Tell Qasîle: Preliminary Report. *IEJ* 1:61–76, 125–40, 194–218.
1952 Yurza—Tell Jemmeh. *PEQ* 1952:48–51.
1954 Gath and Gittaim. *IEJ* 4:227–35.
1975 *Cities and Districts in Eretz-Israel* [in Hebrew]. Jerusalem: Bialik Institute.
1986 The Philistines and the Rise of Israel and Tyre. In *The Early Biblical Period: Historical Studies*, ed. S. Aḥituv and B. A. Levine, 63–82. Jerusalem: Israel Exploration Society.

Mazar, Eilat
1990 A Horsemen's Tomb at Akhziv. *Qadmoniot* 23:104–9.
1993 Akhziv. *ESI* 12:5–6.
2001 *The Phoenicians in Achziv, the Southern Cemetery: Jerome L. Joss Expedition, Final Report of the Excavations, 1988–1990*. Cuadernos de arqueología mediterránea 7. Barcelona: Universidad Pompeu Fabra.
2004 *The Phoenician Family Tomb N. 1 at the Northern Cemetery of Achziv*. Cuadernos de arqueología mediterránea 10. Barcelona: Universidad Pompeu Fabra.

Mazow, Laura B.
2005 Competing Material Culture: Philistine Settlement at Tel Miqne-Ekron in the Early Iron Age. Ph.D. diss., University of Arizona.

Meehl, Mark W., Trude Dothan, and Seymour Gitin
2006 *Tel Miqne-Ekron Excavations 1995–1996, Field INE East Slope Iron Age I (Early Philistine Period)*. Ed. S. Gitin. Tel Miqne-Ekron Final Field Report Series No. 8. Jerusalem: W. F. Albright Institute of Archaeological Research and Institute of Archaeology, Hebrew University of Jerusalem.

Messika, Natalie
1996 Terracotta Figurines from Acco in the Persian and the Hellenistic Period (Sixth-First Century B.C.E.). Master's thesis, Hebrew University.

Metzger, Martin
2004 Two Architectural Models in Terracotta. In *The Phoenician Cemetery of Tyre-Al Bass: Excavations 1997–1999*, ed. M. E. Aubet, 420–36. Bulletin d'Archéologie et d'Architecture Libanaises, Hors-Série I. Beirut: Ministère de la Culture, Direction Générale des Antiquités.

Meyers, Carol
1987 A Terracotta at the Harvard Semitic Museum and Disc-holding Female Figures Reconsidered. *IEJ* 37:116–22.
2007 Terracottas without Texts: Judean Pillar Figurines in Anthropological Perspective. In *To Break Every Yoke: Essays in Honor of Marvin L. Chaney*, ed. R. B. Coote and N. K. Gottwald, 115–30. Sheffield: Sheffield Phoenix.

Mitchell, W . J. Thomas
1991 Iconology and Ideology: Panofsky, Althusser, and the Scene of Recognition. In *Image and Ideology in Modern/Postmodern Discourse*, ed. D. B. Downing and S. Bazargan, 321–30. Albany, N.Y.: State University of New York Press.
1995 What is Visual Culture? In *Meaning in the Visual Arts: Views from the Outside. A Centennial Commemoration of Erwin Panofsky (1892–1968)*, ed. I. Lavin, 207–17. Princeton, N.J.: Institute for Advanced Study.

Moore, Andrew D.
1988 The Large Monochrome Terracotta Figures from Mycenae: The Problem of Interpretation. In *Problems in Greek Prehistory: Papers Presented at the Centenary Conference of the British School of Archaeology at Athens, Manchester, April 1986*, ed. E. B. French and K. A. Wardle, 219–28. Bristol: Bristol Classical Press.

Moore, Andrew D., and William D. Taylour
1999 *Well Built Mycenae: The Helleno-British Excavations within the Citadel at Mycenae, 1959–1969.* Fascicule 10, *The Temple Complex*. Oxford: Oxbow Books.

Moorey, P. R. S.
2003 *Idols of the People: Miniature Images of Clay in the Ancient Near East.* The Schweich Lectures of the British Academy, 2001. Oxford: Oxford University Press.

Morgan, Charles H.
1935 The Terracotta Figurines from the North Slope of the Acropolis. *Hesperia* 4:189–213.

Moscati, Sabatino
1973 *The World of the Phoenicians*. Translated by A. Hamilton. London: Cardinal.

Mountjoy, Penelope A.
1986 *Mycenaean Decorated Pottery: A Guide to Identification.* SIMA 73. Göteborg: P. Åström.

Müller, Valentin K.
1915 *Der Polos, die griechische Götterkrone*. Berlin: G. Schade.

Mylonas, George E.
1956 Seated and Multiple Mycenaean Figurines in the National Museum of Athens, Greece. In *The Aegean and the Near East. Studies Presented to Hetty Goldman on the Occasion of Her Seventy-Fifth Birthday*, ed. S. Weinberg, 110–21. Locust Valley: J. J. Augustin.
1966 *Mycenae and the Mycenaean Age*. Princeton, N.J.: Princeton University Press.

Myres, John L.
1897 Excavations in Cyprus in 1894. *JHS* 17:134–73.

Naᵓaman, Nadav
1979 The Brook of Egypt and Assyrian Policy on the Border of Egypt. *TA* 6:68–90.
2003 Ekron under the Assyrian and Egyptian Empires. *BASOR* 332:81–91.
2005–06 *Collected Essays*. 3 vols. Winona Lake, Ind.: Eisenbrauns.

Naᵓaman, Nadav, and Ran Zadok
1988 Sargon II's Deportations to Israel and Philistia. *JCS* 40:36–46.

Nakamura, Carolyn, and Lynn Meskell
2009 Articulate Bodies: Forms and Figures at Çatalhöyük. *Journal of Archaeological Method and Theory* 16:205–30.

Nakhai, Beth Alpert, J. P. Dessel, and Bonnie L. Wisthoff
1987–88 Tell el-Wawiyat—1986. *ESI* 6:100–2.

Naveh, Joseph
1958 Khirbat al-Muqannaᶜ—Ekron: An Archaeological Survey. *IEJ* 8:87–100.

Negbi, Ora
1966 *A Deposit of Terracottas and Statuettes from Tel Ṣippor.* ᶜAtiqot 6 [English series]. Jerusalem: Department of Antiquities and Museums.
1976 *Canaanite Gods in Metal: An Archaeological Study of Ancient Syro-Palestinian Figurines.* Tel Aviv: Institute of Archaeology, Tel Aviv University.

Nicholls, Richard V.

1952 Type, Group and Series: A Reconsideration of Some Coroplastic Fundamentals. *BSA* 47: 217–26.

1970 Greek Votive Statuettes and Religious Continuity, c. 1200–700 B.C. In *Auckland Classical Essays Presented to E. M. Blaiklock*, ed. B. F. Harris, 1–37. Auckland: Auckland University Press.

Nicholson, Ernest

1998 *The Pentateuch in the Twentieth Century: The Legacy of Julius Wellhausen*. Oxford: Clarendon Press.

Nilsson, Martin P.

1968 *The Minoan-Mycenaean Religion and Its Survival in Greek Religion*. 2d rev. ed. Lund: C. W. K. Gleerup.

Noort, Ed

1994 *Die Seevölker in Palästina*. Kampen: Kok Pharos.

Noth, Martin

1960 *The History of Israel*. 2d ed. Translation revised by P. R. Ackroyd. New York: Harper & Brothers.

1971 *Das Buch Josua*. Tübingen: J. C. B. Mohr.

O'Bryhim, Shawn

1997 The Sphere-Bearing Anthropomorphic Figurines of Amathus. *BASOR* 306:39–45.

Ochsenschlager, Edward

1974 Mud Objects from al-Hiba: A Study in Ancient and Modern Technology. *Archaeology* 27/3:162–74.

Ohata, Kiyoshi, ed.

1967 *Tel Zeror.* Vol. II, *Preliminary Report of the Excavation, Second Season, 1965*. Tokyo: The Society for Near Eastern Studies in Japan.

Ohly, Dieter

1940 Frühe Tonfiguren aus dem Heraion von Samos I. *AM* 65:57–102.

Olsen, Barbara A.

1998 Women, Children and the Family in the Late Aegean Bronze Age: Differences in Minoan and Mycenaean Constructions of Gender. *World Archaeology* 29:380–92.

Oppenheim, A. Leo

1955 Babylonian and Assyrian Historical Texts. In *Ancient Near Eastern Texts Relating to the Old Testament*, ed. J. B. Pritchard, 275–317. Princeton, N.J.: Princeton University Press.

Oren, Eliezer D.

1973 *The Northern Cemetery of Beth Shan*. Leiden: E. J. Brill.

1978 Esh-Shari^{c}a, Tell (Tel Sera^{c}). In *EAEHL*, ed. M. Avi-Yonah and E. Stern, 4:1059–69. Englewood Cliffs, N.J.: Prentice-Hall.

1982 Ziglag—A Biblical City on the Edge of the Negev. *BA* 45:155–66.

1993a Ethnicity and Regional Archaeology: The Western Negev under Assyrian Rule. In *Biblical Archaeology Today, 1990*, ed. A. Biran and J. Aviram, 102–5. Proceedings of the Second International Congress on Biblical Archaeology, Jerusalem, June–July 1990. Jerusalem: Israel Exploration Society.

1993b Sera^{c}, Tel. In *NEAEHL*, ed. E. Stern, 4:1329–35. Jerusalem: Israel Exploration Society and Carta.

Oren, Eliezer, et al.

1991 Tell Haror—After Six Seasons. *Qadmoniot* 24/1–2:2–19.

Oren, Ronit

2002 Figurines. In *Tel Kabri: The 1986–1993 Excavation Seasons*, by A. Kempinski, ed. N. Scheftelowitz and R. Oren, 349–55. Tel Aviv: Emery and Claire Yass Publications in Archaeology.

Ornan, Tallay.

2005 *The Triumph of the Symbol: Pictorial Representation of Deities in Mesopotamia and the Biblical Image Ban*. OBO 213. Fribourg: Academic Press.

2007 Labor Pangs: The Revadim plaque type. In *Bilder als Quellen* (= *Images as Sources: Studies on Ancient Near Eastern Artefacts and the Bible Inspired by the Work of Othmar Keel*), ed. S. Bickel et al., 215–35. OBO, Sonderband. Fribourg: Academic Press.

Özgüç, Tahsin

1963 An Assyrian Trading Outpost. *Scientific American* 208:96–106.

Panitz-Cohen, Nava

2010 The Pottery Assemblage. In *Yavneh.* Vol. I, *The Excavation of the "Temple Hill" Repository Pit and the Cult Stands*, ed. R. Kletter, I. Ziffer, and W. Zwickel, 110–45. OBO, Series Archaeologica 30. Fribourg: Academic Press.

Panofsky, Erwin

1939 *Studies in Iconology: Humanistic Themes in the Art of the Renaissance*. New York: Oxford University Press.

1955a Introduction. The History of Art as a Humanistic Discipline. In *Meaning in the Visual Arts: Papers in and on Art History*, ed. E. Panofsky, 1–25. Garden City, N.Y.: Doubleday.

1955b Iconography and Iconology: An Introduction to the Study of Renaissance Art. In *Meaning in the Visual Arts: Papers in and on Art History*, ed. E. Panofsky, 26–54. Garden City, N.Y.: Doubleday.

1955c Epilogue. Three Decades of Art History in the United States: Impressions of a Transplanted European. In *Meaning in the Visual Arts: Papers in and on Art History*, ed. E. Panofsky, 321–46. Garden City, N.Y.: Doubleday.

Paraire, Dorothée J.
1980 Figurines. In *Tell Keisan (1971–1976): une cité phénicienne en Galilée*, ed. J. Briend and J. B. Humbert, 331–52. OBO, Series Archaeologica 1. Fribourg: Éditions Universitaires.

Paz, Sarit
2007 *Drums, Women, and Goddesses: Drumming and Gender in Iron Age II Israel*. OBO 232. Fribourg: Academic Press.

Perdrizet, Paul
1908 *Fouilles de Delphes*. Tome V, *Monuments figures: petits bronzes, terres-cuites, antiquités diverses*. Paris: École Française d'Athènes.

Perlman, Isadore, and Frank Asaro
1969 Pottery Analysis by Neutron Activation. *Archaeometry* 11:21–52.

Persson, Axel W.
1938 The Finds. In *Asine: Results of the Swedish Excavations, 1922–1930*, ed. O. Frödin and A. W. Persson, 199–431. Stockholm: Generalstabens Litografiska Anstalt.

Petersen, William
1974 On the Subnations of Western Europe. In *Ethnicity*, ed. N. Glazer and D. P. Moynihan, 177–208. Cambridge, Mass.: Harvard University Press.

Petrie, W. M. Flinders
1928 *Gerar*. London: British School of Archaeology in Egypt.
1931 *Ancient Gaza*. Vol. I. London: British School of Archaeology in Egypt.
1932 *Ancient Gaza*. Vol. II. London: British School of Archaeology in Egypt.
1933 *Ancient Gaza*. Vol. III. London: British School of Archaeology in Egypt.

Petty, Alice
2006 *Bronze Age Anthropomorphic Figurines from Umm el-Marra, Syria: Chronology, Visual Analysis, and Function*. BARIS 1575. Oxford: Archaeopress.

Phythian-Adams, William J.
1923a Reports on Soundings at Gaza, etc. *PEFQS*:11–36.
1923b Report on the Stratification of Askalon. *PEFQS*: 60–84.

Picard, Charles
1948 *Les religions préhellénique (Crète et Mycènes)*. Paris: Presses Universitaires de France.

Picard, C. G.
1967 Sacra Punica: étude sur les masques et rasoirs de Carthage. *Karthago* 13:1–115.

Pike, Kenneth L.
1954 *Language in Relation to a Unified Theory of the Structure of Human Behavior*. Vol. 1. Glendale: Summer Institute of Linguistics.

Pilafidis-Williams, Korinna
1998 *The Sanctuary of Aphaia on Aigina in the Bronze Age*. München: Deutsches Archäologisches Institut.
2009 The Mycenaean Kourotrophos Figurine at the Sanctuary of Aphaia on Aigina. In *Encounters with Mycenaean Figures and Figurines*, ed. A. L. Schallin and P. Pakkanen, 113–24. Papers Presented at a Seminar at the Swedish Institute at Athens, 27–29 April 2001. Stockholm: Svenska Institutet i Athen.

Pilz, Edwin
1924 Die weiblichen Gottheiten Kanaans. *ZDPV* 47: 129–68.

Pinch, Geraldine
1983 Childbirth and Female Figurines at Deir el-Medina and el-ᶜAmarna. *Orientalia* 52:405–14.
1993 *Votive Offerings to Hathor*. Oxford: Griffith Institute, Ashmolean Museum.

Pisano, Giovanna
1999 Jewellery. In *The Phoenicians*, ed. S. Moscati, 418–44. New York: Rizzoli.

Popham, Mervyn R.
1974 Sellopoulo Tombs 3 and 4, Two Late Minoan Graves Near Knossos. IV. The Jewellery Including Sealstones. *BSA* 69:210–25.

Popham, Mervyn R., and Irene S. Lemos
1996 *Lefkandi*. Vol. III, *The Toumba Cemetery: The Excavations of 1981, 1984, 1986 and 1992–94. Plates*. Athens: British School at Athens.

Prent, Mieke
2005 *Cretan Sanctuaries and Cults: Continuity and Change from Late Minoan IIIC to the Archaic*

Period. Religions in the Graeco-Roman World 154. Leiden: Brill.

Press, Michael D.
2007 Philistine Figurines and Figurines in Philistia in the Iron Age. Ph.D. diss., Harvard University.
2011 A Problem of Definition: "Cultic" and "Domestic" Contexts in Philistia. In *Household Archaeology in Ancient Israel and Beyond*, ed. A. Yasur-Landau, J. R. Ebeling, and L. B. Mazow, 361–89. Leiden: Brill.
2012 (Pytho)Gaia in Myth and Legend: The Goddess of the Ekron Inscription Revisited. *BASOR* 365:1–24.
forthcoming Zoomorphic Vessels. In the Iron Age I volume of the Ashkelon Series. Winona Lake, Ind.: Eisenbrauns.

Pritchard, James B.
1943 *Palestinian Figurines in Relation to Certain Goddesses Known Through Literature*. American Oriental Series 24. New Haven, Conn.: American Oriental Society.
1954 *The Ancient Near East in Pictures Relating to the Old Testament*. Princeton, N.J.: Princeton University Press.
1975 *Sarepta: A Preliminary Report of the Iron Age. Excavations of the University of Pennsylvania, 1970–72*. Philadelphia: University Museum, University of Pennsylvania.
1988 *Sarepta*. Vol. IV, *The Objects from Area II, X. The University Museum of the University of Pennsylvania Excavations at Sarafand, Lebanon*. Beirut: Publications de l'Université Libanaise.

Pritchard, James B., ed.
1969 *Ancient Near Eastern Texts Relating to the Old Testament*. 3d ed. Princeton: Princeton University Press.

Pruß, Alexander
2002 Ein Licht in der Nacht? Die Amuq-Ebene während der Dark Ages. In *Die nahöstlichen Kulturen und Griechenland an der Wende vom 2. zum 1. Jahrtausend v. Chr.: Kontinuität und Wandel von Strukturen und Mechanismen kultureller Interaktion*, ed. E. A. Braun-Holzinger and H. Matthäus, 161–76. Kolloquium des Sonderforschungsbereiches 295 "Kulturelle und sprachliche Kontakte" der Johannes Gutenberg-Universität Mainz, 11 –12. Dezember 1998. Möhnesee: Bibliopolis.
2010 *Die Amuq-Terrakotten: Untersuchungen zu den Terrakotta-Figuren des 2. und 1. Jahrtausends v. Chr. aus den Grabungen des Oriental Institute Chicago in der Amuq-Ebene*. Subartu 26. Turnhout: Brepols.

Raban, Avner
1991 The Philistines in the Western Jezreel Valley. *BASOR* 284:17–27.
1999 *Archaeological Survey of Israel: Map of Mishmar Ha-ᶜEmeq (32)*. Jerusalem: Israel Antiquities Authority.

Rainey, Anson F., et al.
2006 *The Sacred Bridge: Carta's Atlas of the Biblical World*. Jerusalem: Carta.

Redford, Donald B.
1992 *Egypt, Canaan, and Israel in Ancient Times*. Princeton, N.J.: Princeton University Press.

Rehak, Paul
1995 Enthroned Figures in Aegean Art and the Function of the Mycenaean Megaron. In T*he Role of the Ruler in the Prehistoric Aegean*, ed. P. Rehak, 95–118. Proceedings of a Panel Discussion Presented at the Annual Meeting of the Archaeological Institute of America, New Orleans, Louisiana, 28 December 1992, with Additions. Aegaeum 11. Liège: Université de Liège.

Rehak, Paul, and John G. Younger
1998 Review of *Aegean Prehistory*. Vol VII, *Neopalatial, Final Palatial, and Postpalatial Crete. AJA* 102:91–173.

Reich, Ronny
1980 On the Identification of the "Sealed Karu of Egypt" [in Hebrew with English summary]. *EI* 15 (1981):283–87.

Renfrew, Colin
1981a Questions of Minoan and Mycenaean Cult. In *Sanctuaries and Cults in the Aegean Bronze Age*, ed. R. Hägg and N. Marinatos, 27–33. Proceedings of the First International Symposium at the Swedish Institute in Athens, 12–13 May 1980. Stockholm: P. Åström.
1981b The Sanctuary at Phylakopi. In *Sanctuaries and Cults in the Aegean Bronze Age*, ed. R. Hägg and N. Marinatos, 67–79. Proceedings of the First International Symposium at the Swedish Institute in Athens, 12–13 May 1980. Stockholm: P. Åström.
1985 *The Archaeology of Cult: The Sanctuary at Phylakopi*. London: British School of Archaeology at Athens.

Riis, P. J.
1949 The Syrian Astarte Plaques and Their Western Connections. *Berytus* 9:69–90.

Riis, P . J., and Marie-Louise Buhl
1990 *Hama. Fouilles et recherches de la fondation Carlsberg 1931–1938.* Vol. II.2, *Les objets de la période dite syro-hittite (âge du fer)*. Copenhagen: Nationalmuseet.

Sahlins, Marshall
1983 Other Times, Other Customs: The Anthropology of History. *AA* 85:517–44.

Sass, Benjamin
2002 Wenamun and His Levant—1075 B.C. or 925 B.C.? *Ägypten und Levante* 12:247–55.

Saussure, Ferdinand de
1916 *Cours de linguistique générale*. Paris: Payot.

Schäfer-Lichtenberger, Christa
2000 The Goddess of Ekron and the Religious-Cultural Background of the Philistines. *IEJ* 50:82–91.

Scheepers, Anne.
1991 Anthroponymes et toponymes du récit d'Ounamon. In *Phoenicia and the Bible*, ed. E. Lipiński, 17–83. Studia Phoenicia XI. Leuven: Peeters.

Schiffer, Michael B.
1972 Archaeological Context and Systemic Context. *American Antiquity* 37:156–65.
1976 *Behavioral Archaeology*. New York: Academic Press.
1985 Is There a "Pompeii Premise" in Archaeology? *Journal of Anthropological Research* 41:18–41.
1987 *Formation Processes of the Archaeological Record*. Albuquerque: University of Mexico Press.

Schipper, Bernd U.
2005 *Die Erzählung des Wenamun: Ein Literaturwerk im Spannungsfeld von Politik, Geschichte und Religion*. OBO 209. Fribourg: Academic Press.

Schloen, J. David
2001 *The House of the Father as Fact and Symbol: Patrimonialism in Ugarit and the Ancient Near East*. Studies in the Archaeology and History of the Levant 2. Winona Lake, Ind.: Eisenbrauns.

Schmid, H. E.
1967 Frühgriechische Terrakotten aus Kreta. In *Gestalt und Geschichte. Festschrift Karl Schefold, zu seinem 60. Geburstag am 26. Jan. 1965*, ed. M. Rohde-Liegle, H. A. Cahn, and H. C. Ackermann, 168–73. Bern: Francke.

Schmid, Hans H.
1976 *Der sogenannte Jahwist: Beobachtungen und Fragen zur Pentateuchforschung*. Zürich: Theologischer Verlag.

Schmidt, Gerhard
1968 *Kyprische Bildwerke aus dem Heraion von Samos*. Samos Band VII. Bonn: R. Habelt.

Schmitt, Rüdiger
1999 Philistäische Terrakottafigurinen. *Ugarit-Forschungen* 31:577–676.

Schoinas, C.
1999 Εικονιστικη Παρασταση σε Οστρακα Κρατηρα απο την Αγια Τριαδα Ηλειας. In *ΗΠΕΡΙΦΕΡΕΙΑ ΤΟΥ ΜΥΚΗΝΑΙΚΟΥΚΟΣΜΟΥ.* Vol. 1, ed. H. Phroussou, 257–62. Diethnes Diepistemoniko Symposio, Lamia, 25–29 Septembriou 1994. Lamia: Ephoreias Proistorikon kai Klassikon Archaioteton.

Schroer, Silvia
1989 Die Göttin auf den Stempelsiegeln aus Palästina/Israel. In *Studien zu den Stempelsiegeln aus Palästina/Israel*, Vol. II., ed. O. Keel, H. Keel-Leu, and S. Schroer, 89–207. OBO 88. Freiburg: Universitätsverlag.

Shavit, Alon, and Assaf Yasur-Landau
2005 A Bronze and Iron Age Settlement at Netiv Ha-ᶜAsara. In *Salvage Excavation Reports*. No. 2, ed. B. Sass and I. Roll, 59–92. Tel Aviv: Sonia and Marco Nadler Institute of Archaeology, Tel Aviv University.

Shelmerdine, Cynthia W.
1997 Review of *Aegean Prehistory*. Vol. VI, *The Palatial Bronze Age of the Southern and Central Greek Mainland*. *AJA* 101:537–85.

Shennan, Stephen
1994a Introduction: Archaeological Approaches to Cultural Identity. In *Archaeological Approaches to Cultural Identity*, ed. S. Shennan, 1–32. London and New York: Routledge.

Shennan, Stephen, ed.
1994b *Archaeological Approaches to Cultural Identity*. London and New York: Routledge.

Sherratt, Susan
1998 "Sea Peoples" and the Economic Structure of the Late Second Millennium in the Eastern Mediterranean. In *Mediterranean Peoples in Transition, Thirteenth to Early Tenth Centuries B.C.E.*, ed. S. Gitin, A. Mazar, and E. Stern, 292–313. Jerusalem: Israel Exploration Society.

Singer, Itamar
1985 The Beginning of Philistine Settlement in Canaan and the Northern Boundary of Philistia. *TA* 12:109–22.
1994 Egyptians, Canaanites, and Philistines in the Period of the Emergence of Israel. In *From Nomadism to Monarchy: Archaeological and Historical Aspects of Early Israel*, ed. I. Finkelstein and N. Naʾaman, 281–338. Jerusalem: Israel Exploration Society.

Ska, Jean-Louis
2006 *Introduction to Reading the Pentateuch*. Translated by P. Dominique. Winona Lake, Ind.: Eisenbrauns.

Skupinska-Løvset, Ilona
1976 *The Ustinov Collection: The Palestinian Pottery*. Oslo: Universitetsforlaget.
1978 *The Ustinow Collection: Terracottas*. Oslo: Universitetsforlaget.

Smith, Joanna S.
2009 *Art and Society in Cyprus from the Bronze Age into the Iron Age*. Cambridge: Cambridge University Press.

Solá-Solé, J. M.
1966 Nueva inscripción fenicia de España (Hispania 14). *Rivista degli studi orientali* 41:97–108.

Spyropoulos, Theodoros G.
1969 Το Μυκηναϊκόν Νεκροταφείον της Τανάγρας. *AAA* 2:20–25.
1970 Ανασκαφή εις το Μυκηναϊκόν Νεκροταφείον της Τανάγρας. *AAA* 3:184–97.
1971 Funèbre mais sensationnelle découverte à Tanagra. *Connaissance des Arts* 230:72–77.

Stager, Lawrence E.
1985 Merneptah, Israel and Sea Peoples: New Light on an Old Relief. *EI* 18:56*–64*.
1991 *Ashkelon Discovered: From Canaanites and Philistines to Romans and Moslems*. Washington, D. C.: Biblical Archaeological Society.
1998 The Impact of the Sea Peoples in Canaan (1185–1050 B.C.E.). In *The Archaeology of Society in the Holy Land*, ed. T. Levy, 332–48. London: Leicester University Press.
2000 Another Mould for Cakes from Cyprus: In the Queen's Image. *Rivista di Studi Fenici* 28:6–11.
2006a Chariot Fittings from Philistine Ashkelon. In *Confronting the Past: Archaeological and Historical Essays on Ancient Israel in Honor of William G. Dever*, ed. S. Gitin, J. E. Wright, and J. P. Dessel, 169–76. Winona Lake, Ind.: Eisenbrauns.
2006b New Discoveries in the Excavations of Ashkelon in the Bronze and Iron Ages [in Hebrew]. *Qadmoniot* 39:2–19.
2006c Biblical Philistines: A Hellenistic Literary Creation? In *"I Will Speak the Riddles of Ancient Times": Archaeological and Historical Studies in Honor of Amihai Mazar*, ed. A. M. Maeir and P. de Miroschedji, 375–84. Winona Lake, Ind.: Eisenbrauns.

Stager, Lawrence E., Daniel M. Master, and J. David Schloen, eds.
2011 *Ashkelon*. Vol. 3, *The Seventh Century B.C.* Winona Lake, Ind.: Eisenbrauns.

Stager, Lawrence E., J. David Schloen, and Daniel M. Master, eds.
2008 *Ashkelon*. Vol. 1, *Introduction and Overview*. Winona Lake, Ind.: Eisenbrauns.

Steindorff, Georg
1939 The Statuette of an Egyptian Commissioner in Syria. *EA* 25:30–33.

Stern, Ephraim
1978 Phoenician Masks and Pendants. *PEQ* 108:109–18.
1982 *Material Culture of the Land of the Bible in the Persian Period, 538–332 B.C.* Warminster: Aris and Phillips.
1989 What Happened to the Cult Figurines? Israelite Religion Purified after the Exile. *BAR* 15/4:22–29, 53–54.
1995 *Excavations at Dor, Final Report*. Vol. IB, *Areas C and D: The Finds*. Qedem Reports 2. Jerusalem: Institute of Archaeology, the Hebrew University of Jerusalem.
2000 The Settlement of Sea Peoples in Northern Israel. In *The Sea Peoples and Their World: A Reassessment*, ed. E. D. Oren, 197–212. Philadelphia: University Museum, University of Pennsylvania.
2001 *Archaeology of the Land of the Bible*. Vol. II, *The Assyrian, Babylonian, and Persian Periods, 732–332 B.C.E.* New York: Doubleday.
2003 The Phoenician Source of Palestinian Cults at the End of the Iron Age. In *Symbiosis, Symbolism, and the Power of the Past: Canaan, Ancient Israel, and Their Neighbors from the Late Bronze Age through Roman Palaestina*, ed. W. G. Dever and S. Gitin, 309–22. Proceedings of the Centennial Symposium, W. F. Albright Institute of Archaeological Research and American Schools of Oriental Research, Jerusalem, May 29–31, 2000. Winona Lake, Ind.: Eisenbrauns.
2006 The Sea Peoples Cult in Philistia and Northern Israel. In *"I Will Speak the Riddles of Ancient Times": Archaeological and Historical Studies in Honor of Amihai Mazar on the Occasion of His Sixtieth Birthday*. Vol. 1, ed. A. M. Maeir and P. de Miroschedji, 385–98. Winona Lake, Ind.: Eisenbrauns.

2010 *Excavations at Dor: Figurines, Cult Objects, and Amulets, 1980–2000 Seasons*. Jerusalem: Israel Exploration Society.

Stewart, Andrew
1990 *Greek Sculpture: An Exploration*. New Haven, Conn.: Yale University Press.

Stone, Bryan J.
1995 The Philistines and Acculturation: Culture Change and Ethnic Continuity in the Iron Age. *BASOR* 298:7–32.

Stone, Linda
1977 East Indian Adaptations on St. Vincent. In *Ethnic Encounters: Identities and Contexts*, ed. G. L. Hicks and P. E. Leis, 37–47. North Scituate: Duxbury.

Strange, John
1966 The Inheritance of Dan. *Studia Theologica* 20:120–39.

Sugimoto, David T.
2008 *Female Figurines with a Disk from the Southern Levant and the Formation of Monotheism*. Tokyo: Keio University Press.

Szabó, Miklós
1994 *Archaic Terracottas of Boeotia*. Studia Archaeologica 17. Rome: "L'Erma" di Bretschneider.

Tadmor, Hayim
1958 The Campaigns of Sargon II of Assur: A Chronological-Historical Study. *JCS* 12:22–40, 77–100.
1966 Philistia Under Assyrian Rule. *BA* 29:86–102.
1969 A Note on the Sabᵓa Stele of Adad-nirari III. *IEJ* 19:46–48.

Tadmor, Miriam
1982 Female Cult Figurines in Late Canaan and Early Israel. Archaeological Evidence. In *Studies in the Period of David and Solomon and Other Essays*, ed. T. Ishida, 139–73. First International Symposium for Biblical Studies, 1979. Winona Lake, Ind.: Eisenbrauns.
1996 Plaque Figurines of Recumbent Women—Use and Meaning [in Hebrew with English summary]. *EI* 25:290–96.

Talalay, Lauren
1993 *Deities, Dolls, and Devices: Neolithic Figurines from Franchthi Cave, Greece*. Bloomington and Indianapolis: Indiana University Press.

Tamvaki, Angela
1973 Some Unusual Mycenaean Terracottas from the Citadel House Area, 1954–69. *BSA* 68:207–65.

Tappy, Ron
1998 Review of *The Judean Pillar-Figurines and the Archaeology of Asherah*, by R. Kletter. *BASOR* 310:84–89.

Tatton-Brown, Veronica
1982 Two Finds Allegedly from Rantidi. *RDAC* 1982:174–82.

Taylour, William D.
1969 Mycenae, 1968. *Antiquity* 43:91–97.
1970 New Light on Mycenaean Religion. *Antiquity* 44:270–80.
1995 *The Mycenaeans*. Rev. ed. London: Thames and Hudson.

Teixidor, Javier
1975 A Note on the Phoenician Inscription from Spain. *HTR* 68:197–98.

Thalmann, Jean-Paul
1978 Tell ᶜArqa (Liban Nord) campagnes I–III (1972–1974), chantier I. Rapport préliminaire. *Syria* 35:1–153.

Theocharis, M.
1961 Iolkos. *Ergon* for 1960:55–61.

Theodossiadou, Maro
1995 Representations of Furniture on Cylinder Seals from Late Bronze Age Cyprus. In *Klados. Essays in Honour of J. N. Coldstream*, ed. C. Morris, 249–60. Bulletin of the Institute of Classical Studies Supplement 63. London: University of London, Institute of Classical Studies.

Trigger, Bruce
1989 *A History of Archaeological Thought*. Cambridge: Cambridge University Press.

Tsountas, Christos
1888 Ανασκαφαί τάφων εν Μυκήναις. *Ephemeris*: 119–79.

Tufnell, Olga
1953 *Lachish (Tell ed-Duweir)*. Vol. III, *The Iron Age. Plates*. London: Oxford University Press.

Ucko, Peter J.
1968 *Anthropomorphic Figurines of Predynastic Egypt and Neolithic Crete with Comparative Material from the Prehistoric Near East and Mainland Greece*. Royal Anthropological Institute Occasional Paper No. 24. London: Andrew Szmidla.
1996 Mother, Are You There? *CAJ* 6/2:300–4.

Uehlinger, Chirstoph
1997 Anthropomorphic Cult Statuary in Iron Age Palestine and the Search for Yahweh's Cult Image. In *The Image and the Book: Iconic Cults, Aniconism,*

and the Rise of Book Religion in Israel and the Ancient Near East, ed. K. van der Toorn, 97–155. Leuven: Peeters.

Uziel, Joe
2007 The Development Process of Philistine Material Culture: Assimilation, Acculturation and Everything in Between. *Levant* 39:165–73.

Van Beek, Gus W.
1983 Digging up Tell Jemmeh. *Archaeology* 36/1:12–19.
1993 Jemmeh, Tell. In *NEAEHL*, ed. E. Stern, 2:667–74. Jerusalem: Israel Exploration Society and Carta.

Van Buren, E. Douglas
1930 *Clay Figurines of Babylonia and Assyria*. New Haven, Conn.: Yale University Press.

Vance, Donald R.
1993 Literary Sources for the History of Palestine and Syria: The Phoenician Inscriptions. *BA* 57:110–20.

Vandenabeele, Frieda
1985 L'influence phénicienne sur la coroplastie chypriote. In *Phoenicia and Its Neighbours*, ed. E. Gubel and E. Lipiński, 203–11. Studia Phoenicia III. Leuven: Peeters.
1986 Phoenician Influence on the Cypro-Archaic Terracotta Production and Cypriot Influence Abroad. In *Acts of the International Archaeological Symposium "Cyprus Between the Orient and Occident," Nicosia, 8–14 September 1985*, ed. V. Karageorghis, 351–58. Nicosia: Department of Antiquities, Cyprus.
1991 The Terracottas of the Cypro-Geometric Period. In *Cypriote Terracottas*, ed. F. Vandenabeele and R. Laffineur, 57–68. Proceedings of the First International Conference of Cypriote Studies, Brussels-Liège-Amsterdam, 29 May-1 June, 1989. Brussels and Liège: A. G. Leventis Foundation.

Van den Berghe, Pierre L.
1974 Introduction. In *Class and Ethnicity in Peru*, ed. P. L. van den Berghe, 1–11. Leiden: E. J. Brill.

Van der Toorn, Karel
2002 Israelite Figurines: A View from the Texts. In *Sacred Time, Sacred Place: Archaeology and the Religion of Israel*, ed. B. M. Gittlen, 45–62. Winona Lake, Ind.: Eisenbrauns.

Vanschoonwinkel, Jacques
1999 Between the Aegean and the Levant: The Philistines. In *Ancient Greeks West and East*, ed. G. R. Tsetskhladze, 85–107. Leiden: Brill.

Van Seters, John
1975 *Abraham in History and Tradition*. New Haven, Conn.: Yale University Press.

Vaux, Roland de
1972 Les Philistins dans la Septante. In *Wort, Lied und Gottesspruch: Festschrift für Joseph Ziegler*. I. *Beiträge zur Septuaginta*, ed. J. Schreiner, 185–94. Würzburg: Echter Verlag.
1978 *The Early History of Israel*. Translated by D. Smith. Philadelphia: Westminster.

Verdery, Katherine
1994 Ethnicity, Nationalism, and State-making. *Ethnic Groups and Boundaries*: Past and Present. In *The Anthropology of Ethnicity: Beyond "Ethnic Groups and Boundaries,"* ed. H. Vermeulen and C. Govers, 33–58. Amsterdam: Spinhuis.

Vermeule, Emily
1964 *Greece in the Bronze Age*. Chicago: University of Chicago Press.
1965 Painted Mycenaean Larnakes. *JHS* 85:123–48.

Vermeulen, Hans, and Cora Govers
1994a Introduction. In *The Anthropology of Ethnicity: Beyond "Ethnic Groups and Boundaries,"* ed. H. Vermeulen and C. Govers, 1–9. Amsterdam: Spinhuis.

Vermeulen, Hans, and Cora Govers, eds.
1994b *The Anthropology of Ethnicity: "Beyond Ethnic Groups and Boundaries."* Amsterdam: Spinhuis.

Voigt, Mary M.
1983 *Hasanlu Excavation Reports*. Vol. 1, *Hajji Firuz Tepe, Iran: The Neolithic Settlement*. University Museum Mongraph 50. Philadelphia: University Museum, University of Pennsylvania.

Waldbaum, Jane C.
2011 Greek Pottery. In *Ashkelon* 3:127–338. Winona Lake, Ind.: Eisenbrauns.

Wapnish, Paula C.
1985 Animal Names and Animal Classifications in Mesopotamia: An Interdisciplinary Approach Based on Folk Taxonomy. Ph.D. diss., Columbia University.

Ward, William A.
1996 The Goddess within the Facade of a Shrine: A Phoenician Clay Plaque of the 8th Century B.C. *Rivista di Studi Fenici* 24:7–19.

Wheeler, R. E. Mortimer
1954 *Archaeology from the Earth*. Oxford: Clarendon Press.

Wiggermann, F. A. M.
1991 *Mesopotamian Protective Spirits: The Ritual Texts*. Cuneiform Monographs I. Gronigen: STYX & PP.

Wilson, John A.
1955 Egyptian Myths, Tales, and Mortuary Texts. In *ANET*[3], ed. J. B. Pritchard, 3–36. Princeton, N.J.: Princeton University Press.

Winter, Nancy A.
1996 The Terracottas. In *The Sanctuary of Apollo Hylates at Kourion: Excavations in the Archaic Precinct*, ed. D. Buitron-Oliver, 89–137. Jonsered: P. Åström.

Winter, Urs
1983 *Frau und Göttin: exegetische und ikonographische Studien zum weiblichen Gottesbild im alten Israel und in dessen Umwelt.* OBO 53. Freiburg: Universitätsverlag.

Wolff, Samuel R.
1998 Archaeology in Israel. *AJA* 102:757–807.

Wolff, Samuel, and Alon Shavit
1999 Tel Ḥamid [in Hebrew and English]. *Hadashot Arkheologiyot—Excavations and Surveys in Israel* 109:68*–70*, 104–7.

Wright, G. Ernest
1939 Iron: The Date of Its Introduction into Common Use in Palestine. *AJA* 43:458–63.
1966 Fresh Evidence for the Philistine Story. *BA* 29:70–86.

Yasur-Landau, Assaf
2001 The Mother(s) of all Philistines? Aegean Enthroned Deities of the 12th-11th Century Philistia. In *Potnia: Deities and Religion in the Aegean Bronze Age*, ed. R. Laffineur and R. Hägg, 329–43. Proceedings of the 8th International Aegean Conference/8e Rencontre égéenne internationale, Göteborg, Göteborg University, 12–15 April 2000. Aegaeum 22. Liège: Université de Liège.
2002 Social Aspects of Aegean Settlement in the Southern Levant in the End of the 2nd Millennium B.C.E. Ph.D. diss., Tel Aviv University.
2010 *The Philistines and Aegean Migration at the End of the Late Bronze Age.* Cambridge: Cambridge University Press.

Yeivin, Shmuel
1961 *First Preliminary Report on the Excavations at Tel Gat (Tell Sheykh ʾAhmed el-ʿAreyny). Seasons 1956–1958.* Jerusalem: The Gat Expedition. 1971 *The Israelite Conquest of Canaan.* Istanbul: Nederlands Historisch-Archaeologisch Instituut in het Nabije Oosten.

Yeivin, Shmuel, and Aharon Kempinski
1993 ʿErani, Tel. In *NEAEHL*, ed. E. Stern, 2:417–22. Jerusalem: Israel Exploration Society and Carta.

Yon, Marguerite, and Annie Caubet
1988 Un Culte Populaire de la Grande Déesse à Lapithos. *RDAC* 1988, part 2:1–16.

Yorkoff, Hildreth
1972 Concerning "A Mold from Mari and Its Relations." *JANES* 4:81–84.

Young, John H., and Suzanne H. Young
1955 *Terracotta Figurines from Kourion in Cyprus.* Philadelphia: University Museum, University of Pennsylvania.

Younger, John
1995 The Iconography of Rulership: A Conspectus. In *The Role of the Ruler in the Prehistoric Aegean*, ed. P. Rehak, 152–211. Proceedings of a Panel Discussion Presented at the Annual Meeting of the Archaeological Institute of America, New Orleans, Louisiana, 28 December 1992, with Additions. Aegaeum 11. Liège: Université de Liège.

Zadok, Ran
1978 Phoenicians, Philistines, and Moabites in Mesopotamia. *BASOR* 230:57–65.

Zenner, Walter P.
1996 Ethnicity. In *Encyclopedia of Cultural Anthropology*, ed. D. Levinson and M. Ember, 2:393–95. New York: Henry Holt and Company.

Zevit, Ziony
2001 *The Religions of Ancient Israel: A Synthesis of Parallactic Approaches.* London and New York: Continuum.

Ziffer, Irit
2010 The Iconography of the Cult Stands. In *Yavneh.* Vol. I, *The Excavation of the "Temple Hill" Repository Pit and the Cult Stands*, ed. R. Kletter, I. Ziffer, and W. Zwickel, 61–104. OBO, Series Archaeologica 30. Fribourg: Academic Press.

Ziffer, Irit, and Raz Kletter
2007 *In the Field of the Philistines: Cult Furnishings from the Favissa of a Yavneh Temple.* Tel Aviv: Eretz Israel Museum.

Zschietzschmann, Willy
1928 Die Darstellung der Prothesis in der griechischen Kunst. *AM* 53:17–47.

INDEX

CATALOGUE ENTRY INDEX